ENGLISH WARFA
1511–1642

English Warfare, 1511–1642 chronicles and analyses military operations from the reign of Henry VIII to the outbreak of the Civil War. The Tudor and Stuart periods laid the foundations of modern English military power. Henry VIII's expeditions, the Elizabethan contest with Catholic Europe, and the subsequent commitment of English troops to the Protestant cause by James I and Charles I, constituted a sustained military experience that shaped English armies for subsequent generations.

Drawing largely on manuscript sources, *English Warfare, 1511–1642* includes coverage of:

- the military adventures of Henry VIII in France, Scotland and Ireland
- Elizabeth I's interventions on the Continent after 1572, and how arms were perfected
- conflict in Ireland
- the production and use of artillery
- the development of logistics
- early Stuart military actions and the descent into civil war

English Warfare, 1511–1642 demolishes the myth of an inexpert English military prior to the upheavals of the 1640s.

Mark Charles Fissel is Associate Vice President for Academic Affairs and Professor of History at Augusta State University, USA. His previous books include *The Bishops' Wars: Charles I's Campaigns Against Scotland, 1638–1640* (Cambridge, 1994).

WARFARE AND HISTORY
General Editor: Jeremy Black
Professor of History, University of Exeter

ENGLISH WARFARE, 1511–1642

Mark Charles Fissel

London and New York

FOR RALPH J. WALLER
VERITAS, LIBERTAS, ET RELIGIOS

First published 2001
by Routledge
11 New Fetter Lane, London EC4P 4EE

Simultaneously published in the USA and Canada
by Routledge
29 West 35th Street, New York, NY 10001

Routledge is an imprint of the Taylor & Francis Group

© 2001 Mark Charles Fissel

Typeset in Bembo by Florence Production Ltd,
Stoodleigh, Devon
Printed and bound in Great Britain by
Biddles Ltd, Guildford and King's Lynn

British Library Cataloguing in Publication Data
A catalogue record for this book is available from
the British Library

Library of Congress Cataloging-in-Publication-Data
Fissel, Mark Charles.
English warfare 1511–1642 / Mark Charles Fissel.
p. cm. – (Warfare and history)
Includes bibliographical references and index.
1. Great Britain—History, Military—1485–1603.   2. Military art
and science—Great Britain—History—16th century.   3. Military art
and science—Great Britain—History—17th century.   4. Great
Britain—History, Military—1603–1714.   I. Title.   II. Series.
DA66.F57 2001
355'.00942'0902–dc21   00-065332

ISBN 0–415–21481–5 (hbk)
ISBN 0–415–21482–3 (pbk)

CONTENTS

CONTENTS

ILLUSTRATIONS

PREFACE

Did an 'English art of war' exist during the century that preceded the civil wars of 1642–9? When Englishmen fought Englishmen at Edgehill (October 1642), how expert were they in the practice of arms? Were Tudor and early Stuart English soldiers inferior to their continental counterparts? This book examines English land warfare from 1511 to 1642, blending narrative with thematic explorations of topics such as the military obligation and logistics.

For all the controversies about, and criticisms of, English warfare that appeared in English print during the century and a half before 1642, debate raised the question of how to defend the realm. Diversity of English opinion stemmed from the varieties of continental military practices. What weapons, tactics and organisational frameworks best served England? England was not Europe. The relationship between country and Crown, between the shires and the court, was distinctly English, and affected how soldiers were pressed from the populations of the towns and countryside, and how the lieutenancy managed local defence.

Fernand Braudel suggested that geography is the key to understanding the sixteenth century. Geography (and, implicitly, culture as a result) shaped the English art of war. As an independent island kingdom, England faced threats from a number of places on the Continent. Flotillas sailing up from Iberia might assail any of the many harbours on the southern coast. Holland, Flanders, Normandy, and even Brittany could be used as jumping-off points for invaders. The medieval struggle with Scotland, with the attendant logistical problems of waging war in the North, meant that the Borders had to be secured. Finally, but not least of all, Ireland made the west coast of England, and the Welsh principality, vulnerable to attack. That every shire was reasonably proximate to the sea meant that the responsibility of the defence of the realm fell to all inhabitants. Exercise of the military obligation was thus consensual and channelled through traditional patterns of local autonomy and patronage, which meant that mobilisation rarely could be achieved unilaterally or immediately. Similarly, English governments relied upon decentralised supply systems. Unless these arrangements were made with a certain thoroughness (as in dealing with the shires) the victuallers, arms manufacturers and ordnance officers could not assemble the *matériel* requisite for victory. Several times English military ventures failed because logistics were handled hastily, not because the English did not know how to fight. One intriguing truism, which deserves further research, is that English arms usually prevailed when they had access to artillery. The judicious use of cannon may be the salient development in English land warfare as it is in the emergence of English naval power.

At the end of the day, what *was* English warfare? The English approached warfare with eclecticism and adaptability. Except for a few bellicose anomalies, few Englishmen relished going to war; it was an arduous and disagreeable task that had to be done, and done rightly, so that the realm might return to peace. The fluidity with which the English moved from fighting upon the seas to fielding land armies resulted from geography – there were many theatres that required defending. When in those theatres of war, the English did their best to assimilate the style of combat that suited that terrain and enemy. The English art of war was more than the sum of the parts – rather it consisted of the manner in which foreign innovations and practices were synthesised with English practice. Problems there were. Muddy strategic thinking could confound the best efforts of English soldiers and their suppliers. The local communities put their own interests ahead of national security rather often. But by the time of the Civil War, England had remained free from foreign oppression. The cost was high, and a review of the military actions that occurred between 1511 and 1642 dispels any notion of an England living blissfully at peace through the era of the wars of religion.

The writing of this book is a tale of three universities. The initial typescript was written at Boğaziçi University, in a campus house nestled behind the Rumeli Hisar (the fortress raised upon the European shore of the Bosphorus by Mehmet the Conqueror prior to his seizure of Constantinople in 1453). Teaching and writing in Istanbul challenged my eurocentric biases, and a debt is owed to Boğaziçi's History Department, particularly to Selçuk Esanbel, Edhem Eldhem, and Selim Deringel, who shared with me their offices overlooking the Asian shore. Tony Greenwood, the American Research Institute in Turkey (Istanbul branch), and the Fulbright Commission, also provided encouragement. Special thanks go to Süreyya Ersoy and Ülkü Inal.

If books could be dedicated to Colleges, Harris Manchester College of the University of Oxford should be the recipient of such a designation from the author. Twice during the 1990s the Fellows of Harris Manchester graciously tolerated an early modernist thorn amongst the medievalist roses. Citing each individual would be most difficult, but the following must be thanked explicitly: Lesley Smith, Rowena Archer, Frances Walsh, Judith

Nisbet, John Sloan, Bill Mander, Sister Benedicta Ward, Howard Oliver, and Roger Trigg. Margaret Sarosi's endless patience and enterprise in ordering and locating books in the Tate Library were phenomenal. The College staff, especially Anita, Pat, Sally, and Ann, shared their computing equipment and pleasant surroundings. Thanks are also due to Stuart and Anne White, and Donald and Joan Tranter. The greatest debt is owed the Revd Dr Ralph Waller, Principal of Harris Manchester College. To dedicate a book about warfare to a gentle and compassionate scholar who has devoted himself as much to the propagation of religious toleration as to the pursuit of academic excellence may seem strange. But *English Warfare* charts part of the story of the preservation of the reformed religion, ensuring the eventual rise of toleration. The 'Christian soldiers' discussed herein helped us along the circuitous route to 'Veritas, Libertas, et Religios'.

Archives in the United Kingdom continue to provide highly efficient services to scholars of all nations, in spite of escalating operational costs. Deserving high praise are the Public Record Office (where Richard Elvin was especially helpful), the British Library, the Institute of Historical Research, the Scottish Record Office, the Lambeth Palace Library, the Corporation of London Records Office, the National Library of Scotland, the John Rylands Library, the Tate Library of Harris Manchester College (Oxon), the East Suffolk Record Office, the Somerset Record Office, the Wiltshire Record Office, the Shropshire Records and Research Centre, the Centre for Kentish Studies, the Norfolk Record Office, the Bristol Record Office and the Staffordshire Record Office. There is no finer place on earth than Duke Humfrey's Library in the Bodleian Library of the University of Oxford. The Department of Western Manuscripts was particularly gracious in making those pleasant days and evenings in Duke Humfrey productive. Grateful thanks are extended to Martin Kauffman, Michael Webb, W. G. Hodges, and the staff in Duke Humfrey.

The idea for this book grew from conversations with Tom Barnes in the late 1970s. Since then many have contributed to the work's compilation, purposefully or sometimes unaware. Jeremy Black, as series editor, created a niche for such a volume. The section on impressment owes much to Buchanan Sharp. David Trim and Peter Edwards shared their work during their visits to Harris Manchester College. The United States Military Academy, West Point, hosted a colloquium that focused on the theme of this book. Major Brad Gericke, Colonel Scott Wheeler, Cliff Rogers, and the USMA History Department shed much light on the subject. The medieval and early modern warfare seminar of the Department of War Studies at King's College London, chaired by Jan Willem Honig, commented upon a draft of the final chapter. The Sociedad Española de Estudios del Renacimiento Inglés hosted a similar paper. The Hargrett Library of the University of Georgia made available the resources of their A. L. Rowse collection, and made many useful suggestions regarding illustrations available in their rare book collections. Linda and Morton Rosenberg, historians in their own right, provided a base for operations in London. Thanks are due also to Simon Adams, Richard Aquila, Brian Awty, Michael Braddick, Tom Cogswell, Pauline Croft, Cliff Davies, Peter Donald, Anthony Fletcher, Edward Furgol, Ian Gentles, Raymond Gillespie, Matthew Glozier, Dan Goffman, Fernando Gonzalez, Steve Gunn, John Guy, Paul Hammer, Simon Healy, Ian Heath, Caroline Hibbard, Paul Lockhart, Dan Lutz, David Marini, Michael P. Maxwell, John Morrill, Kathleen Noonan, Phillip Norris, Bev Pitts, Jim Pyle, Brian Quintrell, the Earl Russell, Elizabeth Russell, David Scott, Barbara Weaver Smith, Erica and Willi Steiner, Richard Stewart, R. H. Teel, Andrew Thrush, Warren Vander Hill, Sterling Warner, the late Bruce Wernham, John Tofts White, Austin Woolrych, and Mike Young.

The third haven is my new home, Augusta State University. President William A. Bloodworth, jun., Vice President for Academic Affairs Bill Bompart, the Reese Library, and the Department of History and Anthropology, have been gracious. Tiffani Hampton Jones inherited the task of preparing the final draft. Darlene Scarff located books and Jennifer Onofrio contributed her photographic skills. Emily Linderman inserted changes to the original typescript. Kim Hart, Tammy Brewington, Rhonda Small, and Heather Rogers helped in many ways. Hilary Walford made suggestions regarding style. James Nyce brought to bear the imposing artillery of cultural anthropology and peer instructional design upon the sections on military architecture. Connie McOmber created several original maps. Roger Lockyer and Addison Wesley Longman publishers granted permission to reprint maps of the Isle of Rhé and Cadiz, originally published in Dr Lockyer's *Buckingham* (1987). M. L. Bush and Arnold publishers allowed the reproduction of a map of garrisons that appeared in *The Government Policy of Protector Somerset* (1975). Last, but never least, one's family plays a part in sustaining a work through completion. Thank you, Chuck, Vecenta, Jodi, Christina Maria and Jules.

Although this book is aimed at undergraduates and all students of English history, it also attempts to make an original contribution. Manuscript sources are cited and quoted liberally because history is best served when contemporaries speak for themselves. As this work is longer than Routledge would have liked, abbreviations have been used wherever possible. The continuing microfilming of manuscript collections, which will overlap with digital reproduction of archives (thus helping to preserve irreplaceable historical records), poses some problems in citation. For example, the State Papers Domestic Charles I were microfilmed systematically after I had consulted many of them in the late 1970s. Thus the end notes occasionally lack the modern foliation numbers assigned during microfilming. This is also true of a few British Library categories. Where possible I have rechecked the sources and provided foliation. In cases of double (sometimes triple) foliation, especially prevalent amongst certain British Library collections, I have tried to provide 'old' and 'new' citations in an effort to guide students to the proper folio. Some manuscripts entirely lack foliation at present (such as PRO, E 407/12), but will no doubt be foliated in future during digital reproduction. Consequently, some manuscript references may be incomplete by the standards of twenty-first-century scholarship.

Finally, Routledge editors Victoria Peters and Gillian Oliver enabled this book to see the light of day. Their efforts, and those of many at the Press, are appreciated. Susan Leaper and Sue Edwards of Florence Production formatted and polished the final product.

ABBREVIATIONS

ALC   Sir Roger Williams, *The Actions of the Low Countries*. Two versions are used in this volume, most often the D.W. Davies edition (Ithaca, NY 1964), and on occasion the John X. Evans edition in *The Works of Sir Roger Williams* (Oxford 1972)

APC   *Acts of the Privy Council* 1542–1631, J. Dasent, ed., vols 1–32; E. Atkinson, ed., vols 33–4; J. Lyle, ed., vols 35–43; R. Monger, ed., vol. 44; P. Penfold, ed., vols 45–6 (London 1890–1964)

Ashley, B.Litt.   Roger Ashley, 'The Organisation and Administration of the Tudor Office of the Ordnance', Oxford University B.Litt. thesis (1972), on deposit in the Bodleian Library

Bain, ed., *Calendar*   Joseph Bain, ed., *Calendar of the State Papers Relating to Scotland*, vol. 1 (Edinburgh 1898)

Barnes, *Somerset*   T. G. Barnes, *Somerset 1625–1640. A County's Government During the Personal Rule* (Oxford 1961)

BL   British Library

Boynton, *EM*   Lyndsay Boynton, *The Elizabethan Militia, 1558–1638* (London 1967)

CCSP   O. Ogle and W. Bliss, eds, *Calendar of the Clarendon State Papers preserved in the Bodleian Library*, vol. 1 (Oxford 1872)

CKS   Centre for Kentish Studies, Maidstone, Kent

Colvin, ed., *KW*   H. M. Colvin, D. Ramseur and J. Summerson, eds, *The History of the King's Works*, vol. 4 (1485–1660) pt 2 (London 1975)

Cogswell, *HD*   Thomas Cogswell, *Home Divisions. Aristocracy, the State and Provincial Conflict* (Stanford 1998)

Cruickshank, *EA*   Charles W. Cruickshank, *Elizabeth's Army* (2nd edn, Oxford 1966)

CSPD   *Calendar of State Papers, Domestic* 1547–1643, Edward VI, Mary, Elizabeth I and James I (12 vols, London 1856–72); Charles I (18 vols, London 1858–87)

CSP Foreign   *Calendar of State Papers, Foreign* Elizabeth I (1558–89), J. Stevenson, ed., vols 1–7; A. Crosby, ed., vols 8–11; A. Butler, ed., vols 12–16; Butler and S. Lomas, eds, vol. 17; Lomas, ed., vols 18–21 pt 1; Lomas and A. Hinds, eds, vol. 21 pts 2–4; R. Wernham, ed., vols 22–3 (London 1863–1950). For post-July 1589 Elizabethan State Papers Foreign, see *L&A* below

CSPI   *Calendar of State Papers, Ireland* 1509–1647, Henry VIII, Edward VI, Mary and Elizabeth I (11 vols, London 1860–1912); James I (5 vols, London 1872–80); Charles I (2 vols, 1900–1)

CSP Venetian   *Calendar of State Papers, Venetian* 1509–1643, R. Brown, ed., vols 2–6; Brown and G. Cavendish-Bentinck, eds, vol. 7; H. Brown, ed., vols 8–12; A. Hinds, ed., vols 13–26 (London 1864–1925)

CW   Council of War

Davies D.Phil.   C. S. L. Davies, 'Supply Services of the English Armed Forces, 1509–50', University of Oxford D.Phil. thesis (1963)

Davies, ed., *ALC*   D. W. Davies, ed., *The Actions of the Low Countries* (by Sir Roger Williams), (Ithaca, NY, 1964)

Dietz, *EPF*   F. C. Dietz, *English Public Finance, 1558–1641* vol. 2 (New York 1932)

DL   Deputy Lieutenant

DNB   *Dictionary of National Biography* (Various dates and publishers)

E   Exchequer

EconHR   *Economic History Review*

EHR   *English Historical Review*

Eltis, *MRSC*   David Eltis, *The Military Revolution in Sixteenth Century Europe* (London 1995)

Evans, ed., *ALC*   John X. Evans, ed., *The Works of Sir Roger Williams* (Oxford 1972)

Falls, *EIW*   Cyril Falls, *Elizabeth's Irish Wars* (New York 1950)

Fissel, *BW*   M. C. Fissel, *The Bishops' Wars: Charles I's Campaigns Against Scotland, 1638–1640* (Cambridge 1994)

Fissel, ed., *W&G*   M. C. Fissel, ed., *War and Government in Britain, 1598–1650* (Manchester 1991)

Forbes, ed., *Transactions*   Patrick Forbes, ed., *A Full View of the Public Transactions in the Reign of Queen Elizabeth* 2 vols (London 1740–1)

Hale, ed., *CDM*   J. R. Hale, ed., *Certain Discourses Military* (by Sir John Smythe) (New York 1964)

Hale, *WSRE*   J. R. Hale, *War and Society in Renaissance Europe 1450–1620* (London 1985)

Hayes-McCoy, *IB*   G. A. Hayes-McCoy, *Irish Battles. A Military History of Ireland* (Belfast 1990)

Haynes, ed., *SP*   Samuel Haynes, ed., *A Collection of State Papers . . . From the Year 1542 to 1570*, vol. 1 (London 1740)

HEH   Henry E. Huntington Library, San Marino, Calif.

HJ   *The Historical Journal*

HMC   Historical Manuscripts Commission

Hoyle, *MSG*   R. W. Hoyle, ed., *The Military Survey of Gloucestershire, 1522*, Bristol and Gloucestershire Archaeological Society, Gloucester Record Services vol. 6 (Stroud 1993)

IHS   *Irish Historical Studies*

JBS   *Journal of British Studies*

JP   Justice of the Peace

JSAHR   *The Journal of the Society for Army Historical Research*

LB   Lieutenancy Book

LL   Lord Lieutenant

L&A   *Lists and Analysis of State Papers Foreign* Elizabeth I, August 1589–December 1595, R. B. Wernham, ed., vols 1–6 (London 1964–93)

L&P   *Letters and Papers, Foreign and Domestic, of the reign of Henry VIII*, 1509–47, J. Brewer, ed., vols 1–4; J. Gairdner, ed., vols 5–13; Gairdner and R. Brodie, eds, vols 14–21 (London 1862–1910)

Loades, *TN*   David Loades, *The Tudor Navy: An Administrative, Political and Military History* (Aldershot 1992)

LPL   Lambeth Palace Library

McGurk, *ECI*   J. J. N. McGurk, *The Elizabethan Conquest of Ireland. The 1590s Crisis* (Manchester 1997)

Nolan, *SJN*   John Nolan, *Sir John Norreys and the Elizabethan Military World* (Exeter 1997)

Northants Lieutenancy Papers   J. Goring and J. Wake, eds, *Northamptonshire Lieutenancy Papers and other documents, 1580–1614* (Gateshead 1975)

NRO   Norfolk Record Office, Norwich

Oman, *AWSC*   Sir Charles Oman, *A History of The Art of War in the Sixteenth Century* (London 1937)

PC   Privy Council

P&P   Past and Present

Phillips, *ASW*   Gervase Phillips, *The Anglo-Scottish Wars, 1513–1550* (Woodbridge, Suffolk 1999)

PRO   Public Record Office, Kew

Quintrell, ed., *MLB*   Brian Quintrell, ed., *The Maynard Lieutenancy Book, 1608–1639*, Essex Historical Documents 3, Essex Record Office Publication 123 (Chelmsford 1993)

QS   Quarter Sessions

RO   Record Office

Russell, *FBM*   Conrad Russell, *The Fall of the British Monarchies 1637–1642* (Oxford 1991)

Russell, *PEP*   Conrad Russell, *Parliaments and English Politics 1621–1629* (Oxford 1979)

Sadler Papers   A. Clifford, ed., *The State Papers and Letters of Sir Ralph Sadler* (several editions)

Scottish RO   Scottish Record Office, General Register Office, Edinburgh

Sharp, *Memorials*   Sir Cuthbert Sharp, ed., *Memorials of the Rebellion of 1569* (London 1840)

Somerset RO   Somerset County Record Office, Taunton

SP   State Papers

Stearns, *CMS*   S. J. Stearns, 'The Caroline Military System, 1625–1627. The Expeditions to Cadiz and Ré', U. C. Berkeley (1967) Ph.D. dissertation.

Stewart, *EOO*   Richard Winship Stewart, *The English Ordnance Office 1585–1625* (Woodbridge, Suffolk 1996)

Tallett, *WSEME*   Frank Tallett, *War and Society in Early Modern Europe, 1495–1715* (London 1992)

TRHS   Transactions of the Royal Historical Society

Webb, *EMS*   Henry J. Webb, *Elizabethan Military Science. The Books and the Practice* (Madison, Wisconsin 1965)

Wernham, *ATA*   R. B. Wernham, *After the Armada* (Oxford 1984)

Wernham, ed., *1589*   R. B. Wernham, ed., *The Expedition of Sir John Norris and Sir Francis Drake to Spain and Portugal, 1589*, Navy Records Society vol. 127 (Aldershot, Hants. 1988)

WO   War Office

WRO   Wiltshire County Record Office, Trowbridge

1

THE EARLY TUDOR
ART OF WAR ON THE
CONTINENT

Francesco Petrarca, the fourteenth-century humanist who so very perceptively reconfigured the European conception of time and periodisation, had views on the English and warfare. Although an unmilitary people who had been pummelled recently, at Bannockburn, by the 'wretched Scots', the English had proved fierce and adept at warfare once drawn into the European theatre.[1] Six hundred years later, American GIs were advised not to be misled by the English 'tendency to be soft-spoken and polite. If they need to be, they can be plenty tough.'[2] From Crecy to Goose Green, the English often projected, with some justification, an air of invincibility. Outnumbered, they gained victory in a manner that, to the spectator, implied they regarded war as something of a sporting event. The English affectation of understatement, wry wit, and reserve even in the face of crisis, bred such an image.

And then there was the English technological edge that brought victory to the few over the haughty many. In 1415, the longbow; in 1940, radar. The English military tradition, however, with its resolute 'thin red line', has not blinded some contemporary historians to the weaknesses of English warfare, even if these were often overcome spectacularly.[3] The vitality and success of the English 'amateur military tradition' provoked disparaging remarks from those who believed the study of war should focus on professional military establishments and standing armies.[4] Furthermore, characteristics deemed 'English' in the early modern period may in fact be more applicable to English Hanoverian and Victorian cultures (though national characteristics by definition have some longevity). It has been suggested recently that Tudor and early Stuart Englishmen had the ability to assimilate, adapt, and absorb remarkably, and this study underscores that assertion.[5]

English flexibility in varying operational conditions, in combination with the 'stiff upper lip', or English pluck in dangerous straits, was sometimes explained by environmental determinism. According to an anonymous Elizabethan,

What hathe ben the Auncyent vertue of the Englishmen . . . yt is that many great parsonages hathe wrytten the truthe, of the feates

1

of warre. . . . People whiche be borne in the coulde region under the heavens, have more force and strengthe, and are lesse of Policye and counsaile, on the othersyde. Those which aproche nerer the sonne, be more subtile and craftye and less of courage. England is so set that for her situation she holdethe of bothe temperatours, and is for the most parte so moderate, in suche sorte, that neither force nor hawtenes, of courage, vertue, counsaile, or wisdome, can not fayle theis people . . . in all tymes hathe shewed themselves to take Armor so lyvelye, and in mannor so hardilye and corragiouslye, as any other people in the world.[6]

Geography and culture distinguished the English art of war from continental military practices. The strategic predicament of the realm, a direct result of geography, dictated English military culture and how the English prosecuted their wars. A mid-sixteenth-century Venetian analysed English military capability:

These troops, although armed, not being experienced and trained soldiers (because there would be few among them who would know how to move under arms, and to handle the pike, harque-buse, or other sort of weapon, it not being the custom in that kingdom for the inhabitants to perform any sort of exercise with similar arms), yet having veterans for their comrades, and many of the English themselves being experienced soldiers, as like other nations they go abroad and take part in one war and the other, they, at any rate, would produce great effect, and make a stout defence, from their natural disposition and tendency as common to them all, for which reason the recruits in like manner would stand firm, as everybody knows there is not a nation in the world that fights with less regard for danger and death than the English.[7]

Given that England's best defensive weapon was the sea, it is somewhat unnatural to examine land warfare without giving due regard to naval developments. Tudor and early Stuart strategists treated naval power as an appendage of land armies,[8] and no decisive battles were fought at sea. The Armada engagement of 1588 ushered in a decade of invasion scares and certainly did not seem decisive to contemporaries. On his accession Henry VII inherited half a dozen 'royal' vessels and a minimum of naval bureaucracy. The medieval navy (like Parliament) was 'less an institution than an event'.[9] The marriage of firepower and flotilla would be consummated slowly through the sixteenth century, and English strategists thought of their navy in terms of the delivery of land armies. Ships, like men, were readily pressed into service by indenture, and were converted into transport for troops and the increasingly useful arm of artillery, as, for example in the amphibious operation against Scotland in 1497.[10] This was the style of naval warfare, as in 1544–5, 1596, 1625, 1627, and 1639, to name but a few operations.

Land warfare for the English has been largely defensive, at least in terms of strategy. Throughout their history the English have usually found more constructive activities than building machines and bureaucracies for war. In Sir Geoffrey Elton's words, 'by the early sixteenth the English were not a martial people, or at least not a military one; a call to war found no ready response among them'.[11] The rule of the Tudors, with the exception of Henry VIII's obsession with emulating Henry V,[12] saw English strategic concerns remain primarily defensive. The Reformation increased England's vulnerability as a 'beleaguered isle',[13] for religious divisions exacerbated inter-national political rivalries and made England a target for continental aggres-sors, especially under Elizabeth I. One would have had difficulty convincing a Scot at Bannockburn or a Roman Catholic Irishman at the Boyne that the English were not aggressors. But intervention on the Continent, and in Scotland and Ireland, served to protect England's territorial, dynastic, and reli-gious integrity. There were notable exceptions, of course, particularly in the period following the Norman invasion up to the mid-fifteenth century. The territorial ambitions of English monarchs, which fuelled the French wars, resulted from the Norman Conquest of 1066 and thus in some ways were brought on by French dynastic struggles, a long-term consequence of the death of the last Saxon king.

While Henry VII wisely eschewed designs upon French territory, his reign coincided with some of the more salient technological develop-ments of the military revolution: the proliferation of the matchlock firing mechanism, the use of trunnions by artillerists, and the construction of bastioned defence systems.[14] Henry VII's 1496–7 mobilisation against Scotland exhibited the classic elements of English warfare. Within two years of Charles VIII's march through Italy, which so dramatised the potential of the artillery train,[15] Henry Tudor had cast 28 falcons from Weald iron. With his siege pieces, the King placed under his standard harquebusiers and an 'ord-nance corps' of 1,000 men and 600 horses, along with traditionally armed sol-diers. Dutch gunners were recruited, and the new royal cannoneers perfected their gunnery at Mile End upon 'a specially built proving ground of gun emplacements and butts'. Besides light ordnance and Renaissance art, the King appreciated the printing press. His ordinances of war appeared in printed form in 1492. Strategically defensive, tactically flexible, technolog-ically innovative, resolute, and imbued with the quality of leadership, Henry VII personified English warfare. The first Tudor did not covet war, but would fight if forced to it. His success at Bosworth Field in 1485, indeed, had elevated his trial by combat in battle to 'a status akin to a religious act'.[16]

Of the rulers whose reigns are encompassed in this study, the only one who loved war, and could afford it, was Bluff King Hal. Young Edward VI, contrary to the images on his later coinage, lacked the stamina and blood-lust of his father.[17] Mary I had more pressing matters at hand, such as the succession and her religion. For Elizabeth I, whose gender was supposed to keep her off the battlefield but whose appearance at Tilbury proved otherwise, war was a last resort: expensive, unpredictable, and fatal. Chivalry in its military guise cast little spell on her, as she struggled to pay adequately her soldiers and mariners upon discharge.[18] Royal personality and politics determined the frequency of campaigning, as geography affected the nature of warfare and strategy.

Early Henrician expeditions to the Continent

Henry VIII's foreign and domestic policies were often dictated by his appetite for war.[19] That appetite grew from a hunger for territory, for the acquisition of continental lands that would legitimise his imperial vision of himself and his dominions. Henry coveted the prestige and wealth that conquests bestowed. The King's fascination with war imbued his Privy Chamber with a rather militarised character, and the gentlemen pursued their personal relationship with Henry VIII by donning armour and fielding more soldiers than even some of the nobility might have boasted. Henry determined to pluck military resources from church and citizenry. Indeed, the King transformed his Gentlemen Pensioners and Privy Chamber into 'military Powerhouses'.[20] The Court's martial vigour infected even Thomas Cromwell and remained fashionable throughout the Henrician era, culminating in the great campaigns of the 1540s.[21]

The major armed conflicts fought during the reign of the second Tudor demonstrated the impressive potential of English warfare, for armies on that scale were not seen again until the days of William III. Henry VIII succeeded in assembling comparatively gargantuan armies, first because he was willing to expend the ample financial resources available to himself, and, second, because he possessed two recruiting systems, one calcifying gradually and the other budding slowly. Commissions were issued to lords to raise contingents, a privilege not often granted by the Tudors, and country lads were tapped for overseas service. Magnates calculated the sizes of their contingents and types of weaponry according to Crown formulae based upon real proprietary holdings.[22] The King could compel military service as part of the allegiance due the Crown. In 1544,

> The old acts of Henry VII that all who had grants of land from the king or who held any office or annuity must attend the king in person on his military expeditions were again enforced; but persons desiring to compound for such attendance were enabled to do so.[23]

So the King got money as well as troops from the military obligation.

In 1511 English soldiers marched the Continent toting their favoured weapon, the longbow. Fifteen hundred archers under Lord Darcy, hoping to fight the Moors alongside Spanish allies, never launched their arrows, as the Spanish King shifted strategies and cancelled the campaign. The anticlimax may have been a blessing, for in the following year's expedition (under the Marquis of Dorset) only a couple of hundred of the force's 8,000 longbows were judged usable.[24] More effective proved the 1,500 soldiers under Sir Edward Poynings, who served at the siege of Venlo against the forces of the Duke of Guelders. Margaret of Savoy, the leader of the alliance, confided to her father, the Emperor, 'The English acquit themselves very well and make more war on the enemies than any other'. As operations dragged into late October 1511, she reported to Maximilian that the commanders planned a three-day battering of Venlo's walls, followed by an 'assault, in which the English offer to take first place'. Even at this early date the English showed aptitude for gunnery. The defenders had mounted one of the town's towers and rained projectiles upon the English camp. The English retaliated by erecting a mound, positioning their artillery, and managing partially to demolish the offending structure. Margaret regarded her English troops' performance as 'better than the rest of the army'.[25]

Henry was learning, too, that naval transport and victuals made the difference between victory and defeat. The Guines campaign of midsummer 1512 faltered because the Spanish victuallers failed their allies. Henry received encrypted reports on his soldiers' predicament and the cost of victuals.[26] Mutinies broke out. The inconsistencies of the expeditions of 1511–12 explain why such great pains were taken subsequently, and preparations made, when the royal personage accompanied the expedition (numbering between 24,000 and 35,000 soldiers) sent to France in 1513.[27] The Tudor governmental apparatus operated well largely due to the efforts of talented administrators. Thomas Wolsey, humble in origins but rich in administrative skill, turned his attention from matters ecclesiastical to logistics in 1512–13. With due attention to macromanagement, such as the transferral of troops from naval duty to the landing force, and to cavils such as what wage trumpeters would receive, Wolsey oversaw the mobilisation with a vigilant eye and active pen.[28]

Sir Thomas Wyndham, the army's treasurer (who recruited and conducted sailors as well as soldiers), and Sir John Daunce (who acted as a liaison with the victuallers) performed as well as Wolsey. Wise personnel choices, sufficient resources, and planning could indeed bring victory, a point that had been equally well made during the Hundred Years War.[29] 'The roast beef of old England' kept her soldiers marching. The manner in which meat was supplied to the forces, decentralised, privately contracted, royally supervised, and as much in conjunction with naval forces as the land army, illustrates the Henrician approach to logistics. In 1513–14 the supervisor of the King's Custom House, John Heron, being familiar with trade and royal accounting, set about getting beef for the royal army. Working with £3,000 issued under the signet,[30] Heron aimed to find sufficient meat for a 10,000-man force. Working with the Lord Admiral, he used several ports – Lynn, Boston, Sandwich, and London – as depots from which barrels of salted meat could be shipped. 'Oxen fatte and wynterfede' were herded from Lincolnshire, Holland, and elsewhere, and slaughtered at designated spots. Salted and packed in barrels, the victuals found their way to port by water. For example, a salting and packing operation in Wisbech conveyed the barrels to Lynn upon small craft. London slaughterhouses used the lighters of the metropolis to waft the food down the Thames, though the costs of 'Cranage and portag to the Watersyd' were relatively high. Heron's suppliers disposed of the hides and tallow at a profit, but these transactions were noted in Heron's accounts.[31]

The fray near Bromy on 16 August 1513, dubbed the 'Battle of the Spurs' because of the haste with which the French gendarmerie fled, was essentially a foiled attempt to victual the besieged town of Thérouanne. Seeking only to deliver provisions, for the most part slabs of bacon, the French neither wanted nor expected a confrontation with the English. Through superior intelligence and a little luck, the English surprised the French column. The latter found themselves facing a numerically superior force that included cavalry ardent for a brawl, light artillery on a hillock to their left, and dismounted horse archers planted on their right. These bowmen could not wait to emulate their forefathers and launched arrows as soon as the French were in range; the French suffered losses before they could work out any tactical response. Retreat was, in fact, the only solution. Henry and the Emperor Maximilian were perhaps less than a mile away with their infantry, marching briskly in anticipation of bloodshed. The King later described the action without acknowledging his absence at the inauguration of violence:

> news came that all the French horse at Blangy were moving, some toward Guinegate, the others to the place where Lord Talbot was stationed before Terouenne to cut off supplies. A skirmish took place and there were taken on his side 44 men and 22 wounded. The French, thinking that the English were still beyond the Lys, considered they would not be in time to prevent them revictualling the town. The English horse however passed by Guinegate and confronted the French, who were three times their number. Several encounters took place and men were wounded on both sides. After this, in the Emperor's company, they advanced straight against the French, causing the artillery to be fired at them, whereupon they immediately began to retire, and were pursued for 10 leagues without great loss to the English.[32]

Whilst the casting-off of armour and weapons in the flight disgraced the French, at least a few distinguished themselves, such as Pierre Terrail, the Seigneur de Bayard, whose holding action at a narrow bridge saved lives and blunted the English offensive.

> Although there was no vast slaughter as there had been at Agincourt, it was the English archers that started the rout. Secondly, the speed with which the French panicked and fled suggests that there may have been a good deal in the contemporary belief that they had an innate fear of the English.[33]

However much the skills of the English artillerists were vaunted (for example, at Venlo), there were not enough to meet the Crown's needs. The King recruited the force under Lord Lisle from captains and soldiers currently serving in the navy. These were supplemented with cavalry, including 700 'Almains' (probably Germans) under Sir William Sandys and Sir Maurice Berkeley. In 1513 Wolsey's gun crews were almost entirely Flemish, and their cannon had been cast in the Netherlands. The pikemen in the 1513 French expedition were invariably *landesknechts*, and the calivermen were foreign as well. Given the Crown's dependence on Dutch transports, Henry would have been hard pressed to field an effective fighting force had not military resources been available on the open market.[34]

The greatest flaw revealed by the 1513 French campaign was England's unconvincing posture as a European military power. Were fiscal and logistic successes to be squandered on misguided and ill-conceived strategies? Was the English army no more than an appendage of an alarmingly unfocused English diplomacy? Henry certainly envisioned the 1523 expedition as an extension of foreign policy and spelled it out in the warrants for musters:

> We shall put a good and comieyente army in a redynes to bee sente for pressing of thennemy and the constraynyng of hym the rather to come unto reason to the weale of all christpendom in cace we cannot induce hym thereunto by suche good meanes as bee alredy set furthe.[35]

But these questions arose with the expeditions of 1522 and 1523, again undertaken in unison with faithless allies, which made incursions into France and in the latter campaign nearly took Paris, with the Duke of Suffolk showing some degree of skill in command and the English soldiers distinguishing themselves. The English displayed tactical competence, and particular deadliness with artillery. They made short work of several French strongholds. At Bray in 1523 the English positioned their guns under cover of night, commenced close range firing, and 'beate downe great gape in the walles the bred[th] of a carte' in only two hours.

The same artillery tactics were repeated at Montdidier with similar devastating effect a week later. A barrage erupted at 6 p.m., and by 2 a.m. the English ordnance had been positioned, again camouflaged by darkness, within 40 feet of the walls. Four salvoes 'brake downe the Walles a great bredith, hard by the myghtie stronge bolwerke, the strongist that evyr I saw. . . .' By 7 a.m. Montdidier had surrendered rather than face the English troops, who had been chanting 'assault! assault!'[36] But these stirring actions must have been accomplished with the assistance of non-English gunners, for, as in 1513, foreign artillerists were recruited with some desperation.[37]

Henry VIII's command of logistics, though inconsistent, reflected the monarch's expensive strategic goals. His personality as much as his resources spurred royal servants to achieve logistical successes unmatched, really, until the post-Restoration period, possibly even until the armies of William III. Henry was more inclined to take victualling, for example, under the umbrella of his royal government, more so than other English sovereigns of the early-modern era. Lacking a professional bureaucracy qualitatively, administratively, and numerically, Henry's ministers fashioned an *ad hoc* administration out of household and ecclesiastical servants, who channelled their energies into solving logistical problems.

Unfortunately, substantial expenditure did not always make for bureaucratic efficiency. In the expedition of the summer of 1522, the logistics in regard to carts and cannon were particularly badly managed.[38] The exertions of 1522 and 1523 illustrated why many in England preferred fighting defensive wars. The 10,000-man army sent against France in July 1522 required more than a dozen royal vessels, plus Spanish transports and mariners, in addition to the wholesale subcontracting of private English ships from Calais, Harwich, Hull, and 'Dertmouth' (the most common entry). The convoy, organised under Wolsey and in the pay of Sir Thomas Wyndham, under the latter's authority as treasurer of the royal army, brought the shipmasters and their employees, along with mariners and gunners, into royal pay along with the soldiers they accompanied. This included 'dedshares', a form of seagoing dead pay. In spite of the strenuous efforts to transport the army, still not enough wagons and artillery made it to the front.[39]

Henry VIII and an armed citizenry

From the outset, Henry VIII staked his dynasty and physical safety on the armed citizenry of England.[40] On 3 July 1511 the King proclaimed against retainers; two days later he enforced the Statute of Winchester (1285). Military power was best entrusted to local communities, not to cliques of nobles, although Henry was keen on building relationships individually with lords, provided their loyalty was unquestionable.[41] When the Crown mustered the nation's forces in 1511 it was probably more than anything else to enforce the statutory obligation and oil the mechanism for mobilisation. Perhaps the King mulled over the French expedition taking shape in his imagination. Henry set about ascertaining the number of soldiers at his disposal.[42] The military experiences of 1511–13 disclosed the limits of English warfare, and the renewal of hostilities in the early 1520s compelled Henry to investigate England's resources.

The thoroughness of the subsequent muster of 1522 and the conceptualisation behind its information gathering should be credited to Cardinal Wolsey, who determined that 'every man may be assessed to contribute to the furnisshing of harneys in sufficient forme for the preparydnes of the kings subjects. . . .' To that end the commissioners were to have a 'substauncial boke made and engrosed. . . .'[43] The muster regarded all able-bodied males, aged 16 to 60, as potential soldiers. No policy of selection based on weaponry, social standing or capacity for training, was observed or even contemplated, unlike the Statute of Winchester before or the trained bands after.[44] While the survey of wealth and manpower that has come to be known as the General Proscription of 1522 failed for the most part to classify the able-bodied, it did create other categories. Although categorisations separating out lands, goods, weapons, and able-bodied men might convey some notion of compartmentalisation, and thus multi-purpose use, one must recall that the three major periods of intensive taxation (1512–16, 1522–5, 1542–7) that comprised the Henrician war years 'conflated military resources with fiscal needs'.[45]

The 1522 survey has been described as 'first and foremost a military affair.' In fact, the 1522 musters may have more in common with the history of forcible conscription than the local defence obligation of the militia. The Crown was interested in what citizens could provide for England, not in what the Crown could do to protect the shires. In Henry VIII's vision, there was no militia *per se*, but simply county forces that might one year repel invasion in the guise of a militia and the following year be shipped to France as an expeditionary force. Statistics from nearly thirty counties reported 128,250 able men.[46] Like the Statute of Winchester, the 1522 survey assumed a correlation between an inhabitant's wealth and the weapons he maintained.[47] But, as much as the 1522 Proscription recalled earlier musters, it is alleged to have been a cynical attempt to raise revenue, a ploy by Henry and Wolsey 'to obtain new assessments by subterfuge, under the pretext of holding musters'.[48] Data regarding personal wealth and lands are more abundant and consistent than information about armour and weapons. Although some parishes gave bare descriptions of the ability of the men (marked 'able' or not at all), selection and suitability for service was not regarded as important a source of information as wealth. As for weapons, many parishes were so badly supplied it was not worth asking.[49] The pressing need for data on weapon availability prompted the commissioners to catalogue equipment.[50] However, Buckinghamshire at least seems to have been an exception in the latter respect, whose commissioners, regarding information on weapons and armour as of only minor importance, allowed slack and incomplete recording by their subordinates.[51] The Crown may have been pursuing a mixed agenda, for '. . . returns for the whole country may never have been collected centrally'.[52] England was treated as an arsenal and treasure house:

> The possession of weapons and harness was noted after the dwelling place of the owner but, whilst such entries occasionally record bills and bows, there is no indication of equivalent ways in which the earlier scribes pin-pointed in the left-hand margin which men were skilled as bowmen or archers.[53]

The lack of specificity in the Buckinghamshire lists suggest these provided little immediate usefulness for the defence of that shire.

Regional patterns of military preparedness (and local administrative vigour) emerged in the 1522 musters and continued on through the seventeenth century. Border counties such as Cumberland, Northumberland, and Westmorland no more answered the call in 1522 than they did in 1638. No certificates were forthcoming in either year. It has been argued that these northern shires, like Yorkshire, Lancashire, Nottinghamshire, and part of Derbyshire, were so involved in Scottish war precautions that they had not the time for surveys. Their proximity to the frontier dictated that their degree of preparedness should have been high, and military action on the Borders would have made clear the strengths and weaknesses of the parishes, wapentakes, and hundreds of the Border shires.

Was the 1522 General Proscription a response to the eroding military power of the nobility? The query posed by the central government, as to whom various potential soldiers 'belonged', implied a sense of obligation and 'ownership' that was feudal in character. If the medieval system was breaking down, with whom lay allegiances and personal connection in the shires? What was occurring was not exactly the eclipse of one system by another; rather this was an enquiry as to how gentry families had garnered the loyalties of the country, and how the gentry and their 'quasi-dependents' fitted into the old scheme of things, cast in terms that were not at variance with the Statute of Winchester. When responses generally 'failed to record tenurial relationships', the cause was not just suspicion related to taxation. Very probably new agrarian relationships with copyholders and cottagers did not translate easily into a military obligation. Indeed, the rise of copyhold spelt a cash nexus rather than service (including a military component). The commissioners for Surrey indicated to tenants (as did those for Berkshire) that demands for men and weapons could be 'refined' and made more equitable. 'Steps were taken to rationalize the distribution of armour, to secure a better match between those who possessed it and those who were able to use it'. Those who supplied weapons were not necessarily the ones who would use them. One encounters in Suffolk and Gloucestershire instances of those of modest wealth pooling their resources to acquire harness.[54] By disclosing information, 'honest subjects were encouraged by purchase to meet their statutory obligations'.[55]

The 1522 survey, which turned up weapons we would describe as medieval (harness, bows, arrows, swords, daggers, slings, jacks, splints, sallets, almain rivets, bills, and the stray 'hand gunne'), sheds light on the military revolution.[56] If the focus of the military revolution is how resources were managed by a central authority (as John Lynn has argued), then we should not see the 1522 survey with binary vision, delineating military and fiscal functions. The conjunction of two elements that to the Tudors were equally indispensable, money and weapons, made up a military force. Inseparability imposed an obligation. The manifestation of the fulfilment of the citizen's obligation varied, as it should have, for there were different ranks of people in society. The obligation to the Crown was universal but not necessarily equitable. Just as in the matter of military theory (as we shall see), the Tudor view of the nature of society integrated aspects of civic life, not subject to modern categorisation and hair-splitting. 'Fiscal' and 'military' were different sides of the King's shilling, collected for war.[57] Brooks and Heard point to '. . . the long-standing failure of [English] governments to tap the real wealth of the country, a failure related to popular resistance to innovation in taxation,' for example, in 1381 and 1497.[58] Had Henry been able permanently to boost his resources for war through non-parliamentary taxation, the character and scope of English warfare might have changed. The scale of the 1540s campaigns owed much to wealth that had once belonged to the English Church.

In summer 1522, the hastily planned amphibious operation against Le Havre stretched English resources to the maximum. Sir Thomas Wyndham, as treasurer, hired private vessels (as was usual) to supplement the royal transports and even had 'maryners Spanyards' on his crews. And, of course, the English vessels required gunners. So the French campaigns necessitated the diversion of soldiers and sailors on a large scale, and, even if the victualling responsibilities were assumed (though not very efficiently) by allies, the combined operations absorbed England's entire resources, except for those that were positioned on the Scottish borders. Practical separation between army and navy did not exist in Henrician England, given the Crown's financial and organisational arrangements during overseas campaigns.[59] Too often Henrician expeditions incorporated unreliable allies and merchants. In 1522 the Earl of Surrey's perambulations through France failed to achieve the strategic goal, for the Habsburgs again proved untrustworthy; indeed they even begged victuals from the English fleet.[60]

In the 1523 campaign, though some of the siege actions proved successful, once again strategy and supply were not sufficiently well worked out. Interestingly, Henry seemed to have learnt from the previous year's failure and successfully predicted the strategic failures that ultimately crippled the campaign. But Wolsey and the King's allies pressed on. Once across the Somme, the army's money ran out. The French recovered and cold weather set in. English handling of the siege guns was expert, but Henry's soldiers could not be victorious if the campaign's strategy was doomed. A participant described the strategic predicament with Welsh candour. The French King

> did not make much haste to turn back to drive the English from his kingdom since he was sufficiently familiar with them to know that they would do no harm in the world, only take their sport in strolling around the countryside eating wheaten bread and meat and fish and drinking wine, which was a great treat for the English common people. And as soon as winter came it was sure for that they would keep to their custom

of retreating to the familiar comforts of Albion.[61] The tantalising prospect of a Paris coronation had slipped from Henry's grasp, and the Tudors never again aimed so high. In Steven Gunn's words, '1523 might justly be seen as the watershed between medieval and modern strategy'.[62]

The 1539 national musters, a reaction to a reconciled Holy Roman Emperor and King of France now capable of using Henry VIII's excommunication as a pretext for an invasion of England, demonstrated the backwardness of English weaponry and the Tudor notion that 'militia' were fair game for overseas service. The letters patent appointing Commissioners of Array specified that the citizen soldiers 'so armed, arrayed, inspected, and furnished, henceforth from time to time may be ready and prepared to serve us as often as, and when it shall be needful and requisite'.[63] The phraseology indicates that defence of the realm was just that, and the terms of military obligation were defined by the Crown's prerogative. Further, the use of Commissioners of Array, the officers through whom medieval contract armies served, indicates Henry VIII's conviction that all able men between the ages of 16 and 60 were liable for overseas service. Thus the distinctions between 'voluntary' militia service within the realm and contractual overseas service that had emerged in varying degrees in the Middle Ages were conflated under the Tudors, to resurface in demands for definition under the early Stuarts.

As for weaponry, still in 1539 the English countrymen relied upon bill and bow. The returns revealed a dearth of firearms. Yet that is not surprising, for the Spurs seemingly justified the bow as the battle of Flodden (also fought in 1513) did the bill. These infantry weapons, with an artillery train and some tactical imagination, seemed the implements of the Englishman's art of fighting. Guns and swords (which are rare in the certificates) were perhaps 'not within the scope of the muster'.[64] This would confirm that Henry VIII never considered the 'English Army' a complete force; it would have to be supplemented by professional (i.e. foreign) harquebusiers and heavy cavalry. England's security would be further buttressed by a system of coastal defences. Fortifications complemented the militia system entrenched behind them. As the Henrician navy's duties consisted largely of skirmishing and providing an escort service for troops and merchants, the defence works on England's southern coastline created strong points that provided shore fire in support of naval vessels.[65]

The French campaign of 1544: Henrician strategy and royal finance

The 1544 French campaign was the 1513 expedition writ large, its strengths and failures identical. Intelligence-gathering proved reliable, even though the army was operating on foreign soil. English ordnance performed well, and the skirmishing around Boulogne demonstrated tactical skill.[66] Henry's 1544 expedition signified the final chivalric enterprise against France and ushered in the new era of English warfare. It constituted 'the last hurrah for the royal affinity in war and encouraged a new phenomenon: armies composed of levies and officered by gentlemen whose patronage ties created military clienteles'.[67] The King got his last chance to prove that English warfare rested on the decisiveness of battle. Most striking was the unashamedly offensive character of the Henrician continental grand strategy. If Henry's long-range objectives were not always clear, his tactics were to give battle at all costs.

> Battle was the greatest test of honour. The dominance of pitched battles in European warfare between 1450 and 1530 sprang largely from dominance of chivalric aspirations in the military mind. This could give English strategy an appearance of aimlessness, as armies roamed across France offering battle.[68]

Strategic goals could be achieved through manoeuvre and attrition. In spite of the perilous state of the realm, particularly after the Reformation, Henry VIII envisioned massive continental interventions in the 1540s, even fighting on two fronts. The King knew war well by this time. During the previous year Sir Henry Wallop's contingent of 5,000 men had fought alongside the imperial army, with reports posted regularly to the King. Further, Henry had his personal experiences of 1513 to draw upon. So the allied army that intended to take Paris in late summer and autumn 1544 should have been organised and supplied with great thoroughness, and on the English side it most certainly was. The logistical ingenuity and skill that had upon occasion characterised earlier Henrician forays into France were exhibited again. It was recommended, for example, that the requisite 1,200 carriages be imported from England rather than hired out in Flanders.[69] Mobile brewing and baking companies marched with the army, stocked with foodstuffs obtained through private contractors, household victuallers, and the shires.[70] The Duke of Norfolk, who commanded the vanguard, attended the smallest details, such as ensuring that the hoys' beams below deck were sufficient to accommodate horses safely. The Crown paid coat and conduct money. Although the invasion force would pass through rich areas of France, no chances were to be taken regarding victuals. Royal purveyors were to supply the army with sufficient provision to get the entire army from Calais to the Somme, with an additional ten days' food for operations after they had reached that point. The shires did carry much of the burden, however. Horses, carriages, and carters were assessed upon the counties. For example, Buckinghamshire provided 43 carriages (with 2 carters and 7 horses per carriage), Cambridgeshire 26, Bedfordshire 29, etc. The shires contributed 1,974 horses, 282 carriages, and 564 carters. Country gentlemen sponsored cavalry and infantry for a projected total of 3,684 horsemen and 31,955 foot soldiers.

While the mechanism for financing and supplying expeditionary forces was being perfected, still the Henrician strategy that those logistical advances fulfilled remained suspect. Thomas Cromwell hit on the essential flaw in Henrician continental campaigns: poor strategic thinking. Cromwell had warned against logistical vulnerability even should the English achieve their objective and occupy Paris or a portion of northwestern France.[71] Apart from the fact that the financial and logistical achievements were, ironically, undermined by poor diplomacy, some counselled against military escalation for fear of financial exhaustion. 'Henry's VIII's 1544 invasion of France was estimated at £250,000 and turned out to be nearer £650,000.' The King debased the coinage, sought benevolences, borrowed from the Mint, solicited loans from foreigners, and 'became indebted to foreign bankers, including the Fuggers, to the tune of 3 million pounds'.[72] As arbitrary taxation, Henry VIII's benevolences and forced loans were more oppressive and exacting than those of Charles I.[73] Treasurer Thomas Wriothesley's desperation in seeking adequate funds for the war efforts led him to the Mint, First Fruits and Tenths, the Court of Augmentations, and elsewhere, and was now 'at his wits end how to shift for the next three months'.[74]

The enterprise of Boulogne, all things considered, cost the Crown a million pounds, from the mobilisation of 1544 to the 1550 occupation. If one adds the expenses of the occupation of Calais and Guines from September 1538 to August 1552, another £370,000 should be appended. 'Sea charges' (naval costs) added £96,000 during the latter Henrician and Edwardian years. Counting in the journey to Landrécies, with its soldiers and equipment in 1544, a further charge of £36,500 can be reckoned in.

Figure 1.1 The Henrician campaigns of the 1540s, though strategically dubious, were very often triumphs of logistics. Here the English army encamps at Marquison, France, in July 1544.

Source: The Boulogne Campaign 1544: Henry VIII's encampment at Marquison, reproduced by permission of the National Army Museum, Chelsea.

Thus, *excluding* the ambitious domestic fortification programme and the expensive Scottish wars, the European adventures of the 1540s consumed a million and a half pounds. That money was not easily come by. The reserves of various receivers revealed a deficit of £116,000. Crown lands were listed (another £10,000), and money from English merchants and merchant strangers (£10,000 more apiece).[75] Henry necessarily sought news of new infusions of cash to keep his war machine operating, as when on 25 July 1544 Catherine Parr wrote that Clement Higham, 'High Treasurer of Your Graces warres', was sending £40,000 to the royal army.[76]

The army that Henry VIII sent into France in early summer 1544, including foreign auxillaries, numbered at least 38,000, perhaps as many as 50,000 men. Another 4,000 men had been placed on alert, to serve the King on one hour's notice. Further, 'generall mustars' had been ordered for all England.[77] If indeed 36,000 native English soldiers crossed the Channel in 1544, then Henry's army constituted the largest force ever to do so. Its ultimate tactical achievement, the capture of Boulogne, determined subsequent English strategy, for the expenditure of so much upon Boulogne necessitated, in the King's mind, that he retain the city, hence England's massive naval activities in 1545.[78]

The 'new' warfare which revolved around gunpowder and developed in Italy in the late 1400s and early 1500s made siegecraft emblematic of the military revolution.[79] And although the English had not picked up very quickly on the infantry weapons of the military revolution, cannon figured largely in their operations throughout the sixteenth century. When the English neglected to bring a sufficient artillery train, their operations foundered.[80] At the siege of St Dizier (August 1544) the science of reducing a stronghold was once again performed by the English with a certain confidence. Intelligence gathered from deserters indicated French victualling problems and dissension amongst the defenders. As much as the English relished an assault to display their skills, there was no need to risk life or limb against a weakening garrison. The invaders held a logistical superiority. The garrison of St Dizier slowly, but steadily, deserted. It started as a trickle,

> first a laborer or pionnier, and a daye or two after one of the soul-
> diours, and sithe that a drumslare. Their talis agree muche that in
> the towne they lacke fleche and wyne, wheate in nough they have,
> but lacke meale. . . . They are so weryed within with watche, warde,
> and contynual laboring abowte the fortifycation of the towne, that
> dyvers aventre to escape with danger of their lyfis.

The English knew the lay of the land, the condition of their enemy, and calculated how long they the besiegers could stay in the field.[81] Henry VIII was told in November 1543, perhaps with hyperbole, that the

Figure 1.2 Henry VIII's French campaigns taught the English much about contemporary siegecraft.

Source: The Boulogne Campaign 1544: Henry VIII's encampment at Marquison, reproduced by permission of the National Army Museum, Chelsea.

... light horssemen of the North were with the formost and best
skyrmysshers ... puttyng theym in ordre of skrmysche, after the
maner used uppon your Majesties Border toward Scotland, the
which was well praised by the light horssemen Imperiales that
where there. In the which skyrmysches were slayne dyverse, and
taken about fortie, of the Frenche part. . . .[82]

Weakness in several arms persisted: the heavy cavalry, pikemen, and harquebusiers.[83] As in 1513, deficiencies were made up by the recruitment of
foreigners, including the Irish.[84]

In the evolution of a distinctively English form of warfare, continental
influences upon military architecture had to be adapted to English geography and building practices. Continental field operations also promoted
the usage of some kinds of weapons over others, as well as the integration of cavalry with infantry in battle. Another manifestation of continental
warfare in English military practices was the presence of the foreign mercenary, or auxiliary, on English soil. As English warfare developed through
the 1500s, continental influences waned in favour of a more peculiarly
English approach to waging war. Contemporary English military theorists
clashed over this trend. These international exchanges where foreign military engineers and European soldiers served England benefited the English
in the long run, as it gave them personal association with practitioners of
the continental military art, especially when those troops had fought in
the more progressive Italian theatre of operations. The integration of foreign
mercenaries into English armies would reach its peak under Edward VI,
and the accounts of the rebellion of 1549 would draw particular attention
to the presence of these strangely clad and accoutred interlopers.[85]

The employment of auxiliaries and mercenaries was necessitated by the
strategy of military intervention on the Continent. Exchanges of troops,
and the financing of multinational forces, demanded the recruitment of
foreign soldiers. In some ways, auxiliaries were part of international diplomacy. Henry VIII and the Holy Roman Emperor hammered out complex
collaborative ventures that involved troop transferrals. Henry provided the
Emperor with '20 thousande crownes; so as thEmperour ... wold sende
to serve His Majestie in the North partes agaynst Scotland [a] thousande
Spanyardes harquebusiers.'[86]

Possessing a sufficient army, with an imposing artillery train, Henry did
win a prize in Boulogne. Ironically, these efforts were wasted by poor
strategy and diplomatic blunders. In spite of its occupation, Boulogne[87]
was ultimately given up to the French. English units were drawn into
Flemish adventures because Boulogne kept English interests alive in that
part of the world. The worsening relationship with France broke into war
in April 1549, which led to the loss of Boulogne and English participation in the siege and battle of St Quentin (1557). After the raising of

Charles V's year-long siege of Metz, English bands were dispersed into Picardy and not long after found themselves fighting in engagements between imperial forces and the Duke of Vendôme's Frenchmen. The English drew first blood:

> the English bande provoked the skirmishe, and so the bloodie broile began hotter and hotter . . . and came to hande strokes, where many a Launce was broken, and many a man laie grovelyng on the ground, some under their horses, and some strike from their horses backes, suche was the terrour of the tyme, and the furie of the fight.[88]

These 'hot skirmishes, and good leaping of dikes' educated the 'sundrie English bands' in the contemporary art of war and ensured that a cadre of English warriors brought first-hand experience of mid-sixteenth century continental warfare to the courts of Mary I and Elizabeth I.[89]

The post-Henrician military dilemma

The military experiences of 1557–9 underscored the immense cost of continental land war. If any had forgotten the expeditions of the 1540s, the latest French wars served as a painful reminder. The forced loan of summer 1557 amounted to £109,000, in comparison with £112,000 (1542) and £120,000 (1545). The two parliaments that convened in 1558 struggled mightily with military taxation and defence. Ultimately the Crown got £168,000, a subsidy of four shillings on the pound on land and 2s. 8d. for goods, bringing in an initial £140,000, a fifteenth and tenth later rounding out the sum. Human costs forced a reconsideration of the forms of recruitment and organisation of the militia. The confluence of high mortality rates with the ambiguity of the military obligation made impressment difficult and maintenance of the militia problematic. Both kinds of soldiers (conscripts and militiamen) struggled to find adequate weapons.[90]

The apparent need for reform of the military 'system', so that the English might compete with continental foes, prompted far-sighted remedies such as statutory legislation reorganising the militia.[91] There occurred the predictable knee-jerk reactions to the Calais débâcle: a bellicose naval policy, the reinforcement of Berwick (as a 'northern Calais'), stockpiling of imported arms, and negotiations with mercenaries.[92] An English monarch wedded to Philip II, a ruler who full well appreciated the Braudellian problems of distance and logistics, realised the inseparability of naval power and land warfare. Thus Mary initiated the flurry of dockyard activity that occurred around the time of the loss of Calais.[93] Against this backdrop of fruitless continental warfare, the accession of Elizabeth signified a fresh start. Gloriana and her courtiers were only too eager to engage in reform that prompted the Canon of Windsor to proclaim, 'Elizabeth arms England, which Mary had left defenceless'.[94] The Elizabethan 'trained bands' that would evolve from the early Tudor militia would be a defence force based largely upon coastal communities; 'the twelve seaboard countries from Yorkshire round to Gloucestershire were assessed for two-thirds of the nation's trained foot and for over one-half of its horse'.[95] Until a Protestant party ruled Scotland, however, a 'southward-looking' defensive system remained vulnerable.

The sense that Scottish matters might indeed be of greater import than the Continent began to divert the royal eyes northward. This realisation underscored the observations of Thomas Cromwell who had counselled, 'who that intendeth France to win, with Scotland let him begin'.[96] The 'British problem' could not be ignored. Significantly, the French wars coincided with Scottish conflicts, in 1513, in the early 1520s, and in 1542–4. The Henrician art of war invariably entailed fighting on two fronts, if not always simultaneously, at least close enough for logistical arrangements to overlap. This might somewhat account for the Henrician predilection for contracting out of the household and into the private sector, thus decentralising supply. The utility of the Treasurer of the Chamber in financing military endeavours, which Sir John Heron accomplished under Wolsey, gave Henry close rein over war-related expenditure, and flexibility as well as thoroughness.[97] Logistics, especially victualling, were not only paramount in land–sea operations against France. Provisioning was even more critical in Scotland, where no continental allies existed to share the burden of supplying carts, horses, and food. Ireland would emerge as an increasingly important theatre for English strategy, and logistics would prove to be the key to mastering Ireland.

2

THE EARLY TUDOR
ART OF WAR IN THE
BRITISH ISLES

Henrician warfare and the Scots

Scotland had proved England's greatest military challenge, and the late fifteenth century had seen numerous Border confrontations, such as Edward IV of Scotland's sabre rattlings in 1481–2. Yet another Scottish monarch, James IV in 1496 and 1497, threatened England, forcing Henry VII to send 8,000–9,000 soldiers across the Tweed in July 1497. So Henry VIII should have realised the strategic importance of Scotland. The folly of pressing ancient claims to French territory nearly became tragedy in 1513. No firmer indictment of Henry's strategic blundering exists than the decision to embark on a chivalric tour of France while James IV of Scotland was forging a weighty instrument with which he would hammer the North of England. In Sir Charles Oman's words, 'the army collected outside Edinburgh on August 13 was the largest that Scotland ever put in the field'.[1] Henry VIII knew of the Scottish preparations yet launched the French expedition anyway, leaving England without the presence of a King and his best soldiers, save for one.[2] The Earl of Surrey, a grizzled septuagenarian, now got his opportunity and made his contribution to the legend of English tactical invincibility.

Flodden Field, like Dunbar 140 years later, was a battle Scotland should have won.[3] Having taken Norham Castle (bypassing Berwick, as would Leslie *en route* to Newburn in 1640), James IV dug in upon Flodden Edge, southeast of Coldstream, pitched tents, and waited for the English. Although some Scots had toted their plunder back home, James should have had 40,000 men at his disposal, though by this juncture his forces probably numbered about 30,000. Surrey, riding north and gathering up levies from the northern and midland counties, effected a rendezvous with 1,000 of the Lord Admiral's men, via an amphibious landing similar to the Marquis of Hamilton's action in 1639. Now, with perhaps 15,000 men (the English figures are ambiguous), Surrey approached the Scottish bivouac from the east. With extraordinary daring the Earl pushed northwards, divided his outnumbered and famished troops and crossed the River Till, now manoeuvring southeast, placing the English armies below the Tweed and to the north of the elevated Scottish camp. In response, James IV, possessing excellent artillery and pikemen, and with the English outnumbered and on perilous ground, won the first action by smashing Surrey's flank.[4] A Scottish victory seemed imminent. At this critical moment, those wavering English troops, with the Scots attacking them, the Tweed at their rear, commanded by an (apparently) reckless old noble, their King oblivious to their plight while indulging in a narcissistic romp across the Channel, managed to reverse the fortune of battle. They stood ground against the furious assault led in person by the Scottish King. In the early 1500s pikes were clearly superior to bills. But pikemen often got only one chance. If they did not splinter their opponents' formation, the *landesknechts* were compelled to fight at close quarters, their momentum lost. By withstanding the first collision, the English decided the issue by mêlée.

The superiority of the Scottish artillery, too, was cast aside, for, by attacking downhill, its advantage was minimised and wasted, just as the strength of the Scottish formations and terrain was lost in the impulsive charge downhill. The English archers, like the billmen, found their somewhat antiquated weapons useful, as they severely harassed the Highlander light infantry that succoured the Scottish King. James IV was lost, along with most of his nobles. The English suffered fewer than 1,000 casualties, in spite of savage hand-to-hand fighting. The Scots left 5,000 or more upon the field.[5] In analysing Flodden one observes the speed and efficiency of Surrey's mobilisation, and the logistical success of herding scattered forces to the Borders (though, on the eve of battle, the English troops must surely have craved food and drink). Further, the tried weapons of bill and bow proved, almost amazingly, effective. And the tactical brilliance of Surrey was matched by the tenacity of his fighting men. Wisely, the Earl did not resort to innovations that his weary and probably inexpert army would have found difficult. He relied on 'traditional' English warfare, whereas the Scottish King had attempted to fight in the German style.[6]

The safest way to deal with the Scottish strategic challenge was to ensure that a force like that of James IV never again crossed the Borders. The Scottish threat needed to be neutralised: options included invasion by a substantial English army or occupation by garrisons. In the 1520s Henry's policy towards Scotland responded to his designs against France. And the logistical complexity of sending large numbers of infantry against Scotland, through northern England, could not be overcome if France were considered the primary theatre of operations and Scotland a secondary one. Nevertheless, Henrician strategy led to fighting on two fronts simultaneously, in 1523, as had been the case in 1513. Raiding escalated to siege warfare when the Earl of Surrey (inspired perhaps by the comparatively mobile artillery trains used in continental warfare) set about reducing Scottish strongholds on the Borders. Even without the *trace italianne*, Scottish fortifications, most utilising extensive

Figure 2.1 Despite the Scots' artillery and emulation of the Swiss–German style of
warfare, English tactical ingenuity and tenacity won the Battle of Flodden,
9 September 1513.

Source: The Battle of Flodden, 9 September 1513, as depicted in a Burgkmair woodcut.
Reproduced by permission of the Hargrett Library, The University of Georgia.

earthworks, held up well. Gervase Phillips judges the English experiment
with ordnance on the Borders largely a failure: 'The heavier guns required
to batter thick walled fortresses into submission were too cumbersome for
Border warfare, whilst the lighter, more mobile, pieces lacked the necessary
punch to end sieges unaided by more traditional means of assault.'[7] Objectives
were taken, however, for example Jedburgh. But selective devastation did not

Britain, 1511-1642

INSET 1

Firth of Forth
Inchcolm
Aberlady
Tantallon Castle | **Hailes Castle**
Dunbar
Leith (1560)
Edinburgh
Haddington
Lintonbridge
Prestonpans
Coldingham
Pinkie (1547)
Musselburgh
Duns

Legend
✕ Siege/Battle/Skirmish
⊠ Castle
■ Town

Broughty Castle

SCOTLAND
Drumlanrig (1548)
Solway Moss (1542)
Naworth Castle
Morpeth
Newcastle-upon-Tyne
Newburn (1640)
Carlisle
Tynemouth Castle
Durham
Appleby
Bowes Castle
Hartlepool
Kendal
Piercebridge
Barnard Castle
Northallerton
Gilling East
Richmond Castle
York
Kingston-upon-Hull

North Channel
North Sea
Irish Sea

IRELAND
Dublin
Holyhead
Manchester
Selby-upon-Ouse
Doncaster
Chesterfield
Chester
Newark
Nantwich
Boston
Melton Mowbray
Grantham
Craig
King's Lynn
Norwich
Wisbech
Ludlow Castle
Lichfield
Great Yarmouth
Bosworth Field (1485)
Leicester
Bury St. Edmunds
Bardwell
Coventry
Daventry
Harwich
Landguard Fort
Edgehill (1642)
Towcester
Colchester
Witham
Woolwich
Powick Bridge (1642)
Oxford
St. Albans
Hounslow
Brentwood
Tilbury
Gravesend
Maidenhead
LONDON
Medway
Canterbury
Reading
THAMES
Rochester
Margate
Newbury
Strood
Sandwich
Marlborough
Chatham
Dover
Chippenham
Marshfield
Rye
Deal Castle
Barnstaple
Portsmouth

Fishguard
St. George's Channel
WALES
Bristol
Melcombe Regis
Yarmouth Castle
Sandgate Castle
Milford Haven
Padstow
Pendennis Castle
Plymouth
Totnes
Weymouth
Portland Castle
Hurst Castle
Truro
St. Mawes Castle
Dartmouth Castle
Falmouth

Miles
0   50   100

INSET 2

R. Severn
Warminster
Duns
Paxton
The Birks
Berwick-upon-Tweed
Wark Castle
Goswick
Bridgwater
Marshalls Elm (1642)
Coldstream
Norham Castle
Holy Island
FISHERTON ANGER
KING'S MOOR (Kingsmore)
Kelso (1639)
Branxton
Flodden (1513)
Tintinhull
Abbas Combe
Branxton Hill
Flodden Hill
Montacute
Babylon Hill (1642)
Ancrum Moor (1545)
Haddon Rigg (1542)
Jedburgh
INSET 3
Alnwick Castle

Crossed swords denote a military engagement.
These include select battles, skirmishes,
and sieges, and are dated.

C. McOmber, Cartographer

Figure 2.2 Britain, 1511–1642.
Source: Connie McOmber and the author.

guarantee strategic security. In the autumn of 1523, James IV riposted by besieging Wark Castle. But neither could the Franco-Scottish force secure the Marches, and the siege was raised.[8] The pattern of Border warfare during Henry VIII's reign, then, was raiding on a grander scale, including the deployment of cannon and, ultimately, improved fortifications.

A proposal put forth in the early 1540s recommended that Henry 'inlarge his frontyers' to the Firth of Forth and build fortresses, in effect creating an occupation zone from which to launch a future war of conquest. Deployment of an army of 18,000 foot and 6,000 horse would suffice. The whole enterprise including garrisons, border light horse regiments, bakehouses, etc., would cost £99,568.[9] There was no shortage of those eager to absorb Scotland. Surveys and reconnoitrings were presented to the King, assessing the strength of castles, and distances between towns, and laying out routes for the English army.[10]

In summer 1542 Henry VIII sought the decisive blow that would conquer Scotland or at least reduce the Lowlands and neutralise the strategic threat posed by a francophile and Roman Catholic Scotland, but got instead a clumsy incursion by Sir Robert Bowes on 24 August. Several hundred English, including Bowes, were captured, along with documents allegedly disclosing Henry's design. Without hesitation the King accelerated the mobilisation, hurling against James V an army that drew soldiers from as far south as Suffolk. Throughout September the Duke of Norfolk grappled with the great bane of Scottish campaigns: logistics. Victualling proved a nightmare and transportation of men and equipment a daunting task.[11] Through Sir Ralph Sadler, Henry's Treasurer-at-War, sufficient conduct money reached the regional commanders (although at least one, Lord Maxwell, had to borrow £100). Beef and mutton from Norfolk and Oxfordshire, and Berkshire corn, as well as Essex butter and cheese, found their way north.[12]

In November 1542 a Scottish army estimated at 10,000–12,000 marauded the Borders, often plundering their own countryside because of the 'great scarctie of victualle, and such hunger among them by reason of the great wast[e] don[e] by' the English. Consequently, the poorer infantry deserted: 'the Comons of Scotland beying retyrned to ther houses and ther tents taken uppe. The Lords and gentlemen remain together entending as it is thought to make some invasion in Ingland.'[13] The same problem afflicted the English. Norfolk told the King that

> . . . your maistie doth mervaille we wold so soudainly Dissolve tharmy without knoweing your pleasure first therein. Thonly cause therof was for lack of victailles as we have before written . . . in case we had had plentie of victailles to have kept tharmy togethers . . . and penetrated further into the realme of Scotland.[14]

The Scots, Norfolk contended, could do little without further provision, for the 'skarsitie of vitayle' had immobilised them.[15] The Warden of the West March, Sir Thomas Wharton, was not so easily lulled into a sense of security. James V now turned to his nobility and mobilised 18,000 soldiers and an artillery train. Their incursion towards Carlisle was met by Wharton's 3,000-man force and hastily summoned groups of cavalry. The English had won at Flodden by virtue of tactical ingenuity, and such would again be the case at Solway Moss (24 November 1542). As the invading army advanced upon marshy ground, skirting the bogs of the River Esk, Sir William Musgrave struck the Scottish flanks with 700 cavalry. Surprised and unsteady, the Scots infantry veered towards the river. As at Flodden, the Scottish ordnance was rendered useless, and disordered infantrymen scattered quickly.[16]

While victory in 1513 and 1542 had been the result of superior tactics, still the English were troubled (as Norfolk's letter to Henry attests) with the logistical challenge of gaining ascendancy on the Borders. The outfitting of war involved considerable behind-the-scenes organisation. Apparently, the Crown (not the shires) absorbed the cost of coating.[17] The Crown assumed 'provision of Cootes,' as well as substantial sums for victualling. In the 1542 campaign against Scotland, Henry's government fed the entire retinue, from the Earl of Southampton to the humblest baker, including 3,345 horsemen and 14,407 infantrymen. In addition to providing coats and wages for soldiers, the Crown even paid the nobles conduct money 'from diverse places of this realme into yorke by Sundrye distaunce of miles.' By warrants from the Lord Lieutenant, captains received 4d. per mile, and, though their inferiors received less, the total cost to the central government was more than £3,000. Over £6,000 was disbursed to get the officers and troops home after the dissolution of the army. The aggregate cost of diet, wages, coats, and conduct amounted to over £25,000. Sir John Harrington and his entourage of clerks and carters transported the King's 'treasure', protected by a military escort of two dozen white-liveried soldiers. They relayed the army's money to where coin was most needed and kept track of the various revenue sources from which they collected funds.[18]

Although we find episodes, such as that when Wriothesley ordered 4,300 coats, there is evidence that the localities sometimes uniformed their men, perhaps with reimbursement. When the Duke of Norfolk assembled his vanguard in that shire,

> ev'y souldier [was] to have a cote of blew clothe garded with redde, after suche ffacon as all ffotemen be made at London that shal s've the Kinges Maiestie in this jorney. . . . Ev'y man to p'vyde a payer of hose for ev'y of his men, the right hose to be all redde and the left hose to be all blewe. . . .'[19]

The assumption of the costs of war hinged upon whether the action was deemed offensive, or defensive. The Borderers still owed service, including the supply of victuals, when in a defensive posture – as, for example, in the aftermath of Solway Moss. The report of the 'gathering up gret powers within the Realme of Scotlande' obliged the communities at their own expense to see that 'all Men betwen Sextie and sexteyn shuld with fyve dayes victuall be redy to folowe the King uppon one houres warnyng' when signalled by 'Beakin' from a nearby crag.[20]

The 'rough wooing' in 1544 and after aimed at battering Scotland into surrendering the infant Queen Mary Stuart. In the spring, the Earl of Hertford (the Prince of Wales' uncle, Edward Seymour, who would master-mind only three years later England's most successful invasion of Scotland) descended upon Scotland by sea, landing his army in less than three hours at Grantham Crag, west of Leith. Their objective was Leith haven, where they might disembark 'Suche hoyes and crayers as weare laden with our greate peaces of artillery'. Hoping for some advantage of surprise, the English hurried towards Leith, pulling along their light cannon 'by force and strength of men'. Within a mile of the beach they encountered 5,000–6,000 Scots, in formation with ordnance positioned. In retrospect, the defenders should have repulsed the English at their initial landing, when the invaders were most vulnerable. Without hesitation the English engaged, both sides fir-ing cannon as they pressed towards each other. The English 'forward' section of the traditional tripartite battle order sought out the largest body of Scots, deployed along a brook near the Edinburgh road. Hertford later described the action for the King:

> We approached them so fast, and pressed them with our shot, as well of the hackbutiers as [of the] archers, that we beat them from the said brook and having put them to flight, and scared them from their ordnance turned towards the other passage besides Legh [Leith] because the Scots shot their ordnance from thence very hotly upon your men. And yet, when the said Scots perceived the forward turn towards them [no sooner did they see that], than they all left that passage with their ordnance; and the hackbutiers, being in hot chase of the Scots, which fled from the further passage towards Edinburgh, had no regard to the forward when the same turned to the other passage towards Legh as aforesaid, but followed the first chase; whereupon, the battle being at hand, [we] made towards the said hackbutiers, and sent out a good number of archers to back them, and retired the said hackbutiers without losing of any man, and brought away the Scot's ordnance.

Those 'hackbutiers' were probably Spaniards, commanded by Pedro Michaelea, and Hertford told the King those infantry had done 'right honest service'.[21] Although the strategic and tactical operations went well, the weaponry of the English was the usual motley assortment of infantry: 'hackbutiers' and archers, along with the odd pole weapons.

In spite of fairly good defensive preparations, the inhabitants of Leith fled rather than face bombardment, and the city was taken, enabling the English to unload their victuals and heavier guns. By 18 March 1544 Hertford's army had returned to Berwick, having devastated the Lowlands. Entire towns and villages, sometimes including their civilian populations, had been burned. Holyrood was destroyed, and Jedburgh sacked.[22] Victualling proved decisive in this case, and with the English advantage in logistics they ravaged the southern Lowlands.[23] A further 'triumph' was the Henrician government's ability to keep its soldiers in pay; which made possible the disciplined deployment of the army. The Earl informed the Council regarding the

> grete lacke we have of Money; we have not so moche left at this present as woll furnishe the Payment of the Monethes Wages now expired of the Capteynes, Souldors, and Maryners . . . which now uppon theyr Arryvall here do loke for Money both for their said Wages, from the 21st Day of Marche . . . not doubting but your Lordshippes doth remember that for the Furnyture of this Enterprise appoynted thirty thousand Pounds . . . by Reason of the long tarrying of the Shippes for lack of Wynde, the Armye hath unfrutefully consumed her one Monethes Wages; which, if the Shippes had come in Tyme, had advanced a grete pece of this Enterprise, so that we shulde haue had no suche lack as we have at this present . . . put to your helping Hands for the Supplie of this lack of Money; for if, at the Retourne of the Armye out of Scotland, we have not Money to paye them such Sommes as shall be then due to them for their Wages, with also Conduct Money to depech [despatch] them hom withall and for Tonage of the Shippes, the longer we kepe them togither, the more Charge it shalbe to the King's Majestie. And also what Money Mr. Uvedale hath for the Payment of the Garrison we did lately advertise your Lordships, which also must neds be supplied in Tyme. . . . Fynally, we have sent one with Money to Chester for the Conduction hither of the four hundred Kerne. . . .[24]

Hertford's bidding was obeyed. It is a measure of England's ability to wage war in the 1540s that Hertford's request was granted in spite of the costly mobilisation for the French expedition, under way as well during that spring of 1544. The accounts show prompt and efficient payment of wages, including conduct money. As they straggled into Newcastle after a successful raid on the Lowlands, the soldiers were paid by company up to their last day of service and discharged almost immediately. The Earl issued a certificate, signed by the company commander, verifying disbursement, and then sent the captain off to Sir Ralph Sadler for the men's final payment.[25] England, then, was mastering the logistics of fighting a Scottish war, but still the strategy of the *chevauchée*, where Scotland was brutalised into submission, remained unsound, for it merely invited a Celtic reprisal when the English army withdrew.[26]

Scotland obtained revenge at Ancrum Moor on 27 February 1545. Tactical brilliance and lessons gleaned from Bannockburn (the schiltron[27]) and Agincourt (cavalry traps[28]) combined to rout the English. Feigning a cavalry retreat along a Roman road bordered by marsh, the Scots lured the invaders into an impulsive rush down the avenue, whereupon the horses stumbled into pits and were then surprised by an infantry 'hedgehog'.[29] As had happened to the French infantry at Agincourt, the foot soldiers could neither form up nor avoid their own retreating horsemen and the enemy. As at Flodden and Solway Moss, superior numbers did not bring victory, though it was the turn of the Scots to savour it.[30] Emboldened by their triumph at Ancrum Moor, the Scots joined with the French to mobilise an army that would invade England.

Edwardian actions against Scotland in 1547

It is tempting to ascribe the impressive military efforts of the Henrician period to the King himself. Henry's resolve provided leadership that meshed with increased expenditure. But the Scottish campaigns of Edward VI demonstrated that a system of organisation and recruitment outlived Bluff King Hal. Lord Protector Somerset's campaign of 1547 benefited from the experiences of the 1544 Scottish adventure and showed how a successful Scottish war (a) coordinated land forces with a naval presence in the Firth of Forth; (b) took full advantage of artillery, both field guns and ship-borne cannon; and (c) supplied adequate victual by inducing soldiers to carry their own provisions for several days' campaigning (while ample reserves remained safely on board ship in the Firth). The 1547 campaign proved English proficiency at mastering logistics and assembling a balanced expeditionary force inclusive of substantial horse as well as foot.

Also perfected was the Henrician practice of seasoning the English ranks with foreign mercenaries, predominantly from Habsburg dominions. Although auxiliaries could still be recruited through international exchange, sometimes their recruitment followed the procedure perfected in Italy. A captain engaged his band for a given campaign, for which they received a fair monthly salary (as opposed to the daily pittance paid to English conscripts). Hertford had not hesitated to salute foreign troops. Twice he lauded his Spanish harquebusiers in Scotland – in 1544 and 1545.[31] In the latter campaigning Spanish troops fought alongside large contingents of 'Almaignes'

Figure 2.3 As Earl of Hertford in 1544, Seymour excelled in fighting Scottish wars. His 1547 combined operations against Scotland proved the efficacy of English warfare.

Source: Sir Edward Seymour, later Viscount Beauchamp, first Earl of Hertford, first Duke of Somerset, and Lord Protector (author's collection).

and two smaller bands of Italians under Morgan Mansron and Captain Muskovito. Later, in 1549 Peter Sanga led his Albanian light horse against the western rebels, while Captain Spinola and Jacques Germyn commanded Italians.[32] Kett's Rebellion, too, was extinguished by foreign troops – Conrad Pennick's *landesknechts* and the Spanish light cavalry under Carlos de Guavarra and Pedro de Gamboa.[33] However, not all were convinced by the evident successes of continental arms wielded by foreign professionals. Sir John Smythe, the xenophobic advocate of archery, claimed that

> The archers of the rebels did so behave themselves with their volleys of arrows against divers old bands harquebusiers Italians and Spaniards that they drave them from all their strengths, as from banks, ditches, hedges, and other advantages of ground, to the great mischief of many of those strangers. And of these great effects of archers against harquebusiers I have heard the Lord of Hunsdon aforesaid (who was there an eyewitness) very notably report. Besides that, many years past I have heard Captain Spinola, an Italian, who was a very brave soldier and wounded with arrows in those services and actions, give singular commendation of the archery of England.[34]

Smythe cannot have been pleased that no fewer than ten foreign mercenaries had been knighted, and so made his social equals, between 1546 and 1550.[35] Continental influences upon English warfare were not only felt, but applauded, Smythe notwithstanding.

Somerset assembled borderers, shire levies from the Midlands and south, mounted continental mercenaries, and sizeable contingents of aristocratic horse under Grey and Warwick. The force amounted to around 16,000–18,000 soldiers.[36] Having learned the paramount importance of victualling from the lean and stillborn 1542 sojourn, Somerset's common soldiers carried their obligatory four days' provisions. Upon exhaustion of that food, and then and only then, would the army partake of the victuals laden on the carts and wagons. Two days before the march, the Admiral, Lord Clynton set sail carrying munitions and more foodstuffs. He was to rendezvous with the land forces along the Firth, supplying them as necessary. Somerset set forth on 4 September 1547, moving northwest, then east, in a route paralleling today's railway line between Berwick and Edinburgh.[37] Although tarrying to secure Dunglass and Innerwick, the force kept pace with the fleet, occasionally catching sight of English sail, and maintaining regular communications with the Admiral via coastal dispatches.

The first action of the campaign occurred when the Earl of Warwick's horsemen skirmished with several hundred Scots near Hailes Castle, from which the inhabitants harassed the marching English with a cannonade. In spite of harrying tactics by the Scottish cavalry, the column reached the River Esk, and the English commanders set about reconnoitring the Scottish positions and the surrounding terrain, sending forth the thousand or so light horsemen brought along for this purpose. In the process, a brisk equestrian contest occurred on 9 September. Sir Ralph Bonner and some gentlemen volunteers, supported by 300 light horse, tested the Scottish defences. In the resultant skirmish, the English slew or captured several hundred Scots, though Bonner and some of his party were captured during the six-hour struggle.[38] English tactics, outflanking both ends of the Scottish cavalry line, proved decisive.

The Scots sat in a highly defensible position, blocking the road to Edinburgh, with the Firth covering their left flank, and a marsh their right. Dug in upon high ground, Scottish artillery had the advantage.[39] In 1544 the Scots had eschewed battle, ultimately seeking refuge in Edinburgh Castle while the English had plundered at will. In 1547 the Scots, like the English, learnt from their mistakes. Though the 1544 campaign had to a certain extent been a failure, as the English had not succeeded in seizing Edinburgh castle, and so had failed to establish hence any long-term presence in the Firth, nevertheless great damage was inflicted, including the burning of Holyrood. This time the Scots were determined to meet the enemy. Somerset predicated his strategy upon the Scots entrenching and waging a defensive struggle. He could not have been more surprised when the Scots advanced from their works on Edmonston's Edge on the morning of 10 September.

The Scottish commander Arran had mistaken movement in the English camp for a general retreat, when in fact the English were mustering to assume an advance position upon the hill of Inveresk church, overlooking the River Esk and the Scottish emplacements beyond. Perhaps Arran sought to deny the English this defensive posture, and so leapt into action: '. . . the Scots preventyd us of the sayd church, merchynge the hyghe way toward us in battayle raye, devyded in 3 great wards. . . .'[40] It was Arran's crucial error, for, like James IV at Flodden, the Scots at Pinkie Cleugh abandoned the higher ground in the hope of exploiting the enemy's apparent withdrawal with a sudden attack. Descending into the low ground surrounding the river, they exposed themselves to fire from English inshore vessels, whose barrages made possible the ultimate flanking of the Scottish infantry.

> The Scots thowght to have passed us to an hyll . . . on our left hande, which of we preventyd them, so they havyng the fote of the hyll and we the tope, ordynaunce shotyinge continually on bothe syds of the lord Gray Wilton with his men of armes and dimilancis, and Sir Nicolas Strange with his hargabussiers on horsbake entryed valiantly with their vayword which wer all pyke men.[41]

In the collision the demi-lances broke many of their lances and the mounted harquebusiers unleashed their fire. The Scottish schiltron still held firm, and the configuration compacted. Still pressing forward 'very stoutly', the Scots moved towards the Lord Protector's position, while the English light horse (demi-lances and harquebusiers) regrouped.

Advancing within 'an arrow shot' of Somerset, the Scots perceived that the English position betrayed no weakness, and they hesitated. The Scots' formations now stationary, the English guns above played upon them with devastating effect. A combined missile attack of artillery, harquebuses and arrows thinned the Scottish ranks, and they wavered, especially the Earl of Argyll's Irish (who could 'abyde no goneshot'). The tactical mistake in itself would not have doomed the Scots had not the English forces been balanced, well supplied, of high morale, and in combined operation with their fleet. When a salvo from the latter routed the Highland bowmen assigned to protect the northern flank of the Scottish army, the Earl of Huntly's troops were pushed inland, thrusting them against the main body spearheading the advance. Consequently, the Scots were comparatively densely arrayed as they trudged up the incline on the eastern bank of the Esk, at the top of which the English hurriedly assembled for the unanticipated frontal assault. Had Arran's forces continued moving headlong into the still unsettled English battle lines, they might have rectified their commander's initial miscalculation. But the slowness of the Scottish ordnance (the few they had, drawn, as Patten says, by men not steeds), and the slope, slowed their march enough to allow Somerset to complete the flanking manoeuvre. Somerset's investment in mercenary cavalry and his recruitment of noble horsemen proved wise, for a series of charges (which must have appeared as folly to the Scots) further impeded the advance. Simultaneously, English cannon positioned themselves to tear at the Scottish flanks, exposing the Scots to the flotilla's bombardment and the volleys of the field ordnance, supplemented by firearms and bows. The withering effect of the fire forced a retreat that precipitated a rout.[42]

The decisive factors in the outcome of Pinkie Cleugh were the English artillery, the wise choice of ground in the initial stages of the fight by the English tacticians, and the poor decision by the Scots in leaving their fortified position only to be wedged between the cannon of the fleet and ordnance planted on the southern hills. Like Newburn ninety-three years later, the movements of the cavalry and foot soldiers were dictated by pressure applied by artillery barrage. But at Newburn the Scots would place their ordnance at the best vantage points and catch the English off balance, whereas at Pinkie the English ordnance was deployed to greatest advantage and the Scots were caught moving from their encampment to a position of attack.

Pinkie Cleugh comprised 'the last full-scale battle in which a predominantly English army was involved until the Civil Wars. . . .'[43] The campaign demonstrated that an army of 16,000 could be fielded against Lowland Scotland, that victualling problems could be surmounted, that a balanced force (cavalry and infantry; shock and missile) could be mobilised with adequate leadership and resources, and that synchronisation of a fleet with an expeditionary force was feasible, weather permitting. Less apparent, but equally true, Pinkie Cleugh underscored the great paradox of waging war against Scotland. Triumph upon the field of battle did not ensure the subjugation of the Scots. Although the 1547 campaign improved greatly upon the efforts of 1542 and 1544, it still failed to achieve domination of the Scottish Lowlands. Realising this, Somerset pursued an alternative to intermittent border raids or major invasions seeking battle. Garrisons, Somerset surmised, could anchor English power in the North.

The logistical challenge: garrisons, victualling, and fortresses

From 1541 the English central government grappled with the Scottish problem. A number of solutions had been tried: the abysmal 1542 mobilisation, the plunder of the Lowlands in 1544, a savage stroke against the Borders in 1545, and finally a substantial incursion in 1547. Still Scotland stubbornly charted its independent political and dynastic course. The garrison experiment had commenced with hostilities, not as their result. The English planted garrisons in Scotland before the reign of Edward VI, but on an *ad hoc* basis. The Jedburgh and Coldingham garrisons mustered in 1542. Three years later the Privy Council embraced the general idea of the programme: 'His grace never thinketh to come to his purpose of keeping the country in subjection until he shall lay garrisons amongst them. . . .'[44] In the wake of Pinkie, garrisons studded the disputed lands of the Borders, on the coastline from Berwick to Aberlady. English control of the Firth was to be facilitated by garrisons on the islets of Inchcolm and Inchkeith, two sites that Hamilton would seize in 1639. The purpose of the garrisons was 'to offer protection to the assured Scots and to apply military repression to the remainder as an incentive to assure.' Their role was political and, as M. L. Bush shows, simply substituted for the old formula of raids and intimidation. Worse, the garrisons remained vulnerable to that greatest of problems, victualling.[45]

In spring 1548 an unknown strategist laid before Edward VI and his advisers an analysis of the comparative fiscal dimensions of invading Scotland by land and sea. He concluded that the costs were roughly equal, and emphasised the importance of seaborne logistical support for any English army operating in the Lowlands:

> provision to be in the Frythe afore Tharmy shall entre into Scotland for tharmy may not tary for the Victuall but the Victuall may tary for them . . . sende in no mayne Army farre into Scotland and to tarry there anywhere withoute Revictualing by see for greate abounance and excesse of carrage.[46]

The Scottish wars from September 1542 to the end of April 1550, including garrison accounts and victualling contracts, cost nearly a million pounds (£954,135).[47] The central government pressured the victuallers of the army to moderate their prices, and no doubt the reputation of ruthless Henrician government aided such efforts.[48] From 7 June 1557, when the

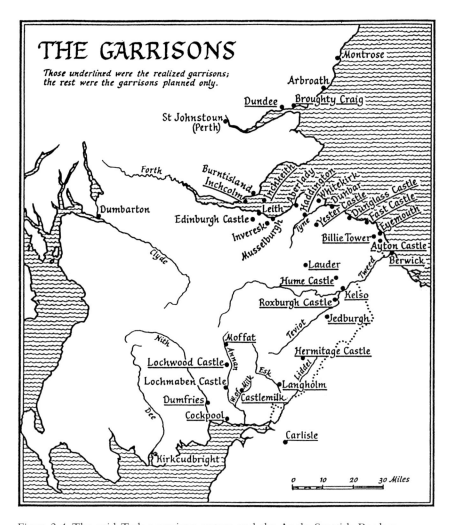

Figure 2.4 The mid-Tudor garrison system and the Anglo-Scottish Borders.

Source: English garrisons planned and established in Scotland after Somerset's 1547 conquest. Reproduced by kind permission of M. L. Bush and Arnold publishers. Reprinted from the former's *The Government Policy of Protector Somerset* (Arnold 1975).

conflict with France began, the Scottish theatre of war smouldered again, occasioning sieges at Haddington, Broughty Crag, and Aberlady, which met with mixed results because of 'lacke of succour out of Englande'. English forces fought spirited actions against the French in the Firth of Forth. While trying to intercept supplies going into Broughty Crag, the French galleys found themselves up against English seamanship and longbows. Although the French vessels (which vastly outnumbered the three English ships) managed to topple a mast or two whilst Lord Admiral the Earl of Lincoln struggled to position his minuscule fleet, the full force of English firepower ultimately devastated the galleys and forced several aground. '[W]ee were so nere them, that our bowemen shot into their gallies, and our cannons made a great murther, and havoke emong the poor slaves, whose leggs, armes, and ores I saw flie about. . . .'[49] England's essentially defensive approach to warfare used pre-emptive expeditions and naval power to neutralise foreign aggression before Albion's garrisons and fortresses were tested. The problem with the garrison strategy was that occupation of foreign territory was incongruous with the defensive *mentalité* of the English, though in Ireland an exception was made.

The strategic designation of key fortresses in England, the style in which they were constructed, and the number of soldiers who manned them, fluctuated under the Tudors and early Stuarts. Whereas the southern coastal fortifications received great attention under Henry VIII, the northern border castles became increasingly important under the latter three Tudors. With the Union of Crowns, Channel defences resumed their precedence, only to see a shift northwards again in 1638. Military architecture, too, followed an uneven evolutionary pattern. The taming of the nobility by Henry VII encompassed the sleighting of castles that might be used by upstart lords. But civil disorder in England was in no way as destructive as was warfare on the Continent. Fewer fortifications were attempted and European designs were not introduced very quickly. At the accession of Henry VIII, England possessed fortifications of the predictable medieval style. Only gradually did continental military architecture exert its influence, and ultimately it would do so within a genuinely English context.

The earlier Tudors drew selectively from the culture of Renaissance Italy. Henry VII's admiration of the court of Urbino and his recruitment of Pietro Torregiano accompanied his embracement of the new artillery warfare of the 1490s. Italian advances in geometry and engineering, reflected in the construction of Brunelleschi's dome for Santa Maria del Fiore and the art of creating gridworks that rendered accurately the topography of the Earth in the mapmaker's workshop, were part of the scientific revolution that included a military revolution as well. Fittingly, Niccolò Tartaglia presented his work on propulsion and the trajectory of falling bodies as revealed in the science of gunnery to Henry VIII via one of the latter's gentlemen, Richard Wentworth.[50] Gunpowder now determined the design and remodelling of English fortresses. Ordnance, however, lay side by side, almost literally, with the older tools of war in Henry VIII's Tower of London. The ordnance officers inventoried bows, arrows, and bowstrings as they made room for the 'howsyng for Ordynaunce'.[51] The stockpiling of royal artillery had been a priority under Henry VII, and the second Tudor simply continued the dynastic tradition.[52]

The high Cromwellian years initiated defence on a comprehensive basis. Henry VIII, conceiving himself the equal of a Roman emperor, planned on a gigantic scale: large expeditions were complemented by extensive defensive schemes. In 1539 he chose twenty-five sites in England that would be fortified against reprisal from Roman Catholic Europe.[53] In that year Henry personally spearheaded a military construction programme unprecedented since the reign of Edward I. The architectural design of the fortifications that garnished the shores were distinctly English and bore the imprimatur of the Tudors. The Englishness of the coastal defence system derived from several factors: its defensive strategic inspiration, the fact that the enormous cost could be borne by the consequences of the English Reformation, the unique design of fortresses such as at Deal and Sandgate, and the advances in English cartography and surveying.[54] Henry's coastal forts emphasised height and firepower, not tactical defensibility and siegeworthiness. They represented a transitional military architectural form bridging the crenellated medieval castle with the Italianate bastion. Its efflorescence was possible only at this time in the evolution of English warfare: just as the English Reformation necessitated the construction of defensive works on the English sea coast, so it also generated the money the Crown needed to undertake such a programme.[55] The Henrician cylindrical artillery tower stood on dismantled monasteries.

The continental bastion assumed a paradigmatic position in the late Tudor and early Stuart periods, not only because certain nations had introduced the feature with good effect, but also because 'pure defence' became an almost Platonic ideal. It was possible to apply the cerebral principles of mathematics to achieve a geometric perfection that shifted Plato's world to the grim abode of Aristotle, to an ideal (and hence impregnable) fortification that addressed the peculiarities of the individual situation.[56] By the mid-1500s England had spawned her own school of geometry through the Oxonian Leonard Digges.[57] The application of surveying and mathematical calculation to English warfare was achieved by Leonard's son, Thomas, who joined theory and practice by writing military treatises while serving as Elizabeth's Muster-Master General in the Netherlands.[58] The concentric circles of Henrician military architecture, deemed overly 'aggressive' in terms of potential firepower as opposed to the more defensive bastion, contrast with the angular and sharp features of the *trace italienne*.[59] Both embody the confident 'geometrical formalism' of the Renaissance.[60] But theory was always tempered by reality, as one can see in the building programme at Berwick-upon-Tweed that commenced in 1558 under Mary, and was inherited in due course by Elizabeth.[61]

Most often the new military architecture had to accommodate existing medieval fortifications, whose elimination or modification might expose the town and garrison to attack during construction.[62] Rarely did a military engineer have the luxury of starting from scratch, upon pristine terrain. At

Berwick the centuries-old crenellated circuit of medieval walls could not withstand the artillery that Scottish kings had collected in the early sixteenth century. The Scots' reduction of Norham Castle during the Flodden campaign underscored the vulnerability of northern defences. During 1522–3 earthworks were thrown up around Berwick.[63] Although the 1530s saw piecemeal construction, clearly a comprehensive building programme needed to be undertaken.[64] But what Berwick lacked in defence was made up for at least partially in the offensive capability of its ordnance. Although enamoured with French conquests, the young Henry VIII saw to Berwick's defences and maintained the gunners.[65] A survey of January 1539 revealed 18 bronze cannon of varying size, 22 iron cannon, and many iron handguns within Berwick's defensive works. Although the fortifications could have incorporated more ordnance, the limiting factor was the medieval design of the towers, the decrepit condition of many of which prevented the disposition of firepower.[66]

Mary Tudor deserves credit for initiating major reconstruction, and for recruiting in 1557 Sir Richard Lee, who served as the Earl of Pembroke's trenchmaster with the English army in combined operations with the Duke of Savoy's Spaniards in the Low Countries.[67] He marched in numerous Tudor campaigns, and his Scottish exploits earned him a knighthood, while his resourceful defence of Boulogne in late 1544 won him the accolades of a grateful Henry VIII. The demand upon Lee's talents meant that, from 1558 on, when he supervised the rebuilding of Berwick's fortifications, his attention was divided, as he travelled about improving England's defences in several locations. But he pressed on and in 1565 was still actively engaged at Berwick. Lee's continental experiences impressed upon him the advantages of the *trace italienne*. Bastions had been proposed for Berwick before, as in the reign of Edward VI, but no appreciable advances had been made, save for the massing of earthworks at key points. But earthworks were a good start. A further problem for Berwick (and other strategic sites) was that, although all might agree that improvements were requisite, the Tudor–early Stuart state was liable to run short of cash, so that the project was delayed, leaving the town vulnerable and ultimately increasing the cost of adequate defence. So, in 1569 construction stopped short of its goal and was not resumed with any urgency until the First Bishops' War (1639).[68] Deputy Surveyor Rowland Johnson, with the help of Sir William Drury, strove to maintain the bridges and fortifications while the building programme was 'stayed', even though they laboured under reduced salaries and with sparse work crews.[69]

After her accession, Elizabeth found the realm's fortifications had deteriorated. A survey of 1559 disclosed that the ambitious programme of twenty years earlier had stalled, leaving defensive works unfinished, with insufficient firepower and personnel. It would take decades to erect military architecture suitable to withstand the offensive capabilities developed by European powers in the 1570s and 1580s.[70] By abandoning its isolation and embarking on a strategy of continental intervention, England faced an expensive and comprehensive rebuilding of defences. With the introduction of the *trace italienne*, England also had to come to terms with recent developments in artillery. New fortifications and new guns had their impact on garrison size and the strategic potential of military installations.[71] The confluence of the rising cost of fortifications and the high prioritisation of the continental theatre meant there was less money for erecting defences on the Scottish border. As a result, *ad hoc* garrisoning had to secure the North.

> [I]t was not the failings of the [royal] surveyors, but the Crown's refusal to spend the necessary money which explains the weakness of the North. Although the equation was early appreciated that weak fortifications necessitated larger and more expensive garrisons, the money was only fitfully forthcoming. Even the most sustained intelligent attempt to make the North secure, the major Elizabethan construction at Berwick, ultimately failed in its purpose because the funds to complete it were not provided.[72]

A Tudor garrison was a self-sustained, almost 'urbanised' community capable both of defending itself and of launching substantive incursions into neighbouring territories. Often this meant establishing a townscape where geography and demography had not created one. Garrisons were more than soldiers in strongholds. They counted among their number those that brought in the victuals and operated the bakehouses and brewhouses: 'clevers of woode for the backehouse', 'syfters of meale and branne', 'turners and casters of grayne', 'kepers of bere', 'dryvers of the mylhorses', and clerks to keep track of it all. Long-term contracts with merchants were negotiated to bring wheat flour, rye flour, beans, malt, hops, bran, biscuit, loaves of bread, beer, salt, sea coals, casks, horse meat, and other provisions to the Border garrisons, often shipped in Newcastle merchantmen.[73]

The English have usually regarded peacetime soldiers as a nuisance and sometimes as a threat. Thus the immediate strength of particular garrisons reflected the international political situation. Garrisons were intended to occupy Scotland under Edward VI, but, apart from that experiment, garrisons were not expected to operate semi-autonomously. In other words, the troops garrisoned in a locality were expected to resist an invasion as best they could and alert inland counties so that an army might mobilise to meet the threat. The King and his nobles, many of the latter assuming regional commands, would converge upon the invaders and drive them back. The garrisons, then, were to inflict as many initial casualties upon the enemy as possible and engage them in operations that allowed sufficient time for mobilisation. Berwick-upon-Tweed shouldered an additional responsibility. As the 'jumping-off point' to Scotland, that garrison often served as a staging area for offensive operations. Expeditionary forces of 12,000–15,000 might billet in Berwick. In 1522, 1523, 1542, 1547, 1557, and 1560, entire English armies resided temporarily at Berwick.[74]

From 23 August 1542 to 30 August 1547, John Uvedale, the treasurer for payment of garrisons and crews on the Scottish border, recorded disbursements for the military activities of the central government. The Crown absorbed significant costs in maintaining security on the Borders. Money, allotments of £3,000 or more, was escorted to the North, and deposited at York, Durham, or Newcastle, in temporary receivership of the Archbishop of York or the Bishop of Durham. From thence the treasure was shuttled by cart and wagon to Berwick and Alnwick, where payments were made, generally to the lieutenant, including men such as the Earls of Hertford and Shrewsbury, the Dukes of Suffolk and Norfolk, and Lords Parr and Lisle. The central government paid all expenses and there were many pockets to fill: watchmen, post riders, heralds, trumpeters, gunners, mariners, pressed infantry, officers, victuallers, ironworkers, woodcutters, engineers, and Irish auxiliaries. In cases where the shires expended funds in fielding forces and providing resources, the Exchequer reimbursed them. Diet, wages, coats, and conduct were supplied by Henry VIII's administration. Border counties could ill afford to pay for their own security, but the rest of the realm, for whom the Border shires provided a buffer, paid little or nothing as well.[75]

In November 1542, Henry VIII personally directed that, of 150 gunners assigned to garrison duty on the Borders, 60 go to the East and Middle Marches. The Duke of Norfolk supervised their installation and that of the 4,000 men that 'his majesties pleashr is shold be resiaunt [resident] uppon the borders.'[76] The King envisioned the equivalent of four regiments with sufficient artillery to safeguard the North. Among those garrison troops were some if not all of 3,000 Spanish, Italian, and Albanian troops under Pedro de Gamboa, whose services had cost £21,880 for the Scottish campaign of that year.[77] The declared accounts of the garrison treasurers reveal funds coming from the Mint, First Fruits, and Tenths, various augmentation and land-revenue courts, as well as 'loans and benevolences'. Transports were fitted out at Hull and grain was imported from Yorkshire to sustain English soldiers at Berwick and Carlisle from 1542 to 1547. Clearly the maintenance of the garrisons drew money from numerous sources at a time when the Crown was scrambling for liquid capital. By the time of Ancrum Moor, English operations on the Borders were suffering from financial exhaustion.[78] The cost of victuals guaranteed that their timely transport and delivery had strategic ramifications, as when the Duke of Norfolk groaned over the proposal to establish a garrison in Scotland, for which he could not even guarantee that the troops would even get fresh 'horsmet'.[79] Nevertheless, by the time of the death of Mary I, efforts to buttress the Berwick fortifications and sort out the garrison had been accomplished, if not spectacularly.[80]

The earlier Tudors in Ireland, 1520–53

The strategic predicament posed by Ireland owed much to English ambivalence regarding how best to deal with the threat that that island posed. Ireland occupied a tertiary sphere of importance. While the Continent and Scotland occupied the highest levels of English strategic imperatives respectively, Ireland was left for last. Irish expeditions rarely got the support they deserved. For example, when the Earl of Surrey led an incursion into Ireland in 1520, his operations were dogged by logistical and financial problems, in spite of the fact his 'army' comprised only 500 men. Surrey's two-year operation cost about £18,000.[81] One can only wonder at the course British history would have taken had the Crown been as generous in its support of the forces in the Irish theatre as it was to the French and Scottish campaigns.[82] From the distance of Westminster, the English underestimated the armament and number of the Gaelic Irish, at least until 1598. Individually, Irish lordships could rarely raise more than a few hundred horsemen. Their infantry were lightly armed. Still, the native Irish used artillery and firearms whenever they could lay hands on such weapons, and exploited gunpowder technology with skill. The Anglo-Irish were comparatively stronger and thus held the advantage in pitched battle. But guerrilla warfare favoured the Gaels, whom even the English light horsemen could pursue only with the greatest difficulty.[83]

Lord Deputy Skeffington's military operations of the 1530s signified that not only would numerous English soldiers be needed to maintain the Crown's authority in the Pale, but an English administration as well. English siege artillery was shipped into Ireland.[84] The Gaelic lords ensconced themselves in their mighty keeps and both sides employed gallowglasses and kerne. Mobility dictated that traditionally English kinds of warriors kept steeds. Mounted archers rode with the 'spears', cavalry recruited mostly from Cumberland and the Scottish Borders. But gunpowder, which was making such an impact upon the Continent, demolished medieval warfare in Ireland. The campaign of 1534–5 included many sieges. Maynooth Castle, defended by artillery and sixty 'gunners', fell to systematic battering as Skeffington blasted the bulwarks and took the base court and ward, followed by the breaching of the keep.

Near Limerick, the rebel O'Brien thought to give battle, but

> . . . went into the mountains from us, for fear of ordnance; and when he heard tell that we had no ordnance, then he restored his men into his castles again with such ordnance as he had of his own; and without ordnance to beat the one pile we could not enter well into his country.[85]

Traditional weaponry still predominated (requests for bows, bowstrings, and arrows continued, along with grumbling about the quality of the bows that had been requisitioned from the Ludlow Castle arsenal). Lord James Butler's host of more than 300 gallowglass and 200 kerne boasted but five handgunners.[86] But cannon were being used in innovatory ways, such as aboard ship-boats and in field engagements, on a scale unprecedented. Henry's demi-cannons, hurling 30 pound rounds, were triple the size of the guns that his daughter would use in her Irish wars.[87]

The Gaels abandoned strongholds for mobility and harassing tactics. The importation of heavy siege ordnance into Ireland led the Irish to fight a defensive war with another gunpowder weapon – the harquebus. English arms would be hard-pressed to counter Gaelic mobility and increasing fire-power.[88] And much of Ireland found itself more sympathetic with rebellion against England because the 1534–5 hostilities led to 'an insidious militariz-ation of government in Tudor Ireland'.[89] Armies of occupation proved more reliable than indirect rule through nobles, a lesson underscored more than sixty years later with O'Neill's Rebellion. English rule rested upon a standing army it could ill afford. The King condemned falsified muster returns and corrupt captains, as would Elizabeth in her time. Of 1,600 soldiers disem-barked in a 1534 landing, fewer than 400 actually carried weapons.[90] Coupled with the campaign against native religious orders, the era of the Kildare War (1534–40) heightened the Crown's sense of the danger that Ireland posed to England's religious independence, now proclaimed by the Act of Supremacy (1534).

Though the strategic importance of Ireland was increasingly recognised, the requisite money for the troops was insufficient: only £7,000 was avail-able in June 1536, which in effect ended major operations for that year. Ultimately, Thomas Cromwell settled for a garrisoned Pale. The English became defensive. They hacked through Irish forests to secure perimeters around English settlements. Garrisoned soldiers received leaseholds in border areas.[91] Wracked by mutiny and the allegedly corrupt practices of English captains, the establishment continued to rot. Although well short of a thou-sand effectives by autumn 1536, Lord Deputy Grey was compelled by sheer poverty to discharge another 500–600 soldiers. His King declined to shore up the tottering finances of the Irish establishment, and the English captains sheltered in towns rather than lie in the field with their troops. 'The season of yere approcheth whereing Inglishmen cannot travaile to do service'.[92] Still, the rebellion had been extirpated, and if the fiscal crisis could be remedied, operations could resume in the spring.

By 1538–9 a token force of 340 soldiers garrisoned English-occupied Ireland, as across the Irish Sea England's shires mustered, in anticipation of Charles V's incursion into Ireland as the first step in a wholesale invasion of heretical England.[93] The diminutive Irish Ordnance Office 'in Dwblyng at the black fryares' was no more than a warehouse for the storage and distribution of weaponry imported from the Tower of London.[94] Neverthe-less, in August 1539, at the battle of Bellahoe, Lord Deputy Grey defeated

O'Neill and O'Donnell. Although the light 'campaigning guns' of the English often provided the margin of victory in the field, siege cannon were requisite against any serious Irish fortifications. Misfortune could easily neutralise the English edge in artillery, as at Grey's taking of Dangan Castle in 1537, when his only 'battery piece' was disabled. A replacement was begged from King Henry personally. Unfortunately, the paucity of good powder and substantial cannon persisted into the mid-1540s, doubtless because Scotland and France were deemed more critical in the Henrician grand strategy.[95]

The infiltration of Jesuits after 1541 made Ireland's strategic position critical. The stabilisation that occurred under the leadership of Lord Deputy Sir Anthony St Leger permitted (indeed, encouraged) the siphoning-off of 3,000 Irish kerne to Henry VIII's French and Scottish wars of 1544. Garrisons of mixed troops kept the peace in Ireland.[96] Irish infantry were absorbed into the English forces, mastered firearms, and acquitted themselves well.[97] The advent of Edward VI's Protestant regime necessitated an increased English military presence to Ireland.[98] The battles of the late 1540s and 1550s were sporadic, more like raids, with the greatest bloodshed resulting in 200 Irish casualties in 1547.[99] In spite of some military successes, attrition strained governmental resources as it had in the 1530s. Articles sent to the Lord Deputy on 29 November 1552 reveal the Privy Council's ignorance of the English military establishment in Ireland. They not only enquired as to the political situation but demanded an account of soldiers, ordnance, and fortifications.[100] According to Stephen Ellis, 'By 1552 . . . the privy council was becoming aware of the appalling cost of its military strategy in Ireland.' The inflationary pressures of Edward's reign and the accession of a Roman Catholic in 1553 shrank the English army of Ireland to 500 men.[101] Nevertheless, in spite of Mary's pledge to restore the 'old religion' she determined to safeguard her royal military interests (however reduced they had become) against Scottish interlopers and rebel provinces. The Irish Ordnance Office was to submit yearly accounts and inventories, and the Marian Privy Council expressed particular interest in the manufacture of bows and pikes from native wood. The army was similarly to be small but efficient, well-armed and disciplined. The old rule about ethnicity (regardless of religious sentiment) remained in effect under Philip and Mary. '[T]he men of warre not to be of the nation of Irland above the numbre of ten in evry bande of an hundreth.'[102] It would be those soldiers, marching rapidly, carrying firearms, and supplying garrisons that were to be the mainstay of English warfare, not siege artillery.

Tudor ordnance

The Ordnance Office[103] provided the tools with which England waged war, and clearly this 'first permanent military establishment in England' emerged under the Tudors.[104] The office was originally there to oversee the armour and weapons of the knights of the royal Household in the fourteenth century. A more systematic supervision of arms came about when the Privy Wardrobe dedicated to military accoutrements found its way to the Tower of London. The campaigns of the 1300s, which brought organisational and procedural definition to the Exchequer and to Parliament, imposed separate accounting of military stores and semi-autonomous funding. As cannon became part of the royal army, they too fell under the supervision of the Privy Wardrobe, the Keeper acquiring the title of 'Keeper of the Artillery'. In the fifteenth century a Master of the Ordnance was patented. Although patents exist for 1414 and 1435, probably the earliest Masters (like the earliest Lords Lieutenants) received commission for a current campaign rather than as a term of office.[105] The institutionalisation of the Ordnance out of the Household was symptomatic of the militarisation of the monarchy during the era of the Hundred Years War and was thus part and parcel of the greater fluency found in the operations of the Exchequer and the scope and extent of parliamentary statute.

Henry VII thus inherited an institution staffed with personnel whose duties were delineated, but flexible enough to incorporate widening responsibilities such as the manufacture, storage, and deployment of firearms. Henry VII, always attuned to trends in Renaissance Italy, set his Clerk of the Ordnance upon the task of acquiring artillery shortly after Charles VIII of France's celebrated march through the Italian peninsula. The French King's demonstration of the utility of cannon in 1494 was not lost upon Henry Tudor. The Ordnance Office, for example, received a royal order 'to make provision for us of such parcells of ordenance as be conteyned in a bil herein closed. . . .' William Fourneys, Clerk of the Ordnance was 'to husband us in the buying ther of at as litle price soo the stuff be good. . . .'[106] Although the advent of the declared account in the Ordnance Office marked a more pragmatic and institutional approach to military supply, the personal element, wherein a trusted servant of the monarch gave personal assurance for the discharge of his duties in mobilising men and *matériel*, remained a component of this procedure. An energetic Master of the Ordnance, or later his Lieutenant, might provide the initiative to accommodate the increasing infiltration of gunpowder weapons into what was essentially a late medieval institution.

The English artillery 'industry' had been born within the precincts of the Tower, as a by-product of the Hundred Years War. Henry VII recruited gunners from the Continent so that, whereas in 1489 30 had served there, by 1497 nearly 50 toiled in the Ordnance Office, sharing their knowledge of metallurgy and casting alongside native English founders. Operations were established in Ashdown Forest, where foundries cast iron shot and, later on, guns, in the French fashion. An influx of Dutch gunners in the spring of 1497 saw to it that by midsummer Henry had 200 gunners employed in his realm, the majority of whom were Englishmen who had adapted continental practice to English circumstances.[107] Although Henry VIII's campaigns drew heavily from foreign arms manufacturers, including orders placed for Flemish guns, the demand still encouraged (certainly after 1543) domestic manufacture of cannon, with Italian as well as Low Countries craftsmen bringing their skills to England. The second Tudor nurtured a domestic iron 'industry' by proffering government contracts to English founders and monitoring production.[108] Indeed the wars of the 1540s saw guns cast whole, rather than in detached segments, evidence of an improved English product.[109]

By the reign of Edward VI, his grandfather's and father's investments had reaped handsome rewards, placing England at the apex of the cannon-founding industry. Above all, the English mastered vertical casting of ordnance, which brought impurities to the surface, refining the metal, especially at the critical breech-end of the piece. No comparable gun-casting facility existed on the Continent until 1604. Boosting artillery production and improving design through the mid-Tudor period, the English kept pace with continental innovations, such as standardising bore, introducing 'straight bore', and improving reloading procedures and equipment. The latter facilitated the famed rapidity of fire of English vessels, and English ore, combined with moulding techniques and vertical casting, made gun-founding one of the premier English 'arts' of war.[110]

The key to effective deployment of guns was planning, ensuring that sufficient ordnance, accompanied by powder and accoutrements, arrived at their destination in timely fashion. Delay in transportation or omission of requisite accessories (often powder) could upset a siege's timetable and immobilise a campaign. Too often commanders made the decision to invade a town abruptly, forcing the *ad hoc* transport of batteries piecemeal. Without depots and facing hostilities at sea and upon rivers, the besiegers could never be sure when they would be able to breach the walls of their objective. The immensity of the theatre of general war in the 1500s and 1600s, coupled by the demand for powder and guns by naval and mercantile interests, made it unlikely that munitions could lie about idly, making no depot 'safe'. Armies vied for scarce cannon, powder, wagons, horses, pioneers, and sappers. Allies quarrelled over who would supply munitions and pay. Resource availability often determined the victor. Not surprisingly Gloriana was justifiably niggardly in 'loaning' coveted English cannon to her not-so-trustworthy continental allies, however noble the cause. The Dutch and Henry IV could too easily squander guns that might be needed sometime to defend the Thames, the Medway or even the shires themselves.

English gunpowder was valued as highly as English iron ordnance, and the Crown likewise exercised central control over that burgeoning industry. The 'saltpetremen', who scoured dovecotes and privies in search of nitrates, had governmental sanction to excavate property on the basis of national interest. Central regulation of the marketing of gunpowder and arms rested upon the same justification.[111] Commissioners of Saltpetre and Gunpowder answered to the Privy Council, who coordinated their activities with the Ordnance Office. Individual illicit gunpowder manufacture was noted in the Council Registers amid national business of the greatest significance. Indeed, even the sanctity of private property was overridden by the 'salt-petremen'.[112] They oppressed entire shires by requisitioning carts and carriages to haul their foul diggings, tying up land transport and some-times fixing charges on the locality.[113] Exactions upon the countryside rested upon precedents set by Henry VIII. Gunpowder was not so easily and quickly manufactured, and Elizabeth's Ordnance Office on occasion was obliged to import powder from Antwerp and Hamburg.[114] Under-standably, the wise monarch parcelled out with great discretion the precious store of arms. As well appointed as was Essex's expedition to Rouen, he brought no siege guns. Henry IV informed the Queen of what ordnance he had, but implored her for supply of 'double cannon', which would be matched by allies in Flanders if only Elizabeth would loan some great guns for siegecraft. Additional requests for artillery and munitions came from the Governor of Brest. Had the Queen's surname been Krupp, it is doubtful she could have satisfied all the appeals for armaments from the Continent.

Under Elizabeth I the Ordnance Office entered into a period of 'con-solidation'.[115] The merger of land-based artillery management and naval ordnance administration through the Tower from 1569 onward helped to centralise, and make coherent, the role of artillery in English warfare. Symptomatic of the military reorganisation that Elizabeth imposed on the shire militias on the eve of the Rebellion of the Northern Earls were the increasingly bureaucratised activities of a small army of gun-founders, carpenters, sawyers, smiths, bowyers, blacksmiths, fletchers, masons, joiners, and wheelers, who could now be mobilised systematically at depots such as Portsmouth, Woolwich, Chatham, and elsewhere, administered from the centre, the Tower. Stores of armour, though similarly dispersed amongst royal depots, continued to be managed by the Office of the Armoury.

The Tudors monitored closely the possession of arms, particularly armour, to the point of recording the names of gentlemen who possessed a single mailed shirt. Secured in royal arsenals (Berwick, Portsmouth, etc.), corse-lets and helmets were sold to nobles (and sometimes shires) in the event of rebellion or threatened invasion.[116] Although the royal reserves remained modest by continental standards (15,000 'Almaigne Corsselets' and an equal number of morions and burgonets), sufficient stores and artisans came from Henry VIII's transplanted establishment to make English armour a valuable commodity in the international arms market. Rumours in the Germanies that English armour was being marketed in Muscovy and then sold to the Ottomans prompted a stern denial from the Crown in 1561.[117] The Armoury supplied £2,600 worth of breastplates, swords, and helmets (along with armourers' tools) on at least one occasion during Elizabeth's escalation of the Irish war.[118] The Crown and Privy Council had centralised the management of weapons within an arsenal located only miles away and directly accountable to them.[119] The intrusion of the Privy Council into new areas was part of the process.[120] This system of ordnance management continued into the 1580s and beyond.[121] The centralisation of ordnance management made possible an account of the weaponry at the disposal of the Crown. A comprehensive survey begun on 21 July 1589 and completed in 1591 catalogued not only guns, shot, and powder but, 'pikeheddes' and 'battleaxes' as well. Counting in timber and other habiliments of war, the value of the Queen's arsenal was reckoned at £166,630 17s. 2d.[122]

An English art of war

The English mastered logistics well, fielded large numbers of men in spite of a hybrid recruitment system, had good tactical sense, handled their artillery expertly, and enjoyed a superior sense of morale. Their weaknesses included weaponry. Contingents of heavy cavalry were becoming increasingly difficult to obtain. As for infantry, they had yet to exploit firearms and pikes fully, still being enamoured with tried and trusty bills and bows. Perhaps the greatest challenge faced by the English was the sheer variety of venues in which their troops fought. Given the strategic predicament, the English had to be adept at more than one 'art of war'. Bureaucratic innovations, from the militarisation of the Privy Chamber to the establishment of public and private supply systems, were undertaken. If the English came to terms with the military revolution differently from the Europeans, and if in fact the geographic seclusion of the British Isles[123] meant that angle-bastioned fortifications were rare and bows ubiquitous, still that did not necessarily prove the inferiority of English warfare against a universal standard dictated by a host of contemporary and somewhat idiosyncratic military theorists. Lack of resources inhibited the introduction of the new military architecture on both sides of the Borders. With the 1547 expedition, however, the erection of bastions commenced. English engineers such as Thomas Petit (and the aforementioned Sir Richard Lee) constructed Italian-style fortifications, especially circa 1547–50.[124]

English commanders and their troops occasionally made a muddle of it. But in general, from 1511 to 1642, they achieved success on their own terms.[125] The campaigns of 1542–7 proved that England was indeed still a military power, and an improving one. Not only did Henrician and Edwardian governments assemble large armies, but they also managed to achieve their immediate objectives, such as the taking of Boulogne and the invasion of Scotland. These successes were accompanied by a maturing bureaucracy and budding naval power. Clifford Davies points out that in 1512–13, 1522–3, and 1544–5 the English fleet and the land forces they transported carried out their missions successfully in intervening on the Continent, keeping the Channel, and operating against Scotland. Breaches in English defences did occur, such as the French amphibious incursions in 1545 and 1548. The latter, with its attack on Haddington, exhibited how fragile was the Tudor strategic situation.[126] The essentially defensive imperative emphasised the readiness of shire forces, so that military power was spread throughout the realm. In October 1536 (as in 1642–5) that decentralised system threatened the Crown rather than protected it. The rebels of the Pilgrimage of Grace for the most part commandeered the northern militia to muster an 'impressively weaponed and well-horsed' host, 'with many of the troops experienced in war through service on the northern border'.[127] Part of the post-Henrician military dilemma was the paucity of dependable veteran units kept in close promixity to Whitehall. Consequently, during the unstable reign of Edward VI there occurred experiments with a royal standing army.[128]

Henrician military success proved illusory. Strategic accomplishments fell short of its ambitious diplomacy. Although the army of 1544 impressed by sheer numbers, being the largest foreign expeditionary campaign until the war of the Spanish succession, size did not translate into achievement. England was no more capable of holding continental territory in the early 1500s than it had been in the late 1300s or early 1400s. A gargantuan army might coalesce for a campaign season (and often late at that), and at great cost. But long-term sustenance of forces operating abroad came only with Elizabeth I. The 1544 army of the French theatre may indeed have counted 48,000 soldiers, but 11,500 were non-English recruits. The 27,000 English infantry and 4,000 cavalry reflected the residual military strength of lords and gentlemen who had fielded forces in fulfilment of royal writs. England's manpower in the 1500s, as in previous centuries, served the nobility and gentry. As for *matériel*, saltpetre, copper, and cordage, those most requisite habiliments of war were largely imported from Europe, as was most weaponry. And what was produced in Henrician England was crafted largely by aliens. Finally, foreign transport, especially from the Netherlands, made the Channel crossing possible. Henry VIII might survey ranks bristling with bills, pikes, and pennants, but that brave show was made possible by the obedience of his nobles and money from the Exchequer.[129]

In the half-century or so before Gloriana's accession, steps were taken toward national self-sufficiency in the production of military wares. 'Ynglysh Iron' emerged in increasing quantity and improved quality from furnaces in Sussex and elsewhere, operations in many ways patronised and encouraged by local lords and the Crown.[130] Although gunfounding's aggregate impact must not be exaggerated,[131] still demand from the central government fired the furnaces and gave impetus to the scientific study of artillery, hence an English art of war. Thus the iron cannon industry grew alongside a gunpowder manufacturing sector that saw the appearance of 'saltpetremen' in even the more remote corners of England. Natives of the island mastered the skills of gunmaking and swordmaking, and all these crafts began to export to the Continent. And as far as the fighting men of England were concerned, a medieval office, lieutenancy, evolved in unexpected ways in the late Tudor and early Stuart periods, and a measure of how effective lieutenancy had become by the era of the Civil War was the institution's centrality in the confrontation between King and Parliament in 1641–2.

3

THE DEFENCE OF THE SHIRE
Lieutenancy

How lieutenancy worked: the Lords Lieutenants

Lieutenancy was born of English warfare. As long as kings ruled by the sword, lieutenants were needed to assist their sovereign in maintaining and exercising royal authority. While lieutenants possessed no civil authority, they did much to keep the king's peace. In wartime the Lords Lieutenants mobilised forces in their sphere of influence, whether the inhabitants were connected with the Lord Lieutenant through landholding, or simply residents of that part of the realm lorded over by that particular lieutenant. A good lieutenant moulded available manpower into a fighting contingent to be placed at the king's disposal, either for defence of the realm or for an expedition abroad. Lieutenancy, then, was an integral part of English monarchical government. And when kings began to rule with their pens, having sheathed their blades after 1485, lieutenants continued to serve their royal masters. By the era of the Restoration, when lieutenancy with monarchy was revived, the Lords Lieutenants most often did battle with reams of paper.

A commission of lieutenancy might encompass a single shire or several, or be shared with another lord. Some counties lacked a lieutenant. In the early sixteenth century it was not a 'system' as such, but simply the traditional application of noble patronage for the use of the monarchy. England might be ruled by a dynasty, but it was made up of shires that for the most part cared for themselves.

Lords Lieutenants publicised, with their deputies' assistance, the orders and concerns of the central government to their neighbours. They supervised 'mustering and excercising in martiall feates' the local forces, and organised them into bands. 'The Office of Leuitenaucy doth not consist only in attendance at the Musters, but doth require our Care through the whole yeare fore excercisinge the Soldiers, punishinge Offenders, procuringe payment of Money for the Charge of the Musters, settlinge of Armes and diverse other particulars touching the Militia'.[1] Accounts of available manpower (ages 16 to 60), weapons, and wealth were kept. Captains of

50

horsebands were chosen and their cavalry reviewed. The topography of the shire was surveyed, fortifications and beacons maintained, and the defensive posture of the locality evaluated, especially in regard to potential invasion sites in the coastal counties. Should war come, the lieutenancy had to have a contingency plan for gathering victuals and providing carriages and horses.[2]

Lieutenancy inherited from the Statute of Winchester and medieval military organisation a dualistic system of local defence that neither the Tudors nor the early Stuarts fully sorted out. Rolls of the shires' military resources distinguished the simply able-bodied from wealthy citizens who, by statute, maintained stores of weapons. Theoretically, every man of 17 years or older kept a bow and arrows, that Henrician statute being buttressed by proclamation as late as 1628.[3] But horses, cuirasses, and muskets were too expensive to be widely owned. A highly localised system of accounting developed, down from the Statute of Winchester, through the experiment of the 1522 proscription, and in the pages of lieutenancy books and rolls kept up to the eve of the Civil War. Clearly yeomen were expected to defend the shire in person, carrying a weapon they had purchased or inherited. But many a sturdy lad expected a local gentleman to supply his pike and helmet, or a caliver and powder flask. The problem lay in how to coordinate the swift distribution of the arms of the stock-pilers and sponsors with the men who were able-bodied but lacked weapons. Thus the compilation of lists had to be supported by some plan as to how this tangled pattern of arms ownership could be mobilised in a matter of hours should an emergency arise.[4]

T. G. Barnes has written that early Stuart England's 'institutions are the shadows of men'.[5] Given the amateur nature of English local government, this was particularly true. The personality of the ruler shaped national policy and, in bureaucracies such as the Ordnance Office, the rigour and tempo of the institution were determined by who happened to be the Lieutenant of the Ordnance and the kind of men he recruited (or inherited). But the 'personality factor' was particularly acute within the shires, especially in the case of non-resident Lords Lieutenants. The county community school of historiography has classified the lieutenants as a bridge between Court and Country. Lieutenants reconciled the nation's military needs with localism. However, Lords Lieutenants were more than the Council's mediators with regionalism; they were nobles in their own right. It is therefore something of a misnomer to write of lieutenancy's 'inception', for monarchs traditionally delegated authority, particularly during campaigning, to a trusted noble.

'The *office* of the Lord Lieutenant was wholly a Tudor creation'.[6] The increasing institutionalisation of lieutenancy reflected the centralising tendency of later Tudor and early Stuart monarchs, yet lieutenancy remained rooted in the countryside and ultimately (by the time of the Civil War) represented the interests of the locality as well as the Crown. Meshing with the extant jurisdictions of the shire was part of the process of institutional maturation. For example, the lieutenants supplemented the authority of royally sponsored commissioners of musters, with the latter staying on in many areas in cooperation with the lieutenants. Likewise lieutenancy reconciled itself with magistracy and shrievalty. The Justices of the Peace and the sheriffs, individuals as well as institutions, had to be brought within the new system. All of these posts were filled by the social élite, so egos and reputations were at stake as well as bureaucratic boundaries. Lieutenancy affirmed that power resided in real property, that the nobility were the natural leaders of society, that a 'great chain of being' still connected the monarch with his lords and gentry in maintaining the peace of the realm, and that all government, local and central, was grounded in cooperation, consent, and tradition. A well-managed lieutenancy exhibited all the finer qualities of English paternalism.

Some remnant of feudal overlordship persisted in lieutenancy, because the magnate was presumed to have some territorial jurisdiction over the citizens who dwelt within his shire or shires. After the bloody assault on Leith in 1560, the Lord General the Duke of Norfolk wrote to Burghley '. . . if you doo levie any more Men (as of Necessytie you must doo, and that no small Number) they are not to be hadd within thes Countrees within my Lieutenauncie'. East Anglia had been bled dry. Norfolk anticipated the Queen perfectly, for, before his letter reached Court, she had ordered, '. . . where yow haue taken order to levy within your Lieutenancy two thousand new Men, we meane also to send with all spede two thousand moo[r], out of the Shyrees that lye next to your Lieutenancy'.[7]

In correspondence with his deputy lieutenants, who carried out his orders, the Lord Lieutenant often referred to his subordinates as 'friends'. Bound by kinship and ancestral ties woven within the county community, lieutenants comprised an extended brotherhood that shared bloodlines and 'class' interest. The Earl of Pembroke and Montgomery could express his orders to the deputies in terms of his 'cosen the Lord Paulett and to the rest of my very lovinge freinds and Cosens my deputie Leiuetenants'.[8] These men were unpaid local administrators. No cash nexus sullied their relationship. Orders were carried out as a point of honour and respect. The Lord Lieutenant reached out his hands and joined court with country. In doing so he helped unify the realm and fulfilled that especial confidence placed in him by a grateful sovereign. He was a man whom citizens as well as princes could trust.

Prior to the regimentation of commissions of lieutenancy under Elizabeth, lieutenants were only as powerful (and ubiquitous) as the monarch wished. Henry VIII got good service from them. Fighting on two fronts, in France and Scotland, demanded commissions with some autonomy and discretionary authority. The disorders of the reign of Edward VI justified liberal use of commissions of lieutenancy. Indeed, the Lord Protector Earl of Northumberland probably planned to make lieutenancy a permanent institution of local government.[9] Under Mary I, however, commissions of lieutenancy were issued begrudgingly, even in time of civil disorder. When she mobilised forces from Kent, Sussex, Surrey, and Middlesex to consolidate her defence of Guines, she used the traditional 'Commysshons' rather than depend upon a Lord Lieutenant.[10] The nobility's disaffection with the Queen is partly to blame, and soon she realised that alienation extended beyond the élite. The comprehensiveness of lieutenancy, in Mary's hands, worried some of her gentry. The lieutenancy's displacement of the sheriff as the conductor of troops, the pre-eminence of the post over all others, and its comprehensive jurisdiction sparked complaint.[11] Lieutenants were preferred over the constabulary. The Crown considered deputy lieutenants, especially when assisted by the Justices of the Peace, to be less susceptible to negligence and localism.[12]

Professor Stater summarises it:

> The Tudor lieutenancy had allowed the crown to go a step beyond 'overmighty' lords. Lords lieutenant and their deputies continued to enjoy considerable autonomy, but from 1604 it was an authority cloaked in the king's prerogative. The compromise was satisfactory all around; the crown gained an element of control hitherto unknown over its greater subjects, and aristocrats gained the additional cachet that royal favor bestowed. The bargain was equally beneficial for the relationship between province and capital. The crown created a cheap form of administration, which provided both military and civilian services. This service was paid for at the price of limited central control. The government could never push its claims too hard, for the survival of the system depended upon local cooperation.[13]

Deputy lieutenants

Deputy lieutenancy illustrates how English society rested upon social co-operation rather than class conflict. The nobility bestowed some of their authority securely on the shoulders of the gentry. Although of differing social orders, and often possessing different economic interests, nobles and gentry comprised the realm's élite. But this was not exactly the medieval great chain of being. There was no explicit contract binding the Lord Lieutenant to the lesser nobles and gentlemen of the deputy lieutenancy. Rather, lords and gentlemen each possessed rights and responsibilities for the maintenance of order in rural society. Lieutenancy might raise gentlemen to the highest level of service to their community. 'A deputy lieutenancy was the pinnacle in the hierarchy of county offices'.[14] The deputy lieutenants occupied a world rather different from that of their noble superiors. The latter generally had a court connection, or at least kept an eye on that influential circle. In time of Parliament a Lord Lieutenant would hurry to Westminster to sit in the House of Lords. His jurisdiction could comprise several counties and give him a perspective that looked beyond shire boundaries. But the deputy lieutenant's authority was by definition grounded within his shire of residency. He was, more than the Lord Lieutenant could be, the county's man.[15]

In recruiting the 'first' deputy lieutenants, the Crown drew from the ranks of the Justices of the Peace. Elizabeth was careful, however, that the lieutenancy did not confound the powers of shrievalty. The offices of sheriff and deputy lieutenant were kept separate and no man might hold both, though a deputy lieutenant might remain a Justice of the Peace. No potential conflict of interest was seen between magistracy and lieutenancy. In the early stages of the Elizabethan Lord Lieutenancy, the Crown exerted control over the appointment of deputy lieutenants, naming them at Westminster, by the Queen's personal choice. In June 1585 Chancellor Sir Thomas Bromley, at the Queen's behest, composed a new genre of commission of lieutenancy.[16]

A single deputy lieutenant assumed precedence over his fellows, in practice if not in law. This chief deputy saw that the work was done.[17] Within a given shire, three or four deputy lieutenants exercised authority, though in some cases half a dozen might share the responsibilities.[18] Together they orchestrated county affairs, possessing a familiarity with the locality and the authority of the Crown via the Lord Lieutenant, who could well be non-resident for much of the year. The monarch's conception of England's military might rested on the diligence of the deputy lieutenants, for they kept the 'perfect books of all armour, warlike weapons and furniture' and oversaw the captains and muster-masters.[19]

In the 1570s the Crown wrestled with military deficiencies: lack of armour, a dearth of horses, and insufficient firepower. Assessments revealed misappropriated moneys. The muster commissioners and lieutenants had faltered in remedying defects, and thus the shrievalty experienced a rejuvenation of its authority in the musters of the 1570s.[20] Constables and bailiffs kept possession of the weapons, and the commissioners (mindful of the charges of corruption) assured the Council that 'no Somes of money but such as was for the provysyon of the Armour above wrytten, was leveyed taxed or gathered. . . .'[21] The Crown intended to train one-tenth of the quarter million males eligible for the military obligation. By the mid-1570s no fewer than 12,000 citizens had received instruction in the English art of war, and behind them stood 62,462 militia bearing weapons but possessing little practical sense of how to use them.[22] When militia rating and mustering of trained soldiers was resuscitated (in 1614 for example), the deputy lieutenants coordinated the constables and militia captains so that a general rendezvous might be effected. Deputy lieutenants' lists of ratepayers and select horse and foot were based upon personal inspection. Their authority lay behind the installation of a new muster-master, and assured the latter's pay.[23]

Assessments for light horse and infantry shed light on the financial ability of the shires to field forces, and the supervision of the return of horses, armour, and weapons to owners disclosed details about private arms possession. Through the summer of 1570 the Lords Lieutenants harnessed all the agents of local bureaucracy (sheriffs, commissioners of musters and Justices of the Peace) in supplying certificates to the Privy Council.[24] In 1573 the Crown created the 'trained bands', citizen-soldiers selected for drilling in the 'modern' art of war.[25] Training took place throughout the year, roughly ten days (four in Easter week, four more in Whitsun week, and two in Michaelmas) in small groups supervised by Justices of the Peace and commissioners of musters. The latter rated and taxed the shire and localities, seeing that the most affluent paid, 'hauing regarde not to charge the pore sort of howsholders nor specyalye the cotagers'. The commissioners themselves contributed, but 'The menour sort not to be burthenede, nor none that was not reated at the last subsydie aboue vli in goodes, exept the kepers of taverns or ale howses.' Although the emphases of the trained-band initiative were uniformity and modernity, with training in the use of firearms being the major focus, the harquebus was not expected to replace the bow, and archers were excluded from the trained bands not out of contempt but out of concern for their preservation.[26]

By spring 1576 Suffolk had still not complied with the 1573 order to produce trained-band certificates on musters.[27] Although the increase of harquebuses remained a high priority, the number of longbows equalled or exceeded the handguns and calivers in the ranks of the militia. In 1577, 1,128 longbows, but less than a thousand firearms, were in use in Suffolk.[28] In 1577–8, the shires came closer to grips with firearms, and gunpowder was bought in quantity, measured out, and distributed to the budding marksmen of the trained bands. The expense, elaborate preparations for target-shooting, and requisite paraphernalia cost the locals a pretty penny.[29] Local officers were instructed 'to have a care that those that be the trainers doe principallie spende their time in seing the persones appointed to be trayned to shoote with the bullet at a marke as is proscribed in the said Instructions'. The cultivation of firearms remained at the centre of the trained bands' purpose.[30]

The need for the trained bands, arming and drilling with modern weapons, was indisputable. Too often, however, the Queen had to negotiate and rescind the troop levels her government deemed requisite from a given shire. Musters remained sporadic, and patchy in attendance and equipment. Substantive improvement occurred in the 1580s.[31] The Crown's stubbornness, and the intrusion of muster-masters, moved the shires to greater efficiency. Cumberland and Westmorland, perhaps the most diffi-cult shires to muster, assembled their bands in 1580–1, demonstrating the range of the Queen's reach as she improved her militia.[32] In Kent the noted soldier-author Thomas Churchyard was dispatched 'especially' by Her Majesty. In the early 1580s training was to be enhanced by the assistance of 'corporalles' in marksmanship exercises.[33] Still, 'a chronic shortage of suitable firearms' existed. The Northamptonshire muster of November 1586 brought out only 88 calivers among the western divisions' 1,063 able militiamen.[34] Exactly one year later, the shires' ability to defend themselves was scrutinised closely by the Privy Council and a board of 'Experiencede Captaines' whilst formulating strategies to foil a Spanish invasion of England.[35]

Defending against the Armadas

In late May 1574, the transport of Spanish troops through the Channel had alerted the newly trained bands in the southern counties. With English volunteers fighting in the Low Countries, the shires militias faced the prospect of Catholic retaliation.[36] While the many fronts upon which the enemy might encroach (the Low Countries, northern France, Ireland, Scotland) compelled the English to be adept at very different kinds of warfare, the sheer number of theatres of conflict also deflected the popish hammer. Elizabeth had to engage in operations throughout the globe, but so did her enemies, Philip of Spain, the Pope, the Guises. The thaw of winter 1587–8 ushered in an era of direct confrontation with Spain.[37] The defence of the island comprised the strategic predicament in micro-cosm. With limited forces and facing the logistical problem of moving to the point of invasion rapidly, how would the Council deploy and configure the militia? Should the trained bands be dispersed? Should the Spaniards be allowed to establish a beachhead, so that regional forces might consol-idate and riposte? Was it 'better to geve an Invador present battaile, or to temporize' and mobilise sufficient troop strength to staunch the influx of Catholic soldiers wading ashore?[38] 'Almost at the eleventh hour, the mistaken policy of diluting the effectiveness of the country's strength over too wide a front was replaced by a large-scale canalisation of troops towards the major ports'.[39]

Militiamen never battled the *tercios*,[40] the best troops in Europe, and thus had no opportunity to dispel the Earl of Leicester's contempt for citizen-soldiers. But lieutenancy and the Privy Council did prove their competence during the mobilisation of 1588. The cultivation of the trained bands through the 1570s, spurred on periodically through the 1580s, gave Elizabeth an assiduous (if untried) national army by April 1588.[41] In Northamptonshire at the time of the Armada, the captains' companies of 150 men cost £225 or more to raise, including 15s. per soldier's coat and 10s. conduct each.

The considerable cost of weapons had been paid earlier. And the locals paid for more than local defence: 400 Northamptonshire infantry were earmarked for service at 'court' in June, and in July this was increased to include 'launces', 'light-horsemenn', and 600 'foote'. The total cost for all the companies and training was £6,220.[42] Of the roughly 120,000 men available, two forces of 30,000 were to be deployed, on the coast and around London respectively. Ultimately, a third force under the ailing Earl of Leicester would be gathered, giving the Crown greater tactical flexibility in the southeast, where Spanish forces under the Duke of Parma would probably disembark. When the alarm came on 30 July 1588, the lieutenants (backed firmly by the Council) deftly overcame localism and coordinated a mutually supportive network of communities in fielding forces for a truly national defence. Though the Tilbury rendezvous, illuminated by Gloriana's dramatic appearance, exemplified the mobilisation, the 22,000 militia, supported by a substantial train of equipment and powder, who marched eastward paralleling the Armada's progress, showed that shire boundaries could be ignored in the defence of the realm.

Despite the counties' occasional vociferousness against the Crown's military programmes, the effective deployment of the militia demonstrated that the mustering indeed had produced an army, although a somewhat autonomous and self-conscious one. For example, Norwich's mobilisation built upon solid foundations laid through the 1570s, and especially since 1584, with municipal musters. Twenty pounds expended on more powder in November 1587 was followed by a £100 purchase of gunpowder on 17 August 1588. The muster of spring 1588 included 'skirmishing' and the discharge of 'great ordnance' (the latter exercise requiring a reward of 'wyne and cakes for the gooners'). The presence of Sir Thomas Leighton, a continental veteran who was shoring up fortifications and reviewing militia at the behest of the Privy Council, lent a ceremonial air to Norwich's mock battles and drilling. Leighton received a 38 ounce gilt cup, and various captains got decorative scarves and gratuities. Throughout the realm, the 1588 muster was conducted with fanfare and occasional panache.[43]

The defence of the Queen's person, too, placed national interest over the defence of home and family.[44] More artillery protected Her Majesty than was allocated to the army that would square off against the invaders. A half-dozen of each type of ordnance was appointed to 'Gurrd' the Queen: full cannon, demi-cannon, culverins, demi-culverins, sakers, and minions. The troops expecting to engage the *tercios* hauled, for example, only four demi-cannon, four culverins, a pair of minions, etc.[45] Elizabeth had 4,081 cavalry and 41,381 infantry in attendance. If one adds the army under Leicester (which included servants of the royal household, the Pensioners, as well as militia from Kent and various shires), an additional 18,049 men swelled the army to 63,511 effectives who could be marched within a few days to the vicinity of Margate, the location that Parma had picked as his penetration point.[46] What England lacked in combat-experienced troops and bastioned fortifications it compensated in numbers.

Meanwhile, the northern militia, especially the Yorkshire bands, kept Scotland in check. In fact, the adaptability of lieutenancy had been demonstrated in the North in Elizabeth's early years – for example, when the Earl of Bedford had assimilated the forces of the Bishopric of Durham while he was Governor of Berwick and fashioning a border defence system. Not only did Bedford prevail over the Palatine's traditional independence, but he did so as an outsider and agent of the Crown, not primarily upon status as a regional magnate.[47] In 1588 the same principles applied. Keeping the realm in a posture of defence required exertion beyond the Crown's resources. The northern border bands had to be propped up as England awaited the Armada.[48] From Lord Burghley's quarters, where he fretted over deficits of thousands of pounds, trying to keep the Fleet victualled in mid-July 1588, to the town wardens of Bardwell, Suffolk, taking pennies from the 'towne boxe' to feed and coat 'sowgers', all parties contributed to the mobilisation.[49] National defence transcended shire borders and county authority, even beyond the exalted authority of lieutenancy.

A legacy of the ancient world, particularly imperial Rome, was the notion that military power might naturally emanate from spiritual authority. Regardless of what might be read in the gospels, the pope and his bishops, like an emperor and his generals, raised armies to buttress their authority.[50] The mitre bestowed martial might. The Reformation did not profoundly alter this arrangement, and the young Protestant Edward VI could require his Archbishop of Canterbury to field forces, especially cavalry, for royal campaigns.[51] Edward's sister Elizabeth, at various times the personification of Protestantism's will to survive, also called upon clerics when Catholic Europe drew its sword against England.[52] The survival of the ecclesiastical component of the defence of the realm underscores conservatism and continuity in the Elizabethan militia reforms. The linkage of parallel systems of recruitment (lords along with their tenants and dependants, the shire trained bands, untrained reserves, 'freeholder' bands, pressed riff-raff, and the clergy's contingents) spread the military obligation and drew military resources from virtually every corner of the kingdom. These obligations were not to overlap, and the clergy's obligation (as would have been the case in the feudal system) was entirely distinct from the musters of the laity. Archbishop Whitgift was reminded that

> those Forces which shalbe by you furnished maye not be taken out of the trayned and enrolled Bandes whiche already are prepared by the Countrey, the which otherwaies your Lordship knoweth should be noe augmentacion of Forces, but weakeninge and deminishinge of the Bandes alredy erected by her Majesties appointment.[53]

Figure 3.1 The Counties of Tudor–Stuart England and Wales.
Source: Connie McOmber and the author.

Although obliged to maintain trained soldiers within their dioceses, the clergy were also liable to provide men for the press – for example, for Ireland and the Low Countries.[54] Bishops, as the ecclesiastical counterparts to the peers of the realm, possessed financial resources sufficient to fund cavalry, particularly light horse, petronels (a type of carabinier), and lancers. Benefices would be rated for arms, as would any private citizen, though the declining wealth of the Elizabethan clergy made them less capable of funding riders.[55]

The noble and medieval characteristics of the clergy's obligation were displayed splendidly in the banners, ensigns, and guidons flown by Archbishop Whitgift's troopers in late 1599. As 'Black Jack' had changed his coat-of-arms from gold and azure to silver and sable, new standards were crafted of silk, taffeta, and damask. His arms had to be emblazoned with sufficient accuracy and style so that these flags would not be confused with the standard of a 'private gentlemans'. They were 'to be wrought in oyle upon the silke, to endure the weather. ...' Whitgift's prerogative included dressing his men in distinctive colours; he chose 'Tawney or Blewe' for their coats.[56] But the clergy bands cannot be dismissed as episcopal bodyguards, for they made up a percentage of the realm's cavalry. The southern bishoprics fielded no fewer than 469 horsemen in 1588, though the clergy required prodding from the Privy Council. It is illustrative of English warfare that interest groups and collective bodies did their best to shunt responsibility elsewhere. The clergy were no exception, as they claimed benefit of their status, whereas the Privy Council (in Reformation spirit) pointed to their 'sufficient livinges' as a means to contribute to the defence of the realm.[57]

The participation of the Church in the defence of the realm dovetailed with the militia's view of the defence of the shire as part and parcel of the Protestant cause. The threat posed by international Catholic aggression reconciled (at least for the 1580s and 1590s) local interest with national security. In an era where decisiveness rarely resulted from frequent conflict, where even victory in the rare major battle did not often secure larger strategic aims, and diplomacy conducted in the name of God evidenced secular cunning and deceit, the English claimed righteousness and divine judgement in the engagement fought in the Channel in 1588. They had earnestly sought peace with Spain at the Gravelines negotiations. The Queen's commissioners then discovered that their six months' work had been wasted upon a Spanish ruse, and England now faced imminent invasion. But 'Almighty God showed His power against Philip in the rout of his great Armada and in the success of the English fleet, which did not lose a ship or have a man taken prisoner.'[58] The inherently defensive nature of the Armada year victory fit perfectly into the English strategic vision. But sustained defensive measures nevertheless placed the realm on a semi-permanent war-footing.

By 1599 the successive invasion scares and siphoning-off of resources into Ireland had infected the bishops as much as the rest of England with war weariness. The number of cavalry appearing at the clergy's musters had decreased markedly.[59] The bishops of Lincoln, Worcester, Norwich, Oxford, and Ely all mentioned the Irish presses as deleterious to their military preparedness, with armour and horses as well as men disappearing into that theatre without being replaced. The clergy felt themselves hemmed in by the Privy Council's excessive ratings and the localities made concerted attempts to divert demands for increased military costs on to the ecclesiastics.[60] The parallel and largely uncoordinated systems of military obligation coexisting and sometimes quarrelling within the shires, coupled with the exhaustion of the 1590s, suggest that, in spite of the very real potential for lieutenancy to harness the inherent military power of the countryside, the decentralised system made domestic defences dangerously weak.

The militia as defender of the realm

By the mid-1590s the cost of English warfare weighed heavily on the community. For example, at Newark the locals brought together communal weapons ('Comons armores') assessed upon the townships and wapentake as well as 'somes of money' to pay militiamen participating in the four-day general muster. These trained men were joined by 'pryvate Armor', individuals who were to 'cause ther severall Armors and weapons to be likewise broughte upon the backes of them selves or some other'. Daily wages of 8d. were paid to all soldiers, and the burden fell largely on private contributors:

> they who are charged with private Armors do beare the whole charge of ther men to be trayned with ther private Armors and be likewise contributorye with ther towneships for the Commone Charge of Comon armor . . . besides the viiid aforesaid for evry comon souldier to bring [with] him thes somes of money which here under are severally assessed uppon evry townshipe which is to be imployed for bullet, matche and powder. . . .[61]

Throughout the Tudor and early Stuart era, communities asserted the amateur and citizen-soldier identity of the militia. The locality insisted that the trained bands did not become a professional or standing force. When militiamen in the tithing of Abbas Combe, Somerset, 'demaunded allowance . . . for every daie of their Muster and trayninge' and maintenance in future, their neighbours protested, insisting these troops 'beare their owne charge'. The matter was brought to the bench at Quarter Sessions by sixteen citizens.[62] Trained-band soldiers, it could have been argued, required no wages because they were substantial citizens, 'sifficient and able men to be chosen, of those of the better qualitye, as Freeholders, Farmers, owners of Lands, householders. . . .'[63] The militia was, therefore, affordable, but ill-designed to sustain itself on a long-term footing.

War weariness infected even the most exemplary communities in spite of the exhortations of the lieutenants. At the beginning of Elizabeth's reign, the City of Bristol repaired its armour, and sent its men to general musters in uniform; with assertion of corporate independence in the 1560s, the municipality 'became markedly more lavish, investing, for example, in a pair of drums, and a dozen ells of fine silk for an ensign in the municipal colours of red, blue and yellow, embellished with gold buttons and tassels'. In the 1570s Bristol dutifully mustered its contingent of 160 militiamen, laced sleeves and all, at a cost of £65. Members of the Common Council provided corslets and muskets and substantial citizens incurred a 20s. penalty if the soldier they clothed and sponsored failed to muster and review. The Queen herself witnessed Bristol's martial vitality in 1573, as the town's 400 infantry staged three days of mock assaults, resplendent with explosions and glittering armour. Elizabeth endured it all, and the citizens expressed satisfaction at exhibiting for their sovereign their military prowess. Civic pride in Bristol's preparedness for war was indisputable, and the tradition carried on into the reign of James I, when Bristol's 'gallant fellows' stood at attention in 1608, and when Queen Anne christened the revival of the militia in 1613 by attending a muster of trained-band soldiers who were garbed in dress fit for officers.[64]

But November 1597 had seen a different spirit. Captain Docwra had been sent down by Whitehall to ensure that the Bristol men fought as well as they looked. Alarm over the threatening Spanish fleet was not terribly evident in Bristol. The Privy Council raged over 'a greate want of care in the officers and townsmen', who were 'altogether unarmed and unwillinge to be at the chardge to be furnyshed'. Genuinely surprised, and outraged, at the town's 'carelessnes for theire owne defence', the central government chastised the mayor:

> those men you presented unto [Captain Docwra] after manie delaies were altogether unarmed, and that he found very small care or feeling in you ... your slender regard deserveth muche to be blamed, especially in theis tymes of daunger, and now do mervell greatly you have bene so negligent ... to have no trayned nombers. ...[65]

Perhaps the siphoning-off of trained-band soldiers to the Continent and frequent Irish presses had brought home the reality of war to Bristol, and rehearsing for combat was no longer seen as a stirring municipal event.

The nature of the English militia and its military obligation was determined by the relationship between Englishmen and the state. One problem in studying warfare before the era of nationalism is that the motives and obligation for entering into military service are comparatively inchoate and diverse. The English trained soldier of the Tudor and early Stuart period did not exactly serve England. The locality, be it a wapentake, a hundred, a village, or most broadly, a shire, was his home. If he defended his patch of ground successfully and others did similarly, then England was safe. As logical as the countryman's reasoning might be, it did not come to terms with the threat of strengthening continental monarchies. The Crown's adversaries, France and Spain, were formidable states; the English locality could not perceive these macrocosmic realities and saw its place in the world within the context of country and city. Resistance to the Crown's military demands reflected not so much opposition to the regime as a myopic concern that levies of men and money would damage seriously the vitality of the local community. The strategic predicament of the monarch largely escaped the denizens of village and shire.

The Crown had to convince the localities of the necessity of learning a new art of war to face the realities of a new state system. An example of such an effort occurred in 1567, more than a year before the 1569 rising precipitated military reforms.[66] Proposals circulated at Court, their aim being to increase English firepower by the establishment of units of highly trained harquebusiers. These corps could be used *en masse* in offensive operations or broken down for purposes of proliferating training in the use of firearms amongst the shire militia. The immediate cause of the submission of these proposals stemmed, again, from the realm's strategic predicament. The arrival of a major Spanish land force in the Low Countries, which heightened England's vulnerability, dictated rapid assimilation of firearms to bring England up to continental standards of military expertise.

Most interesting is *how* harquebusiers were to be raised and maintained, for the proposals comprised imaginative innovations in the thorny political negotiations between ruler and subject over military obligations.[67] By 1567 towns were richer, and the Crown harder pressed financially (because of inelastic ordinary revenue and the decreased value of parliamentary subsidies owing to inflation), than during the reign of Henry VIII. Militia bands had drawn largely upon agricultural labour, taken from the yeomen of the countryside. The anonymously proposed harquebusier project of 3 November 1567 laid the burden on the towns. Half of the 4,000 expert marksmen were to be recruited from London. The rest were scattered among the towns, Bristol (300 harquebusiers) and Newcastle (200) being the largest. A truly national entity, the force represented a new line of thinking about the defence of the realm.

The anonymous proposal broke with tradition in several ways. First, the fiscal military burden was shunted upon 'Citties and townes', and away from the countryside. Second, it suggested a more effectual use of the knowledge of English veterans, the 'skilful souldier', focusing on training an élite using a specific weapon. Third, men between the ages of 18 and 25 were selected – the best investment of training, prefiguring the preference of modern systems of conscription. Yet, traditional elements persisted. The author appealed to 'gentylmen and honnest yomen' as the bulwark of English security, who would underwrite the project, though the Crown would do its part by supplying powder and munitions and, in a suggestive item, providing tax immunity, particularly from parliamentary fifteenths, in return for service and weapons purchases by the urban community. A standing army of 4,000 was not the intention, for it was apparently to be assembled *in toto* only on extraordinary occasions sufficiently perilous to warrant the gathering of troops from the far corners of the realm.[68]

Whoever the author was, he may have been connected with the Lieutenant of the Ordnance Office, Sir William Pelham, who promoted a similar proposal roughly simultaneously.[69] Pelham, too, tried to synthesise tradition with sixteenth-century politics and warfare. Expert use of the longbow persisted 'still in villeges cheffly' and should be continued, as the statute for maintenance of that weapon dictated. Unlike later military reformers, he did not see use of the bow as detrimental to the promotion of firearms.[70] But like the anonymous proposal, Pelham saw tax exemption as a means to maintain an élite corps of firearms specialists. Public demonstrations of shooting ability would replace 'sportes' such as 'Robyn Hood' and 'midsomer Lord and Ladyes'. Wagers placed on target-shooting were less convincing components of alternative financing. But many Englishmen desired exemption from the odious general musters of the shire, municipal rates, subsidies and parliamentary grants of tenths and fifteenths, and other expenditures that made devotion to the harquebus an attractive prospect.[71]

Special rates to train harquebusiers were indeed levied. In Somerset in 1577–8, a pair of zealots (apparently dissatisfied with the rate of 3d. on goods and 6d. per pound on land) increased the rate to 5d. on goods and 10d. on land 'without anie conference or Consente of the reste of the Justices'.[72] Here local Englishmen realised that the community's contribution to the defence of the realm had not kept pace with the cost of the art of war. Pelham's proposal had the weakness of summoning older, more substantial, taxpayers to his banner, whereas the anonymous proposal more wisely imposed age restrictions (which guaranteed longevity of training) and prescribed artificers (presumably men with greater dexterity). Clearly, Elizabeth and Sir William Cecil contemplated proposals that would have altered drastically militia service in England, or at the least created striking anomalies, to keep England apace with the art of war in sixteenth-century Europe. But, in spite of the fact that royal confidence in English military preparedness was further shaken in 1569, it would be the revival of the old militia concept, based upon the principle of selection, that triumphed in the 1570s as it would later in the 1630s.[73]

The statute 1 Jac. I, c.25, which eradicated the 1558 legislation upon which Elizabeth's system of musters rested, had little to do with military reform and much to do with politics both international and domestic. The centuries-old evolution of the definition of the individual's military obligation to the English state was halted – indeed, rendered unfathomable. Although a brilliant stroke financially and a shrewd move politically, James I's demobilisation of the English military establishment gambled everything on a European peace. The King proposed isolation as a solution to the strategic predicament of his predecessors, thinking that, if the Scottish Border problem had been solved by his accession, then the continental threat could be neutralised by dynasticism, diplomacy, and the Channel. So confident was James that the expiration of the statutory basis of militia was by default replaced by the royal prerogative, with ultimately disastrous results. The English art of war was sufficiently retarded for Britain not to measure up against continental foes until the late seventeenth century, and then under the leadership of a Dutchman. Allowing the county communities to monitor their own military strength, after the centralisation and onerous tasks of the Elizabethan war years, naturally seduced the shires into a certain torpor. Having relaxed its military demands, the Crown might now seek extraordinary revenue as a sort of quid pro quo. Globally, what more dramatic announcement of the *pax Jacobi* could there be than a general stand-down of the nation's defence system? James's fiscal desperation and genuine desire for European peace overrode any interest in perfecting English arms.

In 1605, and then a few years later with greater conviction, the Crown came round to the realisation that early seventeenth-century Europe remained a dangerous world. The shires were nudged into assessing their armed strength.[74] When the Earl of Exeter wrote to his Northamptonshire commissioners for musters from his home in Wimbledon, he knew full well that the shire had settled into a more comfortable and pacific posture than had been the case under 'our late dread Soueraigne'. A general muster would provide an opportunity to examine the county's horse and foot, check their weapons, make up a 'perfecte role' of contributors and soldiers, and then remedy the defects that had occurred during the hiatus. Exeter expected some insufficiencies ('I suppose there wilbe many'), but was surprised at just how decayed and complacent the mustering had become. Three hundred infantry were reviewed. The accoutrements were incomplete, because 'maney of the saied armes doe remayne with the armorers', so Exeter rejected their certificate. The Lord Lieutenant enquired about their cavalry and the quantity of munition, 'bullett matche and powlder.' Most objectionable, the commissioners failed to provide the proper certificates, with the demographic rationale that 'some men may dye some decay and others alter their places of habitacion. . . .' Exeter commiserated, agreeing that the universe might be in a state of flux, but he wanted a good certificate to give to the Privy Council, who were not so metaphysically minded.[75]

One clever courtier's plan for a 'Refined Militia' proposed to raise royal revenue, remedy the equestrian deficiencies of English warfare, and create a small standing army, predominantly heavy cavalry, based on the chivalric model. Forty-five knights from each shire would prefer £45 for the status of being 'Knights of the Crown', establishing a backbone of military defence throughout the realm and putting £61,340 per annum in the Exchequer.[76] The Jacobean Crown's sputtering policy of defence characterised early Stuart military efforts as inconsistent and cosmetic. The abrupt onset of peace, followed by sporadic outbursts of exhortations and mustering, brought mixed results and the general conviction that complacency would again become the standard. The 1605 instructions, lukewarm and decentralised in enforcement, led to uneven training and review.

While 1608 saw a new surge of energy from the Council, results were mixed. Gloucestershire did splendidly, while Essex dawdled.[77] Norwich compiled a detailed book listing the City's able-bodied by name, for every ward, in 1608.[78] The Council conceded wide latitude to the localities. Mustering the trained and untrained was not to 'require more haste . . . than may be convenient for the people'. Drilling remained optional, and divisional musters were permitted.[79] During these years the stringency with which the trained forces were maintained was a direct consequence of the personal vigour of the respective Lord Lieutenant. Some shires regressed, while others maintained a minimal level of martial proficiency. The Elizabethan war years had exhausted many parts of England and Wales, but by 1600 a generation of expert soldiers had been bred, who had endured continental sieges, fought guerrilla wars in Ireland, adapted successfully to amphibious warfare, and published studies of contemporary conflicts.

When James bought peace for England, he did so at the price of entering the era of the Thirty Years War with his realm at its lowest level of military proficiency in centuries.

> Throughout most of the 1610s and 1620s, the trained bands' importance was more social and political than military. The militia bound local communities together against the omnipresent danger of faction through patronage and the highly charged symbolism of events like the musters. Teaching the finer points of soldiering was not what made the Lieutenancy useful.[80]

The momentum of the Elizabethan war years had been lost. A 'neglecte of necessarie provisions for warr' and 'a great decaie of Armes' had occurred due to the 'happie times of peace we have inioyed sithence his Majesties comeing to the Crowne'.[81] James's government had had great difficulty ascertaining its military strength at home and abroad. By the second decade of the 1600s the lack of data regarding ratepayers, stores of weapons, and trained men should have unnerved even the most complacent Privy Councillor. The reactive nature of the Jacobean military dictated resumption of serious mustering when, as a response to rumours of an O'Neill conspiracy and Spinola's continental campaigning, the strategic situation was deemed sufficiently grave by the government. From the period 1613–14 the ranks of militia again coalesced and local soldiering men emerged. One of the more promising signs of the revival of English warfare was the advancement of the untrained as well as the trained but unarmed militiamen, to the status of the select trained and accoutred élite.[82]

Muster-masters and military charges

Although the central government and Lord Lieutenant ordered a general muster and preferred comprehensive assemblies (to hinder the 'borrowing' of equipment and to facilitate making lists), the deputy lieutenants and constables, with the assistance of the bailiffs, very often spread the mustering out over a fortnight or so, summoning adjacent hundreds to a rendezvous where a deputy lieutenant and the local captain viewed the troops, as was the case in Suffolk in October 1614.[83] Towns continued to muster independently, of course. With the reinstitution of general, national musters in 1612, the revival of training exercises in 1613, and ultimately the modernisation of weapons (replacing calivers with heavier muskets) in 1618, military service became more exacting and hence more expensive. More than ever, local officers sought out the more affluent to contribute, to buy arms, and, whenever possible 'to weare them themselves', reversing the early Jacobean trend by which the less able had infiltrated the ranks.[84] In some counties – Buckinghamshire for example – labourers stood alongside the craftsmen and occasional gentleman, shouldering muskets, calivers, or pikes, and even straddling mounts, and couching lances.[85] The societal ramification of widening the qualifications for militia service meant that people who were feared prone to unruliness were to be trained in the application of violent force.[86] Worse, the majority entirely lacked military skills, in an era where the art of war demanded unprecedented training. In 1619, Leicestershire spent £271 9s. on the general muster, training, equipment, and personnel. Of that, £50 found its way into the pocket of a controversial interloper, the muster-master.[87]

The odium associated with the muster-master within the shire was compounded by the bad reputation of muster-masters on overseas campaigns.[88] The treasurers of expeditions generally quarrelled with their muster-masters over allegations of excusing 'checks' of troop strength, so that more money might be wrung from the treasurer to the benefit of the captains and muster-master. Conversely, the captains despised the muster-master because his musters would reveal excessive dead pay and inflated troop numbers.[89] Thomas Digges, who learnt first-hand the trials of serving as a muster-master abroad, compiled a thinly veiled critique of English military administration that touched on the muster-master, treasurer, auditor, and commanding officers. Appended was a condemnation of fiscal abuses practised in English army administration. Clearly, the contradictions and inefficiency of the management of the English forces in the Low Countries offended Digges as a mathematician, an administrator, and a Protestant patriot.[90] This background of corruption, which led ultimately to the abolition of the office of expeditionary force muster-master on 25 March 1588,[91] tainted the domestic activities of muster-masters later on. Further increasing the muster-master's unpopularity was the transference of his salary upon local government, making him a Crown-sponsored meddler who worked within the Lord Lieutenant's patronage network at the expense of those he bullied.[92] Through lieutenancy the shires might 'absorb' this expensive appendage to the trained bands. Patronage shifted correspondingly, as the lieutenancy, and ultimately the locality itself, assumed control of appointing the muster-master. From a military standpoint, Whitehall lost the one person who might ensure enforcement of the government's military agenda. Now the county and town communities not only had greater say in who might be their muster-master, but also controlled the purse strings so that he might be 'guided' by their vision of military preparedness.[93]

Captain Thomas Panton, a veteran piketrailer, found himself in a classic dilemma as he traversed the circuitous road from London to Somerset. He could have asked for no better patrons for his mission. The Privy Council had selected him, lauding his 'sufficiency and experience in martiall service', and presented him as a muster-master to the Lord Lieutenant, the Earl of Pembroke. Panton was, in the tense war year of 1598, to remedy the military defects of a strategically important shire in which there existed an alarming paucity of deputy lieutenants. No muster-master at all served Somerset, and the trained bands had not been exercised for several years.[94] Panton's predicament existed because a prospective muster-master did not fit comfortably in the court and country dichotomy of lieutenancy. At worst he was an expensive affront to the shire's military abilities. At best he was a citizen who enjoyed the Lord Lieutenant's patronage at the expense of his neighbours. When injected into the locality by a badgering Privy Council, he personified the central government more than any other official. He could easily become the focus of local resentment, which would neutralise any effort he might make, however much it might be above vested interest. Muster-masters threatened to rupture the decentralised linkages surrounding the management of armed force in the locality.

Under the early Stuarts, muster-masters' fees fell under the despised rubric of those charges and impositions that lacked statutory authority. Given James's proclivity towards peace and the lack of a sustained programme of musters, too often the helpless and hapless muster-master found himself penniless. Panton's successors in Somerset were no exception. In 1612 the salary was in arrears to the sum of £112. Sam Norton, a local justice who doubled as the muster-master, must have had sufficient local clout to have the quarter sessions order a special rate collected across the shire. Every level of local government was drawn into the process: the sessions judges compelled the Justices of the Peace to empower the constables to obtain the money.[95] King Charles and his favourite, the Duke of Buckingham recognised that an infusion of non-commissioned officers, supplementing the efforts of a muster-master, could raise the efficiency of the militia, especially if the sergeants had military experience and the support of the local captains. In April 1626, the Somerset deputy lieutenants presented to the trained-band captains the sergeants who were to put the troops through their paces in an elongated summer mustering.

> This bearer is one of the Sargents which is sent downe by the Kinges Majesties direction for the disciplyninge of the Trayned bandes and with him wee send you the trew Copies of his Majesties letter and our Lord Lyuetenaunts: And if you please to imploy him you may have his servyce for Eight weekes to be disposed of in your Regiment. . . .'[96]

The recipient of this 'offer' was Sir Robert Phelips, an indefatigable advocate of local control, and training, of the militia.[97] Phelips, the 'colonell of a regyment,' was incensed, 'I being the oldest colonell of the countrey ne'er heard one word of these directions tyll now'.[98] Speaking as a deputy lieutenant, Sir Ralph Hopton justified the introduction of muster-masters.

   The institution of the muster-master had medieval origins and was in some ways a legacy of the practices associated with the Marian militia statute.[99] Charles I, then, was simply reinforcing his programme of militia reform by bringing in a specialist, in some cases an outsider, in others an arm of the patronage of lieutenancy. The King sometimes objected to the 'election' of a muster-master, but nevertheless authorised 'the levyinge of his paye being £50 yerely and the arrerages thereof'. Justices were to initiate the collection of the money. A 'hundred rate' was to be gathered, and the quarter sessions rolls instructed each hundred to collect. Hopton replied to Phelips regarding the sergeants:

> by reason much of the tyme is spent which is lymitted unto the Sergeants; soe that one of them cannot have tyme to discipline your Regiment, and . . . since . . . all that heard [hold] office under the States ar commanded over to theire places . . . I thinke fitt that the whole number of the .4. Sergeants be imployed in disciplinynge your Regiment for a fortnight, whereof one of them to be wholely imployed in your owne Company, another in Captaine Champines and Captaine Cox, whose Companies lyeth neerest togeather. The Third with Captaine Blancherd and Captaine Ford, the fowerth Captaine Morgan and Captaine Kenne . . . by which Course (if it please you to approve of yt) your Regiment maye have the like tyme of disciplinynge as the rest of the Regiments had, for they had every of them Eight weekes for one sergeants servyce, and you may have the servyce of .4. Sergeants for a fortnight. . . . [F]or questionynge your right of seniority if there be any error in that I pray impute yt to my ignorance in Martiall matters [of course, Hopton, unlike Phelips, was a skilled

veteran commander!]; for I doe conceive that you being Collonell of the last voyde Regiment, that therefore you ar the youngest Collonell, and if I am in the wronge I will answer yt. . . .[100]

Hopton's suspicion that the West Country trained bands needed more rigorous drill was supported by examination of neighbouring Dorsetshire's forces. An 'untrayned rabble of men armed with all sorts of weapons' made up the Dorset militia at the accession of Charles I, or so opined Sir Walter Earle. And the lack of uniformity, he argued, stemmed from inequitable rating.[101]

On 21 May 1626 the Privy Council sent muster orders to the Lords Lieutenants, remarking that previous instructions 'have byn but slackly performed by the Deputy Lyuetenaunts in many Counties'. All horse and foot were to be mustered and reviewed, arms and armour inspected, and returned

> unto us the names of all such persons of what soever qualitty they shalbe deficient whyther by absence or by wante; or insufficiency of Armes, or in what soever other neglect, that they maye be punished with such severitye as they shall apeare to deserve. . . .

The Lords Lieutenants were also to 'call upon the Clergie for performance' of their military obligation.[102] Accordingly, Pembroke ordered the deputy lieutenants on 23 May 1626 to command 'a generall view and muster all the trayned bands', reminding them of 'the safety of this kingedome in these dangerous tymes, which may depend much uppon the serviceable goodnes of the armes and the readines of those which are to use them'.[103]

A similar grievance regarding muster-masters surfaced at quarter sessions in Shropshire. In April 1635 the grand jury raised the issue of the arrears of the muster-master's £50 annual salary. Now Shropshire, located on the Welsh borders, had for centuries taken seriously its military obligation. Shrewsbury, like Bristol, took corporate pride in keeping filled the ranks of bands. In 1579 the town and liberties of Shrewsbury dutifully mustered their forces, though the preponderance of bows, bills, and the occasional spear or dagger, could not have greatly pleased a Crown that valued gunpowder weapons increasingly. Significantly, the corporate bodies (drapers, mercers, shearman, weavers, glovers, etc.) assumed responsibility for arming and mustering defence forces.[104] Despite James I's weakening of the statutory underpinning of the militia's military obligation, Shropshire continued to drill its trained bands and employ a muster-master.[105] The constitutional debate generated by the Parliaments of 1624–8[106] and accompanying military charges of the Caroline war years, culminating in the Petition of Right, made Salopians desirous to control local military activities.

In 1635 a presentment against the muster-master fee was met head-on by Justice of the Peace Timothy Tourneur, a client of the Lord Lieutenant, the

Earl of Bridgwater. When Tourneur chided the jurors, Sir John Corbet (also a justice) defended them, and demanded a reading of the statute book. When the clerk recited the Petition of Right, Corbet drew the audience's attention to the relevant passage.[107] Ultimately, Corbet, the jurors, and others were summoned before the Privy Council and Sir John found himself gaoled. Having browbeaten its critics, the Crown carried on with the business of the Personal Rule. The muster-master (Edward Burton) got his arrears and was still serving in the muster-master's place when the Scottish Rebellion broke out in 1637.[108] The House of Commons during the Long Parliament ultimately avenged Corbet by voting articles of impeachment against the Lord Lieutenant and the Privy Councillors who had imprisoned Corbet. The House also determined that the muster-master's fee was indeed contrary to the Petition of Right.[109] Widespread protest over muster-masters' fees reflected the politicisation of the trained bands on the eve of the Civil War.[110]

Lieutenancy as an early Stuart political issue

Political issues exacerbated provincial conflicts and drove a wedge between what was perceived as best for the country and best for the King. Although Sir Robert Phelips reaped the blessings of peace in Somerset, he had shown little inclination to defend either his neighbours or sovereign. During his years as a deputy lieutenant he had blessed with his presence the shire musters on a solitary occasion, and then for the purpose of harrassing militia captain John Boyse:

> his frequent Neglects or rather contempts of those Services, havinge for these many yeares never bin present at any Musters, but att that tyme, when he brought your Commaunds to dismisse Capt Boyse, unto whome he had a particular Quarrell.[111]

Phelips allegation that he had not been notified of the muster of 1636 was refuted by the deputy lieutenants, who claimed '. . . the truth, is he had theis Letters delivered him by Sir John Stawell [Phelips' enemy of the 1620s], And signed Warrants for the Mustering some of the Regiments but attended them not'.[112]

John Lord Poulett, who had become a deputy lieutenant around 1624 and a peer in 1627, squared up to Phelips. Poulett's 1636 muster provided an occasion for Phelips to resuscitate the grievances of the 1620s and engage in obstructionism that not only confounded the local practice of the Personal Rule, but (more satisfyingly) embarassed Poulett personally. Phelips' machinations fooled no one:

> Lord Poullett as Colonell had the Consent of us all, and warrant from three of us to Muster in Kingsmore [King's Moor], which is a very

equall and indifferent place for his Regiment. And in some respects fitter than any other; why Sir Robert Phillips should account itt within his Circuite and Compasse, Or what is his Circuite and Compasse we cannot imagine . . . it is neither his Land, nor his division, as a Justice of Peace, and about three or foure mile from his house. But the place is within the Precincts where the Lord Poullets regiment is raised, And tis Sir John Stowells Land, within his division as a Justice of Peace, and not above two Miles from his house. . . .[113]

Poulett defended his choice of location for the Kingsmore muster. It was too easy for a cantankerous individual to subvert the promotion of the public good.

My Lord. You knowe Sir Robert Phillipps, and the condicion of the man, and that he hath bin in and out in these Imployments; You have had good proofe of the Temper and Abilities of the rest your Servants, and of their Inclinacions to honnor and serve you; tis all our hopes, that you will not permitt one unquiett Man to troble the rest.[114]

Phelips claimed Kingsmore lay in his division and that it was inappropriate that a muster be held so close, and unknown, to him. Phelips referred to Poulett's 'craftye insinuacion', implying that the muster was a threat to him, physically perhaps or in terms of prestige. Phelips went on to claim that Poulett was 'abuseing my loyalty to his Majestys service', an amazing assertion, since Phelips consistently undermined the King's interest by seeking his own.[115] Lord Lieutenant Pembroke sent transcripts of the responses of the warring sides to each, and wished to mediate: 'howe much I desire Peace and a good Understandinge betweene you.' The Lord Lieutenant would advance the royal service and compose, as he put it, the differences amongst the deputies.[116] By the late 1630s, the Lords Lieutenants were hard-pressed to find common ground between an uncompromising Crown and provincial interests that were local in the extreme.

The case of Roman Spracklinge of Montacute, Somerset, exemplified the provincial subversion of the English military system: evasion of the press through personal connection, personal rivalries that undermined the efficient mustering of the militia, quasi-legal 'borrowing' of weapons, infusion of military matters with local and national political issues, shoddy procedures at musters, and malicious prosecution combined with obstruction of the King's business. In his insatiable quest for recognition and power within the shire, Sir Robert Phelips seized opportunities to peddle influence and exhibit his benign paternalism, especially to his social inferiors. These selfish motives of patronage and image made him oblivious to the service of Crown and country.[117] When a place in the ranks of the trained bands fell open in 1627, Spracklinge made suit to Phelips for the position in order 'to prevent [Spracklinge from] beinge pressed a common souldier'.[118] As militia, Spracklinge and some of his colleagues were not up to standards and to at least one muster they had 'not brought with them their best array furniture and armour' as required. The constable had received a warrant from the deputy lieutenants to commit Spracklinge for absenting himself without excuse from the general muster at Kingsmore. Spracklinge told Phelips that the constable had a warrant to serve on him. Phelips informed Thomas Chaffie, constable of the hundred of Tintinhull, that Spracklinge was blameless

> for not appearinge with hes Armes before the Lord Poulett at the last muster in Kingsmore. I pray for beare to execute that warrant ... let the Lord Poulet know that the fellow hath noe armes, nor is fitt to be charged with any; the Armes which he sometime wore were mine and by me a good while since taken from him, soe that if there be an offence comitted, twas by mee not the poore fellow. . . .[119]

The deputy lieutenants snapped back:

> As touchinge the armes, if Sir Robert Phelipps hath taken them away, it will be his care aswell as ours to gett them or others, in thier steed [stead], to be in readines for his Majesty's service. But as for Spracklin, who stands a trained souldier enrolled, lett Sir Robte Phelippes know, that though he keepe the armes, yet wee expect that Spracklin should appeare and performe that duety. . . . put the same warrant in execucion, as you will answer your neglect thereof at your perill.[120]

Phelips appealed to the Lord Lieutenant: '. . . you may tell the Lord Poulett that I shall be bold under his lordships good favour to protecte the poore fellow from the Gaole untill my Lord Leiutenant shall declare that his pretended offence deserves soe severe a punishment.'[121] Poulett arrested Spracklinge not to enforce military discipline but rather to avenge a dispute with Phelips dating to 1628, over loaned arms. But, in 1636, Spracklinge appeared at the muster late and Poulett departed early, with significant consequences. Phelips was able to liberate Spracklinge and justly accuse the lord of falsely imprisoning a man who had indeed done his duty (if somewhat belatedly). In the end, Spracklinge went free, Poulett received a reprimand, Phelips gloated, and the King's service was largely ignored.[122] This unseemly and self-interested behaviour on the part of the deputy lieutenant was not confined to Caroline Somerset. The Lord Lieutenant, even under Elizabeth, had recognised that deputy lieutenants, too, mediated and negotiated between the Crown and provincial interest.

The decentralised nature and the protocols of patronage that persisted in the Tudor and early Stuart periods and dictated relationships amongst the Lord Lieutenant and his deputies can be seen in Burghley's dealings with his some-times sycophantic deputy lieutenants, Sir Henry Cocke and Sir John Brockett. When Mr Colte was discharged as the captain of Sir John Cutts's band, the deputy lieutenants 'assembled and conferred togeather'. They concluded that within the two hundreds from which Cuttes's band was 'compounded' there were no gentlemen left who were fit for such a charge, other than the names listed and sent to Burghley. Sir Harry Conningsby's company had been con-ferred upon Mr Luke, who accepted the charge. The central government marvelled that Mr Colte, who they considered fit and capable of taking on the company was so unwilling to do so. They suspected he had been discouraged by some. 'But this we knowe, that (excepte his furniture with Armor for himself, and his drumes, and Ensigne untill he shalbe imployed in service) his Charge cannot exceade £5 a yeare.' Burghley had discharged Colte. The deputy lieutenants yielded to Burghley, but expressed their desire to have the place filled quickly,

> whereby he might not onely be well acquainted with his soldiors: But allsoe might enter into the speady trayninge of them. Which for soe longe a wante of a Capten, (beinge happeninge in that time) many of them are verie unskillfull and unexperienced in martiall services.[123]

Colte's exemption meant that he declined not only to do his duty for the Queen, but (perhaps more importantly) to uphold his responsibilities within the community. Implicitly, the deputy lieutenants chided their Lord Lieutenant for excusing a man from carrying his fair share of the burden.[124] The alternative to a consensual military organisation based upon lieutenancy was to centralise, a method agreeable to Charles I.

Centralisation, which exerted itself with fatal consequences in the matter of religion, was proposed as a panacea for the supposed ills that infected England's military system. From the army proposals by the Duke of Buckingham in 1624[125] to the 'Union of Arms' scheme of secretary Sir John Coke, proposals for standing armies much more radical than the Crown's 'per-fect militia' programme surfaced in the political climate created by Charles and Buckingham. The project for the creation of a standing army of 15,000 infantry and 3,000 cavalry, the 'Order of Warrefare', looked backwards in some ways in order to face the dilemma of fielding a modern army.[126] The project eschewed lieutenancy altogether. Infantry arms would be placed in the cus-tody of churchwardens and constables. Excuses for non-appearance at drill would come from the Justices of the Peace. Grounded in the individual parish, that community would pay the soldiers of the Order, musketeers receiving twice the pay of pikemen (12d. per week as opposed to 6d. for drilling, and in time of war 3s. a week). The Crown would supply 'powder and shott' in time of war, and the weapons would be owned by the locality. Muster-masters would instil military discipline, and four armourers would be required of each shire to 'Keepe the Armes Cleane and supply defects'.[127] The cost of the programme was offset by the advantages it brought to the community. The 'yonger sonnes of the gentry' and 'elder sonnes of the yeomanry' would have brave employment. Further, 'since the greatest cullour for impositions at home is the defence of a country, this will for ever take away all cullour of home impositions'.

As the words 'trained bands', 'militia', 'coat-and-conduct money', 'presses', and 'levies' are entirely absent from the tract, and no provision is therefore made to meld this army with the militia, one might take it as a wholesale rejection of the military *status quo* in England.[128] Equally revealing is the author's dualistic conception of strategy that distinguished the Crown's advantages in maintaining a standing army from the benefits to citizens at large. The King might deploy these forces in 'forraine warres' and thus 'give Lawes unto the whole world'. Regarding the English people, the author argues they will be saved from invasion, and that the intervention of the expeditionary force abroad might confound enemies by creating a 'diversion'. The marketing of this project reflected the very different attitude towards war held by Charles I as opposed to the views of his subjects.

The King fancied protecting and promoting élites, such as the Order of the Garter. The proposed lesser Order would sport St George's cross as well. The infantrymen, when going about civilian life, would be entitled to wear a cloth emblem of the red cross on their outermost garments. And in an age of sumptuary laws, the calvalrymen might stroll about with a silk St George emblazoned upon their cloaks. This local military élite enjoyed notable exemptions and privileges unavailable to the inexpert in arms. Protection from creditors and exemption from appointment to unwelcome local office were to be bestowed upon the parish warriors. Should they commit petty crimes, they were not subject to being pilloried or whipped. For more cardinal crimes, decapitation rather than hanging was their lot.[129] Perhaps it was mistrust of the nobility that led the author to keep Lords Lieutenants out, though the lords temporal and spiritual did have roles to play: they would pay the wages of the colonels and the captains, who would be selected by the King.

England's strategic predicament was blindingly obvious in the 1620s. Secretary Coke's 'Union of Arms' proposal recited the Catholic leagues ranged against England and its Protestant allies. Although La Rochelle's peril diverted attention to that corner of Europe, England buttressed the ramshackle collection of Protestant interests; or as Coke put it '. . . England being the marck which is most aimed at.' Though Coke harkened back to Elizabethan bonds of association, his strategic vision owed more to the political machinations of the Parliaments of the 1620s. The pettiness of

Caroline domestic politics undermined Coke's proposal, which digressed from an illuminating analysis of potential Protestant alliances into a cynical discourse on how to coerce Englishmen to open their purses to their protectors and stifle political dissent.[130] All such schemes reacted against the striking autonomy of the shire militias.

The privileges of the English militia

Many English, who may have read Machiavelli, believed that a state was most securely protected by a militia made up of its 'owne naturall subjects'.[131] Unlike the Florentine, however, Englishmen were convinced that the ruler of 'great Brittaine and Ireland' had the bravest men at his disposal. No one could best the English 'in the Tryalls of Warre', though with the caveat that they must first be trained and disciplined. Tangentially, the common laws of England were perfectly suited for the exercising of an armed citizenry. Strategic prudence, natural law, and Englishness all dictated that Charles I create his 'perfect militia', 'malice having found out fiery weapons' necessitated drill, especially with the musket, 'being a weapon of greater difficultie and more curious practice'. The impulse to create an expert defensive arm came from the realisation of England's strategic vulnerability, hemmed in as the nation was from all sides. The 'continuall enterprises of Spaine with active Armes' had forced England into a 'necessarie defensive warre of the Low Countries'. Simultaneously, 'Broyles in France' and incessant campaigning in the Germanies and Italy had endowed warfare with a certain remoteness, so that 'the great blessing of peace in England brings us into such a security and neglect of Armes'. But royal sponsorship and Englishness would, naturally, remedy the situation: for 'there wants nothing but execution of the lawes and custome of trayning bands'.[132] While Whitehall provided the impetus for the military rehabilitation of the realm through a trained-band programme (for example, when the Duke of Buckingham sent Low Countries sergeants into the shires to drill the locals), still the system was highly decentralised in actual operations.[133] The Crown's sergeants were rebuffed on occasion, as in Norfolk, where old soldiers collecting pensions were preferred.[134] Local communities might retain some control of their resources, and manage their own defence, as when Bristol seized the initiative in October 1625 by petitioning to establish their own artillery yard so the town's citizens might perfect the art of war.[135]

Devon in the autumn of 1625 managed its defence almost as if it were a sovereign state. The network of beacons was coordinated with rendezvous points for their eight regiments. A provost marshal, carriage-master and master of ordnance were appointed from amongst local gentlemen, while the inhabitants themselves inspected coastal fortifications, including the repair and positioning of Totnes's 'field peeces.' The regimental colonels

Figure 3.2 Half a century after their forebears had mobilised to face the threat of the Spanish Armada, the English militia had become a more selective and highly trained force.

Source: Detail, the London Trained Bands escort the entourage of the Queen Mother, 1638 (reproduced by permission of the Museum of London).

were local potentates (though the tinners fielded a corporate regiment), and the strategic defence of the shire, with different scenarios anticipated and analysed, was planned by those who knew the terrain, not from Whitehall.[136] The county knew its vulnerabilities best. The Norfolk interests that rejected the Crown's Low Countries sergeants were also the monarch's eyes and ears in the country, and saw through the ruses and excuses of muster defaulters. The deputy lieutenants reported undervaluation of estates to the Privy Council, so that examples might be made of those slack in providing for common security. When William Oliver of Mowlton 'defaulted in his horse and foote armes, coming to serve undecently in raggs', his recalcitrance was reported to Whitehall.[137]

On the eve of the Thirty Years War there dwelt, on paper at least, in the shires of England and Wales roughly some 100,000 to 150,000 militiamen who had received some modicum of training and had access to weapons.[138] By 1642, the Crown could count fewer trained soldiers, certainly fewer than 100,000 in spite of the initiative of the 'perfect militia'.[139] Part of the decline can be attributed to the atrophying and disappearance of the Border militia bands, a process that continued through the first half of the seventeenth century. 'Westmorland and Cumberland were two salient examples of complete neglect; in these counties, the militia seems to have been virtually nonexistent by the 1630s.'[140] Excused by the Jacobean pacification of the Borders, militiamen in the northern shires left their colours. Northumberland had 2,300 able men in reserve for King James, plus contingents of 1,800 armed militia, perhaps 100 pioneers, 8 demi-lances, and 125 light horse. Cumberland accounted for 2,100 untrained but capable men, 1,300 accounted militia, 86 pioneers, 5 demi-lances, and perhaps 100 light horsemen. Westmorland's totals resembled those of its neighbours (2,000, 1,200, 200, 4, 80).[141] Border shires succeeded in reducing their military obligation through the 1620s at a time when the monarch was invigorating the militia in other corners of the realm.[142]

If there were fewer Caroline militiamen than the number that had mustered under James I, the former were better drilled and equipped. Jacobean lieutenants probably made up quantities on paper in order to compensate for what was undoubtedly a lack of military quality. Equally insubstantial was the statutory ungirding of the Jacobean militia. Successive Expiring Laws Continuance Acts, in 1604 and 1624 respectively, eliminated the legal basis of the trained bands.[143] A government bill of 1621 that would have helped standardise the 'Arms of the Kingdom' failed to navigate the Commons.[144] While Charles's accession in 1625 launched England on a bellicose foreign policy, still the monarch could not induce Parliament to invest in a major military build up or a new model militia. By the autumn of 1628, Charles I had failed utterly to coerce Parliament to sustain his military adventures. The modest overseas campaigns of 1625 and 1627 had not achieved their objectives. The county communities had reluctantly pressed men for the royal armies.[145] The Parliament of 1628 had quarrelled bitterly with the King, largely over military charges that rested solely on the royal prerogative. When the Duke of Buckingham's preparations at Portsmouth for a third expedition were cut short by an assassin's knife, Charles saw it (perhaps rightly) as a direct result of the unpopularity of the Caroline war effort.

Rather than negotiating a statutory basis for impressment, lieutenancy, billeting, coat-and-conduct money, and other military grievances, the King decided that the Lords Lieutenants, buttressed by their own aristocratic power and the royal prerogative, would create a 'perfect militia' independent of Parliament and unheedful of the protests in the shires. From 1629 to 1634, the bands were encouraged to raise themselves to a high level of performance, spurred on by a 1631 order to drill regularly (based on the 1623 printed instructions the Crown had distributed throughout the realm).[146] During the period from 1635 to 1638, towns and shires should have been mastering land warfare by drilling their 'perfect militias' and bolstering the royal navy by paying 'ship money', all under the auspices of Charles's 'Personal Rule', sanctioned by the prerogative. When Scotland rebelled in 1637–8, the trained bands faced tests in 1639 and again in 1640. Or did they? The political context of the Bishops' Wars prompted some militiamen to recruit substitutes who were not always given the best military hardware. It has been suggested that the poor showing of Hamilton's 1639 expedition revealed Caroline England's inherent weaknesses for waging war.[147] The problem was, from the very outset of the reign, English warfare remained inseparable from the politics of Charles I. Whether military expenditure in the mid-1620s, billeting in the late 1620s, or the mobilisation of the militia in 1639–40, Caroline politics and English warfare were intertwined, to the latter's detriment.[148]

By the late 1630s, even the most zealous Lord Lieutenant, for example Henry Hastings, the fifth Earl of Huntingdon, who had made Leicestershire's militia the paradigmatic early Stuart trained band, found his efforts to promote the Crown's policies thwarted by his countrymen.[149] Deputy lieutenants had the effrontery to inform the government that they were exempt from sending troops out of their shire.[150]

Hertfordshire militiamen argued that the autonomy and integrity of the trained bands were essential to English security. When threatened with impressment and amphibious service in 1640, they renewed their pledge to defend the King's person, as they had in 1588, 1599, and 1601. In those instances they crossed the shire boundary to Tilbury, London, indeed Whitehall itself, to do their duty. But these actions had not compromised their ancient 'priviledge . . . to be exempted from forraigne service: strange comaunders or to be transported to any place by sea.' Disavowing the Tudor practice of selecting out militia companies for continental service, the Hertfordshire bands proclaimed that 'trained souldiers are the Cheifest strength and glory of this kingdom' and were not to be deployed except by 'necessity'. Implicitly the shires were presuming to dictate strategic priorities to the Council, who 'before one blowe be strucke' had resorted to 'presse the trained bands, as if wee were the meanest and basest of Majesty's subjects'. On the contrary, 'the yeomanry are so free borne as any of the gent' of England. The constitutional implications became explicit, as the military obligation led to discussion of the rights of the freeholder, levying of military charges, the Petition of Right, and Parliament's role in warmaking.

Countrymen turned Charles I's early reforms to their own advantage, arguing that misuse of the militia would lead to the decay of English military strength and (interestingly) the diminution of the Lord Lieutenant's authority. The militia had been exhorted by the lieutenancy to become expert in the use of their weapons so that they might bear the honour of defending the King's person and the integrity of the realm. Impressment of such men cast pearls before swine, to the discredit of England. The petitioners closed quite audaciously by including their refusal to pay ship money (ostensibly because they were already making a significant contribution to the defence of the realm) under the rubric of their privileges.[151] Such rumblings were to be echoed in the militia controversy of 1641–2, and adopted by the loyal Irish self-defence forces when revolt broke out in Ireland in November 1641.[152] The Irish loyalists quickly learned how to whip their army into fighting trim, and dealt with

> the want of discipline and order amongest the new men raised by us. The generall wants which doe now begin to abound amo[n]gest us in all parts of this countie [Down/Antrim], besides those of Armes cloathing and money, have contrained us to resolve on some other Course for the governing of the souldiors then that under which they were at the first raised, and that is by placing them in Regiments and Garrisons where by the authorite of their Commaunders they may be the better trained and Commaunded, for when they lay in Scattered Troopes and Companyes in the Countrey we could not (by any meanes) draw them together, from their owne Townes either to assist one another or to oppose the enemye in any other place, (were the occasion never soe important) were theire owne perculer interests did not evidently press them unto it, upon these groundes we thought it best to dispose the men which by the authoritie graunted unto us by the Lordes Justices and Councell, were raised into 3 regiments. . . .[153]

From the assertion of the rights of a loyal and armed citizenry in 'British Ireland', one can see parallels in the neutralist movements (such as the clubmen) during the Civil War. Indeed, the common-law context of the rights of self-defence mirrored ideologies underlying the American War for Independence. By 1642, subjects (if not their sovereign) distinguished between voluntary defence of the realm by substantial citizens and the coercion involved in the practice (and theory) of impressment.

In 1642 Parliament wrested control of the lieutenancy from the Crown by installing its own nominees as Lords Lieutenants.[154] The history of lieutenancy is the chronicle of its transformation from military command to a form of amateur civil service. Yet the military component continued in its pre-eminence through 1642 as warfare changed drastically. And it was the military component that led Parliament to attempt the circumvention of lieutenancy during the crises of 1641–2, proposing an impressment act that kept the press strictly within the jurisdiction of magistracy. Justices of the Peace and mayors would raise troops by impressment without any interference from the lieutenancy.[155]

4

THE DEFENCE OF THE REALM
Impressment and mobilisation

Members of the tumultuous 1628 Parliament asserted that the Henrician mobilisations of 1511–13 marked a break from earlier, particularly medieval, campaigns. 'Before tertio of Henry the Eight there was no ordinary pressing of soldiers,' proclaimed one member. Sir John Selden presented a sweeping history of forced military service in England. 'No men compellable to take press money unless it be by warrant . . . [B]etween Edward the 2d's time and H. the 7ᵗʰ . . . great men would press their tenants because they would not refuse. The King took example by them.' The King did indeed, though current historical research emphasises the conservatism of Henrician recruitment more than the ruthless exploitation of 'this new way of press money'.[1] Soldiers could be gathered under the royal standard through the agency of nobles or via community levies. In both procedures indentures or some other arrangement would define terms of service. What the Parliament of 1628 regarded as innovatory were the massive 'call-ups' of the 1540s wars, which snared thousands of militia for foreign service. In September 1542, the Duke of Norfolk simply informed the mayor and sheriffs of Norwich that Henry VIII had appointed him 'lieutenant Northwarde' and was gathering an army 'to resiste the malice of Skotts and to have the rule and levying of *all the abill men* of Norfolk and Suffolk'. The City was to 'make due serche' to raise able men, properly harnessed, for the King's war. 'I shall take order ffor prest money ffor them, and cotes to be delyved [delivered]. . . .'[2] Similar procedures were followed for French expeditions of the 1540s.

Early Tudor mobilisations owed much to the practices of the fifteenth century. During the Wars of the Roses military bonds among individual knights and lords had proved a more useful system for fielding armies than negotiating with, or bullying, communities for troops. If the strength of England lay in a free and armed yeomanry, capable of standing against traitors within the realm as well as invaders without, then a wise monarch did not exhaust his citizens with incessant demands for men and weapons. The free commons were the King's best friend in evil times. The old system of array had proved itself from the late 1200s onwards. These systems were never mutually exclusive, and virtually all royal armies remained amalgams of obligations. 'Thus Richard III and Henry VII appear to have made greater use than their predecessors to constitute a select force in readiness to oppose rebellion or invasion consisting of private companies commanded by trusted gentlefolk, about whose terms of service there was prior agreement.'[3] That 'prior agreement', or individual consent, which figures prominently in the English consciousness, was more easily obtained from a noble than from a wapentake or borough. Moreover, the medieval intermediary in the recruiting process, the 'arrayer', was more of a subcontractor than was an eighteenth-century pressman. Captains, many of whom were of humble stock, possessed familiarity with localities and developed working relationships with rural and civic authorities. Conscription was rarely accomplished easily, but the captains and arrayers of the fourteenth and fifteenth centuries constructed a highly efficient mechanism for the mobilisation of royal armies. By the late 1590s, Tudor impressment would prove equally effective. But direct intrusion by the central government, via Privy Council letters, would be (or at least seemed to members of Parliament) a more arbitrary and oppressive method.

Steely-eyed Henry VIII preferred to rely upon people rather than upon institutions. His strategic paradigm for his French and Scottish wars remained essentially medieval, and his inclinations proved similarly traditional when he contemplated mobilisation. In spite of the existence of contracts and indentures that had proliferated since the reign of Edward III, Henry preferred something 'quasi-feudal', an arrangement that was grounded in the tenurial obligation and personal connection that existed between landlord and tenant.[4] When war commenced in 1511, Henry dispatched 'signet letters to a number of landowners and office-holders calling upon them to send in certificates of the number of able men they could recruit within their "landes, auctorities, rowmes and offices"'.[4a] Although anti-retainer legislation still lay in place, it was from private individuals that Henry demanded recruits. Personally directed summonses delivered under the King's watchful eye brought forth soldiers whom Henry then arrayed under hand-picked noble commanders.

The King chose his officers, as Wolsey learned, and Henry called upon his own inner military circle. Coat and conduct money returns[5] disclose that Henrician contingents that served abroad were recruited by noble landlords more than by civic or county affiliation. A lord recruited from his lands across shire boundaries.[6] A countrywide system of musters and recruitment received royal mandate as early as November 1509.[7] Perhaps Henry believed collective responsibility moved less briskly than did an individual. The Crown regarded shires and boroughs as repositories of able men and weapons. Mobilisations for overseas service, complicated by logistics and combined operations with the Navy, were best entrusted to military-minded nobles. In the 1540s, the King's faltering hand replaced by a stamp, summonses to muster called upon his nobility's 'household, servants and tenants' to field an army. 'Henry maintained to the end his predilections for men he had known since his youth, in war as at court.'[8]

The King told nobles and gentry to select recruits wisely, for all answered to their royal master in a very personal way for their soldierly performance. Henrician troops, sometimes literally and sometimes figuratively, bore their landlord's livery. Personal accountability to the Crown meant that lords and gentlemen could not shelter so easily behind the collective excuses later endured by Elizabeth I and Charles I. And obedience was due not only to the monarch, but also to the territorial magnate who ruled that corner of the realm. Royal centralisation and regional familial patronage were confluent in the procedures of impressment.[9] Henry raised groups of men, often numbering 25 to 100, who (significantly) served as units, intact, almost as kinship groups, certainly as neighbours, their officers being of the landlord's family, or a deputy. This did not cease in the later Tudor and early Stuart periods, but was especially prevalent under Henry VIII. Few mutinies occurred amongst Henrician troops, perhaps because the men were rather better led, and hence paid and fed with a greater sense of paternalism, than was the case in later decades.

Officers, the Henrician indentures imply, were not usually outsiders, but men drawn from the leadership of the locality, chosen by birth as much as by office. Commanded by their natural leaders, not interlopers, the troops were known to their superiors, who had marched up with them, fought alongside them, and escorted the survivors home, all in the King's pay, practices that predominated into the early Elizabethan era. Paternalist recruiting encouraged an informed selection of able-bodied men, saw that they were 'jacketed' and conducted to their point of departure for the campaign. The latter expense of 'coat and conduct money'[10] came from the royal coffers, which made Henrician impressment more palatable to the local community. Furthermore, the demobilised men, very often in their original groups, journeyed home under royal pay and subsistence. At a campaign's end it was not only the entourage of the officer that made its way back to Newcastle or Carlisle; even those indispensable Cornish miners, who laboured upon the earthworks, found passage back to Truro through the Tudor government's agency.[11]

Henrician practices survived the massive levies of the wars of the 1540s, and explain why militiamen saw themselves as a second line of defence, after more privately recruited expeditionary forces. Even then arrayers and landlords were giving way to council-appointed captains. Members of Parliament in 1628 may have perceived a dangerous precedent in all this, though Henry VIII's younger daughter certainly had not. The gargantuan size, and splendour, of most Henrician campaigns obscured the sporadic nature of Henrician recruitment. In fact, Elizabeth sent more men to the wars than did her bellicose father. Gloriana carried on Tudor magnanimity, paying discharged soldiers and providing their coats in December 1558.[12] In 1561, the Exchequer was reimbursing coat and conduct money expense for Ireland forces.[13] The Queen wrestled with more formidable military finance, beginning in the mid-1580s and escalating up to the day of her death. She was compelled to institutionalise, creating trained bands in the 1570s (which she used overseas in Brittany and elsewhere) and drawing the localities into collective systems of recruitment, especially for the Irish wars.

Elizabethan levies and the institutionalisation of impressment

The demands of maintaining border and continental theatres of operations in an age of siege warfare made intervention in France by a relatively vulnerable power such as England rather daunting. Sir Richard Lee, arguably the realm's finest military engineer, was sent, with 'all spede', to assist the English garrison at Le Havre in October 1562. He split his energies between Le Havre and Berwick, where at both locations the condition of the fortifications demanded improvement.[14] Pioneers, sappers, and miners were needed in both theatres. The flow of such personnel had been northwards in early 1559, but then these essential labouring men were diverted into Normandy. In mid-January 1559 the refurbishment of the Berwick fortifications necessitated the services of 500 pioneers levied from Gloucestershire, Worcestershire, Nottinghamshire, Derbyshire, Suffolk, and Norfolk. It is likely that many were taken on campaign in Scotland in 1560. But by 1562, with Border fortifications still under construction, the focus shifted to English forces at Calais, Dieppe, and Le Havre, with hurried inspection and improvement of the fortifications of the latter imperative.[15] Two hundred and sixty men of the Berwick garrison reinforced the Normandy companies.[16]

Elizabeth's earlier levies were undertaken in the style of her father. The Duke of Norfolk and other nobles, as well as gentlemen, were entrusted to take 'care in seing the nombers appointed to be good and well given men. . . .'[17] So territorial magnates supervised impressment, especially at the outset of the 1562 intervention. The Earl of Arundel recruited 400 Sussex men and Lord St John 400 soldiers of Hampshire.[18] When 600 pressed men marched to Rye for embarkation to France, a gentleman pensioner, Edward Oremesby, was sent to muster and review the men. He came accompanied with 'armor and weapon' to furnish their defects, but the localities too shouldered the burden: 'the justicees of peace from whence the companyes doo come have sent monny for the same purpoos.'[19] Armigill Waad, a sort of muster-master general, enrolled the names of the recruits and paid out 28 days' wages from the money he had been allocated from the treasurer of war, Sir Maurice Denys.[20] Selecting, equipping, and conducting soldiers fell hard upon the sheriffs and Justices of the Peace.

Though sometimes noble (in Kent Lord Cobham was sheriff) or of gentle status (in Herefordshire Sir Ralph Sadler bore the shrievalty), sheriffs discharged impressment duties as part of their office, not as individuals equipped with commissions of array.[21] Captains for their part were still appointed from within the county, but they clearly served the Queen and answered to royal officers.[22]

Elizabeth's Normandy embroilment saw an increasingly bureaucratic and institutional approach than had earlier Tudor mobilisations. Although levies were overseen, implicitly if not always explicitly, by substantial landlords, it was increasingly the sheriffs and Justices of the Peace who spearheaded impressment. In Hertfordshire and Essex, counties within the Cecil sphere of influence, 200 'pyoners' destined for the trenches of Le Havre were pressed. The sheriffs were not to delay the mobilisation by calling together all the Justices of the Peace, but were to confer with those available. Nor were the sheriffs to wait on money from the Exchequer, regardless of London's proximity. In his own hand, Cecil instructed that, if the shire authorities lacked enough money to pay 'the charges of the prest and conduct', they should find funds within their community, even if 'by way of Lone'. The Crown did not refuse to cover these costs, but the burden of raising the cash (in an environment chronically short of coin), and assuring those from whom it might be borrowed that adequate security for repayment was in place, undeniably now fell to local officers. Slowly the institutionalisation of impressment proceeded, though clumsily.[23]

Troops for Le Havre were pressed in successive waves: one in September 1562, two in the second half of June 1563, and then another around 8 July 1563. The initial pressing occurred in the southern coastal counties. In 1563 the levies were drawn from shires further inland, incorporating the human resources, roughly speaking, of the realm south of the Trent. The 'pioneers' came in stages as well, in late January and then midsummer 1563. The nation had been halved into recruiting zones. The southern half of the nation, including Cheshire and Wales, provided men for the continental wars; the North, as had been the case for centuries, fixed itself on Border defence. Significantly 'Gentlemen' (though lords are included) were appointed, usually three to a shire, to oversee impressment.[24] Prisoners, too, were pulled into the ranks. The commissioners at Newgate prison sorted through the inmates, commenting on each offender's suitability for military service at Le Havre. Though some 'quality control' was exercised, the pressing of prisoners by commissioners reflected increasingly bureaucratic procedure and the admission of less-than-satisfactory soldiers into overseas expeditions.[25]

Sending to the wars able-bodied Englishmen appealed to neither Elizabeth nor Cecil, who were both reluctant to place the Queen's subjects (criminal or not) in harm's way, as well as being apprehensive of embroiling the realm in a continental conflict or provoking an invasion of the homeland.[26]

And the men suffered. The Le Havre garrison imported all its foodstuffs from England, and basics such as bedding and clothing were in extremely short supply. But it is tempting to conclude that upon disbandment things got worse because no local nobleman or gentleman had sheltered these discharged soldiers under his wing; recruits depended on a collective bureaucracy that all too easily failed. Troops disembarked 'without Kaptaynes or officers . . . [and with] no books of the musters nor of the reckonynge of vyctualles.' No conduct money remained and the paymasters were absent, raising the spectre that 'some disorder woll fall owt'.[27] Sir William Kellaway composed a 'booke of sertyfficat of soldiers and Laborers' who had landed at Portsmouth on their way home from Normandy. The troops were not a pretty sight,

> . . . havinge neyther clothes to defend the colde, noo money at all to defend Hunger with nor showes [shoes] hable to hange on their feet, and the poore men affirminge that they were constraynid at new havon [Le Havre] to begg money to paye for their passports. . . .[28]

Increasing Irish military commitments further institutionalised impressment. We find in 1567 50 archers from Lancashire sent to Ireland.[29] In August 1585, the Council ordered Lord Howard of Effingham (coincidentally, the Lord Admiral of England) to press 150 footsoldiers and see that they were 'with weapons'. A royal officer with no local affiliation would conduct them, and the bill would be footed by the community: 'receave such money as shalbe disbursed by the Sheyrs for the coate and conduct money' at the rate established by the Crown.[30] Between 30,000 and 40,000 troops left England and Wales for Irish service between the years 1585 and 1602. Roughly a quarter of these were Welsh, and none were from the shires bordering Scotland. As somewhat more than 68,000 men in all were pressed between 1585 and 1602, the allocations to the continental and Irish theatres were roughly equal. The western maritime shires (Devon, Cornwall, Gloucestershire, Lancashire, and Somerset) fielded the biggest Irish contingents between 1594 and 1602. But the most sizeable levies marched out of London and Yorkshire, 2,269 and 2,160 campaigners respectively.

The greatest intensity of mobilisation occurred in 1598–9 and in 1601. Thus the demand for manpower was spread out fairly evenly geographically, with those shires close to ports of embarkation for Ireland or with sizeable populations carrying the heaviest load. Although equity and allowance for ability was observed, successive presses in April, August, October, and December 1601 (which collared between 8,300 and 12,600 men) followed more than a decade and a half of sustained military activities on several fronts.[31] In autumn 1601 every county in England and Wales pressed men to meet the Hispano-Irish threat. In all, The Nine Years War required sixteen individual presses and laid the heaviest burdens upon London, Yorkshire, the English western maritime shires, and Wales. The Welsh principality yielded up roughly 3 per cent of its population, while English shires, on average, pressed less than 1 per cent.[32]

What did it cost to press, equip, and send forth soldiers? When Bury St Edmunds levied seven infantrymen in 1570, the total cost was £24 6s. 10d. Press money, given to the recruits upon their being taken into the ranks, was not a substantial outlay: 2s. 4d. Conduct money amounted to £3 10s., and the coats 9s. apiece (though that did not include the 3s. 6d. for the tailoring). Three pikes cost 7s. 6d., and four calivers £3 12s. Helmets ('muryons') for the calivermen, corselet body armour for the pikemen, swords, girdles, shoes, and cloth caps for all seven, rounded out the costs. Two years later the township expended £4 10s. on five foot soldiers.[33] Suffolk, however, did it right. They purchased the requisite equipment rather than plunder parish armouries or simply send the men off unarmed and shabbily dressed. Conscripting and equipping recruits for overseas service competed with the localities' efforts to train and arm its militia, men zealously protected from any obligation to campaign.

One might argue that militia could not be spared in vulnerable counties, yet West Country shires gave up their trained soldiers to French expeditions on numerous occasions. The Irish wars, notorious for deprivation and death, might swallow up entire shire militia companies. As desperate as the Irish situation became, and as plaintive as the pleas of commanders sounded, still trained-band soldiers were exempted from that ferocious conflict, until the emergency contingent of 500 London militia departed in 1601. Did Elizabeth regard Picardy, Normandy, or Brittany as more vital to English strategic interests, or was she simply appalled at Ireland's capacity for spoiling company upon company of English soldiers and emptying chest upon chest of treasure? The trained bandsmen had been promised 'They should never be pressed for foreign service'. Should the Crown renege, militiamen would offer the captains £20, £30, even £40, to escape an Irish expedition. Sir Robert Cecil was advised, perhaps warned, '. . . if companies must go from this shire to Ireland, such men as are fittest may be pressed, but our trained bands may be kept for the purpose for which they were first chosen'.[34] Thus, Elizabethan militia often found themselves, reluctantly, off to the Continent, but rarely *en route* to Ireland. Lancashire militia were sent to Ireland in 1580, an anomaly not often repeated until the 1601 crisis.[35]

Fear of impressment discouraged Elizabethans not only from militia service, but also from listing themselves as able-bodied citizens. A 1588 report from York confessed, 'all men here have no liking to be inrolled in a muster book. . . . They are unwilling to come into the muster book, lest they should be called upon for any service in Ireland'.[36] Lincolnshire proved equally recalcitrant. Lord Burghley wrote to his lieutenants in that shire,

... you seem to doubt whether the 700 men ... to be put in readiness in the county for any service that should be needful in the North parts or about the frontiers towards Scotland ... should be of those numbers that were appoitned [*sic*] to be trained ... of the most substantial and personable freeholders and husbandmen and their sons for defence of that shire if any invasion should happen there, or otherwise to serve about Her Majesty's person. The truth is when those instructions were sent there was no intention to employ them otherwise than in either of those two services. But some accidents have fallen out sithence which have given cause to have good regard to the north parts and to the borders there. And because the defence thereof some part of the north so near adjoining and bordering upon that shire is in some sort a good defence to the same it shall not be amiss ... that *the numbers already trained for defence of that county be ready to be employed, if need shall be, for the defence of the north parts so nearly adjacent. ...* [I]t shall be requisite that the ... 700 men so appointed by Her Majesty *be had in readiness for any occasion which may be best supplied of the numbers already trained* for the diminution of the charge which otherwise, you write, would grow burdenous to the country by training of several numbers.[37]

The Crown did not quibble over such details in time of national emergency. In one case the lieutenants were asked to ferret out marksmen, those skilled in the use of fowling pieces. But implicit in the instructions was the caveat that the musketeers and calivermen of the trained bands were to be left alone.[38] The militia were trained amateurs, not professional soldiers.

Part of the Crown's difficulty in securing sufficient recruits (willing or unwilling) for the Irish wars stemmed from the fact that the gravity of the situation on the Continent drew residents of the British Isles into the wars of religion. Men willing to take up the profession of arms often migrated voluntarily to the Low Countries. Fewer men thus remained available for Irish service. The government could transfer units from, say, Dutch service, to the Irish theatre, but such a course was fraught with political complications and not inconsiderable expense. The large numbers of Welsh recruits that flocked to the Netherlandish wars particularly compounded the difficulties of impressment. The exodus of young Welshmen to the Low Countries wars, following in Sir Roger Williams' footsteps, diminished the potential of the Crown's best recruiting ground for Irish campaigns.

Institutionalised conscription and impressment coexisted with private recruitment that was organised along lines of patronage and clientage.[39] To raise men, the Crown would either beat the drum, literally, in the streets of London, or resort to its institutional mechanism of impressment to snare the unwilling.[40] We can discover a great deal about volunteers for continental service, particularly during the reign of James I. Usually in their twenties and thirties, veterans could always find a place on the muster roll. Robert Middleton, serving at The Hague, was 59 years old when he took the oath of allegiance upon crossing the Channel in June 1619. Licences to 'go beyond the sea' reveal men travelling in nuclear groups, often an old soldier with a pair of recruits in their early twenties, or brothers-in-arms (literally) and occasionally fathers and sons. Some were illiterate and unskilled, migrating down from the North and the Midlands, or very often from Wales; others, such as Sackville Crowe, came from good families and were destined for careers in the wars of the 1620s or even commercial ventures overseas.[41] Edward Wattkins, for example, marched in Sir John Norris's relief of Antwerp, as a 'pryvat souldier'. Soon he hooked on with Sir Thomas Knowles, and under the latter's patronage, was transformed from common soldier to ensign to lieutenant.[42] Not all troops served the Protestant cause: 'the Great Exchange', a company under Sir Henry Peyton, embarked to serve the Venetian Republic in spring 1619.[43]

With so many Englishmen and Welshmen serving on the Continent, the drain upon the realm's human resources for sustaining the Irish army necessitated impressment upon many counties that the Crown would have preferred to leave undisturbed. The presses in the West Country may not have diminished appreciably the ranks of the militia, but it was inadvisable for able-bodied men of the western coastal shires to disappear into the void of Eire. Lancashire and Cheshire bore their fair share of recruitment.[44] When impressment stretched inland to Yorkshire, not only were these coastal countries engaged in shore defence as well as the outfitting of expeditionary forces, but the country at the heart of the northern defences now diverted resources to Ireland.[45] War, offensive and defensive, could be waged only upon consent grounded in the country's conviction that the commitment was reasonable and that a region was not unfairly burdened in comparison with neighbouring locales. Drawing upon Yorkshire in the era before the Union of Crowns necessarily weakened Border defences, for able-bodied men were needed to bolster the militia in the event of invasion. As the defence of Berwick and the North came to cross purposes with the build-up in Normandy during the early 1560s, so too the Irish theatre worked against the diversion of scarce resources to protect the south of England. Even Yorkshire, the main bulwark of defence in the North, was second only to London in drumming up men for the Irish wars, sending off 2,160 soldiers between 1594 and 1602.[46]

In Somerset and Wiltshire, a steady stream of soldiers marched out of the shires for embarkation to the Continent. In particular, the Brittany campaigns consumed money, men, *materiél*, and time, occasionally even pulling militiamen out of the ranks of the privileged citizenry.[47] European demands abated just as the acceleration of the Irish conflict reached a critical state. Ireland tied up only a thousand or so English troops before 1578, but by 1584 that figure had doubled.[48] When Somerset and Wiltshire found that after decades of military contributions, offensive and defensive, they would now be recruiting local men for Irish service, it seemed not so burdensome. The first call-up required only 150 able men ('not admitting any Rogues or Vagabounds'), 45 as pikemen, 30 musketeers, and 75 calivermen. The Crown assured 'repayment' of some coat and conduct charges from the Lord Treasurer. Several days later, however, the Crown changed its mind about the conductors. Rather than have local authorities conduct the men to the Plymouth embarkation, the government presumed to send its own captains to inspect the quality of the men and arms, and then shepherd them away. As ominous as these proceedings may have appeared, the Irish service made less onerous demands on the West Country, Somerset and Wiltshire at least, than had the Brittany service.[49]

Striving to spare the militia whilst simultaneously prosecuting Irish and continental wars demanded the increased institutionalisation of the nation's capability to wage war. Although Dr Downing alludes to the 'relatively light' military burdens shouldered by England, one notes Frank Tallett's point, that the 'regional impact of recruiting' cannot always be conveyed by 'crude overall figures'. The western Midland and Welsh counties[50] were bled by Irish wars while the southern counties provided men for most of the continental campaigns, so much so that 4 per cent of Kent's population was drawn into military service from 1591 to 1602.[51] Essex was another shire that felt the bite of the press, where old soldier Sir John Smythe railed against the chronic and deleterious effects of the attrition of late sixteenth-century warfare.

Sir John Smythe, Catholic conspiracy, and the deleterious effects of impressment

Smythe, like the irascible and wilful Sir Robert Phelips a generation later, saw himself as a guardian of wholesome English country life and resented the incursion of the Council and captains into Essex, where they dragged off the lads to probable injury and possible death on a continental battlefield. As something of a precursor of the 1620s protest, Smythe enquired into the legal basis of impressment for foreign service. In 1587–8 Smythe had pursued the question as far as Lord Chief Baron Manwood and had consulted lawyers. Smythe's actions implied that what was best for the countryside was best for the nation, and were related to his proposal to rid the country of rogues.[52] Patterns of impressment had, contemporaries alleged, aggravated social dislocation, and the Crown recognised that the military corridors to and from Ireland imported unwelcome vagabonds to England.[53] Smythe's plan sought to make impressment solve the problems that impressment had created.

If soldierly virtue and character made up the basic stuff of battlefield victory, as the Romans and later English admirers insisted, they would have regarded Sir John Smythe's new recruits, the 'Soldiars Roges', as candidates for a rout. But Smythe insisted,

> ... some of the chief inventors and executors of the newe discipline militarie say that they had rather have three hundred Soldiars-Roges, then five hundred voluntarie soldiors or taken up by commission [pressed] ... Roges can abide more honger, cold, and travaile, and therwithall provide and make better shift for them selves. ...[54]

Smythe may have known that his nemesis, the Earl of Leicester (who had seen that Smythe was sacked from his colonelcy), had expressed similar sentiments in 1585, though the noble Earl stopped far short of advocating the deployment of a host of vagrants.

Precious few Englishmen volunteered for Irish service, and the pressed infantry from the English shires, whose ranks were thinned from disease and desertion, were supplemented by native-born Irish troops. The filling-up of English companies with Irish reinforcements was a great controversy for decades. Leicester valued these men, whatever the English commanders serving in Eire might think. He wanted the Queen to dispatch 600–1,000 of her

> Iresh idell men, such as be not only in her majestyes pay but very mete to be out of that countrey. ... They be hard, and wyll abyde more pains than our men, tyll they have byn well trayned with hardnes. ...

As it was, the Queen declined.[55]

Many dismiss Smythe as eccentric. Leicester had cast doubt on Sir John's mental health after observing him at the 1588 rendezvous: '... at the muster he entered agen into such straunge cryes for ordering of men [?] for the fyght with weapons as made me thinke he was not well. ...'[56] Smythe clearly possessed a volatile spirit and conducted his life with a certain unmanageability. But in fact Smythe's boisterousness verbalised concerns that many harboured silently. What precisely aggrieved Smythe? First, the scale of warfare, which consumed shire levy upon shire levy, not just because conditions for the fighting man were so poor, but also because of the kinds of wars being fought: wars of stalemate and starvation. Further, England lay at the intersection of several wars, so that numerous theatres consumed recruits simultaneously. Second, the longevity of these conflicts; by 1596 it seemed as if the wars had gone on for decades. The 'eternalised' warfare of the Low Countries appalled Smythe and many others, just as the stalemate of the First World War, with its mud, night attacks, 'great guns' (the term was used in both conflicts), disease, and privation, was to shock a later generation. Geoffrey Parker has suggested that the Dutch revolt was in some ways like a global, world war.[57]

Sir John, like Sir Robert Phelips, represented something distinctly English: the local and defensive orientation of the English. These old stalwarts took pride that at various times in English history their ancestors had gone abroad and given the enemy a good thrashing. And it was that decisiveness that appealed to them. Win the war and return home to the shire. English armies had never been designed to stay in the field for years at a time, or to conscript levy after levy. Smythe upheld tradition and the vitality of country life, both of which were threatened by this infernal new military discipline and 'consumed in forren warrs'.[58] Smythe's beloved Essex, like Cheshire and Kent (shires through which conscripts marched regularly), experienced the disorders associated with impressment. For example, on 18 June 1582, pressed soldiers from Hertfordshire, *en route* to the Low Countries via Gravesend, flew their banner at the White Hart in Brentwood, allegedly to 'assemble the most Idle and worst disposede people. . . .'[59] Impressment rent Essex's social fabric.

Such is the background to the events of 12 June 1596. Smythe appeared at the Colchester muster at the very least somewhat inebriated. Coming upon a company of pikemen and archers, being drilled a distance from those using Smythe's detested firearms, Sir John could not resist the temptation to deliver a Roman-style adlocution. Before him stood trained-band soldiers, a square of pikemen flanked on each side by Smythe's beloved bowmen, half a dozen of his 'retainers' probably among them. The militiamen knew that the Crown had been raiding the trained bands for 'ultra-marine' service. Smythe was convinced that not only was overseas deployment of the militia illegal, but that the process of impressment by which any Englishman, trained or not, could be sent off to the foreign wars was in itself illegal. In this he anticipated the controversies of the seventeenth century.[60] His conversations with Sir Roger Manwood, the Lord Chief Baron, and others had convinced him that his objections had some legal merit. He commenced his harangue by lamenting the overseas wars. To personalise this tragedy, Smythe proclaimed that yet another massive levy would be undertaken, with the implication that the trained-band soldiers standing before him were fair game. In a deposition after the fact Smythe claimed that 2,900 Essex men had been pressed of late, yet fewer than 200 had come home. A rumour circulated at the muster that another 1,000 Essex men were to receive the Queen's shilling for a mobilisation of 11,000–12,000 men destined for the Continent.

Although he never mentioned the Queen, Smythe clearly blamed Whitehall for the useless sacrifice of Essex's menfolk. And, in his cups, he fixed the responsibility on the Lord Treasurer, Burghley, with whom he had corresponded for years, seeking the Cecil patronage. If the assembled men wished to stay at home, where the militia belonged, then Smythe pledged to keep them free of the press, provided that they raise their hands and engage themselves with him. To encourage the soldiers, Smythe pointed to the Earl of Hertford's second son, who had accompanied him, saying that here was someone of the blood royal to lead them, and that Smythe would be the young man's lieutenant. Then he denounced traitors at Court, and someone shouted 'God save the Queen'.[61] Young Seymour, Hertford's son, apparently had come along for a drink and a view of the musters, and now must suddenly have realised that Smythe was placing his, young Seymour's, neck on the block. Some soldiers, encouraged perhaps by the few Smythe 'retainers' in the ranks, raised their hands, murmuring over the allegation of treason against the Lord Treasurer. Perhaps as many as fifty, though probably fewer, affirmed their allegiance to Smythe's crusade. More level-headed militiamen asked the volunteers if they were asking to be hanged. Smythe did not get the outpouring he had hoped for.[62] In the ensuing stir, several of the horsemen that had ridden up with Smythe now tried to disassociate themselves from Sir John's conspiracy by galloping off.

When apprehended by the Crown and imprisoned, Smythe answered interrogatories that reveal both the issues in Smythe's mind and the fear amongst the Queen's servants. Sir John's Roman Catholic sympathies and his service under the Duke of Alba justified the government's suspicion.[63] Smythe's habit of stockpiling weapons in his private residence gave credence to the theory that he planned a rising.[64] A treatise on the succession, dedicated to the Earl of Essex (foreshadowing the latter's own treason), and a libel against Burghley, were investigated. Considering Smythe's remarks, which included the observation that the common people of England had too long been oppressed, probably in reference to conscription and war-related taxation, the incident smacked of a harebrained but potentially dangerous conspiracy. And resistance to impressment played a large role, given Smythe's complaint that 'his countrymen had ben used as bond men these 30 yeres'.[65] Not only did Smythe's actions threaten England's ability to wage war by challenging the legal basis of impressment, but Sir John incited the militia, upon whom the Crown entrusted the maintenance of public order in the event of widespread violence (be it insurrection, invasion, or riot). And pressed soldiers were certainly regarded as potential rioters. Mutiny had erupted in Chester amongst the men awaiting transfer to Ireland, and thus the Queen's Council was in no mood to tolerate disorder in the ranks.[66] Militiamen were expected to keep the peace and use violence upon pressed men if necessary, not to sympathise with them.[67] The volatility of this issue, even in the time of Elizabeth I, cannot be underestimated, as it was passed on to the 1620s, the Bishops' Wars, and ultimately the debate over the militia bill in the Long Parliament.

Repeated presses, which funnelled reluctant warriors through the few suitable points of embarkation, led to endemic disorder. Troops destined for Ireland mutinied in the vicinity of Chester in 1574, 1578, 1580, 1581, 1594, and 1596, as well as in Limerick, Towcester, and elsewhere.[68] The conflation of socio-economic disorder with relentless pressing made conscription universally detested. The Stuarts ameliorated institutionalised impressment by capitalising on the Elizabethan victory in Ireland, reducing the standing forces there (from 9,000 troops in 1603 to barely over a thousand in 1606), and then erecting a resident loyalist establishment through plantation and patronage. Extra-parliamentary fiscal and military devices, such as grants of land and the bestowal of baronetcies, braced the modest army of Ireland. For example, Essex gentleman Edward Aleyn purchased the title of baronet for £1,095 and his family's three-year commitment to sustain thirty soldiers in the royal army in Ireland.[69]

Dependence upon pressed men during the wars of religion was a dangerous game, and expensive, too. In 1574, the Crown levied 1,000 men who dwelt in proximity to the ports of the West Country. For some reason only 100 were actually dispatched for embarkation. That company was kept waiting a month, then discharged. The victuals were sold off at a loss.[70] Poor logistical coordination delayed food and reinforcements to the detriment of the army. Even though the mechanisms for transporting troops into the Irish theatre had not yet been perfected in the 1570s, and the recruits often lacked enthusiasm for the task at hand, English pressed men still fared well on occasion. During the Desmond rebellion, English levies distinguished themselves, though with a few notable exceptions.

On 3 October 1579 Sir Nicholas Malby led a thousand troops, some of which were newly impressed reinforcements from England, against a superior Irish force later described by Sir William Stanley (who understood such things) as equal to veteran continental units. Appropriately, the insurgents marched under a papal banner, but the standard did not prevent the English from driving them from their defensive position on the third gallant try. 'Pressed Devon and Cornwall ploughmen showed themselves superior to the professional gallowglasses, as generally happened when the fight was in the open, partly because the former were rather better armed.'[71] Malby personified the development of an English art of war. Under a death sentence for counterfeiting, Sir Nicholas gained a reprieve in the Le Havre expedition and distinguished himself. The Irish wars gave him further opportunity, and his skill in command brought him promotion. Malby was, therefore, the perfect man to spur on pressed rascals.[72]

Sir William Stanley's religious inclinations had not yet overcome his patriotism. Unfortunately the same could not be said of some Lancashire levies already in possession of 'the Queen's shilling' but not yet embarked, who refused to serve against fellow Romanists, even if they were Irish.[73] Even had they obeyed, they might not have been of much use in combat. In the midst of a hot engagement in October 1595 English officers stripped pressed English troops of their muskets and put the guns in the skilled hands

of loyal native Irish troops in an ultimately successful attempt to prevent annihilation.[74] One solution was to import English veterans of the continental
wars, who were accustomed to the rigours of war, had training,
and whose abilities were known to their captains. Veterans of the Low
Countries wars could provide instruction, and thus there was traffic between
the theatres, even if the styles of warfare remained different. For example, the
transfer of Sir John Norris into the Irish conflict marked the Crown's deter-
mination to put to use experienced commanders, who were accustomed to
waging war with raw levies.[75] Given the physical hardships and unorthodox
combat practised in Ireland, English commanders often cautioned Whitehall
from breaking in new recruits through Irish service. Untrained and ill-
equipped pressed men, disembarked in a hostile environment that claimed
more casualties than the locals' hit-and-run tactics, were rendered unserviceable rapidly, necessitating another hasty press and leaving field forces under
strength and in jeopardy of being overrun.

Pressed English soldiers in the Irish theatre

The southern counties found increased demands falling upon them at the
height of the war years, 1597–1602. Kent, which provided the most troops
for continental expeditions with (again) the exception of London, was
obliged to press its residents for the Irish wars. Even before the climax of
the Irish conflict in 1601, Kent's resources were diffused in several directions. Before 1595, Kent frequently reinforced English forces operating in
the Low Countries and France. In summer 1595 the lathes[76] combined to
send expensive heavy cavalry to Ireland. The following year Kent's clergymen raised infantry and cavalry also destined for Ireland. The county
was busy in May and September raising men for the sieges at Boulogne.
In May 1597 the Earl of Essex required 300 fully equipped and drilled
infantry at Calais (at a cost to Kent of £1,200); in July the shire contributed
50 men to the Picardy campaign and 400 to the Ostend garrison.[77]
Hampshire's experiences paralleled those of its neighbour.[78]

Elizabeth's strategic predicament, and the consequent demands upon the
shires, are plainly evident at the beginning of November 1597. Lord Burgh,
Elizabeth's Lord Deputy of Ireland, had died, requiring a reconfiguration of
leadership and military power in Ireland. Simultaneously, the beleaguered
English forces in Ostend cried out for immediate reinforcement. In the
wake of 0Burgh's expiration, and still uncomfortably ill-informed of her
actual field strength and financial commitment in Ireland, the Queen
weighed the danger. The Irish Pale lay vulnerable, with the prospect of an
English garrison being overrun, perhaps massacred. A thousand reinforcements came out of Kent and Sussex. Their impressment violated three
principles of Elizabethan recruitment. Some units were to be embarked and
sent across the Channel, regardless of whether their companion companies

had reached the rendezvous or not. Sending forces piecemeal did not represent economy of effort: it tied up costly and scarce transports. It was usual for the Crown to billet troops on the port until the entire contingent had assembled. But the Ostend garrison could not wait. More surprisingly, the Sussex press came from 'those partes of the shire that are nerest to the porte of Ry, where they are to be imbarqued. . . .' Demography and politics obliged the central government to spread a press somewhat equitably across the hundreds and townships of the county. Again, Ostend could not be kept waiting. Soldiers were 'chosen out of the [Sussex] trayned bands of hable persons and furnyshed with armour and weapons. . . .'[79] Defence of the realm became increasingly complicated for the shires. Though Sussex pressed its hundred men for Irish service in late 1598, the following year the shire had to coordinate the logistics of sending forth 4,000 militia to rescue vulnerable Kent in the event of a Spanish landing.[80]

In the 1540s, even the 1570s, such deployments of the southern coastal militia might, perhaps, have been excused. But in 1597–9, it constituted a clear act of desperation. To deploy outside England strategically located trained men, along with their equipment, powder, and victual, when a Spanish fleet was *en route* to the British Isles, was a dangerous gambit. The absence of their fighting men alarmed locals, but the purveyance of food for the troops, for the Earl of Cumberland's squadron, and to supplement naval stores (all of which were necessities in early November), aggravated East Anglia and the south, which were experiencing grain shortages.

As it was, the Catholic forces abandoned the siege of Ostend, allowing the Queen to cancel her mobilisation orders to Sir Charles Percy (the commander of the relief column). Then on 5 November news arrived that the Spanish fleet had met disaster at the hands of the elements. All of this activity occurred within the space of a week. But no respite came from Ireland, to where the Queen now diverted her Picardy forces, though without letting the piketrailers know their terminus. St Valery had been uncomfortable, but was not as despised as Ireland. Companies withdrawn from French service, under Sir Arthur Savage, were destined for Dover or the Downs. But these veterans were valued in Ireland, so the vice-admiral, Sir Henry Palmer, was instructed to 'waft' them to the Isle of Wight. From Wight they would be transported to Ireland; 'keepe yt secrete untill your men be brought over.'[81]

In July 1598 English commanders in the Low Countries resented losing companies to the Irish theatre of operations, and, worse, their paymasters had to continue paying the transferred soldiers during their billeting in England while awaiting embarkation to Ireland. Ten companies (six at Falmouth, two at Plymouth and a pair at Portsmouth) collected moneys allocated for continental operations. Another fifty soldiers under Sir Nicholas Parker stayed on in England until raw shire levies gathered to accompany them on.[82] During August 1598, in the wake of the defeat at the Yellow Ford, impressment for Ireland was conducted widely throughout England.[83] Increasing the number of fighting men in Ireland to a level that would tip the balance in England's favour had to be weighed against resultant strategic alternatives, such as denuding the defences of the English shires and reducing participation in allied operations on the Continent. Calculating accurately was difficult, because ascertaining the actual field strength of English units in Ireland was even more unfathomable than sorting out the musters of English forces in the Netherlands. When figures were forthcoming, the Queen could not rely entirely on Irish Catholics in the royal ranks, who might melt away or join the enemy in the face of imminent action. The Crown faced such a problem at the end of August 1598. Since the men in Armagh had been saved (survivors of the Yellow Ford), the 2,000 reinforcements being mobilised in England would be an 'unsupportable charge' upon the Irish establishment. But if 2,000 Irish were discharged, then the Queen would encourage their replacement with these 2,000.[84]

Impressment was also costly because of the inefficiency and recalcitrance of the localities. When the Crown, citing 'a late accident fallen out' (a sanguine reference to the Yellow Ford), asked the citizens of Hereford to dig a little deeper in their pockets and levy a further 50 men to follow the 100 they had already pressed, the request failed to trigger an outpouring of patriotism. Elizabeth complained of recruiting that had produced unfit men and shoddy equipment. Poor specimens and equipment undermined the military effort and compounded the cost of war for the Queen and her subjects, for it compelled her to levy more men yet again. Elizabeth wanted stout lads and firepower. The 50 were to be a dozen corseleted pikemen, 25 calivermen and 10 musketeers. There would be no more recruiting of 'such refues of men as the villages desier to be ridd of for theire lewde behaviour'.[85] The Lord Lieutenant, the Earl of Pembroke, berated the deputy lieutenants and Justices of the Peace, scolding them for their carelessness and vowing he would not assume the 'faulte' of their failure. As it was, the cost of raising these 50 soldiers was £180.[86]

Throughout September 1598, soldiers continued to be floated across the Irish Sea. A thousand men were sent over, without captains, under Sir Richard Bingham (who had his own company of 200 Norfolk men), who would fill 'decayed' companies with them.[87] The process continued despite the Earl of Ormonde's warnings about deploying pressed men in Ireland, sent to the Privy Council in the aftermath of the Yellow Ford.[88] Sir Samuel Bagenal arrived in Ireland around 18 September with the remnants of his regiment. Another 1,300 soldiers had landed at Youghal.[89] Simultaneously, the Crown expressed concern about the composition of government forces, insisting upon native Englishmen to discourage desertions to the enemy. Irish defections had forced an additional press of 4,000.[90]

On 3 October, Bingham's pressed cavalry, the 200 Norfolk men, threatened mutiny over their shabby coats.[91] On 11 October, Captain Stafford at Chester reported his 800 men were ill-clad and some would have to march without shoes or stockings. The Buckinghamshire contingent 'were bothe the worste men and worste apparelled' and some of the Londoners were poorly clothed as well: 'all London cassocks made of northern cloathe, which by wett dothe soe muche shrinke, . . . will this winter stande them in little steade'.[92]

In late October 1598, 2,000 more reinforcements embarked at English ports for Irish service. Plans were under way in November and December for the levying of an army of raw men and continental veterans that the Earl of Essex might use to rescue the situation in the coming year. Thus did Elizabeth raise more than 7,000 men in five months during the crisis of the Yellow Ford. But the levies' transport, training, and deployment meant that there would be some months before the tide could be turned in England's favour. By November 1598, the escalation of the war and the time required for pressing Englishmen and transporting them along with victuals and equipment forced the Crown into a defensive war until adequate troops arrived. Accounting procedures for mustering men meant that Whitehall had only a vague notion of actual field strength. From the Privy Council's point of view, it was difficult to anticipate decayed companies and fill the gaps in their ranks with pressed men without some data as to attrition, desertion, and troop-strength projections. This lay at the heart of the disputes surrounding the discharge of the office of the Irish mustermaster. Ormonde was to see that

> Musters be more exactly taken . . . to the end that Her Majesty, knowinge the trewe state of her forces there, may make her levies accordinglye, to fill up such a number as shall be thought convenient for the proseqution of this warr; and that in this Muster, not only the heads of the men in every companie, but the sorts and number of every kinde of Armes, be sett down . . . and to that end is both makinge greate levies of horsemen and footemen in England, as also sending all her olde soldiers from the Low Countreis, with store of vittells, armes, munition, artillerye, and treasure. . . .[93]

In December 1598, 2,000 troops were ordered to be transferred from the Low Countries to Ireland. The Council allocated £6,000 for a levy of horsemen and set about pressing 3,000 infantry to follow the 2,000 already being sent into Ireland. They also authorised £500 for two months' worth of victuals to be used in the transfer of the Low Countries veterans, who would need sustenance in their journey first to Flushing and then as they wafted their way to Ireland.[94] On 15 December 1598, 706 men of the listed 1,000 soldiers in the companies were sent out of England.[95] Reassignment cost £1,583 plus additional transport charges for seagoing vessels.[96] The government's shuffle aimed, at least at some point during the December 1598 mobilisation, to divert some of the shires' raw recruits to the Low Countries and then 'select 2,000 of the olde and Trayned Soldiers of the lowe Countries which wilbee the flower of all the forces', to stiffen the Irish army.[97]

Special skills were sought. Two arms craftsmen found themselves pressed by express command of the Queen and Council, a 'mender' of the 'harquabuz' and an armourer.[98] In 1598 the Council instructed that the commissioners of the musters for Ireland see that among the pressed men sent from England there be '. . . three or 4er carpenters amongest those souldiers and a smithe or two, and one mason yf anie maie be had. . . .'[99]

Pressing craftsmen seemed to locals a waste of talented individuals, given the attrition of the Irish service. The 2,000 soldiers pressed during January and February 1599, and destined to serve under the Earl of Essex, suffered in quality from the virtually unprecedentedly large levy of 5,450 recruits in 1598.[100] On 8 February 1599, Sir Samuel Bagenal wrote to the Privy Council from Kells regarding the condition of his troops. He still had not been fully repaid for raising his horsemen, who had been duly mustered and inspected. He had brought cattle (stolen from O'Neill, in the old rebel's sight) to the garrison at Newry

> which before was so distressed, that myself sawe some of the soldiors of that garrison (drawne out for that service) fall dead in Marchinge with verie povertie and want of victuals. The greatest Enimyes that the Soldiors have yet felt, hath beene hunger and colde, by which meanes they are muche weakned, for they have as yet since their arrivall in this Kingdome, receaved but two monethes Intertaine-ment, onelie they have had victuals in slender allowance, and they lodge one [on] the grounde without Coveringe. Clothes they have none as yet, although they have bene dewe to them longe since, nor can get anie, unles they will take half suits, which by noe meanes they will accepte.[101]

Victuals were distributed inequitably.[102] Bagenal asked Cecil to arrange for payment to be made to Sir Thomas Egerton of the remainder of the money due for raising his horse company.[103] On 13 February 1599, the Privy Council instructed the Mayor of Bristol 'for the finding of 18d. a day for each of the 100 horsemen under Sir Henry Davers during their abode in Bristol for passage. The money shall be repaid on the Mayor's demand.'[104]

On 6 April 1599, Essex informed Sir Robert Cecil that he had 'appointed Babington the merchant' to receive £600 from the counties and city for the levying of 200 men. He directed Sir Robert to pay accordingly, ostensibly from the Exchequer of Receipt. Essex thanked Lord Cobham for his forwardness in supplying the sum that Kent was to contribute. Funds issued by the government, and accounted as a disbursement, probably came from the localities, sometimes via a circuitous route. Did the Earl employ merchants as intermediaries? The government reimbursed them, with money that was collected from the shires. Attorney-General Bankes's investigation years later revealed variation and flexibility in financing pressed contingents. Bedfordshire, Hertfordshire, and Northamptonshire paid directly into the Exchequer of Receipt for provisions and arms for their respective shire contingents sent to the Irish wars in summer 1601. The City of London engaged merchant William Rumler to find liquid capital to pay £1,000 of the £3,500 owed for the 1,000 recruits it sent to relieve Ostend. Lincolnshire's 300 Ostend-bound troops had their provisions paid for through commissions of array. In the following summer, Bankes noted, the Exchequer of Receipt issued coat and conduct money to Lincolnshire, Northhamptonshire, and London for levies *en route* to Ireland. The Attorney-General concluded that for the relief of Ostend, the Crown did not reimburse the shires for arms and apparel, but did supply coat and conduct money. For Irish expeditions the Crown acted as a temporary receiver, the counties paying military expenses into the Receipt, then disbursing the requisite sums via the Exchequer. The fluidity of the financial arrangement obscured who in fact paid for levies, and thus the fiscal ambiguity created a political controversy.[105]

Impressment seemed especially grievous when the men were dispatched to a war that appeared unwinnable with English troops. Essex commented on the nature of the war and compared English recruits with the native Irish:

> . . . this warre is like to exercise bothe our faculties that doe manage it, and Her Majesties patience that must maynteine it. For this people againste whome we fighte hathe able bodies, good use of the armes they carie, boldnes enoughe to attempte, and quicknes in apprehending any advantage they see offred them. Whereas our newe and common sorte of men have neither bodies, spirits, nor practise of armes, like the others [the Irish]. What advantage we have is more horsse, which will command all champions [open ground]; in our order, which these savages have not: and in the extraordinary courage and spirite of our men of qualitie. . . . [T]he rebells fighte in woods and bogges, where horse are utterly unserviceable, they use the advantage of lightnes and swiftenes in going of [off], when they finde our ordre too stronge . . . and as for the laste advantage . . . how unequall a wager it is to adventure the lives of noble men and gentlemen against rougues and naked beggars.[106]

Essex argued that the hostile Irish environment bred better common soldiers than England's hospitable clime. His Darwinian view of English soldiers, which avoided the social issue of pressing the dregs rather than sturdy and useful men, strongly implied that this was an unnatural war fought in an unnatural place. Subtly though perceptibly, Essex's evaluation questioned the wisdom of the Irish war. The English fought nature as well as the Irish, and the Earl's frequent references to the illness of his troops and the unhealthiness of the climate not only sought some rationale for England's disappointing performance in Ireland but also asked at what price Ireland would be conquered. Need England sacrifice her gallants for this piece of ground? The poor showing of English 'enlisted' men in the late 1590s to some extent vindicated Essex's sour assessment. But Charles Blount, Lord Mountjoy, Essex's successor, commanded men of no better quality when they effectively won the Irish war in 1601. They were, however, better led, and that contributed to the victory at Kinsale.[107]

Essex's emphasis on leadership was not misplaced. A valiant tactician might forge the army into a more effective fighting force. This contradicted military commentators such as Barnaby Rich, for it asked the noble commanders to make a silk purse out of a sow's ear. The alternatives were either to press better quality men, or, that equally controversial solution (as Elizabeth would do) to shift veterans from the Continent to Ireland. On 11 October 1599 Loftus, Carey, and other Irish councillors reminded the Privy Council that, in a letter of 4 August 1599, the Queen had allowed a temporary press of 2,000 native Irish for the harvest period. Essex had then reduced the army list by 4,000, bringing the number to 14,000;[108] additionally, the Treasurer borrowed money upon the orders to the Lord Lieutenant (Essex) in August, while campaigning against O'Neill. The question of recruiting Irishmen dovetailed with the problem of obtaining Englishmen via impressment quickly and in sufficient quantities, especially considering that pressed companies invariably arrived understrength because of corruption, disease, desertion, and dead pay. If Essex were right – that Irishmen were better suited to fight Irishmen – and given the expense, difficulty, and controversy surrounding impressment, should an 'Anglo-Irish' army have been used?

Mountjoy, who had earned the right to speak candidly, summarised the problem:

> Where yt pleaseth your Lordships to putt us in mynde, that the leavies of men for this Realm [Ireland] are so greveous to the people there [in England], and the transportacion so chardgeable to her Majestie; as you seeke all means possible to avoyde yt. And therefore would have me the deputy to Reenforce the weake garrisons in the northe from the rest of the Armie: wee concure fully with your lordships touchinge the burdens in leavyinge of

men in England. But as out of our experience seing at eye the Continuall toyles of the army here, being alwayes in accion, so your lordships out of your owne grand consideracions are to thinke that so longe as there is an armie, so longe must supplies be sent to beare yt up specially in such a hard warr as this, where the soldior is still Itinerant and goinge, and subject to lye in the field in all weathers, with little more to Cover him then his owne bare garments, whereby the armie (how strange soever yt may be thought) cannot but be daily Reduced ... there is a Continuall mortalety and death of soldiers by so many extremities. . . .[109]

As the attrition of the Irish wars stretched the Crown's resources, and the conflict was fought in defence of the *ecclesia anglicana* as well as the Tudor dynasty, the clergy levied troops, especially horsemen. Raising cavalry for overseas service posed numerous problems. The sheer cost of the steed and equipment of a cavalryman sent shudders through the local magistrates when they were asked to provide such troops. Further, most levies confined themselves to infantry, so that the request was somewhat unusual for some shires. Light horse had traditionally been an ecclesiastical speciality. But more varied and heavily armed contingents issued from the Church in the late 1590s. In March 1596 Archbishop Whitgift proclaimed the crusade in Ireland 'doeth little less importe England then if this realme itself were invaded'. The bishops were to field from their dioceses 285 infantry and 300 cavalry, to be mustered at Chester and transported across the Irish Sea. 'Black Jack' spelled out the requisite equipment in detail, and lack of such constituted no excuse for delay. If a horseman had no cuirass, he could buy one at Chester for 20 shillings.[110] The mobilisations of forces sponsored by the clergy were monitored at the highest levels of government, between Privy Council and Archbishop.[111]

Between 1598 and 1601 the English shires contributed 720 horsemen and the clergy scores of light cavalry. The precariousness of Elizabethan strategy was illustrated by the fact that Kent, perhaps the most strategic county in the defence of the realm, contributed the most horses, and Kent's clergy also supplied mounts at the Archbishop of Canterbury's direction.[112] The counties supplemented the cavalry, and levied horsemen for service under Sir John Brooke and Sir Anthony Cooke in January 1599.[113] The Privy Council instructed the mayor of Bristol to be ready for the 100 cavalry pressed for Ireland, which would embark at the port. Stables for the horses, billets for the troops, as well as food and transport, were the city's responsibility, and Bristol could expect more – 200 additional cavalry and 2,550 infantry would be embarked in late February 1599. These men would need coin in pocket for their victualling.[114] More troops would follow.[115]

The Irish wars increased the clergy's military obligation from being mostly defensive, to engagement in overseas campaigning. When the churchmen mustered lances, petronels, etc. earlier in the century, their troops enjoyed the status of militiamen. Elizabeth, like her father, had never been overly fastidious in exempting militia from continental service. She, like Henry, would rather not have risked her shire forces for a dangerous expedition, but, if circumstances so dictated, off they went. One must wonder, as has John McGurk, how 'ecclesiastical militia felt when ordered into Ireland'.[116] The Irish wars saw substantial and mixed forces assembled under ecclesiastical sponsorship on a level not seen since Henry VIII's French campaigns.[117] Even with the advent of peace, and the Jacobean reduction of the Irish military establishment, the garrisons required a regular stream of pressed recruits, largely from Cheshire and Lancashire. In Manchester, the 'misegatherers' (elected rate collectors) methodically taxed the locality to provide for recruits destined for the Irish garrisons.[118] When James I boasted, in 1621, that he had redressed the Elizabethan grievance of chronic, institutionalised impressments during his eighteen years on the throne, he conveniently overlooked presses for Irish garrison duty, which continued.[119]

The Royal Navy, too, needed bodies. Pressed forces included sailors as well as piketrailers, drawn all from roughly similar demographies. The Crown treated seafaring men rather differently from soldiers. A royal naval commissioner instructed the constables to give 'warninge' to local sailors 'to apeere before me'. At an early morning assembly the commissioner would 'vewe and take up (the Muster seene) suche men as shalbe thought meet.' He enrolled the names of the selected men and a 'byll' was 'geven unto thos marrinars that be prested' along with a few shillings 'prest and conducte money', the latter sums calculated via tables showing amounts based on the distance of the town of recruitment to the port of embarkation.[120] Mariners were regarded as more skilled, and thus received better treatment and higher wages.[121] But, whereas the Crown needed mariners residing near the ports, loitering soldiers, especially veterans returning from the wars, were unwelcome guests.

Upon discharge, pressed men received a printed pass (or letter from a commander) and conduct money to get them to their home parish, where presumably they would resume their civilian occupation.[122] Despite royal proclamations for the re-employment and resettlement of levied men, the lure of vagrancy and petty crime seduced many, personified by Shakebag and Blackwill in *The lamentable and true tragedy of M. Arden of Feversham* of 1592 and resulting in the 1598 felonisation of vagrancy.[123] Though ostensibly reliable men were pressed, still the Privy Council and the local authorities often sought out idle and masterless men.[124] The severe suppression of sturdy rogues and vagabonds was matched by an attempt at just treatment of discharged soldiers, especially those that might have been swindled by their captains. When thirty disbanded men gathered at the Court gate, Elizabeth prompted her councillors to interview a pair of the unfortunates. The enquiry into the predicament of these penniless piketrailers ultimately led the Council to summon 'all suche souldiers as uppon the last levyes were sent and served in the Lowe Countryes . . . to th'ende that yf they could duly claime and shew many fest [manifest] proofe for any wages behinde and unpaied for their service and centertainement in those countryes, they should upon their repaier to the Court be fullye satysfied. . . .'[125]

When the Privy Council learned that a Gloucestershire gentleman alleged the Justices of the Peace had pressed him despite being a 'Subsyde man of great years', Lord Chandos was asked to look into the matter personally. Although officially sceptical of such charges, the Council admitted '. . . in some places the lyke dealing hath bredd great offence to the subject and both slander and prejudice to her Majesty's service. . . .' Should the good yeoman pay as high a subsidy rate as the best men in the locality, then Chandos was to punish the perpetrators, for Elizabeth 'doth myslyke her authoritie and service should be abused.'[126] Illegal impressment, in the eyes of the Queen, constituted no petty offence, but rather an affront to royal justice and authority. Abuse of royal military charges estranged the Queen's subjects all the more because of the lack of any statutory undergirding for impressment and military rates. Indignation over these apparently illegal measures taken for the defence of the realm was expressed at least as early as 1588, a year in which one would suspect patriotism would have silenced such murmurings. Although a bill of 1601, which would have legitimised the lieutenancy's pressing, rating, and arming of troops, passed the Lords, it was quashed by the House of Commons.[127]

Billeting and impressment under the early Stuarts

When James I resolved to assist in the recovery of the Palatinate, his orders for the impressment of his subjects began with a preamble that resembled those of Henry VIII, justifying the call to campaign upon the Continent.[128] Like Tudor expeditions, the pressing was spread out over most of the shires. Some of the 12,000 men came from London (2,000) and the Home Counties (Middlesex 400, Kent 750), a predictable pattern, given that the embarkations were planned for London and Dover. However, East Anglian shires contributed (Norfolk 600, Suffolk 500), as did the West Country (Devon 300, Somerset 500, Wiltshire 400), though Cornwall was spared. Inland counties pressed contingents as well. Areas near to Ireland were excused, ostensibly because that theatre remained somewhat insecure. No men left Cheshire, Lancashire, or Wales. The North, in theory pacified by the Union of Crowns, should therefore have been freed up to field soldiers. York did indeed do so, mustering 600 men. But the Borders, specifically Cumberland, Northumberland, Westmorland, and Durham, yielded none. Their exclusion was due to the relatively small number of men available in those areas, and the distance (and hence cost) involved in marching men down to the south. In fact, when the rendezvous was postponed until

Figure 4.1 'In the 19. how he (havinge the Pike advanced) shall take the same with left hand higher and at the same tyme charge withal, but if he desire to set the Pike downe againe, he shall doe it as is taught by the figures before. But if (having charged the Pike) he would carrye the same againe advanced, he shall doe it in one posture or motion.'

Source: Pikeman, 1607, from Jacob de Gheyn's *The Exercise of Armes* (author's collection).

the end of November, it was noted that the delay would enable 'the towns of yorkshire and the Northe parts' to muster their troops and set off on the road.[129]

Procedures remained consistent with the previous century. The trained bands were to be kept 'entyre' and not made subject to the press.[130] Nevertheless, Mansfeld's expedition[131] raised clamours even more discordant than those heard by Elizabeth's councillors. James allowed special

Figure 4.2 'In the 33. how he shall lightlye with one hand laye the Musket upon
the shoulder, and yet in the meane tyme hold the rest.'

Source: Caliverman, from Jacob de Gheyn's influential illustrated training manual (author's
collection).

treasurers to disperse funds for the 1624–5 war effort, compromising the
Crown's prerogative in waging war in order to obtain supply from a sus-
picious House of Commons.[132] Misgivings about the Crown's war policy
were enlarged by the vagueness of Mansfeld's strategy and the absence of
a substantial cadre of English officers to herd English soldiers.[133] Evidence
from Buckinghamshire in November 1624 discloses how the deputy lieutenants negotiated with the constables, sparing recruits upon learning they
were tithing men and arranging for extra conscripts in case quotas were
not met.[134] Pressing men remained a tangled and time-consuming chore.
If the shires believed their sovereign was allowing foreign rulers to exploit

English men and money to fight distant, bloody wars, those apprehensions were inflamed when James's successor impressed troops for the King of Denmark.[135] Compared with the 70,000 English and Welshmen pressed by Elizabeth I, the recurrent Danish presses, the 12,000 men for Mansfeld, the 10,000 for Cadiz, and the 6,000 for the Isle of Rhé (not counting reinforcements in the latter case) may not seem excessively burdensome in retrospect.[136] Nevertheless, the unpopularity of impressment was reflected in an unspoken leniency towards deserters.

When John Gilford (and other Wiltshire lads) took 'French leave' rather than risk their necks with Mansfeld, he slipped out of his lodgings at Twisford, six days' march from his house in Marlborough, and headed home in the pre-dawn darkness. His community had upon his conscription laid out for him 'new hose, coate, stockings, shooes, and shirt', not to mention sixpence press money. Now Gilford and his compatriots surreptitiously rejoined their community amid relief, anxiety, and embarrassment. The score or more deserters later apprehended around Marlborough were labourers, tinkers, weavers, and husbandmen, not unskilled vagrants. Indeed the inhabitants of Fisherton Anger protested that the 1624 press had taken from their parish citizens who had been forced to abandon pregnant wives, aged fathers, and dependent children. Eleven men had been pressed from their tithing (not counting hapless strangers). John Brice left a wife and three children; John Miller similarly departed from a spouse and four children. John Rawling's and Robert Bushell's wives were 'greate with Childe'. A score of dependants now fell on the tithing's charge.

Deserters were captured, indicted, and imprisoned. But the quarter sessions rolls rarely reveal prosecutions and penalties. The deserters remain on the calendars of prisoners for a number of terms, and then disappear from the records, suggesting that local officialdom admitted the malefactors back into productive labour as soon as it could be done discreetly. The central government had business to deal with and a few months' imprisonment were sufficient punishment for the deserters.[137] If those deserters committed crimes, it was another matter, however. In 1597 Peter Hatcher, a deserter, was sentenced to death for grand larceny and highway robbery.[138]

Mansfeld plucked up so many Englishmen that the throngs needed for Ireland were not as easily dredged up. In February 1625 a shortage of drummers occurred, 'so many being taken up for Count Mansfeld that the Irish service is likely to be prejudiced'.[139] The Mansfeld expedition not only drew pressed men from across the realm[140] but then billeted many of them in English ports and villages.[141] Billeting became the focal point for grievances against military charges, for 'Not only was it one of the most expensive of all the war demands: it also, in the most literal sense, brought the war home to people'.[142] The impossibility of the billeting situation was laid bare when the Dover commissioners received a reply from the Privy Council commending them for their 'tender care not to erre in the way of shedding bloude without great cause', and instructing them to find ample food from the Dover markets so that the soldiers might eat, and to secure wages. The Dover authorities were 'required' to meet with Count Mansfeld and his officers and devise a way to quiet the soldiery. Such instructions were of little use when, several days later, soldiers threatened to hang the mayor, and pillaged the neighbouring countryside.[143] Shaken by the disorders of 1624–5, the government scrutinised troops pressed for the Cadiz expedition, using the 2,500 men then mobilised as a case study.

In summer 1625, Sir John Ogle, colonel over the forces billeted in the vicinity of Plymouth, commissioned Captain Edward Leigh, Sergeant-Major of the forces in Devonshire to investigate the impressments of each company. He conducted exhaustive interviews, compiled in a 'book of particulars', which has not survived. But Leigh's forty-page summary does, and documents the failings of institutionalised impressment.[144] Simultaneously, Captain Robert Gore went among the billeted companies and drew up tables of the breeches, shirts, stockings, and shoes supplied the soldiers.[145] Roughly 10 per cent of pressed men bargained their way out of the service before reaching Plymouth, who were often replaced by unfortunates who happened to pass by.[146] London-raised companies were especially notorious for snaring visitors to the metropolis, many of whom were engaged in lawsuits.[147] Edward Sterling was *en route* to consult counsel for an upcoming trial, and near Temple Bar asked directions to a solicitor's lodgings. His escorts instead clapped him up in Bridewell prison, where he was pressed.[148]

Leigh's interviews revealed systematic corruption, with the local commissioners conspiring with the conductors rather than overseeing the fairness and quality of the press. Shoes and stockings provided frequently proved substandard. Indeed, Leigh personally drilled the Leicestershire contingent, but was forced to reduce drilling exercises because the men were badly shod. The Leicestershire men were particularly intent on escaping service: three escaped using a counterfeit pass, another offered £5 to be excused (and would pawn his horse if that sum was insufficient), and a tailor of Melton Mowbray paid '2 peeces of gould' for his freedom.[149]

The confluence of the forced loan, coat and conduct money, billeting, and associated military charges had exhausted the Exchequer's allocations by 1626–7. In May 1627, £500 of recusant fines earmarked for works at Landguard were diverted to pay soldiers' wages. The Rhé expedition took precedence over fortifying the coastline.[150] Short of ready money, the Crown relied on citizens to help keep the royal forces intact through billeting. Billeted pressed men easily transformed themselves into vagrants and rioters.[151] Indeed, the ghost of Sir John Smythe strode Essex when riot broke out on St Patrick's Day 1628 not far from where the disgruntled old Elizabethan had been laid to rest.[152] Sir John's grievance of the 1590s, that European wars consumed Essex's male population, was again raised. Recent campaigns had led to the impressment of no fewer than 1,600 local inhabitants.[153] More grievously, in September 1625, 'the raising of 3000 men out of the Trayne bands' to meet an invasion threat outraged the citizens of Harwich, who were to find room for these Essex citizen-warriors, and their militiamen as well, who had been pressed out of their communities and maintained by their captains and themselves, a clear instance of insult added to injury.[154] If Harwich folk thought a strike on Cadiz was stretching the concept of defence of the realm, and hence inter-preting liberally their duty to billet, the English veterans of Danish service soon took up residence and required the collection of loan moneys within Harwich for their maintenance. Essex communities not only had to deal with unwelcome and unruly armed strangers in their midst; they also had to raise funds to keep the soldiers fed.[155]

Essex, like other shires, lacked the apparatus for maintaining soldiers in the midst of a civilian population. Given the political manoeuvrings of the various communities to avoid billeting assignments, the ultimate hosts, in this case Witham, were less capable of quartering men than the more popu-lous towns. In anticipation of another campaign, the Duke of Buckingham kept together numerous companies, one of these being composed of Irish infantrymen, who had distinguished themselves at the Isle of Rhé,[156] under the command of Colonel Pierce Crosby, Captain Rosse Cary, and Sergeant-Major Esmonds. The Irish contingent found itself divided up amongst various dwellings, still armed, but dependent on the mayor and sheriff for sustenance. It was a volatile situation. On 17 March 1628, while the Irish troops 'solemly celebrate[d] in memory of Sainte Patricke their Patrone', some local boys (apprentices and a shoemaker's servant) attached small red crosses, denoting of course the symbol of St George, England's patron saint, on a dog and the town's whipping post.[157]

Incensed at this mockery, the troops gathered, drew swords, charged pikes, and proceeded through Witham's streets, stopping at the home of the shoe-maker who employed one of the boys. Denied entrance, they struck at a lattice-work window. Their lieutenant arrived upon the scene and 'paci-fied' the men. Captain Cary appeared, brandished his sword, and put them in formation. With colours now unfurled and drum beating, he marched them through Witham, in the direction of the London road. Just passing the market cross, the crack of a musket shot echoed and Cary stumbled, grazed across the forehead by the projectile. The constable and his men, who had apparently appealed in vain to Cary, begging him to order his soldiers to put up their weapons, now faced the fury of the wounded captain's troops. The constable and other town folk were injured in the ensuing fray.[158] Although Cary recovered, several soldiers gathered the following morning at the Blue Bell on Beer Street, where they vowed 'they would lose their lyves rather then lose their weapons' and discussed seizing a single building wherein they might all lodge together. A special fate was planned for the constable, should he show his face. Constable

George Lambe was to be 'buttocked' with a sword. Mercifully, cooler heads prevailed and the Privy Council got the Irish out of Witham.[159]

The Witham incident, along with similar disorders in Surrey, Oxfordshire, and Northamptonshire, came to the attention of the Privy Council and before a not disinterested Parliament. It served the agenda of a parliamentary faction to weld together billeting, martial law, coat and conduct money, even arbitrary imprisonment and forced loans, as part of the politicisation of English warfare. For noted parliamentarian Sir John Eliot, 'billeting of soldiers' constituted 'the greatest of grievances', for it bridged liberty of the subject with the matter of rule of law.[160] But, as in the cases of lieutenancy and the militia,[161] local political rivalries could orchestrate what on the national level appeared to be significant constitutional issues. Impressment, with the attendant problems of billeting and martial law, posed thorny political problems for the Crown. The clash in the streets of Witham was not only 'ideological' (and under that rubric one can include ethnicity and religious animosity) but also an exasperated political protest against mounting and increasingly unbearable military charges. The local, and almost personal, anger against Witham's unwelcome Irish lodgers stemmed from Earl of Warwick's attempt to seize the lieutenancy from the Earl of Sussex and a High Church court faction.[162] The West Country endured much of the grief of billeting, as Eliot's words, based on his knowledge of Cornish grievances, conveyed. Likewise Somerset and Wiltshire had reached the limits of their patience. Marlborough's inhabitants claimed to have spent £244 on billeting and conduct money in 1627–8.[163] But the situation was exploited for local political benefit, again by the likes of Sir Robert Phelips and his rivals.

In December 1627 the south of England hosted 7,000 soldiers, all drawn from the lowest ranks of society.[164] Buckingham's soldiers, many of them battered, wounded, sick, emaciated, and angry, descended primarily upon Portsmouth and Plymouth, some being sent off to 'Hospitalls at London' for care. The number of sick and wounded troops in Plymouth alone was estimated at 1,200 at the least, with the toll mounting as soldiers as well as mariners 'daily infect one the other and fall downe', posing a hazard to the health of the port's civilians.[165] Amongst the billeted soldiers was Lieutenant John Felton, who would later assassinate Buckingham in the streets of Portsmouth. Lieutenant Felton was very much involved in disbursing funds for quartering his men and negotiating with civilians. The extent to which this miserable experience further embittered Felton and contributed to his rage towards the architect of these military adventures can only be conjectured at. Felton had served the Protestant cause in the regiments of Sir Edward Cecil and Lord Valentia, and found himself stranded in Munster, his petitions snubbed, after the Cadiz adventure. In arrears of pay after the Rhé expedition and fending for soldiers like himself, the Lieutenant killed Buckingham for the latter's betrayal of the soldiery, as well as for Parliament and Protestantism.[166]

Billeting particularly inflamed anti-military sentiment when soldiers disrupted civilian communities. Disorderly mariners, in February 1628, prompted the calling-out of the London and Middlesex trained bands, to 'repell their insolencies, and assaile them in hostile manner, as rebels to the State. . . .'[167] Marlborough could ill afford £200 expended on pressed soldiers in the first half of 1628. Communities groaned under the strain.[168] From the south coast similar protests were heard. Surrey's deputy lieutenants obeyed their billeting orders but in enumerating the costs reminded the Privy Council of the difficulty in funding ordinary services given the shire's 'smallness and povertie'. The weekly allowance provided the soldiers was 3s. 6d. the man:

> take order, that such as shall march through the said county, be accomodated with lodginge and money for theire dyet, after the rate of 8d. per diem for each man, accounting twelve myles for a dayes march; wee, in discharge of o'dutyes, dow humbly certifie your lordshipps, the great sums of money lately disbursed for the loane to his majestie, and alsoe for the late sendinge out of soldiers to the number of 800, whereof 600 weare coated at the rate of 12s. 6d. the coate, beside the presse and conduct money.[169]

Prompt payment on the local level was essential, as the Crown's agents phrased it: 'This monie is the maine wheele which moveth the whole frame of the business.'[170]

The Bishops' Wars (1639–40) even more so than the 1620s campaigns mobilised men who were then quartered within the realm, and, with the exception of Hamilton's expedition, did not embark and disappear beyond the seas. Rather, the recruits marched the breadth of the shires of England. Thus, failing to outfit the levies properly invited disorder, as when in 1639 the Herefordshire soldiers ('naked poore conditioned people') rebelled against their conductors 'for want of fitt clothinge' and food, assaulting their officers and many deserting.[171] Towns along the route of the march contributed to the sustenance of the pressed men, as Manchester did for Welsh recruits headed for the York rendezvous in 1639.[172] In the 1640 war the Council made every effort to quarter the men within their home county until the great rendezvous in the North was orchestrated fully.[173] Nevertheless, complaints in 1640 were virtually indistinguishable from those of the 1620s:

> the citty of Rochester with the Libertyis and parish of Strowd adiacent is more overcharged with souldiers than any other place in the whole country, having a 100 men that were brought out of the County of Sussex, as also 150 pressed in the County of Kent. The which are like to prove very dangerous and preiducial

to the said citty by reason the same is full of Seamen and Workemen belonging to His Majestys Navy. The souldiers growing daily into many Insolencyes and out rages, and it is to bee feared they will daily increase.[174]

Thus Yorkshire cited the Petition of Right in rebutting the King's and the Earl of Strafford's call to arms.[175] Resentment toward impressment, billeting, and ultimately mobilisation was reflected in the Impressment Act of February 1642. The military obligation was now defined by statute. No citizen was compelled to serve outside his shire except in event of 'the sudden coming in of strange enemies into the kingdom', or unless bound by tenurial contract. The act wrenched from the lieutenancy the right to impress, because a Lord Lieutenant who might obediently levy men for the King might equally obediently assist the King in deploying country forces against the interests of Parliament. Better to trust in Justices of the Peace and mayors, whose loyalties lay squarely with the country. Militia were exempted. Those who refused to take 'imprest money' and serve were to be imprisoned for six months until £10 was paid toward the locality's maimed soldier fund. The money was not to go up to London, to the Exchequer. If no £10 fine was paid, the offender remained locked up for twelve months' additional time. The act imposed a £20 fine on conductors who released conscripts in return for bribes. Rather than abolishing institutionalised impressment, Parliament appropriated the mechanism and, after decades of controversy, sanctioned the press by statute. It did so to defend the realm against the sovereign himself. Less than a month later, on 5 March 1642, the Houses moved to assume control of the trained bands of England and Wales. Such was the astonishing transformation by the monarchy, now perceived as a threat to the citizenry, of the institution that in the hands of the early Tudors had, in spite of its inefficiencies and failures, defended the realm successfully.[176]

ELIZABETHAN WARFARE IN THE NORTH, 1560–73

England's strategic predicament forced Elizabeth into war, even though English arms had perhaps reached their nadir.[1] The dynastic alliance between the Stuarts and the Catholic rulers of France had put a Guise in control of Scotland. When the Protestant Scots rebelled, the English had to make common cause, for the extirpation of the reformed religion in Lowland Scotland would be a prelude to the invasion of England. The English Protestant heresy would be crushed and the injuries of the Hundred Years War avenged. Catholic Spain also looked for an opportunity to take advantage of any English faltering. Regardless of the odds, quick action against the mounting French occupation had to be taken.[2]

Countering the French threat in Scotland, 1560–1

Cognisant of the practices of previous campaigns, especially those of Edward VI, Elizabeth set about dislodging the French. Her preparations were not dissimilar to those of Charles I eighty years later. First, she secured Berwick. Second, she saw to northern defences. Third, she built a Scottish alliance. Fourth, Edinburgh Castle was kept out of the enemy's hands.[3] Facing a grave military challenge at the outset of her reign, the Queen quickly became acquainted with the disagreeable and expensive demands of war. The Scottish campaign of 1560 also set the tone for her entire reign: she preferred to settle matters by diplomacy but would use military force when necessary, even though operational control might be exercised capriciously by her commanders.[4] Elizabeth I, therefore, learned very early on about campaigning. Many old soldiers and sagacious nobles realised survival depended upon the Queen's familiarity with martial matters. One courtier cautioned the young Queen:

> The Duke of Norfolkes granfather was sent by the King, your father, to invade Scotland, well accompanied both with good headds and with a good nombre: an army also by sea went into the Frithe, well furnished with victualles to releive the army by land at theire

comyng to Edenborow, which the army by land was not able to do for lacke, and yet as much was done for the furtherance of the jorney as might be. In the Duke of Somersettes tyme, the victory was not folowed in Scotland for lacke. . . . [D]o considre what an enemy besides the French men, yea, and peradventure the Scotts, first the weather will be to your people and to there horses.

Rulers should understand field operations. This conviction stretched through the Middle Ages back to classical antiquity, but would be lost in the early modern era, as the complexity of war increased. The young Elizabeth was urged to ask tough questions about logistics, supply being the key to successful operations against Scotland. Elizabeth was not to rest satisfied with glib assurances. She had to know for herself.

How they shalbe furnished of victualls both going and comyng.
What store of gunners you may have.
What passage for their ordinaunce and the carriages.
What store of carriages for their munition and victualles.
What maner of encamping is at this tyme of the yeare by the waye.
What forage is to be founde both for the horse of service and for the horse of drawght.
What maner of men be sent into this invasion, and if they should fortune to perishe for lacke of one thing or of another, how much the losse of them will importe to your Matie and to this realme.
. . .
If it be said to your Matie you shall lacke no victualles, you shall have carriages ynough, you shall have horses ynough to drawe your carriages, both of victualles and munition, and like-wise for your ordinaunce, good gracious Lady, be not to ready to beleve yt without you se the proportion in your eye, and knowe where, by whome, and by what tyme, expressely every thing may be furnished, set furth, and come to the place; for we have sene heretofore, in our dayes, the wisest men have failed in their enterprices for the want of good provision of these thinges. I pray God, if your Matie will nedes send it, that you may finde store of these thinges; for I feare, from the further south your folkes come, the worse they will like the aire and ground of Scotland at this tyme of the yeare.[5]

The Duke of Norfolk became Lieutenant General for operations in the 'North partes'. Lord Grey served as second in command. Marshal of the Field was filled by Lord Scrope, who kept sixty light horse and twenty infantry around his standard. Sir James Croft led the English infantry as 'Coronell of the Fotemen'.[6] The Queen exhibited some strategic sense by coordinating the convergence of far-flung contingents on the Borders, hence saving the cost of victualling tarrying troops. But financial arrangements left much to be desired.

> Untill the Horssmen shall arryve at Newcastell, which be appoynted, ye cannot well take in Hand any such Exploit into Scotland. . . . Certen Shyrees, from whence the Nomber of Footmen shold be sent thyther, that as many of the same, as be not passed out of the Contress, shuld not departe before such convenient Tyme, as they may be uppon the Frontyer about the same Tyme. And for such as be gone and ar come towards those Frontiers, we thynk that ye shall doo well to cause them to be layed in severall Bands and Places, so farr from the Borders within the Land, as that they may be both victelled without Expence of such Victell as is provided nigh the Border, and yet may be reddy to be at some convenient Place nigh the Frontyer about the said 30th of January; by this meane shall our Victell be saved for our seruice following, and the Men also better used. And in the meane Tyme ye may doo well to gyve order, that they may be traned and tought to use there Weapons and become hable to serue. As for Money to prest to them afore hand for their Provision, and Payment for there Victell, although Valentyne Broune is in reddynes to depart, yet considering the Carriadg of our Treasure will in this Wynter tyme ask some longer tyme, we praye yow ether to borrow seven or eight hundred Pounds of some Merchants of Newcastle, for fifteen Days at the most, until the Treasure come, or els lett the Tresoror of Berwyk, if, he can possible, forbeare in some payment at Barwyk a lyke Some or less, to emprest to the Captayns of the Footemen, so as they maye be better victelleid.[7]

Norfolk prepared for war amid the snow and sleet at Berwick. He borrowed on his own security £500 from local merchants. His financial worries also included the Berwick garrison, for Treasurer Valentine Browne had explicit orders not to expend any money on the garrison, in spite of the £9,000–£10,000 arrears owed them. These neglected men would be needed for the 'exployt in Scotland', Norfolk believed:

> the Service of the seid Garrison shalbe most meet and necessarie for that Purpose; for that they be well trayned, and for the most Part olde Souldiors, and, as I understand, so skillfull, specially for the Harquebuseries, and for the Pike also, as ther be no better.[8]

The English army, numbering about 6,000, crossed into Scotland on Friday, 29 March 1560, and covered 13 miles, bivouacking at Coldingham.

On Saturday they marched 10 miles and rendezvoused with their cavalry. The sabbath trek took them 'to Lynton bridge, and passynge by dunbar, the Frenche and Englyshe skyrmished and men [were] hurt on bothe sydes'. By 1 April they were at Salt Preston (Preston Pans) and within 7 miles of Leith.[9] The siege began in a highly mobile exchange, with 'Skottes harcquebussiers' and 'Skotts and Inglyshe lighthorsmen' engaging French troops, who included many harquebusiers, in skirmishing on 6 April 1560.[10] English armies that relied heavily on foot soldiers, and drew many carriages into Scotland, found campaigning there difficult. Indeed, late Henrician expeditions had been exclusively equestrian in some operations. The army of 1560 included more than 670 demi-lances and at least 1,120 light horsemen.[11] Equine mobility was essential to the conduct of Anglo-Scottish siege warfare.

During the second week of April, the English army encamped before Leith and encountered 1,000 French harquebusiers backed by 500 pikemen and 50 horsemen. In chivalric Anglo-French tradition, the English commander insisted that the French depart from the field; their refusal was followed by insolencies and ultimately a fusillade: 'The frenche shot all theyr shot into the fild' and a three-hour 'Skyrmishe' erupted.[12] The English drove the French from the advantageous ground of Halke Hill, a crag outside the town, and the contest escalated from an exchange of gunfire to an artillery duel. French cannon from the Leith ramparts pounded at the field pieces the English were manoeuvring against the French skirmishers, who sheltered behind a chapel. As the French began to yield, a charge of English demi-lance then routed the skirmishing party back through the gates of the besieged town, with a loss of about 150–300 on both sides, the French taking the worse. Though the English Lieutenant General pronounced the contest a draw, only days later did the extent of the casualties become known.[13]

The assault on Leith

At Easter, 14 April 1560, Elizabeth's ordnance pummelled the city and her troops again engaged the enemy. Terror became the order of the day, as in most sieges. On that same Easter day, French soldiers disguised as women slipped out of Leith and 'by effemynat facions compassed one of the englyshe scoutes and toke him' for interrogation. When they had finished with him, the French 'stroke of [off] his heade and set it upon theyr churche steple toppe'.[14] The following day an unanticipated sally by 500 French shot and 50 horse surprised the besiegers and raided their trenches. In spite of this tactical triumph, the strategic position of the French disintegrated. On 2 May, the English made a nocturnal encroachment and planted 16 pieces of 'great ordenaunce' on the southern side of the town. At daylight the Queen's forces bombarded Leith's fortifications, moving ordnance closer through the trenches.[15]

Northwestern Leith next felt the encirclement tightening, as 'tooe pieces of artilerie' were planted in the trenches for an attack on the French corn mills; 'fearing oure ordinance', the defenders retired. The English 'sett the milles on fier'. The French suffered now the diminution of their victuals along with a higher percentage of casualties in the skirmishes with the besiegers.[16] On the night of 6–7 May, the English effected a breach. Two 'false' assaults had been launched, in order to locate the French 'flanckees'– those defenders who would pour flanking fire from the bastion against the attacking forces attempting to enter through the breached wall. The English batteries were adjusted appropriately, though the French sallied out against the new ensconcements.

The English planned a 'night camisade', or nocturnal assault, whereby the dark would conceal them and reduce casualties. This would be a combined operation, with the attack including amphibious elements that would converge on Leith simultaneously. The main assault, comprising 3,020 men, would arrive on the breach at 3 a.m. Five hundred 'marines' would, at a pre-arranged signal, penetrate Leith haven. Meanwhile a Scottish force would storm the west side of the town facing the sea. To sustain the momentum of the soldiers in the breach, a second wave, numbering 2,240 men, would charge into Leith shortly after the first assault.[17] The assailants approached the defences, only to find that the walls were in better condition than they had thought, that the English scaling ladders were short by two yards and more, and that mud and water were diverted into the beseigers' ditches by a French redirection of the river that very night.

> For this assault, lewd ladders, vile and nought the souldiours had, which were to shorte God wot. The proofe therof, with bloude the poore men boughte . . . for when they layd ther ladders in the dyke they were to short the length of halfe a pyke. The flankers then murdering holdes that lay went of and slew, God knowes stout men enow, the harquebuz afore hande made foule play.[18]

The historian William Camden related how

> they labour most sharply with their whole Strength to scale and win the Walls: but for that their Ladders were too short, and the Water by stopping of the Sluce very deep, they were beaten back, being over-charged with a multitude of small Shot from above, very many slain, and more hurt.[19]

An hour's battle brought only a few Englishmen into Leith's streets. English losses were perhaps 200.[20] Sir George Howard, commanding the demi-lances, found the skyrmyshe began very hote, and owre men approache fast to thassawlte, which I was not a lytle glad to see . . . but within twoo owrs after it was daye lyght we myght see all thyngs contrarye, for nether was there breache mete for any tassawlte nor allso any scalynge ladder longe enoghe by 2 yards to reache the toppe of the walle no nor never a flanker taken awaye, For wante of whyche thyngs we have sustayned a marvelous greate losse, not onlye that we have all owre worthye capytaynes allmost hurte, but allso we have kylled and hurte I thynke a thowsand men, Whych is not onlye a greate losse unto us, but allso it hathe put suche a feare amonge the soldyers. . . . Owr power dymynyshys dayelye, I thynke we ar wurse then we weare when we came owte of Barwyke by at least 2 thowsand men, beyde all owr greate shott all owre smale [small shot], and other owr munysyon be uttery [utterly] spente . . . owre poore hurte soldyers ar fayne to lye in the streetes and cannot get no howserome [lodging] for money. Owr horsmeate [provender] allso is so dear that owr poore solldyers is not able to lyve on theyr wage.[21]

In the evening of 24 May, two hundred French infantry and a score of cavalry raided the English trenchworks on the western side, towards the sea, with casualties on both sides. French sallies continued through June.[22] After the repulse of 7 May 1560, still no relief from the Continent entered the Firth of Forth. Lack of supplies and no reinforcements made the French receptive to the negotiated settlement worked out at Edinburgh. French capitulation came as a godsend, for the English were grappling with logistical problems that seemed insurmountable.

From the Queen's viewpoint, the siege of Leith achieved its goal – the expulsion of the 4,000 or so French from a potential beachhead for an invasion of England. That strategic success occurred despite tactical blunders. It is paradoxical that the superbly managed 1547 campaign should have failed to attain its end while the 1560 siege witnessed a shameful repulse yet resulted in the desired effect. One could win the battle and accomplish nothing, or lose the battle and secure one's goals none the less through negotiation or default. Where Protector Somerset differed from Elizabeth I (and Charles I) was the prioritisation that the Scottish war received. For 1547, the central government fielded a sufficient and well-supplied expeditionary force. Elizabeth and Charles sometimes fought their wars in half measures, for lurking in their minds was the cheap and relatively painless solution of a negotiated settlement. Resolution had much to do with military success in the North. The campaign of 1560 confirmed the problems inherent in Scottish campaigns. Victualling, pay shortages, slow transport of ordnance, inadequate troop strength, shoddy military engineering, and inexpert command decisions all came into play in the spring of 1560. Bitter lessons, the failings of 1560 convinced Elizabeth to cast a diligent royal eye over military preparations. Providentially, though, English strategic security had been preserved.

Yet the 1560 campaign, with its skirmishing, siegecraft, and ambushes, showed occasional flashes of tactical ingenuity. In the trench warfare surrounding Leith, the English consistently foiled French sallies and inflicted proportionately heavier casualties upon the enemy. Besides meeting the Leith garrison's sallies and preventing the enfilading of their trenches, the English executed a good ambush or two. In late April intelligence reports indicated that the French garrisoned in Dunbar strayed from their defences, so the English laid a trap. Lord Grey ordered Sir Henry Percy's light horsemen to hide themselves by night a mile and a half south of Dunbar. In the morning a dozen English in convoy passed with carriage horses, enticing the French to give chase. The latter were surprised by Percy's 300 men, who ran down the infantry and pursued the fleeing horsemen to a large residence, 'where we lighted, and with our harquebuters on horseback and the harquebutes we had won from the [French] foot, we won the house'. Forty-five prisoners were taken and a dozen French slain.[23]

In 1560 disaster might have struck had not the French contended with the same logistical challenges. The dearth of experienced captains and non-commissioned officers in spring 1560 made training the expeditionary forces difficult, and accounts for why mid-winter exercising was deemed necessary. The central government acknowledged officer shortages in Berkshire, Surrey, Sussex, Hampshire, Leicestershire, and Hertfordshire.[24] The prognostications of old Captain Edward Turnor seemed borne out: '. . . the sacred profession of perfect men of ware ys now by ill training growen to misorder and mischef.'[25] The field generals were quick to cite their soldiers' lack of expertise for the failed assault in early May, which stalled 'by meanes of disorder and Cowardise of our menne except the small number of the bandes of barwick'. The English army was almost entirely 'rawe souldiors'.[26] But, the officers complained not only of quality, but also of quantity. Twelve thousand, probably twenty thousand, men were needed to reduce Leith.[27]

A royal inquest into the campaign failed to get to the heart of the matter. Perhaps Elizabeth simply wished the business closed. Victualling had proved more complicated than in 1547 because of the Queen's inconsistent deployment of the navy. Somerset's successful strategy of linking up the land forces with the fleet at various point along the Firth had not been emulated. Swayed by reports of chronic shortages of provisions at Berwick, the Queen had instructed Admiral Wynter to deliver rations to that garrison town, and then proceed to harass French vessels sailing for Scotland. Her vacillations regarding the role of the fleet placed the expeditionary force at an unnecessary disadvantage.[28] What if, for example, the flotilla patrolled the southern coastline of the Firth, periodically unloading provisions to the land forces and bombarding Leith from the sea? The experience of 1547 had demonstrated that inshore fire could prove most effective. Victuals would have heartened the besieging force and demoralised the French. Wynter estimated that his victuals would last until 13 February at best. Foul weather caused leakage and spoiled the bread; 'besydes ther mealles', the soldiers lacked drink and clothes. Supply from England was tenuous.[29]

The French consumed great quantities of foodstuffs in the vicinity of Leith. Sympathetic (or opportunistic) merchants had sold supplies to the invaders, while disaffected Scots drove off their cattle and evacuated their grain. Consequently, the victuals remaining were priced dearly. With the English fleet otherwise engaged, no 'cheap' food could be transported regularly from Berwick to the besiegers' camp, making them that much more dependent on their own resources and local expensive fare.[30] Adequate pay was especially requisite as the English soldiers tried to obey strictures against plundering, an abuse that would anger the Scots, jeopardising the anti-French alliance. The Queen's commanders' obliviousness to the fiscal limitations within which the Crown operated is illustrated by the remark of Sir Ralph Sadler, poised upon the Borders to attack Leith in spring 1560. He mused to Cecil confidentially, '. . . what is £20,000 more or less in a pryncis purse . . .'[31] Sadler's observation came three and a half months after he had warned the government that timely and sufficient payment was essential:

> . . . have better consideracion of my charges, or ells I shall begger my self in this service. . . . My horsemete [provender] woll eate up the one half of myn enterteynment; all things here be so unreasonally dere. . . . I wolde to God ye had ben more forwarde in tyme. For God's sake put to your helping hande, that money and victuall maybe sent hither with spede, and trust not overmoche to my lord treasourers faire words. . . . The quenes majestie is in debt here at this time £12,000 and odde money . . . as Mr Ingleby, treasourer here . . . hath not one peny left . . . towards the payment there of. . . . Souldeours here do moche complayn . . . if they lacke their wages, they woll serve with the worse will.[32]

The accounts of army treasurer Valentine Browne reveal that Elizabeth's Scottish campaign was leaner than its Henrician and Edwardian predecessors. The money, roughly £133,151, came through the Tellers of the Exchequer of Receipt. Other treasurers, such as those serving in the Duchy of Lancaster, the Mint, and the Court of Wards respectively, all of whom participated in Henry's campaigns, are listed in Browne's account, but with no disbursements made. The Exchequer of Receipt now monopolised military finance.[33] The money did arrive at the front, though not always in the denominations desired, with logistical ramifications. One shipment at the height of hostilities consisted of change: 'pence, twoo pences, and olde testons.' More gold and silver coins would have been useful. The sheer bulk meant that the army's pay could not be carried on horseback, but required carts and horses, which could not navigate the terrain of the Borders without difficulty and dangerous slowness. Norfolk opined that seaborne transport was the best means to convey treasure.[34] Browne delivered the army's pay personally, coming by sea, landing in the haven, and then proceeding to the camp with a caravan of carts on 30 April.[35]

Company-based military organisation also seemed to be emerging, for the accounts were often based on company-sized units of 100–500 men, drawn from all over England – for example, 200 from Chesterfield in Derbyshire and 50 from Richmond. The troops may have been less well taken care of than Henry VIII's warriors. In some cases the cost of food, weapons, and powder was subtracted from their pay. The composition of the army reflects what one would expect of an English besieging force – a preponderance of light horsemen, only a few of whom carried harquebuses, many infantry (half or more of whom were not armed, apparently), and pioneers. In fact, it is likely that unarmed infantry assisted the pioneers and did double duty. These were supported by numerous gunners and ordnance personnel, and companies of demi-lances. The army's weaponry suggests that they did not anticipate a set-piece battle.[36]

Elizabeth's dislike of professional soldiers sometimes placed her at a disadvantage in plotting strategy. By relying upon William Cecil to draw up the initial invasion plan, the number of siege guns was underestimated by the minister.[37] Later in his career, as Lord Burghley, he would become expert at such business.[38] Carriages, carts, and sturdy horses did not abound in the North, which restricted the number of field pieces and siege cannon that could be wheeled into the works surrounding Leith.[39] Elizabeth's unwillingness to use the fleet for inshore barrages against Leith placed that much more reliance on land-based cannon to demolish Leith's outerworks. Considering that the failure to storm Leith resulted from the ordnance's inability to puncture a breach, the deployment of so few guns[40] was a major miscalculation. Increased firepower certainly could have effected an entry into Leith.[41] Too few cannon led to hundreds of casualties in the abortive assault. Likewise, not enough men were mobilised. Theoretically, 9,000 infantrymen stood before Leith.[42] In reality, probably 6,000 were left by 7 May.[43] Twenty thousand troops may have been the requisite number.[44] As Grey refrained from committing a large body of men in the assault (another reason for its failure, it could be argued, since some men actually clambered into the town, though their small numbers forced them to retreat back through the breach), the smallness of the attacking party was a direct result of the wastage of the original force.[45]

As for siegeworks, the diminutive French garrison successfully defended old-style fortifications against the artillery of the military revolution.[46] Finally, the English high command performed badly. Grey's decision to proceed with the assault without ascertaining the strength of his forces at a muster, contrary to the advice of the officers who had inspected the breach, borders on criminal negligence. His quarrel with Lord General Norfolk after the assault's failure betrayed the pettiness, dishonesty, and incompetence of both. Recriminations between Grey and Norfolk, and the scapegoating of Croft, made an ugly scene. The performance of her generals convinced Elizabeth that she would have to question their good judgement (or lack of it). The Queen saw warfare swallow up enormous amounts of money. The logistical problems, the need for carriages, naval support, etc., underscored the precarious timetables involved in campaigning, with consequent ramifications for her freedom of manoeuvre in negotiations and diplomacy. The soldiers themselves were found unsatisfactory, poorly trained (if at all) and insufficiently armed, storming fortifications with bills, bows, and 'sheaf arrowes'.[47]

The northern rising of 1569–70

The 1569 rising was a baronial revolt of the era of the wars of religion. It had more in common with the Wars of the Roses than the Thirty Years War. The Crown was not only moving the kingdom towards a Protestant *via media* but also considering modern weaponry and experimenting with local military administration. The rebellion reminded the government that civil war fomented by the 'overmighty' or conspiratorially minded lord was not a thing of the past. That reality persisted, in some ways, into the conflicts of the 1640s. If Elizabeth had any reluctance to build sizeable militias in the North (or the West Country for that matter), the later example of Charles I justified these sentiments, for military power raised in regions with a history of autonomy (and conspiracy) could very well be turned against Whitehall, as it had been in the mid-fifteenth and would be in the mid-seventeenth century. As long as martial leadership remained associated with aristocracy (and it did so at least into Victoria's reign), then royal control of the armed forces had to encompass manipulation of the nobility. Obviously, *who* commanded Elizabeth's armies was as significant as how many soldiers she fielded, and with what equipment.

In 1569, Elizabeth chose as her commanders the Earl of Sussex, Lord Clynton, and the Baron Hunsdon. Sussex, an intimate of the Duke of Norfolk (around whose schemed marriage to Mary Stuart the conspiracy swirled), and a brother of one of the insurgents, led the reaction force of 7,000 men. Similarly, Sir Henry Percy, brother to the Earl of Northumberland (the main traitor along with the Earl of Westmorland), recruited northern forces for Elizabeth. Other key nobles were obliged to demonstrate their loyalty to the dynasty by either mobilising troops (very often their own tenantry) or passing on intelligence reports. Elizabeth made it clear that the noble houses were divided, and that the North was not united in opposition to the Crown.[48] More revealing was her choice of

Henry Carey, Baron Hunsdon, as one of the field generals of the royal army. Her closest blood relative, the son of Anne Boleyn's sister, Hunsdon would guard the Queen's person at Tilbury in 1588. By appointing Hunsdon as General of the Horse in 1569, she injected her own dynastic and familial loyalties into the command structure.

The stickiness of the situation in suppressing the revolt is reflected in the muster certificates done that very summer. Supervising the commissioners of musters in Yorkshire were the Earls of Northumberland, Westmorland, and Sussex; the latter would be marching against the other two in a matter of months. The perilous irony was nicely encapsulated within the wapentakes of Clarow, Howdenshire, Holderness and Harthill, which answered to the Earls of Sussex and Northumberland jointly. No doubt the able men found their loyalties torn when the rebellion broke out, and they were forced to declare for one Earl or the other. It was even alleged that the Earls had used the general musters of 1569 as an opportunity to spy out the distribution of arms. Their intelligence then allowed them to intercept the militia as they marched to York, 'and eyther caused them to serve them, or ells toke their horse, armour, weapon, and money'. As a result, the muster certificates were no longer reliable as to the men and weapons available to the Crown.[49] The residents of the wapentakes of Allertonshire, Langbaurge, Hang East, Hang West, Gilling East, Gilling West, and Hallikelde[50] faced an even more complicated dilemma at the rising. Assisting the Earl of Westmorland had been Sir George Bowes, whose daring rearguard mobilisation would trap the former and collapse the Catholic strategy.[51]

On 12 November 1569, the Earl of Sussex, the Queen's Lieutenant General in the North, learned that the Earls had armed themselves and ridden towards Durham to celebrate Mass. Sussex resolved 'to mete therewith presently by force', and sent letters under the signet to the Yorkshire gentry 'to levy all the force of horsemen that may be had sufficiently ether horsed and armed with speare and fote armour, or horsed and weaponed with harquebuz or bowe and arowes . . . and to levye 2500 fotemen'. He issued similar orders in Northumberland, the Bishopric of Durham, and 'Richmondshire'.[52] What kind of soldiers turned out? Were they newly mustered militiamen, raw lads, or sturdy tenants? From York, Sussex wrote that his call to arms had been received

> . . . very slackly, we have raised all the forcs in all the wapentaks nereto this Citie, and have chosen owte of them that be come so many hable mene as have ether armour or any kinde of weapen, and the rest we loke for to morow.[53]

In effect, all able men were summoned, and hopefully they carried weapons. The wapentakes mustered all available manpower, both cavalry and infantry.

Sussex worried that the rebels, who had had time to arm themselves and were of necessity desperate, would triumph over his hastily gathered and ill-armed levies. Shortages of riders and mounts disturbed him, as he needed a mobile wing in such an operation.[54] Money, too, came in slowly. Valentine Browne, Treasurer at Berwick, had disbursed all that was available in temporary receivership and had advanced private funds to keep the mobilisation afoot.[55] In the meanwhile, Sussex, Hunsdon, and Sadler strove to make an army. They commanded horse archers but few pikemen. Harquebusiers and light horse were summoned out of the Berwick garrison.[56]

Sussex realised that a reliable body of cavalry, with its mobility and shock, would give him sufficient force to challenge the Earls' horsemen, for he had learned of the rebels' deficiencies in infantry and even jested about '. . . ther pore rascall fotmen, that for feare, come slowly on the one day, go away a pace willingly on the other, so as ther chife force is horsemen, which be well appointed'.[57] Some reports indicated that the rebels had been fairly successful in recruiting infantry. Sir Ralph Sadler reckoned Sussex's loyal forces at 3,000 foot but fewer than 300 horse. The Earls might have as many as 6,000–7,000 foot soldiers and cavalry numbering 1,200.[58] Noble influence over tenants and gentlemen of the shire boosted the forces available to Elizabeth. Lord Darcy, eager to demonstrate his loyalty to the regime, reported glowingly:

> The fourteenth of this instant I receavyed commyssion from my Lord Lieutenant of theis North partes for the levie of all the force of horsemen within the liberties of Strafford, and likewise for levie of 150 fotemen. All which, with thaide of the gentlemen my neighbours joined in the commyssion with me, were not only well fyrnished in every behalf, but also safely conducted and delyveryd at York the eighteenth of the same, togethers with there conduct-money and wages for 21 dayes. [At Doncaster] by force of a second commyssion, I musterd 2000 fotemen and all the power of horsemen that cold everywaies be had aswell of my Freindes as all the gentlemen there servants and tenants within the said liberties. And have taken such order as I retayne 400 fotemen, besydes horse, and depeched the rest to repayer uppon the first warnynge; Manie in effect alltogethers merely destitut both of money and armore, for the causes abovesaid. And yet nevertheless offering themselves, if they had wherewith to sustain nature, to die at my feet; I and my fellow Commissioners have supplied them so far as either lands, goods, or credit will extend.[59]

Recruitment on both sides was wholesale and not terribly systematic. The able-bodied and armed citizens that had received such attention in summer 1569 now got summonses from both sides, and in the Queen's name. The dearth was more evident in weaponry than in bodies, but the Crown rushed to put Yorkshiremen under the royal standard before they could be seduced into the rebel ranks. When the Earls retired to the area where the North and East ridings meet, Sussex told the Queen that their numbers would now cease to grow, for 'all that be hable to serve in these parts be alreadie levied for your majesties service'.[60] Ideologically, the recruits seem to have needed some guidance, and familial patronage, tenurial obligation, and personal connection steered men into the ranks. The Earl of Rutland, a minor and a ward of the Crown, wielded the Manners' family influence to keep the tenants of that noble household on the straight and narrow:

> my servants Bamborow and Thomson are heare and beare office both. Bamborow is seriant-maior, and the Thomson is provost martiall under Mr. Vaughan who is martiall Sigrane and divers other of my gentlemen, who were my fathers men, with a great nomber of my tenants ar heare; and further ther is not one of my tenants as farr as I can lerne I sent is out.[61]

Among loyal nobles equipped with commissions of lieutenancy, the Marshal of Berwick, and loyal gentry, the northern situation would be stabilised at least until a southern army could succour the Queen's northern agents. The south contained England's military strength. Due care was spent in ensuring that rebellion would not raise its head elsewhere – for example, in Wales – and Catholic nobles were dragooned into the Queen's preparations. Cecil increased the number of calivermen and harquebusiers. He seems to have had some confidence in firepower.[62] Ordnance and munitions were transported to Leicester.[63] Two southern armies coalesced, one to safeguard the Queen's person, the other to march northwards. The former numbered 10,000 foot (1,000 from Kent, 2,000 from Surrey, 1,000 Hampshire men, and an impressive array of 6,000 from Sussex), along with 800 cavalry (half of which came from Sussex). The expeditionary force drew from London (4,000 men, half being 'shot', 1,500 pikes, and the remainder bowmen), Middlesex (2,000), Berkshire (2,000), Oxfordshire (2,000), Hertfordshire (1,000), Buckinghamshire (1,500), Wiltshire (500), Norfolk (1,000), Suffolk (1,000), Somerset (2,000), for a total of 20,000 foot. The same shires supplied much-needed cavalry amounting to 2,500. Marginalia in the draft indicate that this ambitious plan was in fact in use.[64]

Organisationally, the army was centred upon the company as the basic unit, underscoring the autonomy and importance of captains at this time.[65] Ultimately there emerged a 14,215-man force led by the Earl of Warwick and Lord Admiral Clynton. They were seconded by Viscount Hereford, Lord Willoughby, Charles Howard and Henry Knolles. Among the captains was Robert Hitchcock, the logistics and victualling specialist.

Hunsdon propagandised as he mobilised Yorkshire, and 'brought the sod-yars that leket well of the Rebbels to thynk very yll of them, and too mysleke theyr dooyngs and too know that the rebbels doo abuse her Majesties name'.[66] But in spite of the commanders' exhortations they had not got the army they needed to defeat the rebellion.

> The force and power assembled here for your Majesty is above the number of 2500 foteman and not above 500 horsemen which is not able to incounter the forces of the rebells being as I am crediblie informed aboute the number of 6000 foteman and 1000 horsemen well appoynted, whereof a grete number of them being serving men, servants, and tenants to the two Erles and to thother gentlemen; their assosiates be pistoliers armed and furnished with shotte, which argueth that this matter hathe long befor hande ben prepared for by the said Rebells.[67]

Elizabeth's generals in the North had to curb their impulse to engage the rebels, for they lacked a sufficiently balanced force to overcome the Earls' cavalry. They needed reinforcements of 1,000 horse, 500 pikemen and 500 harquebusiers to take on the field.[68] Had the northern army been properly armed, there would have been no need for the southern army. Heavy cavalry, harquebuses, and a supply of money would have done the trick.[69] Sussex's experiences suggested an approach to warfare that, sadly, the government did not embrace in subsequent years. Facing a superior enemy ('they be farr stronger both of horseman and fotemen'[70]), he under-stood that a small, trained force armed with the proper combination of weaponry might gain a decisive victory without recourse to bringing a lumbering and expensive force from the south. Although the rebels outmatched the royal cavalry (if the latter might be distinguished with such a description) at a ratio of perhaps four to one, with a motley crew of 1,600 rebel cavalry challenging 400 'ill-equipped' royal horsemen, Sussex planned to thin the enemy's ranks with volleys from mounted 'pistolets' and then ride them down with lancers. The infantry, like the horse, would blend shock and missile. He wanted 500 pikemen, in corselets, 'to make the fronts of my battells' – in other words to anchor a formation that would withstand any attacks from the rebels' main strength, their horsemen. But the strongest blow would be delivered by the 500 'harquebuts'. Sussex wrote,

> I may levye greate nombers of fotemen in this contrye [Yorkshire] but utterlye unarmed and unweponed and therefore I think it better to reteyne a convenyent number of the best furnyshed then to over charge the Queens Majestie with such as be unservys-abell.[71]

By the end of November, Sussex may well have remedied his deficiency in foot soldiers for he estimated his impending muster at 4,000 infantry, while at the same time (28 November) they had fallen back, dividing their forces between the main group that proceeded on to besiege Barnard Castle, and a smaller group that was to take Hartlepool as a potential rendezvous point with the seaborne force of Spanish allies they mistakenly expected to succour them. Belief that continental forces might intervene, bringing much needed money and war material, was not confined to the rebels. Intelligence from Europe alleged that the Duke of Alba would reinforce the rebels, which may perhaps explain the government's strategy of amassing an army of large proportions.[72] The Queen's commanders in the North were not asking the impossible. Hundred-man companies of harquebusiers marched amongst the relieving southern army, two for example under Captains Leonerde Knappe and John Pragell. Further, mounted 'pistolars' and 'harquebuzers' could conceivably have ridden ahead. And money now existed as well, more than £27,000 raised in London and earmarked for the suppression of the revolt. But all this came maddeningly slowly to Sussex and his compatriots, as the precious cavalry, arms, money, and reinforcements mobilised *en masse*.[73]

The 1569 rebellion and the wars of religion

The military resources of the Bishopric of Durham became a prize for both sides. The clergy of the realm ostensibly participated in the revivification of the statutes of Philip and Mary for the ecclesiastical contribution to the stockpiling of the nation's arms.[74] Given the fact that the rebels had celebrated Mass in Durham Cathedral, Cecil was quick to make sure the Archbishop of Canterbury maintained obedience in the clerical ranks, not just to shore up the religious 'legitimacy' of the realm but also to keep the arms and armour (generally for light horsemen and demi-lances) of the clerics at the disposal of the Queen.[75] The Earls did their utmost to muddy the waters, commanding

> . . . in the quenes maiestie name, all and everie Tennaunts, belonginge to the layte supposed Bisshop of Duresme, that they make readye all such rents as were due . . . [and] . . . payde in the accustomed plaice within the Exchequer of Duresme, before Satterdaye next. . . .[76]

From the Palatine Exchequer the coins would find their way into the purses of the rebel soldiers.

As had been the case in earlier Tudor rebellions, commanders had to assess the morale and temperament of the loyal and opposition armies.

Religion indeed confounded the decision to risk battle. Northern sentiment favoured the Old Religion. Sussex strove to dampen popular religious fervour by discrediting the Earls, who 'never had care of conscience, or even respected any religion, but continued a dissolute lyfe, untyll at this present they were driven to pretend a popishe holynesse'. The Queen pointed to the Earls' poverty as a motive for rebellion. Ironically, she had done much to lessen the value of their estates and reputation, in some ways almost daring them to revolt.[77] But the rebels' heinous sin was offending English attitudes towards peace and war. The Queen's Peace entailed more than simply the prevention of crime. As the shepherdess of her people, she determined that her people would not be devoured by the wolves of war. The Earls had brought down the scourge upon their own neighbours, having ignited 'open and actuall rebellion, armyng and fortifying them selves rebelliously in all warlyke manner, and have invaded houses and churches', actions that created turmoil that might be exploited by foreign powers bent on conquering England's green pastures. The blessings of peace, the Queen reminded her subjects, were now jeopardised, for this constituted '. . . the first rebellion and breache of the publique blessed peace . . . whiche now hath continued above eleven yeres, an act horrible against God the only gever of so long a peace'.

Thus counterposed against religious sentiment in the North were peace, prosperity, and stability. Elizabeth not only condemned treason, but also articulated her pacific policies on the domestic and foreign levels. War and violence were literally last resorts.[78] That tradition of English self-defence, where all true English hearts, regardless of religious opinion, worked together to preserve their nation, was also articulated and addressed to the 'poore deceived subjectes of the North Countrey', who were chastised by Cambridge scholar Thomas Norton: '. . . you have lost the iustue name of Englishmen by disturbing the common peace of Englande, with cruell invasion and spoile lyke enimies'. Endemic disorder in the region of the Borders had been largely extinguished, for which the rebels should have been grateful: '. . . they nor their auncesters never knewe it so well ordered'. Indeed, '. . . had Englande ever in our memorie so long so blissed peace bothe at home and abroad . . . ? Was Englande ever better ordered in all degrees, from hye to lowe, till your shameful rebellion hath interrupted the great blessing of God?' Norton boasted of Elizabeth's military preparedness, describing a bristling arsenal that the historian (possessing Ordnance Office records) knows did not exist.[79] In terms that prefigure the divisions of the Civil War, it was remarked,

> . . . if we shulde go to the felde with this northren force onely, they would fight but fayntly in this quarele, for . . . if the father be on this syde, the soon is on the other, and one brother with us, and the other with the rebells.

And in the same missive, a complaint appears that would be repeated by royal commanders in the northern expeditions of 1639 and 1640, that '. . . money, armour, and munycyon sent from thens, is not arryved here, whereof we have great lacke'.[80] Ultimately the military consequences of rebel activities came down to the acquisition of resources. Rather than setting themselves up in unassailable positions and girding for battle, the armies spent their time scrambling about for armour, foraging for sustenance from the 'hollowe harted' inhabitants, and indulging in 'lamentation great for want of pay'.[81]

The weaponry of the southern force, too, betrayed medieval characteristics. There were 2,000 bills but only 500 pikes; 500 harquebusiers to 1,000 archers.[82] The 1569 mobilisation drove home a point made clearly in Somerset's Scottish expedition: operations in the North entailed the supply of more than one army. In 1547, land and sea forces were supplied separately so that they might support one another. In December 1569 the Crown faced not only the supply of Sussex's force, but also the victualling of the defenders of Barnard Castle, the continued supply of the Border garrisons (which were now reluctantly drawn into the suppression of the rebellion) and the mobilisation of the large southern army.[83] That southern army not only lacked weapons but also required training; the two deficiencies were of course related. Although the militia had been 'raided' by the Earls, it was not so much recruits as modern weapons and horses that Sussex needed. So, though the southern army may well have been marginally more reliable on the battlefield because of its immunity to northern religious sentiments, it was not highly trained or properly equipped. Like Hamilton in 1639, Clynton in 1569 hesitated to declare his force operational until he had sorted out the deficiencies in his men's equipment and above all provided training for those carrying firearms.[84]

The rebel Earls had no bureaucracy to sustain an army. Raising a host through a quasi-feudal means was one thing, to sustain the troops much more difficult.[85] Their effort to collect the rents of the Bishopric of Durham was followed by attempts at rating – for example, in the area between Northallerton and Piercebridge, where they directed villages to supply footsoldiers.[86] But even if the service of men could be extorted, wages were not forthcoming, resulting in mass desertion and expressions that the pressed men would rather be hanged than serve the Earls, perhaps realising, too, that they would be hanged if in the pay of the Earls. One reporter alleged that he had encountered groups of dozens of deserters from the rebel army '. . . that sayd their comyng home was for more munny, but thay wold be hangged at home or [ere] thay retorned agayn to sarve withowt wayges'.[86a]

The sieges of Barnard Castle (1569) and Edinburgh Castle (1573)

The rebels' strategic error, perhaps unavoidable, was to allow a royalist force (under the guidance of Sir George Bowes) to get behind them, so that loyal troops fortified themselves within Barnard Castle, compelling the insurgents to lay siege. As a result, the rebel Earls delayed their move south. Bowes's resistance bought time for Elizabeth, so that the desperately needed shot (300 of the Berwick garrison) and cavalry (from the Northumberland militia presumably) might march towards the rebels' stronghold in Durham, while the southern army trekked northwards. Sir George Bowes's occupation of Barnard Castle began simply as an act to safeguard his family and household amid the rumours and clandestine military preparations in the North. Thus the castle's initial possession by a loyalist to the regime was not a deliberate strategic move, yet in the end it would prove to be a brilliant stroke.[87] Those loyal to the Crown, and adhering to Sir George Bowes as his tenants or friends, gathered within the precincts of Barnard Castle. Naturally, Bowes explained,

> . . . in respecte of this castell, I thought yt good to begin th'assem-
> blye here, where ys alredye comed unto me, with greate haste, and
> well appoynted, to serve as light horsemen, the whole gentlemen
> dwellinge upon the ryver of Teyse . . . They brought with them
> yn abowt a hundred lighte horsemen, well mounted, and armed
> with playte coyts and speares, and I have of my owne verye yne
> and hundred light horseman. And therys also assembled nether of
> the countrethes next adjoyning, two hundred able men, armed and
> weaponed with playte coyt, jack, bowes and arrows, and bylls, and
> twenty corslets of my owne, and thirtie harquebusses; the effect of
> which nomber ys a choyse of my owne tenants and others under
> my rewle, of the Quene's Majesties tennants of Barnard Castell
> Lordship. And Most Dewtyfullye and obedyentlye the people yne
> these parts assemble ther styll, whereof the best lyke, in person and
> furnyture I staye, and the reste with thanks, and good words, I
> returne with thanks, and good words, I returne home.[88]

Such was the paternal, local, and decentralised nature of military organisation in 1569. In spite of the reforms of earlier that year, late medieval forms of recruitment based upon familial influence within the shire, grounded in real proprietal relationships, patronage, and local prestige, remained vital, and, in this case, reliable. However, weaponry remained problematic. Bowes's impromptu garrison suffered '. . . a mervellows lack of armour, but specyally of weapone; and can nott tell howe to supply yt'.[89] Nor was Barnard Castle prepared for a siege in terms of victuals, ordnance,

or architecture. Having lain neglected before the revolt, it would be abandoned after the suppression.[90] The Queen's subjects stood ready to serve
but lacked the means to do so. For all the efforts of 1569, the traditional
means of fielding forces came off best, but still could not produce the
required weapons. Some armour lay at Newcastle, but Bowes had no
warrant.[91]

Regardless, Sir George assembled a garrison that brought up his strength
to at least 400 infantry and 200 cavalry.[92] Gathering a modest store of victuals, Bowes recognised his peril, as the rebels rode through the North
intimidating the populace and striving to strengthen their forces. He
requested reinforcements. Given the strategy of the Queen's commanders,
to hold off from battle until they possessed sufficient strength to scatter
the rebels, each loyal commander would have to rely on his own means
until a coordinated effort could be launched.[93] By 29 November, Bowes
strongly suspected that the rebels would 'beseage' him, and news that the
Earls had acquired 'a fawcon and two slyngs' obliged him to ready his
artillery and fortifications.[94] Others, too, reported that the rebels meant 'to
assaulte Sir George Bowes in Barnard Castle, and so to repaier into Tyndale
and Ryddesdall, where they hope to be reinforced with the Scotts, such
as be of the Quene of Scots faction'.[95]

As it was, the royal army came too late. Clynton's forces, which Sussex
urged on to relieve Bowes, had been trudging through December's cold
and muddy fields '. . . in the foule waies with there Armors upon them',
initially marching sometimes twelve miles a day. Greatly wearied, they now
could cover no more than five miles a day. Within a week, Barnard Castle
had fallen.[96] Sussex had exhorted them to carry on, with horse and shot,
not waiting for more heavily armed men, 'lest Sir George Bowes perish
in the meantime'.[97] When the rebels descended on Barnard Castle, they
had little if any artillery, but in the event they needed none. The scarcity
of food within the walls was known to the Earls and they simply starved
out the garrison, encouraging desertion at first ('. . . in one daye and nyght,
two hundred and twenty six men leapyd over the walles . . . thirty five
broke their necks, legges, or armes in the leaping').[98] Mutiny finished them
off, probably because the rebels had taken the first ward of the castle,
driving Bowes and his adherents into the keep. Hard-pressed, hungry, and
unarmed, the 150 or so assigned to hold the gates, and whose loyalty up
to that point had held firm, '. . . did sodenly sett open the gats, and went
to the rebels'. Bowes, 'seing the falshode of his men', agreed to terms, and
left the castle with his arms.[99]

The anticlimax came when the Earls, unable to sustain their modest
gains at Barnard Castle and elsewhere, retreated into Scotland after skirmishing with Sir John Forster's forces. While Sussex disbanded much of
the royal infantry not long after mid-December, the generals exploited
what they had lacked for so long: horsemen and firearms. Forster, with as

much zeal for furthering his own fortunes in the North as devotion to the Queen's cause, set off in hot pursuit of the fleeing Earls, who were travelling fast now that they had discharged their infantry. Forster's thousand horsemen got close, and fought a 'skyrmyshe betwene ther skowtes and his skowtes', though the rebels extricated themselves and found refuge in Hexham.[100] They retreated west, then north, crossing the River Irthing, and rode into Scotland, effectively ending their uprising.

The Queen faced the prospect of maintaining armies that she could not afford. By the year's end the royal army numbered 11,000 infantry and 1,200 cavalry, at a monthly charge (for wages only) of no less than £14,430. In addition, numerous gentlemen and their servants hung on, and required conduct money, carriage charges (including those for transporting ordnance and munitions), and the pay of the high command. 'The sum of the hole' was estimated at £21,030. With only £8,500 paid against this debt, the army required £12,880 more before it could be disbanded adequately. And each day of delay cost a further £300.[101] Perhaps an army of this size would have been necessary had four things, or at least some of them, happened: had the Duke of Norfolk risen, swelling the rebel ranks and widening the revolt geographically; had the Earls of Northumberland and Westmorland succeeded in mobilising their entire tenantry; had shires outside the immediate sphere of influence of the Earls harkened to the denunciation of Elizabethan religious policy; and, finally, had Lord Dacre coordinated his uprising with the Earls. In fact, Dacre launched the most impressive onslaught against the government forces, after his return to Cumberland in January 1570 (he had been detained by a lawsuit in London during the Earls' rising).

English warfare in the North still could revolve around siegecraft, however. The focus shifted from Barnard Castle to Naworth Castle, and then a few years later to Edinburgh Castle. A clash occurred in February 1570 between the rebel Lord Dacre, ensconced in Naworth Castle, and loyal forces under Hunsdon. After marching all night from Hexham, on 20 February Elizabeth's commander found the fortress ablaze with beacons, and '. . . every hyll full of men, bothe horsemen and footmen, krynge and shoutyng, as they had been mad'. Having lost any element of surprise and certain that Dacre had stocked significant munition and ordnance, and positioned soldiers on the heights, Hunsdon elected to march to Carlisle. Dacre offered battle, however, but Hunsdon declined. Undeterred, the rebel lord chased the loyalists for four miles, and upon a heath, Dacre's bellicose infantrymen launched '. . . the prowdes charge upon my shott that ever I saw'. Posting 500 cavalry at his rear, Hunsdon counter-attacked 'with the rest of my horsemen upon his footmen; and slew between 3 and 400' as well as taking prisoners.[102]

The supression of the rebellion revealed dramatically just how pathetic the militia was prior to the invigoration of lieutenancy in the 1570s. The militia had proved to be useless. Bodies were present, but shire arms stores seem to have been virtually non-existent, with the private possession of arms, the medieval model reinforced by the Statute of Winchester, still predominant. Privatised also was the command of levies. Allegiance in the northern countryside remained parochial, and thus recruitment (and hence mobilisation in general) had to proceed through the recognised channels of shire prestige and authority. Nor had the victualling and transport problems of the North abated in the sixteenth century. Food, not religion, undermined the less than steadfast wills of Bowes's impromptu garrison.

In spite of the slowness of the royal mobilisation and the dearth of modern weapons, still Elizabeth's army exhibited during the rebellion the strengths of English warfare: reliable and bold command, tactical ingenuity, and the right application of the right weapon at the opportune time. Hunsdon's nocturnal advance on Naworth Castle was commendable, and, when circumstances appeared unfavourable, he prudently withdrew – a perilous manoeuvre that is almost as risky as battle. When forced to fight, having kept his country folk in order through four miles of provocation, he steadied his men through the initial onslaught, then riposted with daring: '. . . Hunsdon, himselfe in the for frunt of the field, takinge th advantage thereof, gave the charge verie orderlye and valientlie'.[103]

The command of armies, and forms of recruitment that reflected decentralisation, retained medieval structure even if the substance was rather lacking. The procedure by which Sir Ralph Sadler allocated pay to the royal army in the North in 1569 did involve temporary receivers and loans from merchants. Sir Thomas Gargrave disbursed £1,600 of his initial reserve (apparently sent down from London) of £2,000 via warrant. The remaining £400 was given over to Sadler as the Treasurer at War, who also gathered in £2,000 from Chester and £500 that was supposed to be sent to London, the latter sum circumventing the Exchequer (at least in the short run). Sadler also borrowed £400 from the 'honeste merchauntes of Hull, to be repayed at the commying hither of the quenes majesties tresour. . . .' Sadler kept £500 of the £3,300 he had gathered.[104]

The instability in the North in 1569, compounded by the assassination of the Earl of Murray on 22 January 1570, prompted another English incursion into Scottish territory and Celtic politics. Despite the Crown's inability to honour the remaining coat, conduct, and carriage arrears of the army of autumn 1569, 500 harquebusiers of the London militia were summoned to reinforce York, and (perhaps disingenuously) promised 'reddy paye'.[105] Elizabeth ordered clergy and gentlemen to provide light horsemen.[106] Contingents of thirty harquebusiers and a score of pikemen were pressed in Middlesex, Hertfordshire, Essex, Suffolk, Norfolk, Cambridgeshire, Bedfordshire, Buckinghamshire, Oxfordshire, Berkshire, Herefordshire, Wiltshire, Nottinghamshire, and Lincolnshire; a full company of 100 soldiers came out of Gloucestershire.[107] Worcestershire, which had supplied 300 men in the last northern campaign, was spared, perhaps because of the disgraceful practice of Lieutenant William Price, who had excused no less than 67 recruits in exchange for payments amounting to £100.[108] Worcestershire had also fielded 50 cavalry, a contingent larger than any that that 'Little Shire' had sent off since before Henrician times. When the horsemen were discharged at the campaign's end, some of their arms and armour were requisitioned by the 'borderers' who took their places. Given the shortage of arms in the North, the appropriation of the Worcestershire weapons is not surprising. But when the troopers returned home without equipment and (on occasion) horses, those unreimbursed losses made the spring 1570 mobilisation difficult to supply.[109] On 10 April, the Queen proclaimed her decision 'to levie and send an armie to the borders of Scotland'.[110] On 17 April, Sussex and Hunsdon raided Tividale, torched 300 villages, and slated 50 Scottish castles. After a brief retreat across the border, the English army returned to reduce Castle Hume and install a garrison of 200. Between 11 May and 3 June 1570, the Marshal of Berwick, Sir William Drury, marched a force of 1,200 infantry and 400 cavalry through Scotland.[111]

Drury returned in the spring of 1573, but in the guise of English allies determined to root out the 'Castillian', the remnants of the French Catholic faction who held Edinburgh Castle in the hopes of invoking the 'auld alliance' in the form of military succour from France. Devastation of the Scottish countryside, a common tactic of Border warfare, was forbidden, and English soldiers were commanded to treat the Scottish population civilly.[112] The military strength of Berwick garrison, a modest expeditionary force, and the services of siege engineer Sir Henry Lee, were but three aspects of English warfare that the Protestant Scots could count on.[113] The great ordnance arrived via the sea, and the English set about entrenching, laying a mine, and erecting 'a mound platformwise' in late April. Mining proceeded, and one 'Hubbard the myner' managed to get himself 'under the grounde as farre as the Spoore [Spur]'. Drury reported that simultaneously he had positioned sixteen siege pieces 'and thys nyght prepares for the rest and beyng all place I mynd they schall all speake together'.[114] Although the placement of the batteries, especially the main one, consumed more time than anticipated, the besieging force, with its 'gunners expert', began its cannonade 17–18 May,[115] after the Castillians had poured fire upon them. The English pieces

> beat ther defences and then they began the battery in to [two] places which the Castellans at the first having bin cold all this whyle began to Impeche with hott shotting tho in vayne . . . and to no hurt of any of ours with ther great shott but one was slayne, a comon soldier with a smale shott. This stayed a lytle the generalles ordynance from battering and made hem to direct them for the dismonting of these peaces which might otherwise hyndre his

batterye and by this meanes Ser Henry Leys breache was in more forwardnes. . . .[116]

The partial demolition of David's Tower and shrinking powder reserves forced upon the Castillians the realisation that the two dozen or more guns trained on them would ultimately breach their defences. Drury's conduct of the siege contrasted with actions at Leith thirteen years before. Even though his forces were quartered in a city, he avoided the logistical problems of a long siege by moving quickly to take Edinburgh Castle. Not only was the starving-out of the garrison ruled out, but Drury did not tarry for his miners to finish their subterranean encroachment. He combined all offensive elements, mining, bombardment, diverson, and direct assault.[117] On the 26th, an assault captured Edinburgh Castle's spur (abetted by a feint against the rear of the fortress). On 28 May, the defenders surrendered.[118]

The northern wars of 1560 and 1569–70, following the dismal performance of the Le Havre campaign of 1559, gave Elizabeth I a clear notion of the limits of contemporary English warfare and lessons in logistics and siegecraft. The military reforms of the 1570s, reflected in the foundation of the trained bands and a more invigorated attack on Edinburgh Castle in 1573, built on lessons learned in 1559, 1560, and 1569–70. While the 1573 siege, like the 1560 assault, underscored the utility of ordnance, Englishmen still saw value in their traditional weapon of the longbow. The Earl of Huntingdon, helping secure the North during the battering of Edinburgh Castle, recommended 500 'bowes' be supplied to the forces of Yorkshire.[119] The defensive and offensive capabilities of England were seen to be inseparable. More than a few Elizabethan captains and lieutenants got their first taste of piketrailing during the suppression of the Northern Earls. The decade's adventures lured many Elizabethans into military service across the Channel.[120]

6

ELIZABETHAN WARFARE
IN THE NETHERLANDS,
1572–92

Elizabeth and the wars of religion

Elizabeth and her councillors hesitated to embroil the realm in continental wars for nearly a decade following the ignominious retreat of the English garrison from Le Havre in late July and early August 1563. English armies, in Scotland at the siege of Leith (1560) and then in the tentative defence of Le Havre in 1562–3, had not distinguished themselves. Cecil and Elizabeth (if not Leicester and his circle) grasped the strategic dilemma. Had France retaliated and, more frightening, enlisted support from Spain or the German states, England would have been in peril indeed.[1] Furthermore, English fighting men suffered dreadfully in those campaigns, being short of victuals and clothes in both expeditions, and the 1562–3 débâcle made worse by lack of bedding and the virulence of the plague. The decision to intervene on the Continent in 1572 was made with the knowledge that the English art of war had reached its nadir. Elizabeth's coyness, grounded in her realm's vulnerability, prompted her to employ 'voluntaries' in the wars of religion. The depth of English support for continental Protestants was often the story of English warfare.[2] First, England was more deeply enmeshed in the wars of religion than muster rolls would suggest. Second, a higher percentage of English and Welsh soldiers learnt from overseas conflicts than historians have acknowledged, creating a wider base for the development of an English art of war.

The 300 piketrailers who spearheaded the Tudor military incursion in the Low Countries beheld the royal countenance at Greenwich in April 1572.[3] In the ranks stood Roger Williams. Fifty of his comrades would be slain in a sally outside Flushing. Although Williams, like historians later, repeatedly characterised the English forces as inexperienced and ill-trained,[4] the companies under Captain Thomas Morgan showed a fair amount of pluck for citizens of a nation that for decades had been engaged only marginally in continental warfare. Indisputably, the English committed tactical errors in their first actions. But they also displayed discipline under fire, initiative, and a keen sense of honour – as, for example, when venturing

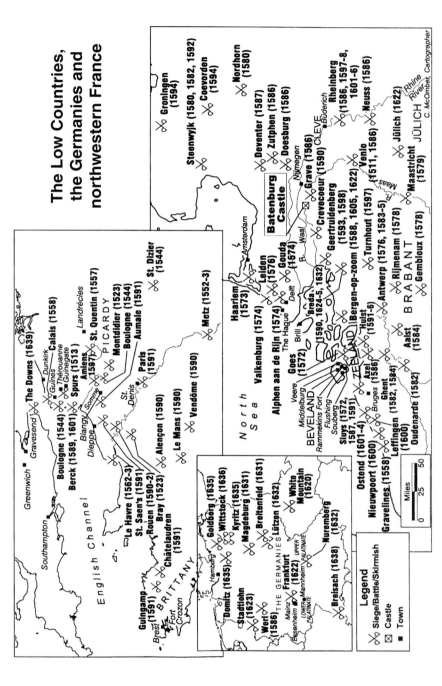

Figure 6.1 Map of the Low Countries, the Germanies and northwestern France. *Source:* Connie McOmber and the author.

out to demolish a mound that the enemy had positioned in the territory between the Flushing garrison and Middelburg. Although the Catholic forces withdrew (perhaps as a ruse, hoping to entrap the rebel force once it set to work dismantling the earthworks), they soon reappeared, led by 400 harquebusiers, who discharged heavy fire. As the Netherlandish forces retired, the English stood so that their allies might make a fighting retreat. Allegedly, Morgan's men inflicted casualties at a ratio of three Spaniards for every Englishman lost. Encouraged rather than intimidated by these initial exchanges with the *tercios*, Morgan's companies sought permission from Flushing's governor to challenge the enemy the following morning. Unfurling their battle colours as a display of bravado, the English came forth from the city, as they often would in the Low Countries wars, in the vanguard. Protecting their flanks marched French, Walloons, and Flemings. Morgan brought his men within musket range of the enemy, formed up his troops, and advanced the shot. The English had not sauntered out of their garrison blindly. They occupied a defensible position on a bridge and made a stand, cavalry on the causeway and infantry fanned out on both sides of the bridge. The Spaniards tested these deployments with an all-out charge. Although outnumbered, the Protestants received the onslaught without breaking formation. Bringing up greater numbers of men, the Spanish poured fire against the Protestant positions, which returned these volleys. At this point Morgan resolutely went to push of pike,[5] which effectively stalled the Spanish advance. The allied commander, Tseraerts, unsure of his losses in repelling the first charge, dared not risk weathering another, and so ordered a retreat. In that manoeuvre the English standard-bearer was captured, but his countrymen rallied and rescued him and his banner. The skirmishes had lasted two hours, the English twice coming to grips with the *tercios*. The Protestant side lost 100 men, half of whom were English; Spanish casualties were reckoned at about 400.

Considering the most recent large-scale English field engagements had been fought nearly thirty years before, one would have expected the performance of 1572 to have been dismal (especially considering Sir Roger Williams' candid confessions that the English practice of arms had declined alarmingly). And, had Morgan's companies been composed of the recently founded trained bands or of pressed rascals from the remote shires, the force might have crumbled in the face of the Army of Flanders. Two clues reveal the identity of the 300.[6] First, Morgan's recruiting went on in London, and Williams speaks of a muster of Londoners. Second, many of the officers had previous military experience, in Scotland, Ireland, and France. How Elizabethan forces were 'seasoned' by the inclusion of experienced soldiers is disclosed in a series of forty-one petitions, drawn up at the end of Elizabeth's reign, providing professional autobiographies of the Queen's old lieutenants and captains.[7] These two score or so old pike-trailers – and they were survivors putting pen to paper in the late 1590s

– represent the professional English mercenary, who campaigned abroad, then signed on for service in another theatre.[8] Many had followings of common soldiers. Although the pressed troops and shire levies that followed were of a different complexion, there certainly existed, even before the 'opportunity' of the Eighty Years War, a sizeable cadre of English military professionals. And should Her Majesty's government so wish, these veterans might train the militia as well as lead her expeditions.

Sir Humphrey Gilbert's 1,500 soldiers arrived a few weeks after Morgan.[9] In one of his earliest actions, Gilbert and his allies attempted the capture of Sluys. The performance of English arms in this and other engagements under Gilbert that year have received abusive comment from Sir Roger Williams and his modern editors. Admittedly, Gilbert and Tseraerts (his co-commander) laid their ambush of the Sluys garrison badly, and then, having been outflanked so to speak, were outfoxed by the governor, who delayed the Protestant assault for four days through feigned negotiation. The Duke of Alba thus had time to rush troops to the vicinity. Embarrassing, but hardly disastrous, the fight was exemplified by the unexpected hail of gunfire the allies received as they marched up to Sluys in expectation of imminent surrender. The diversion to Bruges was equally futile, but such was often the case in the tortuous siege warfare of the Low Countries.[10]

The two successive sieges of Goes constituted more serious defeats, but like most of the frays of 1572–3 simply demonstrated that late sixteenth-century siegecraft, with its logistical complexities, was difficult to manage. The first campaign involved ambushes; the last of these would have snared the wily commandant, Don Isidro Pacheco, and his 400-strong garrison, had it not been for a premature volley from a Protestant Walloon officer. The allies then withdrew from the island, as the supply of artillery and munitions dwindled. Shamed by the natives of Flushing, the English and their allies set off again, camping *en route* at the village of Souborg. The Spanish located them, and still confident from the successful ambuscade upon the English, treated them to a *camisado*, a night assault. But the Spaniards found the recently humbled Englishmen resilient and pugnacious. Not only were the attackers turned back, but many were captured. And in response to the barbarism that they had encountered, the English hanged their adversaries with the very nooses their enemies had brought along to lynch the heretics.[11]

At the second and more consequential siege of Goes, in August 1572, Gilbert and Morgan circumvallated the town. Battery and escalade failed to reduce Goes. Although stalemated, the besiegers controlled the island of South Beveland and thus had some protection against a succouring force, which they naturally assumed would have to secure a safe haven for landing. Not in their wildest imaginations did the English anticipate what next happened: 3,000 Spaniards waded through neck-deep water and, incredibly, traversed the eight or so miles from Bergen-op-Zoom to the island.

Utterly surprised, the English forces panicked and ran; many were cut down by the Spanish. Again, Sir Roger Williams found himself in the thick of the fray.[12] He learnt that to achieve victory over the *tercios* meant assimilating the Spanish art of war. This realisation prompted his decision, years later, to fight alongside them.

In 1574 English troops at Valkenburg (northwest of Leiden) surrendered. Another force at Alphen (southwest of Leiden) was allegedly humiliated as well. Captains Chester and Gainsford, commanding these separate units, were 'disgraced'. 'Surprised' at Gouda and 'routed with a loss of 300 men and three colors taken', the English military reputation suffered.[13] Yet revisionist research by David Trim reveals that the alleged failure of English warfare has been much exaggerated. Gainsford's troops 'beat a retreat against overwhelming odds where they took part in the gallant defence of the city of Leiden'.[14]

In mid-1578 John Norris arrived in the Low Countries, accompanied by his brothers, as well as John North and Henry Cavendish. On 1 August 1578 the English soldiery enhanced their reputation by blunting Don Juan of Austria, the victor of Gembloux. Facing a concerted attack by crack *tercios* upon their trenches near Rijmenam, the English did not break formation when the Spanish tide was turned back, the attackers' ploy being to lure them out on to indefensible ground.

> The victory at Rijmenam on 1 August 1578 was important for a number of reasons, including a real improvement in the rebel States' strategic position, without which they were probably doomed. However, albeit being arguably more significant than Gembloux in its consequences, the battle has never been as well known as the earlier Dutch defeat.[15]

The English demonstrated again that they could work in unison with allies, hold their ground, and, perhaps even more importantly, maintain discipline in the crucible of battle, even against the best forces in Europe.

From 1579 to 1581 English forces proved mobile and reliable as they first fought the States' cause in Flanders and then countered the designs of the traitorous Count of Rennenberg in the northern Netherlands. English warfare in this phase included not only siege relief but lightning cavalry operations and guerrilla tactics reminiscent of Norris's Irish experiences. With the intrusion of the Protestant Duke of Anjou into the Low Countries wars in early 1582, English forces gravitated to his circle. The personal, almost clannish, leadership of English companies diluted their effectiveness as cooperation amongst the commanders (Norris, North, and Morgan) evaporated. Nevertheless the English forces fought a spirited war of manoeuvre revolving around sieges throughout Flanders. Norris's regiment, seconded by Morgan's, fought a stalwart defence at the gates of Ghent on

29 August. Disaffection with the French led Norris back into Dutch service, in spite of Sir Roger Williams' attempts to shore up the alliance with Anjou. Ultimately, the common soldiers chose to follow their captains and colonels, and enlisted under Morgan, Williams, or Norris.[16] These patronage networks governed not only enlistment but deployment, a pattern compounded when the Earl of Leicester intervened in the Dutch revolt in 1585.

The Earl of Leicester's campaign, 1585–6

Elizabeth's commitments to the Protestant cause and the Low Countries' 'war of liberation' were unqualified and firm. Strategic defensive considerations were always more palatable to the Queen than their ideological justification. Naturally she found the abetting of rebels repugnant.[17] But the terms of the alliance, hammered out in summer 1585, were calculated to protect the Queen's prerogative as to how deeply enmeshed she would become militarily and diplomatically and to ensure that England's resources would not be consumed wastefully. On 10 August 1585, Elizabeth authorised General Sir John Norris to command 5,000 foot and 1,000 horse in Holland, holding the cautionary towns (Brill, Flushing, and the Rammekins Fort) as pledges, while she paid £12,526 monthly.[18] The installation of garrisons made the Dutch revolt a chapter in English military history that lasted three decades.[19] Indeed, the occupation of the cautionary towns guaranteed the Queen collateral. This was more lend-lease than escalation of the war. But she was outmanoeuvred by her continental ally, a fate that had befallen her father in his wars, when Leicester was seduced into assuming the title of Governor and Captain General of the States.

Elizabeth strived to retain control over the escalation of the war and the commitment of resources, as her commanders embarked on expeditions and made strategic and tactical commitments without occasion for royal review. For example, on 31 October 1585, while praising Sir John Norris's 'value and good conduct', the Queen reminded him of *her* strategy ('wuld we have liked best, you had remembered our particuler direction geven unto you to stand upon a defensive warr . . .') and second-guessed his tactical judgment ('. . . the place being not assaultable . . .').[20] Had it been possible, Elizabeth I would have kept a close eye on her subordinates. War, that expensive and deadly creature, had a life of its own, which caused her great consternation. It required a stern princely will to heel the dogs of war, and by the 1580s and 1590s Elizabeth had learned from the lessons of the 1560s.[21]

If Leicester was perhaps not the best choice (not just because of his lack of martial experience but also because he felt less restrained by the Queen's orders owing to the place he occupied in her heart) for the senior commanding officer, at least the Earl knew his own shortcomings and enlisted two good and experienced soldiers to command at his side, Count Hohenloe and William Pelham. Sir John Norris made a resourceful colonel-general, even if Leicester trusted him not a jot. The best surprise was Sir William Russell, who developed into a tenacious cavalry commander. Thus English leadership did not exceed that of the Spaniards, probably not even equalled it – but Leicester put some good officers in the field. As for the rank and file, they did their best, facing the finest army in Europe. Leicester's expeditionary force met its first tests in May 1586, which entailed ferreting out an enemy of superior number. Peregrine Bertie, Lord Willoughby, scrambled a modest detachment of 200 cavalry and 400 infantry in order to intercept a Spanish supply train, and succeeded in seizing or destroying the entire convoy and inflicting casualties upon an enemy nearly twice the size of the force under his command.

A similar incident followed not long after. A 3,000-man attack column under Willoughby and Sir Philip Sydney surprised Axel. Several dozen English soldiers swam the moat, scaled the walls, and burst open the gates. Sydney, leading the column, rode in to find the Spanish 'soldiers wer ein armes', and engaged in street-to-street fighting. Perhaps 600 died resisting the English and Dutch. Clearly the English by the mid-1580s were not hesitant to take the initiative against the enemy, utilised rapid movement, and were willing to engage larger forces. Yet in the midst of these stirring actions, English morale suffered. Leicester lamented that it was 'no marvell our men runn fast awaye', for they had little or no food. Five hundred had fled in the space of two days, 'a great manie to the enemye'. Two hundred 'runagates' had been apprehended at the sea coast, no doubt trying to get back to Albion's shore: '. . . divers I hanged before the rest', Leicester wrote. 'Our old roggues ragged here hath soe discouraged our new men as, I protest to you, theie looke like dead men.'[22]

Reclaiming their reputation at siegecraft also motivated the English, especially when their numbers were reckoned insufficient to take on Parma's entire army. A diversion in the form of laying siege to Doesburg in 1586 brought such an opportunity. Within days the English battery pounded out two breaches, one for Norris's English and the other for Hohenloe's Dutch. Before this international contest of military valour could commence, the governor surrendered. The affair recalled Henry VIII's forays in France: chivalric competitions amongst allied nations, devastating English gunnery, and a surrender to forestall a brutal assault and sacking. But the chivalric displays and flamboyance of the English force, personified nicely before Doesburg by Sir Roger Williams dashing about in the trenches, clad in finery and a plumed and gilded morion, would have tragic (and celebrated) consequences at the subsequent action. Displays of English valour upon continental battlefields resuscitated collective memory of past triumphs. Coinciding with Leicester's expedition was the publication of *The Valiant*

Actes And Victorious Battailes of the English nation, which recited the course of English warfare from 1327 to the accession of Elizabeth I.[23]

Perched on the shores of the River Maas, in Brabant, Grave gave the Protestant Dutch some measure of control over traffic upon the waterways. Protected by recently constructed 'modern' fortifications, it possessed a garrison of 800 Protestant natives of the Low Countries. In March of 1586 Leicester, begging both money and men from the Queen (and with very limited success) through the agency of Sir Francis Walsingham, forced the issue by moving against the Spanish forces threatening the town.[24] Around 27 March, Leicester dispatched between 1,300 and 1,500 cavalry, who were followed by 2,000 infantry. He had managed to ship into the garrison victuals and 300 men. Dislodging the Spanish from Mill Fort, about four miles from the beleaguered town, the English forces dug in along the Maas overnight, with 300 foot soldiers working alongside a few pioneers.[25] Three thousand Spanish troops stormed the makeshift works, forcing the English from the yard-high embankments. But a counter-attack, an English speciality, met the attackers: 'other of our troups [those not stationed in foreward positions] to the number of eight or nine hundred . . . gave a fresh charge upon the Spaniardes, drave them over the fortification. . . .' Seven 'speciall captaines' and 500 *tercios* were slain, with one cannon taken. The English lost less than 150 men, though Sir John Norris took the point of a pike in his chest and Sir John Burgh had a finger shot off.[26]

As the English commanders progressed in raising the siege, they needed reinforcements, for they were engaged in a strategem that might rebound upon themselves if they lacked sufficient manpower. The Earl had sent 'as manie English companies as we might spare . . .' but could not expect victory without more 'men and monie'.[27] The systematic eradication of stationary Catholic positions required reliable supply and sufficient infantry and cavalry. The English victory gave impetus to Count Hohenloe to emulate his allies and dislodge several more formidable Spanish strong points, including Castle Batenburg. By mid-April 1586 the siege had been raised, and the town revictualled. But Parma, who reportedly had been rushing reinforcements to his besieging army when news of the Spanish reverse reached him, again took the initiative in the first part of May. Taking advantage of the strategic and tactical complexities of the Low Countries wars, where holding an objective was nearly as difficult as taking it because of the cost of keeping armies in the field, Parma descended upon Grave with 12,000 foot and 4,000 horse. Given a taste of Spanish cannon, the town capitulated. Leicester, 'being as yet unreadie and destitute of all meanes to furnish a campe sufficient to meete with [Parma] on equall ground in fielde', marched nevertheless, at the head of 3,000 infantry and 1,000 horse.[28] Assuming that Grave would hold out for a reasonable amount of time, the Earl began reducing strong points in neighbouring areas. Grave's surrender after a three-hour barrage and the mere 'shew of an assalt' stunned the English and shattered the allies' cautious optimism. One must credit Parma for his rapid deployment and the psychological outwitting of the Grave garrison. Their prompt surrender gave the Spanish a victory with little loss of resources and time.[29]

The war of manoeuvre led Leicester and his foe, Parma, to the vicinity of Zutphen on 21 September 1586, where the English entrenched themselves before the Spanish-held town. To relieve the garrison, Parma sent a supply train, which skirted English positions under cover of fog. Alerted, Leicester had deployed 200–250 heavy cavalry and 300 infantry. A momentary clearing allowed the combatants a glimpse of their respective positions. The Spanish opened fire. Instantly, the English horsemen hurled themselves upon Parma's convoy. They had no intention of waiting for their foot soldiers. When their opponents, mostly Italian riders, were engaged, it became apparent that the mere 200 or so were vastly outnumbered by several thousand enemy, horse and foot, and had exposed themselves to counter-attack.[30] But the attackers had heard tales of the Hundred Years War for too long and the exhilaration of the mad dash ignited their pent-up ferocity.

> . . . the enimies appeered so neere our companies, having planted all their muskets and arcabuzes being 2000 and their pikes being a thousande, very strongly on the high way, as our men . . . received the whole volie of the enimies shot, and passing the very furie of it, gave charge upon the two formost troupes of the enimies horsemen, and drave them backe over their owne trenches, and within their pikes. . . .[31]

The Italians, who counted among their number several fine cavalry commanders, were cut to bits by the possessed Englishmen. Annibal Gonzaga lay dead with a great gash in his head. The Marquis del Vasto narrowly escaped a similar fate: a detachment of Englishmen had ridden directly into his entourage, hacking, hewing, and hoping to decapitate the Marquis. A blow to his head missed its mark and del Vasto fell back to his infantry, as did the rest of the Catholic horsemen. The English riders, who did not simply charge, but held formation as they closed upon their prey, withstood the barrage of harquebus fire and penetrated the Spanish lines, which were not entirely prepared to withstand an assault. Thus the cavalry dashed ahead of the perhaps 1,500-strong infantry units in order to press the advantage. They cut 'through the thickett of harquebuziers' and forced the enemy to flee, though some wagons may indeed have reached Zutphen in the confusion. Volleys from Spanish musketeers forced them to retire, but only after they had wreaked great destruction; the enemy lost 250 men, the English 34. Leicester was pleased, for his men had proved themselves valiant. But valiant was not always wise. In his haste to engage the enemy, Sir Philip Sydney had ridden into battle *sans cuisses*.[32] Wounded in his thigh by a gunshot, the injury ultimately killed him. Risks like this were not confined to Englishmen such as Sydney and Williams. Henry IV was perhaps the worst offender, and even the prudent Parma would be wounded venturing into dangerous avenues.[33]

Mustering English companies on the Continent

Although English piketrailers half expected hard usage from their own government, this did little to assuage their anger at inhospitable treatment from those whom they were in the Low Countries to defend. Muster-master James Digges, whose family members held places in the English military establishment on the Continent, accused the Dutch of systematically defrauding and abusing their English allies.[34] Mustering men in the shires constituted a political issue of the greatest significance, and what was coloured by domestic politics in the countryside was also influenced by international political concerns when similar unfortunates found themselves mustered and reviewed on the other side of the Channel.

The English soldier overseas stood in the centre of a triangle of ostensibly allied, but in reality competing, interests. His captain, who in theory watched over recruits with a paternal eye, sometimes acted against the soldier's prosperity, health, and security. Captains often held back pay, the disbursement of which was both sporadic and occasionally covered by advances directly from the captain's private purse, so that irregularities were not easy to remedy or even to detect.[35] Then there was the matter of the allies – Dutch and French for the most part – who assumed some responsibility for victualling, lodging, and sometimes paying their English contingents. The Protestant forces suffered from a chronic lack of funds, and reference was as often made to the prodigious amounts of silver commanded by Madrid as to the formidable *tercios* themselves. Promises were solemnly set down to aid or underwrite the English expeditionary forces, only to see these commitments reneged upon.

The Crown itself sometimes failed its fighting men. Apparel did not arrive, and tardy payments impoverished loyal soldiers. The consequences were personal and profound: the soldier wasted away, neglected by the very interests he defended. In a broader context, whether there was a military revolution occurring in the 1580s and 1590s or not, the key to victory on the battlefield certainly seemed to be in the allocation of scarce resources for what must indeed have seemed interminable and 'eternalised' warfare.[36] For the States and the covetous captain, survival was the order of the day, and the powerless trooper (unless he mutinied) got short shrift. Ironically, the essential vehicle to military success, the hapless foot soldier, found his needs relegated to the lowest level of priorities by the chain of command above him, from captain to Queen. Despised or not, the common soldier was requisite, and in substantial numbers. Thus the process of mustering, with its inspection and accounting, was a means by which strategic decisions might be made by reckoning the forces at hand.

Henry IV frequently reminded the Queen that troop strength determined strategy. Elizabeth understood and agreed; her problem was how the King of Navarre deployed and treated the English under his command. She found his stratagems sometimes questionable and his usage of her subjects on occasion callous. She critiqued his tactical manoeuvres as readily as she did those of her own commanders. But as Elizabeth, Henry, and the Dutch Estates debated how to meet the Catholic threat, troop strength (with the implicit concern for human and financial resources that came with raising reinforcements) allowed politics to influence matters that should have been decided almost solely upon military consideration. Availability of resources was one side of the coin. The executive authority to set in motion the mechanism of recruitment, and the legitimacy and solvency to commit, field, and sustain forces, comprised the other side. England possessed an advantage, for the Queen ruled a unified realm, assisted by a 'representative assembly' whose usefulness (and, not too far away in the past, survival) lay in assisting the Crown to make war. And Elizabeth did indeed make war, for her letters exhibit a consistent and meticulous monitoring of her forces abroad. She intervened from Whitehall to affect even battlefield decisions in regard to whether her troops could or could not be deployed.[37] The Queen was particularly vocal in commenting on Henry of Navarre's use of English soldiers.

Henry IV lacked the political consensus, and hence the financial resources, of his realm. England's other Protestant ally was not a monarch, but an institution, the Dutch Estates. The potential resources of the United Netherlands constituted a sizeable contribution to the Protestant war effort. But to get at those resources, to apply them to field an army, was a complex political task requiring great patience as the matter moved through committees and readings. The assumption of debt by a representative assembly empowered a state to harness more of its resources by enhancing lender confidence in a collective body taking long-term and aggregate responsibility for governmental indebtedness. Kings in this period might in grandiose and whimsical fashion delay or refuse to satisfy their creditors. But from a sixteenth-century point of view, when the transaction of diplomacy was slowed by distance and unsettled communications routes, monarchs found assemblies exasperating. In their tortuous negotiations with Dutch bureaucrats, Elizabeth's agents threw up their hands and lambasted their allies, that 'all their confusions had resulted from their state falling from monarchy to democracy, or rather anarchy, with multiplicity and equality of commandments'.[38] Thus did Elizabeth find herself supplying forces in alliance with an almost Byzantine assembly and a star-crossed, often penniless, King, and doing her best to keep track of her distant field forces and provide for them as well. Consequently, the business of mustering her men amid combined operations became not only a logistical task of great difficulty but also a political chore that sometimes threatened to poison her strategy.

In the Netherlands, as in Ireland, obtaining accurate muster rolls became impossible. Complicating the situation in the Low Countries were the political and fiscal agreements set by treaty, by which the Protestant forces were sustained. Like their Catholic enemies, allied forces suffered from shortages of pay, victuals, and *matériel*. Contemporaries often blamed the Queen when arrears mounted. Sir Philip Sydney once sniffed, '. . . if the Queen pai not her souldiers she must loos her garrisons. . . .'[39] It was not so simple. While campaigning in the Low Countries in August 1591, Lord Burgh solicited two weeks' lendings for himself and a month's pay for his company of 150. Once they crossed the Waal, relaying pay would be difficult. So the vice-treasurer sent the money 'by a reliable officer of the garrison' of Brill, who had a wife and children there. Burgh learned that he had come within 10 miles of his camp, but then disappeared, as did his military escort. His Lordship surmised, 'I suppose his convoy cut his throat'.[40]

Historians have sometimes blamed the English forces' fiscal problems upon 'parasitic Dutch finance' along with the Earl of Leicester and his cronies.[41] Although it is true that a system of dead pay, and the redirection of funds paid under the privy seal, sometimes lined the pockets of senior officers, expeditions were never adequately financed by the 'ordinary'. Dead pay supported corporals' wages and boosted the pay of valuable musketeers.[42] But, although components of army finance could be justified on utility, the structure of the pay system placed the interests of the Crown and soldiers at cross-purposes with the officers who supposedly served them both. The Treasurer-at-Wars (as he was called), received 1 per cent of the funds he paid out, and thus had no interest in ascertaining whether the actual troop levels matched his lists. Conversely, the mustermaster's job was to perform checks and determine actual field strength, a burdensome and dangerous task that neither the Treasurer nor the captains wanted to see done thoroughly. Take, for example, the case of Thomas Digges, who discharged the duties of muster-master general sporadically from 1586 to 1594.[43] Although a civilian, he brought to bear parliamentary experience, knowledge of fortification and mathematics, and used those skills to apply systematic reforms to English financial administration in the Low Countries wars. He succeeded too well, and 'it was suggested that it might be better for everybody if he were to temper his enthusiasm for saving public funds'.[44] Everyone save the Queen and her common soldiers. Indeed, the abolition of the office of Muster-Master General in 1588 owed much to Digges's reforming zeal.[45] Digges's brother, James, then tried his hand at sorting out the chaos of the musters, but also ran afoul of the omnipotent captains, and was dismissed.[46]

Rooting out padded accounts and investigating fraudulent muster rolls threatened the key officer in the English army, the captain, and took the profit margin from the victuallers and treasurers' officials. The entire weight of the system lay against an honest muster-master.[47] Companies in the Netherlands almost assumed chronic arrears of pay. The captains, burghers, and (occasionally) merchants worked out a system of lending that put brass in the pocket. Only when pay arrived was there a muster, and infrequent musters meant no checks, and no checks meant no accurate muster rolls. And lacking these rolls, how could the Crown formulate strategy upon knowledge of field strength?[48] As the allies pledged to field specific numbers in combined operations and in some cases shared the burden of paying, quartering, and victualling forces, the review of forces in the field was shared knowledge and subject to mutual inspection. The United Provinces saw the compilation of muster certificates as a cooperative exercise with English and Dutch commissaries. The Dutch, in a nice touch for wars of religion, preferred to confine the English garrison troops in a church, so that musters could be taken in a single place, with all companies present, save for one to guard the walls. At Flushing, the English commissary Sydney took umbrage at this, demanded that at least two companies man the fortifications, and complained to Whitehall that it was 'dangerous that the states, at a time of their own choosing, should be thus able to shut up the men of war as if it were in a cupboard'.[49]

During a dispute between a Dutch governor and the English garrisons, the captains refused to provide information on troop strength; consequently 'the muster rolls and books were entirely uncorrected'. When Commissary Coningsby's deputy, Adrian Poyntz, attempted to determine the exact numbers of the English companies, 'he could not directly prove deceit by the captains but he had to muster the men in a small strait place' in a forward position in the siege lines. When a company moved into the English position before a castle, the defenders aimed three or four rounds at them. The captains, who would rather have been paid by the company than by poll, took some amusement in Poyntz's predicament as he attempted to count heads under fire in the squalor of the trench.[50]

Captains and officers had also long practised frauds, mustering men borrowed or hired for one day's wages. On the evening before a muster, according to the new orders of December 1590, after the gates were shut and the watch set, the English commissary, with the Dutch commissary if he would join, was to inform the governor or chief commander that they would review the companies the following morning. The governor was expected to require the captains to have their companies ready by 7 a.m. The clerk of each band delivered the roll from which the names were to be called. This the commissary presented to the governor and compared with the book of the preceding muster. Captains who refused to muster their companies were dismissed.[51]

Captains sometimes slipped artificers, victuallers, pedlars, stragglers, vagrants, and strangers into the ranks. Such charlatans were liable to be hanged by martial law. Corporals could be called to the table and sworn to disclose such frauds. Commissaries were encouraged to discover if any of these had offered to pass muster under other men's names. The commissary conferred his book and delivered copies to the governor. The perfected roll the captain or lieutenant and the commissary signed. Any defect of numbers, arms, officers, gentlemen or musketeers, entitled to have an increase of wages from the dead pay, or any absent without passport or beyond the furlough allocated, was to be duly noted so that the treasurer might adjust the accounts and roll accordingly.[52] The Privy Council therefore insisted that the commissaries within the garrisons take weekly musters and relay those figures to Thomas Bodley, who oversaw the royal forces on the Queen's behalf. Further, Bodley and the commissaries were to proffer such information to the Dutch States General.[53]

On 19 December 1591 the Privy Council ordered Bodley to look into the weakness of units designated for transfer to the French theatre of operations, and in the process remedy the abuses perpetrated by English captains. Bodley was to persuade the Dutch Council of State to assign officers to review English troops periodically. Elizabeth could not trust her own captains. Bodley reminded Whitehall that an agreement regarding muster procedures had still not been reached between the allies. For example, the English allowed dead pay, while the Dutch did not. The deletion of the dead pay would, on paper at least, make the companies look even weaker. However, he could indeed use the Dutch to outfox the English captains. Admitting to their allies that 'the English commissaries were themselves responsible for the deceits', he entreated the Council of State to conduct a simultaneous muster of all English soldiers in the Low Countries, conducted by officers of the United Provinces. The resultant data would then be compared against the old English certificates.[54]

As for the complaint sent to Bodley by Lord Burghley concerning the reduced strength of the companies destined for Rouen, it needed to be pointed out that the whole business of musters and payments had been foisted on Bodley largely because of his role as a liaison officer with the Dutch authorities. 'He had not received copies of any of the orders and instructions that were sent . . . to other officers. . . . The commissaries were to have sent muster books every six months' to Wilkes, Shirley, and the Dutch Council. None had arrived. Bodley's contact with the soldiery was limited to seeing them come into the field in summer (and, even then, he insisted only one-third appeared).

Even with the dearth of information, Bodley had forewarned Whitehall of the diminished state of the companies the Crown wished transferred to

Henry IV's command. A year's wastage and a shortage of supplies inevitably wore down a company, and the redeployment would doubtless occasion desertion. Bodley protested Burghley's unreasonable expectations. '[H]e understood that Mr. Wilkes had a special commission to examine the proceedings of the English commissaries and all matters of musters'.[55] Sir Thomas Morgan retorted in a similar vein when Whitehall criticised the strength of his Bergen-op-Zoom companies transferred to Rouen. Both companies had served in the field for the entire summer and experienced the predictable attrition. Others had been on assignment when the companies departed, while others, frankly, had taken French leave rather than serve before Rouen. Sir Francis Vere, too, reacted to his government's criticism, pointing out that the Privy Council had instructed Vere not to be overly concerned unless a given company's ranks thinned to fewer than 110 men. Sir Francis counted 1,800 active servicemen out of 17 English companies, at the end of a four-month campaign season.[56]

Muster arrangements hampered the strategic initiatives and tactical manoeuvres available to the Crown. Of necessity highly decentralised, the system prevented Elizabeth from doing what she wanted: keeping a tight reign over troop deployments, and determining how and when soldiers were committed to actions undertaken with allies. Commanders rarely knew exactly how many men they had under arms. The situation was unusually unstable in the 1590s. Henry IV's troop strength fluctuated drastically, as French volunteers came and went as they pleased, making him more dependent upon English infantry, whose numbers became a matter of strategic import.

The Dutch, too, plotted their strategies by factoring in English foot soldiers. By holding down key garrisons, English soldiers enabled Maurice of Nassau, Prince of Orange and leader of the Protestant coalition, to commit Dutch troops to field operations. Elizabeth's troops in some ways anchored the operations of the allies. But how weighty were the anchors? The overall quality of English soldiers, especially once they had a year's seasoning in a given theatre of operations, was high. But it was quantity, or lack of it, that troubled the allies. And the number of men was most critically determined by the individual captains. Warfare, on the battlefield or in the maintenance of forces in anticipation of action, rested on mid-level officers, ranging from the colonels to the non-commissioned officers. The captains became the critical linkage, for they ruled their companies with greater effective authority than those above them.

So it was against the captains that the new muster orders aimed, including the elements that tried to circumvent the captains by appealing to the corporals. The good senior commanders, Essex to a degree, certainly Sir Roger Williams and Sir John Norris, knew how to rally their captains together, perhaps indulge them (Norris in fact proved a fine business partner), so as to channel self-interest and survival into a system of patronage. The captains had to believe that their commander understood the nature of the society of soldiers. Mountjoy was the supreme example. Complaints heard in the Low Countries were amplified in the Irish wars. But Mountjoy enjoyed an advantage over continental warriors: his relationship with his officers was neither dependent upon nor interfered with by allies. Commanders then knew what historians are now discovering: the distribution of scarce resources and their effective deployment was the secret of the art of war during the period 1500–1650. Captains ultimately allocated resources, depending upon the relationship they engineered with the commanding officers. In this light, Elizabeth's compulsive tightening of the purse strings meant that the Queen, admittedly far-removed from the mud-spattered piketrailer, understood that resources were the difference between victory and defeat upon the fields of Europe, and in Ireland, for that matter.[57] Given the fiscal and political complexities of the allied 'system' of musters, Elizabeth's tenacity in maintaining her contribution to the Protestant Cause underscores her commitment to the wars of religion, however inefficiently the allies may have managed their armies.

In Ireland the English fought alone, without allies who practised a distinctive art of war or specialised in certain weapons. But if Irish operations more clearly revealed 'English warfare', it was learnt on the Continent, in service as auxiliaries and allies. The old adage that the continental wars served as England's military academy bears truth. They had many schools of war from which to choose. The Low Countries' theatre of war featured siegecraft and combined operations between 'sea beggars' and ground forces. The Netherlands conflicts attracted English military men, while Ireland did not. Sizeable and talented contingents of volunteers left England to be apprenticed in the art of war and to fight the international Roman Catholic threat. These men – the Veres, the Norrises, Sir Roger Williams – carried their expertise back to Albion. In contrast, from 1585 onwards, pressed men from the shires found themselves herded into that amphibious world, and they differed from those 'gentlemen of the religion' who had come before. Though less willing to serve than their predecessors, nevertheless, they too learned to fight effectively.

English warfare, as a nation's conduct of the art of war, can be understood by analysing the actions of groups of men. In some cases, individuals personify the English art of war – as, for example, Sir Roger Williams. Ideologically, he confounds historians, as he declined to follow Colonel Morgan and his 400 expert harquebusiers into Ireland in 1574, where arguably his Queen had most need of him, and instead served the Spaniards for four years. His decision to ride with Julian Romero seems perplexing in the light of the treason of his comrades Sir William Stanley and Rowland Yorke, who forsook English service for the Spanish flag for reasons of religion. When Opslag was taken by Sir Francis Vere in 1592, he hanged three Englishmen he found serving in the enemy garrison, ostensibly on the grounds that they were deserters.[58] Sir Roger harkened back to the foundation of the profession of arms – a *soldato*, one who fought in exchange for money. But the cash nexus did not entirely exonerate English soldiers who switched sides during the wars of religion. Low Countries veteran Captain John Ditcher, currying favour with Burghley, claimed to have spurned a Spanish offer of 1,000 crowns and the command of a company of horse. Ditcher allegedly rebuffed Parma, preferring to be a 'Beggerlye subiecte to her Majestie then a ritche Traytour. . . .'[59] As Sir John Hale pointed out, the 'society of soldiers' operated rather differently from the rest of the world. True, as Williams protested, his sovereign and Philip II were not in 1574 at loggerheads. But the religious undercurrent persisted, and occasionally reared its head in atrocities, such as Alba's slaughter of 2,300 helpless prisoners at Haarlem the year before.[60] It is a measure of how peculiar and unwelcome the fanaticism and ideology of the Reformation and Counter-Reformation must have been to Europe's professional soldiers. If artists could serve whom they chose, taking commissions from rival courts, why could not soldiers practise their trade where they were respected and sought after? Indeed, Julian Romero and Spain seem to have appreciated Williams long before did his royal mistress. But Williams' patriotism was vindicated by the publication of *A Briefe Discourse of War* (1590), which disclosed the author's observations of Spanish military science through the lens of his own martial experience. In Williams, England possessed a warrior who had participated on both sides of the Low Countries wars, and had proved an extraordinary resource when Elizabeth committed her-self formally to intervention in 1585 and after, a key adviser to both her favourites during their campaigns there. In 1588 Williams assisted in Armada preparations and in 1589 sailed with the Portugal expedition. Sir Roger was no mere mercenary, and could not be bribed by his former comrades into betraying Aalst.[61] He embodied the entrepreneurship of the *condottiere* with the chivalric honour of his nationality.

7

ELIZABETHAN AND JACOBEAN ALLIED OPERATIONS ON THE CONTINENT, 1587–1622

The continental reputation of English fighting men

England had a standing army. From the 1580s to the Thirty Years War (1618–48), English companies served abroad continuously. Sometimes the Crown recruited forces for foreign service *en masse*. Additionally, thousands of volunteers individually sought employment by venturing beyond the Channel to serve in foreign wars. This latter group has been somewhat overlooked, for documentary evidence disclosing their identities, ages, destinations, and commanders remains unpublished.[1] The Netherlands garrisons and Irish military establishment were reservoirs of military talent that might be deployed wherever English strategic interests were threatened: Brittany, Normandy, Iberia. Like English supply services, the Crown's standing army was conveniently multi-faceted in its nature – governmental in that these forces could be marshalled from London, private in that many soldiers had volunteered and some officers served at their own expense, and 'foreign' in the sense that they fought cooperatively with continental Protestant allies. In the latter case, the standing army thus did not stand on English soil, and its activities were conducted under the political auspices of another power. The inherent political problems of a standing army, in regard to parliamentary protest domestically or diplomatic objections by Catholic powers to sanctioned English intervention abroad, were somewhat ameliorated by Protestant allies providing occasions when Englishmen took lead roles in fighting 'modern' wars.

The Anglo-Dutch defence of Sluys[2] in summer 1587 tested English military competence severely. Before the Duke of Parma could invest the town, Dutch and English soldiers slipped through the gates with munitions and victuals. Against this garrison of 1,600 men Parma brought a force of 6,000 that boasted some of Philip II's finest infantry. Although the defenders acquitted themselves well, Parma's momentum and willingness to absorb losses gradually but inexorably forced back the Protestant troops to the perimeter of the town, as outlying positions were abandoned and a breach blown out of Sluys's walls. Vigorous sorties slowed but did not halt the Spanish advance. The *coup de grâce* was to be delivered by the *tercio viejo*, Parma's toughest infantry. Blocking the breach with rubble and hastily erected earthworks were the Dutch and their English allies, the latter including Sir Roger Williams, Sir Thomas Baskerville, and Sir Francis Vere (though none as yet had been knighted). Strategy was cast aside. Hand-to-hand combat was to settle the fate of Sluys. Casualties shrunk the defending force from 1,600 to 700, and Parma propelled unit after unit into the breach, day and night. But in the confined space ferocity and tenacity mattered more than numbers (though at least the *tercios* were relieved, and rested, before renewing their assaults).

Parma, impressed by his foes, nevertheless persevered. If he could not burst through the breach he would go under it. But the Anglo-Dutch garrison knew the art of countermining. Massive cellars lay beneath the breach, so subterranean battles erupted as the combatants sometimes encountered each other whilst tunnelling and exploring amongst the chambers. Above, the clashes continued with their daily carnage. When Spanish reinforcements threatened to overwhelm the scanty defences at other points along Sluys's walls, the garrison, whose powder dwindled daily, negotiated with Parma. For eighteen days and nights, the Spanish onslaughts had been turned back at the breach. Spanish casualties exceeded those of Parma's previous campaign, including the fights at Neuss, Venlo, Grave, and Rheinberg. But his disconsolation over the suffering of his men did not prevent Parma from expressing admiration for his opponents, particularly Sir Thomas Baskerville, whom he had observed from afar. The distinctive accoutrements of Williams (gilt morion), Baskerville (white plumes), and Vere (scarlet mantle) made them recognisable. Parma, upon meeting Williams, requested the presence of Baskerville, whose military skill he praised. The English had earned the respect of perhaps the finest general of the time. In fact, it was not that the English were defeated in battle; rather the logistical impossibility, given the shifting tides and resources available to Leicester, of raising the siege compelled the Sluys garrison to surrender on 5 August 1587.[3]

The Dutch, who knew the realities of war perhaps better than any people in Europe at this time, relied heavily upon their English soldiers. Maurice of Nassau found himself manoeuvring against a Catholic army amounting to about 11,000 men under Count Mansfeld in 1589. Of the 1,500 soldiers Maurice mustered to impede Mansfeld's march, 600 were Englishmen. Throughout the campaign, including the siege of Berck, into the 1590s, English companies played an integral role in these wars of religion.[4] Maurice, whose military instincts were unquestionable, prized English troops. He bestowed upon them places of honour, and entrusted them with difficult and important assignments. Maurice's clandestine attempt on Sluys, in August

1591 was a combined operation that relied heavily upon English arms. Robert Sydney and Thomas Bodley were prominent in Nassau's inner circle, as the allied forces snapped up enemy fortresses. When a secret assault on Dunkirk was contemplated, Maurice 'kept it very secret and had told only Vere, Admiral Justinius of Nassau, and Sydney, apart from those sent to view the place.' Of the hand-picked soldiers, most were English.[5] Additional English officers assisted in the enterprise as plans moved forward – Burgh, Poley, Baskerville, and Sir John Norris (who intended to come along with several hundred of his garrison[6]) and at the assault the English made up the vanguard.[7]

English companies were not only highly esteemed but were also reckoned crucial to the success of Netherlandish campaigns. Elizabeth was often badgered for reinforcements, and when Sir John Norris contemplated diverting some of his veterans to the Brittany campaign the Dutch complained that the English soldiers' departure would be a serious political and military setback. The dilution of the army, especially the reduction of quality foreign units, would dampen enthusiasm (and contributions) for the war.[8] Thomas Bodley, who provided confidential strategic assessment to Burghley, figured that the States would and could field a force for seven months, provided the twenty companies of English troops under discussion remained. But should they be withdrawn, Bodley opined, the Dutch would fall into a defensive strategy and dig in.[9] English arms very much determined the outcome, as well as the conduct, of the war. Shortly thereafter Francis Vere's troops seized the fort before Zutphen through a ruse (disguising themselves as local labourers, cloaks over their armour) and made possible the rapid surrender of the town. And immediately after, at Deventer, the English again were selected for the first assault. Clearly in siegecraft and hand-to-hand fighting, the English distinguished themselves.[10]

On 9 October 1588, Elizabeth dispatched Sir John Norris on a mission to the Low Countries.[11] Norris had capitalised on the Queen's anxiety over the expense of her Dutch succours and now the defences mounted against the Armada had reduced her Exchequer to alarmingly low levels. Even before the Armada had sailed, Sir John lamented the 'slender successe' of the Queen's efforts in the Netherlands and ventured the opinion that royal expenses had been £60,000 above the ordinary during the nearly 'twoo yeres' from 10 January 1585/6 to 10 August 1587, efforts during this period costing £500,000, and total expenditure of £812,000.[12] Sir John pandered to Gloriana's mistrust of the administration of her financial accounts, fishing in troubled waters by alleging not only mismanagement but also that a stronghold had been lost to 'treason'. While Norris's figures were mistakenly (or deliberately) inflated, he was correct in his assertion that warfare consumed dangerously the royal treasure.[13] Mid-January 1588 estimates of the Queen's annual charges for the Low Countries war reckoned the cost between £125,000 and £135,000.[14]

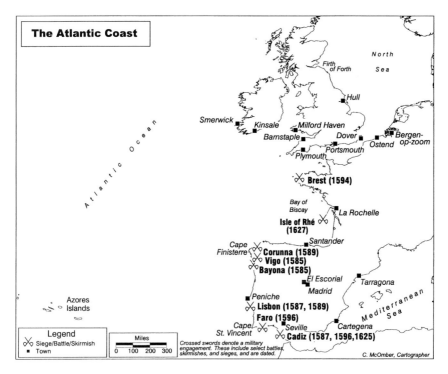

Figure 7.1 Map of the Atlantic coast.

Source: Connie McOmber and the author.

Elizabeth lived 'of her own' on an annual ordinary revenue of a quarter of a million pounds. Before the Spanish conflict she had expended on average £168,000 per annum. War changed all that. By mid-1588 the Exchequer was virtually exhausted, in spite of parliamentary subsidies and a City loan.[15] Strategically, the Armada had been neutralised, even if only temporarily. But Philip II remained wealthy and possessed of forces in Flanders. The English, on the other hand, had expended hundreds of thousands of pounds in their defence. The unwieldiness of the 1588 muster had shaken the confidence of more than a few privy councillors, lieutenants, and courtiers.[16] Defensive considerations continued to dictate English strategy. Some recouping of royal revenue was imperative if the island was to remain on a war-footing. Further, the momentum generated by the crippling of the Armada might be channelled to create offensive opportunities. A blow against Iberia would make the hunters the hunted. It was proposed that a timely voyage to Portugal might foment revolt there, and, steeled by English arms, export the war to Philip's part of the world.

The Portugal expedition of 1589: English warfare on sea and land

The Portugal expedition of 1589 resembled Henry VIII's continental ventures in that it depended upon synchronisation between land forces and naval vessels. The scheme was closely linked with operations in the Netherlands. English forces there would be ferried to invasion points upon the enemy's home soil, a sort of Armada turnabout. Norris would secure the States' cooperation and financial support. Parliament, too, would share the burden. But sixteenth-century warfare was costly. Norris, as usual, schemed to make the enterprise profitable. A group of 'adventurers' would put up most of the capital. Plunder taken at Lisbon, Seville, the Azores, or on the high seas would be divided accordingly. But the 'privatisation' of the expedition made booty the highest strategic priority.

The Queen paid £49,287 as her share.[17] After delays and false starts, the expedition descended upon Corunna, where the 'adventurers' suspected heavily laden Spanish galleons lay at anchor. In fact, scores of Spanish vessels sheltered farther east, at Santander, the very port the Queen had urged her commanders to raid. Had they heeded Her Majesty's strategy, the voyage would have been successful. As it turned out, the Portugal expedition set the model for the Caroline voyages to Cadiz (1625) and the Isle of Rhé (1627). An incoherent strategy underlay the Portugal campaign. The plundering 'adventurers' and the Crown differed over strategic priorities. Elizabeth wished destruction of the Spanish navy first, and a share of booty second, though the inverse was true for Norris, Sir Francis Drake, and the rest of the 'adventurers'. Bad strategy led to poor coordination of the fleet. The Earl of Essex and Sir Roger Williams missed the operations against Corunna entirely. Further lack of coordination resulted in the land forces undertaking unaided the assault on the upper city of Corunna, while their vessels anchored idly. The army lacked a proper artillery train. Unsuccoured by naval gunnery, the infantry miscarried the final attack, though Secretary Anthony Ashley made the peculiar (and perhaps unfair) comment that 'the English common soldier is not well acquainted with matters of breach'.[18]

The English fleet had entered Corunna harbour without bombarding the town or ships there. Expertly, 7,000 soldiers disembarked in 'three howres' but failed to move quickly to assault the town because 'the rayne was soe great'. Positioning themselves within 'musquet shot of the Towne', the English 'lay theare all nighte, and the next nighte assayled the Towne with a Scalado, which was well performed on all parts. Within an howre the Towne was wonne with the losse [of] 500 Spaniards and our men about 20'. The invaders found 'great store of victuals', naval emptions, cannon ('150 peeces of brasse'), pikes, muskets, and calivers. A refreshing discovery was a cache of 'about 6000 pipes of wine wheareof some they spoyled, and spent, and some they kepte'. The gallants toasted themselves liberally, and, in a prefiguring of the 1625 Cadiz landing, imbibed more than discipline should have permitted. Attempts to dislodge the English by local militia were brushed aside almost casually, suggesting that Iberian domestic forces had grown indolent, being far from the wars. Capturing the castle and upper town posed a more formidable challenge. Although a pair of demi-cannon and two culverin pounded out a modest breach, and a mine collapsed part of one of the upper town's towers, still the defenders resisted vigorously.[19] A dual assault was planned. A contingent drawn from the general's foot soldiers and some dismounted cavalry would rush through the breach. With the explosion of a mine, a group 'selected out of divers Regiments' would follow the lieutenant colonel's men.

> All these Companies being in Armes, and the assault intended to be given in all places at an instant, fier was put to the train of the Myne: but by reason the powder brake out backwards . . . the Myners were set to worke againe. . . . [F]ier was given to the trayne of the Mine, which blew up halfe the Tower. . . . The Assailants having in charge upon the effecting of the Myne presently to give the assault . . . but too soone, for having entred the top of the breach, the other halfe of the Tower, which with the first force of the powder was onely shaken and made loose, fell uppon our men: under which were buried 20 or 20. . . . This so amazed our men that stood in the breach, not knowing from whence that terror came . . . two ensigns of Generall Drake and Captaine Anthonie Wingfeild [the author] were shot in the Breach . . . Captaine Sydnam pitifully lost: who having three or foure great stones upon his lower parts, was helde so fast. . . . The next daye being found to be alive, ther was 10 or 12 lost in attempting to relieve him. The breach made by the cannon was wonderful wel assaulted . . . who brought their men to the push of the pike at the top of the Breach . . . the loose earth (which was indeede but the rubbish of the outside of the wall) with the weight of them that were thereon slipped outwards from under their feete. Whereby did appeare halfe the wal unbattered. For let no man thinke that Culurine or Demie Cannon can sufficiently batter a defensible Rampier.[20]

On 6 May 1589, in the midst of the siege of Corunna's upper town, a relief force of local citizens and militia numbering 8,000–10,000 again attempted to drive off the fearsome English. Again a bloody retreat resulted. Outnumbered and tied down in siege activity, Norris gathered up 7,000 troops. Finding the would-be rescuers encamped just beyond a narrow stone bridge approximately 200 yards in length, Sir John charged the bridge, routing the camp and killing several hundred Spaniards. English fatalities were few, allegedly only seven men. But their officers' wounds were notable. Captain Hendar's helmet was blown off and his head slashed in five places by sword blows; Captain Fulford's arm was injured by shot; Captain Barton suffered damage to an eye. Most dramatically, Sir Edward Norris received a gash upon his head, delivered by an enemy swordsman, but was then succoured by his brother the general, hacking his way to his fallen sibling. Sir John apparently had not time to don armour, but none the less plunged impulsively into the fray.[21]

The expedition in general, and this action specifically, suggest that honour-seeking commanders were perhaps too quick to engage and often bullied their men into battle. Certainly the Queen thought so. The will to fight very often came from the upper ranks. English common soldiers may have possessed a sense of honour, but the likelihood that they might garner individual glory and substantial reward from daring combats seems remote. Personal bravery and the recognition of fighting skill meant much, perhaps the most, to the commanders, who sought out occasions in which to distinguish their persons. On the other hand, English officers led from the front. The tactical brilliance of English warfare was a direct result of the officers' unwillingness to shy off from combat. This won battles, even if poor strategy lost the war on occasion.

Having failed to win any strategic advantage at Corunna, the 'adventurers' compounded their mistake by sailing for Lisbon rather than attempting Santander, where significant damage might have been done to Philip's naval capabilities. The English flotilla arrived off the mouth of the Tagus on 15 May 1589. By this time the expedition had been joined by the vessel of two flamboyant soldiers, one expert and the other novice: Sir Roger Williams and Robert Devereux, second Earl of Essex. At the disembarkation the following day, the latter

> was the first man that landed, who by reason the billows weare high waded [up] to the shoulders to come ashoare. Seaven Ensignes with him at that pointe [presente?] wheareto ympeach the landing of our men. Theare weare 5000 Spaniards and Portugals assembled, but in thend they wear by our men driven to flighte, whearen Captains Palmer, Jackson, and Baskervill behaved themselvs very valiently at the push of the pike.[22]

It was reported, to the Queen's horror no doubt, that upon emerging from the surf Essex had sought out hand-to-hand combat with a Spaniard and slain him.[23] Once 6,000 English were ashore at Peniche, they began the 45-mile trek to Lisbon, which would take them six days. The fleet, commanded by Drake, with six infantry companies aboard, would join Norris's troops along the Tagus, near Lisbon. It was hoped that Portuguese rebels would flock to the English column during the march, a prospect that failed to materialise.[24] Twice pro-Spanish forces broke into the English camp by subterfuge, disguising themselves as sympathetic Portuguese. In the first attack, fourteen English were killed, and in the second several officers were shot dead.[25]

When, on 23 May, Norris infiltrated the Lisbon suburbs, the English found themselves in a familiar situation, assailing a fortified town without the requisite artillery. Reduced to 4,000 serviceable men, out of touch with Drake, and lacking Portuguese aid, they moved precariously before Lisbon. All they could do was destroy or consume enemy victuals and stores. They claimed this as a great logistical victory, but the Privy Council was unimpressed. Reports detailed the destruction of Spain's war *matériel*, conveniently overlooking the galleons at Santander and English impotence before Lisbon (ironically due to lack of victuals as well as the absence of an artillery train).[26] By the end of the first week in June, hope of creating a new front in the wars of religion that stretched through the Iberian peninsula, and of devastating Philip II's western ports, had slipped away. Attempts against the Azores were turned back by inclement weather, which drove the remnants of fleet and army back to Albion. Although the judgement of the commanders was open to question, the valour of the soldiers was not. The 'privatisation' of the war sabotaged its strategic purpose, for the generals' priorities (and those of the investors) did not always coincide with those of Her Majesty. The great tragedy was that the Spanish ships survived at Santander, and were refitted, enabling them to renew the marine offensive against England into the following decade.

English warfare in France, 1589–91

In September 1589, Peregrine Bertie, Lord Willoughby (and the ubiquitous Williams), succoured Henry of Navarre, and ultimately the Earl of Essex appeared as well, after an army of 3,000 Englishmen commanded by Sir John Norris arrived in May 1591.[27] The English captains' quest for honour and the maintenance of the essentially defensive Elizabethan grand strategy once again came to cross purposes, in the autumn and early winter of 1589. Strategically, England was involved in five interlocking theatres of operation, through any of which an enemy might descend: the Low Countries, the ports of Normandy and Brittany, Ireland, the Scottish Borders, and the high seas, particularly the Channel. The 1588 Armada defence, and the riposte against Iberia the following year, had depleted English arms, men, equipment, and money. Now, in the late summer of 1589, the wars of religion widened, and Henry of Navarre's predicament was such that Elizabeth feared that Catholic France might extinguish the Protestant revolt and secure ports in northwestern France. These might then be used as the Spanish had planned to utilise the Low Countries' harbours the year before.

With some of her best commanders in disgrace over their mismanagement of the Portugal expedition, Elizabeth looked to a reliable commander in the person of Peregrine Bertie, Lord Willoughby. But he came with baggage. With his reputation unfairly tarnished by the States General's allegation of treachery in the yielding-up of the key town of Geertruidenberg, he pursued vindication more than the nation's interests. Again, the honour of a commander raised its head.[28] Given the dearth of military resources available to the Crown, the Queen hesitated to launch the expeditionary force unless absolutely compelled to do so. The judge of that, her ambassador Sir Edward Stafford, in fact cancelled the campaign in an urgent dispatch that caught Willoughby on the verge of embarkation at Dover. The commander discarded the order and sailed anyway, without advising Whitehall. Thus Willoughby's expedition was as much about honour as the Portugal voyage was about plunder – Elizabethan strategy and the conservation of military resources be damned.[29]

Thus did Henry of Navarre command men who the previous year had guarded the southern coasts against the Spaniard and numbered amongst them English militiamen. Elizabeth took seriously the plight of the never entirely reliable Henry, and had commanded 'certein Companies of the trained bands' to be mustered for foreign service. The strategically crucial areas of Kent, Sussex, Hampshire, and London each contributed a thousand soldiers, some or all of whom were to be trained soldiers of the local militia. Just as the Queen insisted that the officers be acquainted with 'martiall service', so too she ordered trained men into the ranks, even if they were relatively substantial citizens. Probably she had learned from the failures of raw men in earlier expeditions.[30] Some of those skilled amateur soldiers expressed enthusiasm for the campaign. Edward Boys learned that '50 armed men [pikemen] and 30 muskatiers to be taken out of my select band' were destined for Normandy. He asked they be put under command of his son, who had helped to drill them. The elder Boys recommended the service to the young man, because the experience would impart 'further knowledg' of the art of war in 'defence of the gospell'.[31] Those Kentish soldiers mustered and reviewed impressively, though the Sussex and Hampshire contingents were 'ill furnished, ill chosen, and badly armed'.[32] Willoughby's force was seasoned by veterans such as Edward Brewerton, who had started out as a 'pryvat souldier' in the Irish service, promoted to ensign in the Low Countries.[33]

Logistical arrangements and pay schedules were drafted by the Queen's most trusted servants, Burghley and Walsingham. If many of the troops were among the best available, the expeditionary force was designed and supplied by the cogitations of the best minds in the government.[34] Considering that these preparations were undertaken for an expedition that might very possibly be stood down at the eleventh hour (and should have done so), Elizabethan parsimony in things military constituted not simple meaness but calculated conservation of scarce resources. Considering how unreliable continental allies were, Elizabeth showed much good faith and care in organising an expedition of 4,000 troops. That the Sussex and Hampshire men were insufficient says more about the shires than the Crown.

Actually, Willoughby had at most about 3,600 men, given dead pay. The Queen's charge, based upon the month the troops remained in her pay prior to transference to Henry's paymaster, was £6,667.[35] This charge was difficult to bear, given the exhaustion of the Exchequer, which compelled the Crown to sell off lands to meet the recurring costs of war in 1589: £1,232 to T. Perrot and Sir Walter Raleigh for soldiers' wages, £26,000 to Drake and Sir John Norris for defence-related services, £1,932 for defensive works (presumably) at Portsmouth, £5,111 to Drake and Hawkins for the building of fireships to be used against the Spaniards, £6,000 to Thomas Fludd the treasurer for coating, conducting, and wages for the Willoughby expedition, £11,091 to the mayor of Plymouth and others towards the Portugal expedition, £50,909 to the Treasurer of the Fleet, £14,448 to the Surveyor of the Victuals for the Fleet, £20,587 to the Lieutenant of the Ordnance, £300 for the Master of the Armoury, £2,000 for Berwick, £17,757 for the Irish establishment, £571 for Portsmouth and other garrisons, £2,105 to the Lieutenant of the Tower, £77,422 to support the Dutch revolt, and other expenses incidental to the defence of the realm.[36]

Thus before the 1590s had commenced, the 'militarization of the Elizabethan state' was well under way.[37] And the Queen's soldiers sank into poverty with her. Sir Thomas Wilsford, who served in the brave Kentish ranks, lay deeply in debt at the outset of the Willoughby expedition. Willoughby himself would be 'worn out physically and financially' by the end of the campaign, and fewer than a thousand of the troops returned home. The motivation of these men, and their royal mistress, seems to have been heartfelt commitment to Henry's cause, though no doubt there was grumbling amongst the trained bands. The muster-master John Stubbes, who expired before he could fulfil his intended re-enlistment under the French Protestant crusader, remarked 'The King's cause is God's cause. . . . There are few that do not swallow up these incommodities [hardships], thinking it an honor to have been in this jorny'.[38]

Those incommodities were many, and underscore the importance of logistics. More Englishmen were lost on forced marches and bad victuals than in combat. In spite of the wretched conditions endured by Willoughby's troops, the English invigorated Henry's operations and performed admirably. Contemporaries, predictably, claimed that the English intervention had been the salvation of the Protestant war effort; historians have wondered if the 4,000 made a difference at all, from the point of view of strategy.[39] Nineteen towns and castles yielded to Henry while the English comprised part of his army. In which cases the besieged capitulated because they 'feared the English behind them more than the French at the breach' is hard to determine.

But English ferocity and persistence in siegecraft were indisputable, provided that they had the means to attack. The English infiltrated the Paris suburbs without artillery support and would have occupied the university had Henry approved the use of cannon on his Parisian subjects. Willoughby's men negotiated a river and ditches while taking Vendôme in 1590. At Le Mans they drove back the defenders and constructed an ingenious amphibious assault craft fashioned from tuns and ladders. At Alençon, an 'engine' equipped with an iron hook was used to lower a drawbridge. Throughout these exploits the soldiers risked themselves, in spite of the fact that they were liable to be recalled to England because Henry lacked the funds and food to keep them.[40] Elizabeth's soldiers had proved their ability and spirit, but strategically they had little to show for their sacrifices.

Given the crushing cost of English warfare through 1588, 1589, and then into 1590, it was amazing that Elizabeth sustained the Protestant cause through 1591, with significant operations in France and the Low Countries. By the beginning of October 1591, the old Portugal cronies of Norris, Williams, Anthony Wingfield and so on had drawn £28,383 9s. 1d. on the privy seal for the Brittany campaign. Companies were juggled between the Netherlands and France, while Burghley personally kept track of the shipments of victuals.[41] The Queen reckoned she had invested in Henry IV 1,147,119 crowns (roughly £345,000) during 1587–91, including such support as German mercenaries, Willoughby's force, Essex's Normandy campaign of 1591, the Brittany army of 1591, and land and naval forces for Brest.[42] And, if the Queen had become an indispensable paymaster, her soldiers were equally valued at the most crucial points of campaigning. English warfare in the Low Countries and France was in large measure driven by honour, which was why many of the English officers had entered continental service. The casualty rate amongst the officer corps indicates that the stalwart performance of English troops had much to do with their commanders' commitment to victory, even if it was as often personal as ideological.

One tenet of the military revolution theory is that war was 'eternalised' by commanders who avoided the decision of the battle. As defensive warfare dominated attack, manoeuvre (strategic and tactical) promised more, and with greater security, than did combat. The ancient Romans had counselled that the outcome of the clash of armies could not be predicted with certainty, a sentiment echoed by Conway at East Dunkirk that 'nothing under the moon was so uncertain as battle'.[43] Lunar imagery and reference to that 'inconstant orb' were appropriate. Although individual combat affirmed free will and from antiquity had been seen as the greatest opportunity for a man to distinguish himself through his own efforts and sheer will, still the killing field was subject to the whims of the gods. Did survival in battle stem from individual mettle or the sanctification and protection of a superhuman force, including fate? This instilled ambivalence in combat troops.

For some commanders, such as Parma, steeped in the strategy as well as the imagery of the Romans, logistics and manoeuvre were the essence of the art of war, though tactical decisiveness and the bravery to strike full force at the most opportune moment complemented this defensive approach to military science. Others lacked Parma's patience. Henry IV sought battle, strategically because of the preponderance of cavalry in his armies, and more personally because lightning tactics suited his nature. Although adversaries, both the Duke and the King enjoyed success.[44] Contemporaries discussed battle within the context of stereotypical national 'humours'. Henry IV believed his countrymen shared his temperament: '. . . as long as there was hope of a battle they would vanquish all inconveniences, for the French gentry ran to a battle as to a banquet. If there were a battle, victory was certain.'[45] The English did not necessarily share this opinion of French fighting spirit. Though they confirmed Henry IV's bellicosity, they commented sourly on the French art of war: '. . . the King offered many skirmishes, which the enemy coldly entertained. Parma's horse were driven into his trenches, but nothing could draw him to any great skirmish, which he [Parma] feared might bring on a battle.' The result was 'some little skirmishes by French to French . . . but not as a good play at football in England where men's necks, arms, and legs are broken, but here not a man hurt.'[46]

The indecisive campaigning of the 1590s, and contemporaries' anachronistic concept of warfare, prompted chivalric alternatives to battle that offered glory that would be ascribed to the individual warriors rather than to impersonal forces such as the gods, the ground, the weather, the paymaster, or mighty bastions. The Earl of Essex challenged the Spaniards ensconced in Lisbon in the summer of 1589 and would fight any of his quality. If none of that stature hid behind the town walls, then Essex would take on as many inferiors as would face him.[47] Queen Elizabeth was not only unamused, but also incensed when she discovered that offers of individual combat had passed between the Earl and the besieged in Rouen. The Earl challenged Villars, the latter being, in the royal opinion 'a mere rebel', 'a traitor to the French Crown and a conspirator with the King of Spain'.[48] But Gloriana did not regard war in the same light as did her loyal pike-trailers. For the Queen, war was a recurring nightmare of expense and carnage. For the lads of the Court, it was dangerous, but then most English sports are dangerous; and combat afforded them the opportunity to distinguish themselves in that international brotherhood in a way that was impossible at Court or sitting at Council. So Leicester, Essex, and others created knights, issued challenges, postured, and sought a kind of fame and reputation that even the Queen could not bestow. Only when death touched this circle, as in Sir Philip Sydney's sad demise, and in the tragic death of Essex's younger brother, did grim reality overshadow the burnished armour and brightly coloured banners.

During the siege of Paris, which saw more than its share of atrocities, a challenge was exchanged that would have pitted 400 English against an equal number of the Spanish garrison.[49] These displays of masculinity, too, met the Queen's disapproval when she learned 'that a combat was intended between certain hundreds of them and as many hundreds of Spaniards, "altogether without our liking or knowledge"'.[50] Grandiose expressions of chivalric behaviour, even on the battlefield, persisted into the Jacobean era. In 1610 Lord Herbert of Cherbury claimed to have been challenged to display his fencing skills upon the parapet of some trenches, under fire from several hundred Catholics in the bastion opposite. The duellists parried and riposted while bullets whizzed by, neither wishing to appear cowardly by returning to the safety of the trench. Ultimately, they retired, unharmed by the fusillade.[51] Whether interpreted as rites of the society of soldiers or expressions of incipient national character, the conflation of chivalric display with atrocity (equally common in the Hundred Years War as in the Thirty Years War) betrays a certain incoherence in the consciousness of the soldierly profession. The two views of combat were apparently contradictory. In one, violence was pitted against a manifestation of evil, in an expression of knightly virtue, emulating St George. In the other, two humans were sent out like pawns, to act out their states' hostility and suffer for society. How combatants wrestled with this apparent hypocrisy remains mysterious, for soldiers excel in fighting more than in reflection and writing. If the visage of death was sometimes masked behind the image of St George, the description of battle was also sometimes subtly altered to put the best face on a given action. It was not always a matter of bravery, but an attempt to instil bravado *ex post facto*.

Although the report of a contest might have been enhanced to help justify the bestowal of knighthood on certain combatants, a more common cause of any exaggeration seemed to be the necessity of convincing the ruler that her (or his) troops were performing gallantly, meeting success, and making an impact upon the war. In short, correspondents often wished to convince Elizabeth to sustain (or increase) her involvement in a given theatre. Though the growing literature of battle reporting put something of a curb on extreme embellishment (and the fact that Crown and Council got several different accounts that were compared, especially by Burghley), a little special pleading, singling out certain captains or companies, was considered a necessity in a profession where precious few rewards fell to men who had risked their lives. The solicitation of royal favour probably motivated the compilation of a résumé of military feats by Sir John Norris, listing seven major actions in which he had participated as the Queen's general in the Low Countries, followed by four campaigns in Ireland, four in Flanders, and finally nine or more exploits in the most recent French wars.[52] The historian, therefore, who enquires after the behaviour of men fighting in the sixteenth and seventeenth centuries (before combat history became formalised and well documented) should remember that soldiers writing from the battlefield were a vested interest group, not journalists. With that caveat in mind, and the occasional hyperbole excepted, accounts of the English role in continental actions are on the whole consistent and believable.

The continental experience of the English fighting man (in the 1590s at least) can be encapsulated in one trooper's jibe, '. . . the French deal like the Dutch: we are first at frays and last at feasts'.[53] English soldiers, pressed or professional, enjoyed a reputation for pugnacity and ability amongst foreign commanders. They were indeed often in the vanguard, first in the breach, at the point of assault, and in the most perilous trenches. And they rarely got to the feast, their allies neglecting to pay and feed them time and again. As at the Battle of the Spurs, English reputation could put to flight an enemy. When Aumale was surprised in April 1591, the allied forces advanced an English contingent discernible from the castle walls. Sir Roger Williams assembled his 600 men adjacent to a forested area, with his soldiers in plain sight, their ensigns punctuating the foliage, giving the impression that they made up the vanguard of a larger force. Rumours that 3,000 more English had disembarked at Dieppe lent credibility to the ruse. DeChatte dispatched a French courier to the castle, who strongly advised immediate surrender, since their English allies' practice was to slay as many defenders as they could in an assault. Williams gave the French, allies and enemies, good reason to believe it. When the defenders asked if they would send the Duke of Aumale to negotiate, and agreed to surrender peaceably in three days if no relief had been sent, Williams asked DeChatte to cease negotiating and to supply the English with sufficient ladders so that they might attempt Aumale castle at four different points of assault. Sir Roger explained that he and his countrymen despised the Duke. They would take the castle immediately and 'if one Englishman were lost he would cut the throats of all who were in the castle'. Within two hours, the fortress surrendered. English infantry held a certain pre-eminence, in assault or in the open field. Not long after the Aumale episode, forty English pikemen and musketeers held at bay a force of Catholic cavalry reputedly numbering sixty.[54] Praise of English foot soldiers is too ubiquitous to be discounted lightly.

In Henry IV's armies, English infantry were valued for several reasons. The King needed reliable infantry. Henry's penchant for cavalry charges, and the comparative prevalence of horsemen in his ranks meant that he could initiate battle with formidable shock. But sustaining an attack required foot soldiers, and pikemen especially were desperately needed. In sieges, distasteful as they may have been to Henry, Dutch and English infantry were the royal mainstay. English sappers, miners, and pioneers were extremely valuable to the King's war effort.[55] This is not to minimise the contribution of English horsemen, as, for example, when Captain Anthony Sherley's cavalry unit spearheaded the column that put to rout the Catholic forces at Châtelaudren in 1591.[56]

There is reason to agree that the English were very often 'first at frays'. Sir Francis Vere anchored his ambush outside Arnhem on a contingent of Dutch and English infantry, with his countrymen in the vanguard. When the States' cavalry lured Parma's cornets into what became an equestrian brawl, this 'stand of pikes barred the way', preventing a manoeuvre from becoming a rout.[57] At Guingamp, the English overran the suburbs in pre-dawn darkness and then turned their attention to the town:

> An English captain, anxious to shew himself more forward than the rest, then lodged his ensign hard by one of the gates and the garrison captured it, not without some loss, in a sortie. Not more than three English were slain.[58]

Leading the battle held great appeal for the English. So occupying a critical place on the battlefield, or insisting on the honour of commencing an action, was sought eagerly. Not long after Guingamp, Williams's troops could again hardly be restrained from the enemy. On 20 May 1591 the allies descended upon St Saëns, and Williams

> put Capt. Gorge's lieutenant and his own ensign on the right wing with 50 musketeers and 12 halbards; Capt. Dycher's lieutenant and ensign on the left wing with 50 small shot and 12 halbards; placed the pikes and captains in one battalion and the rest of the English shot in two wings, with the rearguard.

The French configured a similar formation and followed, the cavalry and officers trailing. The Catholics planted 300 harquebusiers in ambush behind a barricade. Their volley inflicted little damage on the advancing English. Counter-fire tore into the barricade, while a wing of English infantry waded into the small river flanking the barricade, 'which greatly annoyed the enemy'. The wing overwhelmed the barricaded shot, came to 'push of pike' and forced a retreat, killing 50 defenders. 'The English charged "so hard in their tails" that they stormed the second barricade, slaying another 60, and entered pell-mell into a great church, which was entrenched, killing above six score there'. Four hundred Leaguers fell back on a cloister 'but the English burned the ports of the base court, entered it, spoiled many . . .,' forcing a surrender. The English were not disinclined to fight, and they enjoyed their ancient reputation, which in some bordered on bloodthirstiness. A day and a half's march, including a night trek, did not slow them when the moment of battle arrived. As one Frenchman put it, 'the English showed themselves in no way inferior to their fathers'. As a result, the 'leaguers now so feared the English that they dared not come near Dieppe or into the field'.[59]

When on 22 May 1591 the battering of Guingamp ripped open a suffi-cient breach, Norris 'claimed the point of the assault for the English'. The reader who might harbour some scepticism of the tales of valour spawned by these clashes finds a blunt admission of failure regarding how the attack stalled. English captains Jackson, Herne, and Wolf, under Norris's command, led 200 up the incline, 'but it was too steep to get up and the soldiers did not second them well'. Herne died and Wolf sustained serious injury.[60] One can compare the private correspondence with a contemporary published account, that makes the unpublished account that much more believable:

> [Norris] ... instantly demaunded the pointe and honour of the assault for the English men ... such was the emulation of our commanders and Captaines to winne honour, that all being willing the service, to avoide contention our Generall caused the dice to bee cast, so that it fell to Captaine Iackson and Captaine Heron to lead the first two hundreth to the assault. ... They performed verie valiantly, scrambling up with notable resolution, standing a long halfe houre at the push of the pike in the face of a whole storme of the small shot, especially Captaine Iackson who came to the point of the breach, but not being throughly seconded by the souldiers unable to get up by reason of the steepness of the place, yet were they hardly commanded to retire, performing their retraite with no lesse good order then their attempt to assault, Captaine Heron received a shot in the throate, whereof he presently dyed, and not above twelve others slaine; Captaine Iackson sore hurt. Captaine Wolfe in the top of the breach had three daungerous woundes in the head, and others in his body; Captaine Catesbye a voluntarie gentleman sore hurt in the arme. Also Captaine Whitton. ...[61]

English troops led many assaults during the autumn of 1591. Bringing up English companies and then unleashing a barrage upon the walls was a procedure Maurice of Nassau employed on several occasions, in order to intimidate defenders to parley and surrender.[62]

In the Rouen campaign especially the commanders were perhaps too exuberant. Essex, as well as his subordinates such as Williams and Norris, had a tendency to flamboyancy. In the ill-fated assault on Guingamp, which also daunted the French, who suffered even greater casualties than the English in trying the breach, the English Captain Dennis advanced too far in his reconnoitring of another assault point for a *scalado* and was shot in the gut. The agonising wound finally killed him, at midnight. One must keep in mind that in these campaigns guns were no respecters of rank: both Henry IV and Parma received bullet wounds.[63] The officers' will to battle did not escape Elizabeth's notice. She scolded Essex how little the King regards the hazard of our men and how you, our General, at all times refuse not to run with them to all services of greatest peril but even, like the forlorn hope of a battle, do bring them to the slaughter.[64]

Essex, even before the first shots had been fired, had been judged more in need of a bridle than the spur. His 'friends' at court thought 'the Earl's nature so desirous of martial service'[65] that it is no surprise to find him trailing a pike at one action, much to the Queen's dismay.[66]

English soldiers at Turnhout (1597) and Nieuwpoort (1600)

English warfare was adaptable. The Eighty Years War revolved around defence, punctuated by fierce sporadic fighting, akin to what we have described as a basic tenet of the English art of war. The Spanish Netherlands' terrain could wear down an army (as in the case of Ireland's topography and climate), yet there were also stretches of 'cavalry country' in the south, which invited mobility and provided the landscape for set battles in Hainault and Brabant. Finally, the Low Countries boasted the most modern fortresses in the world, and thus provided a school for siegecraft.[67] Turnhout, Nieuwpoort, and (as shall be seen in the next chapter) Ostend witnessed late Elizabethan soldiering at its best. One third of Maurice of Nassau's hastily fielded army of 6,000 infantry[68] and 800 'pistoleer' cavalry were English, amongst them the Veres, Sir Robert Sydney, Sir Nicholas Parker, and Captain Docwra.

Plotting a mid-winter descent upon the Catholic army bivouacked in the sizeable Brabantine village of Turnhout, the allies executed a forced march and then took advantage of the cloak of night to surprise their foe. But their Spanish prey escaped in the pre-dawn darkness, and Sir Francis Vere, after clearing a bridge of enemy musketeers in a brief firefight, galloped off to intercept and harry the retreating Spanish column, so that the main body under Maurice might catch up and engage the enemy. When Maurice came upon the scene, he had only cavalry at his disposal, apart from the few hundred musketeers that had hurried along with Vere. Staking their fate on the rapidity of their retreat, the Spanish force had not wheeled about and formed up to face their Protestant pursuers. Instead the column had pushed on, towards the town of Herentaéls and safety. Spurring forward his horsemen, Maurice sent cornets speeding along the flanks of the still-marching enemy column. When the Dutch cavalry reached a position parallel to the head of the column, they pivoted towards their quarry and charged headlong, with neither infantry nor artillery support. As the Spanish retreat now halted in an attempt to receive and repel the Protestant horsemen, Sir Francis Vere's troops assailed the Catholic

Figure 7.2
The victory at Turnhout (1597) demonstrated English proficiency in fighting on horseback, as well as tactical ability.

Source: The Battle of Turnhout, winter 1597, reproduced by permission of Bodley's Librarian, from Guillame Baudart, *Second Tome du Livre' intitvle les Guerres de Nassav* (Amsterdam 1616).

TVRNHOVT

Neersche Heyde

Interea lectus ex omni gente cohortes   MAVRITIVS legit peditumq, equitumq, cohortes,
TVRNHOVTI locât ALBERTVS, queis territat Vrbes,   Aty hostem insequitur fugientem, armisq, lacessit.

228

Figure 7.3
'And so we charged their Pikes, not breaking through them, at the first push, as it was anciently used by the men-of-arms with their barbed horses: but as the long pistols, delivered at hand, had made the ranks thin, so thereupon, the rest of the horse got within them.' – Sir Francis Vere.

Source: The Battle of Turnhout, winter 1597, reproduced by permission of Bodley's Librarian, from Guillame Baudart, *Second Tome du Livre' intitule les Guerres de Nassau* (Amsterdam 1616).

rear.[69] A 'British' charge led by Vere, Sydney and Edmondes 'drave the [Catholic] musketiers uppon their owne pikes, from whence arose the beginning of the victorie'.[70] The tactical uses of English cavalry were thus demonstrated, and although it would be an exaggeration to claim the entire victory as wrought by English arms, certainly Vere's instinctive and timely manoeuvre forced the battle, and his falling upon the column's rear assured the enemy's rout.

The battle of Nieuwpoort, fought on 2 July 1600, came about because of a flawed strategy devised by the States General and thrust upon the allied commanders. Prince Maurice realised, rightly, the danger of under-estimating the Army of Flanders, even when wracked by mutiny. To seize the ports of Nieuwpoort and Dunkirk without first controlling their respective inland territories was a dangerous proposition. At the skirmish of Leffingen, the initial collision of these armies on the shoreline near Nieuwpoort, the Protestants were badly mauled, and some units suffered annihilation, largely because of poor tactical positioning. But the main engagement, thanks largely to Sir Francis Vere yet again, was a triumph of land-sea operations, with clever troop movements on broken and unpre-dictable terrain.[71]

The vanguard of the Protestant army included 24 companies of English infantry, along with Dutch and Frisian troops, totalling 4,000 of Maurice's best men, under the Veres. The infantry vanguard was certainly an English-led unit: 'One and fortie Ensignes made the foot vantgard, as were all com-manded by the Generall Sir Francis Veer.'[72] Demonstrating the same rapidity of deployment and eye for ground that had helped him at Turnhout, Vere arranged his troops in anticipation of the Archduke's army's arrival:

> having caused my troops to advance, I drewe from the whole vanguard about one thousand men . . . The English and fifty of the Counts guard I placed on top of a hill that lay more advanced than the rest, which being steep and sandy was not so easily to be mounted. . . .

Behind that hill was another, even higher, joined to the first by a ridge. Ranging his musketeers, harquebusiers and pikemen on this high ground, Vere awaited the Spanish advance.[73]

The enemy marched up the shoreline on a broad front, flinging skirmish-ing cavalry against Maurice's outlying positions. Vere's harquebusiers and musketeers peppered the flanks of the advancing army below. The battle-line stretched across the sand, the ranks becoming increasingly compacted as the tide flooded in. Dutch warships, which had got the Archduke Albert's forces within range as they charted a parallel course, now unleashed a cannonade that in effect created a crossfire, with projectiles hurtling in from the sea and small shot raining down from the dunes. Spanish infantry manoeuvred among the sand dunes and returned fire against Vere's elevated positions. But the combination of the incoming tide and offshore batteries forced the Archduke to shift many of his men inland, and the battle degenerated into a confused exchange amongst the dunes, pikemen lowering their weapons on the slopes while a pair of English demi-culverin positioned on a hilltop fired with devastating effect upon the increasingly compressed Spanish formations.

Vere's troops, which included all the English, had absorbed the attackers' blows for hours and began to waiver, not having been reinforced. 'The enemies Fanterie [foot] fought with better vantage on the Downes, where they tooke one hill after another, from his Excellencies footmen, and did mightily endaunger the ordinance.'[74] Finally the English were driven from the hills, but managed to fall back on their ordnance. Wounded, Vere found his infantry intermingled with the demi-culverin. 'I made them stand . . . and willed the Cannoneers to discharge upon the enemy that now swarmed upon the sands. . . .' Supporting the barrage, Vere hurled all his cavalry along with his brother's foot soldiers. Momentum again shifted and the Archduke's advance was halted and repelled. In the meanwhile Vere's sharpshooters '. . . from the top of the hills, who had kept their place from the beginning . . . plied them with shot: our English souldiers on all hands with new courage resorted to the fight. . . .' Like the lads at Flodden, these stubborn infantry refused to budge and made their commander look brilliant.[75] The Archduke's reserves had already been committed in the exhausting fighting amid the sandhills, and the Spanish army broke. In Sir John Ogle's not disinterested account, the confluence of the English foot regiments launched the counter-attack which sealed the victory and promoted Maurice to cry out (probably apocryphally, unfortunately), 'Voyez, Voyez, les Anglois, qui tournent à la charge' and thereupon commanded his forces to exploit the turn of events.[76]

Nearly one-third of Maurice's army was English, made up of almost all Elizabeth's contingent and placed in the 'vaward'. One can appreciate why the Protestant Dutch dreaded the shifting of English military resources from the Continent to Ireland in the late 1590s. Using the volume of royal revenues to the paymaster of the Queen's forces as an indicator, one can measure the extent of the commitment to the Dutch rebels and how the strategic priority of securing Ireland had diverted resources from that theatre. From the mid-1580s into the early 1590s, the Exchequer of Receipt issued annually an amount ranging from somewhat above £100,000 in 1587-8 to £174,643. After 1591, expenditure fell 25-50 per cent from the level of the seven years beginning circa 1585. Commitment to the Dutch after 1595-6 remained below £70,000 per annum and, at the accession of James I, his initial commitment to the Dutch Protestant cause amounted to merely £6,843. During the late 1580s the figure had been £105,289.[77] The comparative decline of Dutch support by Elizabeth through the 1590s was not

247) *Soubs Philippe III. gouvernant l'Arch. Albert & le Prince Maurice.* 317

Ex hostem ad bellum jamc indulgere furori.
Dux, miles, SCOTUS, pariter manifestus, IBERI

247. Insana suadet victoria prima, cadunt
Perfidia apparet quam mox vindicta sequitur.

Figure 7.4
Tactical manoeuvring
and the judicious use
of firepower
characterised the
successes of English
arms at Nieuwpoort,
2 July 1600.

Source: The Battle of
Nieuwpoort, 2 July 1600,
reproduced by permission
of Bodley's Librarian,
from Guillame Baudart's
*Second Tome dv livre intitvle
les Guerres de Nassav*
(Amsterdam 1616).

248. Nec mora, mox junctis ALBERTUS viribus, ingens   Qui contra hostiles acpias fudére saluti;

Agmen agit properang annis expendere nostros,   ALBERTO fusa fit, capitur MENDOZA superbus.

Figure 7.5

'On our side, in a manner, the whole loss fell upon the English; of whom, nearly 800 were hurt or slain. Eight [English] Captains were slain; of the rest, all but two were hurt, and most of my inferior officers were hurt or slain. .

. . I dare not take the whole honour of the victory to the poor English troop of 1,600 men; but leave it to be judged by those that may give their censure, with less suspicion of partiality.

I will only affirm that they left nothing for the rest of the army to do, but to follow the chase: and that it hath not been heard of, that, by so small a number, in a ground so indifferent, whereof the only advantage was the choice and use of the same, without help of spade or other instrument or engine of fortifying, so great and so victorious an army as the Archduke's had been so long wrestled withal, and so far spent.' – Sir Francis Vere.

Source: The Battle of Nieuwpoort, 2 July 1600, reproduced by permission of Bodley's Librarian, from Guillame Baudart's *Second Tome du livre intitle les Guerres de Nassau* (Amsterdam 1616).

a withdrawal from war.[78] As we shall see, the Irish theatre (one component of global anti-Spanish operations) consumed more and more of her treasure. And, although James may have trimmed expenditures, England was still deeply involved in continental wars.[79]

When James I and Philip III signed Articles of Peace agreed upon 18 August 1604, British soldiers remained in garrison in Flushing, Brill, Rammekins, and elsewhere. And, although these Protestant troops were forbidden by Article VIII from providing war *matériel* to the 'Hollanders', the cautionary towns still lay in British hands, and James's subjects still marched (albeit 'privately') in Protestant armies. The peace with Spain was strategically useful, as direct confrontation between the powers was avoided, and trade restored. But the revolt of the Netherlands continued, with Englishmen still playing an important role.[80] The Brill and Flushing garrisons, for example, contained 1,398 English soldiers in 1607–9. Garrison duty translated into active campaigning when the Cleves-Jülich war ignited, 1610–12.[81] When the castle of Ilsbo ('Elsborow') in Sweden was besieged in May 1612, 'all the englishe companies fell to the assault'.[82] England continued to buttress the Protestant alliance in the wars of religion, alongside her Scottish cousins.[83]

While armed Englishmen defended Dutch Protestants, armed Dutchmen guarded East Anglia. The City of Norwich, in the Jacobean era, incorporated militia companies of Dutchmen and Walloons (the latter sometimes described as Frenchmen) amongst the trained bands. In 1595, the Norwich militia boasted 409 Dutchmen and 358 Walloons/French, serving under their own commanders.[84] In 1611, the commanders included 325 Dutch and 282 Walloons.[85] Under Elizabeth I, in the spirit of the Protestant cause and the diplomatic, commercial, and religious ties between the Netherlands and England, the Dutch congregations had shouldered arms in defence of the beleaguered isle that sheltered them. The practice persisted into the reign of Charles I.[86]

The English school of war

Who were the Queen's professional soldiers? Military history requires a human face, so a dozen or so biographical sketches seem justified. Captain Christopher Levens had gone abroad as a private soldier and fought at St Denis. He appears at the siege of Le Havre, and then inside the Berwick garrison around 1568. The next year's rebellion gave him the opportunity to become a cornet. Garrison duty on the Borders must have been a drab existence for him, for Levens sojourned to the Low Countries and participated in the storming of Brill and other sieges. He was at the revolt of Flushing and moved from garrison to garrison, promoted to ensign and then Sergeant Major of 'Gerttrambarge'[Geertruidenberg], where he developed a reputation as a victualling specialist. Soon he was a vice admiral, through his victualling experience, and captain of his 'owne gallie'. He thus 'continewed by Sea and Land' until the arrival of the Spanish. Levens also served in the Portugal expedition. His extensive service meant that he incurred wounds: he was maimed by cannon shot, suffered an injured arm near Amsterdam around the time of the siege of Haarlem, and sustained various shooting injuries in his back, at the siege of Middelburg and elsewhere.

The rebellion of 1569 also provided an opportunity for Captain Roger Hussey, who after pursuing the rebels into Scotland then signed on for a tour of duty in the Low Countries. As a gentleman volunteer, Hussey accompanied 'Tholde' Earl of Essex into Ireland, and then traversed back to the Continent, serving alongside Sir Edward Stanley in the French King's guard ('at the time of Sir Amias Pallets imbassage'). The Captain returned to Ireland as a horseman under Lord Grey, and then went to France and the Low Countries, and travelled with the Portugal expedition. He rounded off his career in Essex's Normandy campaign. Although thrice wounded, Hussey still begged service of the Queen. Captain Henry Ward perambulated similarly, from Ireland to the Low Countries, and then inherited the captaincy of Chatterton's company when the latter was slain.

Lieutenant William Mortimer fought for Crown and country for thirty-four years, in Scotland, at Le Havre, in Ireland under the Earl of Sussex, in Berwick garrison, in Ireland again, in the Low Countries, back in Ireland for a third tour, and in France, settling finally in the English garrison at Bergen-op-Zoom as a cavalryman. Lieutenant James Metcalf started out at Berwick, followed a gentleman's troop of horse into Ireland, then embarked for the Low Countries wars, where he rose to ensign and then a lieutenancy. A veteran of the Portugal expedition, he fought in the Normandy campaign. Lieutenant Edward Flood also claimed service in Ireland, the Low Countries, Portugal, and Normandy. Lieutenant Timothie Felding enlisted for the Low Countries, served at Berwick, returned to the Netherlands, signed with Sir Francis Drake for 'Cales' (Cadiz), and became one of Drake's sea dogs. He took part in Portugal, voyaged to Ireland as a gentleman under Sir John Norris, went to Normandy, and 'after that in the voyage for Sir Walter Raleigh Knight from the beginning to the ending'. Injured at the defeat of Don Juan of Austria, Felding also received wounds fighting the Spaniards in the Narrow Seas, personifying the marine warrior of the Elizabethan era.

Sergeant Major James Johnson saw first blood in the 1569–70 rebellion, also fighting in Ireland, the Low Countries, Normandy, and Brittany, including a stint in the Polish army. Lieutenant Richard Fletcher, too, gained his initial experience in 1569–70, going on to the Low Countries and serving Sir Roger Williams among others. After the Portugal expedition, he became one of Sir Francis Vere's gentleman soldiers in the Low Countries. Lieutenant Richard Newell, too, mixed theatres – the Low Countries, Portugal, and Brittany. Lieutenant William West fought his way through the

Low Countries, under Sir John Norris, Willoughby and others, moved into Flanders and the Brabant, fought with Essex in Normandy, and was then promoted to Provost Marshal under Sir Roger Williams. His shoulder was broken at the siege of Bergen-op-Zoom, and he reinjured it in the French campaign. Lieutenant John Price followed a similar tour: he went to the Low Countries, joined Willoughby's force in France, became a Lieutenant in the Irish theatre, and 'after that trailed a pike' under Essex in Normandy.

Lieutenant Rowland Hempson wandered from Ireland to Bergen to Ostend and on to France. Lieutenant Robert Deckham's career also showed the amphibious nature of Elizabethan soldiers. Rising through the ranks in Ireland to become a sergeant, he signed for Captain Cecil's 'Indians voyage' and subsequently for another journey to Santo Domingo. Liking the salt air, he joined on with Sir Francis Drake for a while, later participating in another voyage 'off Cartagena'. After the Portugal campaign, Deckham 'served voluntarily' under Sir John Norris in Brittany. Lieutenant James Jones, too, went from land service in the Low Countries, Ireland, and France to participate in an 'Indians voyage'. Numerous lieutenants under the Earl of Essex in Normandy had extensive Irish, Dutch, and Portuguese experience. Lieutenant William Wood was one of these, counting two years' cavalry service in Ireland, a stint as a sergeant to Sir Henry Norris, before being promoted to ensign and then lieutenant. As one of Leicester's horsemen in the 1585 Low Countries expedition, Wood went on to serve Willoughby and Sir Francis Vere, though shot and injured numerous times.

Sir Roger Williams, like Essex and the Norrises, seems to have collected such men under his banner. When he recruited Lieutenant Richard Eures, the latter boasted experience in the Low Countries, Portugal, France, and then Normandy under Williams. Ensign George Orrel signed on to go to Nuremberg, then latched on to Sir Philip Sydney, abandoning the Low Countries later, first for the Portugal expedition and then for a voyage with the Earl of Cumberland as a 'marine'. Ensigns and sergeants, like the captains and lieutenants, peregrinated from theatre to theatre, from land to sea and back. Often they were following a given captain. These men provide specific evidence that a mobile and enterprising cadre of English profes- sional soldiers made its impact on warfare in the late 1500s.[87]

Veterans personified English warfare as they spent their final years amongst their neighbours, supported by maimed-soldier funds that, significantly, were financed by the community not the Crown. In Wiltshire, 85-year-old Robert Rolls, a disabled veteran of Low Countries wars, and Sergeant George Smythe (who had fought his way through Ireland, the Denmark campaign, the Palatinate relief efforts, Cadiz, and the Isle of Rhé) served as reminders that the Personal Rule followed decades of brutal warfare, a peace for which each English community had paid a price in blood.[88] One of Captain Wigmore's troopers had also fought in Ireland and the Low Countries, then fell at Jülich: Thomas Hamelyn was 'hurt with a shott' at the assault on Jülich. Both men spent the following years as maimed soldiers, living in Wiltshire at the public cost.[89] Serving Protestant allies might have been seen by the Crown as 'having done the dutie of honest men', but upon return to England, the volunteers were best kept out of sight and out of mind. The men were ordered out of the metropolis and back to their own shires, as was the policy with pressed men. The invisibility of the continental veterans was promoted by regimes that were never entirely comfortable with martial men and the changing nature of English warfare.[90]

English 'voluntaries' and mercenaries (for contemporaries observed a distinction), under acclaimed commanders such as Sir Horace Vere, participated actively in continental wars in the decade preceding the outbreak of the Thirty Years War[91] and later. When James I contemplated sending 20,000 infantry, 5,000 cavalry, and a score of cannon to the Palatinate in January 1621, it was to Vere and his compatriots that he turned for advice.[92] Vere made peace, as a general in the service of the King of Great Britain, before the citadel of Mannheim on 2 November 1622.[93] By 1622, then, English arms had played a crucial, probably indispensable role in the survival of Protestantism. Britain had escaped foreign invasion, and in the process, since 1572 especially, the English had learnt a great deal about the art of war, particularly logistics and artillery.

8

ORDNANCE AND LOGISTICS, 1511–1642

The English and continental siegecraft

It is now commonplace to contrast the crenellated medieval fortified wall, comparatively high and thin, with the squat yet formidable bastion of the military revolution. So when Sir John Smythe in the 1590s, contemporaneous with the Duke of Parma's glory days, compared Edward III's siege of Calais (September 1346–August 1347) with Parma's circumvallation of Antwerp (July 1584–August 1585), he might have drawn contrasts between medieval and modern siegecraft. But Smythe, who had never read Michael Roberts' 1956 military revolution lecture, stressed the universality of the military predicament. For all the furore surrounding the development of siege ordnance, Smythe queried just how much it had in fact altered the nature and outcome of warfare. Improvements in the offensive power of cannon had been matched, indeed, overcome, by innovation in fortification that harnessed artillery's power for defensive purposes. But that did not necessarily mean that warfare had entered a new era. Synthesis returned siegecraft to its starting point, proving that noble Roman, ambitious Plantagenet, and the modern commander still shared the common concern: to take the stronghold with as few casualties as possible. In spite of the improvements in the defensive nature of warfare afforded by the adoption of the bastion, offensive capabilities increased correspondingly. The angled protrusions that extended from the bastion provided protection for musketeers and cannoneers to lay down devastating enfilading fire. Attacking infantry found themselves cut down by flanking fire on both sides. Thus the defence of a bastion was offensive in its infliction of a high rate of casualties upon besiegers.[1]

Gunpowder exploded the old cyclical conceptualisation of the art of war, exalting the grimy artilleryman as the personification of 'modern warfare'. But, because the evolution of practice and field application was slow, almost imperceptible to some old soldiers, some asked whether or not cannon indeed made military conflict 'decisive'. Sir John Smythe conceded that '. . . the Cannon and Culverin, and other peices of batterie do exceed and excell the effects of Rams, and other such auncient Engines against the fortificacion of these times. . . .'[1a] Henry VIII's French sieges, and the combined operations of Maurice of Nassau with his English allies in the 1590s, showed how ordnance in the hands of a determined commander could reduce a town or fortress in dramatic fashion. The incorporation of the offensive capability of artillery into a defensive scheme made possible the *trace italienne* with its gun platforms and thicker walls. But that transformation did not render the besieger impotent; it simply increased the time and material necessary to batter and/or intimidate the besieged to surrender. Smythe went on to make a historical comparison. The investment of Calais by Edward III constituted classic medieval siege-craft, while the Duke of Parma's fourteen-month circumvallation of Antwerp was an example of contemporary warfare. In spite of the availability of increasingly destructive artillery, both Edward and Parma chose to pursue a strategy '. . . rather by famine than by approaches and consumption of their people'.[1b] Advances in offensive capability were met by corresponding improvements in defence: 'from the first creation of the world until now the very same, the disposition of the people only varying in the difference of weapons, engines, and instruments, which have been invented'.[2] A wise general did not waste good infantry in a siege, and cannon had not changed that reality. In both eras, these exemplary commanders starved out the garrison of a fortified place, rather than waste the lives of their soldiers. The fact that siege guns were greater in Parma's time, and defences more formidable, had not changed a basic fact of warfare.

Smythe's emphasis on defence, on fortification over artillery, recalls Machiavelli,[2a] which underscores how much English military thinkers (even those labelled as idiosyncratically English in the extreme, such as Smythe) were imbued with a neo-classical view of war.[3] The 'moderns', from Sir Roger Williams to Geoffrey Parker, though opining that gunpowder had qualitatively changed warfare forever, recognised that the Low Countries wars revolved around defensive engagements. But the implication that the predominance of defence made war 'indecisive' is far from a logical conclusion. Machiavelli's celebrated remark that 'No wall exists, however thick, that artillery cannot destroy in a few days' was made in a very specific context, based on slim historical experience. Besiegers had to worry over defence of their works as much as did the besieged. English forces before Berck in June 1601 took pride in making their encroachments unassailable.

> As our approaches toward the counterscarp have been leisurely carried forward, so are they made in stronger and more defensive fashion than the oldest soldier amongst us can remember: double trenches, with rampart and parapet, and every 60 paces a court of guard, flanking every curtain of the trench, so that the enemy have

never been so hardy as to attempt forcing the trenches; twice or thrice they sallied, but finding us prepared upon our first volley made retreat. . . . The enemy, in the heat of his admirable courage, sallied some 200 on a battery; had they not been stoutly resisted they had gained much honour. The works are admirable to my experience, neither have I redd of the lyke to have bene made by any butt Caesar.[4]

The English, whose strategical goal was defensive, delighted in their skill in making siegeworks perfectly defensive.

What made the English so adept at siege warfare were (1) English ordnance, (2) Anglo-Welsh miners and sappers, (3) English assault infantry, (4) English gunpowder, and (5) English field leadership. The English proved splendid allies for a siege-centred war. The engineering expertise of John Rogers, Sir Richard Lee, and Sir Henry Lee[5] had, by the 1590s, matured into an English school of military fortification, best personified by Paul Ive, who not only constructed defences (for example, at Pendennis Castle in 1598–9) but proliferated knowledge through succinct and widely circulated publications.[6] The flexibility that characterised the English art of war meant that other nations turned to England for pioneers who could be recruited for mining (especially from the West Country), shock troops for assaulting breaches, and infantry and cavalry easily transferred from garrison to field duty. And even more than men, English powder and artillery were sought after.

Although siegecraft varied amongst theatres, the Low Countries wars, which Smythe so reviled, were instructive, as were England's combined operations with Henry IV. The example of Sluys has been discussed above. The treachery and trap at Bergen-op-Zoom (1588) showed the face of this guerrilla war that sometimes pitted Protestant Englishmen against Catholic Englishmen in the trenches. Vere's relief of Rheinberg (1597) and occupation of Breda illustrated different aspects of English siegecraft, including the taking of the fort at Büderich. Steenwyjk (1580–2) and Coevorden (1594), too, demonstrated English expertise. At the latter action, English troops forced the Spanish to abandon high ground. The successes in and around Crevecoeur (1590) and Geertruidenberg (spring 1593) owed much to the mobility of Protestant artillery, and the bombardment's intensity in routing Spanish infantry from entrenched positions.[6a]

In the spring of 1593, the English took the southern approach to the fortifications at Geertruidenberg. Following extensive circumvallation, a relief column appeared in late May. Six hundred English troops (with the assistance of a thousand Frisian infantry) met the Catholic forces, turned them back, and compelled the town's surrender. Sir Francis Vere then marched his men northwards out of the Brabant, repelling Spanish attacks, and settled into winter quarters, where a siege of Groningen was planned.[6b]

Through the spring of 1594 the English continued to prove their expertise. The Groningen campaign exhibited those characteristics that made Low Countries warfare so gruelling: rapid deployment and mobility (in which infantry could not lag too far behind the horsemen) from troops forced to endure the sedentary weariness of garrison duty in a theatre of war where night assaults (*camisados*), urban conspiracy, and long sieges were common. Vere's soldiers scrambled into action often, in joint operations with non-English Protestant units and sometimes with the English garrison of Ostend.[6c] These manoeuvres were intended to configure Prince Maurice's forces for siegecraft, in this case an investment of Groningen.

The action at Groningen also saw heroics from the Scots, who swarmed upon the defenders after the subterranean demolition of a ravelin. In fierce hand-to-hand combat, those not slain by explosion were dispatched by Scottish blades or drowned. Substantial carnage occurred in the English trenches, too. A sally by the besieged cut off Captain Wray's company and virtually annihilated it, along with the commander. Sir Edward Brook was shot 'through the point of the right shoulder. The bullet cut out at his back, which when he was opened was through his lungs.' Captains Bell and Swan also received wounds from the gunfire. And two of Vere's company captains met their end. The siege claimed the blood and lives of many 'lieutenants, ensigns, and gentlemen'.[7] War in the United Provinces was brutal and dirty, and the high percentage of casualties suffered by unit commanders (and no doubt non-commissioned officers as well) gave the war the nasty reputation cited by Sir John Smythe.[8] As Sir Philip Sydney discovered, artillery and firearms brought down the best of men in grisly fashion. Vere himself was to be severely wounded at Ostend.[9]

The notion that siege warfare had removed war from the immediacy of the field of battle into the mire of the trenches, thus making combat 'indecisive', obscures the dynamism of so-called defensive warfare. The siege of Ostend (1601–4)[10] exemplifies the frenetic pace of siege operations. Days and nights were filled with desperate preparations and actions, and, even when the combatants' positions remained fairly stationary, victory (hence 'decisiveness'), was still within reach, almost daily. The siege

> was almost as uncertain at the last day as at the first, to which side victory did incline. The besieged never wanted fresh succours by Sea [though Vere's famous 'parley' proves otherwise] nor did the besiegers at any time cease advancing by Land [though moving at a snail's pace at times]. Infinite were the Batteries, the Assaults infinite; so many were the Mines, and so obstinate the Countermines. . . .[11]

Hostilities at Ostend dragged on for three years, because both sides were close to victory. At various junctures (for example, the assault of 7 January 1602) the confrontation might have been decided by the sword.

In the summer of 1601 Ostend became the focal point of the Eighty Years War.[12] Strategically, Catholic Europe took a great risk when it lavished hundreds of thousands of ducats (and tens of thousands of soldiers) upon Archduke Albert, hoping he would evict the Ostenders from Belgic soil. It was not certain that Ostend could be isolated, and hence the naval and commercial strength of the Protestants neutralised. To lay a siege when succour from the sea could not be prevented meant that the enemy's avenues of supply might sustain the garrison indefinitely. Ironically, the concentration of the resources of the contending sides upon a single point on the map should have brought a decisive outcome to the war. Even prolonged struggles such as the Hundred Years War experienced turning points (e.g. Agincourt) that did much to decide the outcome of the struggle.[13] As the siege consumed ever more human beings and *matériel*, the United Provinces stubbornly grasped their last foothold in the Flemish Netherlands. Equally resolutely, the Catholic forces determined to rid that land of heresy and turn the tide against the Protestant Low Countries. The Auditor of Ostend, Phillip Fleming, a careful and honest observer, estimated Catholic losses by the spring of 1603 to have reached 18,000 men, and the besieged between 6,000 and 7,000.[14]

The first phase of the siege can be described fairly as an English engagement because of the participation of several thousand English troops and the supervision of a distinguished English commander. Sir Francis Vere formulated Ostend's strategic defence, and the tempo of its struggle with the besiegers, from the moment of his arrival. On 5 July 1601,[15] Vere landed 12–14 veteran English companies on the beach of Ostend. With 29 Dutch companies already ensconced, the garrison numbered about 3,500.[16] English reinforcements, and English beer, were factors in the decision to hold Ostend at all costs. Since spring the States had pestered Elizabeth for 3,000 London recruits who would 'be in the Low countreys' by 10 May 1601.[17] The Queen did not disappoint her allies: 1,500 in 'red cassackes' arrived at Ostend in late July, and were assigned duty amongst the veteran companies. The troops dug in, in a fashion that precursed the First World War: 'The English men made the greene market place within the Towne hollow, fitting themselves with cabbines and lodgings in the earth, and they made hollow another void place vpon the Southwest'. Two thousand more men came from England on 20 August. Along with soldiers arrived a stream of victuals. With Vere's defensive improvements, 200 ships could shelter, their masts drawn down for safety, within the moat or 'ditch' before the town.[18]

In response, the Archduke showered Ostend with 'fiery Bullets', 'Flints', 'artificiall Bullets', 'little vesselles full of Nailes and Bullets chained together', though many wounds seem to have been caused by cannonballs carrying away pieces of defenders' bodies. '50 great peeces of brasse' fired 35,000 rounds by 17 August, 'yet could never make a breach'.[19] On 10 September the youthful nobleman Chatillon, who had fought gallantly at Nieuwpoort, stood on the high bulwark of the Porcupine fort, and '. . . had his head strooke of [off] with a Canon shotte aboue the teeth, his braines flew against the left cheeke of Colonell Vehtenbruch [Uchtenbroek], and made hime to reele a little. . . .'[20] A testament to the thunderous barrages at Ostend is the petition of gunner Richard Sommer, who sought relief (upon certificate from Sir Francis Vere) in his native Wiltshire. Sommer had gone deaf from the 'noyse of the gonne shottes' at the siege.[21]

Ostend's interlocking defences utilised tides, sluices, ordnance hidden in counterscarps, countermines, and daring sallies against the attackers, all of which owed much to the wisdom of Vere, as he was happy to acknowledge. Scores of vessels navigated the Ostend haven, and they not only carried reinforcements and victuals, but took ordnance out of the town for repair, returning with refurbished cannon, powder, shot, and all the habiliments of war. In fact, the besieged had better guns, and more guns, and they were able to repair theirs with greater facility than Archduke Albert could maintain his batteries.[22] Contrary to Cardinal Bentivoglio's account, the ships plying the waters between Ostend and the Protestant world were sometimes unable to enter the haven for weeks at a time. The Catholic gunners, despite the proximity of their emplacements to the shipping channels, rarely sank or even damaged the relief vessels, unless of course the boats ran aground. But the sea, which battered all fortifications and drowned a goodly number of men on both sides, seems to have kept the supply ships at bay, sometimes for weeks. The conduct of the defence included, too, counter-intelligence and deception, which ranged from the kidnapping and interrogation of enemy sentries to Vere's celebrated 'anti-parle' with the Archduke.[23]

Vere's 'parley' came about two days before Christmas 1601, when contrary winds had debarred reinforcements and supplies from Ostend harbour. Attrition had reduced the English contingent to about 800 soldiers, and the allies, too, found their companies seriously understrength. Consequently, the Archduke's forces had crept steadily forward, infiltrating and seizing the outworks. Alerted to the likelihood of a major assault on the night of the 23rd, Vere grasped at a ploy that might rescue the garrison from being overrun in a matter of hours. Conferring with his allies, he proposed to enter into negotiations with the Archduke, realising that, if the Spanish forces could take Ostend without further loss, they might jump at the chance. In all fairness to Vere, who might be accused of dealing in something less than good faith, it should be recollected that the Spaniards had perpetrated a much greater fraud in 1588, proffering peace while the Armada made ready. After presenting two English hostages, Captains Ogle and Fairfax, Vere protracted the negotiations to 25 December. A 'Protestant wind' then blew three Dutch warships, loaded with troops and what would be Christmas dinner for Ostend, into the harbour. The Catholic hopes were dashed; Vere recovered his hostages and resumed the defence. The point is that wily leadership on Vere's part (and he was more a field commander than a specialist in siegecraft) saved Ostend.[24]

An enraged Archduke Albert on 7 January 1602 assaulted all fortified positions simultaneously (Sand Hill, the Porcupine, the East and West Ravelins, South Carre, etc.).[25] Vere, having repaired and remanned his outerworks, now steeled the garrison for the predictable assault. Hand-choosing the units that would hold the critical forts, he laid traps for the stormers, who by darkness scaled and enfiladed their way into Ostend. With the tide low and some of the positions deliberately left vulnerable to entice the enemy, the Protestants waited quietly. Four thousand enemy soldiers swarmed up the works of the Sand Hill fort, and groups similarly equipped with iron scaling ladders and weapons for hand-to-hand fighting mounted other key works. On Vere's signal, fires were ignited, illuminating the assault. The besieged opened fire upon the massed attackers, with devastating effect.

An eyewitness recorded the carnage:

> Generall Vere had caused two double canons to be planted that day vpon the flankes of the West port, with some other peeces that were there before, the which with others, did scoure along the Sand-hil and the West Rauelin, and played vpon the comming and returne of the enemies, and whilest the assault continued, they charged them with chaines and nailes, and little sacks full of Musket Bullets, which made a great slaughter, so as there was a pittiful crie of hurt men and dying, and the Souldiers fell one vpon an other pel mel. The enemie being hotte at the assault, and the water risen, Generall Vere caused the sluces to be taken vp, the which did coole the enemies courage: and he (growing more and more assured) charged them and put them to flight, recouering all their ladders, bridges and other instruments. . . . All about the Sand-hill euen vnto the old Church, and all about the Porke-espike [Porcupine], in the West Raulein, and in the English trenches, all was full of dead bodies: I speake not of those that were slaine going and comming by the Canon charged with chaines and small shot, nor of those that were drowned, some of whose bodies were carried along the shoare euen vnto Calais.[26]

The Spaniards who had been permitted to capture Ostend's half-moon outerwork were now cut off and massacred. Fifteen hundred corpses littered the ground, and, with an estimate of another 500 drowned or carried away by comrades, 25 per cent of the Archduke's army had been obliterated. Vere's 'murthering peeces caused the enemies to fall, as rotten ripe apples from the trees in a mighty storme'.[27]

The siege of Ostend demonstrated that Europeans regarded the English as respected colleagues in the science of siegecraft. Given the English record during the wars of religion, and the popularity of English guns, powder, and pioneers, the English gained a reputation in this kind of warfare, and there was a proliferation of English works on artillery (such as those of the Digges family and later Robert Norton) that paralleled the continuing manufacture of cast-iron ordnance in Sussex and elsewhere. English specialisation in the manufacture and use of cast-iron guns stemmed from that weapon's affordability and local provenance. Swedish and Danish cannon, cast from inferior iron, were not worth the investment. Henrician militarisation of trades such as carriagemaking and shipbuilding manifested itself in domestic production of armour[28] and, perhaps most dramatically, the proliferation of English iron cannon amongst European armies.

English ordnance was exported duty-free, with permission of the Crown, by warrant under the Sign Manual.[29] For example, in August 1590 the States General asked licence to purchase 200 English iron guns. Zeeland wanted 150 tons for their ships and pinnaces that guarded streams and the Flemish coast, but 100 tons would probably suffice. The factors thought that the States General would be satisfied with 80 sakers, to be exported now, and 20 falcons (about 100 tons in all) and Zeeland with 60 sakers, 60 minions, 40 falcons (also about 100 tons). As for unlicenced entrepreneurs in England, in the summer of 1590, for example, English gun-runners smuggled iron ordnance into Flushing and elsewhere from Sussex and Kent. A small vessel would lay cannon in its hold, then cover the contraband with timber or some other bulk export. Dutch magistrates urged leniency in allowing artillery to be shipped to the Protestant-controlled Low Countries, and protested that merchants would sell cannon elsewhere. The Queen would gain nothing fiscally and militarily. Sixty pieces came to Middelburg and 19 to Veere in late 1590, sold by Thomas Burbride of Sandwich, who had become a sort of artillery broker. Edward Nicholls of Newhaven in Sussex shipped 17 sakers and minions, and a ton of shot, to Flushing.[30] If artillery was the most progressive branch of what has been called a 'military revolution', then the English were certainly keeping abreast of contemporary military science.

The Ordnance Office and English military architecture

Drawings, tables, and treatises set forth the types of contemporary ordnance, and those distinctively English received attention as a unique category of ordnance, for example in Robert Norton's *The Gunner*, which drew upon (and subsequently generated) a literature of English artillery.[31] Roger Ascham's *Toxophilus*, editions of which appeared in 1545, 1571, and 1589, expounded an art of gunnery, which was then advanced by William Bourne.

Treatises said little about institutional organisation, logistical problems (how to transport cannon over muddied roads, for example), the organisation of artillery trains, or how to store powder and prevent accidental ignition. There existed instructions on how troops should be apparelled and transported, and the duties of artillery train officers, etc. The emphasis lay on responsibilities and regulations rather than upon practical problems.[32] Authors were more intrigued with historical context, geometry, mathematics (designing tables and diagrams), defining nomenclature, testing and positioning ordnance, manufacturing gun carriages, and identifying types of ordnance. Reading contemporary artillery treatises and comparing their recommendations about cannon with the inventories of English fortresses provides a glimpse into the hardware of English warfare under the Tudors and early Stuarts. At the same time that Norton's treatises were being written, considerable attention was being paid to the mounting and positioning of artillery in royal fortresses, reprising Henry VIII's notion of establishing gun platforms along the southern coast.[33]

To apprehend how military architecture and fortification reflected the nature of English warfare, one might select examples from opposite ends of the kingdom: the Tower of London and Berwick-upon-Tweed.[34] To understand the Office of the Ordnance[35] and how it was situated in the changing world of warfare, one must start at the Tower of London.[36] A symbol of the universality of English warfare, its Roman and Norman heritage made it the nucleus of English martial manufacture, storage, and consciousness, to the degree that a decentralised system of defence can have a centre. Despite its strategic location, the Tower complex served more as a storage facility, administrative hub, and symbolic presence than as a defensive structure. Tower accounts record repairs on the 'Bullwarke' and 'Battlements', but under Elizabeth and James, essential maintenance (such as reinforcement of walls and flooring) occurred, but no modernisation of the fortifications on the continental model.[37] In 1607, the Venetian ambassador sniffed at the Tower's defences and its lack of bastions.[38]

In 1620, as today, the Tower celebrated its place at the heart of the Crown's military organisation. In that year, that most gentle of kings, James I, attempted the urban renewal and restoration of the Tower precincts. The Privy Council's statement of its intent deserves quotation at length, as it describes the Tower, warts and all, and demonstrates the edifice's centrality as a manifestation of England's ability to wage war:

> Whereas the Tower of London being his Majesties Royall Castle, one of the principall and most eminent Forts of this Kingdom, a great strength and Ornament to the Citie, the Chiefe Storehouse and Magazen of Warlike provisions of this Kingdom hath annciently been fortifyed, not only within the Walls, Ditches and Wharfe of the same, but also such care taken in the Minorits [Minories] and

other neigbouring places, as well for the Lodging and receipt of the principall officers of the Ordenaunce, as likewise for Artificers, Gonmakers, Wheelers, and other whose Trades be appropriate to Military ends as nothing was there almost wanting which was fit for the State to provide. . . . [I]n these latter times either through the evill Example or tolleration of some Lieutenants of the Tower or by abusing of Trust reposed in some Officers, who have particular relation to that place there hath insensibly crept in divers abuses and encroachments whereby the antient Lymitts of the Tower and those other habitants and storehouses appointed for publick use are now perverted to private profitt, the Splendor and magnificence of the said Royal Castle, being by that meanes defaced, and the place it self as it were beseiged in the Wharfe, Ditches and Liberties thereof.[38a]

The Tower comprised a complex community, though its reputation as a prison and place of death may well have tainted its military function. Elizabeth I never set foot there during her long reign, presumably because the edifice housed traumatic memories for her. Nor was it the kind of architectural space that would have attracted cerebral monarchs such as the first two Stuarts. It must have been a place of cold stone, muddy boots, clanking metal, and damp. With prison keepers intermingled with military craftsmen and administrators, it was the haunt of pragmatic and deliberate men.

The White Tower, or Caesar's Tower as it was sometimes known before the Civil War, lay entirely within the control of the Ordnance Office, it being '. . . in use for the cheife Battery and Storehowse for the Magazine'.[39] The rows of bronze and iron ordnance that spelt the end of medieval fortification sheltered inside the old Norman keep, along with barrels upon barrels of powder. As inventories grew, additional space for storing cannon was found in the Minories, the lanes and shops surrounding the Tower, where workmen and artisans carried on munitions-related crafts.[40] The contents of the Tower in 1620 included 348 bronze ordnance, ranging from 20 great guns (with a bore of 7–8 inches), 16 demi-cannon (with a bore of 6½ inches), 36 culverins, to miscellaneous artillery. Of cast-iron ordnance, 90 guns lay about, probably on the ground floor of the White Tower. Whereas the bronze cannon were 'mounted' and 'serviceable', the iron guns were 'dismounted'. As for small arms, the office possessed 8,209 muskets, 2,577 'furnished' calivers, 18 old harquebuses, and 484 'Long French Pistolls'. Long pikes numbered 9,102, short pikes 3,908. Edged pole weapons, shot, tools, and the usual accoutrements were stored up as well, plus more miscellaneous firearms, and 'unserviceable' arms (which included 4,048 bows and bowstaves).[41]

The Master of the Ordnance 'lodged in the Brick Tower,[42] adjoining the Armoury'. The clerk who kept accounts for the Lieutenant of the

Ordnance resided near a 'green mount' in the vicinity of Martin Tower. Beside the chapel stood a tower named after the Ordnance Office itself, with two 'London-style' towers behind, though it is not clear in what capacity the latter pair were used. The chapel area was situated near the Beauchamp (sometimes called 'Cobham') Tower. Also within the precinct was an 'Artillery tower', which may have safeguarded the records of the Ordnance Office, as it was also known as the 'Records Tower'.[43] These documents were kept not far from the 'Bluddy tower' (also known as the Wakefield Tower, where more documents were housed).[44] Manuscripts were also kept in the Chapel of St John and elsewhere. The practice of storing arms and records within the Tower precinct had gone on for centuries. During the reign of Henry VI a more systematic approach to storage and administration was proposed in a petition, recommending that '. . . as ther is noon housing certaynly assigned for youre ordenaunce to be kept, for lak wherof their hath growe grete hurt and dayly doth unto the said ordenaunce and other stuffe [be]longing to his said office. . . .' As a result, Henry VI granted a sizeable area from the shore, from the 'Traitors' Gate' (Watergate) to St Catherine's Tower, for the use of the Master of the King's Ordnance. The actual offices of the Ordnance lay behind St Peter's Chapel, in the northwest corner of the precincts. Sadly, during the reign of James II renovations dismantled these edifices.[45]

The walls of the Tower, kept sturdy under the eye of the Clerk of the King's Works (or Surveyor), encircled the most precious royal resources, save for the person of the monarch (as few used it as a royal residence any longer). The Crown's plate, jewels, weapons, and coinage lay within precincts whose military architecture remained almost intact during the period covered by this book. The Crown jewels were dangerously close to the stores of powder and shot. It was suggested, in 1623, that the magazine be relocated.[46] Oddly enough it was Henry VIII, whose designs for the southeastern castles had resisted so stubbornly the influence of the *trace italienne*, who undertook the building of bulwarks at the northern corners of the Tower's outer ward, during the first two decades of his reign. An inventory of 1531–2 records their restoration, including the reference, 'The bullwark as aforsayd to be new rough caste with mortar, the which for said bulwark stondith be hynde the Mynte.' The roof of the White Tower was also used as a gun platform during the reign of the Tudors.[47] The outlying bulwarks were fifteenth-century additions that possibly even pre-dated the accession of the Tudors. Even if this is the case it emphasises the conservative nature (and idiosyncrasies) of English military architecture.

The improvement of the residential quarters of the Master of the Ordnance reflected the growing importance of the Office, and provided an incentive for the Master to dwell at the Tower. As long as the bureaucratic apparatus of the Office necessitated the signature of the Master, his presence within the precincts sped up the paperwork and improved efficiency. 'Apart from the reconstruction of the Brick Tower as a residence for the Master of the Ordnance, which probably took place during the decade 1510–20, only one tower is known to have been entirely built or rebuilt between 1485 and 1660.' The upsurge in the tempo of military activity in 1511–12 is also evident in the Tower. The Master of the Ordnance (Sir Sampson Norton) and the deputy lieutenant of the Tower collaborated in 'the repairing amending and finishing of a tower standing on the back syde of the house of the Ordnance within the Tower of London'.[48] The Ordnance House, by that we assume is meant what in the 1641 survey was labelled the Ordnance Tower, was at the forefront of Henry VIII's attempt to restore England as a great military power.

Sea power and artillery, increasingly closely linked through the sixteenth century, required maturing bureaucratic establishments.[49] Henrician government in the 1540s made full use of committees, and the delegation of collective leadership translated into more permanent military establishments. The essential structure of the Ordnance Office, with the Master, Lieutenant, Treasurer, Surveyor, and Clerk, mirrored the institutionalisation of the Navy Board. Synchronising the timetables of the Ordnance with the needs of the Royal Navy became increasingly complicated, and from the period after the massive expeditions of the 1540s up to the year of the Portugal expedition (1589) the Navy enjoyed a liaison, a Master of the Naval Ordnance, who linked the Navy Board with the Ordnance Office. From 1546 to 1589, the Navy exercised greater autonomy in obtaining guns and munitions, but the centralised system drew the Navy back to administration from the Tower.[50] A central foundation made possible regional outposts such as local arms depots and dockyards. Yet, even institutions at the centre remained remarkably decentralised.

The Ordnance Office practised a curious form of subinfeudation, or incestuous subcontracting, via its system of patentees and patronage. Bailiwicks were created, split, alienated, and absorbed. The line between official association with the Crown's military establishment and private enterprise was predictably blurred in the Tudor fashion. Bureaucrats carved out niches within the administration similar to the way in which wheelwrights and foundrymen erected shacks and workshops propped up against the walls of the Tower. Sir Roger Dallison, who had been Lieutenant of the Ordnance, had negotiated a 60-year lease in his own name on various houses in Minories ('mynoritts') and then rented them out to private persons engaged in the arms market. Sir Thomas Monson, Master of the Armoury, had done likewise in the Tower wharf, Tower ditch, portcullis and postern gates. In effect they created their own 'company town', where the gunmakers, wheelers, and the like occupied (and in some cases, erected) domiciles and workshops, for which they paid rent to the very same men for whose offices they manufactured habiliments of war. These arrangements bred corruption and a plethora of unsightly and flammable shops. The Council and judges ruled the leases void and cleared the area.[51]

The proliferation of small arms, particularly handguns, spawned by 1576 an 'office of the keeper of the small guns', which became a sinecure of the Paulfreyman family in the late Elizabethan–early Jacobean period. Richard Paulfreyman's tenure (1599–1610) saw him retain his £20 per annum position as a clerk within the Ordnance Office (the keeper's salary was £50 per annum). The actual maintenance of the pistols and the like fell to a pair of £12 per annum assistants, though much of the work was consigned to London gunmakers. Thus pluralism, nepotism, and dependence upon the private sector (with the predictable complications regarding fixed rates, commissions, and bribes) kept the Ordnance Office from becoming 'professionalised'. The keeper of the small guns, and the Office of the Ordnance in general, regularly endured charges of corruption, price-fixing, and embezzlement as a result.[52]

The crux of the problem was resources. Perhaps the resilience of medieval institutionalism and the longevity of a royal-household approach to administration, which could be (under optimal conditions) both cheap and efficient, obliged England to keep its military establishment decentralised. Until the Civil War it worked remarkably well. But the management of a decentralised system meant that adequate time and sensible strategies had to be taken into consideration when preparing for war, especially campaigning. In this way, Elizabeth's deliberate and piecemeal escalation of the war effort in fact suited the system, though it drove her generals mad and often brought her forces to the brink of disaster.

The Lieutenant of the Ordnance received ordinary revenue from the Exchequer of Receipt via privy seal. All disbursements were then centralised under him and conducted within the Tower, at the 'paiehouse of thordynaunce', under the scrutiny of the Surveyor and Clerk of the Ordnance. Purchases and expenses were 'entrde particulerlie into Two faire Lierger books', today preserved in the Public Record Office. The autonomy of these transactions made the Office vulnerable to charges of embezzlement and concealed bookkeeping.[53] Consequently, the officers tended to act in unison in response to external bureaucracies. Despite the blemishes and erratic performances of its employees, the Ordnance Office got the job done, even with its minuscule budget. Most often, the cannon were delivered and the powder was supplied. Supplying food and clothing to English soldiers, however, was best accomplished by a decentralised system.

Victualling and logistics, 1550–1640

The English practice of arms reached a high level of efficiency in regard to logistics in the years between 1543 and 1550. The gargantuan invasion of France in 1544, coupled with Scottish operations, was followed by

Edwardian successes in the North, including amphibious invasions and the victualling of mobile armies and garrisons on a grand scale. After 1550 the Royal Navy evolved further its permanent infrastructure, such as a commissariat, while land armies dispersed without leaving bureaucratic remnants as institutional legacies.[54]

Clearly the vitality of English agriculture was an advantage, as too were the prosperous port towns and numerous waterways. The English ability to utilise waterborne transport created unusual problems. In a benign and politic attempt to spread the demand for victuals throughout the realm and, perhaps, allow contractors to take advantage of more competitive prices through access to a national rather than strictly regional market, the Crown gathered food throughout England. Although purveyors overcame the Braudellian challenge of distance, they could not guarantee freshness and wholesomeness of their victuals in an age before refrigeration. Thus commanders in Ireland begged Whitehall to compel contractors to purchase cheeses in Cheshire rather than bring them in from the home counties, for too often food spoiled and made ill their troops.

Centralisation of supply was virtually impossible. England managed to fight on many fronts, especially circa 1594–1603, due to the devolution of logistical tasks on a variety of outports and the laying out of a network of land transport routes. The main recruiting grounds for troops for Ireland were London and Yorkshire, and although the western maritime shires also recruited from their inhabitants extensively, the distances involved in getting men and *matériel* aboard ships from Barnstaple to Liverpool, meant that a varied and difficult terrain had to be traversed from the interiors of those shires to the seacoast. Many outports accommodated the shipping of troops and freight beyond their commercial capacities.

English military might was thus delivered into Ireland through ports whose abilities to accommodate government forces and stores varied widely: Chester (the main outport), Bristol (the runner-up), Barnstaple, Plymouth, Southampton, Rochester, Milford, Weymouth, Fowey, and Padstow. But marshalling municipal resources to store temporarily foodstuffs, gather vessels, and lodge unruly soldiers, was only part of the story. The 'Irish Road', or, more accurately, 'Roads', snaked through the English countryside. Wagon trains of ordnance and victuals, as well as columns of disgruntled men, made their way through England's green hills towards an uncertain fate on the other side of the Irish Sea. London contractors and conductors *en route* to Chester probably followed the post road, to St Albans, Brickhill, Towcester, Daventry, Coventry, Lichfield, and Nantwich. Getting to Bristol, convoys meandered through Hounslow, Maidenhead, Reading, Newbury, Marlborough, Chippenham, and finally, Marshfield.[55] Military corridors radiated out from the ports. In 1598 the Norfolk and Northamptonshire contingents surely travelled different routes from, say, the London and Berkshire companies in getting to Chester. Once they were within the municipality, the mayor billeted and fed them, and arranged transport to Ireland.[56] The mayor and municipal authorities assumed an unusual military function when the troops and stores awaited shipping across the Irish Sea. Escorted by halberdiers, the mayor became 'a military agent of the privy council'. He coordinated logistical arrangements, including the capture of deserters. Not only was this a horrific administrative burden; it was physically dangerous, as the mayor of Bristol discovered when rowdy troops stoned him.[57]

Seafaring men and shipowners proved equally unmanageable, for there was usually more to be earned from commercial maritime enterprise than from ferrying soldiers to Ireland. To assist the mayors in browbeating sailors and merchants, the Privy Council appointed what were effectively government transport supervisors, who monitored vessel availability and intervened to requisition crews and sturdy craft.[58] Barnstaple specialised in scrounging up transports, a task that benefited the town's depressed maritime economy. But Barnstaple appears to have been anomalous. The continental wars had disrupted trade with European ports at a time when England was venturing into the lucrative carrying trade. A combination of the vitality of London's merchant companies, and sporadic piracy near the West Country and eastern ports, contributed to the declining fortunes of these coastal towns. Most often the employment generated by the government's Irish campaigns compensated poorly for the loss of trade. Masters of ships operating out of Barnstaple got two to four shillings per ton per month for serving as military transports. In Bristol an arrangement to charge ten shillings per soldier for transport to Ireland was disapproved of as being too expensive. The private sector made money from the Irish Wars, but shipowners and crews got a pitiful percentage of the profits.[59]

The mayors sometimes found themselves at cross purposes with private contractors. The multiple system pitted municipal government against Crown agents drawn from the private sector as all parties scoured the countryside competing for foodstuffs for the royal army.[60] For example, in 1560 Roger Johns, the mayor of Bristol, stockpiled wheat and malt from Somersetshire, Gloucestershire, and Monmouthshire. The victuals were transported along with 200 soldiers under Captain Cust directly to the Lord Deputy, the Earl of Sussex. The money to requisition the food had been put up by the Queen and paid through John Aylworthe, Her Majesty's Receiver of Revenues for West Country shires. Though Johns ultimately accounted for his expenditures through the Exchequer of Receipt at Westminster, temporary receivers enabled mayors to purchase grain without compromising municipal revenues.[61] In November 1598, one William Watham served as a temporary receiver on behalf of the Mayor of Weymouth-Melcombe Regis, the latter having expended funds for shipping 400 soldiers 'attending the commoditie of winde and weather' for safe passage to Munster. The Lord Treasurer, Lord Buckhurst, instructed by the Privy Council to reimburse the mayor to the extent of £100, and had a Mr Skinner (probably a Teller of the Receipt) issue the money. Skinner was similarly employed nearly two years later, obtaining at Buckhurst's orders reimbursement of coat and conduct money expended by Dorset authorities, which Skinner issued to Roger Keate, a gentleman acting as a temporary receiver.[62]

Victory required not only supplies and personnel, but timely distribution of resources. English commanders sometimes complained of bad food, late delivery, barefoot infantrymen, shrunken jackets, and dishonest victuallers. Although both systems (centralised and 'multiple') ultimately worked, the more centralised ordnance supply performed better:

> . . . the most effective of the supply systems for the provision of the three basic necessities of war – food, clothing, and arms – was that system mainly run by a centralised agency, the Ordnance Office, rather than the other two which were in the hands of civilian contractors.

Although the Ordnance Office's wares were not as perishable, nor its cash outlay as large, as the freightage of the private contractors, still the sustained labours of that administrative network became increasingly regularised and efficient through the Nine Years War and by force of circumstance, not because of strategic planning or even by deliberate policy at Whitehall.[63] In January 1600, Lord Justice Loftus spoke his mind on this issue to Sir Robert Cecil, as much to acquaint that rising star at Court with the Irish situation as to obtain adequate support for the armies that fought there. Loftus applauded the arrival of a new president to Dublin and a renewed commitment from Whitehall to extirpate the rebellion. Now would come 'men, money, victuals, apparel, and all other means necessary for that prosecution, which yf it had bene at first done, it would have saved the lives of may [many] tall souldiers'.[64]

The capture of foodstuffs and the burning of crops constituted tactics for both sides. English commanders filled their reports not only with the number of rebels slain but with the head of cattle taken and the location of fields scorched. The Irish wars, which fluctuated from 'a garrison war' to search-and-destroy operations on the part of the English, were fought with proportionally less food for the marauding soldiers than, say, many continental campaigns. Indeed, the European practice of invading hostile territory largely to plunder the foodstuffs of the enemy and thus keep one's army together and operational did not quite translate to Ireland. For English and Gaels desperately needed the assistance of civilian populations, especially in the cities. The confusing ethnicity of the Irish theatre muddied the distinction between friendly and hostile locals. The Pale obviously favoured English troops (though the citizens' niggardliness in reaching into their purses to help was bitterly resented by the forces sent there to protect them). But elsewhere, depending on clan politics, familial succession, inheritance questions, the percentage of Anglo-Irish in the neighbourhood, and the very personal quarrels among Irish native leaders, it was difficult to determine whether the army was quartered upon a potentially useful ally or was consuming food destined for the rebels.

Although cost determined what English fighting men ate, the Privy Council and commanders took an active interest in the nutrition of the men that were so expensive to transport to, and maintain in, Ireland. The diet, not surprisingly, was mainly carbohydrates and fatty proteins: a pound of biscuit or similar grain product per day, supplemented by a half-pound of butter and 2 pounds of cheese weekly. Pork and fish rations punctuated the monthly menu. Supplements of fish from Irish waters failed disastrously, largely because of the enlisted man's distaste for large amounts of the stuff, and due to preservation problems. A soldier's diet in Ireland varied over the weeks, depending on the availability of rations and their cost. The ideal daily 'menu' would have included some of the following items, around the year 1585:[65]

Bread, 1 lb	1d.
Biscuit, 1 lb	1d.
Fresh beef, 2 lb	2d.
Salt beef, 2 lb	2d.
Butter, ½ lb	2d.
Herrings (8)	2d.
Claret wine, 1 qt	2d.
English beef, 2 lb	2½d.
Beer, one pottle	1d.
Cheese, 1 lb	2d.
Sack, 1 pt	2d.

A daily minimum requirement might be set at:

Bread, 24 oz	1d. Ir.
Beer, 1 pottle	1¼d.
Beef, fresh, 2½lb	1¾d.
or salted, 2 lb	1¾d.

'Fish day'[66] victuals included:

Bread, 24 oz	1d. Ir.
Beer, 1 pottle	1¼d.
Herrings, 8	2d.
Butter, ½ lb	2d.
Cheese, 1 lb	2d.
Newland fish ½	[cost omitted]

We know the English soldier's diet because the Crown demanded certificates that detailed the quantity and quality of provisions loaded for the troops serving in Ireland. The contractors swore that the food, when it was put aboard ship, was 'swete whollsom and good'.[67] The problem for the historian is the same as that which the Crown pondered. If the victuals were palatable upon export, why were there so many complaints from Ireland? Victuallers in England might compromise the quality of their produce with some impunity, for the English and Irish Privy Councils had to make manifest in the hinterland their displeasure. But Irish victuallers found distributing bad food were penalised summarily, as on 25 August 1581, when the Irish Council fined the Dublin company of bakers £200 for 'ill-baked biscuit, furnished to the army, and short measure'. The three bakers who should have inspected the victuals were clapped up in gaol.[68]

Governmental steadfastness determined the fate of war in Ireland more than a particular bureaucratic structure. As food and clothing posed the greatest cost in keeping an army in the field, supply, even through the more chaotic, semi-privatised 'multiple' system, was the key to taming Ireland. How the supplies got there was of secondary importance.[69] This view clashes with the theory that centralised, professional, departmentalised bureaucracy had to develop before a military machine might subjugate Ireland. Still, Mountjoy succeeded. O'Neill's rebellion was broken. Further, there existed a level of centralisation, or at least some measure of centripetal force. The comptroller of the victuals in Ireland, George Beverley,[70] had to proffer a 'perfect certificate' to the Privy Council every sixty days. This requirement was symptomatic of Whitehall's efforts to ascertain the strength and condition of the English army. Similar certificates were demanded by the Queen herself from the comptrollers of musters. Invariably, the arrival of the certificates in London lagged, not so much because the comptrollers strove to hide any irregularities as much as that even in Dublin the monitoring of storehouses and garrisons proved extremely difficult. The terrain of Ireland and the smallness of the English logistical bureaucracy (the latter of which should not surprise us, as not even enough combat troops were available) made even rough estimates of supplies dubious. Thus, when a commissary expressed ignorance of what lay in his stores, it was as likely to be because of logistical problems as of any alleged corruption in his office.[71]

One drawback that plagued the multiple system of supply, with its civilian contractors and government comptrollers, was that, with so many participants conflicts of interest were bound to erupt and interrupt the supply of victuals and apparel.[72] In the autumn of 1602, George Beverley, whose victualling contracts were numerous, poked around in the bakehouses in the magazine at Dublin. Finding the bread too coarse, he reprehended the master baker, Joseph Crewe. Not long after, a libel appeared in the Dublin streets, ostensibly published by the English soldiery, that the best quality food in the undertakers' (private contractors') stores made its way into the public markets of Dublin. Not only were the soldiers thus robbed of good food, but the local merchants' buying and selling were undermined by 'black market' victuals. Beverley, in his sleuthing, had discovered privately-owned grain and governmental stores suspiciously intermingled. In a letter to the Lord Treasurer, Beverley suggested that, once foodstuffs were in the magazine, the good grain was sold off privately, regardless of owner, and the bad stuff fobbed off on the troops. To allay complaints by soldiers who might have unravelled the scheme, Crewe was 'sometimes employed to relieve the soldiers with beer'. John Jolles and William Cockayne, private contractors for the victualling of the royal army, tried to put Beverley on the defensive by presenting information against him to the Privy Council.[73] The entire arrangement seems to have been contentious and on occasion corrupt. Beverley's investigation cast most aspersion on commissary Robert Newcomen, with whom Jolles and Cockayne had tangled several years before.[74]

On 23 July 1602 the Privy Council asked Newcomen to victual the entire royal army in Ireland, and he responded by offering to supply the Leinster forces, the most profitable market, given its proximate location, unlike the more distant provinces of Ulster and Connaught, which necessitated higher transportation costs.[75] Munster was apparently not discussed in these negotiations. Ultimately, Newcomen, Jolles, and Cockayne agreed to victual the soldiers in Leinster, Connaught, and Ulster, receiving as recompense 5d. per man per day. Half of the money was issued out of the London Exchequer and the rest from the Treasurer in Dublin. The Lord Deputy and Council in Ireland carried the responsibility of inspecting the victuals through commissaries appointed by them. Newcomen, Jolles, Cockayne, and their employees accounted for everything spent, bought, and issued. Most foodstuffs came from England, but the beef and corn were Irish. Examinations taken upon oath were to be administered to the bakers. Finally, the Queen reimbursed the undertakers for items such as biscuit bags (at 12d. apiece). These sensible partnerships between private enterprise and the Crown depended entirely on the product at the end of the line: the victuals placed in the hands of the English fighting men. The Crown had gone to great expense to press, equip, transport, and deploy soldiers.[76] These efforts would be in vain if nourishment did not reach the troops. Once in the field, the Commissary General took over, as was the case in early English armies.[77]

Because the Crown constructed new victualling systems with each campaign, and because each theatre of operation posed unique supply problems, victualling administration had to be flexible. Overseas operations, as in 1513, 1544–5, 1596, 1625, and 1627, best coordinated victualling in close cooperation with the Navy. Such was the case with the voyage to Rhé in 1627, when Treasurer of the Navy, Sir Sackville Crowe, supervised provisioning of the expedition. Having managed Buckingham's personal finances, Crowe belonged to the Duke's circle. Courtly and commercial connections helped in fitting out the expedition and securing victuals, for a single man scheduled the supply of the vessels and the disbursement of funds. Working with Sir William Russell (who later succeeded Crowe) and the financier Philip Burlamachi (with whom Crowe had negotiated the pawning of the royal jewels at the Hague years before), Sir Sackville supplied food for a 12,000-man expeditionary force at various ports and coordinated refitting and departure of the respective naval vessels.[78]

The Duke's expedition boasted an administrator whose expertise encompassed gun-founding, provisioning, financing, and logistical arrangement: 'Sir Sackvile Crowe who is to sett hence to morrowe to give some direcions for the followinge supplies of shippinge and victualls will bringe likewise order and some monies for the better satisfacion of the Countrey' (i.e. pay to the localities the sums owed them for contributions, food, supplies, and services, made to the expedition).[79] Insufficient capital meant victualling was too often done on a scale and in a manner that produced poor-quality provisions. Bad diet had in turn created epidemic-like conditions amongst troops billeted in Plymouth. Seven famished soldiers died in the city streets on 21 December 1625, while corpses were 'contynually throwen over board' from the ships. Infantry captain Bolles died as well, as starvation showed no respect for rank.[80]

Mass production of soldiers' apparel received great impetus when the Crown placed orders for quantities of winter and summer clothing for its garrisons in the Low Countries. Entrepreneurs could count on large orders at regular intervals, and thus could shift from piecemeal manufacture of clothing toward a crudely 'industrialised' off-the-shelf kind of supply.[81] But those victualling Charles I's armies in the 1620s usually incurred more debt than profit: witness the unsettled debts that dogged the survivors of Burlamachi, Apsley, and Bagg.[82] In fact, few entrepreneurs could, or dared, plunge into the business of military supply. Linen draper Robert Swann employed 300–400 clothworkers to make shirts for the soldiers of the Earls of Oxford and Southampton, Count Mansfeld, and for Sir Edward Cecil's sailors, during the mid-1620s. Discrepancies between the original orders placed and the actual number of men pressed left him with bolts of cloth and unused shirts in his inventory.[83]

In the late sixteenth and early seventeenth centuries, as English trade expanded globally, risks taken on capital invested in trading-company ventures offered greater profit than military enterprise. It is amazing that the Crown, especially in the reign of Charles I, could convince any speculator, especially in the light of the fiscal crisis and parliamentary protests, to risk hard currency on these dubious royal endeavours. During the Scottish rebellion the King's usually amenable victuallers actually refused to supply the Royal Navy unless proffered ready money.[84] Suppliers the Crown called upon in 1638–40 had had difficulty with government reimbursement in the 1620s.[85]

During the 1620s campaigns, a motley group of contractors had to be managed and coordinated in timely fashion. Deputy victuallers who regularly supplied the Navy moved into action. However, the needs of a 12,000-man expeditionary force strained even the largest producers, which pulled less regularly used, and probably less reliable, wholesalers into the process. The scale of the expeditions must also have made life difficult for the Admiralty officers, who customarily administered food purchases and deliveries to the ports. Equally unsettling was the reality that the infantryman's ration was markedly inferior to that of the English sailor.[86] Experiments with drawing nutrition from the sea failed. The 'fish allowance' was despised on the 1620s expeditions, as in Ireland.[87] Although codfish or ling remained weekly staples for soldiers as well as sailors in the mid-1620s, efforts were made to balance the troops' diet with a dish made from pork and peas, and a kind of gruel made from oil, rice, and oatmeal.[88]

English armies were to subsist upon supposedly symbiotic early modern market economics. Victuallers' factors were to locate the best markets and buy at just prices, passing on these bargains to the soldiery.[89] However, inflation and cyclical poor harvests buffeted Caroline food prices, which, for example, jumped 20 per cent between 1636–7 and March 1638. Biscuit, beef, pork, peas, butter, and cheese cost more for the wholesalers, with only the loathsome fish ration actually falling in price. Beer prices skyrocketed from £1 16s. per ton to £2 2s. (not including cask).[90] In 1639 English soldiers received the daily ration of 2 pounds of bread and 2 quarts of beer. A 20,000-man army, the victuallers reckoned, needed more than 80 quarters of 'Bread Corne' per day (a quarter contains 8 bushels, with a bushel weighing 60 pounds). Thus during a six-month campaign against Scotland, that 20,000-man force would eat 675,000 pounds of bread, a lot of food in an England prone to chronic food shortages.

Fresh bread required ovens, so portable ovens were developed – one, for example, which baked 2,400 pounds of bread in a day. Made of copper, these ovens could be transported two or three to a wagon. Modelled upon army ovens used in the Netherlands, they each weighed 700–800 pounds.[91] Nevertheless, even on English soil, the army ran out of bread. While encamped at Goswick,[92] between Newcastle and Berwick, a bread shortage precipitated mutiny.

> . . . the greatest ennemy wee could heare of (at our retourne to Anwick) was hunger, which had soe assaulted the campe then at Gosswick, that there was a mutine in the army for want of bread, and if wee had gone on it was feared wee shoulde have sufferd with them and emboldned theire disorder with our companie. This

was probably the occasion of our command back, because wee mett divers cart loades of bread the dayes following goeing to the Army from New Castle, Morpitt and Anwick and all the county about, which carriadges, with the King and campe's remooval before, soe overlaboured the countrey's cattell that many of them dyed, and the rest were soe feeble and the people soe unwilling to come in upon summons (knowing how they were abused by the master waggoner, who would sometimes send out warrant for 500 carriadges when hee wanted but 200, making his profitt by the rest), their allowance being but 2d the mile, that the King was constrained to stay a day longer at Anwick than hee intended for want of carriadges.[93]

In an age when the transportation of grain might provoke food riots, the central government regularly rounded up victuals for the Royal Navy. The Surveyor General of HM Marine Victuals coped with 'the dearnesse of all kinde of victualls'.[94] The Surveyor operated out of the navy victualling establishment's equivalent of the Ordnance Office's Tower: the East Smithfield depot and Mansion House. Housed therein were mills, bakeries, slaughterhouses, and a 'biskett loft'. As at the Tower, shops and sheds clustered around the royal establishment. Under the early Stuarts, the East Smithfield facility had deteriorated. But Caroline reform had come with the new Surveyor, John Crane. Like the Ordnance officers, Crane struggled to remove the clutter of appurtenances that literally attached themselves, leech-like, to the walls of his institution. The navy victuallers complained that 'there is noe roome or space left now or which way any workemen or Labourers may come to amend and repair the deceayes of the wall of the said Mancion house'. Fire posed a great danger that might consume royal stores.[95] The subsequent improvements in the London facilities did much to help issue stores from the metropolis to the field. The marches through the North in 1639 and 1640 showed that relaying supplies from Hull, and gathering food and arms at Newcastle and Berwick, however, was still problematic.

A system of 'Competent Magazines' was seen as the only way to guarantee the sustenance of the men, not even counting the hay and oats necessary for forage for the cavalry and transport horses.[96] In winter 1638–9, the bakeries and granaries of Berwick were repaired.[97] In February 1640, breweries were planned for Berwick and ovens were being readied at Carlisle.[98] Through the agency of lieutenancy, the shires of central England (Derbyshire, Northamptonshire, Cambridgeshire, Lincolnshire, Leicestershire, Lancashire, Cheshire, Huntingdonshire, Warwickshire, Rutland, and Nottinghamshire) pooled 400 horses and 133 carts to haul ammunition. With barely a fortnight's notice, the respective Lords Lieutenants recruited horsedrivers, carters, and their steeds, and paid their expenses until they all entered royal pay upon arrival at the royal army's rendezvous at Newcastle-upon-Tyne on 20 April 1639.[99] The predicament was more acute than usual due to a succession of dry summers that had depleted Yorkshire's 'fodder grasse'. Expensive fodder meant fewer and more expensive oxen for hauling carts. That Yorkshire communities bore much of the charge for wagons and drivers increased tensions between William Grosvenor (the royal purveyor) and the locals.[100] Bridge boats, too, increased the cost of land warfare, not just because they cost £10 apiece, but rather because of the accoutrements required to fashion them into bridges, such as rope, anchors, and lumber.[101]

The Nine Years War that suppressed Ireland had proved that caravans of war *matériel* could be organised into a network that spanned England and Wales.[102] But ground transport nevertheless remained costly and complicated. 'Roust wagons' for hauling ammunition cost £13 6s. 8d. apiece, and because of the variety of bores of cannon, all sorts of different sized shot had to accompany an artillery train.[103] Each officer demanded a fitting number of wagons: the Lord General 30, the Provost Marshal 2, the Muster-Master General a pair, the Treasurer-at-Wars half a dozen, and so on, so that for the First Bishops' War the officers' train counted 72 wagons. Infantry captains paired up to share a wagon, and thus 30 foot regiments required 330 wagons. Each cavalry troop possessed a wagon. The army's carriage, excluding the artillery train, cost over £3,330.[104] In 1640 various shires had to rustle up 1,100 horses[105] for the artillery train and 300 steeds more to pull carts piled high with tents. The carts cost £5 apiece.[106]

During the First Bishops' War the aforementioned shortage of carts and horses had hindered victuals and tents from keeping pace with the army. As a result, living conditions had deteriorated rapidly. Troops camped under open skies, not in tents or huts.[107] Suffering from cold and exposure, the soldiers were often very hungry, their hunger being exceeded only by their craving for drink.[108] Bad weather, illness, and dearth of victuals drove Hamilton's men on Inchkeith to mutiny, 'in which Rage they killed your Grace's 3 oxen and some sheep, which they shared amongst them'. The officers, who had hid themselves, later restored order. Discipline might be maintained 'provided that their Beere hould out'. Unfortunately the 'badness of the cask' had allowed substantial leakage, and resupply was strongly urged.[109]

Soldiers' pay likewise had to be packed and transported,[110] though in the cases of 1639 and 1640, wages were as scarce as were weapons.[111] Arrears of pay also prompted mutiny, for example, at the Berwick garrison.[112] The murders and disorders of the summer of 1640 have overshadowed the soldiery's mischief of 1639, much of which had to do with victualling and wages. After the defeat at Newburn (27 August 1640), when the English army fell back on Yorkshire, the commissariat had so collapsed that the Lord Mayor of York daily dispatched rations (including gratis broken loaves) of bread as well as cheese, which were distributed among ten regiments and scattered companies. For example, the Lord Mayor hired nine carts, loaded food upon them, and sent them off to depots at Topcliffe and Tollerton.[113]

The army had marched by regiment, spreading the burdens of billeting and quarter throughout the North, especially upon Yorkshire, and, in both Bishops' Wars and their aftermath, the supply arrangements in that shire provoked conflict. Troops helped themselves to provisions, sometimes forcibly.[114]

> Some of Sir Jacob Asheley's regiment were quartered about South Sheilds neare New Castle, and there were courteously used by a bayliffe of Sir Nicholas Tempest's (whose demeasnes adjoined to their quarter) but they ill requited his pitty of them, with stealing his cattle and other outrages, which moved him to complaine to their colonell, who having severely punished the offendours, it begot such a rancour in one of their hearts, that hee onely to please himselfe with an unchristian and unprofitable revenge upon the steward, fyred with his match a great stake of his master's hay (valued by report at 40*l*.) This villaine, when hee was found out, was on Monday, the 20th of May, while all the army marched by, executed upon a new gibbett newly erected for him at the south end of Stannington towne, framed of some of the burnt timber of the fired houses, and this inscription fixed on the poast: 'for willfull and malicious burning of a stack of hay'. This was the first exemplary justice done in the army, and noe question but this and the strict martiall lawes published in printe was a bridle to base mindes onely awed with feare of punishment.[115]

Colonel Fielding believed his regiment purloined sheep because they lacked money to buy food.[116] If farm animals could not be found, the soldiers poached deer.[117] Civilians offered up (voluntarily or with persuasion) bread, cheese, fodder, and animals, to the occupying Scots in the autumn of 1640. Local officials reimbursed citizens from their own pockets for billeting expenses.[118] The occupation of the North imparted the bitter experiences of quartering and requisitioning on English citizens, a plague they would endure through 1641 until the fall of the Major-Generals in the 1650s.[119]

Billeting arrangements at York in 1639 had separated civilians, cavalry, and infantry to avoid the 'disorder which common souldiours are apt to occasion in great townes.' Only the King's servants and courtiers lodged within the walls of York, while the horsemen camped at Selby-upon-Ouse, 10 miles from the city. Foot soldiers were scattered amongst villages. There was contact between the services, however. John Aston, one of the King's Privy Chamber men, recorded in his diary that some infantrymen intermixt with the horse, which bred some disorders and quarrells (yet without bloud-shed), there beeing ever an aemulation betweene the horse and foote for presendecy, the auncient dispute reviving, especially in their distemper with wine, the foote then not contented that common opinion should bee theire umpire.[120]

This rivalry was exacerbated by the ill will between the third Earl of Essex, the lieutenant general of the infantry, and the Earl of Holland, commander of the horse.[121] An intriguing and violent argument erupted at York in April 1639 between two officers responsible for the supply of the army: Captain Hunnywood, a quartermaster for the infantry, and Wilmot, Commissary General for the horse. Wilmot drew his sword upon one of Arundel's captains for allegedly encroaching upon his office, and was gaoled by Colonel Goring.[122] It appears that the dispute arose over the functioning of the commissariat and the duties and privileges of the officers. The Earl of Rutland entered in his diary under 8 April that a Council of War had been called 'Upon a difference that happened betwixt Hunnywood, Quarter-Master Officer to the General, and Sir Wilmot, Commissary of the horse'. Goring, the lieutenant general of the cavalry, was to investigate the matter, and, after Hunnywood's examination, the captain was committed 'by the Kinge and Councell of War'.[123]

Reliance upon the militia had encouraged localities to be as self-sufficient as possible in arms procurement, and more attention was paid to the contents of the county stores than inventories in the Ordnance Office. Royal disappointment with the quantity and quality of pikes in parish armouries and militia stockpiles prompted the Privy Council to search for ash timber, and to press pikemakers at the very height of the First Bishops' War.[124] Royal arms had been distributed to the localities to improve shire militias, and were accordingly marked with the King's initials (and the counties were told to mark communal weapons).[125] Infantry weapons in the summer of 1640 were shipped by sea from London to Hull, and then hauled overland to the various regiments.[126] These efforts in 1640, along with the assembling of an artillery train for the North, were thwarted because of the failure to secure adequate ground transport at Hull.[127] Viscount Edward Conway, upon whom had fallen tactical command of the royal army, complained in summer 1640, 'There are noe flaskes nor hornes for the souldiers to carry their powder. . . . There are some cartriches to carry charges for the carabines, but not one quarter enough.'[128] Powder and lead were laid up in Newcastle, but bullet moulds had been forgotten, so that the supply proved to be virtually useless during the crisis of autumn.[129]

It has been alleged that England in the sixteenth century was profoundly backward in the science and practice of artillery; that it was so inferior in knowledge and in its arsenal that it had to rely upon superior European allies. As a corollary, it is suggested that logistics were similarly misunderstood, and that English engagements against the Irish were somehow an inferior type of warfare because the European bastion was not widespread in Eire. In this view, a backward English warfare was pitted against primitive Irish warfare.[130] But Ireland was an innovatory theatre of operation, and, if not as progressive as Italy (and who *was* in the fifteenth and early sixteenth centuries?), witnessed significant military innovations. From the very outset the Tudors had embraced gunpowder weapons, which they did not regard as antithetical to the practice of the longbow. Henry VIII did assemble a stable of gunners, foreign and domestic, especially at Berwick.[131] As early as 1515 the Gaels employed siege guns. The English, too, hauled large artillery pieces through Ireland in the 1530s and 1540s. In the 1590s Limerick boasted bastioned defences.[132] Limerick Castle exemplified the British assimilation of the military revolution. By 1611 a 'new Bulwark capable of [elevating] five or six great peeces', an angled bastion, had been incorporated into the medieval defences, providing flanking cover for the adjoining towers of the curtain wall. Older English fortifications accommodated themselves to 'modern' siege warfare, and the diary of the defence of Limerick Castle from May to June 1642 reads much like accounts recorded at Ostend in 1601–4: vigorous mining and counter-mining, subterranean skirmishes, the use of artillery to repel seaborne relief efforts, grisly civilian casualties, contests of gunnery, etc.[133] Ireland may have seemed a backwater to Europeans. But from a British perspective, it was increasingly a crucial theatre of operations from the Reformation onwards. And the arts of war, English and Gaelic, improved each decade until their destructive power utterly ravaged that island during 1641–50.

9

HIBERNIAN WARFARE
UNDER THE TUDORS,
1558–1601

At mid-sixteenth century, the English military establishment in Ireland showed characteristics of permanence.[1] Edward III, Henry V, and others had intended that English dynastic dominance be maintained indefinitely in France. But the immensity of France made a native English occupational force out of the question. Ireland was another matter. Ireland could be held, so it seemed, whereas France had proved itself unmanageable. Lord Deputy Anthony St Leger's instructions of July 1550 bade him 'sett furthe God's service . . . in the English tounge' and 'cause the Englishe to be translated truly into the Irish tongue, unto such tyme as the people maye be broughte to understand the Englishe'. Until the Anglicisation of Ireland was achieved, caution was to be exercised. A modest Ordnance Office was erected, and local production of bows and pikes, fashioned from Irish wood, undertaken. The companies who carried these weapons were to be overwhelmingly English: 'the men of warre not be of the nation of Irelande, above the number of tenne in every bande of a hundreth'. Fortifications were sketched out, military justice instituted, and shipping arranged.[2]

Administrative commitment was assumed, as was manageability of scale. The smallness of the English military establishment meant it had to play the various Irish and Scottish factions off against one another, a strategy that also kept mid-Tudor military expenditure low. Elizabeth's Irish military presence cost roughly £30,000 per annum, and did well through the 1560s–70s.[3] In 1559, 1,150 English soldiers served in Ireland (824 infantry and 326 cavalry), not counting Irish kerne auxiliaries. This level remained fairly consistent: 1,100 English troops in 1562, and 1,483 in 1569. The Desmond rebellion raised troop strength to 8,892 in 1580, and O'Neill's rebellion escalated English military commitment to 18,000 men at reign's end.[4]

England's perilous strategic situation meant that large numbers of veteran piketrailers could not be diverted from the Continent to the Irish theatre.[5] English expeditions and standing forces were of necessity smaller and more inexperienced in the face of the rigours of Irish warfare. Welsh, Scottish, and continental campaigns had, historically, entailed the deployment of large English armies. But the military establishment in Ireland, unlike any operational arrangement on the Welsh Marches, the northern Borders, or in France, grew steadily through the sixteenth century. Logistically, fighting the Irish posed the greatest challenge the Crown had faced in transporting foodstuffs, apparel, men, arms, and money. The problem was not so much distance as wind, weather, and currents. In Reverend Silke's account, Spain faced a more formidable supply problem because King Philip's Biscayan depots were further afield than Bristol or Chester. But in the dead of the Irish winter the wind rarely blows from the east, to hasten supplies from the English coast. Instead, a 'Catholic wind' comes out of the west or southwest, favouring vessels from the Atlantic coast. Although galleons were impracticable in Irish waters in winter, the sea lanes still favoured the Spanish invaders. The reason the Spaniards did not gather superior forces and more cannon was because of political and military decisions taken at the Court of Philip II, not because of the proximity of English ports.[6] Throughout the Irish wars, ill winds disadvantaged the English by holding up victuals, powder, and other supplies, often jeopardising an entire campaign. A typical case was that of the *Salaman*, which in April 1599 attempted to carry war *matériel* from Barnstaple to Ireland, but was forced back to port 'by fowle weather and Contrarie Wynds'. There she sheltered until May, when the cargo was discharged and the mission abandoned.[7]

English warfare in Ireland, 1561–95

Although the rebel Shane O'Neill had defeated English troops at the Battle of Red Sagums on 18 July 1561, Lord Lieutenant the Earl of Sussex for the most part kept O'Neill on the defensive until the English divide-and-conquer strategy ultimately succeeded, when the Macdonalds assassinated Shane. Lord Deputy Sussex convinced Whitehall that firepower, mobility, and increased garrison strength were requisite, and got reinforcements of archers and harquebusiers who carried no supplemental equipment or armour, save sword or dagger.[8] But it was Irish warfare, not English warfare, that toppled Shane at the battle of Farsetmore (18 May 1567), though his severed head became an English trophy.[9] Sir Henry Sydney (who succeeded Sussex in 1566) 'saw the period of military rule as a transitional stage between Gaelic and English forms of government'.[10] English troops would be necessary only for an indefinite period. The Lord Deputy intended war, always on a manageable scale, as part of a gradual pacification. The comparatively substantial commitment of £6,000 for the subjugation of Ulster made possible Sydney's celebrated march of 17 September–12 November 1566. Even in his second stint in 1575, troop strength remained at merely 1,600 men.[11]

English military domination was woven into the localities, with resident lords and gentlemen cementing their loyalty to the Crown by maintaining retinues of horsemen and/or foot soldiers.[12] The Celtic complexion of Tudor armies of this period was evident at the battle of Shrule (24 June

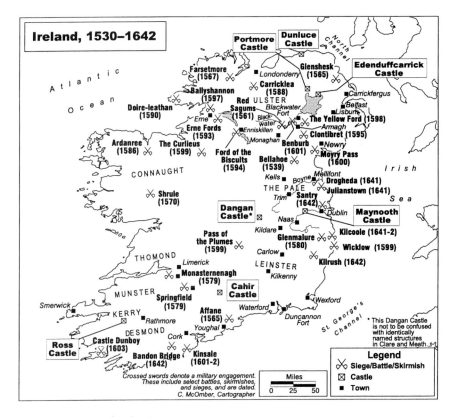

Figure 9.1 Map of Ireland, 1530–1642.

Source: Connie McOmber and the author.

1570), a set-piece battle, rare in Ireland. The main contingents of the rebel and royal armies were gallowglasses (Celtic heavy infantry), usually mailed and carrying axes. In spite of a barrage of English shot and arrows, the insurgents nearly swept Sir Edward Fitton's force from the field. But the English cavalry, so useful against Celtic warfare on the Anglo-Scottish borders, rescued the Lord President's infantry by flanking Shane MacOliver's foot soldiers.[13] The shock and mobility of English horsemen would be proved again, more than three decades later, at Kinsale.

Suppressing the Fitzmaurice rebellion (1568–73) and fighting Desmond[14] necessitated the creation of an Irish military establishment that matured through the 1570s and 1580s, paralleling Elizabeth's programme for improving the administration and performance of the English trained bands. But whereas the shire militia's supervision and equipment remained rooted in the countryside, Irish military operations asked much more from a less affluent population. So in Ireland the Crown footed the bill for military expenditures on timber and victuals, something that was unusual within England with the exception of the Berwick garrison.[15] When the Desmond rebellion called for an enlarged army, Sir Henry Wallop arrived in Dublin as the new Treasurer at War.[16] Sufficient financing of the English establishment was essential, for Irish warfare entailed enduring attrition and privation. Burghley had tried to prune the Irish establishment to 884 infantry, 326 cavalry, and 300 kerne in May 1559. Shane O'Neill's rebellion proved the folly of such measures,[17] as did the Fitzmaurice and Desmond revolts, for the rebels' strategy was consistently 'resort to violence'. A 'fundamental dependence upon force'[18] by both sides necessitated keeping men in arms for extended periods.

To master Ireland, then, the English created a bureaucratic apparatus unlike anything in their native land.[19] A semi-permanent military establishment, replete with a standing army, had to be constructed upon the modest foundations of Irish governmental revenues. Composition moneys paid by the inhabitants of the Pale and the provinces of Connaught and Thomond could be added to imposts and fines to finance an army,[20] but the bulk of funds came from London. From the 1579 rebellion until 30 September 1584, the establishment consumed well over a quarter of a million pounds sterling, perhaps as much as £350,000 sterling, largely from the English Exchequer of Receipt and close to £40,000 of Irish internal governmental income.[21] These funds drained into parallel supply systems, governmental ('Mynisters of Victualles') and private, which had been developed under Sussex and Sydney.[22] Even the English clergy were drawn into the Irish fiscal whirlpool. To suppress Desmond and 'foraine forces sent by the Pope and his confederates', Elizabeth demanded armour and horse from her bishops and their subordinates.[23]

Sir Nicholas Malby wrote to the Protestant crusader the Earl of Leicester, from Dublin,

> Religion is now the quarrel. . . . Some do think there I do use the sword too much. If her Majesty do not use her sword more sharply, she lose both sword and realm. The expectation of foreign forces [by Desmond's rebels] is not out of their heads.[24]

In fact, an Hispano-Papal force had ensconced itself in 1580 in Kerry, in the harbour of Smerwick, to succour Desmond and to divert Elizabethan forces from the Netherlands wars. Numbering 300–400, the force faced an English army of 800, the latter soon reinforced by 1,500 Irish under Thomas Butler, the eleventh Earl of Ormonde (whom Elizabeth had appointed recently the governor of Munster), and a small English naval force. After a battery lasting four to five days, during which the defenders sallied forth often and skirmished vigorously, the garrison offered to parley. Suspecting a trick, the commander, Lord Grey, was worried that Desmond's forces might cut his lines of supply. Grey demanded that the defenders lay down their arms; whether quarter was promised has become a matter of debate. The English forces, seeing the garrison partially disarmed, massacred the occupants except for a select group. The taking of Smerwick has been cited as evidence of the cruelty of the English soldiery, though research by one of the more virulent Irish nationalist historians suggests that the Catholic commander may have tried to hide the alleged cowardice of his surrender by arranging to have the besiegers murder his garrison, sparing only his hand-picked confederates.[25]

The fate of the citizens of Antwerp in 1576 was well known to the English, and Elizabeth's soldiers had heard of the massacres of Protestant garrisons. The savagery and religious animosities of the Irish conflict mirrored the barbarity of the Low Countries wars and precursed the Thirty Years War. The English adopted the treachery and bloodthirstiness of Irish warfare. A fine example can be found in the normally mundane declared accounts, where an officer had his defalcation (allowances for supplies advanced by the Crown) balanced out by rewards for decapitating Shane O'Neill.[26] In May 1595, the severed heads of 36 of Feagh McHugh's adherents were carried to Dublin.[27]

The extirpation of the Desmond revolt levelled out expenditure on the Irish establishment. In the mid-1580s, it cost about £45,000 sterling annually.

Figure 9.2 From the 1570s to the 1590s, the English strategy of occupation was based upon destructive marches, to succour garrisons and strike fear amongst the population. Terror was exercised by both sides.

Source: An English force on a 'search-and-destroy' mission in Ireland, 1575–76, from Derricke's *The Image of Ireland* (London? 1581), reproduced by permission of the Hargrett Library, the University of Georgia.

Figure 9.3 A characteristic of English warfare was the assimilation of the techniques of the enemy the English faced in that particular theatre. Here English soldiers engage in the Gaelic practice of taking the heads of their adversaries.

Source: Detail of heads, from *The Image of Ireland* (London? 1581), reproduced by permission of the Hargrett Library, the University of Georgia.

From 1587 to the outbreak of O'Neill's rebellion about £25,000–£30,000 underwrote annual operations.[28] Even during a period of relative peace, revenues were insufficient. In late May 1590, Sir Thomas Norris's veteran garrison at Limerick mutinied and marched on the government in Dublin Castle. The seventy-seven soldiers had not been given victualling money for months, and had been denied further credit in their garrison community. They had to choose between starvation and mutiny. The arrival of new levies in Ireland, who were paid in full, weekly, exacerbated the situation. Mindful of the hardships suffered, and of the service rendered, they marched on the Lord Deputy's residence, accompanied by fife and drum. This was a mutiny in the contemporary European sense – giving voice to a grievance and negotiating over a contract unfulfilled. Standing at arms outside Dublin Castle, the soldiers were dispersed, temporarily. On Sunday morning, 28 May 1590, they returned and lined the bridge that led into the Castle's keep. An angry Lord Deputy Sir William Fitzwilliam very nearly cleared the bridge with chain shot, but thought better of it. The mutineers in fact refrained from violence and even trespassing within the precincts of the Castle. When they attempted to accost the Lord Deputy, riding upon his horse across the bridge, it was Fitzwilliam who confronted a shouting soldier. The musketeer held up his firearm (the match was unlit) against the Lord Deputy's rearing horse, and seized the bridle with his free

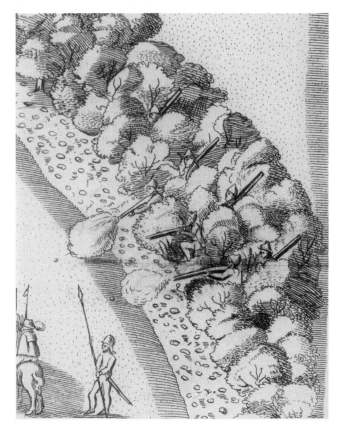

Figure 9.4 The Irish were quick to adapt firearms to the terrain of Eire.

Source: Partially-concealed Irish sharpshooters fire on the English (*Pacata Hibernia*, reproduced by permission of the Hargrett Library of the University of Georgia).

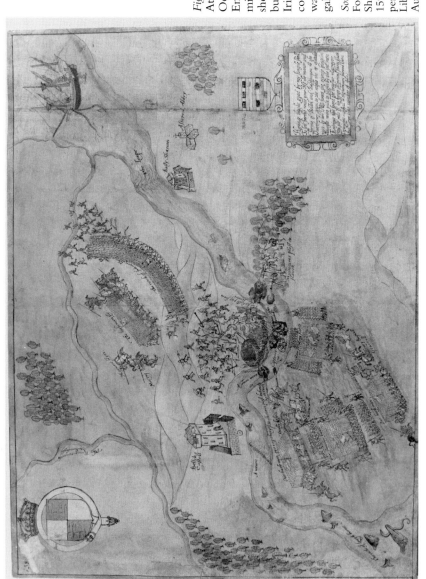

Figure 9.5
At Erne Fords (10 October 1592) the English brought to bear missile (musketeers) and shock (sword-and-buckler men) against an Irish force that contained traditional warriors such as gallowglasses.

Source: The Battle of Erne Fords (Belleek, Bally Shannon), 10 October 1593, reproduced by permission of the British Library (Cottonian MS Augustus I/ii, f. 38).

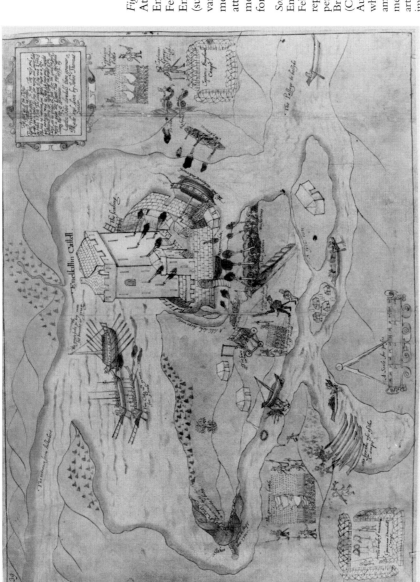

Figure 9.6
At the siege of Enniskillen Castle in February 1594, English batteries (supported by various other siege mechanisms) attacked Irish medieval fortifications.

Source: The Siege of Enniskillen Castle, February 1594, reproduced by permission of the British Library (Cottonian MS Augustus I.ii, f. 39), which depicts amphibious assaults, medieval fortifications, artillery, and heads impaled upon stakes.

hand. Incensed, the mounted Fitzwilliam drew his dagger, prompting the gentlemen of his entourage to brandish their rapiers and the mutineers to raise their weapons. Still unwilling to commit violence against their superiors, the mutineers submitted and were disarmed, sixty-one of them being gaoled subsequently. Two salient points may be made. First, despite their hard usage, the common soldiers still deferred to the government, in contrast with the more serious military disorders of the early and mid-seventeenth century. Second, and most important, the English military establishment struggled even to sustain its garrisons. Field operations would have been well nigh impossible.[29]

As the Irish theatre was thus pacified so very tenuously, English military commitment to continental Protestant allies escalated. War broke out in Ulster in 1593, with garrisons as the focal points. The English military objective was to safeguard the Ulster garrisons, a logistical and strategic problem that England had faced in Lowland Scotland and in the Netherlands. In 1595 the pendulum swung back, placing Irish strategic defence over continental intervention. Hugh O'Neill's initial success escalated and ironically improved the English mobilisation when he proved that Irish troops could master the weapons and tactics of the late sixteenth century with devastating effect. Victualling problems that had stymied operations and cost English lives in the process, could no longer be tolerated.[30] The vulnerability of relief columns was exploited by the Irish, so that surprise attacks and ambushed marches were the hallmarks of the wars of the 1590s – for example, the English rout at the 'Ford of the Biscuits' (so-called because of the victuals abandoned in the hasty retreat), an unsuccessful attempt to relieve the Enniskillen garrison.

The rebellion of Hugh O'Neill, Earl of Tyrone, 1595–1601

By obliterating Blackwater fort (the key to the security of Ulster) in February 1595, Hugh O'Neill, Earl of Tyrone, made the rebellion his.[31] On 24 May 1595, Sir Henry Bagenal marched from Newry with between 1,500 and 1,750 infantry, and 250 horsemen, intent on delivering supplies to the garrison at Monaghan. In command of several companies of Brittany campaign veterans as well as raw recruits from England,[32] Bagenal did not anticipate serious combat. O'Neill, however, harried the entire march, alarming the English when in camp as well as when navigating narrow roadways. The Irish made good use of firearms, eliciting from an English commander the begrudging compliment that nowhere had he seen 'more readier or perfect shot'. Many of the Irish cavalry and shot had been trained by the English years before, when the Earl of Tyrone had been a loyal subject of the Crown. After chasing an Irish force from the vicinity of Monaghan, the English replenished the garrison's victuals and changed the ward. Now marching home, Bagenal's force had expended a good deal of the ten barrels of powder they had brought. Allegedly, when confronted on the eve of the march by a Brittany captain protesting about the marginal amount of powder supplied, Lord Deputy Russell had sniffed that this was Ireland, not Holland.[33] Escort service through Ulster was simply a matter of showing one's colours on the march.

A shortage of officers likewise diluted Bagenal's force, and of those present many were lost in skirmishing and, ultimately, on 26–7 May 1595, in battle.[34] O'Neill's hit-and-run tactics against the marching column bore fruit when, with his 2,000–4,000 troops, he started a 'running fight' with Bagenal's English column that lasted seven or eight hours, on 27 May. O'Neill's troops pummelled the hapless column at will. Both sides afterwards disguised their casualty figures. Yet it is clear that each side lost several hundred men. Bagenal's soldiers, though intimidated and upon the defensive, extricated themselves from disaster. Had the Irish had a little more ammunition they might have found the stamina to overrun the English. The royal soldiery, particularly the old companies and Brittany veterans, held their ground well. The raw men under Captain Cuney (who bore the brunt of attacks on both 26 and 27 May) ultimately held their ground, and at Crossdall (four miles from the Blackwater Fort) advanced to a strong defensive position. The battle of Clontibret underscored the need for leadership, for the absence of colonels (in general) and captains (specifically, in the units under attack) was even more damaging than the shortage of powder.[35] As it was, an individual act of daring, Seagrave's charge across the river to grapple individually with O'Neill, nearly changed the outcome of the battle and Ireland's future. Seagrave came within inches of slaying the Irish leader, though he himself lost his life in the mêlée. Subsequent defeats, particularly the Yellow Ford, painted Clontibret as a worse defeat than it actually was.

Between Clontibret and the Yellow Ford (14 August 1598), the Crown experimented with proven continental soldiers to check O'Neill's military skill. Sir John Norris's Brittany veterans, though not the commander himself, made little difference at Clontibret, though their experience may have saved lives in that they did not break and run. Troops from other theatres of operation were diverted to Irish garrisons. Some Border troops, specifically garrisonmen from Berwick and levies from Yorkshire and Northumberland, found themselves in Ireland. Continental veterans were recruited or rerouted, and committed sometimes over the objections of senior officers. The contingents taken from Sir Francis Vere demonstrate the government's shifting priorities in taking continental troops over the blatant obstruction of their commander. Survivors of the Portugal, Brittany, and Picardy campaigns found themselves stiffening companies of pressed men in the very different military world of Ireland[36] – for example, when in 1597 Sir John Norris was sent into Ireland with 1,300 Netherlands veterans.[37] At least 2,000 seasoned men were transferred to Ireland in the aftermath of the Yellow

Ford.[38] Unfortunately Sir John's predilection for quarrelling and politicking was as evident in Ireland as it had been in the Netherlands, and he made no headway in mobilising enough English resources to topple O'Neill.[39]

Another Low Countries import was the diligent muster-master Maurice Kiffin, whose investigations into muster abuses in the Netherlands qualified him to root out corruption in Ireland. He found abuses, but he also judged Connaught garrison in June 1597 to have attained an impressive level of military preparedness.[40] While the practice of garrisoning may have improved in the 1590s, still field operations foundered. Whilst Kiffin toured the garrisons, Lord Deputy Burgh launched a campaign against the rebels in Ulster. At the head of 3,000 infantry and 500 cavalry, Burgh aimed to take Armagh, and then Portmore in July 1597. Simultaneously, the new President of Connaught, Lord Clifford, would strike at Ulster via the Fords at Ballyshannon, with both English armies rendezvousing at Lough Foyle. But both forces were stymied by the rebels' spirited resistance, and Burgh fell back on the defensive strategy of planting garrisons, erecting a string of forts from the Blackwater to the Pale.[41]

On 18 June 1597 Belfast Castle was surprised, and 'all the Inglishe men in the warde wear hanged, and their throots cutt, and their bowels cutt oute of ther bellyes. . . .' Newly appointed governor of Carrickfergus, Sir John Chichester, recaptured the stronghold less than a month later in a bold amphibious operation. In late July, 700 rebel infantry, seconded by 300 cavalry, challenged the garrison and Chichester sallied out with 250 foot and 30 horsemen and confronted them. The English held fire while the rebel calivermen peppered their ranks. When the advancing Irish line was close enough, Chichester unleashed a volley, tearing the Irish line and sending the rebels running. Sir John not long after took Edenduffcarrick Castle as the result of a reconnaissance-in-force. These successes, all based on tactical ingenuity, buoyed English confidence.

The MacDonnels, whose loyalty to the Crown remained suspect, possessed cannon that allegedly had been salvaged from Armada wrecks. When Chichester learnt that James MacDonnel had exploited the turbulent times by plundering in the vicinity of Carrickfergus, a parley was arranged, and both forces squared off, adorned for battle, if necessary, on 4 November 1597. However, the English foot soldiers had not fully recuperated from an exhausting march, a journey which had dampened much of their gunpowder. When Chichester's vanguard discovered the Scots-Irish occupying a hill, it was decided, initially, not to provoke a fight. But the arrival of the English main force, despite its smallness, prompted Chichester to challenge the odds again. A body of sixty pikemen, flanked by forty horse approached the hill, preceded by a forlorn hope of nine pikes protecting roughly a dozen calivermen. Three wings of shot spread out to provide supporting fire, especially for covering the English cavalry. When MacDonnel's force began to melt away, descending from the hill, Chichester

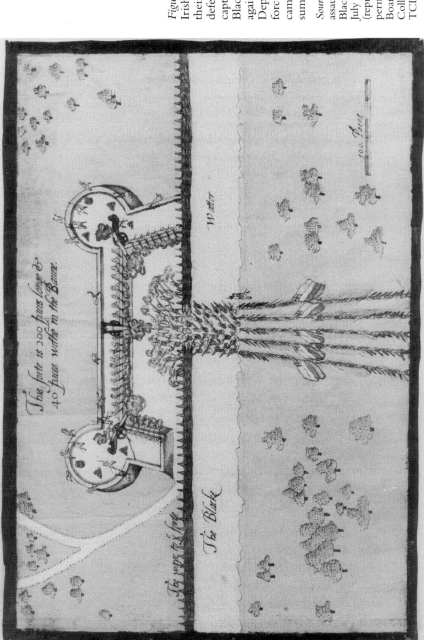

Figure 9.7
Irish forces mass
their firepower to
defend the
captured
Blackwater Fort
against Lord
Deputy Burgh's
forces during the
campaign of
summer 1597.

Source: Lord Burgh
assaults the
Blackwater Fort, 14
July 1597
(reproduced by
permission of the
Board of Trinity
College, Dublin,
TCD MS 1209/34).

ordered his horsemen to charge, which manoeuvre was not performed with alacrity.

At this point, the Scots-Irish wheeled about to meet the stillborn advance and cut down the wings of English calivermen. The lieutenant leading the forlorn hope fell, as did virtually all the sergeants, and the momentum of MacDonnel's horse and shot swept away the centre of the English position. In the rout, numerous commissioned and non-commissioned officers, including Chichester, were slain. Later, intelligence disclosed that this striking reversal of fortune on the field of battle owed as much to a Scots-Irish ruse as to bad execution by the English horse. Allegedly, MacDonnel's allies, the McSorleys, had quietly reinforced the rebel position, bringing the host to perhaps 1,300–1,500 soldiers, 500 of whom were expert in the use of firearms. When MacDonnel ascended the hill, '. . . he showede of horsse and foote aboute 700 fightinge men; yet havinge lefte about two myle beehinde him in certaine shrubs an ambushemente of Irish shotte and Scotche bowermen with sloughes [edge weapons], swords, and pikes, in all 800.' In broken formation, and with whatever dry powder had remained now expended in skirmishing, Chichester's small force was overwhelmed, and the casualty list of lieutenants and sergeants testifies to the garrisonmen's inability to respond tactically and save themselves.[42]

Sir Henry Bagenal, whose resolve outstripped his comprehension of how Irish warfare had changed in the 1590s, attempted to resupply the Blackwater Fort on 14 August 1598 with a force not dissimilar to that which had been mauled at Clontibret. The ensuing ambush and fight, known as the 'Battle of the Yellow Ford', shook confidence in English warfare for decades. Continental veterans (the old Brittany bands and newly arrived troops from the Picardy campaign), the standing companies, and nearly 2,000 recently pressed English, made up a relief column of 3,900–4,000 infantry and 300–320 cavalry, complete with artillery, including a saker.[43] Divided into regiments, the column would close ranks in the event of being attacked and fight in the traditional tripartite of forward, vanguard, and rearward – a challenge, given the hilly ground that made up the four and a half miles from their camp to the Blackwater Fort. Musketeers and calivermen marched partially detached from the column, as 'sleeves', in anticipation of enemy action.

Bagenal's plans could not smooth the undulating ground over which his men would march. Nor could he diminish the level of martial skill that the Gaels had achieved under O'Neill. When the English came under fire, the regiments engaged rapidly, throwing out shot so that the Irish might not fire with impunity. Though this tactic did not prevent repeated attacks, it did occasion firefights that slowed, and then divided, the progress of the column. Once separated among the hills over which the road wound, the English units (the vanguard of which hauled the heavy saker) found themselves isolated and vulnerable. Hemmed in between the Irish, they had little

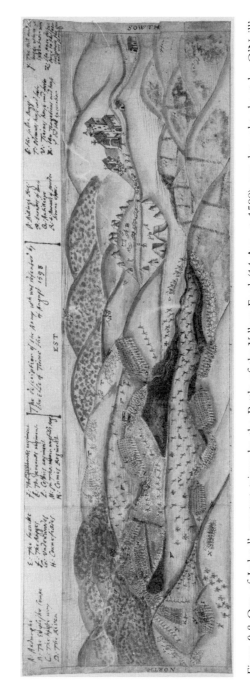

Figure 9.8 One of Ireland's greatest triumphs, the Battle of the Yellow Ford (14 August 1598), was brought about by O'Neill's tactical brilliance and use of firearms, and an unsound English strategy of garrisons and relief columns.

Source: The rout of the English forces at the Yellow Ford, 14 August 1598 (reproduced by permission of the Board of Trinity College, Dublin, TCD MS 1209/35).

room for manoeuvre. Pikemen and musketeers had difficulty coordinating their defensive efforts, and ultimately an English soldier inadvertently exploded a couple of barrels of powder with a lit match. When the marshal, Bagenal, received a fatal shot in the face, the morale of the harried troops unravelled, and a rout (not unlike that at Clontibret) occurred. However, as in that earlier action, the surviving commanders rallied their units and shepherded them back to camp, escaping wholesale slaughter.[44] True enough, the Yellow Ford was the greatest triumph Hibernian warfare had ever enjoyed over English warfare. In spite of English losses, which approached 50 per cent, annihilation was avoided. Credit goes to Wingfield, whose bold rescue of Cosby's men saved perhaps 13 per cent of the army. But O'Neill refrained from massacring the fleeing troops at Clontibret and Yellow Ford, perhaps because he sensed that such a resounding blow might escalate the war and increase the number of English troops destined for Ireland.

Eire could never defeat a fully mobilised England; rather, the Gaels sought to wear out (and hence not to enrage unduly) their opponents. Ireland benefited from England's strategic predicament, much as would America in the late 1700s and early 1800s. England had bigger fish to fry. Ireland did not, and never did, feel the full military force of England. Thus the ideal solution to the pacification of Ireland – the planting of substantial garrisons and the deployment of a sizeable highly mobile expeditionary force – could not be achieved given the military resources allocated by the Crown. Indeed, England's adversaries believed it 'impossible for Her Majesty longe to contynue the warrs heere for wante of money'.[45] The utter subjection of Ireland by fire and sword was a strategy consistently avoided by the Tudors. Sir John Perrot, in the 1580s, officially rejected such an approach. Garrisoning in Ireland, like garrisoning in Scotland and the Borders, entailed a monstrous financial commitment. Lacking alternatives, as Ciaran Brady has shown, the English employed 'general hostings', expeditions that marched the countryside on search-and-destroy missions. The ineffectiveness of this latter strategy in the second half of the 1590s led to the precipitous escalation of the war.[46]

In 1598 it was proposed to levy 11,000 Englishmen to safeguard Ulster.[47] Having spent £250,000 on the Spanish war before the year 1598 had even begun, the Crown was compelled to lay much of the 1599 mobilisation on the shires.[48] Unfortunately this kind of decentralised mobilisation filled the ranks of the Queen's Irish army with the raw recruits whose lack of training had hobbled the English columns in the reverses of 1595 and 1598. But with impressment for Ireland doubling and tripling over previous years, Elizabeth had no choice.[49] The supply systems, as well as the financing, of the Irish military establishment therefore had to be transformed. A virtually professional army had to be integrated with the English amateur defence forces. The 1599 Irish mobilisation coincided with the creation of an army to safeguard England itself during the late summer. Drawing upon the lesson of the 1588 mobilisation, 6,400 infantry and over 1,000 horsemen coalesced into a centralised rapid deployment force.[50] If the O'Neill rebellion proved the Irish could fight effectively, it also demonstrated that England, even under severe fiscal pressure, could organise a system of supply (from governmental and entrepreneurial sources) that was sufficient to sustain the army. That experience, honed later by Strafford and Christopher Wandesford, would reach ever greater levels of logistical potential in 1642 and after. A new treasurer, in March 1599, Sir George Carey, realised almost immediately the insufficiency of Exchequer funding.[51] Victory would cost nearly half a million pounds, all of which passed through Carey's busy hands.[52]

Cognisant of the threat posed by O'Neill's rebellion, Elizabeth dispatched her most daring courtier to quell the revolt, in the spring of 1599. The Queen now faced an unenviable fiscal problem. By the end of the century she had been compelled to 'sett the King of France in his Kingdome, to protect all the Low Countries, to encounter the King of Spain, and all his Forces, and to have spent her Men and Treasure in Conquering Ireland'. Ireland's annual governmental revenue rarely exceeded £13,000.[53] Consequently, the English military establishment in Ireland required substantial monetary supplements as well as arms, wagons, and men. The treasurer, Sir Henry Wallop (who died upon Essex's arrival in April 1599), and his successor, Sir George Carey, were accused of misappropriating funds. For more than two decades Wallop grafted revenues from the Pale – for example boeves[54] – on to the royally financed military establishment.[55]

The forces, money, and supplies given to Essex constituted a major military effort: 16,000 infantry (costing £228,246 annually) 1,300 cavalry (£31,408 per annum) plus officers and logistical support staff.[56] Essex, occasionally a talented strategist,[57] felt overwhelmed by the logistics of fighting in Ireland. Bemoaning what he regarded as a dearth of draught horses, arms, troops, carts, and money, the Earl dared not march into the heart of Ulster. Clontibret and the Yellow Ford had not been forgotten. Essex knew the strength of English warfare when practised in the Irish theatre: cavalry and leadership. But the foot soldiers had 'neither bodies, spirits, not practice of arms. . . .' The rebels, however, possessed 'able bodies, good use of the arms, boldness enough to attempt, and quickness in apprehending any advantage. . . .' Celtic warfare held sway.[58] The Lord Lieutenant, discontented that he could not launch his forces into Ulster straight away, or so said Essex and his subordinates, would delay the direct suppression of that province until logistically possible.[59]

Essex's doubts regarding English military ability seemed confirmed when Sir Henry Harrington, on garrison duty in County Wicklow with 400 foot soldiers and 50 horsemen, completed a reconnaissance in late May 1599. Upon breaking camp, the Gaels pursued the marching English, a successful tactic in the 1590s. The English superiority in cavalry aided the withdrawal, with periodic charges (punctuated by volleys from Sir Henry's 'loose shot', or skirmishing musketeers) as the horsemen's actions provided a margin of safety. The persistence of the Irish harrying tactic, hanging on the inevitability of the English encountering a difficult bit of terrain, bore fruit, however. Though the English soldiers acquitted themselves well through the first few miles of the march, a surge by the rebels elicited a volley from the English shot covering the rear of the column. Apparently, a 'rolling fire' had kept the attackers at bay. But the general discharge of musketry left the shot temporarily vulnerable and several score musketeers bolted, threw down their pieces rather than reload, and abandoned their pike-toting comrades. What appears to have been a weakness of English warfare as practised in Ireland may have come into play at this point. A dearth of (and perhaps the inexperience of) junior officers prevented the steadying of the column, especially amongst the rearward. As had been the case, especially since 1593, a retreating English column became fair prey for the rebels.[60]

A greater disaster occurred at the Curlieu hills, under similar circumstances, on 5 August 1599. The musketeers of an English column once again expended much powder in defensive skirmishing, which ultimately created an opportunity for the Gaels to break the English ranks and precipitate a rout of the nearly 1,500 English infantry and 200 horse. Ten senior and junior officers died along with 231 enlisted men. A further 196 pike-trailers and a dozen officers sustained injuries.[61] Essex's own perambulations in Munster, displaying the banner of the cross of St George, achieved some small successes in skirmishes and at sieges (e.g. Cahir Castle), but these actions could not disguise the fact that English strategy and tactics had still to contend successfully against O'Neill's modernised Celtic warfare.

At the end of 1599, English forces settled into their respective garrisons, diminished and disheartened.[62] A sizeable army had been assembled to suppress the rebellion and instead the Lord Lieutenant had fallen back on a defensive war-footing. Garrisons obsessed the English strategists, and thus groups of three to five companies would be tied to a fixed location, sufficient perhaps to defend themselves but unable to take the initiative against a wily enemy. Should those several hundred, or even several thousand, men march forth, they invited the Gaels to fight precisely the kind of war that the latter preferred. The Queen, who had too often seen her commanders squander opportunities to achieve a decisive victory in the Low Countries and, worse, in the bungling of the Portugal expedition of 1589, gnashed her teeth as disappointing news, complaints, and excuses arrived from Ireland. What could have been done? Marginal garrisons would have had to have been abandoned, freeing up larger numbers for search-and-destroy missions. The concept of transferring Low Countries veterans was sound, provided that the newly pressed men who joined them had some modicum of training. Thus either the trained bands would have to be transported to

DEVEREUX Earl of *ESSEX* 1601.

Figure 9.9 The Earl of Essex saw military success as a key to furthering his ambitions at Court. Although possessed of some martial ability, winning the Irish War was beyond his means. His abandonment of that theatre in September 1599 doomed his political ambitions.

Source: Robert Devereux, second Earl of Essex, executed for treason, 1601 (author's collection).

Ireland or the process of impressment changed. When Essex threw up his hands and abandoned Ireland, it was in no small part frustration in failing to outfox Irish strategy and tactics.

While exhausting the English, forcing the occupiers to march the countryside, expend treasure, and allowing weather and illness to take their toll, the Irish rebels pursued another stratagem, of solicitation of help from Rome and Madrid to pressure the English at home as well as in Ireland. The most direct avenue of assistance from the international Roman Catholic community was invasion. This had led to the Smerwick massacre in 1580. Not all Roman Catholics advocated a Spanish stroke, for the Pope sought to balance Catholic power, not to promote single and potentially dictatorial hegemony that might result in the manipulation of the papacy itself. But Philip II, and his son after him, saw the humbling of England as a point of national honour as well as of religious vindication. The landing of the Spaniards at Kinsale (County Cork) in 1601 transformed the strategic situation: a decisive confrontation became likely in a war that had it remained a strictly Anglo-Irish duel, could well have become a stalemate. The global capabilities of Spain, combined with operations in the Low Countries, against England itself, or on the high seas, elevated the Irish theatre in terms of international strategic significance. Spanish intervention meant that the English would obtain the confrontation they had long sought, and the Irish, who excelled in guerrilla fighting, now had to contemplate set-piece battles and, worse, siege warfare. The future of Eire was to be settled by English warfare, not Irish warfare.

From the Yellow Ford to Kinsale

If Irish warfare laid bare English weaknesses, it gave occasion for the emergence of the qualities of English military skill that brought victory on Christmas Eve 1601: tactical skill, a product of resourceful and occasionally daring command, and the persistence of the soldiery under adverse conditions. Steady and accurate gunnery, too, made its impact, more impressive considering that the Spaniards were equally skilled with artillery. The English overcame a talented and resolute foe. And, finally, the effective conjunction of land forces with naval vessels distinguished Mountjoy's campaign, in spite of appalling weather conditions. The Spaniards had choice of ground. Mountjoy's campaign strategy could not develop fully until after the invaders had gained a foothold and dug in, for news of their arrival, location, and numbers had to reach him and then be confirmed. Don Aguila, the invasion's commander, should have gone to Cork but instead chose Kinsale.[63] The Catholic forces still had the advantage. No better opportunity to throw off the English had occurred. O'Neill's army had attained a level of training and size unprecedented in the Anglo-Irish conflict. Further, the English had continually to disperse their forces.

Strategically, garrisons required protection more than ever, for the presence of a continental enemy in the south provided ample opportunity for Gaelic risings elsewhere. Garrisons proved a liability when Irish warfare found the means to waylay English relief columns. Even though the war was now transformed into a contest of siege, and ultimately battle, the garrison system still hampered English warfare by tying up fighting men in remote corners. The English could not gather their full strength. Tactically, once Mountjoy had besieged the Spanish, O'Neill might attack him at a disadvantage, for the English trenches and platforms kept them at least partially stationary and fixed upon Kinsale, anticipating a Spanish sortie from the city.[64] The key was to join the Irish and Spanish forces to annihilate Mountjoy's numerically inferior army, and then turn upon the English garrisons. Ireland would be Roman Catholic and the Spaniards would have numerous ports from which to assault England.

That did not happen, because the English deployed themselves with near perfect tactical sense, and the Irish did not, leaving a gallant band of Spaniards to fight a siege alone. O'Neill was no fool. To circumvent pitched battle, keeping the English off balance and apprehensive as they consumed their supplies and sickened from the climate, had been a successful Irish ploy. The Kinsale siege obliged the Irish to fight the kind of war in which they could be beaten. Having verified Spanish landfall at Kinsale, Mountjoy chose Cork as his operational staging area. Three considerations occupied the Lord General as he made his way south: victualling, disposition of troops already in Ireland, and coordination of his army with seaborne reinforcements and supplies. He shared the Spanish commander's vulnerabilities. His central government had not allotted sufficient resources to get the job done, and his subordinates would second-guess any errors the commander might make and certainly share those criticisms with the royal council.[65]

On 28–9 September 1601, the rival forces skirmished, though they probably had little idea of each other's actual strength. While the Spanish had ensconced themselves securely in Kinsale town, their lack of horsemen prevented them from spying on the English army's approach.

> Captaine George Flower . . . was sent with certaine Companies to view the Towne of Kinsale. . . . [H]ee no sooner approached the Towne, but the Spaniards sallied, our men beate them into the Towne, and were so eager in pursuit, as they came to the Port, and would have set fire unto it, if Flower had not drawen them off.[66]

The Spaniards had committed 5,000 soldiers[67] at the maximum, but probably more like 3,800 in Ireland,[68] although Spanish sources put the figure at around 3,300–3,400.[69] The 3,500 estimated by a pair of French deserters was close to the mark.[70] English forces, even more scattered, can be reckoned at 7,500 effectives.[71] Under Mountjoy's command were listed 6,800 infantry and 611 cavalry.[72] But garrisons in Munster and elsewhere could not be denuded of troops, and supply lines and transportation systems required manpower. So probably Mountjoy's column that marched out of Cork on 16 October, *en route* for Kinsale, counted only 4,300 able soldiers.[73]

Both commanders expected reinforcements, but with favourable winds blowing, Mountjoy's were closer at hand and definitely on the way.[74] The Spanish Crown failed to commit sufficient men, especially cavalry, with dispatch. Thus the English, as of mid-October, brought a slightly greater force in the field against a veteran and resolute band of Spanish defenders. But, given the strength of O'Neill's insurgents, especially with the Spanish catalyst considered, the massive rebel army might have overwhelmed the besiegers. In October 1601, O'Neill's force, the numbers of which will always be somewhat clouded owing to the lack of 'lists' and 'establishments' similar to those of the Spaniards and English, amounted to perhaps 6,000 infantry and 520 cavalry.[75]

Finally, in terms of the quality of fighting men, the advantage lay with the Catholic forces. The martial excellence of Don Juan del Aguila and his comrades was of the calibre one would expect of the *tercios*. They fought splendidly against the English, and maintained their dignity in defeat. As for the Irish, much depended upon what kind of war would be fought. As individuals and irregulars, they proved deadly foes. Their success against marching columns was impressive. Irish armies had improved noticeably from the mid-1590s, largely through O'Neill's leadership, for he knew English arms well, having served in the royal forces in 1572–4, 1579–83, and 1593. The caliver became a deadly weapon in Irish hands and was adapted to Gaelic combat. Marksmanship was valued, and O'Neill paid calivermen more than other infantry. His pikemen also received training and, when Spanish arms shipments arrived, the Earl quickly appropriated imported pikes for his best men.[76] Considering that the latter weapon was suited for the pitched battles that Irishmen rarely fought, its adaptation signifies O'Neill's selected borrowing from English warfare, even to the extent of marching and uniforms. At Clontibret the Irish harquebusiers and others 'marching in red coats' had been a sight to behold, for such soldiers were 'not usually seen before that time amongst the mere Irishry.'[77] But tactics of harassment, rapid deployment, surprise, and sporadic attack were distinctly Irish. Thus, by the time of Kinsale, Irish armies were, potentially, at the very apex of their development.[78] They handled pikes, drilled, learnt formations. The Irish charge, which became a devastating tactic in subsequent centuries, originated in this era, and increased O'Neill's formidability.[79]

The English position at Knochrobin Hill (a mile from Kinsale town, and near the inlet of Oyster Haven) on 17 October lay rather exposed, the men 'having not the meanes to entrench', with their artillery still *en route*. Seizing the advantage, the Spaniards launched a counter-attack when the English tested Kinsale's defences on the nights of 19 and 20 October: 'Sir John Barkley was this night apointed to give an Alarm to the Town, who bett [beat] in all the guards . . . into their Trenches.' But the following night a thousand or so Spaniards occupied a hill above the English camp 'to cutt of [off] some of the Skouts or guards, or to attempt somewhat upon that quarter'. A patrol in force, lying between Kinsale and the camp, discovered them and a battle erupted in the darkness, though with few casualties. The Spaniards withdrew into the garrison.[80] These actions resembled the Low Countries wars, combat familiar to both sides.

The tactical wisdom of reducing these outlying strongholds quickly may have been obvious, but these manoeuvres were executed well in spite of vigorous resistance from the Spaniards.[81] As munitions and victuals piled up, the English conducted the siege as if they were in the Netherlands. On 25 October another nocturnal raid occurred, when sixty chosen 'pikes and targetts, to be the better undiscovered', infiltrated the outworks of Kinsale. The use of 'targets,' short-sword-and-buckler men, was a Spanish innovation drawn from ancient Roman practice, well suited to trench fighting and illustrative of the eclecticism of English warfare.[82] The Gaels themselves had used short-sword-and-buckler men at Clontibret.

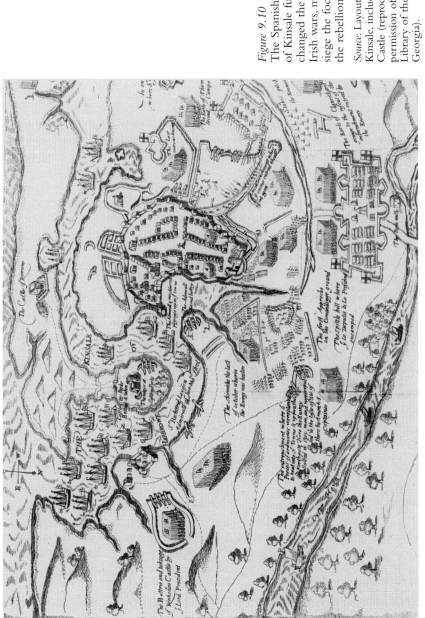

Figure 9.10
The Spanish occupation of Kinsale fundamentally changed the nature of the Irish wars, making the siege the focal point of the rebellion.

Source: Layout of the siege of Kinsale, including Rincorran Castle (reproduced by permission of the Hargrett Library of the University of Georgia).

Mountjoy shifted his tactics fluidly, contemplating an assault on Kinsale when that seemed the best course, then starving out the garrison when threatened from the rear. He capitalised on O'Neill's indecisiveness,[83] seized the initiative, and drove out the Spanish. At least three weeks before O'Neill resolved even to move on Munster, the English compromised the Spanish defences decisively. Quickly the Queen's troops, in conjunction with her navy, disembarked artillery,[84] got it into place, and sighted it. The English fired on the Spanish outpost at Rincorran Castle, a key fort near to Kinsale that could prevent the English from encircling the town and from navigating the harbour with impunity.[85] By 2 November the fortress had been taken, despite a Spanish sortie.

In the midst of the cannonades against Rincorran (directed by Sir George Carew, who regarded himself the most expert artillerist amongst the Queen's forces), furious skirmishing continued. The Kinsale garrison sallied forth to disrupt the bombardment, and several English 'broken companies' scrambled to meet the threat. The Spaniards poured musket fire into the hundred or so English who had left their defensive positions, and a hot exchange raged on open ground. Before the Spaniards could draw up their pikes fully to crush the English shot, reinforcements came up and the English charged headlong, pushing back the enemy, only to be peppered by Spanish musketeers hidden amongst the buildings of Rincorran. By the 4th, Rincorran had become an English gun-platform, lobbing shot into Kinsale and battering its walls. The Spanish abandoned their trenches and held on to the castle park peninsula. The tactical fluidity of the situation stemmed from the penchant of both sides to attack and counter-attack unexpectedly. [86]

In November Mountjoy consolidated his gains and gave up, momentarily, the tactic of bombardment in anticipation of a breach followed by assault. He rested content with confining the Spaniards, safeguarding against sorties against his trenches and artillery platforms. Now he prepared earthworks at the north of his encampment, anticipating Irish relief, against which Carew gathered 1,000 infantry and 250 cavalry and set off to intercept the Gaels.[87] Mountjoy, like O'Neill and Aguila, remained cautious. He knew that the tactical advantage would lie with the army that reacted quickly to altered circumstances, be they enemy redispositions or changed weather.

Again in a 72-hour period (21–23 November) Mountjoy brought to bear seven artillery pieces to effect a breach of Kinsale. Rebuffed by Aguila when the Spaniards were called upon to surrender, the English launched a sizeable attack on 1 December, the latter regarding it as a reconnaissance in force, Spanish sources calling it a failed assault. Either way, Kinsale's walls could not be penetrated.[88] The spirited resistance encountered by 2,000 English prompted Mountjoy to change tactics again. The English camps now constructed another fort, even closer to Kinsale, tightening the circumvallation. This pressure spurred another Spanish sortie.[89] An hour after dusk on 3 December 1601, the Spaniards sallied forth, perhaps 1,500 strong, overran the eastern trenches, and took the newly built fort. They intended to destroy the gabion trench system and spike artillery. Savage fighting raged and, ultimately, the Spaniards withdrew (though several captains later claimed that they did so only at the command of Don Aguila). Casualty figures varied widely, as each side claimed hundreds of enemy dead.[90] Most likely each force lost sixty men, and the spiked guns were repaired.[91] Though he could not have broken the siege, Aguila was buying time, time that might see succour from his countrymen. English reinforcements continued to arrive. As the Spaniards showed no inclination to surrender, Mountjoy wisely refrained from attempting another assault. He would batter and starve his foes. The beleaguered, on the other hand, hoped for a Spanish fleet that would sink Elizabeth's ships in Kinsale harbour and fire upon the English emplacements.

At Castlehaven a half-dozen Spanish vessels had appeared with 1,000 reinforcements, artillery, and food. But these Spaniards, as redoubtable as Aguila's troops, were wasted tactically, as were the cannon. General Zubiaur, the commander, pursued a grandiose strategy: the establishment of several Spanish strongholds in Ireland that would lead to the invasion of England itself. But Kinsale's walls were battered and the Irish had yet to strike a good stroke. In spite of the diplomatic successes he had had with the rebels, Zubiaur failed to swell their ranks with Spaniards and speed them off to relieve Kinsale. Nor did he break through to Aguila and deliver the much-needed ordnance and a morale-boosting contingent of reinforcements. Instead he dug in in various castles and forts, so intractably that Sir Richard Levenson's fleet could not blast him out of Castlehaven. Both sides suffered losses in the artillery duel and the English vessels returned to Kinsale harbour.[92]

At a time when an effective conjunction of a combined force under O'Neill and Zubiaur with the Kinsale defenders might have overwhelmed Mountjoy's forces, now dwindling rapidly because of the harsh conditions in the trenches, neither the Irish nor the Spanish commanders were willing to modify this grand strategy (or perhaps more realistically, compromise a safe defensive position) to break through to Aguila's courageous garrison and possibly win the war. O'Neill's army of 6,000 infantry and 800 cavalry, supplemented by 250 Spaniards, encamped 5 miles from the besieged Aguila.[93] And for ten days he sat, ignoring pleas from Spanish and Irish advisers to take the field. Aguila promised to sally forth once the besiegers were engaged, joining with an Irish contingent and driving the English from the trenches.[94]

English soldiers, though more experienced with traditional warfare than the Irish, were still unaccustomed to the rigours of a winter siege, particularly in Ireland. Further, Mountjoy was working with raw men in many cases. The dutiful ones had died from exposure in the siegeworks, and the wicked ones had deserted. Recaptured runaways were executed, and at one point

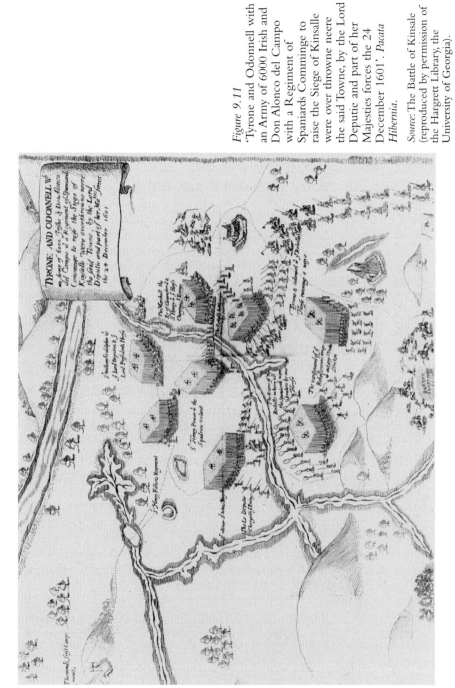

Figure 9.11
'Tyrone and Odonnell with an Army of 6000 Irish and Don Alonco del Campo with a Regiment of Spaniards Comminge to raise the Siege of Kinsalle were over throwne neere the said Towne, by the Lord Deputie and part of her Majesties forces the 24 December 1601'. *Pacata Hibernia.*

Source: The Battle of Kinsale (reproduced by permission of the Hargrett Library, the University of Georgia).

200 were in custody at Waterford awaiting judgement.[95] The undermanned trenches lay vulnerable, especially should they be attacked from Kinsale and at their rear simultaneously. In any event, the English tacticians exploited the slightest advantage, while the Catholics squandered a strategic opportunity, and failed to take any tactical initiative. Ultimately, O'Neill took the offensive, for, while he dallied, Mountjoy resumed artillery fire against Kinsale. In spite of the weather, Spanish marksmen, and mud, the siegeworks had developed sufficiently, with enough cannon in place to effect a breach. If O'Neill did not commit, Mountjoy might storm Kinsale, slaughter the garrison, and turn upon O'Neill, who would have the northern garrisons at his back. O'Neill would be the hunted one. Cutting the English supply line was no longer enough. The Irish would have to fight, and in formation. On the night of 23 December, the Catholic forces lumbered into action.

The attack in three bodies was organised (under O'Neill, Tyrell, and O'Donnell). Captain Richard Tyrell's vanguard would force its way through a gap in the English lines lying between the Earl of Thomond's camp and the fort covering their western flank. From this place, Tyrell was to signal Kinsale, prompting a sally from Aguila's men. Together they would attack, in unison with the main body of Irish under O'Neill and O'Donnell. But the latter commander had had enough of Hugh O'Neill and his restraint. O'Donnell refused to march as the rearguard, and instead wheeled his men abreast of O'Neill's main battle. Gallant and rebellious as the gesture might appear, it had fatal consequences, for the Irish advance became unsynchronised and thus O'Donnell was out of position when battle commenced. O'Neill, too, erred, for he did not engage before dawn, as he had told the Kinsale defenders. Illuminated by early morning, there could be no surprise. Mountjoy's troops opened fire from their positions, and O'Neill pulled off to safer ground. Meanwhile, Tyrell failed to occupy the ground agreed upon, rendering the Kinsale garrison impotent.

Mountjoy, quickly apprehending the tactical situation, divided his forces. The main English army consisting of infantry steadied their siegeworks to repel a sortie from Kinsale. Mountjoy's three regiments of cavalry, in two brigades, were hurled against O'Neill. From amongst his shivering infantry, Mountjoy sent forth three regiments of foot to support the horsemen.

> [T]he Marshall beinge advanced with the horse neere unto the Ford ... perceived the Enymy in some disorder. ... [T]he Marshall as soone as a Winge of the Foote of the Vaunt guard was come uppe unto him, and Sir Henry Power with his Regiment drawn over the Ford, advanced with some *100* Horse ... and gave occasion of skirmishe uppon the bogg side, with some hundred hargubishers; the Enemy thereuppon putt out some of their loose shott from their battell; and ... offered a charge on a battell of *1000* Foote, and Findinge them to stand firme: wheeled a little about.

Figure 9.12 'Heere the Spaniards made a little stand to gather uppe there forces, but were soone put to execution'. *Pacata Hibernia*.

Source: Detail of the battle of Kinsale; the *tercios* fight the English cavalry (reproduced by permission of the Hargrett Library, the University of Georgia).

More English horsemen arrived and 'charged agayne the Horse and the Reere of the same battell, who presently thereuppon, both Horse and Foote Fell into disorder and brake'.[96] The result resembled something from the French wars of religion – an action of highly mobile and charging cavalry. As O'Neill had not assaulted Mountjoy's main camp, and had often been advised that Mountjoy would be preoccupied with Aguila (which he was), the headlong charge of English cavalry into his force, which had been joined by Tyrell, and considering the English horse's numerical inferiority, probably surprised O'Neill.

The first wave of horsemen was beaten back by the Irish foot soldiers. Wingfield's brigade, undeterred by the repulse of their comrades, crashed into the hastily collected Irish formation and broke it up, cavalry as well as infantry. O'Neill's manoeuvre, which had been a careful retreat to safer ground, now became a rout under the second English charge. Had the Irish cavalry fallen hard upon their attackers, the Irish foot might have been able to stiffen their formation and fight on. But the Irish horse fled, and, with the English infantry now coming on, the Gaelic foot soldiers elected to retire. Although outnumbered, the English attackers pressed on, invigorated with the success of their impetuosity, cutting down the fleeing forces.

> ... the Reere of the enemy beinge in the Retreite, the van went of [off] with fewe slaine but with the losse of many of their Armes their battell beinge the greatest bodie was putt all to the sword, and not above some 60 escaped, the Vantguard who went last of [off] were broken on the toppe of the hill, the Irish for the most parte quitt the Spaniards, whoe makinge a stand were broken by the Lord Deputies Troupe, and most of them killed.[97]

The hapless Aguila had been let down, in spite of his heroic sorties and stubborn resistance. The Irish had only themselves to blame in the defeat, for their leadership and deployment had failed them. Hayes-McCoy's verdict stands: 'The immediate cause of defeat was the failure of the main battle to stand up to Wingfield and Power.'[98] The English cavalry had brought the victory, much as English horsemen had done at Turnhout only a few years earlier.[99]

English warfare proved itself at Kinsale: the tactical flexibility of English forces, even when grossly outnumbered, in the hands of an able commander;[100] expert use of artillery; coordination of horse and foot in a situation where the availability of the latter was limited. The victory proved English competence in siege warfare, even under the most adverse conditions; it also showed that their use of cavalry, in which only some nationalities seemed to excel, was impressive. And, as is so often the case, the common foot soldier did his duty at the crucial moment. Kinsale vindicated English arms at a time when guerrilla warfare had instilled self-doubt from within the ranks to the very highest level of government. English chroniclers, from contemporary army secretaries to Victorian antiquarians and twentieth-century historians, paint Mountjoy's victory in the same tones of inevitability and gallantry used to describe 1588, or 1688. Conversely, we have an account, skilfully drawn from Spanish archival sources, which depicts a warmongering Gloriana. Such a portrait, that is comparable to blaming the carnage of 1939 on Polish aggression, disregards the brutal reality that England was fighting for survival. The year 1601, like 1588 before, and 1688 and 1940 afterwards, brought a seemingly miraculous victory but did not remedy England's strategic vulnerability. Kinsale also proved that English warfare had become competitive with continental arts of war by reign's end.

10

THE IRISH MILITARY ESTABLISHMENT, 1603–42

The early Stuart peace in Ireland

Sir Robert Cecil, whose deft diplomatic touch bridged Tudor England with Stuart Britain, opined in 1602 that 'our affairs ... do for the most part depend upon the success of Ireland'. He saw Ireland as the linchpin that held together England's, then Britain's, strategic security.[1] Fifty years later, after the Irish Rebellion had surpassed the Nine Years War in cost, carnage, and intensity, Ireland's strategic importance had been demonstrated beyond doubt. The enormous burden of the army that subdued Ireland in 1600–1 could not be sustained. Expenditures of £208,000 to maintain the military establishment (1 February 1600), followed by greater expense still, threatened to bankrupt the Crown.[2] The Queen's total Irish charges for the year 1 April 1601 to 31 March 1602 came to £322,500, of which £250,000 constituted the 'establishment'.[3] Private contractors shipped bulk arms and (above all) food to Ireland through the early 1600s.[4]

At the height of the mobilisation, English troops numbered 19,000.[5] The Elizabethan peace was kept by 1,200 horse and between 12,000 and 14,000 foot. James reduced this severely to 1,000 cavalry and 8,000 infantry. By spring 1606 the Lord Deputy, Sir Arthur Chichester, had on the rolls merely 234 horsemen and 880 infantrymen.[6] When faced with disorder, Chichester fielded a militia drawn from the tenantry and patronage of his chief subordinates, as happened in October 1606 and the spring of 1608. In the self-defence tradition of Ulster, groups of men ranging in number from ten to sixty assembled under one of the Deputy's commanders and marched, victualled for a month by the localities themselves, to fight 'wood kearnes' or any other threat identified by order from Dublin Castle.[7]

Sir John Davies, Chichester's Solicitor General, had had the opportunity to view the military predicament in Ireland since late 1603. In 1604, when the army had amounted to roughly 3,700 infantry and 229 cavalry, English power resided in garrison: 900 in Munster, 1,200 in Dublin, the Pale and southern Leinster, 400 in Londonderry, and around 1,300 stationed in a series of forts stretching from Carrickfergus to Ballyshannon.[8] Davies lauded

Mountjoy's achievement, but pointed out that massive military operations of that scale were extraordinary, and that a system must be devised to keep the peace. He critiqued earlier martial efforts succinctly: 'First, the armies for the most part were too weak for a conquest; secondly, when they were of a competent strength, as in both the journeys of Richard the Second, they were too soon broken up and dissolved; thirdly, they were ill-paid; and fourthly they were ill-governed, which is always a consequent [sic] of ill-payment.'[9]

The soldier-administrator that ruled late Elizabethan and early Jacobean Ireland, Lord Deputy Sir Arthur Chichester, had received his training in the continental wars. He started where he would finish: Ireland. Fleeing from trouble in England, young Arthur sheltered under the wing of Sir George Bouchier, who later became the Master of Ordnance in Ireland in 1592. Chichester served aboard ship during the Armada fight of 1588 and later campaigned with Drake and Essex. When Chichester's captain was shot dead at Cadiz (1596), Essex promoted Arthur to a captaincy. As a sergeant major in Baskerville's Picardy contingent, he took a bullet in the shoulder at the siege of Amiens (1597), receiving a knighthood from Henry IV. Settled into garrison at Ostend at the rank of captain with 200 men under his command, Sir Arthur was picked through the intercession of Sir Robert Cecil to escort a regiment of 1,200 into Ireland. Not long after, the Earl of Essex arrived at Chichester's Drogheda garrison to review the troops.

> Sir Arthur haveing drawn his Regiment up in a fayre field and exercised them perfectly (at which he was excelent) they being in close order, the Earle thinking to put a sally on them by breaking thorow them, charged at them with his Galant Cavallrie, but the Coloneill (not being used to receive foyles) [mock attacks in order to show off the skills of the attackers] had so ordered his Pikes as they forc't the Earle to a carry coale [a carracole, a wheeling about of horsemen in preparation of a resumed attack], and upon his wheele a saucie fellow with his Pike prickt his Lordship (saveing your reverence) in the arse, and made him bleed, so, he haveing enough of that smarting sport, he retreated, giving the Collonell and his Regiment high Prayse.[10]

Upon Essex's departure from Ireland, he made Sir Arthur Sergeant Major General of the English army there. The wisdom Chichester had gleaned from continental warfare convinced him that Ireland would be won by garrisons and occupation rather than sporadic raiding and set-piece battles, regardless of the fact that the English were adept at the latter forms of fighting. His application of operational and administrative knowledge to Ireland demonstrated how the 'English art of war' was transmuted from one theatre to another. Rising ultimately to the position of Lord Deputy of Ireland, he provided the continuity necessary in the government under

James I, and coped well with the reduced troop strength available in that era, largely through development of an *ad hoc* Protestant militia built upon a patronage network.[11] The shrunken army was overseen by the Muster-Master General, who also served as clerk of the cheque.[12]

The decline of the Jacobean Irish military establishment was arrested partially by increased expenditure for the suppression of the O'Dougherty revolt in the autumn of 1607; however, the Crown was in no position to pledge itself to long-term funding that might rebuild the Elizabethan establishment. The deteriorating Jacobean establishment was inherited by a new treasurer, Sir Thomas Ridgeway in April 1606. In late 1611 the Irish military establishment cost £7,573. In 1613–16 expenditure from London dropped even more sharply.[13] The early years of the reign of Charles I in some ways approximated the strategic dilemma of the Tudors, particularly Elizabeth's, in that Irish and continental commitments competed for royal resources. The 'Irish Road' continued to function through the agency of the mayor of Chester and others, and companies of pressed men were transported and victualled as their Elizabethan ancestors had been.[14] The imperilled state of Protestant Europe brought, however, intervention from England, and continental strategic concerns forced Irish affairs to a lower rung of strategic priority. The certitude of Charles and Buckingham that war with Spain in 1625 could help restore the Elector Palatine, and reverse the Catholic tide, led them, ironically, to tolerate Irish Catholicism to a greater degree and relax royal control over Ireland. The expansion of the continental war to France prompted further concessions to the old English and the Gaels. The King's bellicosity, which in turn created the need for extraordinary revenue, forced English government to grant Irish constituencies greater autonomy at a time when continental war inclined the Crown to centralise without compromise in England. These European manoeuvres reversed a trend towards more rigorous control of government from London, for the grip of Whitehall had been growing tighter and its reach ever longer through the late sixteenth century onwards; and even if James I had decided to demobilise the English military in Ireland so dramatically, after 1612 he brought 'native' Irish, be they old English or Gaelic, to heel. This process was undone by Charles I's fixation upon European strategies.[15] Early Caroline Ireland was granted economic and jurisdictional concessions and expected to maintain its own security through what was in effect an Irish standing army.[16] The Irish military establishment cost settlers significantly. According to Raymond Gillespie, 'Between 1628 and 1632 Antrim and Down paid £6,978 19s. 5d. toward the maintenance of the army.[17]

Charles's Irish military establishment mirrored the management of his later campaigns in the Bishops' Wars. Military preparations were undertaken without sufficient revenue to sustain them, forcing the Crown into a fiscal crisis. While sitting in the House of Commons in the 1620s, Sir

Thomas Wentworth of Yorkshire had opposed the Duke of Buckingham's European military adventures. In the political realignment following the Duke's assassination, the talented Wentworth got his chance to join the King's government. With the 'Personal Rule' of Charles I came a heightened sense of fiscal accountability, and Sir Thomas, in 1631, took on a challenge that some said not even Atlas could shoulder: Ireland. The new Lord Deputy would not only keep the peace, an achievement that had eluded some of the best Elizabethan viceroys. Wentworth would also balance the books of the military establishment in Ireland. He succeeded beyond belief, making a profit and raising an army. Wentworth's administration created a sufficient fiscal base and strove to avoid having its policies 'translated' through the filter of enforcement and implemented by vested interests,

Figure 10.1 Strafford tamed Ireland and similarly might have extinguished the Covenanters' rebellion had he been given the resources to do so. His military talents have not been accorded full recognition by historians.

Source: Sir Thomas Wentworth, later Earl of Strafford (author's collection).

be they new or old English. Ireland had never been fully integrated into royal strategic thinking. For no one could predict the Irish response to the Crown's initiatives. But the Lord Deputy would make the Irish investment reap some royal dividend. This Wentworthian programme to draw Ireland more closely into the orbit around Whitehall not only made it easier to maintain the security of Ireland but also freed the monarch to arrange a grand strategy in relation to the Continent.

One cannot help thinking that the relatively low place of Irish security in the ground strategies of Henry VIII and Charles owed as much to the island's unreliability as to its meagre resources. Henry lacked Elizabeth's lessons about strategic vulnerability, but Charles I should have known better. Viscount Wentworth did. In fact, his cautions about the impact of continental wars, particularly when unnecessary, were expressed not only in the 1620s, but again in 1637, when rumours of war conjured up a spectre that could very easily have undone all Wentworth had achieved in Ireland since 1634. As much as he personally disliked Roman Catholicism, Wentworth felt less of a compulsion to defend Protestants abroad. His interests were firmly planted in the British Isles. And it was this interest that made him resolve to create 'an army in Ireland'. Sir Thomas's army reforms in Ireland were not his. The Irish committee of 1622 had recommended them; but Wentworth carried them out with vigour and characteristic thoroughness.[18]

> The new lord deputy had to face the same financial problems as his predecessor, which had its origins in the need to provide a standing army in Ireland during time of war. . . . But with the declaration of war against Spain in 1625 . . . Ireland was expected to provide for a greatly increased army out of her own resources. The military establishment was raised to 5,000 foot and 500 horse. Even though ordinary income was double what it had been in 1611 and was now £40,000 it was still insufficient to make ends meet. There was a gap between revenue and expenditure of £50,000 per annum.[19]

Irish policy, especially the expansion of plantation, stymied by frequent bruits of conflict with the Hapsburgs, was jeopardised in 1638 by the Scottish troubles. In addition to keeping any Catholic rising in check, Wentworth kept a wary eye on Scots settlers in Ulster, who sympathised with the Covenanter revolt in Lowland Scotland.[20] As in the 1500s, Ireland was regarded at Whitehall as a theatre of secondary importance, for Charles I looked primarily to Scotland (with an occasional glance at the wars in Europe). With the King secretly arming England, Wentworth looked further afield, to Holland, where he dispatched the Master Gunner of Ireland and a quartermaster with £12,000 to obtain everything from 'Redd Scarfes' for his troopers, to 'brasse' culverins.[21] Wentworth weighed the relative costs of casting cannon in Holland rather than England, and even scavenged metal to keep costs in line:

> . . . these ten peeces now to be cast, with their Carriages may be gon on with all in Holland. In regard a Considerable part of the Mettall was sent over before wee received these letters for the casting of them in England; In regard a great part of the Mettall is belonging to the Citty of Dublin, who desire to have the worke done in Holland, as conceiving it may be gott there better, and better Cheape.[22]

The meticulousness of Wentworth's procurement system contrasted with his royal master's penchant for sending off a hapless diplomat or merchant to find arms in Hamburg or Flanders, only to discover the weapons' defects upon their delivery to the Tower.[23] Dutch weapons purchases, Wentworth reckoned, would arm his expeditionary force of 7,000 infantry and 400 cavalry for deployment by Easter 1639.[24] The cuirassiers raised for the First Bishops' War by James Butler, Earl of Ormonde, received Dutch arms and sought bits, 'girt webb', and saddles from suppliers in Chester.[25] Gunpowder, which would prove such a precious commodity in Ireland during the wars of the 1640s, was stockpiled and allocated carefully. Wentworth's powder reserves in 1638–9 amounted to more than 81,000 pounds (equivalent to 812 barrels or 33 lasts) available to naval vessels as well as land forces. The Irish army consumed ammunition worth £971 annually.[26] The First Bishops' War planned a combined Irish operation in spring and summer 1639, consisting of the Earl of Antrim's men and Wentworth's army. While in the end these troops were never transported to the Anglo-Scottish Borders, still Wentworth had fielded well-equipped forces and squared military expenditure with Irish income. Such success elevated him to an English peerage (the earldom of Strafford).

In 1640 Strafford outdid himself, creating not only a superb Irish army for the Second Bishops' War, but also raising money for the English mobilisation via the Irish Parliament. Again, Strafford purchased arms on the Netherlands market.[27] After the Earl's departure for England in autumn 1639, his procurement system continued to reach abroad. In April 1640 arms, tents, 'an hundred horses of a bigge size', and wagons, were to be ordered from England.[28] Arms purchases, with money often channelled through the Irish Treasurer Sir William Raylton (who dwelt in St Martin's Lane in St-Martin-in-the-Fields), were undertaken independently of English purchases. Ireland possessed its own Ordnance Office, to supply the indigenous army. Under Elizabeth the English Ordnance Office had shipped large quantities of military *matériel* into Ireland in support of English forces operating there. In 1639–40, English and Dutch arms had to be imported into Ireland and then sent back out with soldiers destined for the Anglo-Scottish Borders. The arrival of English forces in 1642 would again reverse the polarity.

The management of the Irish Office of Ordnance, for example, required greater stringency and the presence of an able administrator. No longer could the mastership be treated as a sinecure or an impropriation, as on the eve of the rebellion of 1641.[29] Shipping arms to Ireland was one problem. Inventorying, storage, and disbursement also posed great challenges. First, the Irish Ordnance Office was more prone to sinecure abuse and bureaucratic exploitation for private ends than was its much-maligned English counter-part. Second, the garrison system required small depots, which decentralised the Irish system.[30] Some English had come to Ireland for profit, and the mastership of the Ordnance Office fell into this system of profiteering.

In early 1640 Sir John Borlase negotiated with Sir Thomas Lucas and family to arrange 'joint execution' of the office of Master of the Ordnance in Ireland. Borlase had enjoyed lifetime possession of the office by letters patent under the Great Seal since 1635. For £2,000 he would share his position, along with its perquisites. Both Sir John and Sir Thomas boasted military experience, the latter being another example of a Low Countries veteran transplanted to Ireland.[31] At a crucial time, through the prepara-tions for the Second Bishops' War, the trial of Strafford, and the Army Plot, the matter of the mastership of the Ordnance lay unsettled. In fact, control of the Ordnance was not determined until less than ten days before the outbreak of the Irish Rebellion. As the Borlase and Lucas families hammered out a mutually beneficial agreement, the disposition of artillery, munitions, and arms necessarily suffered from the distractions. Sir Thomas and others even made the pilgrimage to the Tower to consult the imprisoned Strafford. With the Lord Lieutenant's fate uncertain, Lucas refused to put up the money and sign the bonds.

Ultimately, Borlase became a Lord Justice and embroiled in the post-Straffordian political struggle. Lucas did become Master of the Ordnance, but he had to abandon his post as Commissary General of the Horse Troops in Ireland, an office the King in fact regarded as an illegal inno-vation.[32] In 1640, military costs rose, the politics of an Irish parliament challenged Strafford, and unrest amongst Scottish planters in Ulster made unmanageable a situation that had nearly achieved that end. The Bishops' Wars doomed royal control over Ireland at the very moment that royal control over Scotland was proved impossible and England, too, was slip-ping from the royal grasp. At that point, the King turned to Strafford too late, and the 'army in Ireland' that might have saved Charles I instead became Strafford's undoing.[33]

The force Strafford had created in only a few years in Ireland surpassed the English shire militias substantially in terms of training, supply, and cohe-sion. The Earl saw to the proliferation of gunpowder weapons, deploying more cannon, replacing harquebuses with muskets.[34] Given Charles I's attempts to create a 'perfect militia', Strafford's achievement is impressive, for he came much closer to perfection in a theatre notorious for its lack of military sustenance than did the Lords Lieutenants in the fat, pastoral counties of England. Strafford saw armed force as an extension of policy. His army became an appendage of the efficient government he created. His troops marched with the same precision that he expected of the Customs Farm. The Lord Deputy's approach to government, which demanded a level of performance that outstripped the respectable amateurism of English local government, including the management of the trained bands, approached the more modern concept of a professional armed force. That improvement threatened to upset the old balance, vague and 'illegal' as it might have been, between what the Crown might expect and what the subject would render towards the military obligation. The stridence of the charges against the Lieutenant speak for themselves. 'Strafford trayterously and wickedly devised and contrived by force of Armes in a warlike manner to subdue the Subjects of the said Realme of Ireland, to bring them under his tyrannical power and will.'[35]

Strafford demanded his army be fit: well clad, supplied, and trained. By 1636 he had regularised pay and equipment, though not to a level of his full satisfaction. The Earl's inspections of the columns epitomised thoroughness. He eyed each soldier, exercised them in his very presence, and judged their ability by his own standards, not the reports of subordinates.[36] As Strafford was an extension of the Crown, and his troops acted under his direct command, these soldiers embodied the authority of Charles I, and thus were to behave with dignity, obeying the laws like their fellow subjects, 'a company of gallant Gentlemen their officers, fit to serve a great and wise King'. On the march, sufficient money was proffered for food, and plunder was forbidden. Strafford's vision looked beyond the seventeenth century, for he conceived '. . . the army, as of absolute necessity to the government [in Dublin] was rather to be reinforced than at all diminished, as an excellent minister and assistant in the execution of all the King's writts; betwixt the British and the Native, betwixt the Protestant and the Papist.'[37] The army was an instrument of government that promoted policy of state. For that reason it was professional in a sense, and centralised. Little wonder that Parliament found the spectre of the Earl of Strafford leading this army so frightful.

This conception of armed force was carried to the highest level, the English Privy Council, when Strafford transferred his services across the Irish Sea, at his King's request in 1639–40. His arrival in England, where he took his place at the Council table as the recently elevated Earl, allowed the Irish Rebellion to foment and ultimately, in the chambers of Westminster, force the issue of who controlled England's militia, the closest thing to a standing army. The military nature of the Straffordian threat was construed as a treason that encompassed 'by force of armes to compell' the King's subjects into obedience. The Irish army comprised much of that force. The most unjust of the articles levied against the Earl charged that his actions had betrayed '. . . divers of his Majesties subjects to death, his [Charles I's] Army to a dishonourable defeat by the Scots at Newborn, and the Towne of New-Castle into their hands'. On the contrary, Strafford was the one person who might have averted military disaster in 1640, and perhaps even brought victory in 1639.[38] Certainly the Irish army fashioned for intervention in the North of England in 1640 was one of the superior military forces of the early Stuart era. While Britain's King struggled to field an English army to protect England's northern border, Strafford's Irish force (even in his absence) continued to drill and maintain a high level of morale, even if their transport had not arrived and tales were told of chaotic 'newe levyes in Ireland'. A glowing report from the Carrickfergus embarkation point described Strafford's army:

> . . .The coming of the Troop heather [hither] I shall only tell you that thes are not the men that were at Dublinne or Clonnell. For those were poore stinking Rascally sneaks. Thes are brave gallant fellows shuch as a man would cho[o]se if a Crowne lay at stake. There Cloaths are better, there Persons better and there Mettell is better.[39]

It has been suggested that the 1640 war was lost largely because certain treacherous Yorkshiremen delayed the calling-out of the trained bands in defence of the North. The arrival of the Earl of Strafford in that recalcitrant shire, at the head of disciplined Irish troops, might have catalysed the mobilisation.[40] Strafford's planned incursion into Yorkshire represented a politically dangerous reversal of destination, for English troops had always been sent into Ireland, not 'Irish' soldiers into England. The Crown invested heavily in the Irish military, perhaps disastrously so, ironically. In April 1640 half a dozen bronze cannon, 11 pieces of iron ordnance, 2,000 muskets, and 1,500 pikes were ordered to be sent from the Port of London to Dublin.[41] Had those arms gone directly to York, the war might have turned out differently. Ireland, perceived traditionally as a logistical 'black hole' that devoured *matériel* without trace, now became an organisational base for a royal army, a force that required equipment normally shipped from England – for example, bits, saddles, and girth web for the steeds of the cavalry. That the resourceful Christopher Wandesford (Master of the Rolls and, after Strafford's departure, Lord Deputy) was able to equip the army is remarkable.[42] He imposed subsidies for impressment, charges for wagons, and saw that imprests were made to the officers. Chronic victualling problems were met by '. . . letters drawne to the Sheriffes of the severall counties through which the Troopes are to passe to cause provisions to be made for the Souldiers.'[43] What could not be got in Ireland was collected from England: for example, 'an hundred horses of a bigge size' and thirty wagons from London.

The efficiency and vigour characteristic of the Irish Council of War in the absence of its architect demonstrated the efficacy of centralised military leadership for the waging of war by the English in Ireland.[44] A begrudging amazement and genuine fear filled the hearts of English Members of Parliament who complained (after 1640) that

> . . . in the month of May and June last, the said Earle did raise an Army in the said Realme of Ireland, consisting of eight thousand foot, and in their places were a thousand Papists, or thereabouts, put into the said old Army by the said Earle.[45]

It seems inconceivable that Ireland would have erupted in rebellion had Strafford been alive. Had that cataclysm occurred during his tenure, whether he was in Dublin or England, it would have been crushed utterly and ruthlessly. One recalls how he browbeat and shamed the Yorkshiremen in the Second Bishops' War. Strafford was a force to be reckoned with when he had an armed force at his disposal.[46]

According to Edmund Borlase, a Protestant source, '. . . the Earl of Strafford raised 8000 Foot, and 1000 Horse, additional to the Veterane Forces'.[47] How strong were English forces in Ireland in 1640? The Earl of Strafford's celebrated 'army in Ireland' gathered at Carrickfergus in June and July 1640, awaiting deployment in a combined operation with Charles I's English armies, that were supposed to move from their respective shires to the Scottish Borders.[48] A 'Catholic' source reported:

> There have beene 8,000 men of warr in his majesties paie in Ireland before those comotions, as against the Scotts whoe weare in armes against his majestie, but were disbanded by the state, Dublin receavinge theire order for that purpose from the parliament of England.[49]

The articles of impeachment against Strafford stated:

> [In] the moneth of March, before the beginning of the last Parliament, the said Earle of Strafford went into Ireland, and procured the Parliament of that Kingdome to declare their assistance in a warre against the Scots. And gave directions for the raising of an Army consisting of 8000 foot, and 1000 horse, being for the most part Papists, as aforesaid. And confederating with one Sir George Radcliffe, did together with him the said Sir George, trayterously conspire to imploy the said Army for the ruine and destruction of the Kingdome of England.[50]

We can ascertain the cost of the Irish army of 1640 and estimate its size. The annual pay of the officers and transport services was calculated at £11,111.[51] The latter figures compare, at least in terms of rates of pay and allotment of wagons, to a list approved by Parliament in 1641.[52] We can gauge the military demographics at between 6,000 and 8,000 men in the summer of 1640, demobilised to perhaps 3,000 by October 1641, and then swelling (though slowly at first) to between 22,000 and 37,000 mostly Protestant soldiers by 1642.[53] An intelligence report sent to the King on 12 December 1641 estimated 2,000 loyal men confined in Drogheda and a field army of 3,000.[54] The escalation included remnants from the Bishops' Wars – for example, Sir Simon Harcourt, a veteran of Hamilton's amphibious campaign of 1639, who brought over 1,100 English infantry on 30 December 1641.[55] The 1641 list printed by Temple at the eve of the Rebellion accounts for 2,051 infantrymen (at 44 soldiers per company) under 246 officers, with 901 cavalry and their officers (42) making the entire force 3,240.[56] This represents the reduced army, partially demobilised after the Second Bishops' War.[57] The company officers present in 1641 reveal a migration from the disbanded royal army raised in England in 1640. So the officer list of the English army of 1641 is an amalgam of loyal 'Irish' English, many of whom had roots in the post-Elizabethan settlement (Docwra, Coote, Borlase, and Loftus), and men who had served the King faithfully in the Scottish campaigns of 1639 and 1640 (St Leger, Terringham, Price, Byron, and Ogle). Coote was a veteran of Kinsale who bequeathed not only Irish lands but a martial spirit to his son. The conduct of operations under men such as Coote must be evaluated within the context of their perceptions of territory. They fought on what they regarded as their own soil, justified by conquest and further legitimised by tenure based on English forms of real proprietary holding. The Irish Rebellion was not an adventurous expeditionary campaign overseas. Rather, the Irish saw themselves as fighting for the very survival of their families and homes. Indeed, the officer corps carried over from the Second Bishops' War in fact contained some Roman Catholics.[58]

Rebellion and civil war

On 22 October 1641 revolt erupted in Ulster, and the day following the insurgents attempted unsuccessfully to seize Dublin. By 26 October, Armagh lay in the hands of Sir Phelim O'Neill. Ormonde assumed command as Lieutenant General of the royal army on 11 November. On 21 November 1641 Mellifont was sacked by rebels and Drogheda besieged. A week later loyalists foiled an assault on Lisburn, while a column sent to relieve Drogheda was beaten by rebels at Julianstown:

> . . . they sent 500 well trained foote with a troupe or two . . . but the Irish then naked . . . mett them in theire marche at the bridge of Gillam, fell upon soe couragiously that never a one of the foote escaped with life, the horse saved themselves by Icarian flight.

The rebels 'gott well by this daie service, the armes and amunition of these 500 which was noe smale encouragement'. The momentum of revolution propelled the insurgents forward.

> [A]fter the overthrow of the six hundred English at Gillianstown . . . the Irish were lifted up. . . . [F]riars were dispersed among the rebel soldiers, who with tears exhorted and set them to kill the English, whom God had so wonderfully given into their hands, . . . the Irish rebels told him that they admired [i.e. wondered] at the behaviour of the English, being so many and well armed, why they did not at once at least discharge their muskets, and that if they had made but ten shots the Irish would have fled, they concluded that God had taken away the heart of the English, and now they would destroy them all out of the kingdom (their words being '*now we will devour the seed of the English out of the land*'), and they said when they had rid them out of Ireland, they would go over into England and not leave the memorial of the English name under heaven, and some said they would have England as long in possession as the English has possessed Ireland.[59]

'The O'Reillys did much extol themselves for being the destroyers of those 600 English, for that by their valour, as they said, all the Pale before that morning and all Ireland was brought together to be joined in that war.'[60] It was alleged that the mixed contingent within the relief column had faltered at least in part because native Irish troops marched within the ranks, who subsequently deserted to the rebels.[61]

'I have (with as little of apparence as may be, of distrustinge the Papistes,) lookte into the number of the Protestantes of this Regiment; and I finde them to be upwards of 700, besides one companie lately raised of Captain gibsons, that hathe but 3 papistes in it.' Sir Henry Tichborne then requested 'payment of his [Captain Gibson's] souldiors, most of them being of Englishe that have beene Robde, and have little other subsistance.'[62] Tichborne informed Ormonde on 14 November 1641, from Drogheda: 'The Companies heere are compleate; the souldiers cheer full and exceedinge Willinge to goe uppon service, the greater parte, are English or of Englishe parents; 2 partes I am sure if not more are Protestants'.[63]

From the Catholic native perspective, the success of the Covenanting armies of Scotland and an increasingly anti-popish English Parliament placed the Catholic Irish in a dilemma common enough during the wars of religion. People might take to arms before their religion (and the people themselves) could be exterminated. The savagery of the Elizabethan wars was quickly revived and exceeded. The Irish justification for 'raisinge in armes' entailed 'maintaininge the holy religion, defence of his majesties prerogatives and vindication of the free libertie of the Irish Nation'.[64] The Long Parliament responded by attempting to raise a volunteer force of 6,000 foot soldiers and 2,000 horsemen. In negotiations with the Scots to forge joint military actions against the Roman Catholics of Ireland, an army of 10,000 was proposed (to be matched by a similar Covenanter force). Administratively, Parliament seized control of military preparations with unprecedented resolve and relegated the mobilisation and deployment to a committee for Irish Affairs comprised of both Houses. A more specialised commission for the war, assisted by the non-resident Lord Lieutenant of Ireland (the Earl of Leicester), came into being in March 1642. Charles I kept his hand in the business by authorising Ormonde, who commanded the government's forces (though somewhat constrained by Dublin), to appoint officers without reference to the more parliamentary-minded Leicester.[65]

The establishment's fiscal and administrative scale, which had reached such unprecedented levels in 1598–1601, culminating in the victory at Kinsale, increased ominously. Cost matched size. In November 1640 the government's Irish army consumed £1,000 a day and, although partially demobilised and put in garrison, the force still cost the government £6,000 in early 1641.[66] The similarity to the styles of 'national' fighting of the late 1590s was obvious. The English sent forth columns to relieve threatened strategic locations. *En route* the columns plundered supplies and scorched the earth. Although frugal garrisoning had proven reasonably effective in Ireland, the London government, often the King himself, obstructed adequate garrisoning because the early Stuarts remained strapped for cash and regarded Ireland as less of a strategic imperative than had Elizabeth.

The existence of an Irish army, officered by Protestants but inclusive of Catholic soldiers, became a political issue of magnitude in England. That this army had been raised and equipped outside English channels, so to speak, made its supply politically questionable. Against whom would the army fight?

A cynical Parliament and an untrustworthy King hesitated to procure arms for Irish combatants because war might break out in England and weapons would be needed at home. Further, the situation in Ireland was difficult to judge, and in whose hands arms would ultimately end up was a relevant concern. Supply of artillery, powder, shoes, and victuals became crucial to the conduct of the Irish war. The influx of weapons determined the scale of the conflict.

Ormonde proposed immediate action against the rebels, even if that meant denuding strategic defensive areas, such as Dublin. Using arms stockpiled by Strafford for use in the Second Bishops' War, Ormonde planned to rout the rebel infantry with trained companies, supplemented by 'a fine train of field artillery'. But the Lord Justices baulked, the rebels armed, and the momentum shifted in the New Year.[67] Cargoes for Ireland in the winter of 1641–2 confirmed that the English government again had grasped the nature of Irish warfare. Dragoon arms (carbines, belts, swivels, etc.), horses, and wagons, made up much of the consignments, as mobility was paramount in Ireland. Light horse could deliver firepower rapidly, and there were never enough wagons and horses available. Muskets, shot, and powder claimed a high priority as well. Finally, artillery made its way across the Irish Sea in greater proportion than ever.[68]

The rebellion reinitiated a pattern of warfare that resembled the strategy of the 1590s, when Catholics employed hit-and-run tactics to undermine the Protestant garrisons and their scant logistical infrastructure. Another parallel with the Elizabethan wars was England's inability to bring to bear its full military might (and that, of course, included supplies and artillery). Where in the 1590s English units were committed to continental service, in 1641–2 the confrontation between Charles I and his Parliament diverted resources. The militia controversy meant that, regardless of ideological position, English citizens wanted the tools of war within their reach, not at someone else's reach. Likewise the King was understandably reluctant to allow weapons and clothing to leave his English kingdom, while Parliament took care to see that arsenals lay unmolested in London and elsewhere. Thus when civil war erupted in England in 1642, a 36,000-man Protestant army was fragmented throughout Ireland, clamouring for shoes, swords, and biscuit.[69] England may have been spared continental military involvement in 1642, but in fact the wars of religion had already drained significant resources in the Irish theatre.

Strafford's successes instilled short memories at Whitehall. Thus English arms were forced back on the tactics and strategy of the decades before the arrival of Mountjoy. Other parallels between the 1590s and the 1641 revolt were those of logistics and arms procurement, or, more incisively, how cleverly the rebels armed and fed themselves. Irish accounts celebrate treachery – how, for example, the Dublin government, in its fear, armed what were regarded as loyal Irish inhabitants in Westmeath in late 1641, only to have the recipients foment a rising; these were descendants of O'Neill's red-coated sharpshooters. The houses of the great, including the castle of Sir Charles Coote, were stripped of arms.

Two recurrent themes in accounts of the military history of the Irish Rebellion are, first, how the Irish acquired arms, and, second, their *esprit de corps*. In guerrilla fashion the Catholics prised weapons from the enemy and, in spite of the training of the English, seized the initiative. A component of Irish legend is how they used English weapons to take British lives. Similarly, Protestant forces struggled to find sufficient weaponry, fearing that the rebels had gathered all to themselves.[70] Inchiquin, upon landing at Cork in November 1642, looked to Ormonde for weapons, that his 'men shall with Jaw-bones, kill soe many rebbells, as may arme themselves by the spoyle'.[71]

In order to seize the strategic initiative, Gaelic warfare would have to come to terms with continental warfare, specifically contemporary siegecraft.

When Phelim O'Neill set about capturing Drogheda, he arrived in camp without an artillery train. Nor did he construct works of circumvallation, but rather posted troops in key villages in the surrounding area. Discovering a weak link in Drogheda's defences, a decrepit section of wall where 'easy pickaxe work' might 'pierce it', the rebels launched a night attack. However, poor coordination amongst the infiltrators alerted the garrison before the gate could be taken. The attack was repulsed by pikemen and cavalry. The besieged possessed sufficient weaponry, though victuals were not plentiful. The absence of ordnance rendered O'Neill almost powerless, as the inhabitants of Drogheda on occasion sallied out and captured corn and cattle. Ormonde soon arrived with a relief force and dispersed the rebel outposts after a brief battle. The Lieutenant General wished to press the advantage and pursue the Irish forces into the North, perhaps thereby ending the revolt.[72]

On 27 November 1641 Colonel Sir Charles Coote marched to relieve Castle Wicklow with 500 infantry and 50 cavalry.[73] The English forces meted out summary justice that would have been somewhat unusual in other theatres of operation. On the second day of the march, two alleged spies were hanged on the spot. The following day 'men and women' were 'executed'. And when on the 29th the Castle was relieved and revictualled, Coote himself participated in the scouting operations and killed a captured rebel with 'his owne Pistoll'. Sir Charles's zeal inspired some of his men and also contributed to the frequency of atrocity that made the Irish wars as savage as the Thirty Years War.[74] Terror was sown liberally, because the English tactical units, typically small, as were most English forces in Ireland, dared not tarry. Dublin's garrison remained undermanned and vulnerable, and Coote's force returned quickly. First, however, they had to face 1,000 Irish partisans under Luke O'Toole. Irish forces, which had shadowed Coote's march, now

> shewed themselves to our Fronts making ready to fight, and when wee had marched about 2 miles they came downe towards Sir Charles and his men as they were in a narrowe lane, a Bogge being of the one side of them and a little wood on the other, thinking there to have gott the advantage of that place. . . . Sir Charles his men beeing in some little disorder at the First, the Enemies came on boldlie and swiftlie with a great showt after their barbarous manner, but by that time that 2 or 3 vollies of shott were given on both sides Sir Charles and his men recovered the Hill where they found good ground both for Horse and Foote, From which place our musquiteers [fired] on them very feircely and both slew some and hurt a great meany. So that they suddainlie dispersed themselves and fledd toward the bogge and into the woods.[75]

On 1 December 1641 the battle of Kilcoole was fought, and by mid-December Coote had assaulted Santry and Clontarf.

On the eve of 1642, Coote's forays against the rebels and the defence of Drogheda indicated that the Protestant forces were holding their own. The arrival of Sir Simon Harcourt's 1,100 infantry on 30 December 1641 boded well. Combining the 3,000 troops of the government with 4,000 Ulster volunteers, 'loyalist' forces put into the field reasonably well-equipped and trained units. In early February 1642, Parliament debated sending into Ireland all officers of that establishment who were absent, upon pain of being cashiered. The Lord Lieutenant of Ireland answered that '. . . the old companies both horse and Foot doe stand on the Kings List, and there-fore [Parliament] could neither Stop their Pay nor Casheere' them without the King's knowledge. Lord Wilmot fell into that category, and asked Edward Hyde to see that Charles I would permit his confinement to England on grounds of ill health. Wilmot (who had fought at Newburn) had 'had a Troope of horse in Ireland ever since the Bataill at Kinsale'. At present Wilmot's charge was assumed by Sir Edward Povey, 'who hath commanded that troope under me ever since the battell of Kinsale, and is knowne to be an Expert Captaine'.[76] Charles Wilmot too passed this legacy to his son, as did Sir Charles Coote.[77]

While the rebellion spread, therefore, throughout 1642, adequate counter-insurgent armies met the challenge, supplemented by forces from England (George Monck's 1,500 infantry on 20 February 1642, for example). Once in Ireland, these new troops had to be billeted and fed, and thus the Irish establishment, which possessed a minuscule commissariat and Ordnance Office, tackled logistical problems unseen since the Nine Years War. Sir Philip Perceval enumerated the provisioning and quartering difficulties he experienced with the forces about Trim. The companies lay scattered in billets throughout Bermingham county; the army's horses had to be marked and accounted for, and carriages and carts constructed immediately. Caches of hay and corn needed to be stockpiled in newly constructed storehouses. All this required ready money. Disputes over rations and lodgings erupted; horses were stolen.[78]

Coote and Ormonde enjoyed success in the field and in raising sieges. The former gained victory upon victory until killed outside Trim on 7 May 1642. The latter achieved an important triumph at Kilrush on 15 April 1642. Ormonde had ventured forth from Dublin with 3,000 infantry and 500 cavalry to retake strategic castles and towns, primarily in Kildare and Carlow, which would help secure the areas between Dublin and his lands in Kilkenny. As was often the case in Irish warfare, Omonde's column was under greatest threat as it navigated the roads leading to its home base. About twenty miles from Dublin, between Rathmore and Kilrush, a rebel force of perhaps 6,000–8,000, entrenched itself upon high ground to impede Ormonde's march. The Lieutenant General understood that an attack on this numerically superior and well-positioned army was hazardous, and the insurgents probably stayed in the field on this occasion because an English assault on such a position would likely incur staggering casualties. Such a major reverse might well break the back of the Dublin government given that the loyalist army had been reduced to perhaps 2,400 effectives in terms of infantry and 400 horsemen. The latter in particular were exhausted from relief missions in eastern Leinster. Numerous ill soldiers, from the garrisons as well as from the expeditions, slowed the movement of Ormonde's army, burdened as it already was with scores of carriages for hauling ammunition and victuals to outlying castles and town garrisons. Ormonde's attempts to outmanoeuvre the rebel army failed.

True to the practices of Gaelic warfare, the English had been worn down and were ripe for disaster. Although the Lieutenant General and his commanders had studiously avoided any engagement with the formidable army that had dogged their march back to Dublin, the ensconcement of the Gaels lay so close to the roadway that its proximity forced battle.[79] Ormonde drew up his men in formation behind the tree-lined lane, looking across 'deepe plowed ground' and a dry ditch fortification to the heights, upon which sat two bodies of roughly 1,500 infantry each, flanked by rebel horse. To the English right was a bog and upon the left yet another hill, this crowned with two blocks of Irish infantry, perched above the defile, as it wound between the two occupied hillocks. If they had marched any farther, the English column would have been surrounded on both sides as it passed beneath this elevated ground. Five English artillery pieces were wheeled up to the very edge of the lane, punctuating the tree line, their barrels aimed at the earthen bulwarks on the heights directly opposite. Placing the baggage and little munition he had remaining directly to the rear, Ormonde laid out the regiments in two broken lines, with a single reserve, a formation somewhat 'Roman' in its flexible configuration. The firelocks under Sergeant Major Berry, recently arrived from England, anchored themselves directly behind the exposed artillery.

The opening action also showed some 'Roman' characteristics, with some of the firelocks and about 150 musketeers acting as 'velites', using the impact of missile weapons to break up the enemy formation.[80] A cannonade did little if any physical damage to the Irish defensive position. The infantry bearing firearms trudged up the hill, discharged their pieces, provoking the rebels. By this time the opposing 'lines' were within 100 yards of one another, and, with Irish attention focused on the smoke and noise of the advancing English gunmen, Ormonde's cavalry sprang into action, in a flanking manoeuvre. This expert coordination of firepower and shock, and full use of the cavalry, shook the Irish position, prompting some to fall back to boggy ground on the opposite side of the hill. Perhaps sensing that the English might pursue too aggressively, Lord Viscount Mountgarret and Hugh Burne, the Irish commanders, seized this opportunity to plunder the English cannon, wagons, and munition. This right wing of the rebel army had endured the English fusillade. The equestrian displays of Sir Thomas Lucas and Sir Richard Grenville succeeded in routing the Irish left. To meet the right wing Ormonde now marshalled his troop of volunteer cavalry and 300 infantry. A firefight erupted in which the English prevailed, and the rebel right followed the left in hasty retreat. The Irish lost perhaps 700 men, most of whom were overtaken in the rout. Loyalist forces claimed to have suffered fewer than 100 casualties.[81]

Sir William St Leger reported the situation in May 1642, from Cork. Reinforcements at the quayside, awaiting a fair wind to Ireland, were ordered back to London, for the rift between Charles and the Parliament had suddenly grown 'on to a greater and more deplorable distaunce'.[82] The war raging in Ireland by 1642 had become the greatest conflagration ever to ravage that island. As both sides diligently sought arms from Britain, the scope of the war broadened with imported powder and weapons from the more seasoned European arms markets of the Thirty Years War, a process that had been exploited systematically since 1638. By late summer 1642 combined armies of English, Scots, and 'loyal Irish' amounted to 36,000 and were poised to crush the rebellion. But Edgehill (23 October 1642) reversed the polarity of Anglo-Irish conflict, and companies shifted back to mainland British fields of battle, prolonging the Irish Rebellion through the rest of the decade.[83] Vigorous suppression of the revolt depended upon resupply from England. A fortnight after Edgehill, loyalist operations were foundering without supplies, especially money, match, and powder.[84] Captain Tucker described Sir Francis Willoughby's effort against Maynooth:

> He had with him fifteen hundred foot, of which at least two hundred had never a pair of shoes, the horse in worse condition, the train of artillery very meanly provided, the cry and the wants did so pierce me as I could not abide in the field, and, to say the truth, their necessities were so great that I sorrow to think that the state of England should be so much dishonoured in name to employ men, and not given them what is fitting for them.[85]

Just as hostilities broke out in England, at Marshalls Elm, Babylon Hill, and Powick Bridge, loyalist forces were prevailing in Ireland. Inchiquin achieved successes in county Cork in late August, and then in November won the battle of Bandon Bridge. By that time, though, civil war had come to England. Edgehill had been fought, and the show of force at Turnham Green had brought the reality of war home to London and southern England. In late 1642 Arthur Loftus anticipated fighting a rebel force of 7,000 foot, 2,000 horse, and their train of 'four peeces of Batterie'.[86] By mid-1643 too many garrisons were like that at Naas. For nearly a month the soldiers had lived on a ration of three pounds of biscuit, and the clerk of the store demanded immediate payment for that. The subsistence diet left the men 'begging and starving' and prone to pillaging the townspeople. Some captains took drastic action. Fearing the arrival of a besieging force of 1,500 foot and 100 horses, Lord Esmonde found that even as governor of the town of Duncannon he could not restrain captains from taking victualling matters into their own hands. One Captain Weldon took from the fortress store his company's ration and

> locked it upp in his chamber, and would not suffer his companye have anny part of it (they being then in distress of victualls) untill I was forced to comand som officers to breake upp his dore, and soe supplyed his companye.[87]

It was all too reminiscent of the plight of Irish garrisons in the 1500s.[88]

The English Crown and its enemies saw Ireland as one of the theatres in the global struggle between Protestantism and Roman Catholicism, which it was. Irish defeat ensured Dutch survival.[89] Ironically, the culmination of the struggle, the siege of Kinsale, in fact resembled the Dutch wars, and the English and Spanish fought it out as they would have at Ostend, for example. Though Kinsale was anomalous to classic Irish warfare, it demonstrated English military proficiency. The Irish wars bore their own distinctive characteristics: assaults on marching columns, garrisoning which posed greater logistical problems than supplying even those outposts and cities of Scotland and the Netherlands, atrocity and privation. The terrain and geographical remoteness from central supply bureaucracies made it, operationally, a different kind of war from conflicts in the Low Countries.

The period 1595–1601 in fact demonstrated that if the Gaels mobilised sufficient resources and learned English forms of drill and manoeuvre, they could wage war successfully, provided they remained within the context of Irish warfare: hit-and-run tactics and harassing marching columns. When the Irish learnt the English art of war and kept the struggle within their own terrain, they proved themselves to be formidable, not just in 1595–1601, but in 1641–2 and afterwards. The chronology of English warfare synchronises poorly with Irish warfare in the 1640s. Whereas July 1642 marked a decisive point – the shedding of first blood and the commencement of the English Civil War – Ireland had already endured by mid-1642 campaigning on a scale unseen since Kinsale. To terminate our survey in 1642 is to engage in an arbitrary and anglocentric view of 'Celtic' warfare. But, with that caveat, one can see that the Irish Rebellion precipitated a delayed but decisive English response to military challenges originating in Ireland.[90] English warfare in Ireland triumphed in 1601 and 1649 when given priority over other theatres and when driven by the supplies, money, and officers requisite for victory.

11

THE CAROLINE ART
OF WAR

Early Stuart continental warfare and the Cadiz expedition

Hans Huhm, a Brabantine corporal serving in the Governor of Ostend's company during the siege of that city, murdered his sergeant during the night and was summarily executed the following day (23 March 1603).[1] Also shuffling off the mortal coil that day was Gloriana, Queen Elizabeth I. Historians, who tend to compartmentalise eras to make sense of them, draw sharp distinctions between warfare under the last Tudor and warfare during the reign of the early Stuarts. Certainly the accession of James I marked major changes in foreign policy, which affected England's involvement in war. But, in places such as Ostend, British soldiers continued to hold their positions in the spring of 1603 just as they had in the summer of 1601. In short, there existed elements of continuity between the Tudor age and the early seventeenth century. The English art of war was learnt abroad, and thus new dynastic policies that affected the domestic scene in Britain were felt less acutely in the trenches of Ostend. In September 1605, still ensconced in the Cautionary Towns, English units continued to fight the wars of religion. At Bergen-op-Zoom 5,000 Spanish infantry, supported by five horse companies, hurled themselves against the English garrison's defences in a night attack aimed at three city gates simultaneously. Despite the withering defensive fire, the attackers nearly breached a gate using a 'Petarre' device with an extendable/retractable ladder. Nevertheless, Bergen-op-Zoom held out, with the English troops assisted by women and children in barricading the gates.[2]

The Cleves–Jülich war of succession (1610–14), a European dynastic war fought within the context of the bitter religious animosity that followed the assassination of Henry IV of France, posed a significant threat to Britain. The strategic location of the theatre of operations, in relation to the Low Countries and the Germanys, made it a vortex into which the combatants of the wars of religion threw themselves in desperation. Textbooks refer to Jacobean halcyon years, but war fever infected much of southern

England, and the fortunes of 'our Armie' made exciting reading for the contemporary English public. While technically at peace, James participated in the wars of religion, as he 'sent a puissant Armie' to Nassau's aid in 1610, and remained embroiled with continental conflicts, which accelerated with the Bohemian crisis of 1618 that ignited the Thirty Years War. English volunteer companies intervened on Denmark's behalf in its war with Sweden, 1611–13, and Stuart military support of the Danes would continue for more than two decades.[3] It is no coincidence that the period of the Cleves–Jülich war and the succouring of the Swedes generated significant improvements in the rating and training of the Jacobean militia around 1613–15.[4] In September 1614 Prince Maurice's army boasted twenty-nine English companies under Sir Horace Vere, eleven commanded by Sir John Ogle, and twelve companies under Sir Edward Cecil. The latter, along with Sir Charles Morgan (Lieutenant Colonel to Ogle), would see even more action in the latter half of the 1620s.[5]

All this time, Englishmen served in garrisons in the United Provinces[6] and often marched in the field armies of Protestants and, on occasion, Catholics. A stream of English volunteers enlisted in the continental wars from the late Elizabethan period, through the Jacobean 'peace' and into the reign of Charles I.[7] From late 1624 through to 1628, the drum beat incessantly.[8] Even though James I and, to a degree, Charles I had disengaged from theatres of war that had seen incursions of English units during the reign of Elizabeth, these troops remained, in a practical and diplomatic sense, out of reach of the Stuart monarchs. Charles could not easily exercise his right to recall his subjects to serve under the banner of St George, for he would endanger his allies and personal prestige. Thus the campaigns of 1624–5, 1625, and 1627 contained higher proportions of pressed men than would have been advisable.[9]

England's military resurgence came as a reaction to the Thirty Years War: the aborted 1621 expedition in relief of the Palatinate,[10] the defence of Bergen-op-Zoom (1622), the revival of the Council of War, the Mansfeld expedition in late 1624–5, and Charles's military support of Denmark.[11] The King declared in October 1626,

> When the Impriall Crowne of this Realme descended first vpon vs we found our selues engaged in a Warr, vndertaken and entred by our late Deare father . . ., not willinglye, nor vpon light and ill grounded counsell, but that by the many prouocations of an ambitious enemy. . . .

Charles harped on the essentially defensive justification for military intervention on behalf of the Danish King: '. . . otherwise our comon enemy [Spain and the Empire], will in an instant become Master of all Germanye' to the detriment of British trade and security.[12] In a sort of Elizabethan reprise, it was conceived that a lightning stroke against Iberia was a good defence, hence the Cadiz expedition of 1625. The decision to go to war was a royal one, made in concert with the Duke of Buckingham. Flawed foreign policy made for a flawed campaign, and the Cadiz expedition resembled Henry VIII's reckless incursions upon the Continent. But Charles Stuart was not Henry Tudor, and the former (although he did cast the royal eyes upon the preparations) lacked the latter's dynamism, a quality that was desperately needed in the campaign. Buckingham might have brought the requisite leadership skills to the expedition, but entanglement in diplomacy precluded his assumption of command personally.

Historians have dealt mainly with the military administration of the Cadiz campaign, examining institutions and procedures to illuminate the governmental structure of Caroline England. The dismal failure of this exploit generated more than the usual blame for military disaster, and those accusations, which detail muskets lacking touchholes, rotten victuals, and overall poor logistical execution, may lead to criticism of administration in general, rather than individuals. But the Cadiz expedition saw a lapse in command, not uncommon in Tudor–Stuart amphibious warfare, which compounded the customary weaknesses of early Stuart military administration. Parallels with the Portugal campaign (1589) abound.

In mid-September 1625 Charles spent more than a week at Plymouth overseeing the outfitting of the expedition. The King

> . . . went aboard many of the shipps, and . . . tooke a veiwe of the whole Armie, using all dilligence in his owne person to accomodate and send them forth about the intended enterprise and for an incouragement to all men imployed in this service and to testifie his gratious affection towardes the sea and land comanders, bestowed the honor of Knighthood upon divers of the Captaines of his owne shipps and upon some other Captaines of land Companies.[13]

Along with the knighthoods, Charles might have bestowed some instructions about the grand strategy this gallant crew was expected to fulfil. In fact, the expedition was hampered by an 'almost total lack of strategic planning'.[14] Amazingly, even though the Council of War had existed since 1624, strategic objectives were never properly formulated.[15] The fleet put to sea in early October without a consensus as to whether they would hunt the plate fleet or undertake an amphibious assault. They were not even sure where in Spain to strike. And whatever sealed sailing orders the commander, Sir Edward Cecil, had composed (vague as they might be) were not delivered to all the commanders upon setting sail. This strategic incoherence resembled Elizabethan amphibious fiascos.[16]

The English army contained 10,000 infantrymen, 5,000 sailors, and 'tenn peeces of great brass [bronze] Ordinance, to batter withall, and as manie

Figure 11.1 Although a veteran piketrailer, Cecil's lack of strategic vision figured largely in the failure of the 1625 Cadiz expedition.

Source: Sir Edward Cecil, later Viscount Wimbledon (author's collection).

small feild peeces, with 50 horses to draw ordinance'.[17] Dearth of intelligence had been the justification for postponing the targeting of strategic objectives. The commander hoped that luck would bring him into contact with a vessel that would reveal to him the disposition of the Spaniards and the whereabouts of the plate fleet.[18] The lack of focus that characterised Cecil's leadership (and this was his first independent command) infected his under-officers with complacency and ill-discipline. A disrupted chain of command compounded the poor communications amongst the ships and various services.

Reprising the spectacular 1596 raid, appropriately it was the current Earl of Essex and his vessel that first burst into the bay of Cadiz. Miraculously, the Earl achieved some measure of surprise, as news of the existence of the fleet (believed to be still at Plymouth) had arrived at Cadiz only within the last

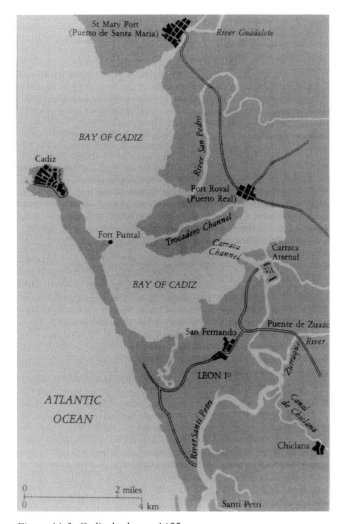

Figure 11.2 Cadiz harbour, 1625.

Source: The Bay of Cadiz, 1625 (reproduced by kind permission of Roger Lockyer and Longman publishers).

twenty-four hours. But Essex's squadron failed to second their commander briskly, and a marvellous opportunity to repeat history and swoop down on Cadiz slipped away.

Cecil further confounded the situation by expressing ambivalence about where the troops should go ashore. Ultimately the citadel guarding the harbour, Fort Puntal, became the focal point of the attack and an artillery duel.[19] Dutch gunnery proved most effective in the bombardment, and, while England's allies showed their seamanship, Cecil struggled with the pressed Newcastle colliers attached to his fleet, 'Threatening and cudgeling . . . crying to them to advance to Puntal for shame and upon pain of their lives.'[20] Fire they did, one round accidentally ripping through the *Swiftsure*. But while sheltering behind the Dutch and royal ships, the privately owned vessels hindered more than helped the assault. The less than courageous performance of the colliers and the talented gunner who had managed to hit one of the King's flotilla brought no swift upbraiding or punishment from Cecil. Cadiz would prove a failure of leadership.

After battering Fort Puntal severely enough to incapacitate its guns, the first wave of English troops disembarked at the foot of Fort Puntal, a tactical blunder that caused numerous English deaths from Spanish musketry.[21] The poor execution of the assault suggests that the poor leadership at the senior level infected junior and non-commissioned officers. When finally the amphibious forces stood on the beach at a safe distance from the fortress, an honourable surrender was negotiated.[22] All this action had been a prelude to a siege of Cadiz (and, as mentioned above, Cecil's forces had ten bronze 'great ordnance'). Anxious at how much time had been wasted, Cecil seems to have panicked when handed a report that a Spanish force was *en route* to repel the English invaders. Hurriedly deciding to meet them, Cecil marched his forces, without sufficient rations, into the hinterland. No reconnaissance or patrol went forth as the newly landed troops trudged off.

Cecil's perambulation through the Spanish countryside has become notorious for his soldiers' festivities on the Monday night of the march. Rations lay aboard the English ships. But the disarray during landing saw, in at least one case, provisions that had been sent ashore returned shipside simply because of bureaucratic confusion. The precipitous departure, too, had prevented the expeditionary force from packing rations in their knapsacks. So the men went hungry. Thirst was an equally pressing problem – until the soldiers discovered a cache of wine, about 200 tuns or 400–500 pipes.[23] The troops slaked their thirst upon empty bellies, and disorder erupted. Tardily, officers stove in casks to restore discipline and some measure of sobriety. But the drunken piketrailers stumbled amongst the broken barrels and pools of wine, gathering up the beverage from the floor with hats, hands, and cups. One particularly inebriated company became so unruly that Cecil's personal guard fired upon their own countrymen.[24] The King might have liked to have known that these men extolled loyalty to the Crown above obedience to their officers.[25] These commanders, surrounded by slumbering and groggy soldiers, quarrelled with Cecil in the morning and arrived at the obvious conclusion. They should retire to the harbour rapidly, gather up rations, and consider taking Cadiz, which was why they had entered the bay in the first place.[26] The most pathetic result of this ill-conceived march was that the Spaniards slit the throats of the incapacitated soldiers, some of them sleeping, who could not march off with their comrades.[27]

Critiques of the Cadiz expedition lumped together virtually all potential causes of failure: logistics ('badd' and 'slow' victualling), recruitment, strategy ('Our going out upon ill-grounded, and uncertaine designs'), and command.[28] They might have added intelligence gathering.[29] Cecil complained that his men were 'so addicted to drinke' that maintaining discipline was virtually impossible. '[S]et a guard upon wyne . . . and the guard will be first drunke'.[30] Cadiz exemplified all that could go wrong in English warfare. Essex and the nine dissident colonels ascribed the calamity to Cecil's personal failure as a commander and to a collapse of the supply system (the latter being at least somewhat a fault of the former).

The apparent insufficiency of English warfare and the strategic predicament occupied the Parliament of 1626 at its very outset. The King's ministers painted a portrait of an island imperilled through no fault of their royal master. A million pounds were needed to keep England safe that year. More than £373,000 had been spent on the Cadiz attack. The forty ships of the royal fleet required £170,000 and the Irish establishment £2,000 a month. Simultaneous military support of the Danes (£30,000 per month), the Palatinate (£20,000 a month for Mansfeld's force), and the Dutch Republic (£9,000 a month) were 'insupportable' on the King's current revenues. Spain possessed 50,000 foot and 5,000 horse across the Channel. The Emperor and Catholic League of Germany might commit 40,000 troops against England. Even Hungary appeared to be a threat from the Crown's viewpoint (Montenegro's 18,000 men), as well as the armies of northern Italy (28,000 soldiers), all of whom might be diverted by Catholic Europe against Britain. The Emperor 'hath made peace with France. So that the forces of Italy are like to fall downe upon us. Spinolae provides strongly for sea, and all the power Spain can make at home is prepared.'[31] Charles's rash commitment of a £30,000-monthly military subsidy towards the mobilisation of 6,000 infantry and 1,000 cavalry for the Danish service foundered when his parliaments refused to cooperate, bringing embarrassment to the young King. With 'tears almost standing in his eyes', he reassured the Danish ambassador of his zealousness to support his uncle. Yet, within months, Buckingham and Charles had changed their strategy, in favour of a French war, leaving Christian IV unsecured and vulnerable.[32]

The Isle of Rhé expedition

If feeble and distracted leadership obstructed the waging of effective war against Spain in 1625, headstrong command and political considerations influenced the siege at the Isle of Rhé in 1627. Contemporary military accounts of the latter action are often thinly veiled attacks on the Duke of Buckingham (the royal favourite) or narratives that put the best light possible on the campaign, hence upon the Duke as well. The English resorted to warfare, it has been argued above, to meet a strategic threat, very often a specific military peril. On occasion, diplomatic manoeuvring prompted the use of force, so that strategic ends were political, not military. Caroline foreign policy in the 1620s, striving to maximise England's influence in continental politics in order to help restore the Elector Palatine, was more akin to Henry VIII's war aims. In these cases, English warfare was truly an extension of policy. Buckingham succumbed to the notion that military success would silence his critics, especially those at Westminster. Perhaps he took absolute command and went in person because of the failure of a subordinated command at Cadiz. But, additionally, Buckingham craved martial glory that might simultaneously justify and legitimise him as a politician. Although under both Charles and Elizabeth English arms were fighting in the cause of the preservation of the reformed religion, Charles's war aims might not seem so justifiable, for he sought war for war's sake in order to achieve cynical political goals. He saw the Duke as fighting on his behalf[33] and Buckingham's royal instructions were to precipitate a war with France whether the Huguenots desired it or not.

VILLERS Duke of BUCKINGHAM.

Figure 11.3 Although blamed widely, especially within Parliament, for the military failure at the Isle of Rhé, still, Buckingham came close to taking the Citadel.

Source: George Villiers, Duke of Buckingham, who assumed personal command of the expedition to the Isle of Rhé (author's collection).

The army of 5,934 infantrymen, supplemented by cavalry and many officers drawn from the Duke's circle, departed from Portsmouth on 27 June 1627. Ideally, the common soldiers should have been mostly seasoned veterans. Survivors of the Cadiz voyage had been billeted along the southern coast, at Southampton, in Devonshire, and elsewhere. Had they been drilled and supplied, the Crown would have possessed the nucleus of a reliable expeditionary force. But the experience of billeting had embittered both soldiers and civilians, particularly one John Felton, who would survive to the Isle of Rhé, return to winter quarters for humiliating quartering upon a resentful countryside, and then put in a final and historic appearance at Portsmouth in 1628, changing the course of English history with his dagger and sending George Villiers, Duke of Buckingham, to a better world.[34]

During the voyage, doubts were expressed as to the sufficiency and quality of the supplies. While money could not be found in sufficient quantities to supply victuals and munitions promptly (so that piecemeal shipments were loaded only shortly before sailing), the Duke lavished £10,000 on his own retinue, including 'Sixe purple velvett Covers for great saddles richly embrodered with silver and a deep silver frindge' costing £200.[35] Logistics – particularly victualling – not guns, decided the campaign.[36] Had the Duke seized the Isle of Rhé (assuming supplies continued to follow him from England), he would indeed have been able to wage war upon Spain and France while simultaneously boosting French Protestant resistance to Louis XIII. The desirability of the objective was assured. The feasibility of taking Rhé, which required a successful assault on the island's Citadel, was another matter entirely. But while the strategic sense of the colonels who strove unsuccessfully to dissuade the Duke from attempting the siege seems confirmed by the campaign's failure, one must note that English forces very nearly compelled a surrender, except for an eleventh hour resupply by the enemy. Mistakes, the Duke may have made. When the French eluded the blockade and resupplied their countrymen, they gained victory through logistical ingenuity and daring, and not by defeating the English army.

The disembarkation site was well chosen, though the landing was poorly executed.[37] As at the 1625 Cadiz landing, the troops did not form up with alacrity nor was a reconnaissance force dispatched, suggesting that by the 1620s English expertise in amphibious operations had diminished. During the three hours in which the troops were whipped into order, the French garrison stealthily placed themselves behind the nearby dunes and launched an attack. The tactical error of failing to anticipate that the enemy would attempt to drive the English into the sea when they were most vulnerable cost lives, especially amongst the officer corps. The clash was later represented as a classic collision between English and French styles of warfare. If the English could withstand the fury of the French cavalry, who '... charged so exceeding furrouslie, and with such a showe of daring',

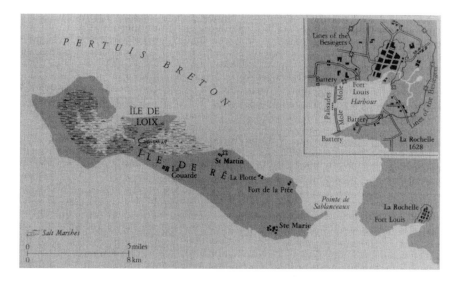

Figure 11.4 The Isle of Rhé and the Siege of La Rochelle, 1627–8.

Source: The Isle of Rhé and La Rochelle, 1627–8 (reproduced by kind permission of Roger Lockyer and Longman Publishers).

then they could hold fast against the French infantry, who invariably proved cowardly. With the momentum of the charging horse absorbed and repelled, then the English foot might counter-attack. As it had been for centuries, so it was at Rhé.

[T]hey charged our Troops with that Antient French Valour, wherewith their Ancestours used to charge the English, when they lost both day and Kingdom. . . . The Horse divided themselves into two Bodies, and marched in the Front of their Foot, when they came within distance of our great Shott, the Horse, (therewith terrifyed) were inforced to advance with such speed that the Foot were cast much short. The Horse now descending to the Plaine and on either side the Neck of Land were forced [at] the highest speed to come on without expecting their Foot to second them. Desperate was the Charge both given and received, for the French were not able to susteyne both the fury of our Ships and Musketiers; Our Men not fully in order were forced to fight as they were, or by flight to loose their Lives by Drowning (the which indeede was the fate of most of our common souldiers that day lost) but the rest bravely standing, had the Killing of many French Horse, till at length the Monsieurs unslaine were forced to run back as fast as formerly they advanced. The French Foot all this while marched, but before they could come to fight, the Dukes Grace in his Barge had advanced to the Soldiers, and with his sword drawn encouraged a Victory by which means our scattered Troops was recollected, and in so good Order that in a short space, the French Foot were constrayned with all dexterity to Lackey it after their Horse.[38]

Buckingham sought intelligence by sending Captain Hart in the *Martha*, a man-of-war, to scout the French coast. The fairly rapid English advance across the island, delayed only briefly by the occasional French posturing or challenge (ostensibly to impede the march in order to buy time for the victualling of the island's main fortress, the Citadel), confirmed that the defenders had placed their faith in their fortifications. The campaign revolved around a single question: could the English, with the resources at hand, take the Citadel? Buckingham's colonels discouraged a siege. Reinforcements and resupply lay in far-off England. The power of Louis XIII resided only a few miles away, upon the mainland. The smaller fort, La Priet, still stood defiant. And most formidable of all was the daunting architecture of the Citadel itself. That the Duke chose to lay siege nevertheless stemmed, once again, from personal honour and political goals. Having committed himself to Rhé, Buckingham had to take the fortress, or retreat. But before berating Buckingham's bellicosity, one needs to realise that the Duke very nearly succeeded in forcing the Citadel to capitulate.

Having secured the town of St Martin's (which adjoined the Citadel) after a brief skirmish in which two French horsemen were slain by the discharge of an English drake, the circumvallation of the fortress began.[39] Buckingham could pursue one of three courses: launch an immediate assault, create a breach with siege guns, or simply isolate the Citadel and let hunger take its course. In the latter case, English naval vessels would have to maintain a blockade. The alternative to this long siege, for which the expeditionary force was unprepared, would mean assailing bastions, ditches, and ramparts – in other words, offensive warfare at its most formidable. Further, the English suspected that they lacked a sufficient ratio of attackers over defenders to make a successful assault.[40]

Buckingham changed tactics during the investment. While entrenched, he encircled the fortress, dug tunnels, planted mines, and pounded the walls. Although his long-term intention was to starve the garrison, he flirted several times with the rash solution, an assault, especially as weeks dragged on and the trenches had still to be completed. The slowness of the English approach to the Citadel now came back to haunt the Duke, as revictualling from the mainland had been carried out with urgency once the intelligence of the coming of the English had been confirmed by their arrival off La Rochelle. Logistics increasingly favoured the French. Supplies and tempers grew short, and the chivalric exchanges between Buckingham and Toiras, the garrison commander, gave way to desperate and vicious strokes.[41] On 30 July the English foiled an alleged assassination when the Duke's servants discovered a 'poysoned dagger' hidden upon the person of a deserter from the Citadel who had asked for a personal audience with Buckingham.[42] In early August, the Duke '. . . gathered together all the Women Papists left in the Towne of St. Martins, which being ledd near the Trenches of the Enemy were there left, either to be taken into The Cittadel, or to perish.'[43] Buckingham even contemplated denying quarter should the garrison not surrender immediately.[44]

By late September the noose slowly but painfully tightened as the Citadel's food supplies dwindled. At this juncture, for all the poor performances by the Duke's engineers and artillerymen, in spite of Buckingham's strategic and tactical sloppiness, the capture of the stronghold seemed imminent. The French knew that the English had received Irish reinforcements. Toiras considered asking for terms of surrender. Then, 'with one stroke', French vessels turned the tide of the siege. A nocturnal relief effort succeeded in wafting supplies through the English naval blockade and beached them just below the Citadel. The defenders hauled in a month's supply of victuals, and in the morning taunted the English by 'brandishing their pikes with turkeys and chickens impaled on the points, in mocking salute to their besiegers below'.[45] This solitary lapse by the naval vessels brought recrimination from the colonels. Reluctantly, the Duke came to terms with the tactical reality. Though it was to be drawn out over weeks, the retreat had begun. The English expeditionary force lacked the resources to carry on for a further period of months.

Still clinging to the hope of victory, Buckingham scheduled a surprise attack on the Citadel, only to have it washed out by torrential rains. With the English soldiers ill, demoralised, and running low on victuals (in spite of a boatload of oxen that had arrived from England seven weeks earlier), the French seized the initiative and transferred 4,000 troops from the mainland. Now the original force and the 1,899 Irish infantry recently landed found themselves outnumbered and vulnerable in withdrawal.[46] In a last attempt to reverse fortune, Buckingham launched a surprise assault on the Citadel, the Duke's worst tactical blunder. With neither an initial barrage of cannon fire nor the element of surprise (for the defenders were ready), the several thousand attackers made little more headway than overrunning the French outworks in some places and leaning scaling ladders against the Citadel.

> Our men being nowe desperate for feare of starvinge . . . went on bravely, but we quickly found, contrarie to the relacion of some villaines, who rann awaie from the Fort, that they had not 400 fightinge men, a resistance fit for 4000 men, and wee nowe scarce 4000. They kill'd above 100 of our men with stones and they might have done the like with our armie without even shootinge

small shott. They blew upp 3 mynes. In all were slaine 400 horse and foote, they tooke some 30 prisoners in trapps which made in their trenches.[47]

Another participant described,

shot flyeing as thick as haile an hour and a halfe together . . . six or seave hundred lost theire lives, and others irrecoverable maym'd and spoyl'd with whole barrells of stones, and great logs of wood, and masts of ships, and such-like instruments of destruction that were tumbled downe from the top as wee were ascending.[48]

Those scaling the walls found their progress impeded by more than falling debris. Lord Herbert alleged that the ladders were short by as much as 20 per cent:

. . . they ranne in two divisions and reared some fourty ladders against the outworks and Cittadell, but finding them not came near the toppe by almost a 5th part. . . . When they almost attained the height of their ladders and had no further means to go on, casting their threatening eies about they remained unmoveable till they were shott and tumbled doune. This hindered not their fellowes . . . falling doune died likewise . . . [and] some were persed [pierced] with 5 or 6 bullets.[49]

The expeditionary force had to withdraw promptly. The Duke's vacillations between attack and retreat had spawned confusion, so that some defensive works that protected a dike, upon which the troops would have to walk, had been razed. Tactical error compounded tactical error. As the English units filed down the path to the anchored ships, over the dike through salt marshes and then across a pontoon bridge, Sir William Courtney drew up three regiments of horse to secure the defile.[50] Not only was his position difficult to defend without the earthworks, but he was expected to repel a superior force with cavalry, when stout pikemen were needed. Predictably, the French advanced.

The Enemy perceiving halfe our Army past the Bridge, with their Musketeers charged our Horse, which by the straitnesse of the Place unable to endure the fury of the shott, were enforced to charge the Enemy, but in their Charge being unable to be seconded by our Musketeers, they were routed whose disorderly Retreate breaking our Foot Rankes, and not only broake Them, but gave advantage to the Enemy to fall into the heart of our latter Regiments; The presse of our flying Troopes, and the Throng of the pursuing Enemy in so straight a Place was such that on either-side our Men were throwne into the aforesaid Salt panns overwhelmed and smothered each by other.[51]

Another veteran wrote, 'Wee came into a straight narrow passage [upon the dike], unavoydable, with salt pits on either side, where wee could march in breast but four or five at most half a mile together'. Suddenly, the French cavalry (as usual) leapt upon the English. The soldiers of the forlorn hope, composed of horse and foot under Lord Mountjoy, fell into disarray, their commander nearly unseated and unable to firm up his soldiers. Fragmenting the English formation, the attackers '. . . beate downe all that were before them, or at least forct them into the salt pits, where they [the English] could make no defence . . . [and] were made a prey for the Enemie, and slaughtered like bruite beasts.' Cunningham's horsemen failed to stem the tide and Sir William was shot dead.[52] Another eyewitness recalled how

> . . . before two Regiments had passed the bridge (beinge verie narrowe) they fell upon our horse in the reare, and put them to rout, and they routed the reare, in as much as none of the foote could chandge; soe all rann awaie, and the enemie had the execution of five whole Regiments, which they put all to the sword except 20 officers and 100 common souldiers prisoners, and those that were drowned, which were many.[53]

In any discussion of English warfare in the Caroline era, a comparison of the Cadiz and Rhé expeditions becomes inevitable. Similarities existed: as amphibious operations, they both faced daunting logistical challenges that were difficult to meet in the political and administrative world of the early 1600s. And, not surprisingly, both landings foundered somewhat and their disembarkations led to confused milling about on the beaches; it then took days to sort out the confusion and put the men into some semblance of battle order. The element of surprise slipped away and the initiative fell to the enemy – for example when the governor of the Isle of Rhé ambushed the disarrayed English forces late in the afternoon of 12 July with a force of 1,200 infantry supported by 200 cavalry. Although the English repulsed the attack, the French drew first blood, which included a dozen of Buckingham's senior officers.

Another parallel was Cecil's and Buckingham's penchant for formulating strategies on the beachhead. Considering both operations lacked coherent strategic goals and were executed with virtually no intelligence as to enemy dispositions, perhaps landing men and equipment safely and only then going about the arduous business of campaigning seemed logical. Unfortunately, that procedure at best gave one's adversary ample opportunity to arrange and improve defences. At worst, it provided time for a relief column to make its way to the scene. The nebulous strategies of the Cadiz and Rhé campaigns made it easy to postpone making decisions about provisioning (and reinforcement). And given the £6,000 yearly budget within which the Ordnance Office worked, it was inadvisable to err on the side of oversupply.

Military failure and 'Personal Rule'

Unsuccessful military adventures in the 1620s did much to delegitimise the practice of arms, and hence shaped English warfare by casting self-doubt on a nation that regarded its soldiers (in the distant field, though not always in the parish itself) as tenacious, brave lads, spirited and sometimes invincible. High politics and religion conspired to besmirch the art of war when Charles I's machinations led members of Parliament steeped in the history of antiquity to see fighting men as potential 'Praetorian Bands', or, in a more contemporary comparison, as 'Janissaryes'.[54] If England had faced trial by combat and failed, false religion could explain English disgrace in war. In the House of Commons Sir Francis Seymour declared, 'If God fight not our battles, the help of man is in vain. . . . The cause hereof is in our defects.'[55] This rhetoric echoed the traditional theme of the defence of the realm. Indeed, the Thirty Years War positively inflamed some Englishmen, including clergymen. The rector of Batcombe, Somersetshire, published an exhortation to his King and countrymen in 1629:

> . . . Great Brittaine is inferiour to no Nation; and that by the prowesse and valour of English and Scots, glorious victories have been obtained. . . . General Norice in the Low Countries; of the worthily honoured Lord Grey in Ireland, of the never dying names of Drake, Furbisher, and Hawkins, of the right famous Earle of Essex, of the deservedly eternized Veres, of the invincible-spirited Greenfield, of the noble Cicill. . . . Weigh your Enemies. . . . Their success is but now of late, consider you the former times; stay and wonder at our incredible victories.[56]

Military failure bore heavily on the King personally. He assumed responsibility for the loss at the Isle of Rhé, and reportedly took no sustenance for two days, agonising over his loss of honour.[57] The following year Charles planned to preside personally over a 'Grand Muster' of northern cavalry at York. Throughout his reign the King used his royal person to coalesce British military power. But English warfare had to be waged collaboratively with Parliament.[58] The degree to which Parliament would shoulder the burden of war remained controversial, and many members of Parliament favoured an amalgam of war, trade, and piracy, as opposed to the disturbingly ineffective, dangerous, and expensive land armies used for allied operations in the Thirty Years War.[59]

Nevertheless, realising that Protestantism lay in peril, Parliament did indeed grant subsidies, though sometimes with strings attached, as in 1624.[60] As armies had become a political issue, domestically as well as in terms of foreign policy, a national English war effort disappeared along with Parliaments as the 1630s began. Charles's dissolution of Parliament in 1629 signified his unwillingness to come to an understanding with his subjects. Instead he accommodated, however tentatively, the Catholic enemy, abandoning an active role in the Protestant cause. The restoration of the Palatinate, the focal point of English foreign policy, was for the Stuarts a dynastic imperative. For the citizens of England, and much of Europe, it symbolised imperilled Protestantism. The birth of the Prince of Wales in May 1630 lessened the dynastic imperative to support militarily Elizabeth the Winter Queen in the reconquest of the Palatinate.[61] The Treaty of Madrid (5 November 1630), however, permitted Englishmen to fight under the banner of the United Provinces (though the increasingly hispanophile inclinations of the Crown made this involvement less threatening to Catholic Europe than had been the case in previous decades), while English naval and mercantile enterprises remained unrestricted.[62]

In mid-November 1630, four English regiments bolstered the forces of the United Provinces, and brought up to strength a virtual standing army of 9,600 Englishmen that included such military luminaries as Sir Jacob Astley, Sir John Ogle, and Sir Nicholas Byron.[63] Such sizeable contingents under an allied banner kept a reservoir of martial talent available to the Crown. The last oblique military intervention came in July 1631, when the Marquis of Hamilton sailed to assist Gustavus Adolphus, taking 6,000 English and 1,000 Scots 'volunteers'. Charles contributed money to launch the expedition, but distanced himself from its financing and command once the force was under its illustrious commander.[64]

By the outset of the Personal Rule, Charles had ceased, temporarily, to play the game of war. Thus the King's apparent aloofness from the wars of religion gave his subjects the impression that Spanish, hence papal, influences had gained ascendancy at Court. The English public were told that warfare raged all round Albion. Nicholas Bourne and Nathaniel Butter published weekly 'avisoes', newsletters brimming with continental military news.[65] But simultaneously Hamilton's close dealings with Gustavus[66] made Catholic Europe doubt that Charles truly desired peace, let alone a Habsburg alliance.

From 1632 to 1635, when England's naval capability grew with the ship money fleet, European powers repeatedly enticed Charles to embroil England in land warfare. The Habsburgs, Gustavus, the French, and the Dutch sought England's military resources. In the final measure, the King drew back. He understood what Henry VIII had not, but Elizabeth I had: that allied land operations rarely achieved English strategic goals. But even if England was not officially engaged in war, still its soldiers continued to perfect the practice of arms – for example, at the siege of Maastricht (10 June–23 August

1632). The plat for that campaign reveals an 'English gallerie' and a fort of the 'Anglois'. Four divisions served under General Vere, and there were other contingents under General Morgan, Colonel Packenham, and Colonel Herbert. Counting the Scots brigades, it would appear that one-third to just less than one-half of the Protestant army was British. With the Earl of Oxford serving in the army as well, the English companies fought the same kind of gritty warfare to which they had been accustomed for decades. Late in the siege, in the early morning darkness of 18 August 1632, the troops kept watch in their works for a night attack. At dawn

> . . . they had scarce layned downe an hower, to take their rest, but wee heard a sudden, and a hott alarum in the trenches. . . . The Enemye sallied out about 400 men, vpon the English trenches, and over the plain feilde fell into our sapps and guards: it was a mistie morning, and so came stealing behinde our centinells, who could not well discover them, and give the alarum so soone as they might. . . . [T]he Enemye fell into our first Corps du Gard, and beate our men out of yt, and so along our righthand sapps, got into the second Corps, and at last assaulted the Colonells Corps. . . . Our men made the best resistance they could, and were at push a pike with them a long tyme: the Enemye gave fire exceedingly from the wall with their ordnance and small shott, and with their firelocks slew many of our men in the Colonels Worke: Sergeant Maior Williamson, received two or three mortall wounds at push a pike and with a shott, that fainting, they puld him downe. . . .[67]

Many English commanders, and their soldiers, still looked squarely upon the face of battle. True, many Englishmen sat safely across the Channel, sampling contemporary military literature. But England's role in the wars of religion was not that of a passive spectator. Allowing European recruiters to absorb the Stuarts' subjects into foreign ranks maintained a nucleus of experienced soldiers who continued to practise their trade, for the better defence of the realm in time of peril, as well as to maintain English involvement in continental affairs, obliging allies from a discreet distance. In 1621, 13,000 Britons still fought alongside the Dutch, which amounted to a third of that nation's standing forces. Many of the English colonels fighting for the King of Denmark in spring 1627 later commanded regiments in the Bishops' Wars.[68] Under the Catholic banner, 4,000 soldiers from the three kingdoms (mostly Irish and recusant English) participated in the wars of the 1620s and 1630s.[69] 'In 1635 England became a focus of attention for all the major protagonists of the Thirty Years War.'[70] At Maastricht, acting as Sergeant Major, Sir Simon Harcourt led his countrymen in the siege. He would go on to lead a regiment in Hamilton's expedition against Scotland in 1639, and in 1642 fall fighting Irish rebels.

Thus was the English art of war learnt on the Continent and then transmitted to the three kingdoms.[71] The early Stuarts had wanted to influence continental affairs, be it through James's mediation and brokerage of the Cleves–Jülich war or Charles's reckless foreign gambles of the 1620s. During the 1630s continental wars of religion – for example, at Maastricht, described above – Scots and English were comrades-in-arms, subjects of the same monarch, and sharing a distrust of Spain and pope. Ancient rivalries had been submerged. Very likely Scots and English had never got on so well. That third Stuart kingdom, Ireland, though not a participant in the Protestant cause, had at least been pacified, and modern research bears out Gardiner's verdict on Strafford's lieutenancy there: 'Never had an [English] army been so completely master of Ireland.'[72]

Beyond the British Isles, the Stuart regime appeared well on the way to creating a centrally financed and truly royal navy, a power the rest of globe would have to reckon with.[73] Personal involvement and symbolism, intertwined in the person of the King, demonstrated Charles's commitment to naval warfare. The launching of the formidably modern *Sovereign of the Seas* made the point in its very name. Charles inspected the dockyards personally, and struck a medal to commemorate the reign in which Britannia commenced to rule the waves. Despite this promising beginning, in practice naval resources were subordinated to land warfare and the sustenance of ground forces. Cadiz and Rhé swallowed up funds that might have built frigates and kept more royal vessels patrolling in the Channel.[74] Ironically, external enemies would not test the capabilities of English arms. War would break out within Britain.

The Bishops' Wars and after

The literature for mobilising and fighting existed, and English veterans were only too willing to help, but apart from Hamilton and Astley there were few if any military men in the King's circle. Military treatises did not occupy the place that did drama and poetry in Court culture. For example, in 1639 Du Praissac's *The Arte of Warre* was translated into English by John Cruso, who had also produced *Militarie Instructions for the Cavallerie* in 1632. Through Henry Hexham, Robert Ward, and others, an English genre of military literature had evolved, still retaining the idiosyncratically English elements (as inherited from Sir John Smythe and like-minded xenophobic Elizabethan soldier-authors) as well as a shrewd eclecticism that allowed the English art of war to extract the best from foreign theorists and practitioners (as had Sir Roger Williams at century's end). Marching with the Prince of Orange's armies, Hexham chronicled Anglo-Dutch military operations, particularly English siege actions.[75]

Operations around Breda became a school of siegecraft for the English, much as Ostend had been for an earlier generation. The circumvallations of that unfortunate city during 1624–37 were described in detail for an English reading public.[76] Hexham, serving as quartermaster in Goring's regiment, analysed the Prince of Orange's taking of the city in 1637, highlighting English contributions and registering British subjects who fell in the Protestant cause.[77] Hexham's efforts to raise public awareness of the exploits of English soldiers and the art of war were seconded by other pamphleteers and newsletter editors such as Weckherlin and Rossingham.[78] Lessons learned and wounds suffered in these engagements bore fruit in the superb *The Principles of the Art Militarie: Practised in the VVarres of the United Netherlands* (London 1637), which expertly delineated the science of siegecraft, depicted firing sequences and the disposition of infantry. Published in the year of the Prayer Book Rebellion, the dedication aimed at one of Charles I's favourites, Henry Rich, Earl of Holland, captain of the royal guard, Privy Councillor, and to be commander of the horse for the First Bishops' War. Oddly enough, Hexham never served in the Scottish wars of 1638–40, and instead shared time between England and the Low Countries. Other Englishmen advanced the Caroline art of war – for example, Robert Ward, whose exhaustive *Anima'dversions of Warre* appeared in 1639.

Had Charles I read merely the first sentence of the first chapter of Cruso's 1639 translation of Du Praissac, he would have been not only a better military man but also a wiser king: 'A Prince being resolved to make warr (be it offensive or defensive) ought to make such provision of men, instruments, money, and victuall, as he shall know to be necessary for his enterprise'. Christ himself had counselled, in another context admittedly, that a ruler ought to 'count the cost' before making war. If the King had not the men or money, then peace should be sought.[79] Explaining England's descent into what has been described as the bloodiest conflict in the island's history up to 1914 reveals a striking irony.[80] When Lowland Scotland rejected in 1637 a prayer book seemingly inspired by Roman Catholic practice and promoted by the Anglican episcopate, Charles responded with political pressure and the threat of force in early 1639.[81] The King then introduced the wars of religion into his own three kingdoms. The mobilisation of Protestant England to coerce Protestant Scotland contradicted and confounded traditional English military policy. The Spanish units that the Scots and English had fought so savagely on the Continent were very nearly imported by the King as allies against the Calvinist Scots. In this scenario, the English militiaman would stand alongside the Catholic *soldado* who for decades had been trying to invade the island. Now the King invited in the Spaniard and made common cause with him in order to suppress the Scots, who loudly and consistently protested their loyalty to the Crown.[82]

Some English subjects who had endured ship money levies, distraint of knighthood, forest laws, and the like, suspected (wrongly) that these 'Bishops'

Wars' were actually another revenue-raising scheme. The King would make peace with the Scots and, conveniently, retain the money that had been raised for the war. As in the case of the ship money fleet's inception, the King cited the defence of the realm as justification for his actions. Yet no Parliament was summoned, even though that institution had been created to support royal campaigns. Not surprisingly, the English nation exhibited little enthusiasm for the war. The sharp-sighted news purveyor Edmund Rossingham reported only days before the rendezvous that Charles's 'perfect militia' would spearhead the campaign:

> . . . the Kinge will expect the Citty should send to the Rendevowe in the north 3000 of their traine bands. This week 8 shipps ready in the river of Thames are to take in out of Essex eleven hundred of the train bands of that County, and one thousand of the traine bands of the County of Kent, to be transported to Newcastle. There are 20 Newcastle shipps also taken upp for transportacion of men. There are now Coronells appoynted to comaund over the traine bands, the first 4 Coronells being to commaund those 6000 men, which are to be prest. . . . Many of the traine souldiers in Essex, rather than they wil goe in person to Newcastle, they will give half they are worth to find an other man in thir stead.

Civil War had come to Britain and only the King and some of his followers believed it necessary. Insistent that each citizen should rally under the royal banner, taking his word that the kingdom lay in peril, Charles extracted military service and money. By using the trained bands (in a way that had been followed under the Tudors but rarely under the Stuarts) as expeditionary forces, the Crown needed to equip only the pressed contingents, the latter amounting (on paper) to 12,000 infantry and 400 cavalry.[83] Style and appearance assumed importance. Sir Edward Dering's summons to the York rendezvous of 1639 dictated that 'The Armes for your selfe are to bee Russett with guilded Nayles or Studds after the fashion of a Curassier, those for your Servant or Servants white and as a Hargobusier.'[84] The nobility for the most part sent their regrets and some money, rumoured to be £30,000–£40,000 destined for the 'Treasorie of the Army'.[85]

The Bishops' Wars stood English strategy on its head. Not since the Rebellion of the Northern Earls (1569) had military intervention of any notable scale been attempted on the Borders. And not since 1560 had a Scottish campaign been mounted, and in that case it was done in unison with Scottish allies against French invaders. Increasingly, the south had become the focus of defence. Further, the King seemed to enjoy entertaining Spanish diplomats and indulging his French Catholic wife. He had deployed the ship money fleet against the Protestant Dutch, and now sought war with his father's good people, who had fought for the Protestant cause

Figure 11.5 'The Severall Formes how King Charles his Armey enquartered in the fields being past New Castle on the march toward Scotland Anno Domini 1639'.

Source: Charles I and his army march against Scotland, 21–27 May 1639 (reproduced from *A History of Northumberland* [1893]).

and survived the same continental Catholic threats. So it came as no surprise when it was rumoured (rightly) that Charles solicited money from the See of St Peter.[86] Now the North, its defences dormant for decades, prepared for a curious Scottish war reminiscent of the Middle Ages and thought until 1638 to be obsolete. In Cumberland and Westmorland, Henry Lord Clifford demonstrated the resiliency of England's military resources, should the King have used them more informedly. R. T. Spence has shown how the loyal and enterprising Clifford revived in a few months atrophied Border defences, which had slept for the most part since the raids that had occurred in March 1603, when Elizabeth I had died.

Abandoned by its garrison in 1621, Carlisle Castle lay in a shambles. Clifford reached into his own purse to make the Castle (which was under his family's lease) defensible. The Cumberland and Westmorland trained bands began looking to their weapons and training, at the urging of the deputy lieutenants, as early as August 1638.[87] These shires presented the greatest topographical obstacles to perfecting a local militia because of their 'remotenes', in the locals' words; as they reminded faraway Whitehall, 'we live in a stormy and mountaynous Countrey'. The slim number of militia-men,[88] the utter absence of armourers and wagonmakers, and the paucity of gunsmiths, left the Borders vulnerable.[89] Spence portrays a Border community that, with Clifford's leadership, put itself in an impressive state of defence despite the contradictory and ignorant orders issued from Court. The towns of Appleby and Kendal, with surprising foresight, had stock-piled ammunition imported from the Low Countries (though Carlisle had none). Clifford dashed about the North, to Newcastle, to Carlisle, wher-ever defences needed shoring up, all the time receiving conflicting, then cancelled, orders from the Crown. Better horses were purchased for his troopers at great trouble and expense, and the result was 'one of the best-equipped and, eventually, well-horsed cavalry units in an army impressively uniformed but noticeably deficient in the essential regard of arms'.[90]

Clifford's subordinates performed with similar alacrity. One of his deputy lieutenants, Sir Philip Musgrave, managed to hurry a trained-band regi-ment into Appleby overnight, and marched in another from Kendal the following day. The rapidity of movement, and coordination with rein-forcements coming from Ireland, with competing instructions coming from York, Newcastle, and elsewhere, demonstrated that even in the weakest shires the spirit of defence of the locality still burned. Cumberland and Westmorland managed all this with inadequate supply from the central government – namely, the Exchequer and the Ordnance Office. Their resources were few: 'In 1639 the borderers could not be called on because they now lacked the means to arm and equip themselves as a result of rack-renting and fining by their landlords over the past three decades.'[91]

Newcastle-upon-Tyne faced a dilemma similar to that of Carlisle: dete-riorated muncipal defensive works. The bridge across the Tyne required a

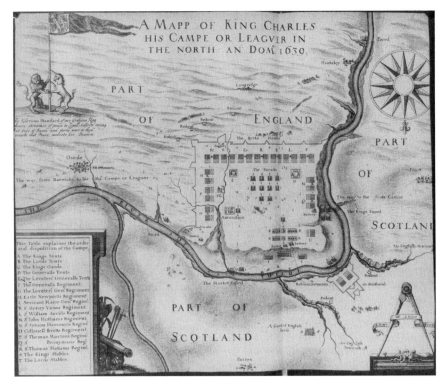

Figure 11.6 Charles I compelled his army to make a brave show on the Borders, but was outbluffed by the Scottish Covenanters.

Source: The English army encamps at the Birks, early June 1639 (reproduced by permission of the British Library, Add. MS 38, 847, ff. 17v–18).

drawbridge, and the shops and houses clustered around it, demolition. Six royal demi-culverins would be positioned on Newcastle's ramparts. Fourteen 'small peeces' could be placed on carriages taken from naval vessels and mounted on the town walls.[92] As for the construction of fortifications for safeguarding the harbour, a midwinter survey found Tynemouth Castle and the surrounding ground to be largely indefensible, and concluded, 'the best safety for this Port in time of Hostilitie wilbe for two of his Majesties shipps to lie neare the harboure mouth'. Although the municipal militia amounted to only 480 men, they claimed that 1,500 able-bodied citizens would help the defence, and an additional 1,000, who would shelter in the city in time of war, could be counted on as well. Of course, the King would have to arm them. The town was indeed augmenting its arsenal with cannon, shot, powder, etc. But not even a solitary gunsmith, armourer, or pistolmaker dwelt in Newcastle, and no one knew how to repair weapons. Besides, the townsmen were short of victuals, and did not export butter and other foodstuffs as often as other eastern ports. Though filled with allusions to their loyalty and willingness, the city's certificate identified the King as being the party most able to safeguard Newcastle. The quarrel over defences continued through 1639 and Newcastle's occupation by the Scots in September 1640.[93]

When the royal army encamped at Birks,[94] upon the Borders, in late May and early June 1639, it numbered 20,000 effectives. Troops arrived over a period of weeks, and units were dispatched out on occasion, making estimations of exact troop strength conjectural. Apart from a brief skirmish between small reconnaissance detachments, the only real action occurred at Kelso, on 4 June. Though no blood was spilled, the royal forces beat a retreat, and, if we concur with contemporaries in calling it a Scottish victory, it was so because of poor command decisions on the part of the English, and excellent Scottish manoeuvring coupled with the cunning of Scottish continental veterans. The English commander, the Earl of Holland, sought out the Covenanters and outdistanced his infantry. When he was confronted by the Scots, who occupied favourable ground outside Kelso, he pondered whether or not he should engage without infantry support. But this was no Turnhout. Holland's decision was made easier because of a trick that Alexander Leslie, the opposing commander, had learned in the Thirty Years War. The wily Scot drew up thin ranks, well garnished with banners and ensigns, and drove cattle behind the soldiers (who were standing at arms). The galloping livestock raised an enormous cloud of dust. Not even Holland's spyglass could see through the ruse, and when the Scots' herald's arrival gave every intimation that, although the Scots remained reluctant to strike against their English brethren, they would oblige the Earl with a good fight, Holland fell back on his infantry and then to the Birks.[95]

England could have fought in 1639, and perhaps won. Delayed mustering, hasty arms purchases, and no parliamentary subsidies, hindered but did not prevent mobilisation. War brought on the crisis that would compel the summoning of the Long Parliament in November 1640, but royal finances during the Personal Rule had been stretched, and poor management of a war, dangerous even for the healthiest of states, overwhelmed a government that ultimately relied upon the cooperation of the ruled in so many ways. One of the more reflective of the King's men, Archbishop Laud, confided,

> It is not the Scottish business alone that I look upon, but the whole frame of things at home and abroad, with vast expenses out of little treasure, and my misgiving soul is deeply apprehensive of no small evils coming on.[96]

Charles had envisioned a 40,000-man army, but later compromised and aimed at around 24,000, with auxiliaries boosting the figure to perhaps

30,000. The Crown fielded between 15,000 and 20,000 (optimistically 25,000) men in 1639. For the Second Bishops' War, directions for arms purchases indicate that as many as 60,000 infantry and 3,000 cavalry were considered as late as December 1639. The chaos of summer 1640 makes ascertaining actual troop strength exceedingly difficult, when the English army reassembled, again hamstrung by a postponed mobilisation and arms shortages.[97] The army had to be large enough to cover the Borders effectively and engage the Scots if necessary, but not so large that it could not be paid or victualled adequately. The cost of sending a sizeable army (25,000–40,000 troops) against Scotland, taking into account the need to supply many ill-equipped soldiers with arms and food, and the logistics of piecing together an artillery train, can be reckoned at roughly a million pounds. Clearly, that sum exceeded the capabilities of the straitened income of the Personal Rule, as the Crown's annual gross receipts rarely exceeded half that amount.

Disbursing large sums when cash remained scarce compounded the complexity of the Exchequer's procedures. The critically needed £160,000 for soldiers' wages, distributed between 28 May and 4 September 1640 (the height of the war) entailed 54 separate transactions between the Treasurer, Sir William Uvedale, and the Tellers of the Receipt.[98] And, this being a 'British' war, the Tellers found warrants thrust at them from every direction, in a manner of speaking: from Ireland, in the person of Sir William Raylton (for Strafford's notorious 'army in Ireland'); from Scotland, embodied by Sir James Lockhart, Sir Patrick Ruthven, the Marquis of Hamilton, and Captain Francis Vernon, who filled Scottish purses, the pockets of Hamilton's English troops and the Edinburgh Castle garrison; and even from across the Channel for arms purchases, negotiated by Sir Thomas Roe, John Quarles, and Sir Job Harby. Then there were the more English recipients: the Ordnance Officers, the Berwick and Carlisle garrisons, contractors for the improvement of fortifications, the Commissary General, the mayor of Newcastle, and, not so insignificantly, the Navy.[99]

Where the Crown should have been focusing was Hull, which had become the logistical bottleneck of the operation. Kingston-upon-Hull had been used as an arms depot in 1638–9, where stockpiling was under way in November 1638, even though the army rendezvous was nearly half a year away.[100] In 1640 the portage of arms to the depots was tardy in spite of the time gained by the delayed mobilisation of the royal army. The artillery never made it to the Borders, for the Covenanters crossed the Tweed, forded the Tyne, and routed a modest detachment of English defenders. Administrative leadership seems again to have been the greatest failing, including the commander in chief, the King. The poorly paid and equipped soldiers were badly deployed, and the artillery (and cannon made a big difference at the battle of Newburn Ford[101]) for the most part lagged behind at Hull.[102]

The rout at Newburn shook confidence in English arms in a way that resembled 1557–69. The royal army never rallied after the battle on the banks of the Tyne, and withdrew; the casualties limping back to the parishes. Thomas Snooke, son of a tradesman in Sutton Mandeville, received a head wound, apparently at Newburn, so severe that 'many peeces . . . of . . . Skull are taken out of his head.' A regimental surgeon pronounced that the wound had 'Perished his Braine.' The return of hurt and demoralised men like Snooke to their localities renewed resentment of the seemingly pointless military charges of the 1620s, including impressment and billeting.[103]

In spite of boasting a militia force that should have amounted to nearly 100,000 men, England had been occupied, by 'foreign' troops.[104] Charles's military reputation, buoyed somewhat by the ship money fleet, now sank with his army's ignominious performance in 1639 and rout in 1640. The Dutch had to smile knowingly when their agent reported that in Wiltshire the 'Trainebands' had refused to be commanded by an officer suspected of popery. The King's religious policies had driven his own soldiers to mutiny.[105] Though the regime might rely on the swift obedience of some of its subjects, such as Henry Lord Clifford, the realm at large mostly resembled the folk in Lincolnshire, who in 1639–40 pushed forward substitutes for their militiamen and expressed misgivings about fighting for their King's policies. In May 1642, when the King proclaimed against assembling trained bands under the parliamentary Militia Ordinance, Charles must have been chagrined to discover that 'very few or none of the trained bands had failed to show up for musters' in Lincolnshire.[106]

Viewing Van Dyck's equestrian portrait of Charles I in the National Gallery, one is liable to be impressed by the sitter's connoisseurship, the scale and quality of this imposing work testifying to Charles's love of art, refinement, and good judgement.[107] But this massive canvas is also a testimony to the King's faith in intimidation based upon the application of English warfare. Having done his utmost to commit England to continental war before he had even ascended the throne (more for personal and dynastic honour than a heartfelt commitment to the Protestant cause), Charles's military adventures dominated the first four years of his reign. He had supported Mansfeld's 1624–5 campaign even though it broke the spirit of the Subsidy Act and spawned parliamentary protests through the last half of the 1620s.[108]

Too often poor royal leadership was mirrored in mediocre operational commands by his senior officers. Having 'lost' two Bishops' Wars, and revealed his disregard for the rule of law and government by consent, Charles blessed the army plots of March–May and July 1641. Totally disregarding the safety of his subjects, Charles emboldened conspirators in 1641 to engineer a military *coup d'état*. The Tower was to be seized and Parliament overawed. The realm that had largely escaped the sword during the bloody era of the wars of religion now became a theatre of operations and home to marauding armies. Charles knew that, given the constraints under which martial law might be imposed, and the militia's unfamiliarity with duties, an unbridled soldiery could not be brought to heel once running amok. The outrages at Dover and elsewhere in late 1624, the disorders of the 1625 and 1627 expeditions, and then the iconoclasm and murders perpetrated by royal soldiers during the Bishops' Wars made it abundantly clear that even native Protestant troops threatened the civil peace.

The presence of 400 soldiers in Charles's company when the King attempted to take by force the Five Members of Parliament (January 1642) was no coincidence. Charles may have been a most unmilitary man, but he placed his faith in the sword, not the law. Military obedience and the cultivation of a paramilitary dramatic personae comprised part of Charles's solution to his political problems. Charles saw royal soldiers as a Praetorian Guard, sworn to personal allegiance to King, not country. The state meant little. Duty to risk one's life in service to the Stuart sovereign was reminiscent of Imperial Rome and Norman England, not 'modern' in a Hobbesian contractual sense. When Sir Simon Harcourt died fighting the Irish rebels in April 1642, the King (then ensconced at York) took the occasion to display his largesse towards those who had sacrificed themselves in the royal cause. After 'much bewayling the losse' of Sir Simon, the King granted the forfeited lands and castle where Sir Simon had fallen to Harcourt's widow and children. Charles made clear that he was honouring Sir Simon's memory for loyal service. The formulation of a creed of loyalty would underlay the recruitment of a royalist army.[109] In Charles's hands, English warfare was turned upon itself and all three kingdoms were put to trial by battle.

12

ENGLISH WARFARE TURNED
UPON ITSELF

An English art of war

The nature of English warfare from 1511 to 1642 was dictated by the predicament of the island kingdom's strategic position. Its defence necessitated expertise in virtually all forms of warfare. Admittedly, the English were like any other European state during the wars of religion in that, first, they favoured certain weapons over others (i.e. the longbow) and, second, they contended with the many innovations in the use of missile weapons (and corresponding defences). But English exceptionalism, and hence an 'English art of war', were products of a culture characterised by fluidity, adaptability, eclecticism and the ability to synthesise a manner of fighting that fit tactical reality.

To survive, the English had to fight and win upon terrain and in situations that often favoured their opponents. Like the similarly vulnerable Dutch, whose lives were so much affected by the sea, the English understood that a strong navy provided an advantage against a hostile Europe. But a fleet could not, on its own, guarantee safety to England. Sea power then, like air power later, supported ground troops. Land warfare upon varying terrains and in concert with shifting alliances was unavoidable in post-Reformation Europe. So the English became expert at siegecraft in Holland, cavalry charges in Huguenot France, amphibious assault in Iberia, guerrilla warfare in Ireland, and set-piece battles where war of manoeuvre gave way to brute force and hand-to-hand combat. The nation at large and its self-conscious communities, the island's geography, and the insularity of its culture (which was a result of that geography) comprised a strategic predicament. Although well suited for defence, island inhabitants had to anticipate potential threats *before* invaders might land upon their shores. Strategic thinking aimed to prevent the beachhead from being established. That meant meeting threats from differing theatres. This defensive mode of thought, coupled with physical separateness of an island culture, led to a distinctly English art of war, characterised by eclecticism and flexibility. The English, like the French and Swiss, specialised in certain forms of combat. The English tenaciously held on to the bow as their national weapon yet simultaneously began to master cannon, especially lighter iron artillery. This eclecticism illustrated how they borrowed from foreign innovations and adapted them to their own art of war.

English warfare drew upon several European arts of war and made their own unique contributions to military science. In an age where 'nations' still specialised in 'weapons' (as had the English in the longbow not so very long before), the English learnt to elevate cannon, set their pikes, charge their muskets, wheel their cavalry in to close with drawn sword, deploy light cavalry to intercept kerne, and, perhaps most arduous of all, master logistics, with the attendant horses, carriages, parchments, biscuits, corned powder, and shoes. English experimentation with the application of gunpowder technology to seaborne warfare brought innovative ship design and, subsequently, more firepower more rapidly, including such devices as truck carriages and lidded gunports.

Contemporaries certainly believed in 'English' warfare – not just Sir John Smythe (with his 'national' weapon) but also his rival, Sir Roger Williams, and later practitioners such as Robert Norton, who recognised that continental practices had to be investigated and explained to English soldier-citizens; they were aware of English 'separateness' from European war, even though England was a more significant participant in the wars of religion than has been acknowledged. An experienced English military profession (officers, non-commissioned officers, and 'enlisted' men) developed and migrated from theatre to theatre, reinforcing the malleability of the English art of war. Survival made inventiveness and adaptability requisite.

The fiscal, organisational, and (ultimately) technological innovations that would make up the English art of war during the military revolution were deeply rooted in medieval practices. Under Henry VI a less ponderous method of auditing accounts developed, where marginal notations indicated the auditing procedure, rather than drafting an entire separate account. These marginal notations were 'the first indication of the changes which led to the regular use of declared accounts'.[1] To a great degree, this process circumvented the tedious extant auditing procedure of the Exchequer, where in effect accounts were 'declared' before the Chamber, rather than processed through the Exchequer. By the reign of Henry VIII, when large sums of money were channelled into military expenditure from 1511 to 1513, English armies and navies reaped the benefits of more efficient military finance much as Renaissance merchants had prospered from the development of double-entry bookkeeping. Interestingly, too, as the English mastered the art of war, they also made the most of new European commercial practices. Adaptability, applied to making money rather than war, lent energy and resilience to the English economic expansion that paralleled these military developments. Before a British imperial paradigm was imposed upon the world, the English absorbed and learnt from that world.

Although the English dress up innovation and change as the maintenance (or restoration) of tradition, the pliability of statute and the utility of Parliament, though sluggishly and unsteadily, created a state that fielded armies in the late seventeenth century that exceeded even those of the Hundred Years War.

Medieval elements in English warfare persisted, as one can see from the accoutrements of those closest to the sovereigns. Throughout 1511 to 1642 monarchs expected their courtiers, officers, and servants to bear arms in time of war. Henry VIII's household and court regarded this as the natural order of things, which of course it was.[2] During the Bishops' Wars, this assumption prevailed still. A different style of rule may have characterised the second Stuart, but a century had done nothing to diminish the conviction that those around the ruler had an almost nuclear role in the mobilisation of an English army. How pervasive was that notion can be seen in the variety of characters who mustered and reviewed from Gloriana's Court in 1569, the year of the rebellion of the Northern Earls. From the Queen's household servants and officers (and the latter category, of course, did not include administrative officials of the Exchequer, Chancery, etc.) there were raised 4 demi-lances, 30 light horsemen, 120 corseleted pikemen, 36 corseleted soldiers with pole weapons (halberds, bills, and pole-axes), 145 harquebusiers, 83 archers, and 118 common billmen.[3] The royal compting house, baking house, pantry, cellar, buttery, spicery, chandrey, confectionery, laundry, kitchen, larder, boiling house, scalding house, scullery, and so on all trotted out personnel to serve as soldiers. The sergeant of the larder, John Heydon, wore a corselet, and supplied a harquebusier. The servitor John Bysshope carried a bill.[4] The various household establishments neither specialised in a single weapon nor fought as a unit.

The conviction that positions in the household carried a military obligation was, of course, feudal. But medieval conceptions and accoutrements long outlasted medieval civilisation. In 1573 a crossbowmaker still practised his craft and sold his wares (though almost exclusively for sporting purposes one must assume) in Chancery Lane.[5] The early Stuarts continued to purchase tilt armour long after the pageantry of jousts gave way to a more refined court culture.[6] Whether in the revival of feudal incidents by Charles I, such as scutage, or in Parliament's search for medieval precedent in the 1620s, the world-view of the Middle Ages survived into eras designated as 'Renaissance' or 'early modern'. Historians, imbued with modern concepts of linear development and (hopefully) some appreciation of narrative, tend to look for beginnings and endings, especially the former. Thus military revolution theories fix on contrasts, and those differences were developmental and linear. One military system was eclipsed by another; one weapon abandoned in favour of a better one. But linear developmentalism, as manifested in the idea of progress, infiltrated the theoretical foundations of the military revolution, and undermined the cyclical conceptual framework which dominated Western thought before the Renaissance.

One notion of cyclical immutability, where certitude in earthly life rested upon universality and changelessness, not only insisted that the great chain of being had designated the social élite as the natural masters of warfare, but steeped any study of the science of warfare in the wisdom of classical antiquity. And the English, on occasion anomalous in their beliefs, were no different from Europeans in their reverence for antiquity. A Mediterranean people they were not, but Caesar had fought upon English ground and Constantine the Great was, arguably, at least half 'British'.[7] Frontinus based (presumably) his *Strategemes* upon experiential reflections of his tenure as a governor of Britain.[8] Lord Burghley stated, in all seriousness, that the Elizabethan 'discipline of embattailing our army is according to the Roman dizeniers'.[9] The scientific underpinnings of English warfare lay in Renaissance and Reformation; the former in its reverence of antiquity, and the latter in the impetus for survival that necessitated humanist writing to justify the Protestant position in the wars of religion.

The universality of soldiering and 'military tourism' obscured temporal and geographic variation. The profession of arms and the experience of battle possessed a certain timelessness. Centuries had passed, but did not the *tercios* resemble the legions, and the Swiss pikemen approximate the Macedonian phalanx? The universality of military science linked itself to the same world-view as represented in the visual arts. Sixteenth- and seventeenth-century paintings of historical events increasingly rendered their subjects more realistically, as archaeology and a more linear conception of time (in which temporal distance implied difference rather than universality) made artists strive to be historically accurate. Albrecht Altdorfer's *Die Alexomder schlacht*, or *The Battle of Issus* (painted 1529), illustrates the transition to a modern concept of time, and in turn, warfare, by conflating sixteenth-century *landesknechts* and heavily plated armoured knights with a fanciful amalgam of 'Persians' conjured up by Ottoman stereotypes and orientalised imagery.[10] This cosmic representation of battle is somewhat in the same vein as Sir John Smythe's advocacy of the superiority of the bow as the infantry weapon *par excellence*. The fact that the stalwart English longbowmen unseated French chivalry with arrows is inseparable from the archery of Egyptians, Turks, Persians, Arabs, and Moors. Saul and Alexander the Great were both injured by arrows, and Smythe recounts other exalted personages humbled by bowmen. Rank was no defence against the bow. The efficacy of that weapon was not limited to a period of history, nor to certain terrains and campaigns.

Victory for most English writers was not confined to weaponry. The virtue of the soldiers, their 'morality' or 'excellence', accompanied the weapon. Thus many writers (though fewer 'pure' soldiers) bowed before the Roman paradigm not just because of the excellent tactics of the legions, but because of the discipline (based on 'morality') that made those tactics possible. To contemporaries, English soldiers possessed expertise, and comparisons as to what nations excelled in what weapons abounded during the wars of religion. At the core was a belief in the universality of martial excellence, grounded in rigorous training and discipline.

Some nations made better soldiers than did others, as one Captain Maria conjectured when he questioned English 'braverie' during a dinner with Sir John Smythe in Antwerp. The day before, the Protestants Egmont and Horn had been decapitated, and tensions were running high. Smythe took umbrage at Maria's scepticism, cited Poitiers, the marauding of Sir John Hawkwood's company in Italy, Richard the Lionheart's success on Cyprus, and other examples. Historical relativism was not at issue: Smythe claimed 'the same vertue of valyauncie' characterised the Englishmen of the present day. Maria dismissed England as a minuscule military power, to which Smythe retorted that England might field a 50,000-man expeditionary force and boasted a 100,000-strong militia, claims not so hyperbolic considering the French invasions of Henry VIII and the potential strength of the Elizabethan militia. When discussion turned to Italian, Spanish, and English 'valyauncie', Smythe offered to put the question to the test. He stood 'readie to prove and mayntayne the same, with my sworde in my hand at anie tyme'. Before blows could be struck, Antwerp's Chancellor and magistrates intervened.[11]

This narrowly averted duel between military veterans of differing religions and nations revolved more around character than expertise. Moral superiority and daring were at issue, not tactical methods or weaponry. Victory was an extension of something internal and human, not external and technological. However much Maria and Smythe disagreed, their view of warfare was universal and not subject to an 'idea of progress'. The new warfare of the sixteenth century created for the soldier as many problems as it solved. The quick decisiveness of artillery 'was neutralised by the cumbrous organisation of their supply trains. Gunpowder, in short, revolutionised the conduct, but not the outcome of wars.'[12] The military revolution involved the use of projectiles and how to defend against them, not the cultivation of virtue or chivalric conduct.

By the 1590s, the military revolution should indeed have been evident. And if ideas are a concern of the new military history, one cannot help but wonder why veterans such as Smythe, whose military career spanned half a century, did not articulate their perceptions of those changes more clearly. Those who perceived the change were, for the most part, artillerists and engineers. Given the emphasis on moral fortitude among military theorists and English commanders, reflected in their adulation of the Romans, it is no surprise that the longbow versus firearm debate in Smythe's hands became linked with charges that bordered on treason and alleged reckless homicide against currently serving army officers. In his desire to refute the efficacy of the 'Fyre shotte of Callyvers and musketts', Smythe muddied the debate by arguing that not only were Her Majesty's commanders wrong about the art of war, but they were also 'evell' men.

The issue of dead pay had long bedevilled relations between the Queen's officers (who insisted upon collecting money for dead pay) and the Dutch Council of State, who disapproved of the practice. English captains (who did indeed enjoy a remarkable degree of autonomy not only in the matter of musters but also often in tactical battlefield initiatives) were keen on distinguishing themselves and sometimes engaged the enemy perhaps too willingly, even recklessly. Smythe attributed the most wicked motives to their zeal. According to one of Burghley's correspondents, Smythe's 'booke doth declare that the sayd captens and leaders of soldyers did leade them sometyme to desperate servyces, to the ende that they myght inioye [enjoy] the dead payes of theyre slayd soldyers'.[13] No wonder Williams and his compatriots reacted so vigorously, knowing that the Queen could not tolerate the libelling of her commanders.[14] In his own defence, Smythe contended

> . . . I have touched with blame no man of warre of vertue and woorthines, of anie sort nor callinge, but only such as uppon their guiltie consciences doe discover and condemne them selves, and therfore finde fault with my booke. But what is he or they that ar so highly offended with my writinge, but only such as have bene the cheefe inventors and executors of that new infernall discipline, not only by me so termed, but also so accounted by the whole Realme. And what effect doth all the worlde evidently see, that they and their newe discipline militarie have wrought, but the dyvertinge of a great part of her Majesties treasure from her intended services, to their owne gaines, and superfluous expenses? Wherof, and of manie other their woonderfull disorders hath ensued [?] their wittinge and willinge consumption of manie and manie thousands of the verie flower and bravest sort of men of this realme.[15]

The injection of morality into the furore over 'modern' warfare obscured an already complex transformation of the art of war. The controversy between bow and firearm comprised more than simply a choice of weapon. Questions regarding strategic commitment, impressment and training, court patronage and country autonomy, were too often rendered inchoate by the muddied conceptual framework (and writing) of the disputants. Humphrey Barwicke, like Smythe, was a hoary veteran; he started soldiering in 1548 and thus, by the end of Elizabeth's reign, had a longer view of contemporary warfare. He reached conclusions different from Smythe's and represented another, almost diametrically opposed, school of English thought. Barwicke threw off the tyranny of the past and dared suggest that contemporaries had synthesised a new art of war that exceeded classical excellence. But he thus misrepresented Smythe's views.

When Sir John Smythe advocated the use of the longbow, was he ruling out the use of firearms? Rather, he was agreeing with Captain Edward Yorke, who had written from the siege of Rouen: 'If half the pioneers had pikes and the other half bows, they might do something beside digging, for "they be natural weapons and therefore need not teaching".'[16] Smythe realised (and this perception was one of very few he shared with contemporary military men) that gunpowder-propelled weapons required substantial training in their proper use.[17] Not only did firearms complicate a soldier's performance, but also the tactical use of guns was imperfectly understood by inexperienced commanders in the Low Countries, a corollary to Smythe's denunciation of English officers serving abroad.[18] Sir John advocated the elegant simplicity of the longbow as a balance to these new infernal machines, for archery was a more 'natural' practice of fighting. But he did not believe guns should be banned. Smythe and others aimed at an English synthesis of tradition with invention. There was a place for the longbow alongside the pike, or in coordination with the musket for that matter.[19] Mastery of Yorke's 'natural weapons' did not entail the drilling (he and Smythe could argue) that these musketeers of the newfangled military discipline needed.

The persistence of the longbow in English armies was not evidence of backwardness. Rather, simultaneous and synchronised use of firearms and bows reflected the eclecticism of the English warfare. Henry VIII recognised that each missile weapon, gun and bow, had unique advantages (and disadvantages) in regard to penetration, rate of fire, trajectory, technical complexity, and cost. Best to combine harquebusiers and archers for tactical utility, which explains the presence of bowmen in English armies into the 1600s.[20] The ambivalence surrounding the efficacy of England's national weapon was illustrated when Charles I put the Henrician archery statute into execution in March 1631 only to revoke it as impractical less than five months later.[21] A government needed to promote a programme of training if any consistency in drill and weaponry were to be achieved. This was especially true during the reign of James I, when periods of decentralised supervision of the militia diluted the already inconsistent quality of the trained bands. Thus in 1623 the lieutenancy sent down into the shires a national drill book. In August, Captain John Preston received his copy and orders to use it:

> I send you here withall a booke intitled Instruction for Musters and Armes, and the use of them, by order from the Lords of the Councill, by which booke you are to bee directed aswell for the Armeing as the disciplineing of your Souldiers.[22]

Even before the Crown rested on Charles's head, he and Buckingham secured the services of 100 English veterans of the Low Countries wars, and assigned them in pairs to each shire 'to be resident' and train the locals.[23]

Success depended not on initiative from above so much as cooperation from below. The municipality of Shrewsbury assessed its citizens diligently and regularly to see that the muster-master received his pay of £3 5s. a year.[24] Simultaneously, in Somersetshire Sir Robert Phelips rejected wholesale the necessity of a muster-master; and in 1615, while Shrewsbury performed exemplarily, the Somerset muster-master found his pay £112 in arrears.[25] Phelips's exchange with Hopton over the sergeant,[26] as with the more spectacular brawl over militiaman Spracklinge with Lord John Poulett, exemplified how lieutenancy might do a splendid job of keeping the peace but often crippled efforts to make war. Too many shires and towns resembled Somerset. Amateur local governors worried for their own reputation in an insular world. When a gentleman's perspective became more national, it did so (such as when standing for Parliament) for personal political motives that translated into county politics writ large at Westminster. In retrospect it is amazing that basic self-defence measures were blithely ignored, as if the Crown were crying 'wolf!' for selfish political motives similar to those held by the leaders of the county communities.

Nor did those in stubborn resistance distinguish Tudor from Stuart. The appalling dereliction of duty in some quarters when Elizabeth faced danger on several fronts indicates an extraordinarily narrow world-view in the country rather than disloyalty to the Crown. At Whitehall England's best interests could be seen clearly, and the bad judgement sometimes exercised there (Henry VIII's useless wars, James I's sanguine hope of a peaceful Europe, Charles I's ham-fisted strategies) discredited in the eyes of the country bumpkin the one institution, the Crown in Council, that knew best when to prepare for and engage in warfare. But, as Elizabeth's enquiries into Irish troop strength and Charles I's attempts at a 'perfect militia' demonstrated, obtaining accurate knowledge at the centre was difficult, and enforcement on the local level was well nigh impossible. Thus that which kept England 'free' in many ways, the strength of local interest steeped in tradition and unabashedly championing country issues at Westminster, came close to allowing the realm to be enslaved by powers far more insidious than anything the Tudors and early Stuarts would have perpetrated on their own subjects. That England refused, then as now, to become in any way a military culture, pliable to the conduct of war and enamoured of using force to settle diplomatic and political problems, meant that its survival was questionable at several junctures in its history. And it is notable that a 'foreign' ruler, William III, brought England up to its full military potential.

Dovetailing with England's reluctance, perhaps inability, to become a militarised culture was the English dichotomy of country and city. Localities exercised a striking amount of autonomy. One can link together the elaborate apparatus of Henrician military administration (with its crew of noble 'retainers', foreign mercenaries, subcontracted mariners, London victuallers, and Cornish miners) with the chaos of 1642, personified by the baffled trained-band soldiers securing the gates of Hull against their King, yet for their King.[27] Growing naturally out of the English version of the feudal system, military power (in other words, men, weapons, horses, and, not the least important, money) was to be found in the countryside before 1642. The centralisation that one might expect on an island dominated by a metropolis and lorded over by ambitious dynasties did not prevail over localism until late 1642. Henry VIII might discard the Pope, but his armies existed by the good graces of cooperative lords and gentlemen, subcontracted transport and victualling services, and mercenaries. Without money, provided by a dismembered Church and a pliant but self-aware Parliament, there would have been few Henrician campaigns of note. Henry not only lacked a standing army; he did not have a militia. The trained bands came about through the efforts of a financially strapped monarch who knew how to make localism work in royal service. And Elizabeth's shrewd management of lieutenancy, for which she owed something to her deceased siblings, on the surface appeared continental and medieval in its delegation of royal authority upon trusted nobles, but in fact was distinctly English in its orchestration of local and royal interests in forging cooperative ventures that safeguarded the Crown as well as the property of the subject.

Indeed, real property and movable wealth (resting on English views of ownership, hence individual rights) shaped English warfare, in that material resources were in the grip of the locality. And the cooperation that monarchy, especially after 1500, expected made such an arrangement acceptable, best illustrated by parliamentary assistance in the financing of government (including the mounting of campaigns). Lieutenancy became the intermediary between the Crown (which formulated national military strategy) and the localities. That was why the government took so seriously Sir John Smythe's drunken ramblings at the Essex muster. He tried to commandeer the trained bands, however amateur they might have been, and thus seize control of the only real military force that existed in England.

English culture did not embrace military values and aggression naturally. Securing a peaceful countryside, which also underlay the desire for political stability, governed the locality. Having survived the continental threat in the sixteenth century, the inhabitants of Albion lapsed back into their peaceful ways, which suited James I admirably. Charles I, oddly enough like Henry VIII in his meddlesome predilection for altering the nation's religion and his misplaced conviction that military force was universally decisive in settling international disputes, did indeed inspire a certain military ardour in some (though very few) of his subjects by launching campaigns in the 1620s, attempting to invigorate the militia, and mobilising one kingdom against another in 1639–40. Charles's attitude to war was as out of step with that of his subjects as he was blind to his people's religious sensibilities. So, although war exercised a certain fascination with Charles, his English subjects preferred to live in peace. The result was the sporadically bellicose King ruling a pacific society. As Conrad Russell points out, 'that England had reached January 1642 with no unquestionably legal method of raising troops is a symptom of this demilitarised condition'. In fact, English warfare had been a victim of its own success, for, although invasion scares sometimes panicked the shires, England's forays into the early seventeenth-century wars of religion were fought on someone else's soil. Mars, though remembered, had been exiled. The trained bands were designed for defence. The nobility no longer summoned significant numbers of obedient armed men to their standards.

> Neither King nor Parliament possessed the money for hiring large numbers of mercenaries, and the professional soldiers who had gathered round the King at Whitehall were numbered in hundreds and not in thousands. There were probably not many countries in Europe where a major panic could be created by a military force costing only £200.[28]

The generally small scale of English military enterprises was characteristic of a strategy of defence. Resources were diverted towards warfare in proportion to the level of danger faced by the realm. English arms thus shined brightest in the midst of crisis. English warfare achieved its greatest strategic successes in 1588–1603, not when the machinery of war was most perfected but when the kingdom's military resources stretched to the breaking point. In the 1590s, when war weariness, which afflicted all levels of society, accompanied the two decades of greatest peril, English arms not only survived, but triumphed against the odds. If only Elizabeth had had her father's armies of 1544–5. Unencumbered by the maintenance of such a large and growing establishment, Henry VIII could afford to devote his considerable resources to French and Scottish campaigns. Henrician mobilisations depended upon subcontractors and mercenaries, especially for modern weapons and transport. Even English recruits were 'decentralised', in that they were raised through lords and gentlemen.[29] Henrician wealth and an energetic, competent royal household circle showed what England was indeed capable of putting on the battlefield. But to what ends? At the very centre of that system stood King Henry, whose strategies were as twisted as his conscience. And much of the administrative machinery had roots in the household. Under the Lord Protector Somerset this system was wielded with skill. But with no powerful monarch at the centre who could coordinate the far-flung reserves of military potential, conquests were undermined rapidly, as happened to the triumphs gained, and garrisons planted, on Scottish soil.

Although English forces operating in Ireland until the later years of Elizabeth were comparatively smaller than contemporary continental armies, still the escalation of the Irish wars cannot be underestimated, particularly in the eyes of the Elizabethans, who found its attrition and expense astonishing. The confluence of continental and Irish conflicts in this context illuminate the thorny political and fiscal dilemma inherited by the Queen. Ironically, when England could most afford massive armies, she least needed them. And when most imperilled, she strained every sinew to field adequate forces to maintain religious liberty and territorial integrity. Martial strength emerged from quarters far from court. Experienced captains stepped forward from the ranks of the continental 'society of soldiers'.[30] The shires, which in reality carried virtually alone the weighty responsibilities of mobilisation and defence, did their duty, if sometimes begrudgingly and shabbily. And when called upon, invariably the localities did things their way. But soldiers, guns, and coats the Queen got.

None of this, such as the infrastructure and products of the cannon-founding industry or victualling systems, came from the central government. 'Private' enterprise and the obstinate county communities, with good generalship and soldiering, brought victory in Ireland, held the Spaniard at bay, checked Catholic advances on the Continent, and over the years inculcated some military experience in the succeeding generation. This was the obverse side of the same shire communities that might grossly inhibit a royal mobilisation if the locals felt that military activities were not in their collective (but sometimes narrow) interests.

Many historians are struck by Elizabeth I's almost obsessive concern with unbridled expense. Her correspondence dwelt as much upon finance as strategy, and the linkage between them did not elude her. The clamouring of unpaid troops and the lamentations of officers underscore the common-place view of 'parsimonious Gloriana'. But a closer look somewhat exonerates her. Parliamentary machinations and attitudes often determined the size, strength, and even deployment of armies under the later Tudors and early Stuarts. With the infrastructure of mobilisation embedded below and geographically distant from the Privy Council, then Members of Parliament, Lords Lieutenants, and local officialdom could pursue the conduct of war more cautiously than the Queen and her councillors wished. Parliamentary yields lessened in value over time because of inflation. So, while the cost of war increased, the value of a parliamentary subsidy decreased; and the Crown was caught between. Politics and parliamentary finances more than anything determined what Elizabeth could or could not do, especially in regard to offensive operations. If the 1596 Cadiz expedition had a piratical dimension, it was not so much that the Queen was unwilling to bear her fiscal responsibility, but rather strapped for ready money. Relations amongst Crown, Commons, and Lords dictated Elizabeth's access to the extraordinary revenues demanded by the exigencies of war. Numerous (and diverse) theatres of operations simply compounded her political dependency upon Parliament and the shire communities. Thus the Queen's strategy was not always hers alone. Even in more oblique financial commitments, such as the supply of transport by coastal communities, impressment, arming, feeding, and clothing levies, the political relationship mediated by the lieutenancy dictated what military support the Council might expect from the shires and cities.[31]

There are parallels between England's development as a military power and the precipitants of the Commercial Revolution. In both cases (and perhaps even also in the matters of the Industrial Revolution and establishment of the Empire), gifted and entrepreneurial individuals provided expertise and initiative with virtually no sustenance from the state. Indeed the state often constituted an impediment. Individual initiatives, in the publication of military treatises by maverick English piketrailers (or in the case of Sir Roger Williams, a lancer) continually reminded the state that military science, as practised on the Continent, continued to move apace. Informed by their martial odysseys, English observers promoted the scientific study of the artillerist. The nimble and decisive tactical manoeuvres of the field commanders were recorded and made sense of by English theorists. English soldiers in general distinguished themselves in the Low Countries. But individuality, in acts of bravery on the battlefield or entrepreneurship in the iron cannon foundry, elevated the art of war. And not just of those whose lives were primarily military; also Justices of the Peace, deputy lieutenants, the mayors of Bristol, Chester, and elsewhere, and others also, made their contributions.

English military history is, clichés aside, individuals doing their duty regardless of obstacles. England muddled through dangerous war years and survived by the skin of its teeth. Duty was done, as in the case of the sentries at Kinsale, who froze to death at their posts in the earthworks. In that sense, nineteenth-century military history still has value, with its emphasis on valour, morale, and mentalité. The denigration of the English art of war by contemporaries and, later, historians, particularly in the areas of the adoption of pikes and firearms with their attendant drill, the 'new' siegecraft and fortification, and the theoretical grasp of the military revolution, suggests that England was a pathetic military power. 'England's major triumphs on the continent, in 1513, 1544 and in the Netherlands in the 1590s were all carried out in association with, or under the command of, experienced Europeans.'[32] But, as often as not, England's allies failed her. In 1513 and 1544 it could be argued that Henry's continental allies in fact hampered his armies' effectiveness. True, the 1523 campaign exhibited poor military ability and unrealised strategic goals, but, as we saw in Chapter 1, English arms achieved significant victories. Nowhere was this more apparent than against Scotland, and later Ireland. Dr Eltis judges these Celtic opponents as less formidable than 'modern' European armies who practised the elements of the military revolution. But Celtic warfare proved the greatest challenge, and, as the century changed, England won its greatest victory at Kinsale, while simultaneously English soldiers took a leading role at Ostend, where they showed themselves equal to Europeans.

English armies and multiple kingdoms

Debate over things military, at least prior to the reign of Charles I, focused on the scale of warfare and its cost. The monarch defended the realm or justified a campaign and expected Parliament to 'do its bit'. But with Charles I, especially within the context of the wars of religion, the ruler became a threat to some of his subjects and threatened to bring down war upon the entire kingdom. The militia, though certainly no standing army, had indeed developed through the transformation of increased firepower in the hands of infantrymen. That civil war, like a bad dream from the fifteenth century, should descend again upon England, was inconceivable. Military preparedness under the Tudors and early Stuarts had never been designed for such a dilemma. Never before had the English army been turned on English society. And the fear that Charles I, if commanding the trained bands through lieutenants loyal to the Crown, might forcibly dissolve Parliament brought the prospect of violence down to its most visceral level amongst the Members of Parliament. The unbelievable was made plausible by the Army Plot and the Irish Rebellion.

In a multiple-kingdom monarchy the armed forces of one realm can impose the royal will on another of the King's possessions, rather as Philip II had used Spanish, German, and Italian forces to suppress the Dutch. The pivotal episode in the struggle over control of the armed forces was the Bishops' Wars of 1639 and 1640.[33] Sending an English army against the Scots could not have been more traditional fare. But the Reformation, in each of the multiple kingdoms, had altered strategic relationships. Since 1558 a religious dimension coloured English warfare. The Elizabethan wars had been waged against popery. Mansfeld's 1624 expedition aimed to recover the Palatinate. Cadiz and Rhé fought international Catholicism. But the Scottish war deliberately struck at Protestantism. Worse, foreign mercenaries would have landed upon the shore of England to assist in the royal campaign against godly religion had not the King lacked financial resources. Those extraordinary resources lay in the hands of Parliament, which saw itself as a guardian of the realm.

Another irony was that the two most proximate 'enemies', the Irish and the Scots, had been brought into apparently unprecedented harmony with England by 1635–7. Within a few years, these kingdoms sparked the conflagration of 1642–9. The Covenanters' apologetic resort to arms became the most successful occupation of northern England achieved in centuries, exalting the power of the sword (even when wielded gently). Irish Catholics saw military revolt as an avenue to religious autonomy, as their covenanting adversaries had achieved in 'loyal opposition' to the Crown. Parliament followed suit. Charles I never learnt the art of compromise and thus it was only through military force that accommodation with Crown policy was achieved. The English learned to manage war in a centralised fashion and brought up a generation of soldiers by fighting within the British Isles. The inclusion of Ireland and Scotland within the multiple kingdom had promised peace but brought division that was settled only by force of arms. When the trained bands met their first real test, it was against neighbours and countrymen.

Charles loosed the horror in 1639 by marching to the Borders without any parliamentary deliberation or subsidy. The subsequent campaign and loss of the North to the Scots brought 'foreign' military occupation. The ensuing disbandment, and payment, of the English and Scottish armies demanded parliamentary involvement in settling the problems of Charles's dominions. Strafford's treason hinged on non-parliamentary use of military force. The first Army Plot in spring 1641 played into the hands of Pym's circle by proving that the King would use force against Parliament. Pym's junto 'undertook a steady course of action to gain control of the military'.[34] If indeed there existed parliamentary conspiracy to seize England's military, Charles I and the Irish rebels (independently) did much to foment it. The King lay under suspicion of importing mercenaries or even inviting a foreign invasion should his political situation deteriorate.

The second Army Plot (July 1641) aimed to shore up Charles's political fortunes though brute force. The English troops raised for Ireland would be marched to London 'if there should bee a disagreement between the king and the people'. The Tower would be seized and Parliament overawed. This conspiracy was revealed on 30 October 1641, and two days later, news of the Irish Rebellion arrived in London.[35] Without the Army Plots, the furore over Irish levies, and then the Irish Rebellion, there would have been no Militia Ordinance in 1642. The outbreak of religious war in Ireland obliged both King and Parliament to restore the peace. But neither Charles nor his critics would allow Parliament to raise forces for the succour of Ireland, suspecting (rightly, it would seem, in both cases) that these soldiers would be employed in England. Such a charade was acknowledged when Sir William St Leger defected to the Royalists in August 1642. 'When I was at York, I feared what sithence is come to pass. That wee (who were pretended for Ireland) should be employed here against our lawfull and most gratious King.'[36]

Figure 12.1 Sir Thomas Lunsford fought at Newburn Ford (28 August 1640) and was embroiled in the Army Plots of 1641. He personified the 'para-militaries' who later provided a foundation for the cavalier army.

Source: Sir Thomas Lunsford, one of Charles's 'para-militaries' (author's collection).

On 14 January 1642 Oliver Cromwell, MP, moved that England and Wales assume a 'posture of defence'. On the 18th followed a resolution that the Lords Lieutenants and deputy lieutenants be designated via parliamentary ordinance.[37] No better illustration that English politics shaped English warfare could be found. Although a nucleus of English professional soldiers had endured through various reigns and two dynasties since 1511, the men were far removed from the seat of English political power, as they plied their trade across the Irish Sea and upon the Continent. As has been shown, 'English warfare' assumed many guises, for it was fought in widely differing theatres of operation. Further, wars often broke out precipitously, so that mobilisation was too often a hurried affair involving the incorporation of resources on a speedy and *ad hoc* basis. And the essentially defensive nature of English warfare (apart from Henry VIII's campaigns) meant that the Crown ruled on its own resources, pursuing a safe peace rather than amassing a war coffer for future conquest. Should war threaten, Parliament had to be approached for extraordinary revenues. And, in doing so, Parliament had become an essential partner in the enterprise of English warfare much as it became a partner in the development and safeguarding of the national religion. Parliament, like the Crown, maintained the centre, in that stretch of ground running from Whitehall to Westminster.

Military power existed outside London, in the ports and localities, where both King and Parliament maintained linkages. Through the institution of lieutenancy, the lieutenants were the key to military power, for the trained bands of the shires constituted the essential military power within the realm, more notable than the clergy's light horse contingents, the informal semi-private bands of the Midland freeholders, and the scattered English 'volunteer' forces abroad.[38] Specialisation, that component of the technologically driven theory of the military revolution, had not been perfected in the militia. Nor were the trained-band soldiers as adept at managing weaponry and tactics as Englishmen fighting abroad. Drill remained sporadic and standardisation of weapons (such as the adoption of a standardised bore for firearms) was an elusive goal. The perfect militia was far from flawless.[39]

What altered the configuration of military power in England was London's emergence as an engine of war, which effectively broke the country's monopoly on the means to make war. London's ascendancy was short lived: 1642–5. The New Model Army, by 1644–7, gained the ascendancy as a formidable political and military force. But in 1642 a collaboration of interest amongst John Pym's junto, 'radicals' within the municipal corporation and professional military men (who had found a haven in the Society of the Artillery Garden), had transformed an amateurish 6,000-man militia into an army of 8,000 that might be deployed offensively in the service of Parliament.[40]

Parliament, whose fiscal support had made possible the Hundred Years War, and whose cooperation with Henry VIII's foreign and domestic policies did much to place the Tudors firmly in control of the realm, ultimately grasped the reins of military power for itself. Hemmed in by a hostile King and a rebellious Ireland, it proved the potential of English warfare by succeeding in 1642 where Charles had failed in 1639 and 1640. Working with the Corporation of London, the City trained bands proved that English military expertise had survived. The reorganisation of the London militia in 1642, and its drilling at the Society of the Artillery Garden, gave Parliament an advantage in the Civil War that Charles never overcame. Any perceived military impotence in the 'perfect militia' stemmed from Charles's mismanagement of the trained bands.[41] Parliament's control of a force roughly reckoned at 20,000 men, even if in collusion with the Corporation of London, posed a thorny constitutional problem and generated scores of pamphlets that debated the issue.[42]

London's gradual assumption of military power during the sixteenth century, eclipsing old centres such as Yorkshire, in 1642 for the first time created a military power within an urban structure, so that Charles was compelled to scour the country to find the means to reduce London. Lords Lieutenants in their rural domains could not be coerced as, say, Crown servants in European countries. For that reason the naming of Lords Lieutenants was a matter of great debate between Pym's junto in the Commons and the circle of Charles I. Lieutenants might slide from one allegiance to another, for who could predict how they would interpret their duty and where they would pin their loyalty in this unprecedented situation? And concern for the country's security took precedence over ideology. Some supported the militia bill hoping to keep the peace, and not initiate hostilities.

The trial of the Earl of Strafford in spring 1641 had raised publicly the danger of the King using troops from one of his kingdoms against subjects in another. In the three-kingdom monarchy, the militia was the only defence against treachery from the other kingdoms. The paradoxical nature of this dilemma emerged in article fifteen of the charges brought against the Earl in his treason trial. Strafford's alleged plan to unleash Irish soldiers against England (when in truth he was speaking of Scotland, though in the generality 'this kingdome') was in effect war against the King as well as the people of England.[43] The Earl, who occasionally advocated lynching aldermen, had no compunction about keeping troops in readiness indefinitely.[44] Thus, when Sir John Hotham locked the gates of Hull against the person of the King on 23 April 1642, denying Charles I access to the garrison, the arsenal, and the fortifications,[45] a dramatic incident acted out the constitutional quandary over deployment of armed forces. In the House's verdict,

> the levying of war against [the King's] laws and authority, though not against his person, is levying war against the King; but the levying force against his personal commands, though accompanied with his presence, and not against his laws and authority, but in maintenance thereof, is not levying war against the King, but for him.

Charles retorted, 'we are the only person in England against whom treason cannot be committed'.[46]

Hotham's garrison troops harboured doubts about the legality of their action, especially after their sequestration dragged on for eleven weeks, a violation of the terms under which militiamen served. William Launsdale and Richard Yeddon, 20-year-old trained-bandsmen of Yorkshire, found themselves herded into Hull and, through Hotham's actions, in rebellion against the King. Sir John warned them to remain in garrison, as Charles

had allegedly sent proclamations to the justices and constables to apprehend soldiers of the Hull garrison and hang them. The two militiamen,
through an intermediary, attempted to defect to the royal standard.[47] To
Laundsdale, Yeddon, and anyone who read the Militia Ordinance, it must
have seemed as if English warfare (which had been developed to defend
the realm against popery) was now turned upon itself. Lord Paget, abandoning Parliament for the King, expressed eloquently why the Militia
Ordinance was the turning point:

> It may seem strange that I whoe with all zeale and earnestnes have
> prosecuted since the beginning of this Parliament the Reformation
> of the disorders in Church and Commonwealth, should now in a
> time of soe greate distracion desert the cause. Most true it is that
> my ends were the Common good. . . . I was ready to lay downe
> my life and fortune. But when I found a reparacion of Armes
> against the King under shaddow of Loyalty I rather resolved to
> obey a good conscience then particular ends.

His fellow nobles at York agreed, pledging to defend the King and his
prerogative 'against the new ordinance of the militia'.[48]

Hotham's decision to bar Charles I from appropriating the magazine at
Hull may be somewhat explicable in the context of Sir John's service in
the Protestant cause during the Thirty Years War. If, as Simon Healy has
suggested, Hotham's soldiering in Bohemia in 1619–20 (which may have
included action at the Battle of the White Mountain) made him more
sensitive to the subversion of the English state by popish conspiracy, Sir
John's radical act at Hull seems understandable. Hotham's 'treasonous'
communication with the Scots in 1639–40 certainly made clear to the
King that Sir John's sympathies lay with militant Protestantism.[49] The wars
of religion had taught the English to look far afield for danger. The variety
of theatres in which English soldiers practised their art of war demonstrated how ubiquitous was the popish threat. 'Defence of the realm' had
become something broader than patrolling the seashore.

The English had been fighting for the survival of their reformed religion,
and the government of which that religion was an integral part, since the
mid-1500s. They felt in 1641–2 more endangered than ever before. It was
difficult, but far from impossible, to transfer that defensive attitude focused
outwards on the Continent, and on Ireland, to a fifth column within. Con-
spiracies and rebellions had a long history in England, and the religious context of 1640–2 made the military situation that much more sinister and liable
to paranoic impression. The Irish Rebellion's atrocities made this fear a reality. Thus this strategic vision of defence was internalised to come to terms
with the impossible: fighting the King to save realm and religion. The law
of nature, survival itself, then, justified the Militia Ordinance.

> ... we who have the greatest part of the world our enemies, may jvstly feare, that they are now plotting and contriving that for England, that is already acted in Ireland ... by reason of the imminent danger which threatens the Common-wealth, the King refusing to settle the Militia, the Parliament may well do it.[50]

The officers of the Ordnance found themselves in the midst of this constitutional struggle when Parliament on 6 November 1641 'enjoyed the yssueing of 1000 Armes for horse, 8000 Armes for Foote', ten lasts of gunpowder and additional munitions for the suppression of the Irish Rebellion. Charles, displeased that the Houses presumed to draw weapons from the royal arsenal upon their own authority, countermanded the order under his sign manual. As the Ordnance officers attempted to maintain the ancient procedures of the Office, the parliamentary commission for Irish affairs unleashed a stream of warrants and orders during early 1642. The confrontation at Hull compounded the dilemma when arms and ammunition from Hotham's garrison were to be transferred to the Ordnance Office's custody in June. The Master of the Ordnance (the Earl of Newport), attending the King at York, stood firmly behind the royal order forbidding the requisition of nearly fifty artillery pieces by Parliament. The Earls of Leicester and Essex, acting on behalf of the Houses and the Irish Committee, bullied the resident officers (Francis Conningsby, Richard March, and Edward Sherburne) and imprisoned them at the outbreak of war in August. The keys were delivered up and parliamentary committees learned the science of logistics and the management of artillery.[51] The intrusion of Parliament into the direct management of war *matériel* changed the nature of English warfare. The struggles for the Ordnance Office stores and the Hull arsenal were mirrored on a smaller scale throughout the county communities. Parliamentary sympathisers manoeuvred against the King's Commissioners of Array to requisition, seize, and intercept war *matérial*, all parties insisting their actions were sanctioned by the law of the land.[52]

A nation, if not always a monarchy, that had (in general) a disinclination towards things military achieved military success. Ireland proved to be the engine that pulled England into more elaborate forms of war, for example in 1599–1601 in terms of supply systems and command, and 1642 in terms of fiscal and military commitment. Even in 1599–1601 and 1642, English national support for Irish wars was begrudging (Parliament proved as recalcitrant as the shires). Ireland ignited England's war of religion; and neither island escaped the curse of the wars of religion. Supporting Dutch independence had aided English security but brought confrontation with Spain, which in turn prompted Spanish succour for a Roman Catholic and independent Ireland. Therefore, the Elizabethan Irish wars constituted a sub-theatre of the Low Countries wars and the Thirty Years War acted out in Ireland, reaching their climax between 1641 and 1649.

Figure 12.2 His father had fought in Ireland and was executed for a treasonous uprising (1601). The third Earl, depicted here, led Parliament's army against the King at Edgehill (23 October 1642). Royalists noted that they were facing the son of a traitor.

Source: Robert Devereux, third Earl of Essex (author's collection).

England's descent into war was painted by those outside the Court of Charles I as a cosmic calamity. War was not a natural state for England, and the outbreak of hostilities was accompanied by unnatural events. A schoolmaster near Knaresborough and his neighbours reported fairies, satyrs, and devils drilling with pikes and muskets (bandoleers about some of their necks) on a hillside on the eve of the First Bishops' War.[53] A continental observer opined that England at long last was drawn into the natural purgation of wickedness through bloodshed:

... it is but yet the beginning of warrs. I wish you had received myne of the last yeare wherein I had written my Judgement of your English hopes for the Palatinate by Ambassage or Peace. There you would see that I had bin a prophet because I did write knowing nothing of the troubles of England that either the English armyes must be beaten in Ireland, or that there must be a Civill war in England. They are no better then other nations and I feare much

Figure 12.3 Lindsey's ancestor, Peregrine Bertie, had served Elizabeth in the French wars of religion. On 23 October 1642, the Earl led the cavalier forces at Edgehill.

Source: Robert Bertie, Earl of Lindsey (author's collection).

the King's children, and the Queen if shee be not converted and that such men as hinder, yea advance not the full Politicall and Ecclesiastical Reformacion must be rooted out. But you will say is there any hope of us poore Germans. Yes very greate, but not by the meanes of Peace but by a most Cruell war. When you see that whole Idollatrus Townes are burnt or killed, then you may hope that a sound peace for Germany beginnith, the warr being translated into Italy which must swim in bloud. Therefore my deare friend have patience, and the Lord will give enough to our children if we can keepe them but alive these 10 yeares. As for the Low Countryes they alsoe must have a thorough purgacion butt it will be very wholesome.[54]

Although a battle had been fought as early as August 1640, at Newburn, the 'thorough purgacion' was postponed by negotiation. But the bloodbath in Ireland after October 1641 fostered a resort to violence in England, at Manchester, Marshalls Elm, Babylon Hill, and Powick Bridge (July–September 1642). When Englishman pitted himself against Englishman, both often from the same community, it was those bickering Somersetshire militiamen who squared off at Marshalls Elm and then Babylon Hill. In the end, they fought. Commanding the victorious Royalists was Sir John Stawell. And at the major engagement of Edgehill (23 October 1642), two veterans led their respective infantries against each other. Sir Jacob Astley and the Earl of Essex, veterans of continental wars who had collaborated so decisively in securing Berwick in the First Bishops' War, now commanded opposing armies, and did so spectacularly. Once comrades-in-arms in the Protestant cause, they now campaigned against each other.[55] The militia and pressed men, Royalists and Roundheads, proved able and expert. The gruesome number of casualties at the opening battle of the Civil War showed how quickly Englishmen assimilated combat skills. Edgehill was not, therefore, a loss of innocence. Rather, it demonstrated, not for the last time, that the English knew very well how to fight when they had need to do so.[56] The tragedy was that, whereas English strategy since the mid-1500s had concentrated upon preventing foreign incursions, in the end England assimilated the military revolution fully by fighting itself and its British cousins.

NOTES

1 THE EARLY TUDOR ART OF WAR ON THE CONTINENT

1 Quoted by Andrew Ayton in *Knights and Warhorses. Military Service and the English Aristocracy under Edward III* (Woodbridge 1994), p. 9; see also D. Thompson, ed., *Petrarch. A Humanist Among Princes* (New York 1971), pp. 184–5.

2 Bodleian Library, *Over There. Instructions for American Servicemen in Britain 1942* (Oxford 1994, reprint of a US War Department pamphlet). I owe this reference to Lesley Smith.

3 A recent denigration of pre-civil war English warfare is *The Military Revolution in Sixteenth Century Europe* (London 1995) by David Eltis.

4 Ian Beckett, *The Amateur Military Tradition, 1558–1945* (Manchester 1991).

5 Daniel Goffman, *Britons in The Ottoman Empire 1642–1660* (Washington 1997), pp. 3–16.

6 BL, Harleian MS 519, ff. 12–12v, 'The institution and dyssepline of a souldier in the Realme of England gathered oute of dyverse auncyent histories very necessarye to be perused in theis perilous tymes'. The author lauds the Romans and analyses the development of English society as well as drawing military wisdom from classical histories.

7 *State Papers and Manuscripts relating to English Affairs, existing in the Archives and Collections of Venice . . . (Calendar of State Papers Venetian)*, R. Brown, ed., (London 1882) vol. 6 pt. 2 (1556–7), p. 1047.

8 For the practice, PRO, E 351/210; for the concept, Thomas Audley's 'A booke of orders in the Warres by see and land', commissioned by Henry VIII and preserved as BL, Harleian MS 309, new ff. 1–14.

9 David Loades, *The Tudor Navy. An Administrative, Political and Military History* (Aldershot 1992), pp. 11, 36.

10 PRO, E 36/7, new ff. 68–104v/old ff. 135–208, 'Ordynaunce and Artillirye sent into Scotlande warde for the warrs', printed in *Naval Accounts and Inventories of the Reign of Henry VII*, M. Oppenheim, ed., (London 1896), pp. 82–132.

11 'War and the English in the Reign of Henry VIII', in L. Freedman et al., eds, *War, Strategy, and International Politics* (Oxford 1992), p. 10.

12 This point is made in Clifford Davies's unpublished paper, 'Henry VIII and Henry V: The Wars in France' (1997).

13 Carol Wiener, 'The Beleaguered Isle. A Study of Elizabethan and Early Jacobean Anti-Catholicism', *P&P* vol. 51 (1971), pp. 27–62.

14 W. Cook, jun., *The Hundred Years Wars for Morocco. Gunpowder and the Military Revolution in the Early Modern Muslim World* (Boulder 1994), p. 60; Simon Pepper and Nicholas Adams, *Firearms and Fortifications. Military Architecture and Siege Warfare in Sixteenth-Century Siena* (Chicago 1986), pp. 3–31.

15 Simon Pepper, 'Castles and Cannon in the Naples Campaign of 1494–95', in D. Abulafia, ed., *The French Descent into Renaissance Italy, 1494–5* (Aldershot 1995), pp. 263–93.

16 Ian Arthurson, 'The King's Voyage into Scotland. The War that Never Was', in *England in the Fifteenth Century. Proceedings of the 1986 Harlaxton Symposium*, ed. Daniel Williams (Woodbridge, Suffolk 1987), pp. 1–2, 5–6, 8–10, 12, 14–15; J. R. Hookes, 'Notes on the Organization and Supply of the Tudor Military under Henry VII', *Huntington Library Quarterly* vol. 23 (1959), pp. 19–31. See Chapter 2, pp. 36, 44–5.

17 Edward contemplated a prototype standing army in 1551. M. M. Norris, 'The 2nd Earl of Rutland's Band of Men-at-Arms, 1551–2', *Historical Research* vol. 68 no. 165 (February 1995), p. 102.

18 Jan Alber Dop, *Eliza's Knights. Soldiers, Poets, and Puritans in the Netherlands, 1572–1586* (Alblasserdam 1981) and Frances Yates, *Astrea. The Imperial Theme in the Sixteenth Century* (London 1975), pp. 88–111. Contrast Sir John Neale, 'Elizabeth and the Netherlands', *EHR* vol. 45 no. 179 (July 1930), pp. 373–96 with Charles Wilson, *Queen Elizabeth and the Revolt of the Netherlands* (Berkeley, Calif. 1970), pp. 127–36.

19 Steven Gunn, 'The French Wars of Henry VIII', in J. Black, ed., *The Origins of War in Early Modern Europe* (Edinburgh 1987), pp. 28–9, 31, 36, 44–7.

20 David Starkey, 'Intimacy and Innovation: The Rise of the Privy Chamber, 1485–1547', in Starkey et al., *The English Court. From the Wars of the Rose to the Civil War* (London 1987), pp. 86–90.

21 Ibid., p. 89.

22 BL, Cotton MS Otho E. XI, ff. 20–27v, 41–49v; Jeremy Goring, 'Social Change and Military Decline in Mid-Tudor England', *History* vol. 60 no. 199 (June 1975), esp. p. 188; Charles Cruickshank, *Army Royal. An Account of Henry VIII's Invasion of France 1513* (Oxford 1969), pp. 196–8; Sir Charles Oman, *A History of the Art of War in the Sixteenth Century* (London 1937), pp. 289–91.

23 F. C. Dietz, *English Public Finance 1485–1558* vol. 1 (New York 1964), pp. 153–4, note 41, citing *L&P*, xix, pp. 626–7, no. 1035 (86 and 87).

24 Cruickshank, *Army Royal*, pp. 3–5; C. S. L. Davies, 'Supply Services of the English Armed forces, 1509–50', University of Oxford D.Phil. thesis 1963, pp. 204–7.

25 *L&P* i, pt. 1 (1509–1513) (London 1920), pp. 463–4, no. 884 and p. 471, no. 919.

26 John Stile's report, quoted by General Sir James Marshall-Cornwall in 'An Expedition to Aquitane, 1512', *History Today* vol. 23 no. 9 (September 1973), p. 646.

27 Davies D.Phil., pp. 206–8.

28 See for example *L&P* i, pt. 2 (1513–1514) (London 1920), pp. 851–2, no. 1869, calendaring a manuscript mostly in Wolsey's hand, dated circa 13 May 1513.

29 See PRO, E 101/56/6, ff. A1–A5, damaged (Daunce) and E 101/56/29, unfoliated (Wyndham). The latter illustrates how closely intertwined were naval and land forces in the government's recruitment procedures.

30 PRO, E 315/4, four accounts kept by John Heron, Treasurer of the King's Chamber, 1513–14, regarding victualling, f. 1v.

31 PRO, E 315/4, ff. 2v–4.

32 *L&P* i, pt. 2 (1513–1514), p. 977, no. 2170, Henry VIII to Margaret of Savoy, 17 August 1513.

33 Cruickshank, *Army Royal*, pp. 116–77.

34 Davies D.Phil., pp. 211–12.

35 BL, Cotton MS Otho E. XI, f. 43.

36 Transcript of BL, Add. MS 10, 110, f. 236, printed in Charles Martin, 'Sir John Daunce's Accounts of Money received from the Treasurer of the King's Chamber temp. Henry VIII', *Archaeologia* vol. 47 no. 2 (1883), pp. 318–19.

37 Davies D.Phil., p. 223, citing *Henrician State Papers* IV, p. 38; *L&P* iii, pt. 2 (1519–1523) (London 1867), nos. 3447 and 3259.

38 See the verdict of Davies, 'Provisions for Armies, 1509–50; A Study in the Effectiveness of Early Tudor Government', *Econ HR* 2nd series vol. 17 no. 2 (December 1964), p. 243; Oman, *AWSC*, p. 323.

39 PRO, E 315/315, Wyndham's accounts, ff. 1–37.

40 PRO, C 82/342, Chancery warrant of proclamation, 20 November 1509, reproduced photographically as plate 2 (between pp. 84–5), citation below.

41 P. Hughes and J. Larkin, eds, *Tudor Royal Proclamations*, vol. 1 (New Haven, Conn. 1964), pp. 84–93.

42 Jeremy Goring, 'The General Proscription of 1522', *EHR* vol. 86 no. 341 (October 1971), p. 683.

43 BL, Cotton MS Cleopatra F.VI, f. 250v, instructions for Durham.

44 BL, Stowe MS 570, new ff. 165–165v/old ff. 182–3; Fissel, *BW*, pp. 178–84.

45 R. W. Hoyle, ed., *The Military Survey of Gloucestershire, 1522*, Bristol and Gloucestershire Archaeological Society, Gloucester Record Service volume 6 (Stroud 1993), pp. ix–x.

46 Ibid., p. xv, citing Goring, 'General Proscription', pp. 694–5.

47 See for example pp. 19–23, 30–1, 35–7, 41–2, etc. in John Pound, ed., *The Military Survey of 1522 for Babergh Hundred* (Woodbridge 1986).

48 *The County Community under Henry VIII. The Military Survey, 1522, and Lay Subsidy, 1524–5, for Rutland* (Oakham 1980), p. 3.

49 For example, see Lis Garnish, 'The Muster Roll for West Berkshire 1522', *Oxfordshire Local History* vol. 2 no. 8 (spring 1988), pp. 267, 281–9.

50 Goring, 'General Proscription', p. 689.

51 *The Muster Certificates for Berkshire, 1522. Introduction and Part Two*, John Brooks and Nigel Heard, eds, published by Oxford Polytechnic, Faculty of Modern Studies Occasional Paper no. 3 (November 1986), p. 6 citing Chibnall, p. 24.

52 Ibid., p. 2, citing Goring's 'General Proscription', p. 687.

53 Ibid., p. 18.

54 Hoyle, *MSG*, p. xv.

55 Brooks and Heard, *Muster Certificates*, p. 7.

56 A. C. Chibnall, *The Certificate of Musters for Buckinghamshire in 1522* (London 1973), p. 73; T. L. Stoate, *The Cornwall Military Survey 1522* (Bristol 1987), p. v; Hoyle, *MSG*, pp. 72–85.

57 The blend of fiscal and military is placed in an historiographical context by Michael Braddick in 'An English Military Revolution?', *HJ* vol. 36 no. 4 (1993), pp. 965–75. The interpretation regarding the 1522 survey set forth here is my own responsibility.

58 Brooks and Heard, *Muster Certificates*, p. 3, citing Goring, 'General Prescription', p. 683.

59 PRO, E 315/315, especially ff. 13v-15, which disclose the presence of the Spaniards.

60 Davies D.Phil., p. 228 citing *Calendar of State Papers Spanish*, vol. 2, p. 145 and *L&P* iii, pt. 2, no. 2442.

61 M. D. Davies, 'Suffolk's Expedition to Montdidier 1523', *Jami'at Al-Qahirah, Kulliyat Al-Adab Majallah/Fouad I University, bulletin of the Faculty of Arts*, vol. 7 (1944), p. 38. Elis Gruffydd describes the English penchant for eating one's way across France, even to the detriment of the campaign. He relates how 'the French seized Englishmen who like fools had been wandering about the country collecting sheep, pigs, and cattle. . . .' (p. 36).

62 'The Duke of Suffolk's March on Paris in 1523', *EHR* vol. 101 no. 400 (July 1986), pp. 608, 616, 625, 628–30.

63 George Wrottesley, 'Muster Roll, Staffordshire, A.D. 1539', *Collections for a History of Staffordshire*, vol. 4, new series (1901), p. 215. For Flodden, pp. 21–3, below.

64   W. P. Baildon, 'Musters in Skyrack Wapentake, 1539, part II', *Miscellanea* (of the Thoresby Society), vol. 9, series 2 (1899), p. 309.

65   See below, pp. 16, 18, 29–31, 37, 40, 183; B. M. Morley, *Henry VIII and the development of coastal defence* (London 1977); Loades, *TN*, pp. 121–2; Colvin, ed., *KW* vol. 4 (1485–1660) pt. 2, pp. 367–90.

66   W. A. Archbold, ed., 'A Diary of the Expedition of 1544', *EHR* vol. 16 no. 63 (July 1901), pp. 503–7.

67   The words are those of Paul Hammer, commenting on the views of Simon Adams.

68   Gunn, 'French Wars of Henry VIII', p. 36.

69   *L&P* xix, pt. 1 (January–July 1544) (London 1903), p. 148, no. 272, item 12, p. 143, p. 142, no. 271, p. 143, items 3, 4, p. 146, pp. 149–56.

70   Davies D.Phil., pp. 265–6.

71   G. R. Elton, 'War and the English in the Reign of Henry VIII', in L. Freedman et al., eds, *War, Strategy and International Politics* (Oxford 1992), pp. 15–16.

72   J. R. Hale, *War and Society in Renaissance Europe 1450–1620* (London 1985), pp. 240, 245; Dietz, *EPF*, vol. 1, p. 155.

73   Goring, 'General Proscription', pp. 681–705; Dietz, *EPF*, vol. 1, esp. pp. 147, 151–8; G. Bernard, *War, Taxation and Rebellion in Early Tudor England* (Brighton 1986), pp. 53–60, 71–2, 150–7.

74   *L&P* xx, pt. 2 (August–December 1545) (London 1907), p. 366, no. 769, 11 November 1545 [SP 1/839].

75   *Calendar of State Papers, Edward VI 1547–1553* (London 1992), pp. 258–63, nos. 721, 723 [SP 10/15/11 and 13].

76   *State Papers Published under the Authority of Her Majesty's Commission, vol. 10. King Henry the Eighth, Part V, Foreign Correspondence 1544–1545* (London 1849), letter 1005, p. 12.

77   Ibid., letter 1005, p. 13.

78   Davies D.Phil., pp. 264–5.

79   For a theory-oriented view of this theme, see David Eltis's *The Military Revolution in Sixteenth Century Europe* (London 1995), pp. 76–94.

80   Davies, 'Provisions for Armies', p. 243 and regarding such campaigns, pp. 122, 158–61, 203, 205–6, 260–1, 266, 278–80.

81   *SPH* vol. 10, letter 1016, pp. 31–2, Sir Henry Wotton to Henry VIII, 10 August 1544.

82   Ibid., vol. 9, letter 925, p. 539, Wotton to Henry VIII, 6 November 1543.

83   Oman, *AWSC*, pp. 332–3.

84   G. J. Millar, *Tudor Mercenaries and Auxiliaries 1485–1547* (Charlottesville 1980), pp. 65–115; D. G. White, 'Henry VIII's Irish Kerne in France and Scotland, 1544–1545', *Irish Sword* vol. 3 no. 13 (1958), pp. 213–25; *L&P* xix, pt. 1 (January–July 1544), pp. 301–3, no. 477, the Justice and Council of Ireland to the King, 7 May 1544; BL, Harleian MS 6989, f. 68, regarding a German mercenary captain, 15 June 1544.

85   PRO, E 351/43, lists of mercenaries employed 17 May 1545 to 28 February 1550/1.

86   *SPH* vol. 9, letter 943, p. 577, PC to Wotton, 4 January 1544. See also pp. 578, 629.

87   John Shelby, *John Rogers. Tudor Military Engineer* (Oxford 1967), pp. 53–85.

88   Thomas Churchyard, *Churchyardes Choise*, f. Biii, from the edition entitled *A Generall Rehearsall of Warres* (London 1579).

89   Amongst the besieged at Metz was the future Lord Charles Howard of Effingham, and with Churchyard in the allied armies of Navarre (along with Burgundians and Flemings) were 'Sir Anthony Storley [Shirley], Captayne Matson, Francis Horsey, Sir William Drury, Captayne Mistchell, Captayne Plankety, [and] Captayne

Hinde'. See pp. 10–11, Thomas Churchyard, *A Lamentable, and Pitifull Description, of the Wofull Warres in Flaunders* (London 1578), which covers the last four years of the reign of Emperor Charles V up to 1578 and the death of Don John of Austria. For a roll call, *HMC Foljambe*, fifteenth report (London 1897), pp. 5–9.

90 C. S. L. Davies, 'England and the French War, 1557–9', in *The Mid-Tudor Polity*, Tittler and Loach, eds, (Totowa, N.J. 1980), esp. pp. 180, 182.

91 Boynton, *EM*, pp. 9–11; Fissel, *BW*, pp. 178–87, esp. pp. 184–5.

92 Davies, 'England and the French War, 1557–9', p. 185.

93 M. Oppenheim, *A History of the Administration of the Royal Navy* (London 1896), p. 110; Loades, *TN*, pp. 178–9.

94 Reverend William Harrison, printed in A. F. Pollard, ed., *Tudor Tracts 1532–1588*, (New York 1964), pp. 396–400.

95 Brian Quintrell, ed., *The Maynard Lieutenancy Book, 1608–1639* pt. 1 (Chelmsford 1993), p. lxii.

96 Quoted by Elton in 'War and the English in the Reign of Henry VIII', p. 16.

97 Starkey, 'Privy Chamber', p. 94.

2 THE EARLY TUDOR ART OF WAR IN THE BRITISH ISLES

1 Oman, *AWSC*, p. 299. Estimates of Scottish strength range from 200,000 (!) to 24,000; 30,000 seems reasonable. See J. D. Mackie, 'The English Army at Flodden', in *Miscellany of the Scottish History Society* VIII (Edinburgh 1951), pp. 47–9 and Davies D.Phil., appendix Q (pp. 335–7) and pp. 217–20.

2 Sanuto's report, *L&P* i, pt. 1 (1509–1513), p. 737, no. 1628, 15 February 1513, and Dacre's report of 24 February, p. 741, no. 1645. Dacre not only reported that James IV attended daily on arms manufacturing, but he also sent to Henry two newly designed arrowheads purloined from the Scottish royal arsenal.

3 For a detailed battle narrative, Gervase Phillips, *The Anglo-Scots Wars 1513–1550* (Woodbridge, Suffolk 1999), pp. 109–32.

4 *L&P* i, pt. 2 (1513–1514), pp. 1005–8, no. 2246 (4441), accounts of Flodden.

5 Paul Cornish, *Henry VIII's Army* (London 1987), pp. 6–9; Oman, *AWSC*, pp. 297–321.

6 The Scots 'cam down the hill . . . in good ordre, after the Almayns maner, withoute spekyng of eny word'. *State Papers Published under Authority of His Majesty's Commission. Volume IV. King Henry the Eighth. Part IV* (London 1836), p. 1; Davies D.Phil., appendix Q.

7 Phillips, *ASW*, pp. 141–2.

8 Ibid., pp. 142–4.

9 PRO, MPF 146; PRO, SP 1/174, ff. 49–53, 'A consutacion for prosecucion of the Warre agaynst Scotland'. Internal evidence in the latter, a reference to 'June next' on f. 49, suggests the manuscript was drafted in late 1541 or late 1542. See also *L&P* xvii (1542), p. 584, no. 1035, cross-referenced to BL, Add. MS 9835, f. 14.

10 PRO, SP 1/174, ff. 54–55v, 'an abstracte for Englissh men to knowe the Reaulme of Scotland through oute'; *L&P* xvii (1542), p. 584, no. 1035, cross-referenced to BL, Add. MS 9835, f. 14.

11 BL, Harleian MS 6989, Council to Norfolk regarding preparations, 17 September 1542 (f. 52); to the Commissioners signifying their diligence in victualling the army, 21 September (f. 53); the King's satisfaction concerning the shipping of grain, 2 October (f. 62); Sir Gainsford Bruce, 'The English Expedition into Scotland in 1542', *Archaeologia Aeliana*, vol. 3 series 3 (1907), pp. 191–212.

12 PRO, E 101/674/2, esp. ff. 2v–4. On Sadler, A. J. Slavin, *Politics and Profit. A Study of Sir Ralph Sadler 1507–1547* (Cambridge 1966).

13 PRO, SP 1/174, ff. 39–40, Norfolk, etc., to the Council, 3 November 1542; *L&P* xvii (1542), p. 579, no. 1025.

14 PRO, SP 1/174, f. 56v, 5 November 1542; *L&P* xvii (1542), p. 585, no. 1037.

15 PRO SP 1/174, f. 93, to Wriothesley, 9 November; *L&P* xvii (1542), p. 595, no. 1058.

16 Phillips, *ASW*, pp. 150–3; *L&P* xvii (1542), p. 617, no. 1121, Anthony Browne on 24 November, citing BL, Add. MS 32,648, f. 156, Hamilton Papers no. 240.

17 PRO, E101/690/20; and this work, other chapters.

18 PRO, Declared Accounts of the Exchequer of Receipt, E 351/212, 9 September to 20 November 1542, Sir John Harrington, Treasurer for the army sent into Scotland under the Duke of Norfolk, unfoliated. The evidence of the declared account is confirmed by the Council's order to Wriothesley 'desiring preparation of money for [4,300 troops *en route* to France] coats, conduct, etc.'; *L&P* xx, pt. 2 (August–December 1545), p. 163, no. 366; and Dietz, *English Public Finance* vol. 1, p. 157.

19 Instructions, drawn up by the Mayor of Norwich (?), for uniforming Norfolk's troops, circa late spring or early summer 1544, printed in *Norfolk Archaeology*, vol. 1 (1847), p. 37.

20 Bodleian Library, Carte MS 206, f. 27v, letter to Lord Lisle.

21 BL, Add. MS 32,654, f. 174. I have made these connections on my own. See the endnote below. Pascual de Gayangos, ed., *Calendar of Letters, Despatches, and State Papers . . . Spain*, vol. 7 (1544) (London 1899), pp. 135–7.

22 'The Late Expedition into Scotland, made by the King's Highness' army . . .', printed in *Tudor Tracts 1532–1588*, A. F. Pollard, ed. (New York 1964), pp. 39–51; BL, Add. MS 32,654, ff. 173–4; newsletter to Lord Russell, *L&P* xix, pt. 1 (January–July 1544), pp. 330–3, no. 533 and p. 333, no. 534, account of the invasion, cross-referenced to BL, Harleian MS 6047, f. 58b.

23 John Guy, *Tudor England* (Oxford 1988), p. 191.

24 Printed in Samuel Haynes, ed., *A Collection of State Papers . . . From the Year 1542 to 1570* (London 1740), p. 30.

25 PRO, E 101/690/20, warrants for conducting soldiers circa April–May 1544. See also *L&P* xix, pt. 1 (January–July 1544), pp. 328–30, no. 532.

26 Phillips, *ASW*, pp. 161, 169. For an overview, Ian Heath, *Armies of the Sixteenth Century* (St Peter Port 1997), pp. 69–80.

27 The schiltron was a medieval Scottish infantry formation in which footsoldiers presented spears to repel attackers. By advancing in a coordinated and deliberate fashion, the bristling points of the spears could also be used offensively. The schiltron drew much from the Macedonian phalanx, with its *sarrisae*, and anticipated the pikes of the *landesknechts* in the fifteenth and sixteenth centuries. Its modern equivalent would be the bayonet charge.

28 A horseman's momentum, which generally provided cavalry such great advantage in battle, could be used to his detriment. At Hastings (1066) some Norman cavalry blundered into a *fosse*, a trench lined with sharpened stakes. At Agincourt, the French *gendarmie* slammed into stakes positioned at 45 degree angles, which were interspersed and obscured amongst Henry V's footsoldiers. The Scots' cavalry trap was a tactical variation on medieval 'cavalry traps'.

29 A hedgehog consisted of a tight infantry formation, predominantly made up of pikemen, with some musketeers interspersed. Usually a square, it proved effective against charging cavalry, but was vulnerable to salvoes from field artillery.

30 Colin Martin, 'Ancrum Moor – a day of reckoning', *The Scots Magazine*, new series, vol. 83 (May 1965), pp. 146–52; Hertford retaliated in September 1545.

31 *L&P* xx, pt. 2 (1545) nos. 169, 205, 216, 308, 317, 359; Pascual de Gayangos, ed., *Calendar of Letters, Despatches, and State Papers . . . Spain*, vol. 7 (1544) (London

1899), p. 137. The former sources verify the presence of Spanish harquebusiers in Hertford's 1545 force; G. Millar, *Tudor Mercenaries and Auxiliaries 1485–1547*, (Charlottesville, NC 1980) pp. 148–50; the Spanish papers, in a letter also in *L&P*, mention a company of 'hackbutiers' under a 'Peter Mecotas', probably Captain Pedro Michale or perhaps Sir Peter Mewtis (David Starkey, 'Intimacy and Innovation. The Rise of the Privy Chamber, 1485–1547', in Starkey et al., *The English Court from the Wars of the Roses to the Civil War* (London 1987), pp. 88–9).

32 PRO, E 351/43, unfoliated, listing foreign mercenaries by commander as well as by nationality, ranging from the mid-1540s to the early 1550s.

33 Millar, *Tudor Mercenaries*, p. 176.

34 J. R. Hale, ed., *Certain Discourses Military*, (Ithaca, N.Y. 1964), p. 96.

35 Millar, *Tudor Mercenaries*, appendix C, p. 191.

36 BL, Harleian MS 540, f. 70; Sir William Patten's 'The Expedition into Scotland of the most worthily fortunate Prince Edward, Duke of Somerset . . .' in Pollard, ed., *Tudor Tracts*, pp. 53–157; W. K. Jordan, *Edward VI. The Young King* (London 1968), p. 254, note 1.

37 Stowe states that the army set forth from the Marches of Berwick at 5 a.m. on Monday 1 September, according to BL, Harleian MS 540, new f. 70.

38 Ibid., new f. 70v.

39 For depictions of the positions of the combatants, see Bodleian Library, MS English misc. C.13 R, 5 foot long paper roll. I am grateful to Dr Martin R. Kauffman of Western Manuscripts, and Bodley's Preservation staff, for arranging for me to view this manuscript; D. Caldwell, 'The Battle of Pinkie', in N. MacDougall, ed., *Scotland and War AD 79–1918* (Edinburgh 1991), pp. 61–94; C. Oman, 'The Battle of Pinkie, Sept. 10, 1547' and C. deW. Crookshank, 'A further note on the battle of Pinkie', both printed in *Archaeological Journal*, vol. 90 (1933), pp. 1–25; M. J. D. Cockle, *A Bibliography of Military Books to 1642* (London 1900), pp. 8–11; Patten, 'The Expedition into Scotland . . .', pp. 114–19.

40 BL, Harleian MS 540, new f. 70v.

41 Ibid., new f. 71/old f. 98.

42 BL, Cotton MS Cleopatra A XI, new ff. 3–16; Harleian MS 540, no. 33, new ff. 70–71v/old ff. 97–98v; Oman, *AWSC*, pp. 358–67.

43 Hale, *AWRE*, p. 40.

44 M. L. Bush, *The Government Policy of Protector Somerset* (Manchester 1975), p. 11, citing *L&P* xx, pt. 1, p. 129.

45 Ibid., pp. 14, 19; Robert Hitchcock, 'The English Army Rations in the time of Elizabeth', *An English Garner. Social England Illustrated* (New York 1964), pp. 115–32, a contemporary account of Berwick victualling.

46 PRO, SP 10/3, ff. 150–4, 'A dispricion or annextymate of the charge of an Army of Fifteine Thowsand fotemen Souldyars to invade by the see not meddeling with the making any extymate for the charge of the furnyture of the said Army by see'; C. S. Knighton, ed., *Calendar of State Papers Domestic Series of the Reign of Edward VI 1547–1553* (London 1992), pp. 42–3, no. 95.

47 *CSP Edward VI*, p. 260; for a slightly smaller figure, see table 2.2 in Bush, *The Government Policy*, p. 33, based on BL, Harleian MS 353, ff. 94b-f.

48 BL, Harleian MS 6989, f. 66, letter of the Privy Council, 15 June 1544.

49 Thomas Churchyard, excerpt from *Churchyard's Choise*, printed in *Churchyard's Chips concerning Scotland*, George Chalmers, ed. (London 1817), pp. 80–1.

50 The 1588 edition of *Three bookes of colloqvies concerning the Arte of Shooting . . .* (Cyprian Lucar, ed.), pp. 3v-4, 'Richad Ventuorth'; Webb, *EMS*, p. 146; Jim Bennett and Stephen Johnston, *The Geometry of War 1500–1750* (Oxford 1996), pp. 20–1.

51 PRO, SP 1/102, ff. 29–31, book of reports compiled for the King, informing him of reorganisation efforts in the Ordnance Office facilities at the Tower, 1536–7.

52 PRO, E 101/690/1, discussed above/below, pp. 2–3, 7–8, 43–6, 192, 283.

53 L. R. Shelby, *John Rogers, Tudor Military Engineer* (Oxford 1967), p. 24 and below.

54 H. M. Colvin, ed., *The King's Works*, vol. 4 (1485–1660), pt. 2, pp. 369–77.

55 See also Martin Brice, *Forts and Fortresses* (Oxford 1990), pp. 78–9.

56 Robert Norwood, *Fortification* (London 1639) illustrates this nicely, especially the section at the rear.

57 Leonard Digges, *A Booke named Tectonicon* . . . (London 1556) explained how measuring and surveying became the basis for the art of gunnery, especially pp. 3–4b, 18–20. The 1592 edition was used for this work.

58 See below, pp. 67, 146, 148–9; *DNB*; Webb, *EMS*, pp. 17–27, 64–6, 142, 146; Nolan, *SJN*, pp. 91–100.

59 B. M. Morley, *Henry VIII and the Development of Coastal Defence* (London 1976), pp. 8–19. Colvin, ed., *KW* vol. 4 (1485–1660) pt. 2, pp. 613–23, 627–41.

60 Although Henrician architecture lies outside its analysis, Jim Bennett and Stephen Johnston's *The Geometry of War 1500–1700* presents the concept of mathematical precision in the 'military revolution' beautifully. A visit to their website is recommended: http://www.mhs.ox.ac.uk/geometry/content/htm

61 Ian MacIvor, 'The Fortifications at Berwick-upon-Tweed', *Antiquaries Journal* vol. 45 (1964), pp. 64–96, and John Summerson's analysis in Colvin, ed., *KW* vol. 4 (1485–1660) pt. 2, pp. 623–6, 641–64.

62 MacIvor, 'Fortifications', pp. 76, 80, 84; I am grateful to Dr James Nyce for constructing an instructional software program that teaches this point.

63 *L&P* iii, p. 1026 no. 2436, cited in J.R. Kenyon, 'Early Artillery Fortification in England and Wales', *The Archaeological Journal* vol. 138 (1981), p. 223.

64 *L&P* v, pp. 678, 691 nos. 1630 and 1670, and vi, p. 98 no. 217, cited in Kenyon 'Early Artillery', p. 223.

65 PRO, E 101/57/13, circa 1515; E 101/57/18, muster book of Berwick gunners circa 1520.

66 The 1539 survey is PRO, E 101/60/3, ff. 10–20, printed in Kenyon, 'AFEW', pp. 223–5; the survey of defences circa 1532–5 is printed in *Archaeologia Aeliana*, new series, vol. 1 (1857), pp. 87–94.

67 *HMC Foljambe*, fifteenth report, part 5 (London 1897), p. 7.

68 MacIvor, 'Fortifications', pp. 62, 65, 93; Fissel, *BW*, pp. 10–17, 40–4.

69 BL, Harleian MS 4943, new f. 62/old f. 69 – new f. 62v/old f. 69v, letters to Drury and order to the Treasurer of Berwick, 1 April 1571.

70 J. R. Kenyon, 'An aspect of the 1559 survey of the Isle of Wight: *The State of all the Quenes Maties Fortresses and Castelles*', *Post-Medieval Archaeology* vol. 13 (1979), pp. 61, 76.

71 The seminal work is Sir John Hale's 'The Early Development of the Bastion: An Italian Chronology c.1450–c.1534', in *Renaissance War Studies* (London *c.* 1983), pp. 1–29; the most influential application, Geoffrey Parker, *The Military Revolution. Military innovation and the rise of the West, 1500–1800* (Cambridge 1990), pp. 7–16, 24–32; best case study, Simon Pepper and Nicholas Adams, *Firearms and Fortifications. Military Architecture in Sixteenth Century Siena* (Chicago 1986); Eltis, *MRSC*, pp. 76–94.

72 Colvin, ed., *KW* vol. 4 (1485–1660) pt. 2, p. 611.

73 PRO, E 351/123, account of George Stonehouse and others.

74 Colvin, ed., *KW* vol. 4 (1485–1660) pt. 2, pp. 395, 614.

75 PRO, E 351/211, 23 August 1542–30 August 1547.

76 PRO, SP 1/174, f. 84.

77 PRO, E 351/211.

78 Contemporary evaluation by Wriothesley, to Paget, 11 November 1545, in *L&P* xx, pt. 2 (August–December 1545), p. 365, no. 769; J. J. Scarisbrick, *Henry VIII* (Berkeley, Calif. 1972), p. 456; M. D. George, 'Notes on the Origin of the Declared Account', *EHR* vol. 31 no. 121 (January 1916), pp. 42, 45, 47–9, 56.

79 PRO, SP 1/174, f. 93, to Wriothesley, November 1542; *L&P* xvii (1542), p. 595, no. 1058.

80 See above, pp. 19, 38–9; BL, Harleian MS 168, ff. 252–3.

81 Brendan Bradshaw, *The Irish Constitutional Revolution of the Sixteenth Century* (Cambridge 1979), p. 59.

82 William Palmer, *The Problem of Ireland in Tudor Foreign Policy* (Woodbridge 1994), p. 32.

83 Ian Heath, *The Irish Wars, 1485–1603* (London 1993), p. 9; S. Ellis, *Tudor Ireland: Crown, Community and the Conflict of Cultures, 1470–1603* (London 1985), p. 30.

84 S. Ellis, 'An Indenture Concerning the King's Munitions in Ireland, 1532', *Irish Sword* vol. 14 no. 7 (1980), p. 101.

85 J. Brewer and W. Bullen, eds, *Calendar of the Carew Manuscripts* vol. 1 (1515–1574) (Nendeln, Liechtenstein 1974), pp. 59, 62–5, 70–7, 75–9, 85.

86 Ibid., pp. 61, 76.

87 Ibid., pp. 59, 63; S. Ellis, *Tudor Frontiers and Noble Power* (Oxford 1995), p. 216.

88 See Chapter 9, pp. 213, 216–17, 220–5; G. Hayes McCoy, 'The Early History of Guns in Ireland', *Journal of the Galway Archaeological and Historical Society* vol. 18 (1938–9), pp. 61–3.

89 Ellis, *Tudor Frontiers*, p. 229.

90 J. Brewer and W. Bullen, eds, *Calendar of the Carew Manuscripts Preserved in the Archiepiscopal Library at Lambeth 1515–1574* vol. 1 (London 1867), pp. 80–1, 73.

91 Bradshaw, *Irish Constitutional Revolution*, pp. 112–13, 117–25.

92 PRO, SP 60/3/79, f. 165v; SP 60/3/77, f. 162; SP 60/3/83, ff. 175–177v; SP 60/3/80, f. 167.

93 Ellis, *Tudor Ireland*, p. 133; Palmer, *The Problem of Ireland*, p. 52.

94 Brian Trainor, 'Extracts from Irish Ordnance Office Accounts, 1537–1539', *Irish Sword* vol. 1 no. 4 (1952), pp. 324, 334. No detailed Irish ordnance accounts exist for the period 1540–90.

95 *Calendar of the Carew Manuscript* vol. 1, pp. 124, 126, items 101 and 102, 16 June and 12 August 1537, respectively; G. Hayes-McCoy, 'The early history of guns in Ireland', *Galway Archaeological Society Journal* vol. 18 (1938–9), pp. 56, 60. The Dangan Castle sleighted in 1537 was located in Offaly and had recently been constructed by O'Connor (see Ellis, *Ireland in the Age of the Tudors*, p. 148). This Dangan Castle should not be confused with the more celebrated Dangan Castle located roughly six kilometres south of Trim (County Meath) which served as a boyhood home to the Duke of Wellington. Nor should the Dangan Castle in Offaly be confused with the fortress built by the O'Branans circa the twelfth and thirteenth centuries, located in County Roscommon (and also known as Dagan-I-Birne, Dingan O'Birne, and Dygen Ibyrne), and solidly rebuilt in 1453. Finally, there should be no confusion with two County Clare sites: Daingean Ui Bhighin Castle and Dangan Breac, the latter a fortified tower house northeast of Quin Abbey.

96 John O'Donovan, ed., *Annals of the Kingdom of Ireland* vol. 6 (New York 1966), p. 1497.

97 D. G. White, 'Henry VIII's Irish Kerne in France and Scotland, 1544–45', *Irish Sword* vol. 3 (1957–8), pp. 213–14, 221–4.

98 Ellis, *Tudor Ireland*, p. 230.

99 O'Donovan, ed., *Annals*, vol. 6, pp. 1503–27.

100 Printed in Samuel Haynes, ed., *A Collection of State Papers . . . From the Year 1542 to 1570*, vol. 1, pp. 141–2.

101 Ellis, *Tudor Ireland*, pp. 232–3.

102 PRO, SP 62/1/2, ff. 4–4v, October 1553.

103 See Chapter 8, pp. 188–93.

104 PRO, 'Records of the Board of Ordnance', leaflet no. 67 (London 1987), p. 1.

105 Roger Ashley, 'The Organisation and Administration of the Tudor Office of the Ordnance', Oxford University B.Litt. thesis (1972), pp. 20–6.

106 PRO, E 404/81/4, warrant and attachment, dated 25 July 1495; see also Chapter 1, pp. 2–3.

107 H. Schubert, 'The First Cast-iron Cannon Made in England', *Journal of the Iron and Steel Institute* vol. 146 (1942), pp. 131–5; Ian Arthurson, 'The King's Voyage to Scotland', p. 8; Chapter 1, pp. 2–3.

108 PRO, E 101/12/13; E 101/483/19; E 101/501/3, all of which are printed in *Archaeologia* vol. 69 (1912), pp. 290–311. Henry recruited another group of Italian artillerists in 1523. See following note.

109 Schubert, 'First Cast-iron Cannon', pp. 136–7; Ashley, B.Litt., p. 15.

110 Brian G. Awty, 'Parson Levett and English Cannon Founding', *Sussex Archaeological Collections* vol. 127 (1989), pp. 133–5, 139–42.

111 PRO, SP 45/10, new ff. 18–20, 57–8, 90–2, 115–17, 128, 137, 291–2, 358–60, 399–400; J. Larkin, ed., *Stuart Royal Proclamations Charles I* vol. 2, Royal Proclamations of Charles I 1625–1646 (Oxford 1983), pp. 16–19, 69–70, 116–19, 136–7, 157–61, 174–5, 180, 207–8.

112 PRO, PC 2/50, ff. 308, 370, 403; PRO, SP 16/404/42.

113 Walter Rye, ed., *State Papers relating to Musters, Beacons, Shipmoney, etc., in Norfolk, from 1626 . . .* (Norwich 1907), pp. 232–3.

114 Bodleian Library, Rawlinson MS A 204, ff. 58v, 90v, 94v, 98v.

115 Ashley, B.Litt., pp. 56–80.

116 BL, Harleian MS 7457, ff. 1–20v, accounts circa January 1546 to December 1561; PRO, SP 12/18/11, ff. 25–6.

117 PRO, SP 12/18/11, f. 25; SP 12/17/42, ff. 93–93v, Sir William Cecil's revisions, including the insertion of a ban on artillery exports.

118 PRO, E 407/12, undated account signed by John Lee, amongst the bundle marked 'miscellaneous documents regarding troops for Ireland, 1565–1603'.

119 Bodleian Library, Rawlinson MS A 235/1, accounts for payment of wages to artificers and labourers in the Ordnance Office at the Tower, Minories, and dockyards in 1571, ff. 1–3v, 6–8, 12–15v, 18–21, 24–7, 30–2, 36–38v, 41–4, 47–50, 53–55v, 58–60, 64–7. The annual cost of these artificers and their transportation amounted to £1,797 2s. 10d. for calendar year 1571.

120 Michael Pulman, *The Elizabethan Privy Council in the Fifteen-seventies* (Berkeley, Calif. 1971), pp. 196–201.

121 Bodleian Library, Rawlinson MS A 207/1, ff.1–10v, account of all the ordnance stores found in the Tower, Minories, the artillery garden, royal ships at Chatham, Upnor Castle, Rochester storehouses, and at Woolwich, surveyed July–August 1589, and an account of stores provided 19 July 1589 to 20 April 1591.

122 Ibid., esp. ff. 9–10v.

123 Phillips, *ASW*, pp. 42–103.

124 Iain MacIvor, 'Artillery and Major Places of Strength in the Lothians and the East Border, 1513–1542', in D. Caldwell, ed., *Scottish Weapons and Fortifications 1100–1800* (Edinburgh 1981), pp. 146–8.

125 These conclusions contradict David Eltis, *The Military Revolution of the Sixteenth Century*, i.e. pp. 99–140, which the author based upon a largely theoretical military literature and secondary sources. See Geoffrey Parker, 'Parade-ground Practice', *Times Literary Supplement* no. 4863 (14 June 1996), p. 26 (1).

126 'The Administration of the Royal Navy under Henry VIII', *EHR* vol. 80 no. 315 (April 1965), p. 281.

127 Michael Bush, *The Pilgrimage of Grace. A Study of the Rebel Armies of October 1536* (Manchester 1996), pp. 407–8, 418–24.

128 R. Braddock, 'The character and composition of the Duke of Northumberland's Army', *Albion* vol. 6 no. 4 (1975), pp. 344, 353–4; M. M. Norris, 'The 2nd Earl of Rutland's Band of Men-at-Arms, 1551–2', *Historical Research* vol. 68 no. 165, (February 1995), pp. 100–6.

129 Davies D.Phil., pp. 9–10, 15, 57, 59, 61–2.

130 PRO, E 101/12/13; E 101/483/19; E 101/501/3, all of which are printed in M. Giussepi, 'The Accounts of the Iron Works at Sheffield and Worth in Sussex, 1546–1549', *Archaeological Journal* vol. 69 (1912), pp. 290–311.

131 Davies D.Phil., pp. 88–96.

3 THE DEFENCE OF THE SHIRE: LIEUTENANCY

1 Somerset RO, DD/PH 222/19, f. 34, DLs to LL, 3 October 1636; BL, Lansdowne MS 155, new f. 325/old f. 322, new f. 333/old f. 300 – new f. 336v/old f. 333v, new f. 353/old f. 350 – new f. 355v/old f. 352v.

2 PRO, SP 12/59, pt 2, f. 208.

3 PRO, SP 45/10, new f. 166; BL, Harleian MS 168, ff. 61–4.

4 Bodleian Library, Tanner MS 177, no. 32, ff. 26–27v; J. Goring, 'The general proscription of 1522', *EHR* vol. 86 no. 341 (October 1971), p. 697.

5 T. G. Barnes, *Somerset 1625–1641. A County's Government during the 'Personal Rule'* (Cambridge, Mass. 1961), p. 281.

6 Ibid., p. 98, emphasis my own.

7 Haynes, ed., *SP* vol. 1, pp. 304–5, Norfolk to Burghley (8 May 1560) and the Queen to Norfolk (11 May 1560). Unfortunately, there are no regional identifications of the levies in the figures from PRO, E 351/226.

8 Somerset RO, DD/PH 222/13, f. 24, 11 May 1632. An identical example from Wiltshire: BL, Additional MS 46, 188, f. 19.

9 Gladys Scott Thomson, *Lords Lieutenants in the Sixteenth Century* (London 1923), p. 35.

10 Haynes, ed., *SP* vol. 1, p. 161.

11 Scott Thomson, *Lords Lieutenants*, pp. 36–40.

12 BL, Harleian MS 4271, ff. 7v, 9, 14v, etc.

13 Victor Stater, *Noble Government. The Stuart Lord Lieutenancy and the Transformation of English Politics* (Athens, Georgia 1994), p. 64.

14 Anthony Fletcher, *Reform in the Provinces. The Government of Stuart England* (New Haven, Conn. 1986), p. 297. A zealous deputy lieutenant could hope that his martial rigour would curry royal favour. See Ian Atherton, *Ambition and failure in Stuart England. The Career of John, first Viscount Scudamore* (Manchester 1999), pp. 119–24.

15 Gladys Scott Thomson, 'The Origin and Growth of the Office of Deputy-Lieutenant', *TRHS*, fourth series, vol. 5 (1922), p. 155.

16 J. Wake, ed., *A Copy of Papers relating to Musters, Beacons, Subsidies, etc., in the County of Northampton A.D. 1586–1623*, Northamptonshire Record Society vol. 3 (Kettering 1926), pp. lii–liii; Quintrell, ed., *MLB* pt. 1, pp. l–li, lvii–lviii.

17 Barnes, *Somerset*, pp. 103–4.

18 During the 1620s war years, the Earl of Suffolk relied upon six deputy lieutenants in Cambridgeshire: BL, Harleian MS 4104, f. 2v. See also Gladys Scott Thomson, introduction to *The Twysden Lieutenancy Papers, 1583–1668*, G. Scott Thomson, ed., Kent Archaeological Society vol. 10 (Ashford 1926), p. 7.

19 *HMC Salisbury* pt. 4, pp. 16–18, Burghley's notes, 15 March 1589.

20 Boynton, *EM*, pp. 63–4.

21 PRO, SP 12/68, f. 87, Shropshire return.

22 J. A. Guy, *Tudor England* (Oxford 1988), p. 340, citing HEH, Ellesmere MS 6206B, ff. 14–15, 18–19 and secondary sources.

23 BL, Add. MS 39, 245, 14 August 1614, new f. 13/old f. 31. For the muster-master, see also this work, pp. 54–5, 66–71, 65, 99.

24 BL, Harleian MS 309, old f. 104/new f. 126 – old f. 110v/new f. 132v; PRO, SP 12/68, entire volume comprised of 1570 muster certificates.

25 Boynton, *EM*, pp. 90–125; PRO SP 12/94, muster certificates for all of England and Wales in 1573; SP 12/93/14, ff. 69, 75–101v.

26 Extracts from the Loseley manuscripts, in *Surrey Musters* pt. 1, Surrey Record Society no. 2 (London 1914), pp. v–vii, articles 1, 3, 4, 5, 10, 14, 17.

27 BL Harleian MS 309, old f. 167/new f. 199 – old f. 167v/new f. 199v, PC to LLs.

28 Ibid., old f. 176v/new f. 209v.

29 NRO, NCR, case 13a/9; *Norfolk Archaeology* vol. 1 (Norwich 1847), pp. 1–3, 21; Boynton, *EM*, pp. 117–19.

30 BL, Harleian MS 309, old f. 181/new f. 214 – old f. 183/new f. 216, PC orders of 27 April and 13 May.

31 M. Pulman, *The Elizabethan Privy Council in the Fifteen-seventies* (Berkeley, Calif. 1971), pp. 198–201.

32 J. Bain, ed., *The Border Papers. Calendar of Letters and Papers Relating to the Affairs of the Borders of England and Scotland* vol. 1 (1560–1594) (Edinburgh 1894), items 90–4, pp. 37–66.

33 *The Twysden Lieutenancy Papers*, p. 67; J. Goring and J. Wake, eds, *Northamptonshire Lieutenancy Papers and Other Documents 1580–1614*, Northamptonshire Record Society (Gateshead 1975), p. 18.

34 *Northants Lieutenancy Papers*, pp. xxi, 23–4.

35 BL, Harleian MS 168. ff. 110–14.

36 BL, Harleian MS 309, old f. 150/new f.177 – old f. 151/new f. 178, PC to LL regarding Suffolk musters.

37 For related, though not identical, strategic interpretations, see Wernham, 'Elizabethan War Aims and Strategy', in S. Bindoff, J. Hurstfield, and C. Williams, eds, *Elizabethan Government and Society* (London 1961), pp. 340–68; and W. MacCaffrey, *Elizabeth I: War and Politics 1588–1603* (Princeton 1992), pp. 3–13, 22–35.

38 BL, Harleian MS 132, ff. 2–17v; Harleian MS 6798, ff. 25–41v; Boynton, *EM*, pp. 140–6; Parker, 'If the Armada had Landed', *History* vol. 61 no. 203 (October 1976), pp. 358–68.

39 Boynton, *EM*, p. 145.

40 Hugo O'Donnell y Duque de Estrada, 'The Army of Flanders and the Invasion of England', in M. Rodriguez-Salgado and S. Adams, eds, *England, Spain and the 'Gran Armada' 1585–1604* (Edinburgh 1991), pp. 216–35.

41 BL, Stowe MS 570, new ff. 236–239v, 'an abstracte of the certificates retorned from the Lieutenaunts of the able men furnished and trained men in the severall counties. . . .', April 1588.

42 Wake, ed., *Northants Musters, Beacons, Subsidies 1586–1623*, pp. 20–3. See also the Northants west division accounts for 1588, being PRO SP 12/214/33, printed as appendix I on pp. 189–91, and the east division, SP 12/214/32, ff. 192–4.

43 NRO, NCR case 13a/9; *Norfolk Archaeology* vol. 1, pp. 5–17, 21–4; Boynton, *EM*, pp. 129, 145, 148–9, 155–8, 162–4; Nolan, *SJN*, pp. 108–24 and the tables in William Murdin, ed., *A Collection of State Papers Relating to Affairs in the Reign of Queen Elizabeth, From the Year 1571 to 1596* (London 1759), pp. 594–627.

44 See for example PRO, SP 16/466, old ff. 13–18/new ff. 120–122v, discussed at this chapter's end.

45 Murdin, ed., *A Collection of State Papers Relating to Affairs in the Reign of Queen Elizabeth . . .*, pp. 612, 614. For an exposition on these types of ordnance, see PRO, SP 12/242/64.

46 *HMC Foljambe*, fifteenth report, part 5 (London 1897), pp. 57–8.

47 Scott Thomson, *Lords Lieutenants*, p. 55.

48 *CSPD Addenda* (1580–1625) vol. 12 (London 1872), pp. 237, 239, 258.

49 PRO, SP 12/212/66, old f. 139/new f. 113, printed in N. A. M. Rodger, *The Armada in the Public Records* (London 1988), pp. 48–9; NRO, NCR, shelf 12G/box 1. How the Bardwell accounts got into the Norwich City Records is a mystery. Thanks to Ian Palfrey.

50 D. P. Waley, 'Papal Armies in the Thirteenth Century', *EHR* vol. 72 no. 282 (January 1957), pp. 1–30.

51 BL, Harleian MS 6986, f. 13, 14 July 1547.

52 See John McGurk's pioneering study, 'The Clergy and the Militia, 1580–1610', *History* vol. 60 no. 199 (June 1975), pp. 198–210.

53 Bodleian Library, Tanner MS 78, item 11, old ff. 30–30v/new ff. 20–20v, Queen to clergy, 23 January 1584/5; LPL 2009, ff. 42–42v, letter from Burghley, 4 March 1589/90.

54 Lambeth Palace, Fairhurst Papers 2009, ff. 1–2v, 64–65v, 76, 88–90v, 144v (Ireland) and ff. 5–6v (Low Countries).

55 For example, Bodleian Library, Rawlinson D 317b, f. 172, where musketeers and pikemen are included with petronels in a scheme to tax the clergy for provision of arms.

56 Lambeth Palace, Fairhurst Papers 2009, ff. 108, 110, and 139.

57 Lambeth Palace, Fairhurst Papers 2009, ff. 137–137v for statistics, ff. 9–16v for correspondence circa May–June 1588.

58 *L&A* vol. 2 (July 1590–May 1591), p. 383, no. 670 (F 177).

59 Lambeth Palace, Fairhurst Papers 2009, ff. 137–137v.

60 Lambeth Palace, Fairhurst Papers 2009, ff. 133–134v, 'Defectes and inconveniences alleged by the Bishoppes and others of the Clergie touching this service with horses.'

61 T. Blagg, ed., 'Muster Roll for Newark Wapentake. 1595', *Transactions of the Thoroton Society of Nottinghamshire* vol. 10 (1906–7), pp. 77–8.

62 Somerset RO, Q/SR 37/1, f. 17.

63 PRO, SP 14/78/15, f. 27, 10 October 1614; SP 14/82/113, f. 178; Boynton, *EM*, pp. 220–1; Fissel, *BW*, pp. 200–7, 213–14, 226–32.

64 Boynton, *EM*, pp. 59, 73, 115–16, 213; Thomas Cogswell, *Home Divisions. Aristocracy, the State and Provincial Conflict* (Stanford 1998), pp. 50–1. See also note 72 below.

65 J. Dasent, ed., *Acts of the Privy Council of England, 1597* (London 1903), pp. 111–12.

66 See Chapter 7.

67 This issue is dealt with at some length, from Henry II's Assize of Arms to Charles I's summoning of the Long Parliament, in Fissel, *BW*, pp. 174–90, 215–22.

68 PRO, SP 12/44/35, ff. 78–9.

69 PRO, SP 12/44/60, ff. 124–5, in a hand different from that of SP 12/44/35. On Pelham, see R. W. Ambler, '"Wise and Experimented": Sir William Pelham, Elizabethan soldier and landlord c.1560–87', in A. Ayton and J. L. Price, eds, *The Medieval Military Revolution* (London 1995), pp. 163–81.

70 See Chapter 4.

71 PRO, SP 12/44/60, ff. 124v–125; Boynton, *EM*, pp. 59–60.

72 Bristol RO, AC 02/2, 16 March 1578, re 'trayninge of Shotte'.

73 Fissel, *BW*, pp. 185–7.

74 Boynton, *EM*, pp. 209–11.

75 Wake, ed., *Northants Musters, Beacons, Subsidies 1586–1623*, pp. 118–21. Boynton, *EM*, p. 210 expresses amused scepticism over the claim that much equipment was in the hands of the armourers. However, given the predictable rusting and breakage of armour, and the few practising local armourers in Jacobean England, the excuse is not so far-fetched.

76 Bodleian Library, Ashmole MS 862, ff. 100–4, esp. f. 101, temp. James I.

77 Gloucestershire authorities confessed that their trained forces had dwindled to 2,000 men (in contrast to the 3,500 it fielded in Armada year). The resultant Smith of Nibley survey demonstrated their diligence in disclosing their state of readiness; W. Willcox, *Gloucestershire 1540–1640* (New Haven, Conn. 1940), p. 79; Boynton, *EM*, pp. 210–11; Fissel, *BW*, pp. 193, 201–3. Quintrell writes that 'the problem of generating enthusiasm persisted' in Essex through 1608: *The Maynard Lieutenancy Book, 1608–1639* pt. 1 (Chelmsford 1993), p. lxiv; A. Clark, 'The Essex Territorial Force in 1608', *The Essex Review* vol. 17 no. 66 (April 1908), pp. 98–115, chronicles the muster process, and continuing problems.

78 NRO, NCR, case 13a/14, ff. 104–167v.

79 G. P. Higgins, 'The Militia in Early Stuart Cheshire', *Journal of the Chester Archaeological Society* vol. 61 (1978), pp. 40–1.

80 Stater, *Noble Government*, p. 25.

81 BL, Add. MS 39,245, new f. 7v/old f.20; *HMC Fifteenth Report* pt. 7, p. 59, Seymour letterbook, 30 June 1608; Wake, ed., *Northants Musters, Beacons, Subsidies 1586–1623*, pp. 121–2. According to Wake, p. cxxi, the Spinola scare was in September 1614; Boynton, *EM*, p. 214.

82 NRO, WLS xxvii/2 (box E), Sir William de Grey's folio book, 1606–1663, ff. 9–11, which specify trained and untrained Norfolk men, the Jacobean strategic predicament, and make reference to Spinola. Wake and Boynton both comment on this: *Northants Musters, Beacons, Subsides 1586–1623*, pp. cxviii–cxix, and *EM*, pp. 220–1.

83 BL, Add. 39, 245, new ff. 15v–17/old ff. 36–9. For the clergy, Boynton, *EM*, pp. 222–4.

84 PRO, SP 14/82/113, f. 178, Middlesex DLs to LL, 26 October 1615.

85 HEH, STT Military Box 1 (7), general muster taken at Buckingham, 24 September 1618. The surprising number of lancers fielded persisted in the 1630s: PRO, SP 16/381/66 *ad* SP 16/408/162, certificates of February 1638.

86 Christopher Hill, *The World Turned Upside Down* (New York 1972), p. 16; Conrad Russell, *The Crisis of Parliaments, 1509–1660* (Oxford 1971), p. 244; and in general, Buchanan Sharp, *In Contempt of All Authority* (Berkeley, Calif. 1980), esp. pp. 6, 99, 118–23, 262.

87 HEH, Hastings Military Box 1 (13); for a contemporary's account of the office, see Gervase Markham, *The Muster Master*, edited by Charles Hamilton in the *Camden Miscellany* vol. 26, fourth series, no. 14 (London 1975), pp. 49–76; for context, Cogswell, *HD*, pp. 21–133.

88 For a definition, BL, Harleian MS 168, ff. 123–123v.

89 Sir John Neale, 'Elizabeth and the Netherlands, 1586–7', *EHR* vol. 45 no. 179 (July 1930), p. 388.

90 'A conference of a good and bad Muster master . . .' (pp. 13–16); 'A brief conference of two Auditors' (pp. 20–3); 'Abuses that may be practized . . .' (pp. 24–8); 'The only or best salve . . .' (pp. 29–30); and 'A Briefe Conference of Two Commanders . . .' (pp. 31–F2v), appended to Digges's *A Breife and true report of*

the Proceedings of The Earle of Leycester (London 1590), comprising pp. 1–10. See also Chapter 6, pp. 148–52.

91 Webb, *EMS*, p. 25; *HMC Salisbury* pt. 3 (London 1889), p. 323 no. 667 for the new system, April 1588.

92 Charles Hamilton, 'The Shropshire Muster-Master's Fee,' *Albion* vol. 2 no. 1 (1970), p. 26.

93 Boynton, *EM*, pp. 179–80.

94 *APC 1597*, pp. 232–3, 9 January 1597/8, PC to LL.

95 BL, Additional MS 46, 188, f. 15; SRO, Q/SR 2/1 (1) a, f. 232, item 4, Barnes, *Somerset*, p. 263.

96 Somerset RO, DD/PH 222/7, Hopton and Rodney to Phelips, 25 April 1626.

97 See Barnes, *Somerset*, p. 118, esp. note 43.

98 SRO, DD/PH 222/8, f. 15.

99 Haynes, ed., *SP* vol. 1, pp. 158–9, PC proceedings of 21 July 1553. The Marian text illustrates this nicely: 'Sir Wylliam Drewrye, Sir Wylliam Walgrave, Sir Thomas Stradlyng Knights, Roger Wodbowse, Francis Colbye, John Jenyngs, Esquyers, are appoynted to be Mustere Masters. . . . They shall immediatlye make a Proclamatyon for all Captyens to bringe the Sowdeors to the Musters, and also all Gentlemen to Muster with ther Howsholde Servants. Owte of theise Souldyours they shall chose the hable Mene, and the well furnyshede, and taike the Harnise from the insuffy-cyent, and delyver the sayme to the suffycyent. That in anyweyse they keype the Archers, and dyscharge as fewe of thym as may be. Also that they make a specyall Note of the Horsemene. The Musters accomplished, that they brynge the Naymes of Captyens and there Numbers, the Names of the Gentlemene and there Numbers.'

100 SRO, DD/PH 222/9, f. 17.

101 PRO, SP 16/6/59, 10 September 1625.

102 SRO, DD/PH222/10, f.19; the DLs underlined Pembroke's instructions regarding defaulters.

103 Somerset RO, DD/PH 222/11, f. 21.

104 'The Booke of generalle musters. . . .', printed in 'Trained Soldiers of Shropshire in the Reign of Queen Elizabeth', *Shropshire Archaeological and Natural History* vol. 2, series 2 (1890), pp. 257–83.

105 Shropshire Records and Research Centre, 3365/2561, 'Money due to the muster master for his fee for the yeere ended at michaelmas 1622'. Tony Carr of the SRRC kindly assisted in locating documents.

106 Russell, *PEP*, pp. 145–433.

107 Charles Hamilton, 'The Shropshire Muster-Master's Fee', *Albion* vol. 2 no. 1 (1970), pp. 26–7. In 1982 Esther Cope published 'Politics without Parliament: The Dispute about Muster Masters' Fees in Shropshire in the 1630s,' *The Huntington Library Quarterly* vol. 45 no. 3 (summer 1982), pp. 271–84. Although she cited Hamilton's 1975 edition of Gervase Markham's *The Muster Master*, she ignored Hamilton's pioneering article of 1970, while paralleling his sources and narrative.

108 HEH, Ellesmere MS 7443, table of DLs and muster-masters in Wales and the Marches, 1637.

109 Hamilton, 'Shropshire Muster Master's fee', p. 30; Cope, 'Politics', p. 279.

110 For example, Boynton, *EM*, pp. 180–1, 225–7, 287–91.

111 Somerset RO, DD/PH 222/19 f. 34, Poulett and DLs to LL, 3 October 1636. See above and Barnes, *Somerset*, p. 261.

112 Somerset RO, DD/PH 222/19, f. 35.

113 Ibid. For Kingsmore's (or King's Moor's) location, see Figure 2.2, inset 3.

114 Somerset RO, DD/PH 222/20, f. 36.

115 Somerset RO, DD/PH 222/21, f. 38; DD/PH 222/22, f. 40 is virtually identical.

116 Somerset RO, DD/PH 222/23, f. 42, 9 January 1636/7.

117 Barnes, *Somerset*, pp. 288–9.

118 Somerset RO, DD/PH 212/5. Immediately following the quotation are two lines inked out that apparently bear on the issue of evading the press. On the context of the incident, Barnes, *Somerset*, p. 264. DD/PH 222/24 f. 44, 19 July 1636 transcripts of warrants re the Spracklinge case (discussed in Barnes, *Somerset*, p. 104). On the trained-band exemption from conscription, see Fissel, *BW*, pp. 175, 181–3, 208–9, 222–5.

119 Somerset RO, DD/PH 222/24, f. 44, Phelips to the constable, 5 August 1636.

120 Somerset RO, DD/PH 222/24, ff. 44–44v, 16 August 1636.

121 Ibid., f. 44v.

122 Barnes, *Somerset*, pp. 269–70; Somerset RO, DD/PH 222/24, end of f.44v. Poulett and DLs to constables and keeper of the common gaol at Ilchester, commanding that the warrant for the apprehending of the body of Spracklinge be executed; the latter to be 'conveid unto his Majestys comon Gaole at Ilchester . . . there to remaine without baile . . . for the space of tenn daies' unless he paid 40s. Dated 8 September 1636. Phelips has inserted the marginal note that in reality the warrant was not executed successfully until 22 September 1636.

123 BL, Lansdowne MS 81, f. 26, item 12, 8 May 1596.

124 Ibid., f. 28. Folio 28 follows a slip of paper listing gentlemen from each of the two hundreds, one of which is to be selected as captain of Cutts's company. William Colte, of Caysoe hundred is described as 'a very sufficient Gentleman but his father is Lyvinge' and Dacorn hundred, Sir John Brockett (who had signed a letter with Cocke) is described as 'well provided of all furniture fitt for it, and very willinge to performe his duety therin [then added in another hand] and he is also of good abilitye'. Also, Boynton, *EM*, pp. 167–8, 178–9.

125 Roger Lockyer, *Buckingham. The Life and Political Career of George Villiers* (London 1981), p. 211

126 BL, Harleian MS 1583, ff. 90–93v. The hand resembles that of Sir John Coke. Although undated, I would conjecture 1625–6. The nature of a military proposal such as this would have become increasingly controversial as the 1620s proceeded. It may have some relation to Buckingham's 1624 proposal and Coke's more grandiose projects of 1626 and 1627.

127 Ibid., f. 90v.

128 Ibid., f. 92.

129 Ibid., ff. 91–2.

130 PRO, SP 16/537/44, new ff. 104–106v; for context, Richard Cust, *The Forced Loan and English Politics 1626–1628* (Oxford 1987), pp. 76–7; A. Thrush, 'Ship Money', in Fissel, ed., *W&G*, pp. 150–1, 160 (note 105) with reference to SP 16/527/44, which Thrush dates as pre-summer 1627.

131 John Nolan suggests an intriguing connection between the concept of the trained bands and Spanish and Italianate influences: 'The Militarization of the Elizabethan State', *The Journal of Military History* vol. 58 (July 1994), p. 399.

132 PRO, SP 16/522/122, old f. 128. A more sinister, and Machiavellian, aspect of the proposal is how the militia could suppress social disorder by 'poore handicrafts men and poore Cottagers', old f. 229.

133 PRO, SP 16/522/123, old f. 230; BL, Additional MS 46, 188, ff. 81–81v, PC order of 14 January 1625/6 and f. 93, PC to LL, 27 June 1626.

134 PRO, SP 16/33/26, f. 44, '. . . old practised Souldiers of our owne. . . .', 3 August.

135 PRO, SP 16/8/27, f. 42.

136 PRO, SP 16/8/14, old ff. 83–7.

137 PRO, SP 16/533/131, new f. 214.

138 The estimate is based on the table compiled in Bodleian Library, Ashmole MS 792, ff. 30–31v of 'General Musters' that I would date as mid-Jacobean. Barons

'Knevet' and 'Clifton' (created in 1607 and 1608) are mentioned in the volume, so conceivably this could be an early Caroline general muster. The individual shire numbers seem to be more closely aligned to Jacobean figures. However, the total for able men in Northumberland has been mistakenly inflated tenfold by the insertion of what must be an extra nought (f. 31). The figures for armed men exceed able men due to the mistranscription of a '7' for a '1' (f. 31v) so that the true figure should be 487,293 potential soldiers in England and Wales. If Northumberland's able men are 'adjusted', the total should be 466,593 or so foot soldiers ('able' as well as 'armed'), pioneers, and horsemen. This seems unrealistic, however, considering that Elizabeth I had no more than a quarter of a million men at her disposal. See Cruickshank, *EA*, pp. 24–5 and McGurk, *ECI*, p. 64. On training between 1603 and 1608, see Quintrell, ed., *MLB* pt. 1, p. lxvii.

139 Bodleian Library, Clarendon SP, XV, f. 80; PRO, SP 16/381/66; SP 16/408/162.

140 Stater, *Noble Government*, p. 202, note 70.

141 Bodleian Library, Ashmole MS 792, f. 31.

142 Fissel, *BW*, pp. 194–5, esp. note 72.

143 Russell, *PEP*, p. 77.

144 Richard Stewart, 'Arms Accountability in Early Stuart Militia', *Bulletin of the Institute of Historical Research* vol. 57 no. 135 (May 1984), pp. 115–16; Boynton, *EM*, pp. 239–40; Russell, *PEP*, pp. 91–2, 274–5.

145 See Chapters 4 and 11.

146 Barnes, *Somerset*, pp. 259–60.

147 John Scally, 'Counsel in Crisis: James, Third Marquis of Hamilton and the Bishops' Wars, 1638–1640', in J. Young, ed., *Celtic Dimensions of the British Civil Wars* (Edinburgh 1997), p. 24.

148 Fissel, *BW*, pp. xi, 1–73, 129–51, 174–263, 288–9. Hamilton's 1639 adventure is the subject of an essay forthcoming in *Amphibious Warfare 1100–1700*, M. Fissel and D. Trim, eds.

149 Cogswell, *HD*, pp. 255–318.

150 PRO, PC 2/50, f. 12, from Anglesey, 28 April 1639.

151 PRO, SP 16/466, old ff. 13–18/new ff. 120–122v.

152 Bodleian Library, Carte MS 2, ff. 62–63v, to Ormonde, from Callan, 18 November 1641, especially f. 62. 'Wee the Suffraine [sovereign] Burgesses and Inhabitants of the Town of Callan, having mustered our men, doe finde that wee are able and most willigne to mayntaine att our owne Charge within the said Towne, for perservacion of the Kings Majesties undoubted right, and for our owne defence, to our best powers, against all rebells and disloyall people, the number of 30 Muskettyers and 40 pikemen beside a number of other of our inhabitants which are provided with halbeards and brownbills, And doe humbly pray to be admitted to furnish ourselves att our owne charge with 30 newe musketts with bandalyraes and rests for them.'

153 Bodleian Library, Carte MS 2, ff. 203–203v, Sir Arthur Chichester, Arthur Terringham and two others, 28 December 1641, from Carrickfergus.

154 Bodleian Library, Clarendon SP, vol. 20, ff. 167v–168, 'A true and exact list. . . .', broadsheet (London 1641/2). See, however, Cogswell, *HD*, pp. 315–16.

155 The Impressment Act is printed in S. R. Gardiner, *Constitutional Documents of the Puritan Revolution* 3rd edn (Oxford 1906), pp. 242–5.

4 THE DEFENCE OF THE REALM: IMPRESSMENT AND MOBILISATION

1 *Commons Debates 1628* vol. 2 (17 March–19 April 1628), R. Johnson and M. Cole, eds, (New Haven, Conn. 1977), p. 292; Paul Christianson, 'Arguments on

Billeting and Martial Law in the Parliament of 1628', *HJ* vol. 37 no. 3 (1994), pp. 546–7.

2 Printed in *Norfolk Archaeology: or Miscellaneous Tracts Relating to the Antiquities of the County of Norfolk* vol. 1 (Norwich 1847), p. 32.

3 Anthony Goodman, *The Wars of the Roses. Military Activity and English Society, 1452–97* (London 1981), pp. 134–5.

4 For the standard view, see Jeremy Goring's University of London Ph.D. thesis, 'The Military Obligations of the English People, 1511–1558' (1955), where the 'quasi-feudal' concept is developed. For an encapsulation of the history of impressment before 1641, Fissel, *BW*, pp. 215–22. Gilbert Millar's *Tudor Mercenaries and Auxiliaries 1485–1547* (Virginia 1980) is also useful, especially p. 14.

4a Helen Miller, *Henry VIII and the English Nobility* (Oxford 1986), p. 134.

5 PRO, E 101/56/25; E 101/57/13; E 101/56/10/2. See below, note 9, for description.

6 Helen Miller, *Henry VIII and the English Nobility* (Oxford 1986), pp. 134–5, 138–40, 144.

7 PRO, C 82/342, Chancery warrant of proclamation, facsimile printed between pp. 84–5 in P. Hughes and J. Larkin, eds, *Tudor Royal Proclamations* vol. 1 (New Haven 1964).

8 PRO, E 101/62/12/15; E 101/62/12/2; Miller, *Henry VIII and the English Nobility*, p. 158.

9 BL, Harleian MS 6989, old ff. 78–79v, PC to the Duke of Norfolk, late July 1545.

10 Ready money laid out to cover the initial expenses of clothing, feeding, and transporting newly pressed soldiers; Fissel, *BW*, pp. 129–37.

11 PRO, E 101/57/13, instructions and indentures for Sir John Daunce and others to supply coat and conduct money; E 101/56/25, scores of documents regarding coat and conduct money and tabulations of transportation charges, circa 1513; E 101/56/10/2, indentures dating around December 1543, in preparation for the French campaign of 1544, illustrative of how the Crown paid for jackets and transportation; E 101/64/2, f. 74, circa early 1558 (fall of Calais), where miners received allowance for traversing the 360 miles from Cambrai to Truro.

12 PRO, SP 12/1/26, f. 59 and SP 12/1/34, ff. 81v–82, 11 and 15 December respectively; SP 12/2/6, f. 10; SP 12/2/7, f. 12; SP 12/2/8, f. 13, the last three inclusive of 17–20 January 1559.

13 PRO, SP 63/3, f. 204, indenture with a notation of £266 13s. 4d. Irish for 'Coates and Conducte'.

14 P. Forbes, ed., *Full View of the Public Transactions in the Reign of Elizabeth*, vol. 2 (London 1741), p. 104; *Calendar of State Papers Foreign 1562* (reprinted Nendeln, Liechtenstein 1966), p. 528, no. 1217, Dacre and others to Cecil, 9 December 1562, from Berwick; PRO, SP 59/1/62 (513), ff. 223–6, Lee to PC, 20 July 1559, from Berwick.

15 *Calendar of State Papers Foreign 1562*, pp. 503–5, no. 1154, 'A Memorial for Newhaven'. By then Sir Richard Lee had completed his survey of Le Havre and had returned to London, where he met with Cecil. See also nos. 1155 and 1156, the latter being Lee's report, p. 505, no. 1160, 1 December 1562, that the soldiers would have to help the pioneers in order to complete the defences by February–March 1563.

16 PRO, SP 12/24/60, f. 108, circa September 1562.

17 J. Dasent, ed., *APC 1558–1570* vol. 7 (London 1893), p. 116, under 23 July 1562.

18 PRO, SP 70/59 f. 16, entry 12; SP 12/24/35, f. 63 and SP 12/24/36, f. 64, 16 September 1562.

19 Forbes, ed., *Transactions* vol. 2, p. 58, Queen's instructions of 23 September 1562.

20 Ibid., p. 59, the Queen to Wood, 23 September 1562.

21 PRO, SP 70/59, f. 16v, entries 15 and 16, right margin; Forbes, ed., *Transactions* vol. 2, p. 92, the Queen to sheriffs and JPs, 7 October 1562.

22 See the case of Essex, the Queen to Essex sheriffs and JPs, 3 November 1562, in Forbes, ed., *Transactions* vol. 2, p. 171.

23 PRO, SP 12/27/8, f. 14, 8 January 1563.

24 BL, Harleian MS 6990, ff. 44–45v; PRO, SP 70/59, ff. 16–17, especially the far right margin of the table, which lists the men who in effect served as lieutenants.

25 PRO, SP 12/28/63, f. 185; Fissel, *BW*, p. 221. In the latter reference the thirteen prisoners described and then cited in note twenty-five (i.e. John Cundall, etc.) were pressed in 1625, as is footnoted correctly, and not in 1563, as stated in the text.

26 W. MacCaffrey, 'The Newhaven Expedition, 1562–1563', *HJ* vol. 40 no. 1 (March 1997), pp. 9, 19.

27 PRO, SP 12/29/58.

28 PRO, SP 12/27/70, f. 278, to Cecil, 27 February 1563, levies from Staffordshire, Suffolk, Warwickshire, and Radnorshire for Irish service.

29 J. Wake, ed., *A Copy of Papers relating to Musters, Beacons, Subsidies, etc., in the County of Northampton A.D. 1586–1623* Northamptonshire Record Society vol. 3 (Kettering 1926), p. 1.

30 BL, Harleian MS 703, f. 37.

31 J. J. N. McGurk is the pre-eminent authority on Elizabethan impressment. Compare his 1982 Liverpool Ph.D. dissertation, 'The Recruitment and Transportation of Elizabethan Troops and their service in Ireland, 1594–1603', tables on pp. 99, 105, 111, and 107 with the tables in Cruickshank's *EA*, pp. 290–1. McGurk has published his figures in *The Elizabethan Conquest of Ireland. The 1590s Crisis* (Manchester 1997), pp. 52–65.

32 McGurk, *ECI*, pp. 56–60.

33 East Suffolk RO, Bury St Edmunds, C 12/1/1–3, 'papers regarding the provision of soldiers, 1570'; C 12/2, 'Bills for setting forth soldyers, 1572'.

34 *HMC Salisbury* vol. 9, p. 43, cited in Wake, ed., *Northants Musters, Beacons and Subsidies 1586–1623*, pp. xx, cxi; Fissel, *BW*, pp. 225, 232, 240–63, 292. p. 43.

35 J. Harland, ed., *The Lancashire Lieutenancy* pt. 1 (Manchester 1859), pp. 111–19.

36 *CSPD Elizabeth, Addenda 1580–1625* vol. 12 (London 1872), p. 250, no. 99, the Earl of Huntingdon to Walsingham.

37 *HMC Cowper*, Coke MSS, 12th report, appendix, part I, vol. 1 (London 1888), pp. 7–8, 4 January 1587/8. The italicisation is my own.

38 Somerset RO, DD/PH 220, f. 80.

39 S. L. Adams, 'The English Military Clientele 1542–1618', in *Patronages et Clientelismes 1550–1750 (France, Angleter, Espagne, Italie)*, C. Giry-Deloisin and R. Mettam, eds, (Lille and London 1995), pp. 217–75. I owe this reference to David Trim.

40 On drumming up 'voluntaries', see BL, Egerton MS 784, Whiteway's diary, new f. 11v/old f. 20 (March 1620), ff. 42v–3/82–3 (July 1624), ff. 45v/88 (December 1624).

41 PRO, E 157/4, f. 155; on Crowe, see Fissel, 'Law and Authority in the Collection of the Strangers' Consulage, 1621–1651', forthcoming.

42 BL, Lansdowne MS 1218, new f. 131/old f. 143.

43 PRO, E 157/4, f. 55. Though Roman Catholic, the Venetians sometimes allied with Protestant powers. See PRO, SP 16/527/44, f. 104.

44 J. Harland, ed., *The Lancashire Lieutenancy under the Tudors and the Stuarts*, Chetham Society volumes 49 and 50 (Manchester 1859), i.e. in vol. 49, pp. 22–31, 62–6, 75–6, 111–19, 132–8, 144–6, 216, 226–33; PRO, E 407/12, 'Levies of Soldiers for Ireland, 1600–1605', unfoliated bundle, i.e. 28 April, 22 July 1601, where these shires top the lists.

45 BL, Add. MS 36, 293, Lord Eure's letterbook, 1598–1606, ff. 3–4v, 8–13v, 43–4, 45v, 48v, etc.

46 McGurk, *ECI*, pp. 55–6, who suggests that some troops from the Border shires may have been intermingled in the presses.

47 Somerset RO, DD/PH 220, ff. 13–36v, entries from 18 February 1590/1 to 4 February 1593/4.

48 Nolan, 'Militarization', p. 397; also pp. 393, 407, and 413; N. Canny, *The Elizabethan Conquest of Ireland* (New York 1976), pp. 154–9 and this volume, Chapter 7; Canny, whose figure for 1575 is around 1,600 troops in the establishment (p. 157), is useful for his model of the English establishment.

49 On Irish presses within the lieutenancy, see Somerset RO, DD/PH 220, ff. 49v–56v, 63v–67v, 74v–84.

50 For example, the press of 23 December 1601. PRO, E 407/12, 'Levies of soldiers for Ireland, 1600–1605', unfoliated bundle.

51 B. Downing, *The Military Revolution and Political Change* (Princeton, NJ 1992), p. 16; see Tallett's remarks, based on Joyce Youings's research, *WSEME*, pp. 217, 293 (note 204).

52 On vagabonds, see Smythe's proposal in BL, Lansdowne MS 65, new ff. 76v–77; also Hale, ed., *CDM*, pp. xxxvii–xxxviii, lxxxiv–lxxxv.

53 PRO, SP 45/10, old f. 110/new f. 185 – old f. 110v/new f. 186; SP 45/10, old f. 171/new f. 325 – old f. 171v/new f. 326.

54 BL, Lansdowne 65, new f. 177, to Burghley, 23 November 1590.

55 J. Bruce, ed., *Correspondence of Robert Dudley, Earl of Leycester . . .*, Camden Society vol. 27 (London 1844), pp. 26, 93.

56 PRO, SP 12/213/55, f. 93v, letter of 28 July 1588, damaged by damp. Motley and Hale quote the same letter. Composed in haste, several key words were further obscured by water damage. Hale, ed., *CDM*, pp. xxxii–xxxiii, citing J. Motley, *The History of the United Netherlands* vol. 2 (New York 1861), pp. 492–3 and *CSPD 1581–1590*, p. 515.

57 Geoffrey Parker, 'Why did the Dutch Revolt last eighty years?', *TRHS*, fifth series, vol. 26 (1976), pp. 53–72.

58 PRO, SP 12/259/34, f. 84.

59 PRO, SP 12/154/10. The year 1582 is conjectural.

60 Fissel, *BW*, pp. 174–95, 215–63.

61 PRO, SP 12/259/16 I, f. 46; Burghley's notation, f. 46v; 16 II, f. 47; 22 I, ff. 58–62; 34, ff. 84–84v; 57, ff. 136–136v.

62 PRO, SP 12/259/21, f. 56.

63 Charles Wilson, *Queen Elizabeth and the Revolt of the Netherlands* (Berkeley, Calif. 1970), pp. 151–2, note 17.

64 PRO, SP 12/259/21, f. 56v; 22 I, f. 63, deposition of Robert Frost; 27, ff. 69–73, 55, ff. 133–133v, Smythe's examinations.

65 PRO, SP 12/259/56, f. 135, item 5.

66 Nolan, 'Militarization', citing *APC 1595–1596* vol. 25, pp. 331–3.

67 See for example PRO, SO 1/3, f. 188v and also SO 3/12, ff. 111–12. The Nottinghamshire trained bands were to suppress mutinous companies of soldiers passing through their locality and to keep order amongst Nottinghamshire's own men 'prested in that county for the Northerne expedition'. I owe the last reference to Andrew Thrush. See also PRO, SP 16/457/77, George Purefoy, a sheriff of Berkshire to PC, 20 June 1640, and Fissel, *BW*, pp. 279–80.

68 Phillip Thomas, 'Military Mayhem in Elizabethan Chester. The Privy Council's Response to Vagrant Soldiers', *JSAHR* vol. 76 no. 308 (Winter 1998), pp. 231–2, 234, 236–7, 241–2, 244.

69 PRO, E 407/3/2, E 407/3/3, E 407/3/4, E 407/3/5, E 407/3/6, E 407/3/9; PRO, SP 39/27, unfoliated parchment.

70 PRO, E 351/219.
71 PRO, SP 63/69/52, old f. 481/new f. 107 – old f. 482/new f. 107v; Falls, *EIW*, pp. 128–9.
72 PRO, SP 12/24/41, f. 75, the Queen to the London sheriffs, 20 September 1562; G. Lambert, 'Sir Nicholas Malby and his Associates', *Journal of the Galway Archaeological and Historical Society* vol. 23 nos. 1 and 2 (1948), pp. 6–7; *DNB*.
73 PRO, SP 63/76/65, old f. 618/new f. 134, 28 September 1580; SP 63/77/25, new ff. 62–3, 4 October 1580; SP 63/77/43, old f. 167/new f. 103 – old f. 169/new f. 103A, 13 and 18 October 1580; SP 63/79/6, old f. 609/new f. 11 – old f. 610/new f. 11v, 9 December 1580. Falls, *EIW*, pp. 142–3.
74 PRO, SP 63/183/84 I, old f. 248/new f. 276v, 7 October 1595; SP 63/185/3, old f. 697/new f. 5 – old f. 699/new f. 6, 4 December 1595; SP 63/185/10, new ff. 17–17v; SP 63/185 10 I; old f. 595/new f. 21 – old f. 597/new f. 22; SP 63/186/12 II, old f. 319/new f. 34 – old f. 320/new f. 34v, 29 December 1595; Falls, *EIW*, pp. 191–2; on 1596 levies and comparative troop levels see ibid., pp. 193–4.
75 PRO, E 101/65/20; PRO, E 407/12. See Falls, *EIW*, pp. 186–9, i.e. on 31 July 1594 Norris authorised Mr Courtney to take delivery of 150 reinforcements to be embarked at Plymouth.
76 A peculiarly Kentish administrative unit that encompassed several hundreds within itself.
77 McGurk, *ECI*, pp. 82–5.
78 Bodleian Library, Rawlinson MS D. 924, ff. 45v–48v (summer 1600 levies), 55–55v, 56v–58, (spring 1601 press).
79 *APC 1597* vol. 27 (London 1903), pp. 81–9, esp. p. 85.
80 BL, Harleian MS 703, ff. 99, 111v, 115.
81 *APC 1597* vol. 27, pp. 89–91, 97, 98, 144–5.
82 *APC 1598* vol. 28 (London 1904), p. 635, to paymaster William Meredithe; and p. 624; also, pp. 628–30, instructions to the captains.
83 See Chapter 9, pp. 222–3; 23 August: 2000 men levied in various shires PRO, SP 63/204, new ff. 89–90/old ff. 83–4; 25 August: pressed men, horse and foot, at Chester, SP 63/202 pt. 3/38, f. 74; 27 August: minutes for levying troops, SP 63/202 pt. 3/41 and 42, ff. 80–81v; 31 August: the arrival of 2,000 men under Sir Samuel Bagenal, SP 63/202 pt. 3/50.
84 PRO, SP 63/204, new ff. 90–90v, old ff. 84v–85, Cecil to Irish Council, 31 August 1598.
85 BL, Harleian MS 4271, ff. 2–3, letters of 26 and 28 August 1598.
86 Ibid., ff. 3v–5.
87 PRO, SP 63/204, new f. 94/old f. 88.
88 Falls, *EIW*, pp. 219–20, 226–7, 236.
89 PRO, SP 63/202 pt. 3/72, new f. 129. On 20 September, 2,000 more men were levied. See SP 63/202 pt. 3/7, October 1598.
90 PRO, SP 63/202 pt. 3/74 and 75, new ff. 131–133v, 20 and 22 September respectively.
91 PRO, SP 63/202 pt. 3/93, new f. 173.
92 PRO, SP 63/202 pt. 3/111, f. 210.
93 PRO, SP 63/202 pt. 3/184, ff. 401–401v.
94 PRO, SP 63/202 pt. 4/29, old f. 459/new f. 44, Cecil's notes.
95 PRO, SP 63/202 pt. 4/34 IX., old ff. 757/new f.67 – old f. 759/new f. 69 and 34 X., old f. 208/new f. 69.
96 PRO, SP 63/213/28, f. 55; see also above, *APC 1598*, 29–31 July, pp. 628–30, 635; for transport instructions aimed at Devon, p. 624.
97 BL, Harleian MS 703, new f. 111v/old f. 116v.

98 *CSPI* vol. 9 1601–1603, *Addenda* 1565–1654, p. 589, 30 September 1573.

99 *APC 1598* vol. 28 (London 1904), p. 630.

100 BL, Harleian MS 4271, ff. 6v–15v; McGurk, *ECI*, pp. 58–9, table 2. PRO, SP 63/204, old f. 114v/new f. 120v – old f.116/new f. 122; SP 63/204, new ff. 121–122v, old ff. 116v.

101 PRO, SP 63/203/39, f. 82.

102 Ibid.

103 Ibid; SP 63/203/40, f. 84, 8 February 1598/9.

104 PRO, SP 63/204, new ff. 122–122v/old ff. 116–116v.

105 Bodleian Library, Bankes MS 25/2; Fissel, *BW*, pp. 111–51.

106 PRO, SP 63/213/63, f. 9v, 20 May 1599.

107 See Chapter 9, pp. 226–35.

108 Soldiers were paid off when 'cassed'.

109 PRO, SP 63/211/18, new ff. 50–50v/old ff. 357–8, to PC, 28 April 1602.

110 Lambeth Palace Cat. of MSS quoting Fairhurst papers 2009, p. 52, citing f. 64.

111 LPL, Fairhurst Papers 2009, ff. 72, 74, 92, 143, 145.

112 LPL, Fairhurst Papers 2009, ff. 96–134v; McGurk, *ECI*, p. 65, table 4. On Kent's burden, see also this work, pp. 86, 91, 93, 97, 101, 105, 113.

113 PRO, SP 63/204, old f. 111/new f. 117.

114 PRO, SP 63/204, old f. 114/new f. 120.

115 PRO, SP 63/204, old ff. 113/new f. 119 – old f. 113v/new f. 119v.

116 J. J. N. McGurk, 'The Clergy and the Militia, 1580–1610', *History* vol. 60 no. 199 (June 1975), pp. 198–210. For the question of militia service versus impressment see Fissel, *BW*, pp. 188, 208–11, 225, 232, 240–63, 289–90, 292.

117 LPL, Fairhurst Papers 2009, ff. 68–9, ff. 68–9, 88–9, 90–90v.

118 J. P. Earwaker, ed., *The Constables' Accounts of the Manor of Manchester . . .* vol. 1 (Manchester 1891), pp. 2–4, 8; Chapter 10, pp. 236–8.

119 Cogswell, *HD*, p. 15.

120 Bodleian Library, Rawlinson MS A 210, f. 14/27 and Rawlinson MS C 846, ff. 99–115, transcriptions from 1566/7, esp. the latter three folios. PRO, SP 45/10, new f. 397, 5 April 1636.

121 PRO, SP 45/10, new f. 76, 18 June 1626. I am grateful to Dr Andrew Thrush for discussion regarding impressment of mariners.

122 For a printed pass specimen, WRO, Quarter Sessions Autograph Book, f. 29, 16 May 1612, with supporting documentation on ff. 28, 30, and 31; on the procedure, PRO, SP 45/10, old f. 96/new f. 162.

123 Hale, *WSRE*, pp. 87–8, 108–9; J. S. Cockburn, 'The Nature and Incidence of Crime in England 1559–1625', in J. S. Cockburn, ed.,*Crime in England 1550–1800* (London 1977), p. 58.

124 Corporation of London Records Office, *Journal of the Court of Common Council* vol. 22, ff. 278, 304, 328; P. Thomas, 'Military Mayhem in Elizabethan Chester', pp. 226–47; Fissel, *BW*, pp. 217, 221–3.

125 PRO, SP 12/240/61, new f. 94, proclamation of 5 November 1591; SP 12/240/76, new ff. 120–120a; Sir J. Neale, 'Elizabeth and the Netherlands 1586–7' in *Essays in Elizabethan History* (London 1958), citing *APC*.

126 *APC 1598* vol. 28, p. 631.

127 Russell, *PEP*, p. 76.

128 PRO, SP 14/173/88 I, f. 110; SP 14/173/89, f. 113; Bodleian Library, Tanner MS 72, f. 30 (item 14), 5 May 1625.

129 The indentures are in boxes PRO SP 14/178 and 179. See also the figures in SP 14/173/88 II, ff. 111–111v; SP 14/173/88, ff. 109–109v, Sec. Calvert to Sec. Conway, 25 October 1624.

130 PRO, SP 14/173/89, f. 113v; also SP 14/173/93, f. 118, PC to LLs.

131 PRO, SP 84/126, f. 8 (act of the Dutch States General granting levies to Mansfeld, 3/13 March 1625); SP 84/126/22–23 (Parliament to Mansfeld); SP 84/126/70 (Mansfeld to Carlton, 22 March/1 April 1625); SP 84/126/238 (provisions for Mansfeld's levies, 19 April 1625); SP 84/126/266 (English colonels to Carlton, 26 April 1625).

132 Fissel, *BW*, p. 64, drawing upon the views of Mike Young and Stephen Stearns.

133 *HMC Supplementary Report on the Manuscripts of the Earl of Mar and Kellie* (London 1930), pp. 215–16, letters of 7 and 15 December 1624; Cogswell, *HD*, pp. 39–42.

134 HEH, STT Military Box 1 (13).

135 PRO, SP 39/20, unfoliated, Charles's warrant to John Bere to be muster-master to 6,000 troops pressed for Danish service, 25 March 1626 (?).

136 Cruickshank, *EA*, tables 1 and 3, pp. 290–1; McGurk, *ECI*, table 1, p. 55; S. Stearns, 'Conscription and English Society in the 1620s', *JBS* vol. 11 no. 2 (May 1972), p. 4. Stuart presses, like Elizabethan levies, overlapped. For example, in spring 1627, pressed troops were *en route* to Denmark as well as to the Isle of Rhé, with some soldiers being transferred from Irish garrisons. PRO, SP 16/63/91, f. 111; 92, f.112, 92 I., f. 113, and *APC January–August 1627* vol. 42 (Nendeln, Liechtenstein 1974), pp. 281–2, 286–7.

137 WRO, Quarter Sessions Great Roll, Hilary 1625, ff. 63, 144 (Gilford), 180 (prison calendar), 60, 62, 63, 64, 70, 80–3, 96 (indictments) and 152 (Fisherton Anger petition).

138 PRO, ASSI 35/39/7/42, Sussex, I, 1703, 1705, cited in Cockburn, 'The Nature and Incidence of Crime in England 1559–1625', p. 58.

139 PRO, SP 14/184/2, new ff. 3–3v and, Captain Charles Price's company. Price played important political and military roles in Charles's reign. M. Fissel, 'Scottish War and English Money', in *W&G*, pp. 206–7, 222.

140 PRO, SP 14/178 and 179, a pair of boxes filled with indentures from late 1624.

141 L. Boynton, 'Billeting. The Example of the Isle of Wight', *EHR* vol. 74 no. 290 (January 1959), pp. 23–40.

142 Russell, *PEP*, p. 336; PRO, E 351/281.

143 PRO, SP 45/10, new ff. 32–33, 15 May 1625.

144 PRO, SP 16/4/160, new ff. 231–268v.

145 PRO, SP16/4/285, new ff. 68–78.

146 PRO, SP 16/4/162 new f. 272.

147 PRO, SP 16/4/160, new ff. 232v, 233, 235, 239, 242.

148 Ibid., new f. 233.

149 Ibid., new ff. 266–266v.

150 PRO, E 404/234, unfoliated, 3 May 1627; Richard Cust, *The Forced Loan and English Politics 1626–1628* (Oxford 1987), pp. 123 esp. and 56–8, 119–26.

151 PRO, SP 45/10, new f. 132, 25 January 1628.

152 Hale, ed., *CDM*, p. xciv and the *DNB* place Smythe's burial site at the church of Little Baddow. However, the pre-eminent authority on Tudor and Stuart Essex, Brian Quintrell, makes reference to Tudor 'judge Sir John Smyth' being interred in Witham church (p. 121, reference below), who I assume is the author of *Certain Discourses Military* and notorious Essex celebrity of the 1590s, discussed in this work, pp. 31, 91–4, 110, 283, 285–8.

153 B. W. Quintrell, ed., *MLB* pt. 1 (Chelmsford 1993), pp. 70–80, 150–2, 157–63, 171–4, pt. 2, pp. 175–80, 185–8, 210–13; *idem*, 'Gentry Factions and the Witham Affray, 1628', *Essex Archaeology and History* third series vol. 10 (1979 for 1978), p. 125, note 2. See also Gerald Aylmer, 'St. Patrick's Day 1628 in Witham, Essex', *P&P* no. 61 (November 1973), pp. 139–48.

154 PRO, SP 16/6/38, f. 56, LL the Earl of Sussex to PC.

155 PRO, SP 16/66/32, f. 41, 6 June 1627.

156 See Chapter 11, pp. 266–8.

157 PRO, SP 16/96/39, ff. 85, 87, 88, 89v, 91–91v.

158 Ibid., f. 88v.

159 The unruly soldiers descended upon Norfolk, at that shire's expense, which is another story; see Fissel, 'Hamilton's Expedition of 1639', forthcoming, and W. Rye, ed., *State Papers relating to Musters, Beacons, Shipmoney, etc. in Norfolk, from 1626 . . .* (Norwich 1907), pp. 121–4, 132. See also PRO, SP 16/96/39, ff. 90–90v.

160 Quoted by T. G. Barnes in 'Deputies not Principals, Lieutenants not Captains. The Institutional Failure of Lieutenancy in the 1620s', in Fissel, ed., *W&G*, p. 69.

161 Chapter 3, pp. 68–76.

162 Quintrell, 'Gentry Factions', pp. 119, 122–4.

163 See notes 164 and 168 below.

164 WRO, G 22/1/206, Borough Council Records, Marlborough Borough Council, the Chamber of Borough Records, order to JPs to billet Captain Crosby's regiment, marching from Barnstaple to the Cinque Ports, 26 December 1627; Victor Stater, 'War and the Structure of Politics. The Lieutenancy and the Campaign of 1628', in Fissel, ed., *W&G*, p. 90.

165 PRO, SP 16/85/22, f. 32, 22 November 1627; SP 16/85/94, ff. 156v–157, and SP 16/85/95, ff. 158–158v, lists of sick and wounded. The final total of disembarked common soldiers came to 2,989 (f. 157).

166 PRO, E 351/288, f. 5v, when Felton was billeted in Devon in the winter of 1625–6: 'John Felton, Leiuetenante to Capten Lee for money owinge him to John Laynge by a note under his hand 21s', Sir George Chudleigh's declared account; Barnes in Fissel, ed., *W&G*, pp. 82–3, 86; Victor Treadwell, *Buckingham and Ireland 1616–1628* (Bodmin 1998), pp. 294–5.

167 PRO, SP 45/10, new f. 142.

168 Barnes and Stater in Fissel, ed., *W&G*, pp. 58–109; WRO, G22/1/206, Council Chamber of the Borough Records.

169 F. Grose, *Military Antiquities* vol. 2, appendix 8, pp. 30–1, 7 December 1627.

170 PRO, SP 14/181/51, Ogle and St Leger to Conway, 13 January 1624/5, assuring payment in Canterbury and elsewhere for the troops embarking for the Continent under Mansfeld.

171 PRO, SP 16/418/95, though the account is based on hearsay evidence.

172 Earwaker, ed., *Constables' Accounts*, vol. 2, p. 62.

173 PRO, PC 2/54, f. 294, 30 June 1640.

174 PRO, SP 16/461/80, undated (July 1640).

175 David Scott, '"Hannibal at our Gates": Loyalists and Fifth Columnists During the Bishops' Wars – the Case of Yorkshire', *Historical Research* vol. 70 no. 173 (October 1997), pp. 274–5.

176 S. R. Gardiner, *Constitutional Documents of the Puritan Revolution*, 3rd edn (Oxford 1906), pp. 242–5; Russell, *FBM*, pp. 417, 434–5, 464–72, 475–84, 505–13.

5 ELIZABETHAN WARFARE IN THE NORTH, 1560–73

1 The years 1557–72 saw the sharpest decline in Tudor military capability, Italian reports in *CSP Venetian* vol. 6 pt. 2 (1556–1557), Rawdon Brown, ed. (London 1881), pp. 1046–51.

2 Cruickshank, *EA*, pp. 201, 211.

3 On this strategy, especially the latter two points, see Sadler's and Croft's letter to the Earl of Arran and Lord James in *The State Papers and Letters of Sir Ralph Sadler . . .*, A. Clifford, ed. (Edinburgh 1809) vol. 1, p. 626, no. 166, 6 December 1559.

4 Gloriana's expressed wish '. . . to have that matter of Scotlande accorded, rather by communication, than by force of bloodshede' characterised the Elizabethan strategic approach even if on occasion strategy slipped from her grasp, as in the

Netherlands. Should bloodshed occur, the Queen did her best to direct England's involvement, hence the war's intensity. The Queen to Norfolk, undated but probably early April 1560, in *Sadler Papers*, vol. 1, pp. 719–21, no. 236.

5 J. Collier, ed., *Egerton Papers*, Camden Society old series, vol. 12 (London 1840), pp. 32–3, by an unknown courtier, 12 January 1559/60.

6 PRO, Exchequer of Receipt, E 351/226, declared account of Sir Valentine Browne, ff. 2–2v.

7 Haynes, ed., *SP* vol. 1, pp. 217–18, 30 December 1559; *HMC Salisbury*, Hatfield MSS, vol. 1 (1883), p. 160, no. 586, dated 29 December.

8 To Cecil, 10 January 1559/60, in Haynes, ed., *SP* vol. 1, p. 220; Joseph Stevenson, ed., *Calendar of State Papers, Foreign Series, of the Reign of Elizabeth, 1559–1560* (London 1865, reprinted Nendeln, Liechtenstein 1966), p. 277; *HMC Salisbury* vol. 1, p. 167, no. 592.

9 BL, Harleian MS 540, f. 72, John Stowe's account; Cruickshank, *EA*, p. 217, which errs in stating the march was 'uneventful'. Thomas Churchyard derided the French skirmishers as 'a silly band'.

10 PRO, State Papers Scotland, SP 52/3/11 I, old f. 91, marked as '24' in pencil.

11 PRO, E 351/226, ff. 3–4.

12 BL, Harleian MS 540, f. 73.

13 Hayward, *Annals*, pp. 53–65; Bain, ed., *Calendar*, vol. 1 (1547–1563), pp. 365–6, no. 788, Norfolk to Cecil, 18 April 1560. Norfolk later increased the French casualty figures – see p. 371, 21 April 1560. See also the figures on p. 372 as well as p. 371, no. 744. On April 18, from Berwick, Norfolk to Sir William Cecil reports a skirmish with the French before Leith. BL, Harleian MS 54, f. 73. Thomas Churchyard, 'The Siege of Leeth', in *Churchyard's Chips concerning Scotland*, George Chalmers, ed. (London 1817), pp. 95–7.

14 BL, Harleian MS 540, f. 73. Cruickshank and Hayward date this event later in the month. See *EA*, p. 223.

15 BL, Harleian MS 540, ff. 74–74v.

16 PRO, SP 52/3/71, Grey to Norfolk, 5 May 1560.

17 PRO, SP 52/3/74 II, f. 423, the order of assault, and SP 52/3/62 II, folio mounted horizontally, '145' at top. Bain, ed., *Calendar*, vol. 1, p. 393, no. 767 (2), written by Lord Grey's clerk, 2 May 1560.

18 Thomas Churchyard, 'The Siege of Leeth', p. 107.

19 *The History of the Most Renowned and Virtuous Princess Elizabeth Late Queen of England*, Wallace MacCaffrey, ed. (Chicago 1970), p. 49.

20 Hayward, *Annals*, pp. 53–65.

21 PRO, SP 52/3/73, ff. 571–2, 7 May 1560; Bain, ed., *Calendar* vol. 1, p. 398, no. 777; J. Thorpe, ed., *Calendar of State Papers, Scotland* vol. 1 (1509–1589) (London 1865), p. 148; J. Stevenson, ed., *Calendar of State Papers, Foreign* (1560–1561) (London 1865), p. 26, no. 46.

22 BL, Harleian MS 540, ff. 75v–76.

23 Bain, ed., *Calendar* vol. 1, p. 384, no. 753 and pp. 390–1, no. 764, dated 27 and 30 April respectively.

24 Boynton, *EM*, p. 97.

25 PRO, SP 12/3/15, to Sir William Cecil, 6 March [1560].

26 PRO, SP 52/3/74 I., old f. 417.

27 PRO, SP 52/3/75, item 8, folio marked '193' at bottom; *HMC Salisbury* vol. 1, p. 219, no. 699, Norfolk to Cecil, 8 May 1560. See also Cruickshank's discussion of numbers in *EA*, pp. 220, 227–8.

28 Loades, *TN*, pp. 210–13.

29 Bain, ed., *Calendar* vol. 1, p. 308, no. 639, Wynter to Norfolk, 31 January 1560. 'Send by captain Southwick the bearer, 700l., without which we cannot have it,

for relief from Holy Island cannot be expected, and Fife, from Stirling to within 10 miles of St Andrews, is totally wasted by the French. As we lack men, it might please your grace to send us 300 hackbutters and captains. Also money for our men, were it but for one month's wages.'

30 Cruickshank, *EA*, pp. 214–17.

31 *Sadler Papers* vol. 1, p. 715, no. 233, 31 March 1560.

32 Ibid., p. 646, to Cecil, 19 December 1559.

33 PRO, E 351/226, ff. 1v, 12v. The army itself received only £91,000, the balance of the £133,000 going to the Berwick garrison, marine causes, etc.

34 Bain, ed., *Calendar* vol. 1, p. 384, no. 753, Norfolk to Cecil, 27 April 1560.

35 BL, Harleian MS 540, f. 74; PRO, E 351/226, f. 9, entry under Edward Stevenson of Yarmouth.

36 PRO, E 351/226, ff. 4–6Av, 9v, and Valentine Browne's instructions from the Queen, in Haynes, ed., *SP* vol. 1, p. 217.

37 Cruickshank, *EA*, p. 210.

38 See below, pp. 162, 164, 166. A manuscript copy of Thomas Churchyard's 'Scole of warre called the Siege of Leith' can be found in BL, Cotton MS Caligula MS B.V, which was Lord Burghley's personal copy, possibly in Churchyard's own handwriting, according to Bodleian Library, Douce MS 172, the 1817 edn of *Churchyard's Chips concerning Scotland*. The latter volume prints letters from the Lansdowne MSS of the British Library.

39 PRO, E 351/226, ff. 8–8v, at bare minimum accounting for 104 carriages, 308 carters, and 1,078 horses. More of each were added as the campaign wore on.

40 Bain, ed., *Calendar* vol. 1, pp. 400–3.

41 Francis W. Steer, 'A map illustrating the Siege of Leith, 1560', in *Proceedings of the Society of Antiquaries of Scotland*, session 1961–2, vol. 95 (1964), pp. 280–3. See also, Stuart Harris, 'The Fortifications and Siege of Leith. A Further Study of the Map of the Siege in 1560', *idem*, vol. 121 (1991), pp. 359–68.

42 PRO, E 351/226, ff. 4–6Av.

43 Cruickshank, *EA*, pp. 227–8.

44 PRO, SP 52/3/76, old f. 437 (also marked as '115' at top and '195' at bottom), Norfolk to Cecil, 8 May 1560, from Berwick. Printed in Haynes, ed., *SP*, pp. 304–5. And, SP 52/3/75, articles 4, 5, 6, and 7, folio with '193' at bottom.

45 No musters were held, hence figures are speculative. Cruickshank, *EA*, pp. 227–8.

46 According to Christopher Duffy, *Siege Warfare: the fortress in the early modern world 1494–1660* (London 1997), the *trace italienne* had not yet been introduced. Stowe twice mentions a 'bastilian', however, in BL, Harleian MS 540, ff. 74–74v.

47 PRO, SP 52/3/81, f. 453, Gower's inventory, which discloses 220 bows, 234 (sheaths?) of arrows, no black bills and 30 hedging bills, taken within forty-eight hours of the assault; while the commanders were lamenting that their 'stores of bows, bills and arrows was [*sic*] utterly destitute'. SP 52/3/75, item 8 and SP 52/3/74 I, 'our store of sheaf arrowes wholly spent'.

48 The Earls of Bedford and Warwick were also active in the Queen's service, the latter taking the field with a sizeable army. Lord Darcy showed greater discretion than had his grandfather, and the Earl of Derby (of that pivotal Stanley stock) honoured his ancestor by adhering to the Tudor standard in spite of his religious sentiments. These are only a few examples, but the principle held for the peerage at large. See the sampling of letters in *Sadler Papers* vol. 2, pp. 303–24.

49 PRO, SP 15/15/106, 'articles towchinge the affaires and preparacion againste the Rebells in the North 1569', f. 189, 18 December.

50 David Scott kindly advised upon place names and geography. The use of contemporary, rather than modern, spellings in some cases is the author's responsibility of course.

51 See the summary in *CSPD 1547–1580* (London 1856), pp. 335–6. The certificates are located in the muster collections classified as PRO, SP 12/62, items 8, 9, 10, 11 and SP 12/63, items 7 and 8.

52 PRO, SP 15/15/20, f. 34, 13 November 1569, to the Queen and PC. The transcription of the size of the levy in the *CSPD Addenda* has mistakenly been given as 1,500 men, most likely because one minim is much darker than the other on f. 34 of the original manuscript.

53 PRO, SP 15/15/30, f. 55, Sussex and members of the Council of the North to the Queen, 20 November 1569.

54 Ibid., ff. 55–55v, and PRO, SP 15/15/32, f. 60, 20 November, to Cecil.

55 Browne's account is PRO, E 351/229, ff. 1–15. Sussex's request is PRO, SP 15/15/32, f. 60.

56 Sir Cuthbert Sharp, ed., *Memorials of the Rebellion of 1569* (London 1840) pp. 57–8; PRO, SP 15/15/44, f. 79 and SP 15/15/55, f. 107.

57 Sharp, *Memorials*, p. 49, to Bowes, 18 November 1569. See also BL, Cotton MS Caligula B. IX, vol. 2, item 332, new f. 399 (lower right-hand corner).

58 PRO, SP 15/15/35, f. 63, Sadler to PC, 23 November. Once again, the troop figures rendered in the *CSPD Addenda* are inaccurate (p. 115).

59 PRO, SP 15/15/36, f. 65, 24 November, John Lord Darcy to Cecil.

60 PRO, SP 15/15/37, f. 68, John Vaughan to Robert Owenson, 24 November; SP 15/15/44, f. 79v, Sussex, Hunsdon, and Sadler, 26 November, and SP 15/15/45, f. 81v.

61 PRO, SP 15/15/48, f. 86, to Cecil, 26 November.

62 PRO, SP 12/59/23 and 24, memoranda of 19 and 20 November, ff. 113 and 114; see SP 12/59/55, especially the map on f. 184v.

63 See Chapter 6.

64 PRO, SP 12/59/65, f. 212.

65 PRO, SP 12/59 pt. II, ff. 216–217v.

66 PRO, SP 15/15/49, f. 87, Hunsdon to Cecil, 26 November.

67 PRO, SP15/15/46, f. 83v, Sadler to the Queen, 26 November.

68 PRO, SP 15/15/51, f. 90: 'if we may halve [have] one thowsand horsemen 500 pikes armed, and 500 shott owt of those parts [the South] with this power we halve here allredy: we thinke the somme sufficient to fyght with the rebells'. See also SP 15/15/54, f. 105, Sadler to Cecil, 30 November; SP 15/15/55, f. 107, Hunsdon to Cecil, 30 November; SP 15/15/65, f. 119v; and SP 15/15/66, f. 121, Sadler to Cecil, 2 December.

69 PRO, SP 15/15/65, f. 119v.

70 PRO, SP 15/15/51 IV, f. 97, 28 November.

71 PRO, SP 15/15/51 IV, f. 97 and SP 15/15/52, f. 100, both of 28 November; A. Fletcher, *Tudor Rebellions* 2nd edn (London 1979), pp. 95–6.

72 *HMC Salisbury* vol. 1, part I (1883), p. 450, item 1438, G. A. to John Marsh, Governor of the Company of Merchants, 8 December 1569.

73 PRO, E 351/227, ff. 1, 4v–5, 7, account of Sir Ralph Sadler, Captain Raphe Merker commanded the firearms specialists on horseback (f.5). The money, 'a masse of Treasoure' was transferred to Sadler from 'Edwarde Eglenby of Warwickeshire'. The Queen noted that 'theis extraordinarye Chardge' had been 'taken up intereste of our citizens of London' (f. 7).

74 See Chapter 3, pp. 58–60, and the graph depicting the rating of the clergy and their corresponding arms assessment printed on pp. 347–9 in *Documentary Annals of the Reformed Church of England. Being a collection of Injunctions, Declarations, Orders, Articles of Inquiry etc.*, Edward Cordwell, ed. (Oxford 1844), letter from the Archbishop of Canterbury to the Bishop of London, 6 May 1569.

75 PRO, SP 12/60/4, f. 15, memorandum of December 1569.

76 BL, Harleian MS 6990, f. 91, proclamation dated 21 December 1569.

77 Bodleian Library, Arch.G.c.6, Elizabethan proclamations, ff. 132–3 (Sussex's of 28 November 1569) and f. 130, Elizabeth's of 24 November); R. R. Reid, 'The Rebellion of the Earls, 1569', *TRHS*, new series, vol. 20 (1906), pp. 177–182, 194, 196, 200–3.

78 Bodleian Library, Arch. G. c. 6, Elizabethan proclamations, ff. 130–1, 24 November.

79 *To the Quenes Maiesties poore decived subiectes of the North Countrey, drawen into rebellion by the Earles of Northumberland and Westmerland*, printed in a Norton anthology by John Daye (London 1570), pp. Aii, Bviii, and Diii. Norton's writing often elaborated upon this theme, 'that a state knit in unity doth continue strong against all force, but being divided is easily destroyed' (*DNB*). The genuine fear of foreign invasion, grounded in the English strategic predicament, was expressed through popular ballads, such as 'An answere to the Proclamation of the Rebels of the North, 1569', composed by W. Seres, printed in *Newcastle Tracts VI, Biographical II* (Newcastle-upon-Tyne 1843), no. 7, pp. i-27. For the actual contents of the royal arsenal, see PRO, E 101/532/3, 'The Accopte of delyveries and issues of all kyndes of Ordnance shott poudre and stuffe . . .'

80 *Sadler Papers* vol. 2, no. 28, p. 55, Sadler to Cecil, 6 December 1569. Sadler's verdict is backed by Thomas Cecil, who opined that '[I]f these Yorkshire men be not backid with a stronger army of assured men frome the Sowthe, which maye allwayes commaunde them, they will fight butt with loose hartes'. PRO, SP 15/15/70, f. 127.

81 *Sadler Papers* vol. 2, p. 67, no. 24, Sadler to Cecil, 15 December 1569; PRO, SP 15/15/71, new f. 128, Darcy to the Council, 2 December 1569.

82 Sharp, *Memorials*, pp. 84–95; BL, Cotton MS Caligula B. IX, vol. 2, no. 333, f. 400; no. 355, ff. 429–30; no. 340, f. 407; no. 361, f. 439. The latter manuscript, 'Transacta Inter Angelicam et Scotiam 1556–1570', was rebound and refoliated in 1951. To cross-reference with Sharp's *Memorials*, the old foliation is used from this point onward.

83 See Warwick's reminder that even the relief force was short of arms and food. PRO, SP 12/60/6, ff. 19v–20.

84 PRO, SP 12/60/9, ff. 26–26v; Boynton, *EM*, p. 63.

85 BL, Harleian MS 6990, item 43, ff. 89–89v; item 44, ff. 90–90v; item 45, ff. 91–92v two proclamations and one declaration by the rebel Earls. The proclamation on ff. 90–90v is printed in Sharp, *Memorials*, p. 42 and in Fletcher, *Tudor Rebellions*, p. 150. The pertinent documents are: Proclamation of the Earls of Northumberland and Westmorland to the Earl of Derby determining to resist force by force, 28 November 1569. Declaration of the Earls of Northumberland and Westmorland for taking up arms for restoring the popish religion, summoning all persons from 16 to 60 years of age; Proclamation of the Earls, requiring the Bishop of Durham's tenants to bring in their rents, 21 December 1569 by which the earls 'do wyll and commaunde in the quenes maiestie name, all and everie Tennaunts, belonginge to the layte supposed Bisshop of Duresme, that they make readye all suche rents as were due at Martynmas last, so as they maybe undelaydlye payd in the accustomed plaice within the Exchequer of Duresme, before Satterdaye next, as they wyll answere to the contrarie at ther perille . . .' PRO, SP 15/15/73, f. 130, Sir Francis Leek to the Council, 3 December 1569; *Sadler Papers* vol. 2, pp. 62–5, no. 22, Robert Constable to Sadler, 14 December 1569.

86 David Scott kindly shared his knowledge of northern geography. A reading of Allen Mawer's *The Place-Names of Northumberland and Durham* (Cambridge 1920), p. 157, would suggest the 'Percy Bridge' mentioned in the original manuscripts is Piercebridge, County Durham. Dr Scott supplied this reference.

86a PRO, SP 15/15/73, f. 130, Sir Francis Leek to the Council, 3 December 1569; *Sadler Papers* vol. 2, p. 333, Robert Constable to Sadler, 14 December 1569.

87 BL, Cotton MS Caligula B. IX, vol. 2, no. 349, ff. 423–423v; Sharp, *Memorials*, p. 19; Bowes to Sussex, 12 November 1569; the original is BL, with a copy in the Bowes manuscript no. 4. Appendix in Sharp, pp. 409–13; his account of the surrender is on p. 100.

88 BL, Cotton MS Caligula B. IX, vol. 2, no. 342, ff. 410–410v; copy in the Bowes MSS, vol. 2, no. 5, printed in Sharp, *Memorials*, pp. 29–30, to Sussex, 15 November 1569.

89 BL, Cotton MS Caligula B. IX, vol. 2, nos. 341, 342, ff. 408, 410–410v; and a copy in the Bowes MSS vol. 2, p. 45; printed in Sharp, *Memorials*, p. 40.

90 See Sharp, *Memorials*, appendix, p. 413.

91 BL, Cotton MS Caligula B. IX, vol. 2, no. 353, ff. 427–428v; Bowes's copy is no. 6 in vol. 2, at Streatham, printed in Sharp, *Memorials*, p. 47, 17 November 1569.

92 Sharp, *Memorials*, p. 54. See the graph of the 'watch and ward' at Barnard Castle, probably composed just before reinforcements from the west entered the stronghold. The listing of handfuls of men under sponsors (including Bowes's mother) demonstrates the personal and highly decentralised process of mobilisation (p. 53). See also the graph of horsemen quartered there on 23 November (p. 61).

93 PRO, SP 15/15/51 I, new ff. 92–92v, from Alnwick, 25 November.

94 BL, Cotton MS Caligula B. IX, vol. 2, item 358, ff. 436–7, the original, with a copy in the Bowes MSS, vol. 2, p. 10, printed in Sharp, *Memorials*, pp. 78, 80.

95 Sharp, *Memorials*, p. 83, Sadler to Cecil, 30 November. See also Sadler's letter of 2 December, where he is more assured the rebels 'wilbe doing with sir G. Bowes at Barney Castle . . .' *Sadler Papers* vol. 2, p. 52, no. 15.

96 PRO, SP 12/60/24, f. 75, 7 December; SP 12/60/34, f. 98, 13 December.

97 PRO SP 15/15/87, new ff. 161–161v, 11 December, to Cecil.

98 Sharp, *Memorials*, p. 100, 14 December 1569.

99 PRO, SP 15/15/88, f. 163, Sussex, Hunsdon and Sadler to PC, 12 December; Sharp, *Memorials*, pp. 95–8; SP 15/15/91, new ff. 168–168v, Bowes to Cecil, 14 December.

100 Sharp, *Memorials*, pp. 107–9, Sussex to Cecil, letters of 17 and 19 December.

101 PRO, SP 15/15/133 I, f. 232, army treasurer Robert Carr to Warwick and Clynton, 28 December.

102 BL, Cotton MS Caligula C. I, 'Transactions Between England and Scotland 1567–1569', item 384, f. 522v, Sir John Forster's account; Sharp, *Memorials*, pp. 218–22.

103 BL, Cotton MS, Caligula C. I, item 384, f. 522v; Sharp, *Memorials*, p. 221.

104 *Sadler Papers* vol. 2, p. 66, no. 23, 15 December 1569.

105 PRO, SP 12/67/3, ff. 4–5, estimate and declaration of Robert Carre, army treasurer, 4 March 1569/70; SP 12/67/7, William Cecil's draft, 8 March 1569/70. The same harquebusiers had been mustered in December 1569 implying that they were a standing company of militiamen.

106 For clergy, see PRO, SP 12/67/10, f. 25; 15, f. 35; 23, f. 46; for an esquire, SP 12/67/13, guaranteeing coat and conduct for the rider.

107 PRO, SP 12/67/12, f. 28; see also 11, ff. 26–7; 30, f. 61; 31, ff. 64–64v.

108 PRO, SP 12/67/26 I, ff. 54–6.

109 PRO, SP 12/67/26, ff. 52–3.

110 Bodleian Library, Arch. G. c. 6, Elizabethan proclamations, ff. 138–9.

111 'The Rode made by Syr VVilliam Druery . . .', in Thomas Churchyard, *The First Part of Churchyardes Chippes . . .* (London 1578), pp. 38v–45v.

112 *Regulations To Be Observed by the English Army Marching to Besiege Edinburgh Castle* (Edinburgh 1573); BL, Cotton MS, Caligula C. IV, old f. 64; W. Boyd, ed., *Calendar*

of the State Papers Relating to Scotland vol. 4 (1571–1574) (London 1905), p. 551, no. 629.

113 Bodleian Library, Rawlinson MS A 235/2, ff. 69–94.

114 BL, Cotton MS Caligula C. IV, f. 93, to Burghley, 13 May 1573.

115 Ibid., f. 87v.

116 PRO, SP 52/25/46, old ff. 233–233v. Henry Killigrew to Burghley and Leicester.

117 BL, Cotton MS Caligula. C. IV, f. 100v, 28 May.

118 Boyd, ed., *Calendar of the State Papers Relating to Scotland* vol. 4, pp. 552, 558, 564, 567–9, 571.

119 BL, Cotton MS Caligula C. III, new f. 503, 3 May 1573.

120 BL, Lansdowne MS 1218, old ff. 125–52/ new ff. 113–140v, discussed pp. 177–8.

6 ELIZABETHAN WARFARE IN THE NETHERLANDS, 1572–92

1 On Le Havre/Newhaven, see Chapter 4, pp. 85–7; on Scotland in 1560, Chapter 5, pp. 114–23.

2 David Trim, 'The "Foundation-Stone of the British Army"? The Normandy Campaign of 1562', *JSAHR* vol. 77 no. 310 (Summer 1999), pp. 74–81; *idem*, 'The "Secret War" of Elizabeth I. England and the Huguenots during the early Wars of Religion, 1562–77', *Proceedings of the Huguenot Society* vol. 27 no. 2 (1999), pp. 189–99.

3 *Calendar of State Papers, Foreign Series, of the Reign of Elizabeth, 1572–1574*, vol 10, A. J. Crosby, ed. (London 1876, reprinted Nendeln, Liechtenstein 1966), p. 98, no. 324; Davies, ed., *ALC*, pp. x–xi, 57.

4 John X. Evans, ed., *The Works of Sir Roger Williams* (Oxford 1972), p. xv.

5 The phrase 'push of pike' is contemporary and refers to the hand-to-hand combat that resulted when infantry formations engaged, pikes levelled at their adversaries.

6 Williams' *Actions of the Low Countries* is the most accessible primary source, with versions in the *Somers Tracts*, the Davies 1964 edition, and the thoroughly anno-tated Evans 1972 edition. The events of the early 1570s are described in Davies, ed., *ALC*, pp. x–xiv, 57–90 and Evans, ed., *The Works of Sir Roger Williams*, pp. xiii–xv.

7 BL, Lansdowne MS 1218, old ff. 125–52/new ff. 113–40v. This collection's title, written upon a medieval parchment cover, is 'The Booke of the Captaines Livetenauntes and other officers at the Warres'. It is discussed below, at the end of this chapter. See also Simon Adams, 'A Puritan Crusade? The Composition of the Earl of Leicester's Expedition to the Netherlands, 1585–1586', in Paul Hoftijzer, ed., *The Dutch in Crisis, 1585–1588* (Leiden 1988), p. 11.

8 For a Low Countries odyssey, see for example Nicholas Brockman, who had became a lieutenant by the 1590s. 'His first enterraunce into arms was under Sir Thomas Morgan at his firste goeing to Flushinge'. He became corporal under Captain Bowsser, and then signed on successively with Sir Humphrey Gilbert, Sir John Norris, and upwards to the lieutenancy he won in Flanders. Surviving several wounds, he finished off his career on the Earl of Essex's campaign in Normandy. BL, Lansdowne MS 1218, new f. 123v/old f. 135v. See Lieutenant John Lewis (new f. 125v/old f. 137v) for an equally fascinating Low Countries tour of duty.

9 *CSP Foreign* (1572–1574) vol. 10, pp. 155–6, no. 491, 20 July 1572; Duncan Caldecott-Baird, *The Expedition into Holland 1572–1574* (London 1976), pp. 5, 15–16; Davies, ed., *ALC*, pp. xii, 66–70; BL Lansdowne MS 155, new ff. 130v–131v/old ff. 127v–128v; by mid-July 1572, when he took Sluys, Gilbert's Englishmen numbered 1,200, according to *CSP Foreign* (1572–1574) vol. 10, p. 150, no. 478.

10 See Evans's comments in his edition of *ALC*, pp. xiv–xv, though he says little about these encounters. Also, Caldecott-Baird, *The Expedition into Holland*, p. 21.

11 Davies, ed., *ALC*, p. 74; Caldecott-Baird, *The Expedition into Holland*, p. 22.

12 Oman, *AWSC*, p. 546; Davies, ed., *ALC*, pp. 78–9; C. Markham, (Boston, Mass. 1888), *The Fighting Veres*, pp. 46–8.

13 Markham, *Fighting Veres* (New York 1888), p. 48; the predicament of the English garrison at Valkenburg (though apparently not mentioned by name) and the ensuing siege of Leiden is discussed by E. Van Meteren, *A True Discourse Historicall* (London 1602).

14 Personal communication regarding Trim's research. See also R. Fruin, *The Siege and Relief of Leyden in 1574* (The Hague 1927).

15 David Trim, 'Fighting "Jacobs's Warres". English and Welsh Mercenaries in the European Wars of Religion. France and the Netherlands, 1562–1610' (Ph.D. thesis, University of London, 2001), chapter four; *SJN*, Nolan, pp. 33–6.

16 Nolan, *SJN*, pp. 33–66.

17 For Elizabeth's European strategy, see Bodleian Library, St. Amand MS 8, letter no. 5, f. 67, Walsingham to Sir John Norris, 12 May 1585. On the ideological and strategic interplay, see also Charles Wilson, *Queen Elizabeth and the Revolt of the Netherlands* (Berkeley, Calif. 1970), pp. 1–20, 123–36.

18 Bodleian Library, Ashmole MS 816, unfoliated partial sheet at the end of the volume, marked '18' in the corner.

19 Marjon Poort, 'English Garrisons in the United Provinces, 1585–1616', in Paul Hoftijzer, ed., *The Dutch in Crisis, 1585–1588*, pp. 71–83.

20 Bodleian Library, St. Amand MS 8, letter no. 1, f. 59; see the analysis of Simon Adams in 'The Protestant Cause: Religious Alliance with the West European Calvinist Communities as a Political Issue in England, 1585–1630', (D.Phil. thesis University of Oxford 1973, p. 51.

21 See above, pp. 114–36.

22 J. Bruce, ed., *Correspondence of Robert Dudley, Earl of Leycester*, Camden Society, vol. 27, pp. 337–9, to Secretary Walsingham, 8 July 1586.

23 J. R. Hale, ed., *The Art of War and Renaissance England* (Washington, DC 1979), pp. 10–11. The author, Christopher Ocland, could not be accused of warmongering, for he praised 'the peaceable and quiet state of England' under the Queen's rule. Ocland, by ending his excursus at 1558, avoided comment on her campaigns at Le Havre, Leith, and against the northern rebels. Markham, *Fighting Veres*, pp. 84–91.

24 Bruce, ed., *Leycester Correspondence*, p. 178, transcript of BL, Cotton MS Galba C. VIII, f. 63, 20 March 1585/6.

25 Thomas Digges, *A Briefe Report of the Militarie Services done in the Low Covntries, by the Erle of Leicester* (London 1587) pp. B1 recto–B1 verso; Bruce, ed., *Leycester Correspondence*, pp. 188–9, transcribing BL, Harleian MS 285, f. 234.

26 Digges, *Briefe Report*, p. B1 verso.

27 Bruce, ed., *Leycester Correspondence*, pp. 218–19, transcription from Ouvry MSS.

28 Digges, *Briefe Report*, p. B2 recto.

29 Bruce, ed., *Leycester Correspondence*, pp. 257, 265, 270, 280, 284 (esp footnote), 287, and 291.

30 Leicester's letter of 24 or 25 September 1586, printed in G. F. Beltz, 'Memorials of the Last Achievement, Illness, and Death of Sir Phillip Sydney', *Archeologia* vol. 28 (1840), pp. 27–31. For the English charge, casualties, etc., see p. 53 of A. Collins, ed., *Letters and Memorials of State* [Sydney Papers] vol. 1 (London 1746); see also John Stowe, *Annales* (London 1631), p. 738.

31 Digges, *Briefe Report*, p. D1; see also *Archaeologia* above, note 30; Stowe's *Annales*, p. 737.

32 In other words, without plate armour to protect his thighs.

33 On the battle, see notes 30 and 31, above. Parma was wounded spying out the Caudebec defences, according to *L&A* vol. 3 (June 1591–April 1592) (London 1980), p. 262, no. 402 (F624, F628).

34 BL, Harleian MS 287, ff. 157–159v.

35 See Maurice Kiffin's complaint in *L&A* vol. 3 (June 1591–April 1592), p. 211, no. 290 (F276).

36 See John Lynn's 1991 comment, quoted in J. Nolan, 'The Militarization of the Elizabethan State', in *Journal of Military History* vol. 58 no. 3 (July 1994), p. 393, note 11, and B. Downing, *The Military Revolution and Political Change* (Princeton, NJ 1992), pp. xi, 3, 10, 14, 16, etc. Whether Downing's assumptions about the 'relatively light warfare of England' lead him to oversimplify the case of the one nation he permits anomalous status is a matter which this book, hopefully, rebuts.

37 See the advice given to the Queen in 1559–60 on the importance of the sovereign grasping the fundamentals of making war, in Chapter 5, pp. 114–15.

38 *L&A* vol. 2 (July 1590–May 1591), p. 182, no. 209 (H13, H176), Wilkes to Bodley; Tallett, *WSEME*, specifically pp. 212–15, and 193–7, 205–11.

39 BL, Harleian MS 287, f. 1v, to Walsingham from Utrecht, 24 March 1586.

40 *L&A* vol. 3 (June 1591–April 1592), p. 114, no. 66 (H108).

41 Neale, 'Elizabeth and the Netherlands, 1586–7', p. 378.

42 BL, Harleian MS 168, ff. 165–165v; Cruickshank, *EA*, pp. 153–8.

43 *DNB*.

44 Cruickshank, *EA*, p. 138.

45 Webb, *EMS*, p. 25; Cruickshank, *EA* pp. 136–9; *CSP Foreign* (January–June 1588) vol. 21 pt. 4 (London 1931), pp. 87, 449; (July–December 1588) vol. 22, p. 109; *L&A* vol. 1 (August 1589–June 1590), pp. 166–7.

46 *L&A* vol. 1 (August 1589–June 1590), pp. 182–5, nos. 247–52.

47 See Chapter 3, and Neale, 'Elizabeth and the Netherlands, pp. 378, 380–5, 387–90. The latter author ultimately blames Leicester for mismanagement, which was true to an extent. But a modern reading of the article, especially in light of the scholarship of Simon Adams, surely reveals the problem was structural and political, not personal.

48 The problem is catalogued in excruciating detail by Bruce Wernham in the section headed 'Administration, Musters, and Accounts' in each volume of *L&A*; for example, see the list of officers and companies in Bergen-op-Zoom circa January 30, 1586/7 (?) (BL, Harleian MS 287, f. 3v). BL, Harleian MS 168, f. 107v to 109v has instructions for commissioners of musters in the Low Countries, 10 August 1587.

49 *L&A* vol. 2 (July 1590–May 1591), p. 119, no. 80 (H281, H282); vol. 3 (June 1591–April 1592), p. 158 no. 167.

50 *L&A* vol. 3 (June 1591–April 1592), p. 245, no. 367 (F523).

51 *L&A* vol. 2 (July 1590–May 1591), p. 165, no. 182 (H281) 20 December 1590. In the United Provinces muster orders were published by the Queen with the advice of the Privy Council, 'intended to reform abuses in the imprests, payments, and appareling of her troops in the Low Countries; and to take away the victualling which some governors and captains found so offensive'. Orders of 20 December 1590 were supplemented by those of 31 December 1590, *L&A* vol. 2, p. 168, no. 183, esp. article II (H298). The procedures for commissioners of musters for 1585–7, upon which the new orders rested, are BL, Harleian MS 168, ff. 107v–109v.

52 Ibid., articles III, IV, and V.

53 BL, Harleian MS 168, ff. 187–189v, circa 1589–90.

54 *L&A* vol. 3 (June 1591–April 1592), pp. 154–5, no. 159.

55 Ibid., p. 155 no. 160 (H265).

56 Ibid., pp. 155–6, nos. 161 and 162, (H268, H270, H271).

57 One calculation of the drain on the Exchequer of Receipt for auxiliary assistance to Henry IV reckons at £355,000, between Easter 31 Elizabeth (1589) and Michaelmas 39 Elizabeth (1597). The pattern follows the involvement in the Low Countries wars. And initial modes of investment of money were followed by a surge of financial commitment (£44,713 in Easter 33 Elizabeth), settling into a more modest range for the several years ensuing. *L&A* vol. 2 (July 1590–May 1591), pp. 160–1, no. 173.

58 *L&A* vol. 3 (June 1591–April 1592), p. 91, no. 12 (H38); Davies, ed., *ALC*, pp. xiii–xv, 112–13; Evans, ed., *BDW*, p. xvii.

59 BL, Lansdowne MS 66, f. 172, item no. 62.

60 Hale, *WSRE*, pp. 127–52; Oman, *AWSC*, p. 561.

61 Davies, ed., *ALC*, p. xx; *CSP Foreign* (August 1584–August 1585) vol. 19 (London 1916), pp. 50–1, 4 September 1584, Williams to Walsingham.

7 ELIZABETHAN AND JACOBEAN ALLIED OPERATIONS ON THE CONTINENT, 1587–1622

1 The largest source is PRO, E 157/2 to E 157/16, books containing licences to go beyond the seas.

2 Davies, *ALC*, pp. xxvi–xxvii; Bodleian Library, St Amand MS 9 letter no. 1, f. 1, letter from State of Utrecht to the Queen regarding John Norris, June 1587.

3 *CSP Foreign* (April–December 1587) vol. 21 pt. 3 (London 1929), pp. 88, 96–8, 107, 109, 120, 137–41, 146–9, 159–60, 169–70, 172, 174, 184, 188, 191–2, 206–8, 235–6, 254, 287, 320, 366, 409–10, especially pp. 107, 138 and 199. C. Markham, *The Fighting Veres* (Boston, Mass, 1888), pp. 100–11.

4 BL, Royal/King's MS 265, new ff. 207–214/old ff. 407–21.

5 *L&A* vol. 2 (July 1590–May 1591), p. 91, no. 8 (H99) and p. 93, no. 14 (H191).

6 Ibid., p. 94, no. 15 (H191; H194; H201; H202; H206; H207).

7 Ibid., p. 94, no. 6 (H330).

8 Ibid., pp. 97–8, no. 24 (H357; H370).

9 Ibid., p. 99, no. 26 (H404; H417; H426).

10 BL, Royal/King's MS 265, new ff. 212–212v/old ff. 417–8; *L&A* vol. 2 (July 1590–May 1591), pp. 105–6, no. 44 (H514; H522; H524).

11 Bodleian Library, Tanner MS 79, no. 30, new f. 67, recredential letter.

12 Bodleian Library, Rawlinson MS C 836, 'A Discourse by Sir John Norris Concerning the Lowe Countreys. 1588', f. 1v.

13 Ibid., ff. 1, 8v; see also *CSP Foreign* (April–December 1587) vol. 21 pt. 3, pp. 291–4, calendaring a discourse by Norris directed to the Queen, amongst the State Papers Holland in the PRO. Dated August 1587, it resembles a text described by Thomas Tanner in *Bibliotheca Britannica* which he dated as written in 1587. Hence the date 1588 in the handwritten title of Rawlinson MS C 836 is probably incorrect. The figures given for Elizabeth's expenditures, specifically Norris's calculation of £812,000, are puzzling. As it appears in both discourses, C 836 and SP Holland, it is probably a contemporary mistranscription. In reviewing the *CSP Foreign* for the latter half of 1587 in the *EHR* vol. 45 no. 179, in July 1930, Sir John Neale pronounced the figure 'clearly wrong', though implicitly he thought it an error on the part of the modern editors and remained unaware of the possible connection with Rawlinson MS C 836. R. B. Wernham's estimates for 1586 and 1587 put England's Low Countries War costs at £313,000 (*1589*, p. xii). But the error is more complicated than simply that a near-contemporary

wrote '8' for '3' or something of that order. Norris does actually cite a £500,000 expenditure in his discourse. The logical conclusion is that Norris himself got the figures wrong, perhaps on purpose.

14 *CSPD Elizabeth, Addenda* 1580–1625 vol. 12 (London 1872), p. 238, nos. 72–3.

15 See the tables on pp. 84–7 of F. C. Dietz, 'The Exchequer in Elizabeth's Reign', *Smith College Studies in History* vol. 8 no. 2 (January 1923) (Northampton, Mass.) and Wernham's commentary in *ATA*, pp. 17, 77, and Wernham, ed., *1589*, pp. xii–xiii.

16 For the pessimistic view, see Geoffrey Parker, 'If the Armada Had Landed', *History* vol. 61 (1976), pp. 358–68; for a rosier picture, Nolan, *SJN*, pp. 108–38.

17 Wernham, ed., *1589*, p. xxxiii.

18 Ibid., pp. xxxvii–xli, 145–50. The participation of so many Low Countries veterans, where sieges were ubiquitous, makes Ashley's remark questionable in its accuracy. For example, the presence of Michael Bennet, Robert Hollingworthe, Phillip Darnell, John Probart, Barret Saxton, William Mundaye, Francis Daye, John Asheley and others proves that experienced lieutenants, ensigns and sergeants participated in the Portugal campaign. BL, Lansdowne MS 1218, new f. 128/old f. 140 – new f. 130/old f. 147 – new f. 136/old f. 149.

19 Bodleian Library, Tanner MS 79, f. 48, 'Advertisementes from the Groyne the 7 Maii 1589'.

20 Anthony Wingfield, *A True Coppie of a Discourse written by a Gentleman, employed in the late Voyage of Spaine and Portingale; Sent to his particular friend, and by him published for the better satisfaction of all such, as having been seduced by partiall report, have entred into conceipts tending to the discredit of the enterprise and Actors of the same* (London 1589), pp. 20/D2v–21/D3. This book was withdrawn almost immediately upon its publication. Wingfield did not feature his name on the title page and referred to himself in the third person throughout the text. See Wernham's comment in *1589*, p. lxiii.

21 Bodleian Library, Tanner MS 79, f. 48; Wernham, ed., *1589*, pp. xli, 144, 148, 230, 243. The best account is that of Wingfield, *A True Coppie*, pp. 23/D5–25/E. Several accounts relate that Captain Cooper (or Cowper), one of the Corporals of the Field, was among the fallen, suggesting that non-commissioned officers may have experienced a high casualty rate as they followed their superiors in risking themselves at the more dangerous points in battle.

22 Bodleian Library, Tanner MS 79, f. 48v, 'Advertisementes from Castcays in the River of Lisbone the 5 of June 1589'; see also f. 51.

23 Wernham, ed., *1589*, pp. xlvii, 193.

24 Wernham, *ATA*, pp. 117–18.

25 Bodleian Library, Tanner MS 79, ff. 48v, 51; Wingfield, *A True Coppie*, pp. 30/E3v–33/F1.

26 See the letters of Williams and Norris printed Wernham, *1589*, pp. 177–8; Wingfield, *A True Coppie*, pp. 16/C4v–17/D1, a grocery list of sorts.

27 Davies, *ALC*, p. xxxiii.

28 *A Short and True Discourse for satisfying all those who not knowing the truth, speake indiscreetly of hir most excellent Majestie, of the Lord Willughby Gouernour of hir Majesties succours in the united Provinces of the Low countries, and of all the English nation; by occasion of a strange placcat of the 17. of April 1589* . . . (London? 1589), Short Title Catalogue 7597. A reading of *Historical Manuscripts Commission, Report on the Manuscripts of the Earl of Ancaster* (Dublin 1907) suggests a date of May 1589 for the above pamphlet, based on a related manuscript, pp. 282–3, and also pp. 280–1, 284–8. Maurice of Nassau wrote directly to the Queen to calm the furore over the mutiny: Bodleian Library, Add. MS D 109 (Fortescue MSS), ff. 61–2, 7/17 May 1589; *CSP Foreign* (January–July 1589) vol. 23, R. B. Wernham, ed. (London 1950), p. 159, 12/22 March 1589.

29 *HMC Ancaster*, pp. 288–9, Stafford to Willoughby, 26 September 1589; Cruickshank, *EA* (2nd edn), pp. 244–5.
30 PRO, SP 12/226/13, ff. 15–15v, the Queen to LLs, circa 9 September.
31 PRO, SP 12/226/33, f. 39, 13 September.
32 *L&A* vol. 1 (August 1589–June 1590), p. 321, no. 34 (F81).
33 BL, Lansdowne MS 1218, new f. 133/old f. 146. After demobilisation of the expeditionary force, Ensign Brewerton again served in Ireland.
34 PRO, SP 12/226/22, ff. 25–26, Burghley's notes on pay and victualling; SP 12/226/29, f. 33, similarly detailed notes; SP 12/226/36, ff. 45–45v, Walsingham's memorials and calculations on pay, transportation and victuals; SP 12/226/42, ff. 56–7, Burghley's notations on pay and victuals, 18 September.
35 PRO, SP 12/226/23, f. 27; *L&A* vol. 1 (August 1589–1590), p. 321, no. 533 (H99); for all his meticulous calculation, the Lord Treasurer expressed exasperation when monitoring the accounting of the Treasurer-at-Wars, Mr Fludd, who by December 1589 still had 'never sent any declaration of his accounts'. Willoughby's 'statement' makes clear that by 1590 there was still no adequate system for reckoning the charges of English armies in the field: *HMC Ancaster*, pp. 298, 302.
36 Deitz, 'The Exchequer in Elizabeth's Reign', *Smith College Studies in History* vol. 8 no. 2 (January 1923), pp. 100–1.
37 J. S. Nolan, 'The Militarization of the Elizabethan State', *Journal of Military History* vol. 58 (July 1994), pp. 391–420.
38 *HMC Salisbury* vol. 3 (London 1889), p. 420, no. 893, Wilsford to PC, June 1589; Simon Adams, 'The Protestant Cause. Religious Alliance with the West European Calvinist Communities as a Political Issue in England, 1585–1630', D.Phil., Oxford 1973, pp. 121–2, citing BL, Lansdowne MS 43, ff. 51–2.
39 Cruickshank, *EA* (2nd edn), pp. 246, 250–1.
40 Lady Georgina Bertie, *Five Generations of a Loyal House*, pt I (London 1845) pp. 282–4, 296; *L&A* vol. 1 (August 1589–June 1590), p. 322, no. 536 (F116; NL12), no. 537 (NL12), p. 324, no. 542 (NL17; NL15), p. 325, no. 543 (NL15; NL17); Wernham, *ATA*, pp. 172–3.
41 PRO, SP 12/240/31, f. 55, notations in Burghley's hand.
42 *HMC Salisbury* vol. 4 (London 1892), p. 172.
43 *L&A* vol. 2 (July 1590–May 1591), p. 145, no. 137 (H123).
44 For a comparison of their styles consider the confrontation upon the plain of Bondi during Parma's intervention in the French civil war.
45 *L&A* vol. 2, p. 245, no. 352 (F63).
46 *L&A* vol. 3 (June 1591–April 1592), p. 264, no. 405 (F632; F636).
47 Wernham, *ATA*, p. 123.
48 *L&A* vol. 3, p. 359, no. 616 (F358) and H. Lloyd, *The Rouen Campaign 1590–1592* (Oxford 1973), p. 166.
49 *L&A* vol. 3, p. 193, no. 249 (F93; F97).
50 Ibid., p. 343, no. 579 (F241).
51 C. H. Herford, ed., *The Autobiography of Edward Lord Herbert of Cherbury* (Newton, Montgomeryshire 1928), pp. 41–2.
52 Bodleian Library, St Amand MS 9, f. 56.
53 *L&A* vol. 2 (July 1590–May 1591), p. 335, no. 555 (H488).
54 *L&A* vol. 2 (July 1590–May 1591), p. 335, nos. 554 and 555 (F381; H488). This was not the only time the presence of Sir Roger Williams halted a parley over a siege. His appearance before Chartres with 600 English disrupted negotiations between DeChatte and the besieged Catholic Leaguers.
55 Sir Roger Williams put it with characteristic bluster: 'The French King had 3,000 of the bravest horsemen in the world. With the English footmen and God's help he

would doubtless beat Parma out of the field even if outnumbered.' *L&A* vol. 2 (July 1590–May 1591), p. 304, no. 486 (F221); on English infantry at sieges, *L&A* vol. 3 (June 1591–April 1592), p. 248, no. 372 (M6; F649) and more may be found throughout *L&A*.

56 *L&A* vol. 3 (June 1591–April 1592), p. 270, no. 420 (F30; F50).

57 *L&A* vol. 3 (June 1591–April 1592), p. 94, no. 19 (H70; H71).

58 *L&A* vol. 2 (July 1590–May 1591), p. 337, no. 560 (primarily F405, secondarily F401).

59 Ibid., pp. 344–5, nos. 576, 577, 578, (F408; F409; F414; F422).

60 Ibid., p. 345, no. 579 (F416).

61 *The True Reporte of the service in Britanie. Performed lately by the Honorable Knight Sir John Norreys and other Captaines and Gentlemen souldiers before Guingend* . . . (London 1591), pp. A4v–B; Nolan, *SJN*, pp. 184–5.

62 Anon., *Aduertisements from Britany, and from the Low Countries, in September and October* (London 1591), pp. 8/C3–8v/C3v.

63 Lloyd, *Rouen*, pp. 178, 185.

64 *L&A* vol. 3 (June 1591–April 1592), p. 364, no. 630 (F432).

65 Ibid., p. 364, no. 629 (F422).

66 Lloyd, *Rouen*, p. 104.

67 Christopher Duffy, *Siege Warfare. The Fortress in the Early Modern World* (London 1979), pp. 58–66, especially the map on p. 60; G. Parker, *The Army of Flanders and the Spanish Road 1567–1659* (Cambridge 1972), pp. 3–21.

68 Although Maurice may have had as few as 4,000 foot, according to an English eye-witness: Anon., *A True discourse of the Ouerthrovve giuen to the common enemy at Turnhaut* . . . (London 1597), p. 3/Aiii

69 *The Commentaries of Sir Francis Vere* (Cambridge 1657), pp. 72–81, based upon various manuscripts, such as Bodleian Library, Rawlinson MS D 665, ff. 43–7 (incorrectly paginated) and BL, Royal/King's MS 265, new ff. 229v–232/old ff. 452–7; Harleian MS 6798, ff. 10–14v; Oman, *AWSC*, pp. 578–83. The four stages of the battle are depicted in Guillame Baudart's splendid *Second Tome dv Livre intitvle les Guerres de Nassav* (Amsterdam 1616), pp. 241, 245. Illustrated on pp. 171–2.

70 *A True discourse of the Ouerthrovve giuen to the common enemy* . . . , p. 4/Biiii.

71 How much glory should be showered upon Vere? See Edward Belleroche's comments on Nieuwpoort in *The Siege of Ostend or the New Troy 1601–1604* (London 1892), pp. 9–10, and T. J. Borman, 'Sir Francis Vere in the Netherlands, 1598–1603. A Re-evaluation of his Career as Sergeant Major General of Elizabeth I's Troops' (unpublished University of Hull Ph.D. thesis, 1997).

72 William Shute, trans., *The Triumphs of Nassau* (London 1613), p. 273.

73 Vere, *Commentaries* (1657 edn), pp. 88–9; Oman, *AWSC*, pp. 592, 594.

74 Shute, *Triumphs of Nassau*, p. 277.

75 BL, Royal/King's MS 265, new ff. 233–240v/old ff. 459–74; Vere, *Commentaries*, pp. 97, 102–3; Oman, *AWSC*, pp. 596–8.

76 Ogle's account in BL, Royal/King's MS 265, new ff. 241–3/old ff. 475–9 and Vere, *Commentaries*, p. 109. Although the 1657 edition of *The Commentaries* presents a spectacular view of the battle (between pp. 80–1), it is based on the sequence of engravings in Guillame Baudert's *Second Tome dv livre intitvle les Guerres de Nassav*, pp. 317, 319, the last of which conveys nicely the chaos of the engagement's end; *HMC Salisbury* pt. 14 (London 1923), pp. 131–4; C. H. Firth, ed., *An English Garner: Stuart Tracts 1603–1693* (New York 1964), pp. 144–65; Harleian MS 287, ff. 243–55, 259–260v; BL, Harleian MS 6798, ff. 64–69v. The battle is illustrated on pp. 175–6.

77 BL, Add. MS 48,168 (Yelverton MS 180), ff. 8v–9, 'Moneys issued at the Receipt of the Exchequer for the warres in the Lowe Countries . . .'

78 David Trim, '"Fin de siècle." The English Soldier's Experience at the End of the Sixteenth-Century', *Military and Naval History Journal* no. 10 (July 1999), pp. 1–13.

79 BL, Additional MS 46, 188, f. 25 (English reinforcements for the Dutch, September 1624), ff. 26–26v (pay for English regiments in the United Provinces, September 1624), f. 28 (the four regiments' cost), f. 29 (companies comprising Essex's regiment), f. 30 (Essex's dozen infantry companies), ff. 32, 33v (the captains), etc., all in the autumn of 1624.

80 *Articles of Peace, Entercourse, and Commerce* . . . (London 1605), pp. B4–C. Article IV (p. B26) attempted to restrict the service of vassals but failed to be enforced. PRO, E 407/7/148, 149 are contracts for payment and apparelling of the garrison troops.

81 David Trim, 'Sir Horace Vere in Holland and the Rhineland, 1610–12', *Historical Research* vol. 72 no. 179 (October 1999), pp. 334–51.

82 HEH, EL 1641, 'a true reporte of our service by lande'. Simon Healy shared a transcript.

83 See example, Steve Murdoch, 'The House of Stuart and the Scottish Professional Soldier 1618–1640. A Conflict of Nationality and Identity', in B. Taithe and T. Thornton, eds, *War. Identities in Conflict, 1300–2000* (Stroud, Gloucestershire 1998), pp. 37–56.

84 NRO, NCR, case 13a/7, 13a/12/2. 53–60, 75–75v, etc.; i.e. list of 16 June 1602.

85 NRO, NCR, case 13a/15, nos. 1–20.

86 NRO, NCR, case 10, shelf H, no. 11, figures for 1634.

87 BL, Lansdowne MS 1218, old ff. 125–52/ new ff. 113–140v.

88 WRO, Quarter Sessions Great Roll, Hilary 1639, f. 175; Quarterly Sessions Autograph Book, f. 114 (23 September 1638) and ff. 109–11 (Smythe, November–December 1632).

89 WRO, Quarter Sessions Autograph Book, ff. 85–87, 8 June, 29 April, and 25 June 1611, respectively.

90 PRO, SP 45/10, new f. 145, 27 December 1629. The old piketrailers remained overlooked by historians, too. See the comments of C. Atkinson, 'Elizabeth's Army', *JSAHR* vol. 24 no. 99 (Autumn 1946), pp. 139–40. Bruce Wernham did much to bring these men to light.

91 Trim, 'Sir Horace Vere in Holland and the Rhineland, 1610–12', in *Historical Research* vol. 72 no. 179 (October 1999), pp. 334–51, especially Trim's comments in note 79 on p. 349.

92 PRO, SP 14/119/50, old ff. 1–21 and Chapter 11, p. 256, esp. note 10.

93 BL, Harleian MS 6845, f. 127.

8 ORDNANCE AND LOGISTICS, 1511–1642

1 BL, Harleian MS 135, ff. 13v/24–14/25; M. Roberts, *The Military Revolution, 1560–1660* (Belfast 1956); Jim Bennett and Stephen Johnston, *The Geometry of War 1500–1700* (Oxford 1996), pp. 12–13.

1a BL, Harleian MS 135 f. 7v/14.

1b Ibid., f. 13/23.

2 Sir Edward Hoby's edition of Bernardino de Mendoza, *Theorique and Practise of Warre* (Middelburg 1597), f. A4 recto, cited by Webb, *EMS*, p. 181 note 38.

2a Niccolò Machiavelli, *The Art of War*, N. Wood, ed. (New York 1990), pp. 183–201, esp. p. 192.

3 Webb, *EMS*, pp. 4–16.

4 *HMC De L'Isle and Dudley* vol. 2 (London 1934), p. 521.

5 Sir Henry also served as Master of the Armoury during the 1580s and 1590s: PRO, E 101/64/11.

6 *The Practise of Fortification* (London 1589), especially pp. 35–40, where the conversion of medieval walls to the *trace italienne* is expounded.

6a *L&A* vol 4 (May 1592–June 1593), p. 120, no. 3 (H2, H3, H59).

6b C. Markham, *The Fighting Veres*, (Boston, Mass. 1888), pp. 100–90.

6c *L&A* vol. 4 (May 1592–June 1593), pp. 130–1, nos 22 (H63), 24 (H76), 34 (H207, H209), 35 (H211, H233).

7 *L&A*, pp. 146–7, nos. 51 (H280; H283) and 53 (H285).

8 See Chapter 12, pp. 31, 91–4, 110, 283, 285–8.

9 *HMC Salisbury* pt. 11 (Dublin 1906), pp. 322, 336, 338, 342, 346, 349, 353; '. . . Vere was hurt with a peece of a Canon which split . . .', A. U., *A Trve Historie of the Memorable Siege of Ostend, and what passed on either side? . . .*, Edward Grimeston, trans. (London 1604), p. 13/133; W. Dillingham, *Continuation of the Siege of Ostend, from 25 July; 1601, as far as Mar. 1602*, printed in C. H. Firth, ed., *Stuart Tracts 1603–1693* (New York 1964), p. 176.

10 BL, Harleian MS 6798, ff. 70–3; Royal/King's MS 265, new ff. 244–55v/old ff. 481–504.

11 *The History of the Wars of Flanders. Written in Italian by that Learned and Famous Cardinal Bentivoglio, translated by Henry, Earl of Monmouth* (London 1678), p. 340.

12 *HMC Salisbury* pt. 12 (Hereford 1910), p. 34, Sir Robert Cecil's assessment, 28 January 1601/2.

13 In the case of Agincourt, that sweet victory convinced the English that the occupation of France, with all its logistical challenges, was their destiny, thus ensuring a sanguinary contest for decades.

14 *A Trve Historie*, p. 162/Y1v.

15 Old style, being 16 July in the European new style; see Edward Bellaroche's *The Siege of Ostend or the New Troy 1601–1604* (London 1892), pp. 62–3.

16 *A Trve Historie*, p. 7/A4; Bellaroche, *The Siege of Ostend*, p. 62, citing SP Holland.

17 Sir Francis Vere, *The Commentaries* (Cambridge 1657), p. 118.

18 *A Trve Historie*, p. 7/A4; 13/B3; 17/C.

19 Ibid., pp. 13/B3; 15/B4; 26/Dv; 37/E3; 53/G3; for a further example see how all day the besiegers hammered the St Claire's Fort side of Ostend and could not make the slightest breach (p. 13/B3). The Sand Hill Fort proved equally formidable, when the Archduke's cannoneers 'began at the breake of day to shoote against the Bulwarke of Sand-hill, the which (after they had discharged some thousands of shot) seemed to be a wall of Yron, and they might heare the Bullets strike one against another' (p. 14/B3v). Motley discusses rates of fire and fortification on pp. 73–4 in his *History of the United Netherlands* vol. 4 (London 1861).

20 *A Trve Historie*, pp. 25/D – 26/Dv; Motley, *History* vol. 4, p. 74.

21 WRO, Quarter Sessions Autograph Book, f. 33, 1 February 1603/4.

22 *A Trve Historie*, pp. 26/Dv; 31/D4; 46/F3v–47F4; 72/I4; 75/K2; 113/P; 115/P2; 132/R2v–133/R3; 142/53v. It was reported 24 April 1603, when the Archduke had encroached substantially upon Ostend, thirty-two ships entered the harbour and only a single mariner was slain (pp. 165/Y3v–166/Y4), though of the twenty vessels entering 4 June 1603, three were indeed sunk (pp. 173/Z3). On 3 January 1604 two dozen sail went forth of Ostend with impunity (p. 190/Bb3v).

23 The episode is encapsulated in the anonymously written *Extremities Vrging the Lord Generall Sir Francis Veare to the Anti-parle with the Archduke Albertus . . . Written by an English Gentleman of verie good account from Ostend* (London 1602).

24 *Extremities*, pp. A2/3–A2v/4, A4/7–B3614, C/17–C/18; Bellaroche, *The Siege of Ostend*, pp. 29–30; *A Trve Historie*, pp. 95/M4–101/N3; Motley, *History*, vol. 4, pp. 75–85.

25 Anon., *A Breefe Declaration Of that which is happened aswell within as without Oastend sithence the vii. of Ianuarie 1602* (London 1602), p. 2/A2v.

26 *A Trve Historie*, p. 107/02; Motley, *History* vol. 4, pp. 88–90.

27 Motley, *History* vol. 4, p. 92; 'The declaration of the desparate attempt made since, by the sayde Archdukes forces, for winning of the ould Towne', appended to *Extremities*, pp. C2/19–C3v/232.

28 The London Armourers claimed, perhaps with hyperbole, that the 'armour that is here made is accompted far better than that which cometh from beyond the Seas' on 13 July 1590. BL, Lansdowne MS 63, no. 5, printed in Charles Ffoulkes, *The Armourer and his Craft* (New York 1988), p. 185.

29 *HMC Salisbury* pt. 3 (London 1889), p. 332 no. 682, a dozen cannon for Middelburg, 27 June 1588. See also *CSPD Addenda, 1580–1625*, vol. 12 (London 1872), p. 254, warrant of 16 August 1588. It is noteworthy that Elizabeth honoured her commitment to the Dutch, providing artillery to them even though her own realm now lay in great danger. Illegal export was inhibited by Crown inventories of ordnance in private hands: PRO, E 101/67/1.

30 *L&A* vol. 2 (July 1590–May 1591), pp. 178–9, no. 202 (H83; H88; H99; H100; H148; H175).

31 *The GVNNER shevving the vvhole Practise of Artillerie* (London 1628). Compare p. 52 of that work with PRO, SP 12/242/64. See also the drawings of Christopher Lad circa 1586, preserved in the Bodleian Library's Rawlinson collection and presented in modernised rendering in A. Caruana, *Tudor Artillery 1485–1603* (Bloomfield, Ont. 1992), pp. 18–36. For the survival of similar works into the Civil Wars era, see http://www.portsdown.demon.co.uk/ord.htm

32 For example, BL, Harleian MS 168, ff. 118–23.

33 PRO, SP 16/13/89.

34 Compare the sections in Colvin, ed., *KW* vol. 3 (1485–1660) pt. 1, pp. 262–77 and vol. 4 (1485–1660) pt. 2, pp. 613–64; on Berwick see Chapter 2.

35 See Chapter 2, pp. 43–7.

36 R. Allen Brown and P. E. Curnow, *Tower of London* (London 1984), pp. 31–6, 70–81. Earlier sources are: John Charlton, ed., *The Tower of London. Its Buildings and Institutions* (London 1978); *Authorised Guide to the Tower of London* (London 1924); and John Bayley, *The History and Antiquities of the Tower of London. With Memoirs of Royal and Distinguished Person, Deduced from Records, State-papers and manuscripts, and from Other and Original and Authentic Sources*, 2 vols (London 1821–5).

37 For example, PRO, E 407/59, ff. 12 (May 1602), 16–16v (October–November 1602), 20v (December 1602–January 1602/3), 28 (June–July 1603).

38 C. Russell, 'The Scottish party in English parliaments, 1640–2', *Historical Research* vol. 66 no. 159 (February 1993), p. 39, citing *CSP Venetian 1603–7*, p. 502 and Pauline Croft.

38a BL, Harleian MS 5913, f.2.

39 BL, Harleian MS 1326, f. 120.

40 Edward Tomlinson, *A History of the Minories* (London 1907), pp. 130–3; R. W. Stewart, *The English Ordnance Office 1585–1625* (Woodbridge, Suffolk 1996), pp. 52–3.

41 The 1641 description is ff. 28–28v in BL, Harleian MS 5913.

42 According to a survey in the early 1530s, 'The wall from Burbedge Tower unto the Mr. of th'Ordynance lodgyng, callede the Bryck Tower, conteynyng in lengthe 53 foote, the whiche forsayd wall parte of it to be ventyde, capyde, and crestyde, and the wall under fote pavyd with Cane stone [stone quarried in Caen, in Normandy], and also rough castede. . . . The Bryck Tower, the Maister of th'Ordynance lodging new repayrede with bryck, safe at the foundacion, a little p'ysshe to be mendyd with Cane stone and rough cast. . . . The wall from the said Bryck Tower, where the Mr. of Ordynance lyeth, unto the nexte tower which

we canot name, that stondith at the northe easte ende. . . .' Printed in Bayley, *The History and Antiquities of the Tower* vol. 1, p. x.

43 See Bayley on the Record Tower in *The History and Antiquities of the Tower* vol. 1, pp. 218–31; 235–46. See also the Martin Tower (p. 269). For Henrician survey descriptions, see Bayley's appendix to vol. 1: Bell Tower (p. viii), Beytcham (Beauchamp) Tower (p. ix), Robyn the Devyll's Tower (p. ix), Bowear's (Bowyer's) Tower (p. ix), Burgege Tower (p. x), Constable Tower (pp. x–xi), Julyus Sesar Tower (White Tower) (p. xi); the New Tower (p. xi) the wall from which extending to 'the tower of the Kyngs records'. . . 'the same tower where the Kyngs records lyethe' (p. xii).

44 BL, Harleian MS 1326, ff. 120, 125.

45 Bayley, *The History and Antiquities of the Tower* vol. 1, contains additional information from the Henrician survey: Garden Tower (p. xii), Bell Tower (p. xii), Outer Ward towers (pp. xii–xv), with reference to St Martin Tower and the Lion Tower.

46 BL, Harleian MS 5913, ff. 2v–3v. The jewels lay near the 'office of Records'. The end of the report reads 'Also the offyce of the Juells hous to be newe made, with sertayn other houses of and appteynyng for th'Ordynaunce behynde the Mynte' (Bayley, p. xv).

47 PRO, SP 12/33/63. The 1564 estimate mentions placing artillery in the vicinity of three towers near the Ordnance Office (the rebuilt area behind St Peter's Chapel?).

48 Colvin, ed., *KW* vol. 3 (1485–1660) pt. 1, p. 263.

49 C. S. L. Davies, 'The Administration of the Royal Navy under Henry VIII. The Origins of the Navy Board', *EHR* vol. 80 no. 315 (April 1965), p. 278.

50 Andrew Thrush, 'The Ordnance Office and the Navy, 1625–40', *The Mariner's Mirror* vol. 77 no. 4 (November 1991), p. 343.

51 BL, Harleian MS 5913, f.3v.

52 Stewart, *EOO*, pp. 17, 39.

53 BL, Harleian MS 309, old. f. 41/new 53, orders signed by Burghley and Mildmay, 8 March 1572 and old f. 42/new f. 54, Lichfield's declaration. PRO, SP 16/206/29, f. 104.

54 C. S. L. Davies, 'Provisions for Armies, 1509–50', *EconHR* 2nd series, vol. 17 no. 2 (December 1964), pp. 234–6, 244–5, 247.

55 Pioneering works are Richard Stewart's 'The "Irish Road": military supply and arms for Elizabeth's army during the O'Neill Rebellion in Ireland, 1598–1601', Fissel, ed., *W&G*, especially pp. 24–5 and J. J. N. McGurk, 'The Recruitment and Transportation of Elizabethan Troops and their Service in Ireland, 1594–1603', Liverpool Ph.D. thesis 1982, pp. 275–375, and recently in *idem*, *ECI*, pp. 137–91.

56 PRO, E 407/12, accounts relating to the billeting of the men of Captains Garrat Dillan and Fraunces Stafford, among the bundle marked 'Letters, Receipts, Certificates, etc., of the Mayor of Chester, relating to expenses incurred for the army in Ireland, 1559–1602', unfoliated and unnumbered.

57 McGurk, *ECI*, pp. 142, 168; PRO, E 407/12, 'Letters, Receipts, Certificates, etc. of the Mayor of Chester'; E 407/12, 'Acquittances of Conductors of Troops paid by the Mayor of Bristol', unfoliated bundle; P. Thomas, 'Military Mayhem in Elizabethan Chester', *JSAHR* vol. 76 no. 308 (winter 1998), pp. 231–6, 239–41.

58 McGurk, *ECI*, p. 149.

59 PRO, E 407/12, 'Accounts of the Mayors of Barnstaple for expenses incurred in victualling and transporting troops for Ireland, 1596–1602', i.e. contracts for 1599; McGurk, *ECI*, pp. 170, 174–8.

60 PRO, E 351/123; E 351/147, dated *c*. 1560 and includes the Mayor of Bristol's accounts for provision of men and food; E 351/148; E 351/149; E 351/162,

1 October 1588–30 September 1594, account of G. Beverley regarding victualling of Irish garrisons; E 351/164 and E 351/171, Irish victualling temp. 1598–1606; E 351/164, 14 June–20 August 1598, account of J. Jolles and others for victualling troops in Ireland; E 351/165, 1 October 1598 to 30 April 1601, M. Darrell and J. Jolles, ditto; E 351/166, 7 November 1598–30 April 1600, account of J. Jolles, ditto; E 351/167, 20 March 1599–20 July 1602, J. Jolles and W. Cockayne, ditto; E 351/168, 26 January 1599/1600–5 November 1604, account of J. Wood, ditto; E 351/69, 20 July 1602–28 September 1604, J. Jolles and others, ditto; E 351/170, 30 September 1603–1 April 1606, account of U. Babbington (*per executrix*) and R. Bromley, contractors for clothing troops in Ireland; E 351/171, 1 January 1604/5–31 March 1608, account of Sir R. Newcomen for victualling troops in Ireland; E 351/162, 1 October 1588–30 September 1594, G. Beverley, victualling the garrisons of Cork, Limerick, Waterford, and Galway. See also *APC* vol. 30 (1599–1600), pp. 185, 189; Brian Pearce, 'Elizabethan Food Policy and the Armed Forces', *Econ HR* vol. 12 no. 1 (1942), pp. 39–46; Captain Robert Hitchcock, 'The English army rations in the time of Elizabeth', *An English Garner* (New York 1964), pp. 115–32; Falls, *EIW*, p. 63.

61 PRO, E 351/147.

62 BL, Egerton MS 1525, letters 15 and 17, ff. 25–26v and 29–30v.

63 Richard Stewart, 'The "Irish Road"', in Fissel, ed., *W&G*, p. 31.

64 PRO, SP 63/207 pt. I/34, new f. 83/old f. 243.

65 PRO, SP 63/213/18, new ff. 31–31v/old ff. 685–6; SP 63/213/16, old. f. 403–4/new f. 28–28v. The spelling has been modernised. According to the editor of *CSPI*, troops consumed bread at this rate of a ration of 56 lb per a month of 28 days. The cost of converting grain into bread was 8d. per bushel of wheat. Transport from Chester (2d. freight and 1d. landing) cost 3d. 'The total is 4s. 5d. [*sic*] which is clearly a mistake for 3s. 5d., but the rest of the calculation is based on it. The bushel of wheat costing 4s. 5d. the 24 oz. of bread should be, in proportion, 1s. 3/4d. Her Majesty issuing the same at 1d. there is a loss on every soldier's bread of 3/4d. a day, or per month of 1s. 9d.'. Compare with SP 63/179/73, f. 162.

66 See below, p 201.

67 PRO, E 407/12, 'Certificates of army stores shipped by contractors for the army in Ireland, 1600–1605', letter dated 29 April 1602.

68 D. B. Quinn, ed., 'Calendar of the Irish Council Book', 1 March 1581–1 July 1586, *Analecta Hibernica* vol. 24 (1967), p. 121, item 91. The explosion in the Record Treasury in the Irish PRO on 30 June 1922 destroyed the original. Earlier records of the Irish Council were lost in 1711.

69 Fissel, ed., *W&G*, pp. 2–3.

70 For an account, literally, of Beverley's activities, see PRO, E 351/159, 4 February 1594/5–31 March 1597, victuals, clothing etc. sent to Chester and Liverpool for troops to be dispatched for Ireland.

71 PRO, SP 63/205/57, new f. 88/old f. 145, 10 May 1599, where George Beverley describes the remoteness of provincial magazines.

72 For the contracts, PRO, E 407/12, 'Contracts for victualling troops in Ireland, 1600–1602'.

73 PRO, SP 63/212/143, new f. 346/old f. 623, 2 March 1603.

74 PRO, E 351/166, 7 November 1598–30 April 1600, and E 351/167, 20 March 1599–20 July 1602, John Jolles and William Cockayne victualling abstracts; PRO, SP 63/211/30, new ff. 89–90/old ff. 423–5, 13 May 1602; SP 63/204, new f. 168/old f. 162, 16 May 1599, PC regarding complaints of Jolles and Cockayne; SP 63/205/10, new ff. 15–15v, 4 April 1599, certificate regarding victuals shipped 27 March and 3 April.

75 PRO, SP 63/211/91, new f. 254/old f. 285.

76 PRO, E 407/12 certificates of army stores shipped by contractors for the Irish army 1600–5, (unfoliated and unnumbered bundle) and contracts for the victualling of troops in Ireland 1600–2 (another unfoliated and unnumbered bundle).

77 Stearns, *CMS*, p. 223.

78 PRO, SP 16/66/31, f. 40, 5 June 1627 (?), Crowe's notes. For more on Crowe, see Fissel, 'Law and Authority in the Collection of the Strangers' Consulage 1621–1647' (forthcoming).

79 PRO, SP 16/84/30, f. 40, Secretary Conway to the Earl of Holland, 6 November 1627.

80 PRO, SP 16/12/38, Sir John Eliot to Conway.

81 PRO, E 407/7/150, clothing for royal garrisons in the United Provinces, circa 1609. Peter Edwards's *Dealing in Death. The Arms Trade and the British Civil Wars, 1638–1652* (Stroud 2000) provides background, pp. 127–31.

82 Stearns, *CMS*, pp. 222–3, 227.

83 PRO, SP 16/34/112.

84 HEH, EL 7837.

85 For example, John Quarles: PRO, SP 16/12/21 I and PRO, E 351/2711.

86 Stearns, *CMS*, pp. 224–6, citing SP 16/68/68.

87 Ibid., p. 225, and his citation of J. Glanville, note 90, p. 53. See also above, note 74.

88 PRO, SP 16/1/87 shows that the fish ration consisted of 'Lings' (*Molva molva*, a large European ling whose size is demonstrated by the allocation of one quarter fish per man *per diem*), 'Codd' (*Gadus morhua*, the now endangered Atlantic cod), and 'Newland fish' (most likely *Gadhus morhua*, small fish, perhaps from the waters of Newfoundland, dried and salted). Veteran fisherman T. G. Barnes provided information on the fish ration; see also SP 16/1/111 and SP 16/5/120.

89 PRO, SP 16/404/137.

90 PRO, SP 16/385/13; see also SP 16/385/50 I and SP 16/386/14.

91 PRO, SP 16/414/107; PRO, E 351/579, f. 2, Commissary General Pinckney's account.

92 The King's army camped at Goswick between 24 and 27 May. For a map of the encampment and identification of the regiments, see Figure 11.5, this book, p. 275.

93 John Aston, *Iter Boreale*, p. 15. *Iter Boreale*, a journal kept by one of the King's Privy Chamber Men Extraordinary, chronicles the First Bishops' War. It is preserved in the British Library, as Additional MS 28,566, and is printed in the Surtees Society volume for 1910, edited by J. C. Hodgson. See also Scottish RO, GD 406/1/1186; Centre for Kentish Studies, U 1475 C 114/4, Sir John Temple to the Earl of Leicester from Berwick, 29 May 1639; HMC *De L'Isle and Dudley* vol. 6 (London 1966), p. 167.

94 PRO, SP 16/403, old f. 40, 12 February 1638/9.

95 PRO, SP 16/386/72, old f. 134.

96 PRO, SP 16/413/79, old f. 151, 23 February 1638/9.

97 PRO, E 351/579.

98 PRO, SP 16/445/5; SP 16/444/24 II.

99 PRO, SP 16/415/67, PC to LLs, 29 March 1639. The Council insisted upon shire cooperation: PRO, PC 2/50, f. 268.

100 F. Barber, ed., 'The West Riding Session Rolls', *Yorkshire Archaeological and Topographical Journal* vol. 5 (London 1879), p. 373, citing order book A, f. 6. See also ibid., pp. 387–8, 395.

101 PRO, SP 16/412/73, 8 February 1638/9.

102 Richard Stewart on the 'Irish Road' in Fissel, ed., *W&G*, pp. 16–32.

103 PRO, SP 16/412/54, 6 February 1638/9.

104 PRO, SP 16/412/22, old f. 51, 3 February 1638/9.

105 PRO, SP 16/417/18; Peter Edwards, *The Horse Trade in Tudor and Stuart England* (Cambridge 1988). Horses not only lugged ammunition but also sustained communication through a system of post-riders. These steeds, too, were requistioned as post-horses, greatly aggravating their owners and triggering a few brawls.

106 PRO, SP 16/448/26 and 26 I, 18 March 1639/40.

107 The most likely reason tents were not issued in 1639 is that several thousand pounds were needed to supply tents to the army, PRO, SP 16/412/136. According to an estimate of the costs of the originally proposed 30,000 man army, 7,500 tents were to be supplied at a cost of £9,350. Bodleian Library, Rawlinson MS B 210, f. 41v: '. . . the Corporalls and comon souldiers lye on the bare ground most of them without any strawe under them and greene sodde under their head, and little or noe shelter. . . .'

108 Bodleian Library, Rawlinson MS B 210, anonymous eyewitness account of the First Bishops' War, who wrote that the soldiers 'are soe putt to itt for drinke that they are in greate necessitie. 6 shilling Beere, or Beere smaller than itt is sould after the Rate of 30 shillings: per Barrell for they give 3 pence a quarte for itt, and some would give sixpence if they could have the favour to gette it. Itt is a pitty Brewhouses and Bakehouses were not provided before hand in these partes for this occasion. The Springs are few here, and they drincke them up as fas as they can Springe. It was ill forecast not to have severall shipp loades of Beere come downe before the Army, and alsoe with Pales to make their shelter against Rayney weather' (ff. 40v–41). The author continues by describing how a shipload of bread was spoiled.

109 Scottish RO, GD 406/1/11147A, Pennington to Hamilton, 14 June 1639; also Fissel, 'Hamilton's Expedition', forthcoming.

110 Overland transport of coin, even within Britain, remained hazardous due to the depredations of thieves and 'scattered rougs'. Scottish RO, GD 406/1/1178 and Fissel, *BW*, pp. 143–4.

111 Fissel, *BW*, pp. 24, 113–17, 140–51. For context, PRO, SP 16/438/11, Nicholas' notes.

112 PRO, SP 16/451/14. See M. Fissel, '*Bellum Episcopale*: the Bishops' Wars and the end of the "Personal Rule" in England, 1638–1640', University of California D.Phil. thesis (1983), p. 178.

113 PRO, SP 16/466/8, old f. 8; SP 16/466/9, old ff. 14–15.

114 PRO, SP 16/456/64; SP 16/456/2; Fissel, *BW*, pp. 18, 271 note 23, citing SP 16/459/95.

115 John Aston, *Iter Boreale*, pp. 12–13.

116 Scottish RO, GD 406/1/1282.

117 PRO, SP 16/459/36.

118 PRO, E 101/668/16.

119 Ronan Bennett, 'War and disorder: policing the soldiery in Civil War Yorkshire', in Fissel, *W&G*, pp. 248–73.

120 John Aston, *Iter Boreale*, p. 6.

121 C. Wedgwood, *The King's Peace 1637–1641* (New York 1969), pp. 264–5.

122 PRO, SP 16/417/110, Rossingham to Conway, 16 April 1639.

123 *HMC Rutland*, p. 505, 8 April 1639. It is noteworthy that the dispute occurred between a captain of Arundel's infantry and an officer of Holland's cavalry, for there was a degree of animosity between the respective generals as well as amongst cavalry and infantry.

124 PRO, PC 2/50, ff. 373–4; SP 16/421/132.

125 PRO, SP 45/10, old ff. 83–83a/new ff. 143–4, 9 March 1627/8.

126 Staffordshire RO, Dartmouth MSS D (w) 1778/I/i/8; D (w) 1778/I/i/5.

127 Fissel, *BW*, pp. 58, 60, 107–10, 116, 293; Russell, *FBM*, pp. 142–3.

128 PRO, SP 16/450/103, Conway to Northumberland, 17 April 1640.

129 Bodleian Library, Clarendon SP, vol. 19, f. 175v, Lord Conway's narrative of his conduct in the action at Newburn.

130 Eltis, *MRSC*, pp. 1, 4, 99–122, 136–9.

131 PRO, E 101/57/18, muster book; E 101/57/20; E 101/57/13.

132 Rolf Loeber and Geoffrey Parker, 'The Military Revolution in Seventeenth Century Ireland', J. Ohlmeyer, ed., *Ireland from Independence to Occupation 1641–1660* (Cambridge 1995), pp. 67–9.

133 'A Relation or Dyary of the siege of the castle of Limerick by the Irish from May 18 until June 23, 1642', printed in *Journal of the Royal Society of Antiquaries* vol. 34 (1904), pp. 164, 171, 173, 177, 186.

9 HIBERNIAN WARFARE UNDER THE TUDORS, 1558–1601

1 For an excellent overview, see Steven Ellis, 'The Tudors and the Origins of the Modern Irish States. A Standing Army', in T. Bartlett and K. Jeffrey, eds, *A Military History of Ireland* (Cambridge 1997), pp. 116–35.

2 J. Collier, ed., *Egerton Papers*, Camden Society, vol. 12 (1840), pp. 14, 17, 20–2.

3 Cruickshank, *EA*, 2nd edn, p. 283.

4 Bodleian Library, Rawlinson MS A 237/5, ff. 37–53v, accounts for 1560–2; Falls, *EIW*, p. 47; tables in Nolan, 'Militarization', p. 418 and Cruickshank, *EA*, pp. 290–1.

5 See, Chapters 4, 6, and 7.

6 Mahaffy's comments in R. Mahaffy, ed., *Calendar of State Papers relating to Ireland 1601–3* vol. 11 (London 1912), pp. xxxii–xxxiii; J. Silke, *Kinsale. The Spanish Intervention in Ireland at the End of the Elizabethan Wars* (London 1970), p. 124.

7 PRO, E 407/12, accounts of John Delbridge and others, including successive mayors of Barnstaple, of expenses incurred in victualling and transporting troops for Ireland, 1596–1602, unnumbered and unfoliated bundle; P. Thomas, 'Military Mayhem in Elizabethan Chester', *JSAHR* vol. 76 no. 308 (Winter 1998), p. 230.

8 BL, Lansdowne MS 155, new f. 336v/old f. 333v.

9 PRO, E 351/230, credit against a debt as a reward for 'the takinge of Shane Oneles head' on f. 2v; Sir Henry Wallop's account from 10 October 1579 to 30 September 1584; Hayes-McCoy, *IB*, pp. 68–86.

10 N. Canny, *The Elizabethan Conquest of Ireland: a pattern established, 1565–76* (New York 1976), p. 49.

11 Ibid., pp. 59, 157.

12 J. Brewer and W. Bullen, eds, *Calendar of the Carew Manuscripts, preserved in the Archiepiscopal Library at Lambeth* 1515–1574 (reprinted Nendeln, Liechtenstein 1974), pp. 391–5.

13 Falls, *EIW*, p. 108.

14 On the nature of the revolts, see Steven Ellis, *Ireland in the Age of the Tudors 1447–1603. English Expansion and the End of Gaelic Rule* (London 1998), pp. 295–300, 312–15, and below, pp. 95, 207, 209–11.

15 PRO, E 351/150, timber for Ulster and other charges 10 May–28 June 1575, account of Sir F. Knollys, who received £230 7s. 2d.

16 PRO, E 351/230, f. 1.

17 F. C. Dietz, *English Public Finance 1558–1641* vol. 2 (New York 1932), p. 430, citing BL, Add. MS 4767, f. 129.

18 Ciaran Brady, 'Faction and the Origins of the Desmond Rebellion of 1579', *IHS* vol. 22 no. 88 (September 1981) p. 292.

19 However, consider M. Noonkester, 'The Third British Empire. Transplanting the English Shire to Wales, Scotland, Ireland, and America', *JBS* vol. 36 (July 1997), pp. 251–84.

20 PRO, E 351/230, ff. 18v–19v.

21 Ibid., f. 99v; Dietz, *EPF* vol. 2, pp. 431–2.

22 PRO, E 351/230, f. 1v.

23 LPL, Fairhurst Papers, vol. 2009, ff. 1–4v.

24 LPL, Carew MS 619, f. 48, 7 September 1580.

25 Alfred O'Rahilly, 'The Massacre at Smerwick (1580)', Historical and Archaeological Papers no. 1 (1938), Cork Historical and Archaeological Society, who tells us that the papal force had landed 'to secure peace and religious toleration' (p. 30). O'Rahilly's audacity in claiming to have written the definitive and objective account without touching a manuscript is matched by his allegation of English atrocity, which was part of a propaganda campaign based on complicity between the Irish Republic and Hitler's Reich. See the preface by S. O'Riordan, which announces their intention to take the story to a wider public.

26 PRO, E 351/230, ff. 2v–3.

27 PRO, SP 63/179/82, f. 180.

28 Dietz, *EPF* vol. 2, p. 432.

29 *Calendar of the Carew Manuscripts* (1589–1600) vol. 3 nos. 76, 78–80, pp. 31–7; Nolan, *SJN*, pp. 162–3.

30 Richard Stewart, 'The "Irish Road". Military Supply and Arms for Elizabeth's Army During the O'Neill Rebellion in Ireland, 1598–1601', in Fissel, ed., *W&G*, pp. 16–37.

31 Hayes-McCoy, *IB*, pp. 90–3.

32 L. O'Mearain, 'The English Army of Clontibret, 1595', *Irish Sword* vol. 2 no. 9 Winter 1956, pp. 368–71, printing the muster lists.

33 PRO, SP 63/179/96, ff. 243–243v; Hayes-McCoy, *IB*, p. 95;

34 *Calendar of the Carew Manuscripts* vol. 3 no. 154, pp. 109–10; Hayes-McCoy, *IB*, pp. 92–5.

35 PRO, SP 63/179/95, ff. 240–240v; Hayes-McCoy, *IB*, pp. 96–102.

36 Evidence of an individual nature regarding Englishmen who migrated between service on the Continent (especially the Low Countries) and the Irish theatre can be found in the many petitions by 'maimed' or aged soldiers preserved in local record offices. For instance, see WRO, Quarter Sessions Autograph Book, f. 26 (Walter Howard, 26 September 1614) and f. 85 (anonymous, 8 June 1611). See also Chapter 7, pp. 178–9 and BL, Lansdowne MS 1218, new ff. 115, 117, 118, 119, 120v, 121v, etc.

37 Bodleian Library, Ashmole MS 816, folio at end of volume, marked in pencil as '18'. T. G., *The True Exemplary, and Remarkable History of the Earl of Tirone . . .* (London 1619), p. 19.

38 PRO, E 351/238, f. 3v; on the Norrises, ff. 18, 20, 24v, etc.

39 E. Van Meteren, *A True Discovrse Historicall* (London 1602), pp. 145–54; Nolan, *SJN*, pp. 218–33.

40 Falls, *EIW*, p. 201.

41 M. O'Baille, 'Brough's Campaign (1597)', *Studies* vol. 40 (June 1951), pp. 224–5.

42 W. Pinkerton, 'The "Overthrow" of Sir John Chichester, in 1597', *Ulster Journal of Archaeology* vol. 5 (1857), pp. 189–96, 199–200, which contains transcriptions of original sources.

43 Hayes-McCoy, *IB*, p. 117; Falls, *EIW*, p. 215.

44 PRO, SP 63/202 pt. 3/28 II, f. 51; SP 63/202 pt. 3/28 III, ff. 55–55v; SP 63/202 pt. 3/34 I, ff. 63–64v; SP 63/202 pt. 3/56, ff. 99–100.

45 PRO, SP 63/205/187, f. 355v.

46 C. Brady, 'The captains' games: army and society in Elizabethan Ireland', in Bartlett and Jeffrey, eds, *A Military History of Ireland*, pp. 140–4.

47 PRO, SP 63/202 pt. 4/83, ff. 263–9.

48 Stewart, 'Irish Road', pp. 19–21; McGurk, *ECI*, pp. 51–76.

49 McGurk, *ECI*, table 2, pp. 58–9; Nolan, 'Militarization', p. 418, table which shows 1596 and 1597 impressment figures at 5,000–6,000 annually to 10,000 in 1598 and 17,000 in 1599. See also Chapter 4, pp. 87–91, 96–104.

50 Dietz, *EPF* vol. 2, p. 92, citing PRO, E 351/264, Stanhope's account.

51 PRO, E 351/238, 1 March 1599–31 March 1600.

52 Dietz, *English Public Finance* vol. 2, p. 432.

53 PRO, SP 63/205/246, old f. 197/new f. 470.

54 PRO, E 351/238, ff. 12v–13; PRO, SP 63/205/184, old f. 361/new f. 349 – old f. 362/new f. 350, 'For her majestey's speciall benefitt'.

55 Dozens of Wallop's accounts, especially in the Exchequer of Receipt, survive. For purposes of sampling, this study focused on PRO, E 351/230 and SP 63/126/II, new ff. 3–8, formal declared account and 'Briefe viewe' of the Treasurer's accounts circa 1 October 1579–30 September 1584, supplemented by SP 63/126/39, new ff. 101–26, accounts for 10 August 1583–30 September 1586.

56 PRO, E 351/238, entire roll; McGurk, *ECI*, p. 201, table 16, drawn from *Calendar of the Carew Manuscripts* vol. 3, pp. 288–9.

57 L. W. Henry, 'Essex as a strategist and military organiser, 1596–7' *EHR* vol. 68 no. 268 (July 1953), pp. 363–93.

58 PRO, SP 63/205/63, f. 92; see J. M. Hill's general assessment in *Celtic Warfare 1595–1763* (Edinburgh 1986), pp. 22–41 and G. Hayes-McCoy, 'Strategy and Tactics in Irish Warfare, 1593–1601', *IHS* vol. 2 (1940–1941), pp. 255–79.

59 PRO, SP 63/205/44, f. 204; SP 63/205/63, f. 92; SP 63/205/65, ff. 98–98v; SP 63/205/109, ff. 205–206v, p. 92.

60 PRO, SP 63/205/108, letter, is ff. 195–195v; SP 63/205/108 I, battle of Wicklow, is ff. 197–197v; SP 63/205/108 II, ff. 201–2; SP 63/205/108 III, ff. 203–4.

61 PRO, SP 63/205/130, old f. 285/new f. 247 – old f. 286/new f. 247v: Falls, *EIW* pp. 242–3.

62 PRO, SP 63/206/68 III, old f. 189/new f. 185 – old f. 189v/new f. 185v.

63 Father Silke describes expertly the controversy over the selection of a landing site, as well as other fatal choices made during preparations in Spain. *Kinsale*, pp. 87–8, 98–103, 108–22.

64 O'Neill did have to worry about the northern garrisons at Londonderry, Donegal, and Carrickfergus – see Mahaffy, ed., *CSPI* (August 1601–March 1603) vol. 2, pp. xliii–xliv.

65 The quarrels amongst the Spaniards are dissected in Silke, *Kinsale*, pp. 42–5, 92–107; Mountjoy had a good working relationship with Carew, whose professionalism he trusted. But as a courtier, Carew envied Mountjoy and on one occasion questioned his patriotism. Mahaffy paints a very different picture of Carew than that found in Falls.

66 Thomas Stafford, *Pacata Hibernia. Ireland Appeased and Reduced* (London 1633), p. 198

67 Mahaffy, *CSPI* (August 1601–March 1603) vol. 2, p. xv.

68 Falls, *EIW*, p. 293.

69 Silke, *Kinsale*, p. 110.

70 PRO, SP 63/209 pt. 2/177A, new f. 146/old f. 397; *Pacata Hibernia*, p. 199

71 Hayes-McCoy, *IB*, p. 158.

72 Silke, *Kinsale*, pp. 116–17 disputes Falls, *EIW*, p. 295.

73 Mahaffy, ed., *CSPI* (August 1601–March 1603) vol. 2, pp. xiv–xv. Carew's letter of 24 October 1601 is PRO, SP 63/209 pt. 2/160, ff. 101–1025v. List of infantry companies – SP 63/209 pt. 2/159, f. 98.

74 See Chapter 4, pp. 102–4, for levies destined for Ireland.

75 PRO, SP 63/209 pt. 2/169, new. f. 129/old f. 655.

76 PRO, SP 63/205/84, f. 141, 19 June 1599.

77 Ian Heath and David Sque, *The Irish Wars 1485–1603* (London 1993), pp. 12–15.

78 For a grand portrait of O'Neill as a sixteenth-century Trotsky or Mao creating the people's army through paternalism, see *The Irish War of Defence, 1589–1600*, M.J. Byrne (ed.) (Dublin, 1930), pp. 31, 33.

79 J. Michael Hill essay in Jeremy Black, ed., (New York 1999), *European Warfare, 1453–1815*, pp. 201–23.

80 PRO, SP 63/209 pt. 2/177A, ff. 146v–147; *Pacata Hibernia*, p. 203.

81 See also Falls, *EIW*, pp. 295–6.

82 PRO, SP 63/209 pt. 2/177A, f. 148; *Pacata Hibernia*, p. 204.

83 See Silke, *Kinsale*, pp. 121–2, based on O'Faolain's analysis.

84 Falls, *EIW*, p. 296.

85 *Pacata Hibernia*, pp. 205–6 and Mahaffy, ed., *CSPI* (August 1601–23 March 1603) vol. 2, pp. xviii, xx.

86 *Pacata Hibernia*, pp. 204–9; Silke, *Kinsale*, p. 123 and J. Brewer and W. Bullen, eds, *Calendar of the Carew Manuscripts 1601–1603* vol. 4 (London 1870), pp. 179, 182.

87 Falls, *EIW*, pp. 296–7; Silke, *Kinsale*, p. 125.

88 *Pacata Hibernia*, p. 220.

89 Silke, *Kinsale*, pp. 129–30, Falls, *EIW*, p. 299.

90 Mahaffy, ed., *CSPI* (August 1601–23 March 1603) vol. 2, p. xxvi; Silke, *Kinsale*, p. 130; Falls, *EIW*, p. 299.

91 *Pacata Hibernia*, p. 222.

92 Mahaffy, ed., *CSPI* (August 1601–23 March 1603) vol. 2, pp. xxvi–xxviii; Silke, *Kinsale*, pp. 131–5; Falls, *EIW*, pp. 300–1.

93 *Pacata Hibernia*, p. 230.

94 Father Silke's account justifies O'Neill's sluggishness by suggesting he was hoping attrition would further weaken the English. But the Irish and Spanish were starving and freezing as well, and no succour from Spain or the Irish was forthcoming. Had O'Neill listened to Aguila and Ruiz de Velasco (a Spanish captain at O'Neill's side) victory might well have been his. See *Kinsale*, pp. 136–7 and *Pacata Hibernia*, p. 231.

95 Mahaffy, ed., *CSPI* (August 1601–23 March 1603) vol. 2, p. xxix.

96 PRO, SP 63/209 pt. 2, ff. 377v–378v; *Pacata Hibernia*, p. 234.

97 PRO, SP 63/209 pt. 2, f. 379; *Pacata Hibernia*, p. 235.

98 The cavalry and infantry commanders respectively. 'The Tide of Victory . . .' *Studies*, (September 1949), p. 317 note 1; Mahaffy, ed., *CSPI* (August 1601–March 1603) vol. 2, pp. xxxii–xxxvi; Silke, *Kinsale*, pp. 141–5; Falls, *EIW*, pp. 304–7.

99 See Chapter 7, pp. 170–3.

100 Note how Mountjoy gave leave to the Marshal to charge the Irish at his discretion. Essentially, the delegation of that decision allowed the English to seize the initiative, and victory. PRO, SP 63/209 pt. 2, f. 377v.

10 THE IRISH MILITARY ESTABLISHMENT, 1603–42

1 *HMC Salisbury* part 14 (London 1923), p. 207, and ibid., part 12 (Hereford 1910), pp. 33–4.

2 PRO, E 407/3/1, f. 1 bottom, parchment roll from the Exchequer of Receipt Miscellaneous.

3 PRO, SP 63/210/82, new ff. 300–300v.

4 PRO, E 407/12, certificates of army stores shipped by contractors, 1600–5, unfoliated bundle.

5 John Nolan, English troop levels table 1585–1602, printed in 'The Militarization of the Elizabethan State', *Journal of Military History* vol. 58 (July 1994), p. 418.

6 Fissel, ed., *W&G*, pp. 6, 13.

7 Bodleian Library, Rawlinson MS A 237, miscellaneous papers relating to Ireland, ff. 2–2v.

8 S. R. Gardiner, *History of England* vol. 1 (1603–1607) (London 1900), p. 382, citing army list of 1 October 1604.

9 *Discovery of the True Causes Why Ireland was Never Entirely subdued and brought under obedience of the Crown of England, until the Beginning of His Majesty's Happy Reign* (1612), printed in H. Morley, ed., *Ireland under Elizabeth and James I* (London 1890), pp. 248–9.

10 Sir Faithful Fortescue, *An Account of the Right Honourable Sir Arthur Chichester, Lord Belfast, Lord Deputy of Ireland*, Lord Clermont's edition (London 1858), pp. 8–12.

11 Bodleian Library, Rawlinson MS A 237, letters of 1606, 1608, and 1619, ff. 2–3v; J. Lodge, ed., *Desiderata Curiosa Hibernica* (Dublin 1772) vol. 1, pp. 46–52, patent for mustering and training the undertakers in Munster and Cannaught in 1615, and Gardiner's comments in the *DNB*.

12 *Irish Patent Rolls of James I*, Irish Historical Manuscript Commission (Dublin 1966), pp. 88, 144–5. Thanks to Andrew Thrush for this reference.

13 PRO, E 407/3/6, f. 1; E 101/533/1; E 407/3/2, account of 1 September 1616; F.C. Dietz, *English Public Finance 1558–1641* vol. 2 (New York 1932), p. 434; E 407/3/9, account of 1 April 1623.

14 PRO, SP 16/1/79 I, Mayor Peter Drinkwater's account of 23 April 1625; SP 16/4/12 I, account for June 1625.

15 V. Treadwell, *Buckingham and Ireland 1616–1628* (Bodmin 1998), pp. 271–93; Hugh Kearney, *Strafford in Ireland 1633–41. A Study in Absolutism* 2nd edn (Cambridge 1989), pp. 18–28.

16 Bodleian Library, Tanner MS 72, item no. 74, ff. 154–155v, 22 September 1626.

17 *Colonial Ulster* p. 78, note 53, citing Sheffield Wentworth Papers vol. 1 ff. 8, 32.

18 See Kearney, *Strafford in Ireland*, p.xviii in his 1989 introduction.

19 Ibid., pp. 32–3. Note that in economics, too, Ireland was a 'pawn in the game', pp. 139–42. Kearney's figures do not square entirely with the sources cited above, note 13.

20 Sheffield City Library, Strafford MSS (Wentworth-Wodehouse Papers) vol. XIa, ff. 129–30.

21 Sheffield, Strafford MSS vol. XIa, f. 133; Bodleian Library, Carte MS 66, f. 32; Resolutions of the States-General, cited in Jan Piet Puype and Macro van der Hoeven, eds, *The Arsenal of the World. Dutch Weapons Trade in the Golden Age* (Amsterdam 1993), p. 15.

22 Sheffield City Library, Strafford MSS vol. XIa, f. 131.

23 Fissel, *BW*, pp. 98–100; PRO, E 351/2711, Quarles's purchases; E 351/2712, Harby's purchases.

24 Bodleian Library, Carte MS 66, f. 32v.

25 Bodleian Library, Carte MS 1, ff. 169, 178v.

26 Sheffield City Library, Strafford MSS, vol. 6 pt. II, ff. 24–6.

27 Scottish Record Office, Hamilton MSS, GD 406/1/803, ff. 2–3, dated '24th of Marche. 1639' but clearly 1640 from internal evidence.

28 Bodleian Library, Carte MS 1, ff. 179–179v, resolutions of the Irish Council of War.

29 Bodleian Library, Carte MS 1, ff. 467–470v.

30 On the latter point, Stewart, *EOO*, pp. 116–17.

31 *DNB*.

32 Bodleian Library, Carte MS1, ff. 467–470v, 476–477v; Carte MS 54, f. 415.

33 Kearney, *Strafford in Ireland,* pp. 187–9.

34 Bodleian Library, Carte MS 66, f. 31, Wentworth to the King, 17 October 1638; R. Loeber and G. Parker, 'The Military Revolution in Seventeenth Century Ireland', in Ohlmeyer, ed., *Ireland from Independence to Occupation* (Cambridge 1995), p. 72, note 26; that Wentworth was able to provide arms, including artillery, during the Bishops' Wars, shows his diligence in accumulating modern armaments.

35 Article XV in *Depositions and Articles against Thomas Earle of Strafford, Febr 16 1640* [1640/1] (London? 1641) p. 25. See also p. 26 where soldiers were billeted upon his opponents and ordered to expel people from homes and castles.

36 Thomas Carte, *Letters* vol. 3 (1735), p. 7, Wentworth to Wandesford, 25 July 1636.

37 Ibid. The historian must balance Wentworth's self-congratulatory assessment of his achievement with historians' jaundiced view of the exact militia that existed contemporaneously in England's counties.

38 See articles V and VIII along with the charges in article XXVIII (alleging that the Earl had forced Conway to engage at Newburn in spite of the latter's numerical inferiority and had failed to take sufficient precautions about Newcastle), *Depositions and Articles*, pp. 1–4, 44. See also related military issues pp. 14, 25–6, 29–30, 36–7, 39, 41–5 (42 and 43 have been omitted – page 41 is followed textually by page 44). Compare these articles with Fissel, *BW*, pp. 22, 37–49, 51–4, 69, 77, 86–7, 90, 110, 288.

39 Bodleian Library, Carte MS 1, f. 211, Wandesford to Ormonde, 30 June 1640, and ff. 214–215v, William St Leger to Ormonde, 21 July. The late Gerald Aylmer, Toby Barnard, Raymond Gillespie, and Michael Webb made up a remarkable confluence of Ormonde specialists in Oxford in 1996–7. The author thanks all four for stimulating discussions.

40 See below, pp. 279–80.

41 PRO, SO 1/3, f. 176, Signet Office Irish letter-books.

42 Bodleian Library, Carte MS 1, f. 178v, note in Ormonde's (?) hand that 'bitts', 'girt webb', etc. were needed and might be available in Chester, circa April 1640; f. 194, on the transport of provisions and navigating rough seas, 16 May 1640; Carte MS 63, f. 108v, on the dangers of failing the King by not providing for the army, 6 May 1640.

43 Bodleian Library, Carte MS 1, f. 179, acts and resolutions of the Irish Council of War since the departure of Strafford for England, 10–20 April 1640.

44 Ibid., ff. 179–80.

45 Article XVIII, *Depositions and Articles*, p. 36.

46 Bodleian Library, Carte MS 77, new f. 458/old f. 187, speech of 22 August 1640; David Scott, '"Hannibal at our Gates". Loyalists and fifth-columnists during the Bishops' Wars – the Case of Yorkshire', *Historical Research* vol. 70 no. 173 (October 1997), pp. 269–93.

47 *The Reduction of Ireland* (London 1675), p. 220; Loeber and Parker, 'The Military Revolution in Ireland', p. 73. Also, see vol. 1, pt 1, of J. T. Gilbert, ed., *A Contemporary History of Affairs in Ireland from 1641 to 1652* (Dublin 1879), pp. 332–7.

48 Fissel, *BW*, pp. 42 (map), 170–1.

49 Gilbert, *A Contemporary History* vol. 1, pt 1, p. 13.

50 Article XXII, *Depositions and Articles*, p. 36.

51 Bodleian Library, Carte MS 40, f. 668/406.

52 Bodleian Library, Carte MS 54, ff. 415–417v. This list was apparently that authorised by the Lords and Commons: see f. 417.

53 The latter figure is taken from Dr Ohlmeyer's chronology in *Ireland from . . .*, p. xix.

54 Sir John Temple to the King, 12 December 1641, from Dublin Castle. PRO, SP 63/260/50, new f. 193/old f. 279, '. . . (besides the 2000 men under the command of Sir Henry Tichburne new beseiged [sic] in Tredagh [Drogheda]) they are not able to bringe into the field above 3000 men both horse and foote, most of them citizens, many of them Irish whom wee have just cause to suspect will upon the first encounter desert this cause and carry over those [sic] armes to the Rebells. And in this posture wee daily expect to be beseiged in this place by strange multitudes of people who have already come from all partes and have on all sides encompassed this city which is of it selfe no wayes defensable'. He writes that the Castle is defensible unless the rebels get 'pieces of Battery' from Waterford. Presently they had none.

55 On Harcourt see Fissel, 'Hamilton's Amphibious Expedition of 1639', forthcoming; Fissel, *BW*, pp. 83, 253–4; and below, pp. 271, 281.

56 One may compare the list printed on p. 26 of Sir John Temple's *The Irish Rebellion* (1646, Dublin edition of 1724) with the officers named in PRO, E 351/293, declared account of the Exchequer of Receipt for the 1640 campaign.

57 M. Perceval Maxwell, *The Outbreak of the Irish Rebellion of 1641* (Montreal 1994), pp. 180, 325.

58 PRO, SP 16/473/53, ff. 104–107v; Fissel, *BW*, pp. 88–9, 264–86.

59 Gilbert, *A Contemporary History* vol. 1 pt 1, pp. 12–13, 15.

60 Mary Hickson, *Ireland in the Seventeenth Century or The Irish Massacres of 1641–2* (London 1884) vol. 2, p. 391.

61 Bodleian Library, Carte MS 2, ff. 130–130v, the Lords of the Council to the Earl of Leicester, 30 November 1641.

62 Bodleian Library, Carte MS 2, new f. 47/old f. 24, Henry Tichborne to Ormonde, 15 November 1641, from Drogheda.

63 Ibid., new f. 43/old f. 22, Tichborne to Ormonde, 14 November 1641, from Drogheda.

64 Gilbert, *A Contemporary History*, vol. 1 pt 1, p. 14.

65 Ian Ryder, *An English Army for Ireland* (Leigh-on-sea 1987), p. 5.

66 Perceval Maxwell, *Outbreak*, pp. 180, 325.

67 Thomas Carte, *The Life of James Duke of Ormond* vol. 1 (Oxford 1851), pp. 4–5 (Book III 68–9).

68 PRO, SP 28/139/15, itemised list of supplies for Irish operations, December 1641–May 1642; SP 28/170, ff. 25–27v, 31v, 34–34v, 37v–38v, 42, 49v, etc., warrants for 1642. Peter Edwards shared his transcripts of these manuscripts.

69 S. Wheeler, 'Four Armies in Ireland', J. Ohlmeyer, ed., *Ireland from Independence to Occupation* (Cambridge 1995), p. 45, note 6.

70 Gilbert, *A Contemporary History*, pp. 17, 18, 21, etc.; also *HMC Ormonde* vol. 2, p. 33, a turncoat company from Kildare.

71 Bodleian Library, Carte MS 4, f. 10.

72 Richard Bellings, *History of the Irish Confederation and the War in Ireland 1641–1643*, J. Gilbert, ed., vol. 1 (Dublin 1882), pp. 46–50.

73 'A Breviarie of the Services done about Dublin', Bodleian Library, Clarendon SP, vol. 20, f. 14, which contains a minutiae of detail in its eleven folios (ff. 14–19). Other sources, not surprisingly, give slightly different figures, i.e. Coote departed 29 November and his horsemen numbered eighty, but the account herein accepts the 'Breviarie's' figures. Certainly the section regarding Coote was written by an eyewitness, for on f. 14 he describes how 'wee marched'.

74 Bodleian Library, Clarendon SP vol. 20, f. 14; see also Gilbert, *A Contemporary History* for an Irish view of Coote on this marauding campaign, including his alleged approval of the decapitation of a 'litle babe', whose head was sported on a trooper's lance, p. 13.

75 Bodleian Library, Clarendon SP vol. 21, f. 14. Garrison planted at Newcastle (see Temple's *Irish Rebellion*).

76 Bodleian Library, Clarendon SP vol. 20, f. 163, item 1558, 9 February 1641/2.

77 *DNB* entries for Charles and Henry Wilmot.

78 *HMC Ormonde*, new series, vol. 1 (London 1902), pp. 47–52.

79 See Wenzel Hollar's contemporary engraving of the disposition of the forces, printed in Gilbert's edition of the *History of the Irish Confederation*, vol. 1, between pp. 80–1.

80 On Roman influences on English warfare, see Chapter 12, pp. 285–7. Garrisoning a subject territory was in itself a somewhat Roman design, as Ciaran Brady points out.

81 Edmund Borlase, *The History of the Irish Rebellion, Traced from many Preceding Acts, to the Grand Eruption . . .* (Dublin 1743), pp. 98–100; Carte, *The Life of James Duke of Ormond* vol. 1, pp. 246–52.

82 Bodleian Library, Carte MS 3, f. 186, 18 May 1642. I owe this reference, and much more, to Peter Edwards.

83 S. Wheeler, 'Four Armies in Ireland', pp. 44–5. But see also Ryder, *An English Army for Ireland* (Leigh-on-sea 1987), p. 14, where he suggests Protestant forces reached a level of 42,800–44,800, based upon the evidence of the Commons' *Journal* and *HMC Ormonde*; Edwards, *Dealing in Death*, pp. 32–5, 36–7, 74, 119, 125, 131–6, 145–6, 149, 168, 192–6, 207–10, 232, 235.

84 J. Hogan, ed., *Letters and Papers Relating to the Irish Rebellion Between 1642–46,* (Dublin 1936), pp. 121, 125, Council of War notes of 5 September and letter to the Speaker, 12 September.

85 Quoted by Gilbert, *History of the Irish Confederation* vol. 2, p. xix.

86 Bodleian Library, Carte MS 4, f. 30, to Ormonde, November 1642.

87 Bodleian Library, Carte MS 4, f. 24. Esmonde to Ormonde, 8 November 1642.

88 *HMC Ormonde*, new series, vol. 1 (London 1902), pp. 59–61, order of the Lieutenant General and Council of War on 16 May 1643 and presentation of grievances dated 10 June 1643.

89 Hiram Morgan, *Tyrone's Rebellion* (London 1993), p. 221.

90 Contrast Stewart and Wheeler in *W&G*, pp. 1–2, 16–56.

11 THE CAROLINE ART OF WAR

1 A. U., *A Trve Historie of the Memorable Siege of Ostend*, E. Grimeston, trans. (London 1604), p. 163/Y2.

2 *A True Reporte of the Great ouerthrowe lately given unto the Spaniards in their resolute assault of Bergen op Zoam, in the Lowe Countries* (London 1605), pp. A3, A4v–B, B2v.

3 PRO, SP 75/15, new ff. 298–298v, 300–2; HEH, EL 1641.

4 BL, Additional MS 46,188, ff. 1–1v; Boynton, *EM*, pp. 219–21. English citizens perceived the need for preparing the trained bands through reading pamphlets such as *The Wars in Germany, With the taking of the seuerall townes by the Marquesse Spynola . . .* (London 1614), which detailed the Imperial mobilisation and the 'Army of the Popes' (p. 15/C2). Also, Chapter 3, pp. 64–7.

5 Henrie Peacham, *A Most Trve Relation of the Affaires of Cleve and Gvlick . . . Vnto the breaking up of our Armie in the beginning of December last past 1614* (London 1615), pp. B4, D3–D3v.

6 The English presence in the Low Countries is documented by the Jessup Papers, especially a list dated tentatively around December 1624, which identifies colonels down to ensigns. The names reappear in the Denmark services lists of the early

1630s, and then again in the Bishops' Wars declared accounts, 1639–40. BL, Additional MS 46, 188, ff. 50v–51v.

7 PRO, E 157/16, licences to go beyond the seas.

8 PRO, SP 45/140, new ff. 49, 54, 56, 60–1, 82, 85, 96–7, 148, 159–60.

9 See Chapter 4.

10 PRO, SP 14/119/50, old ff. 1–21; BL, Royal King's MS 265, new ff. 256–7/old ff. 505–7 and Add. MS 46, 188, ff. 11–11v, conference amongst PC and 'persons of knowlege of experience' to plan the relief of the Palatinate, 13 January 1620/1; Barbara Donagan, 'Halcyon Days and the Literature of War: England's Military Education before 1642', *P&P* no. 147 (May 1995), p. 83.

11 British regiments in Charles's pay still served the Danish King into the 1630s: BL, Add. MS 4106, new ff. 177–177v, where colonels disbursed funds from the English Auditor of the Imprests; Paul Lockhart, *Denmark in the Thirty Years' War, 1618–1648* (London 1996), pp. 143, 150–1, 187; E. Beller, 'The Military Expedition of Sir Charles Morgan to Germany, 1627–9', *EHR* vol. 43 no. 172 (October 1928), pp. 528–39. BL, Additional MS 46, 188, ff. 105–6. I owe knowledge of the latter reference to Barbara Donagan.

12 W. Rye, ed., *State Papers relating to Musters, Beacons, Shipmoney, etc.* (Norwich 1907), pp. 35–6.

13 John Glanville, 'The Voyage to Cadiz in 1625', in A. Grosart, ed., *Camden Society* (London 1883), pp. 3–4. The King should have known a lot about his soldiers. See Chapter 4, p. 109.

14 Stewart, *EOO*, p. 114.

15 The Council of War's commission of 1624 (PRO, SP 14/163/19) is transcribed as appendix A in Stearns *CMS*, pp. 328–9. See also chapter four of that work.

16 R. B. Wernham, 'English Amphibious Operations' in Fissel and Trim, eds, *Amphibious Warfare*, forthcoming.

17 Stearns, *CMS*, p. 39; Glanville, 'Voyage', p. 3.

18 PRO, SP 16/10/67, ff. 122–122v.

19 PRO, SP 16/11/66, f. 135.

20 Quoted in Stearns, *CMS*, p. 47.

21 PRO, SP 16/8/59, ff. 93–93v; Glanville, 'Voyage', p. 45; Stearns, *CMS*, p. 48.

22 PRO, SP 16/10/67, f. 123v.

23 Glanville, 'Voyage', p. 59. A tun is 216 imperial gallons or 252 US gallons; a ton is a measurement of weight (not capacity); a tonne is a metric measurement of weight.

24 PRO, SP 16/10/67, f. 124. See the discussion in Richard Stewart's, 'Arms and Expeditions. The Ordnance Office and the Assaults on Cadiz (1625) and the Isle of Rhé (1627)', in Fissel, ed., *W&G*, pp. 112–32, esp. p. 114 where Gerald Aylmer is cited at length. The most thorough account remains the unpublished Ph.D. dissertation (1967) of Stephen J. Stearns, *CMS*.

25 Edward Cecil, Viscount Wimbledon, *A IOVRNALL, And Relation of the action . . . vpon the Coast of Spaine, 1625* (London 1626), pp. 16/C1–19/C3; Glanville, 'Voyage', pp. 59–60. This account deserves quotation: '. . . the Soldiers of his Lordship's speciall favor having obtayned a competent proporcon of a Butte of wyne for every Regiment, therewith to refreshe themselves, were so disordered in the expence thereof, that some of the worser sorte, being first distempered therewith, sett on the rest and grew to demand more wyne, in such disorder and with such violence that they contemned all command. . . . Noe words of exhortation, noe blowes of correction would restrayne them, but breaking with violence into the roomes where the wines were, cryeing out that they were King Charles his men and fought for him, careing for noe man els. They claymed all the wyne as their owne, due to them for their service, and proceeded to distemper them-

selves therewith still more, till in effect the whole Army except only the Comanders, was all drunken and in one Comon confusion: some of them shooting one att another amongst themselves.'

26 PRO, SP 16/11/66, f. 135v; SP 16/8/59, ff. 93–94v; SP 16/10/67, ff. 124–124v.

27 BL, Harleian MS 1583, f. 39; PRO, SP 16/8/59, f. 94; SP 16/11/66, f. 135v.

28 BL, Add. MS 41,616, f. 26. There were significant lapses, i.e. 'noe pickaxes' for siegeworks – BL, Harleian MS 1583, f. 39.

29 BL, Add. MS 48,168 (Yelverton MS no. 180), Sir William Monson's account, f. 52v, '. . . the carrying of a Sea action depends principally upon secresy and concealing their Intencion, but it seemes this fleete proclaymed the place they were bownd to for all passengers in the sea to tak notice of'. As it turned out the defenders of Cadiz were almost as unaware of the attackers as vice versa.

30 BL, Harleian MS 37, old f. 112/new f. 107; Stearns, 'Conscription and English Society in the 1620's', *JBS* vol. 11 no. 2 (May 1972), pp. 7–8.

31 Bodleian Library, Carte MS 77, ff. 274–274v, Francis Staresmore's report, 23 March 1626; G. Johnson, ed., *The Fairfax Correspondence, Memoirs of the Reign of Charles I* (London 1848), vol. 1, pp. 26–7; C. Russell, *Parliaments and English Politics, 1621–1629* (Oxford 1979), p. 270.

32 Beller, 'The Military Expedition of Sir Charles Morgan, 1627–9', pp. 528–9; Lockhart, *Denmark in the Thirty Years' War*, pp. 137–8, 141, 196, 212.

33 BL, Harleian MS 6988, ff. 1–31v, especially royal letters of 13, 25 August, 2, 20 September, 10 October and 6 November 1627.

34 See Chapter 4, pp. 111–12.

35 PRO, E 351/205, f. 2; Stewart, 'Arms and Expeditions', Fissel, ed., *W&G*, pp. 122, 132 note 35.

36 That theme dominates the account given in BL, Additional MS 4106, ff. 161–5.

37 BL, Harleian MS 6807, f. 287v.

38 BL, Add. MS 9298, ff. 169–169v; *A Continued IOVRNALL of all the proceedings of the Duke of Bvckingham his Grace in the Isle of Rhee* (London 1627), pp. 5–8; BL, Additional MS 4106, ff. 161–161v.

39 Bodleian Library, Tanner MS 303, f. 95v; Ashmole MS 824, f. 188v.

40 At the outset Buckingham had a 2:1 superiority with his nearly 6,000 infantry. See Stearns's discussion of strategy and tactics in this operation, *CMS*, pp. 87–90.

41 BL, Stowe MS 151, ff. 7–7v, Toiras to Buckingham. Toiras, on 13 July, had invited Buckingham to breakfast. The Duke responded to the messenger that '. . . hee would conquer them aswell by curtesie, as the sword, [and] stood complementinge with the Page with his hat in his hand, and returned him with twentie peeces for his message, and the trumpet with five.' Bodleian Library, Tanner MS 303, f. 91v.

42 Bodleian Library, Ashmole MS 824, f. 189v; Tanner MS 303, f. 98.

43 BL, Add. MS 9298, f. 173.

44 Stearns, *CMS*, p. 92.

45 Ibid., p. 97, regarding French nocturnal resupply.

46 PRO, SP 16/85/94 for Irish troop strength; Bodleian Library, Rawlinson MS D 117, f. 10 for the fortuitous arrival of the oxen around 24 August, confirmed by Tanner MS 303, f. 97v. Exactly one month later another supply ship docked, ibid., f. 102; Stearns, *CMS*, pp. 97–100. The belated dispatching of four ships under the Earl of Holland on 13 October 1627 came too late to succour Buckingham's force (PRO, SP 39/20, unfoliated warrant).

47 Bodleian Library, Tanner MS 303, ff. 105–105v; BL, Harleian MS 6807, f. 288v.

48 Bodleian Library, Rawlinson MS D 117, f. 27.

49 Quoted by Stearns, *CMS*, pp. 101–2.

50 The entire operation is discussed expertly by Stearns, *CMS*, pp. 103–5.

51 BL, Add. MS 9298, f. 186.

52 Bodleian Library, Rawlinson MS D 117, ff. 29–30.

53 Bodleian Library, Ashmole MS 824, f. 192v; Tanner MS 303, ff. 106–106v; Carte MS 77, f. 328, 'Verses in defence of the late acsion at the Isle of Ree' compares Rhé casualties with the 300 Spartans at Thermopylae; BL, Harleian MS 6807, ff. 289–289v; Add. MS 12, 496, old f. 43/new f. 47.

54 Russell, *PEP*, p. 358, note 3, and pp. 380–2.

55 Ibid., pp. 406–7.

56 *The Bible-Battells. Or the Sacred Art Military. For the rightly wageing of warre according to Holy Writ* (London 1629), pp. 6–6v.

57 Kevin Sharpe, *The Personal Rule of Charles I* (New Haven, Conn. 1992), pp. 44–5.

58 Simon Adams, 'Spain or the Netherlands? The Dilemmas of Early Stuart Foreign Policy', in H. Tomlinson, ed., *Before the English Civil War* (London 1983), pp. 88, 90–1.

59 Russell, *PEP*, pp. 217–26, 323–89.

60 L. J. Reeve, *Charles I and the Road to Personal Rule* (Cambridge 1989), pp. 230–2.

61 F. Harding. 'Defence and Security Measures in the County Palatine of Durham chiefly in the 17th Century from the Evidence of the Mickleton and Spearman Manuscripts.- I', *Durham University Journal* vol. 16 no. 2 (1955), p. 83.

62 Reeve, *Charles I and the Road to Personal Rule*, p. 254.

63 BL, Royal/King's MS 265, new ff. 26v–28/old ff. 46–49.

64 S. R. Gardiner, *The Personal Government of Charles I* vol. 1 (London 1877), pp. 214–22; *APC* (June 1630–June 1631) (London 1964) p. 264, no. 754, open warrant to 'leavy' 6,000 'voluntaries', 23 March 1631, and p. 376–8, no. 114, thirty warrants for the levying of volunteers, naming captains and territories/shires; *HMC Hamilton* eleventh report, appendix, part 6 (London 1887), pp. 69–81; *HMC Hamilton Supplementary* (London 1932), pp. 10–19; Hamilton receives ordnance, *CSPD* (1631–1633), p. 102 no. 26, and provisions, p. 103, and equipment, p. 109, and the levies, p. 113 no. 91; *CSPD* Addenda vol. 23 (March 1625–January 1649), S. Lomas, ed., (London 1897), pp. 414–15, names of officers; PRO, SP 16/533/43.

65 Usually printed weekly in London as *The Continuation of Ovr Forraine Avisoes*. See Short Title Catalogue item number 11178.

66 *HMC Hamilton*, pp. 70–81, items 28–61.

67 Henry Hexham, *A Journal of the taking in of Venlo, Roerment, Strale, the memorable siege of Mastricht* . . . (Delft 1633), action described on p. 27/D2.

68 I base this on a comparison of the 22 March 1627 list of regiments (BL, Additional MS 46, 188, ff. 105–6) and the declared accounts of 1639 and 1640 (PRO, E 351/292 and 293).

69 Adams, 'Spain or the Netherlands?', p. 85.

70 Sharpe, *The Personal Rule*, p. 510.

71 Hexham, *A Journal of the taking in of Venlo* . . ., pp. 4v; 25/D; 35/E2.

72 *The Personal Government of Charles I* vol. 2, p. 308; J. F. Merritt, ed., *The Political World of Thomas Wentworth, Earl of Strafford 1621–1641* (Cambridge 1996), pp. 1–23, 109–229.

73 On the mechanism for creating this navy, see Andrew Thrush, 'Naval Finance and the Origins and Development of Ship Money', in Fissel, ed., *W&G*, pp. 133–62, and Alison Gill, 'Ship Money during the Personal Rule of Charles I. Politics, Ideology and the Law, 1634–1640', unpublished Sheffield Ph.D. dissertation, 1990.

74 Andrew Thrush, 'In Pursuit of the Frigate, 1603–1640', *Historical Research* vol. 64 (1991), pp. 29–45, esp. 37 and 45; Brian Quintrell, *Charles I, 1625–1640* (London 1994), pp. 69–72.

75 Henry Hexham, *A Historicall Relation of the Famous Siege of Busse* . . . (Delft 1630), especially pp. 2, 5, 11–12, 14, 19–21, 23–7, 29–31, and the appendix, 'A List of

our Noblemen, Vollunteirs, and Gentlemen of our Nation which bore armes and trayled pikes at the Siege. . . .'

76 Herman Hugo's latin account of the siege of Breda was translated for an English-speaking audience by C. H. G., in a licensed edition that acknowledged Hugo's authorship (Short Title Catalogue 13926). Less gracious in attribution was the Catholic translation by Gerrat Barry, *The Seige of Breda by the Armes of Phillip the FOVRT. . . .* (Louvain 1627), a captain in the Earl of Tyrone's regiment, and dedicated to Spinola (STC 13926a/[1529]). See also J. R. Hale, *The Art of War and Renaissance England* (Washington, D.C. 1961), pp. 26–7.

77 Henry Hexham, *A Trve and Briefe Relation of the Famovs Seige of Breda. . . .* (Delft 1637), last two pages of the unpaginated preface, 1–7, 10–46 and last four pages of unpaginated appendix at the very end of the book. Hexham sometimes showed too much diligence in providing detail, as when he mentioned 'my Lord Morgan shott through his britches, which bullet grazed upon his buttock. . . .' (p. 12).

78 R. Weckherlin, *A Short Description of the Marching forth of the Enemie out of Breda. . . .* (London 1637).

79 Du Praissac, *The Art of Warre, or Militarie discourses,* J. Cruso, ed., (Cambridge 1639), p. 1/A4; *Luke* 14:25–33 especially verse 28.

80 See the remarks of Michael Braddick in reference to Charles Carlton's statistical analysis of the Civil War, in 'An English Military Revolution?', *HJ* vol. 30 no. 4 (1993), pp. 965–6, esp. note one.

81 Peter Donald, *An Uncounselled King Charles I and the Scottish Troubles 1637–1641* (Cambridge 1990), pp. 119–71.

82 Fissel, *BW*, pp. 162–6.

83 PRO, SP 16/401/63, f. 178, Nicholas' summary of 12 November 1638; PRO, War Office, WO 49/100, unfoliated, under 'Moneyes to be spared for the present, out of the Estimate for the compleating of armes for 12000 foote and 400 horse' (January 1639?). The men could expect some arduous labour, for entrenching tools (shovels, spades, pick-axes, hurdles, and baskets) were ordered in this account, indicating that the King was still, at this stage, bent on a serious campaign and not a show of force.

84 BL, Pembroke-Stowe MS 743, letter from Whitehall, 3 February 1639, new f. 130. This was not an isolated example. See also new f. 128.

85 BL, Add. MS 11,045, f. 8, Scudamore papers, letter of 26 March 1639; the Essex men would have been even more reluctant had they known the true destination of their particular voyage was not Newcastle, but 'enemy' territory: the Firth of Forth.

86 Caroline Hibbard, *Charles I and the Popish Plot* (Chapel Hill, N.C. 1983), pp. 104–8, 121, 151–2, 168, 179.

87 'Henry, Lord Clifford and the First Bishops' War', *Northern History* vol. 31 no. 31, pp. 139–40. Clifford practised what he preached. At the very outset of the troubles he had obtained better firearms from London and undergone training from his brother, Captain George Clifford: ibid., pp. 138–9; M. McCarthy, H. Summerson, and R. Annis, *Carlisle Castle. A Survey and Documentary History* (London 1990), pp. 194–5.

88 In 1638, 250 foot and 100 horse protected Cumberland, while Westmorland maintained an identical number, according to Bodleian Library, Clarendon State Papers, vol. 15, f. 80; PRO, SP 16/381/66 and SP 16/408/162.

89 PRO, SP 16/409/216, the Cumberland DLs on Captain Henry Waites's enquiries, 23 January 1639.

90 Spence, 'Henry, Lord Clifford,' pp. 143–7; on the problems of keeping horses in the north, see Peter Edwards, *The Horse Trade of Tudor and Stuart England* (Cambridge 1988), pp. 135–9.

91 Spence, 'Henry, Lord Clifford,' pp. 141, 148, 151.

92 For the consequent placement of the artillery in 1639, see PRO, MPF 287, which is

also printed in C. S. Terry, *The Life and Campaigns of Alexander Leslie First Earl of Leven* (London 1899), between pp. 292–3.

93 PRO, SP 16/409/164 and certificate, 164 I, 21 January 1639.

94 BL, Add. MS 38, 847, ff. 17v–18.

95 Fissel, *BW*, pp. 22–31.

96 Quoted by Brian Quintrell in *Charles I 1625–1640*, p. 110, who reminds us that Laud's '. . . experience as a Treasury commissioner 1635–36 had taught him much about the fragile state of the King's finances'. See also Fissel, *BW*, pp. 111–29.

97 PRO, SP 45/10, new f. 442; even assuming the rough approximation of numbers in early modern armies, calculating the size of the forces in the Bishops' Wars is difficult because many contingents, gentry cavalry for example, did not take the King's shilling, and therefore appear not in the declared accounts. Given the corruption rife in 1639–40 one suspects that the pressed infantry units were likely under-strength. Fissel, *BW*, pp. 5, 31–3, 100, 111, 207–8, 225, 247.

98 PRO, E 405/285, f. 143v, Pells declaration book.

99 The myriad of accounts is listed in Fissel, *BW*, p. 303; a succinct view of the problem can be found in the Pells declaration books (i.e. PRO, E 405/285, ff. 101v, 102, 143–146v) but these do not convey the sense of competition of interest as do the issues and order books of the Auditor of Receipt, E 403/2813. For these procedures see Fissel, *BW*, pp. 137–51.

100 Bodleian Library, Clarendon SP vol. 15, f. 38, no. 1151, 16 November 1638; PRO, E 351/579.

101 '[T]hey beate upon the Kings army with their ordnance. Some troupes of our horse went out to skirmish, notwithstanding the disadvantage of their [the English] ordnance, but the Scotts stood. . . .' Centre for Kentish Studies, U 1475/C 132/148, Hawkins to Leicester, 3 September 1640; *HMC De L'Isle and Dudley* vol. 6, p. 323.

102 I should here clarify my previous account of Newburn, on p. 58 of *BW*. The Covenanter infantry participated, belatedly, in the battle. But the Scottish cavalry carried the day. See the Covenanters' own account, in National Library of Scotland, Advocates MS 33–4–6, ff. 4–9, which will be discussed in Brad Gericke's forthcoming Vanderbilt Ph.D. dissertation.

103 WRO, Quarter Sessions Autograph Book, ff. 121–3, including the surgeon's certificate and Snooke's petition.

104 On the militia, see Chapter 3; for the statistics, Bodleian Library, Clarendon SP vol. 15, f. 80; PRO, SP 16/381/66 and SP 16/408/162.

105 BL, Add. MS 17,677Q, f. 207v, Joachimi letters, 1639–40; Fissel, *BW*, pp. 264–86, especially p. 285.

106 Clive Holmes, *Seventeenth Century Lincolnshire* (Lincoln 1980), pp. 137–8, 146.

107 The classic work is Roy Strong, *Van Dyck. Charles I on Horseback* (New York 1972).

108 Michael Young, *Charles I* (New York 1997), pp. 27–9, 36–42, 51, 54.

109 C. Russell, 'The First Army Plot of 1641', in *Unrevolutionary England 1603–1642* (London 1990), pp. 281–302; *idem*, *FBM* pp. 274–303; M. Fissel, 'Army Plots', in *Historical Dictionary of Stuart England, 1603–1689*, R. Fritze and W. Robison, eds (Westport, Conn. 1996), pp. 27–8; Bodleian Library, Clarendon SP vol. 21, f. 24, no. 1587, Conway's letter of 10 April 1642; J. Malcolm, *Caesar's Due. Loyalty and King Charles 1642–1646* (London 1983).

12 ENGLISH WARFARE TURNED UPON ITSELF

1 Public Record Office, Kew, E 351 shelf catalogue, p. 1.

2 See pp. 4, 52, 83–4.

3 PRO, SP 12/60/66, conflating the figures on ff. 192v and 193v. This document was drafted most likely before the worst of the 1569 rebellion and should perhaps be seen as symptomatic of both the 'reforming' zeal of the 1569 spring and summer muster preparations, as well as of the concern for the security of the Queen's person in the latter half of 1569. See Chapter 5, pp. 123–34.

4 Ibid., ff. 187, 190, 191.

5 PRO, SP 12/93/1, account of a brawl outside Lewes's shop, which occurred 30 November 1573.

6 PRO, SP 16/206/31, f. 106.

7 M. C. Fissel, 'Tradition and Invention in the Early Stuart Art of War', *JSAHR* vol. 65 no. 23 (Autumn 1987), p. 134.

8 *The Strategems, Sleghtes and Policies of Warre* was translated for a Tudor audience in 1539. Frontinus served in Britain AD 75–78. See also Webb, *EMS*, p. 6.

9 Fissel, 'Tradition and Invention', p. 134. A Dutch observer noted after the defeat of the Armada that Elizabeth, '. . . imitating the ancient Romans, rode into London in triumph. . . .' Emanuel van Meteren, cited by Barnes and Feldman, eds, *Renaissance, Reformation, and Absolutism 1400–1600* (Lanham, Md. 1979), p. 136.

10 Pinakothek, Munich. J. R. Hale, *Artists and Warfare in the Renaissance* (London 1990), pp. 182–96.

11 PRO, SP 70/104 B, ff. 39–39v, appendix, Flemish correspondence, 6 June 1568. Smythe told Maria that if he ventured into England he would encounter a 'brave and stowte people'; Hale, ed., *CDM*, p. xix.

12 J. R. Hale, 'Gunpowder and the Renaissance. An Essay in the History of Ideas', in *From the Renaissance to the Counter Reformation*, C. H. Carter, ed. (New York 1965), p. 115; R. Wolper, 'The Rhetoric of Gunpowder and the Idea of Progress', *Journal of the History of Ideas* vol. 31 no. 4 (Oct–Nov 1970), pp. 589–98.

13 BL, Lansdowne MS 64, f. 153.

14 Note Elizabeth's disapproval of Smythe in her letter of 14 May 1590 (?), in BL, Lansdowne MS 64, ff. 105–6v.

15 BL, Lansdowne MS 65, f. 175.

16 *L&A* vol. 3 (June 1591–April 1592), p. 219 no. 309 (F328). The observation is that of Sir Edmund Yorke, who also advocated the use of arrows with 'great bows' against Rouen (p. 200, no. 266, F176, F183).

17 Most recently, Eltis, *MRSC*, pp. 8, 14–15, where he contradicts Michael Roberts.

18 Ibid., p. 121.

19 PRO, SP 45/10, old f. 166/new f. 303 – old f. 166v/new f. 303v; A. G. Credland, 'Bow and Pike' and 'Fire Shafts and Musket Arrows', *Journal of the Society of Archer Antiquaries* vol. 29 (1986), pp. 4–14 and 34–51 respectively; Fissel, 'Tradition and Invention', pp. 133–47.

20 Gervase Phillips, 'Longbow and Hackbutt. Weapons Technology and Technology Transfer in Early Modern England', *Technology and Culture* vol. 40 no. 3 (July 1999), pp. 577, 580–3.

21 J. F. Larkin, ed., *Stuart Royal Proclamations Volume II Royal Proclamations of King Charles I 1625–1646* (Oxford 1983), pp. 329–30; PRO, SP 45/10, old f. 145/new f. 260.

22 Somerset RO, Hippisley MSS, DD/HI, Box 9, from Poulett, 28 August 1623. Few copies of the work, *Instructions for Musters and Arms, and the Use of Thereof,* have survived, with only one (apparently) extant in the UK, BL 534/2 e. 14; Fissel, *BW*, p. 193; Barnes, *Somerset*, pp. 248, 347; Boynton, *EM*, p. 240.

23 BL, Egerton MS 784, Whiteway's diary 1618–34, f. 56/109, January 1626, just prior to the coronation.

24 Shropshire Records and Research Centre 3365/2561, muster-master accounts for

1609, 1619, 1621, 1622 and others in that series; C. Hamilton, 'The Shropshire Muster-Master's Fee', *Albion* vol. 2 no. 1 (1970) pp. 26–34.

25   Somerset Record Office, Q/SR 2/1 (1) a, f. 232 no. 4; Barnes, *Somerset*, p. 263.

26   See Chapter 3, pp. 69–70.

27   For the soldiers' insightful petitions see Bodleian Library, Clarendon SP vol. 21, ff. 79–83v, nos. 1614 and 1615. See also below, p. 298–300.

28   Russell, *FBM*, pp. 455–6.

29   See BL, Cottonian MS Otho E XI, f. 32.

30   Hale, *WSRE*, pp. 127–52. For the manuscript evidence see BL, Lansdowne MS 1218, old ff. 128–152/new ff. 113–40v and PRO, E 157/2–16.

31   See above, pp. 55, 57–8, 61–8, 84–103, 123–34, 142, 146–52, 156–8, 162–4, 174, 177.

32   Eltis, *MRSC*, pp. 121–2.

33   Suggested by John Adamson, 'England Without Cromwell', in N. Ferguson, ed. *Virtual History* (London 1997), pp. 95–101.

34   L. V. Matthews, 'Anglo-Irish Relations. The English Militia and the Irish Rebellion 1640–1642', McGill University MA thesis (1983), p. 105. The author anticipated the royalist interpretation that characterised some historiography from the mid-1980s to mid-1990s; compare with Russell's *FBM*, however.

35   *HMC Portland* vol. 1 (London 1891), pp. 15–23, esp. p. 17.

36   Bodleian Library, Clarendon SP vol. 21, f. 120 no. 1633, 11 August 1642.

37   Russell, *FBM*, p. 464; A. Fletcher, *The Outbreak of the English Civil War* (New York 1981), p. 244.

38   C. Russell, 'The Scottish Party in English Parliaments, 1640–2', *Historical Research* vol. 66 no. 159 (February 1993), pp. 40–7.

39   This theme, developed in Fissel, *BW*, owes much to T. G. Barnes's *Somerset*, pp. 244–80 and contrasts with the rosy picture painted by L. Boynton's *EM*, whose chapter on the subject drew heavily from Barnes but inexplicably reached a different conclusion.

40   Lawson Nagel, '"A Great Bouncing at Every Man's Door". The Struggle for London's Militia in 1642', pp. 68–72, 77–8, 80–3; Keith Roberts, 'Citizen Soldiers. The Military Power of the City of London', pp. 89–90, 102, 111, both printed in S. Porter, ed., *London and the Civil War* (London 1996).

41   See the essays by Nagel and Roberts in Porter, ed., *London and the Civil War*, pp. 65–116.

42   A pair of works exemplify this furore: *Militia Old and New. One Thousand six hundred forty two*, which concluded 'No more then were the statute giving power unto Justices of Peace to enquire of a riot doth exclude the power of Kings Bench, which no man will affirme. And therefore the ordinance of the Militia is legall' (p. 7); *An Answer to the Booke Called Observations of the Old and New Militia*, the royalist counterblast, followed in September 1642. Bodleian Library, Godwin pamphlets 976, State Tracts 1626–1643, nos. 27, 28.

43   C. Russell, 'The Theory of Treason in the Trial of Strafford', *Unrevolutionary England*, pp. 102–3.

44   CKS, DeLisle and Dudley, MSS, Sydney Papers, U1475 C85/5, notes taken, 2 January 1640. See also Russell, *FBM*, p. 285.

45   PRO, SP 16/490/77, ff. 193–193v. The loss of Hull was more than symbolic. The arsenal possessed 49 bronze cannon and 7,238 muskets. See also Ian Ryder, 'The seizure of Hull and its magazine, January 1642', *Yorkshire Archaeological Journal* vol. 61 (1989), pp. 139–48.

46   Russell, *FBM*, p. 507, citing Rushworth's *Historical Collections* vol. 3 no. 1, p. 585 and the *Lords' Journals* vol. 5, f. 52.

47 Bodleian Library, Clarendon SP vol. 20, ff. 78–80v, items 1613 and 1614.

48 Bodleian Library, Clarendon SP vol. 21, f. 89, 17 June 1642.

49 Simon Healy, David Scott, and Andrew Thrush of the History of Parliament Trust graciously shared their files.

50 Bodleian Library, Ashmole Pamphlets 1048, *An Argument or Debate in Law: of the Great Qvestion concerning the Militia* . . . (London? 1641), pp. 12, 20.

51 PRO, State Papers Domestic, Charles II, SP 29/6, ff. 189–190v. I owe knowledge of this reference to Michael Maxwell.

52 *HMC Portland* vol. 1, pp. 31, 46–7, 50–3.

53 Bodleian Library, Tanner MS 67, no. 28, f. 54.

54 Bodleian Library, St Amand MS 36A, f. 127.

55 Fissel, *BW*, pp.15–16; for Powicke Bridge see True and happy Newes from WORCESTER (London 1642). Astley had sought Essex's patronage, in 1628, writing, '. . . I hope to live the day to see your Lordship the Cheefe directour att the heade of an Army, in some brave Imployment. . . .' in which Sir Jacob might serve. Astley, of course, got his wish, but found himself in arms as Essex's adversary, on the field of Edgehill. BL, Additional MS 46, 188, f. 110, letter of 10 July 1628; also discussed in Donagan, 'Halcyon Days', p. 70.

56 Bridgadier Peter Young, *Edgehill* (Kineton 1967); Austin Woolrych, *Battles of the English Civil War* (London 1971); Charles Carlton, *Going to the Wars* (London 1994). One might cite, in a tangential context, Simon Jenkins' remark, that 'Britons are good at wars. We do what matters, which is to win them'. *Sunday Times Books*, 27 October 1996, p. 1.

BIBLIOGRAPHICAL ESSAY

Chapter 1

As background, Ian Arthurson's 'The King's Voyage into Scotland: the war that never was', *England in the Fifteenth Century. Proceedings of the 1986 Harlaxton Symposium*, D. Williams, ed. (Woodbridge, Suffolk 1987) builds nicely upon J. R. Hooker's 'The organization and supply of the Tudor military under Henry VII', *Huntington Library Quarterly* vol. 23 (1959), pp. 19–31. In 1963, Clifford Davies completed his Oxford D.Phil. thesis, 'Supply Services of the English armed forces, 1509–50', which led Davies to write a series of superb articles on early Tudor military organisation: 'Provisions for Armies, 1509–50; A study in the effectiveness of early Tudor Government,' *EconHR*, second series, vol. 17 no. 2 (December 1964), pp. 234–48; 'The Administration of the Royal Navy under Henry VIII: The Origins of the Navy Board', *EHR* vol. 80 no. 315 (April 1965); 'The English People and War in the Early Sixteenth Century', in Duke and Tamse, eds, *Britain and the Netherlands* vol. 6, *War and Society* (The Hague 1977), pp. 1–18. Also during the mid- and late 1960s another Oxford scholar, Charles Cruickshank, produced two volumes which chronicled Henry VIII's first major campaign and its aftermath: *Army Royal. Henry VIII's Invasion of France* (Oxford 1969) and *The English Occupation of Tournai 1513–1519* (Oxford 1971). Oxford continues to produce excellent scholarship on the Henrician art of war. Steven Gunn of Merton College has emerged as the foremost historian of warfare under the early Tudors, and places military activities within broader dynastic, political, and social contexts. Of his many publications, of particular note for English warfare are 'The French Wars of Henry VIII' in Jeremy Black's *The Origins of War in Early Modern Europe* (Edinburgh 1987), and 'The Duke of Suffolk's March on Paris in 1523', *EHR* vol. 101 no. 400 (July 1986), pp. 596–634. Another Oxford product, though more illuminative of theory than practice, is David Eltis's *The Military Revolution in Sixteenth Century Europe* (London 1995), based upon a D.Phil. written about English military theorists in the Tudor period, and paralleling Henry Webb's *Elizabethan Military Science the Books and the Practice* (Madison, Wisconsin 1965). These two works, like contemporary treatises, struggle to reconcile the idealised conceptual world of military theory with the realities of English warfare. A rare example of such a synthesis is *John Rogers, Tudor Military Engineer* (Oxford 1967), an illustrated tome on how the art of military architecture was implemented in various theatres of war, a fine work from the pen of L. R. Shelby. Early Tudor fortification is superbly integrated into English architecture history by Colvin and Summerson in their massive research on *The King's Works*. B. M. Morley's *Henry VIII and the Development of Coastal Defence* (London 1976) is a useful introduction, as is the relevant chapter in Eltis (pp. 76–94)

The versatile David Loades produced, in 1992, *The Tudor Navy: An Administrative, Political and Military History*, which overlaps nicely with the classic by Michael Oppenheim, *History of the Administration of the Royal Navy to 1660* (London 1896). A superbly broad view is rendered by N. A. M. Rodger, *The Safeguard of the Sea, A Naval History of Britain 660–1649* (New York 1997); Penn, *Navy of the Early Stuarts* remains the best available study.

At Cambridge, the grand don of Tudor studies during the post-war era, the late Sir Geoffrey Elton, also made a fine contribution to the study of English warfare with his 'War and the English in the Reign of Henry VIII' in L. Freedman, et al., eds, *War, Strategy, and International Politics* (Oxford 1992); An aspect of the 'Tudor Revolution in government' espoused by Sir Geoffrey was the extensive mustering of 1522, which is well documented for students of military and social history. J. J. Goring published 'The General Proscription of 1522' in *EHR* vol. 86 no. 341 (October 1971), pp. 681–705, which elicited numerous local studies through the 1970s and 1980s. That work is ably summarised and used to explain the fiscal system that undergirded Henrician campaigns in Richard Hoyle's *Tudor Taxation Records. A Guide for Users* (London 1994). Those who wish to plough through a 1522 muster survey may find specimens close at hand. *The Military Survey of 1522 for Babergh Hundred* (Woodbridge 1986), edited by John Pound, provides what Hoyle judges as 'perhaps the most elaborate of the surviving military surveys' (p. xv). A. C. Chibnall's *The Certificate of Musters for Buckinghamshire in 1522* (London 1973) is accessible, while other excellent editions by T. L. Stoate (for example, on Cornwall) were published locally and are not commonly available overseas.

Chapter 2

Again, the work of C. S. L. Davies is an excellent starting point. A new synthesis has appeared, Gervase Phillips' *The Anglo-Scots Wars 1513–1550: A Military History* (Woodbridge, Suffolk 1999). As for Henrician and Edwardian armies, Gilbert Millar's *Tudor Mercenaries and Auxiliaries 1485–1547* (Charlottesville, N.C. 1980) discloses the nature of the King's forces. For

Edward VI's campaign, M. L. Bush's *The Government Policy of Protector Somerset* (Montreal 1975) delivers more than the title intimates. Bush's more recent *The Pilgrimage of Grace: A Study of the Rebel Armies of October 1536* (Manchester 1996) reveals much about English military potential as mobilised in suppressing the rebellion. Steven Ellis has much advanced our understanding of Tudor Ireland, and has addressed military historical issues as well. His 'The Tudors and the origins of the modern Irish states' appears in *A military history of Ireland*, T. Bartlett and K. Jeffrey, eds (Cambridge 1996), pp. 116–35.

Chapter 3

The study of lieutenancy was mightily advanced by the opening of local record offices after World War II. Gladys Scot Thomson, in the 1920s and 1930s, had provided a national perspective in her edited works (i.e. *The Twysden Lieutenancy Papers 1583–1668* [Ashford 1926]) and her monograph, *The Lords Lieutenants in the Sixteenth Century* (London 1923). The spate of scholarship based upon the shire produced not only regional case studies of lieutenancy but made available to the student the edited correspondence of lieutenants and their deputies. Some of the better lieutenancy collections are Jeremy Goring and Joan Wake, eds, *Northamptonshire Lieutenancy Papers, 1580–1614* (Northants 1975); W. Murphy, ed., *The Earl of Hertford's Lieutenancy Papers 1603–1612* (Devizes 1969); Brian Quintrell, ed., *The Maynard Lieutenancy Book, 1608–1639* 2 vols (Chelmsford 1993); and Ann J. King, ed., *Muster Books for North & East Hertfordshire 1580–1605*, Hertfordshire Record Society Publication vol. 12 (Cambridge 1996). As very few 'lieutenancy books' seem to have been kept during the upheavals of 1640–60, students will find that the scholarship on lieutenancy tends to be divided between pre-civil war and post-restoration. A notable exception is Victor Stater's synoptic *Noble Government. The Stuart Lord Lieutenancy and the Transformation of English Politics* (Athens, Ga. 1993). A new work is Tom Cogswell's *Home Divisions. Aristocracy, the State and Provincial Conflict* (Stanford 1998).

Chapter 4

Impressment under the Tudors and Stuarts can only be understood in light of the medieval precedents for conscription. One should begin with Arthur Noyes's *The Military Obligation in Mediaeval England* (Columbus, OH 1930) and Michael Powicke's *The Military Obligation Medieval England* (Oxford 1962) and then move on to more recent works. N. B. Lewis has produced some excellent and succinct studies, for example 'The Organization of Indentured Retinues in Fourteenth Century England', *TRHS*, fourth series, vol. 27 (1945), pp. 29–39. The literature for the early modern period is not as plentiful as for studies of medieval mobilisations. For the Tudor period, see C. G. Cruickshank's *Elizabeth's Army* (second edn) (Oxford 1968), pp. 1–40 and John McGurk's *The Elizabethan Conquest of Ireland* (Manchester 1997), pp. 51–134. For the Stuart era, Stephen Stearns's 'Conscription and English Society in the 1620s', *JBS* vol. 11 no. 2 (May 1972), pp. 1–23 has been recognised as a seminal work in the field. The latter two works are based on excellent doctoral dissertations which contain more details than the published works they spawned. For the civil war, see Ronald Hutton, *The Royalist War Effort* (London 1984), and Joyce Malcolm, *Caesar's Due. Loyalty and King Charles 1642–1646* (London 1983).

Chapter 5

The campaign of 1560 is summarised in the second edition of Cruickshanks's *Elizabeth's Army*, pp. 207–36. The expedition deserves a monograph. Anthony Fletcher's *Tudor Rebellions*, third edition (London 1993), provides a succinct account of the 1569 rising, placing it within the longer tradition of civil disorder. For a single volume, Sir Cuthbert Sharp's *Memorial of the Rebellion of 1569* (London 1840) contains a wealth of detail. An account of the 1573 campaign has to be pieced together from the various textbooks on Elizabeth's reign.

Chapter 6

Bruce Wernham's trilogy dramatises the strategic predicament for the entire Tudor period: *Before the Armada: The Emergence of the English Nation, 1485–1588* (New York 1972), *After the Armada* (Oxford 1984), *The Return of the Armadas* (Oxford 1994). A good read for the enterprising student is Wernham's *List and Analysis* series, which edited and presented Elizabeth's state papers foreign in a thematic format. The result is a surprisingly readable series of volumes, rich in historical detail and enlivened by anecdote. Wernham's prolific mining of the archives made him his generation's pre-eminent scholar of Elizabethan foreign policy and sea-going enterprise. Simon Adams, produced an insightful Oxford D.Phil. thesis, 'The Protestant Cause', which bridges Elizabethan foreign policy with Jacobean embroilment on the Continent.

Chapter 7

Sir Roger Williams' celebrated account of *The Actions of the Low Countries* is published in an easily readable form in the 1964 Folger Shakespeare Library version, edited by D. W. Davies. The 1972 Oxford University Press version (John X. Evans, ed.) boasts the inclusion of Williams' *The Breefe Discourse of Warre* and an extensive commentary by Evans. A focused modern history of

English exploits during the Dutch Revolt has yet to be written, but there is good reason to believe that David J. Trim's research in foreign and British archives will yield such a study. John Nolan's *Sir John Norreys and the Elizabethan Military World* (Exeter 1997) takes a biographical approach to English involvement in the wars. Motley's *History of the United Netherlands* 4 vols (New York 1861) provides a narrative history. Some campaigns of this era are the subject of solid campaign histories: Bruce Wernham's *The Expedition of Sir John Norris and Sir Francis Drake to Spain and Portugal, 1589* (London 1988) and Howell Lloyd's *The Rouen Campaign 1590–1592* (Oxford 1973).

Chapter 8

C. S. L. Davies again has done yeoman service in illustrating English application of logistics and the proliferation of cannon (see above, chapter 1). A. Carvana's *Tudor Artillery 1485–1603* Historical Arms Series no. 30 (Bloomfield, Ontario 1992) depicts English artillery as set forth in the Lad brothers' drawings of 1586. Its incomplete and inconsistent references, however, limit its usefulness. The expertly researched (and, unfortunately, unpublished) B.Litt. dissertation of Roger Ashley, 'The organisation and administration of the Tudor office of the ordnance' (1973), is well worth a journey to Oxford to read. A sequential study, Richard Winship Stewart's *The English Ordnance Office 1585–1625*, is as useful as Ashley's preceding study, and equally well-researched. A particularly lively and original work is that of Jim Bennett and Stephen Johnston. Both scholars were involved in an exhibition at the University of Oxford's Museum of the History of Science, and they consequently published *The Geometry of War 1500–1700* (Oxford 1996) and established websites: http://info.ox.ac.uk/departments/hooke/geometry/title/htm and http://www.mhs.ox.ac.uk/geometry/essay.htm. The development of a centralised system of supply from a semi-private, decentralised 'multiple system' can be traced by contrasting Richard Stewart's 'Irish Road' piece and Scott Wheeler's analysis of Cromwellian logistics in Ireland, in *War and Government in Britain, 1598–1650*, M. C. Fissel, ed. (Manchester 1991), pp. 16–56.

Chapter 9

For a half century, Cyril Falls's *Elizabeth's Irish Wars* (New York 1950) has remained the standard narrative text for Tudor forays into Eire. Overlooked, comparatively speaking, have been the pithy, ground-breaking essays of G. A. Hayes-McCoy. His accounts of the battles of Knockdoe (1504), Farsetmore (1567), Clontibret (1595), Yellow Ford (1598), the Moyry Pass (1600), and Kinsale (1601), comprise a unique thread within the fabric of Irish military history (*Irish Battles. A Military History of Ireland* [Belfast 1990], pp. 48–173). More analytical are 'The Army of Ulster, 1593–1601',

Irish Sword vol. 1 (1950), pp.105–117 and 'Strategy and Tactics in Irish Warfare, 1593–1601', *Irish Historical Studies* vol. 2 (1940–1), pp. 255–79. A less objective, if more detailed, work is *Kinsale. The Spanish Intervention in Ireland at the End of the Elizabethan Wars* (New York 1970) by Father John Silke, who combines good research with occasional Jesuitical nonsense. Transcending ideology is Ciaran Brady's insightful essay on the administrative and social context of the sixteenth-century occupation, in 'The captains' games: army and society in Elizabethan Ireland', *A military history of Ireland*, Bartlett and Jeffrey, eds (Cambridge 1996), pp. 136–59.

Chapter 10

The field of Stuart Irish historical studies has never been stronger, with major studies under way by Raymond Gillespie, Jane Ohlmeyer, Mike Webb, Scott Wheeler and Toby Barnard, amongst others. Students may expect some insightful scholarship to be published in the new millennium. A stunningly original work is a collaborative effort between Geoffrey Parker and Rolf Loeber, entitled 'The Military Revolution in Ireland', presented in Jane Ohlmeyer, ed., *Ireland from Independence to Occupation* (Cambridge 1995), pp. 66–88. In the same volume may be found Scott Wheeler's 'Four Armies in Ireland', pp. 43–65, which bridges the military situation in pre-civil war Ireland with Cromwell's campaign, helping to make sense of the operations from 1642–9, and beyond. Tangential to Wheeler's essay is the brief but suggestive study by Ian Ryder, *An English Army for Ireland* (Leigh-on-Sea 1987). A recent narrative is *Confederate Ireland 1642–1649* (Portland, Oregon 1999) by Mícheál O'Siochrú.

Chapter 11

One of the best studies of warfare under Charles I has, unfortunately, never been published, Stephen Stearns's *The Caroline Military System: The Expedition to Cadiz and Rhé, 1625–1627*, a 1967 University of California Ph.D. dissertation written under the supervision of Tom Barnes. See also E. Beller, 'The Military Expedition of Sir Charles Morgan to Germany 1627–9', *EHR* vol. 43 no. 172 (October 1928), pp. 528–39. The resurgence of the Royal Navy under Charles I has attracted much attention, though no comprehensive study of ship money (the revenue from which it was built) has yet to appear. Evidence that University presses, even the best ones, are eager to exploit this gap can be seen, for example, in the publication of *Ships, Money and Politics: Seafaring and naval enterprise in the reign of Charles I* (Cambridge 1991), a tangle of mismatched and occasionally misinformed essays that presumes to provide some coherent view of the Caroline naval situation. More reliably, Andrew Thrush's work has perhaps best illuminated the Caroline navy. See for example his 'In pursuit of the frigate', *Historical*

Research vol 64 (1991), pp. 29–45; 'The Ordnance Office and the Navy, 1625–40', *Mariner's Mirror* vol. 77 no. 4 November 1991, pp. 339–54; 'Naval Finance and the Origins and Development of Ship Money', *War and Government in Britain, 1598–1650* (Manchester 1991), pp. 133–62. In the same volume, see Richard Stewart's view of the campaign of the 1620s (pp. 112–32), where he emphasises administrative resilience.

Considering that much of the opposition to Charles I reacted to military charges, the student might peruse studies which intersect political history with military history. The relevant passages in Conrad Russell's *Parliaments and English Politics, 1621–1629* (Oxford 1977) are pp. 70–84, 260–301, 323–89. Military history between 1629 and 1637 consists largely of the story of English units serving on the Continent and the development of the shire militias (on the latter, see Chapter 3). With the outbreak of the Prayer Book Rebellion in Scotland (1637), the descent into war can be followed until Charles's execution on the scaffold in 1649. Again, Russell sketches out the wider military context, in *The Fall of the British Monarchies 1637–1642* (Oxford 1991), pp. 62–146, 274–329, 373–99, 454–532. The present writer's *The Bishops' Wars: Charles I's Campaigns against Scotland 1638–1640* (Cambridge 1994) follows the Russellian formula of placing English warfare within a political context.

Chapter 12

An imaginative study is *Going to the Wars: The Experience of the British Civil Wars, 1638–1651* (London 1994), by Charles Carlton, which applies the John Keegan 'face of battle' methodology upon the war of the three kingdoms. Carlton's taste for literature and anecdote make this an eminently readable book. P. R. Newman, whose biographical research of royalist officers has produced *The Old Service. Royalist regimental colonels and the Civil War, 1642–46* (Manchester 1993), addresses the question of the military experience of those who fought the civil war. Ronald Hutton's *The Royalist War Effort 1642–1646* (London 1984) explains how the King got his army. And as for combat, Austin Woolrych's *Battles of the English Civil War* (London 1971) remains a standard. Martyn Bennett's *The Civil Wars in Britain and Ireland: 1638–1651* (London 1996) weaves a brisk narrative of the conflicts.

Squaring theory with military practice is extremely difficult, if not impossible (see Sir John Hale's review of Henry Webb's *Elizabethan Military Science the Books and the Practice* in *EHR* vol. 82 no. 323 [April 1967] pp. 383–4). The most successful attempt has been Barbara Donagan, 'Halcyon Days and the Literature of War: England's Military Education before 1642', *P & P* no. 147, pp. 65–100. The literature itself is presented concisely by Sir John Hale in *The Art of War and Renaissance England* (Washington, D.C. 1961). War's reflection in contemporary literature has been captured in Nick de Somogyi's *Shakespeare's Theatre of War* (Aldershot 1998).

INDEX

Page numbers in *italics* refer to the illustrations